Critical Theory Today

"Lois Tyson's *Critical Theory Today* is an accessible introduction to many of the major schools of literary interpretation. She provides clear explanations and illuminating cross-comparisons that work very effectively in the undergraduate classroom."

Elizabeth Renker, *Professor of English, The Ohio State University, USA*

"For anyone who wants to understand contemporary cultural theory, *Critical Theory Today* is the undisputed starting point for that understanding. No other introduction to theory presents each theory on its own terms in the way that Lois Tyson's indispensable work does. She combines penetrating clarity with theoretical sophistication in order to create a book that everyone can learn from. The welcome new third edition provides a keyhole into what's going on right now in the rapidly changing world of contemporary theory."

Todd McGowan, *Associate Professor, The University of Vermont, USA*

This thoroughly updated third edition of *Critical Theory Today* offers an accessible introduction to contemporary critical theory, providing in-depth coverage of the most common approaches to literary analysis today, including: feminism; psychoanalysis; Marxism; reader-response theory; New Criticism; structuralism and semiotics; deconstruction; new historicism and cultural criticism; lesbian, gay, and queer theory; African American criticism and postcolonial criticism.

This new edition features:

- a major expansion of the chapter on postcolonial criticism that includes topics such as Nordicism, globalization and the 'end' of postcolonial theory, global tourism and global conservation
- an extended explanation of each theory, using examples from everyday life, popular culture, and literary texts
- a list of specific questions critics ask about literary texts
- an interpretation of F. Scott Fitzgerald's *The Great Gatsby* through the lens of each theory
- a list of questions for further practice to guide readers in applying each theory to different literary works
- updated and expanded bibliographies

Both engaging and rigorous, this is a "how-to" book for undergraduate and graduate students new to critical theory and for college professors who want to broaden their repertoire of critical approaches to literature.

Lois Tyson is Professor Emerita of English at Grand Valley State University, USA

Critical Theory Today

A user-friendly guide

Third edition

Lois Tyson

Routledge
Taylor & Francis Group

LONDON AND NEW YORK

Third edition published 2015
by Routledge
2 Park Square, Milton Park, Abingdon, Oxon OX14 4RN

by Routledge
711 Third Avenue, New York, NY 10017

Routledge is an imprint of the Taylor & Francis Group, an informa business

First edition published in 1998 by Routledge
Second edition published in 2006 by Routledge

British Library Cataloguing in Publication Data
A catalogue record for this book is available from the British Library

Library of Congress Cataloging in Publication Data
Tyson, Lois, 1950–
Critical theory today: a user-friendly guide / Lois Tyson. – 3rd edition.
pages; cm
Includes bibliographical references and index.
1. Criticism. I. Title.
PN81.T97 2014
801'.95–dc23
2014005974

ISBN: 978-0-415-50674-8 (hbk)
ISBN: 978-0-415-50675-5 (pbk)
ISBN: 978-1-315-76079-7 (ebk)

Typeset in Perpetua
by Taylor & Francis Books

I gratefully dedicate this book
to my students and to my teachers.
I hope I will always have difficulty telling you apart.

Contents

Preface to the third edition   xii

Preface for instructors   xiv

Acknowledgments   xvi

1   **Everything you wanted to know about critical theory
    but were afraid to ask**   1

2   **Psychoanalytic criticism**   11

The origins of the unconscious   12

The defenses, anxiety, and core issues   15

Dreams and dream symbols   18

The meaning of death   21

The meaning of sexuality   23

Lacanian psychoanalysis   25

Classical psychoanalysis and literature   33

Some questions psychoanalytic critics ask about literary texts   36

"What's Love Got to Do with It?": a psychoanalytic reading of
    The Great Gatsby   38

Questions for further practice: psychoanalytic approaches
    to other literary works   48

For further reading   48

For advanced readers   49

3   **Marxist criticism**   51

The fundamental premises of Marxism   51

The class system in America   52

The role of ideology   54

Human behavior, the commodity, and the family   59

Marxism and literature   62

Some questions Marxist critics ask about literary texts   65
You are what you own: a Marxist reading of The Great Gatsby   *66*
Questions for further practice: Marxist approaches to other literary works   76
For further reading   76
For advanced readers   76

4   Feminist criticism

Traditional gender roles   81
A summary of feminist premises   87
Getting beyond patriarchy   88
French feminism   91
Multicultural feminism   100
Gender studies and feminism   103
Feminism and literature   112
Some questions feminist critics ask about literary texts   114
" ... next they'll throw everything overboard ... ": a feminist reading of
    The Great Gatsby   *115*
Questions for further practice: feminist approaches
    to other literary works   125
For further reading   126
For advanced readers   126

5   New Criticism

"The text itself"   129
Literary language and organic unity   131
A New Critical reading of "There Is a Girl Inside"   137
New Criticism as intrinsic, objective criticism   141
The single best interpretation   142
The question New Critics asked about literary texts   143
The "deathless song" of longing: a New Critical reading of
    The Great Gatsby   *144*
Questions for further practice: New Critical approaches
    to other literary works   157
For further reading   158
For advanced readers   159

6   Reader-response criticism

The house passage   162
Transactional reader-response theory   165
Affective stylistics   166
Subjective reader-response theory   169

Psychological reader-response theory   173

Social reader-response theory   176

Defining readers   178

Some questions reader-response critics
ask about literary texts   180

Projecting the reader: a reader-response analysis of
The Great Gatsby   *181*

Questions for further practice: reader-response approaches
to other literary works   193

For further reading   194

For advanced readers   195

7   Structuralist criticism   **198**

Structural linguistics   201

Structural anthropology   203

Semiotics   205

Structuralism and literature   207

The structure of literary genres   209

The structure of narrative (structuralist narratology)   212

The structure of literary interpretation   217

Some questions structuralist critics ask about literary texts   220

"Seek and ye shall find" ... and then lose: a structuralist reading of
The Great Gatsby   *221*

Questions for further practice: structuralist approaches
to other literary works   231

For further reading   232

For advanced readers   232

8   Deconstructive criticism   **235**

Deconstructing language   235

Deconstructing our world   241

Deconstructing human identity   243

Deconstructing literature   244

A deconstructive reading of Robert Frost's "Mending Wall"   246

Some questions deconstructive critics ask about literary texts   251

" ... the thrilling, returning trains of my youth ... ":
a deconstructive reading of The Great Gatsby   *252*

Questions for further practice: deconstructive approaches
to other literary works   264

For further reading   265

For advanced readers   266

9   New historical and cultural criticism   **267**

New historicism   267

New historicism and literature   276

Cultural criticism   280

Cultural criticism and literature   282

Some questions new historical and cultural critics
    ask about literary texts   285

The discourse of the self-made man: a new historical reading of
    The Great Gatsby   *287*

Questions for further practice: new historical and cultural
    criticism of other literary works   297

For further reading   298

For advanced readers   298

10   Lesbian, gay, and queer criticism   **302**

The marginalization of LGBTQ people   303

Lesbian criticism   308

Gay criticism   314

Queer criticism   319

Some shared features of lesbian, gay, and queer criticism   324

Some questions lesbian, gay, and queer critics
    ask about literary texts   326

Will the real Nick Carraway please come out? A queer reading of
    The Great Gatsby   *327*

Questions for further practice: lesbian, gay, and queer approaches
    to other literary works   338

For further reading   340

For advanced readers   340

11   African American criticism   **343**

Racial issues and African American literary history   343

Recent developments: critical race theory   350

Basic tenets   352

African American criticism and literature   368

Some questions African American critics ask about literary texts   377

But where's Harlem? An African American reading of The Great Gatsby   *379*

Questions for further practice: African American approaches
    to other literary works   392

For further reading   393

For advanced readers   394

12 Postcolonial criticism 398

Colonialist ideology and postcolonial identity 399
Foundational postcolonial debates 406
Globalization and the "end" of postcolonial theory 409
Postcolonial theory and global tourism 412
Postcolonial theory and global conservation 416
Postcolonial criticism and literature 421
Some questions postcolonial critics ask about literary texts 425
The colony within: a postcolonial reading of The Great Gatsby *428*
Questions for further practice: postcolonial approaches to other literary
    works 440
For further reading 441
For advanced readers 442

13 Gaining an overview 448

Index 454

Preface to the third edition

Since the second edition of *Critical Theory Today: A User-Friendly Guide* was published in 2006, the field of critical theory has continued to evolve in a number of ways. For example, an interest in critical theory, sometimes under the rubric of *cultural theory*, continues to facilitate cross fertilization among a number of different educational fields that are often divided into separate university departments – such as literature, history, anthropology, philosophy, and sociology – and continues to inform the educational programs it helped create, including women's studies, gender studies, and studies in popular culture. So it is not surprising that the use of one or more of the theoretical perspectives addressed in this book has become a staple of undergraduate courses in these areas or that most graduate level programs in these fields assume that their students will arrive with some degree of theoretical knowledge. A relatively recent development, however, is that an interest in critical theory – which is largely a production of western or westernized educational systems – has grown in many non-western, non-English speaking countries that have their own respected traditions of knowledge. For example, university presses in China, South Korea, and Saudi Arabia are currently in the process of translating the second edition of *Critical Theory Today* into their own languages for use by their own students and teachers.

One thing that hasn't changed, however, is the purpose of this book. It is still an introduction to critical theory written by a teacher of critical theory and literature. And it is still intended for teachers and college-level students who want to learn about critical theory and its usefulness in helping us to achieve a better understanding of literature. As in the case of any new edition of a textbook, you'll find in the third edition of *Critical Theory Today* new theoretical concepts and vocabulary, some expanded discussions of foundational theoretical issues, and, at the end of every chapter, updated and expanded bibliographies "For further reading" and "For advanced readers." You'll also find a reorganized and expanded chapter on postcolonial criticism that includes, among other additions, new sections entitled "Globalization and the 'end' of postcolonial theory," "Postcolonial theory and global tourism," and "Postcolonial theory and global conservation," which reflect recent developments in this field. Because I am a teacher writing for teachers and students, the third edition also contains clarifications wherever my own students have had repeated difficulty, over the years, in understanding a particular concept addressed in the book. Thus you'll find, to cite just a few representative examples, a clarification of the relationship among the operations of the *ego*, *id*, and *superego* in the chapter on psychoanalytic criticism; an expanded explanation of the concept of undecidability in the chapter on deconstructive criticism; and, in the chapter on lesbian, gay, and queer criticism, additional discussion and literary examples of the concept of *homosocial bonding*. Indeed, my own two copies of the second edition, which I've used in my classes, contain innumerable little page markers where a clarification, word change, or additional concrete example was deemed helpful, and all of those small changes also have been made.

As I've so often told my students, a better understanding of the world in which we live, it seems to me, automatically comes along for the ride when we study literature, and the study of critical theory makes that enterprise even more productive. I believed that proposition when I wrote the first and second editions of the book you now hold in your hands, and I've come to believe it more with every critical theory class I've taught. I hope that your experience of the third edition of *Critical Theory Today* also leads you to find that small truth to be self-evident.

Preface for instructors

The writing of this textbook was the product of a sense of pedagogical frustration that I suspect many of you may share. Over the last few decades, critical theory has become a dominant force in higher education. It is now considered an essential part of graduate education, and it plays an increasingly visible role in the under-graduate classroom as well. Yet many college students at all levels, as well as some of their professors, remain confused by much of this jargon-ridden discipline, which seems to defy their understanding. As one colleague said to his students, "Critical theory is a bus, and you're not going to get on it."

Anthologies of essays often used in critical theory courses – which generally include pieces by such frequently arcane theorists as Lacan, Derrida, Spivak, Benjamin, and the like – and books that offer high-tech summaries of these theorists' views don't help the majority of students who are unfamiliar with the basic principles one must understand in order to understand these texts. Conversely, many of the theory textbooks that are written in accessible language are too limited in scope to offer an adequate introduction to this complex field.

Critical Theory Today: A User-Friendly Guide attempts to fill this gap by offering an accessible, unusually thorough introduction to this difficult field that will (1) enable readers to grasp heretofore obscure theoretical concepts by relating them to our everyday experience; (2) show them how to apply theoretical perspectives to lit-erary works; and (3) reveal the relationships among theories – their differences, similarities, strengths, and weaknesses – by applying them all to a single literary work: F. Scott Fitzgerald's *The Great Gatsby* (1925).

I've chosen *The Great Gatsby* for this purpose for several reasons. In addition to lending itself readily to the eleven theoretical readings I offer, the novel is fairly short, quite readable, and familiar, both in terms of its treatment of common themes and in terms of readers' prior exposure to the work. In fact, many of my colleagues who teach critical theory have indicated that they would prefer a text-book that uses *The Great Gatsby* for its literary applications because of their *own* familiarity with the novel.

Aimed primarily at newcomers to the field, each chapter explains the basic principles of the theory it addresses, including the basic principles of literary application, in order to enable students to write their own theoretical interpretations of literature and read with insight what the theorists themselves have written. Thus, this book can be used as the only text in a course or as a precursor to (or in tandem with) critical theory anthologies. Each chapter has grown out of classroom practice, has been thoroughly field tested, and has demonstrated its capacity to motivate students by showing them what critical theory can offer, not only in terms of their practical understanding of literary texts, but also in terms of their personal understanding of themselves and the world in which they live. In a very real sense, this textbook is a "how-to" manual for readers who will probably come to their study of theory with some anxiety, whether they are first-year theory students or college professors who wish to familiarize themselves with theoretical perspectives with which they have not yet become thoroughly acquainted.

Chapters are sequenced for a specific pedagogical purpose: to demonstrate how critical theories both argue and overlap with one another, sometimes overturning, sometimes building on the insights of competing theories. Nevertheless, each chapter is self-explanatory and was written to stand on its own. Therefore, this textbook can be customized to fit your own instructional needs by assigning the chapters in any order you choose; by eliminating some chapters entirely; or by assigning only certain sections of particular chapters, for which purpose chapter subtitles should prove helpful. Similarly, the "Questions for further practice" (which follow each reading of *The Great Gatsby* and can serve as paper topics) encourage students to apply each theory to other well-known, frequently anthologized literary works, but you can have your students apply these questions to any works you select.

However you choose to use *Critical Theory Today,* I hope you will agree that, if critical theory is a bus, it is one our students have every reason to climb aboard. And if this book does its job, they will even enjoy the ride.

Acknowledgments

My most sincere thanks go to the following friends and colleagues for their helpful suggestions and moral support: Hannah Berkowitz, Bertrand Bickersteth, Pat Bloem, Kathleen Blumreich, Linda Chown, Gretchen Cline, Brian Deyo, Michelle Disler, Diane Griffin Crowder, Michelle DeRose, Milt Ford, Jeremy Franceschi, David Greetham, Chance Guyette, Karen Hammes, Michael Hartnett, Alan Hausman, Roseanne Hoefel, Bill Hoffman, Jay Hullett, Howard Kahane, Stephen Lacey, James Lindesay, Rosalind Srb Mayberry, Corinna McLeod, Scott Minar, Joanie Pearlman, James Phelan, Rob Rozema, Sue William Silverman, Veta Smith Tucker, Jill Van Antwerp, Megan Ward, Brian White, and Sharon Whitehill.

Special thanks also go to Grand Valley State University for its generous financial support of this project – especially to Dean Fred Antczak; the late Dean Forrest Armstrong; Professor Jo Miller; and Nancy Raymond, formerly of the Zumberge Library. I would also like to express my sincere appreciation to the wonderful staff of the Loutit District Library in Grand Haven, Michigan, especially to the Interlibrary Loan Department, which is to say especially to Julie M. Williams. At Routledge Press, I am gratefully indebted to Ruth Hilsdon and Elizabeth Levine for their advice and support throughout this project and Polly Dodson and Christina Taranto for their prompt and gracious assistance always. Fond gratitude is still offered to Phyllis Korper, formerly of Garland Press, for her unflagging enthusiasm for the first edition.

Finally, the deepest gratitude is expressed to Mac Davis, the only brave heart who read every word of every chapter of every edition, and to Lenny Briscoe for his invaluable spiritual guidance.

1 Everything you wanted to know about critical theory but were afraid to ask

Why should we bother to learn about critical theories? Is it really worth the trouble? Won't all those abstract concepts (if I can even understand any of them) interfere with my natural, personal interpretations of literature? These questions, or ones like them, are probably the questions most frequently asked by new students of critical theory, regardless of their age or educational status, and such questions reveal the two-fold nature of our reluctance to study theory: (1) fear of failure, and (2) fear of losing the intimate, exciting, magical connection with literature that is our reason for reading it in the first place. I think both these fears are well founded.

With notable exceptions, most theoretical writing – by the big names in the field and by those who attempt to explain their ideas to novices – is filled with technical terms and theoretical concepts that assume a level of familiarity newcomers simply don't have. And because such writing doesn't seem to connect with our love of literature, let alone with the everyday world we live in, it seems that theory's purpose must be to take us into some abstract, intellectual realm in which we try to impress one another by using the latest theoretical jargon (which we hope our peers haven't heard yet) and dropping the names of obscure theorists (whom we hope our peers haven't read yet). In other words, because knowledge of critical theory has become, over the last decade or so, a mark of status, an educational "property" for which students and professors compete, it has also become a costly commodity that is difficult to acquire and to maintain at the state of the art.

Indeed, I think the anxiety that most of us bring to our study of critical theory is due largely to our initial encounters with theoretical jargon or, more accurately, with people who use theoretical jargon to inflate their own status. To cite just one example, a student recently asked me what *"the death of the author"* means.

He'd heard the phrase bandied about, but no one explained it to him, so he felt excluded from the conversation. Because the meaning of the phrase wasn't evident in the context in which he'd heard it used, the student felt that it must be a complex concept. Because those who used the phrase acted as though they belonged to an elite club, at the same time as they pretended that everyone knew what it meant, he felt stupid for not knowing the term and, therefore, afraid to ask about it, afraid to reveal his stupidity. In fact, "the death of the author" is a simple concept, but unless someone explains it to you the phrase makes little sense. "The death of the author" merely refers to the change in attitude toward the role of the author in our interpretation of literary works. In the early decades of the twentieth century, students of literature were taught that the author was our primary concern in reading a literary work: our task was to examine the author's life in order to discover what the author meant to communicate – his or her message, theme, or moral – which is called *authorial intention*. Our focus has changed over the years to the point that, now, among many contemporary critical theorists at least, the author is no longer considered a meaningful object of analysis. We focus, instead, on the reader; on the ideological, rhetorical, or aesthetic structure of the text; or on the culture in which the text was produced, usually without reference to the author. So, for all intents and purposes, the author is "dead." It's a simple idea, really, yet, like many ideas that belong to a particular academic discipline, it can be used to exclude people rather than to communicate with them. This situation is especially objectionable because it results in the exclusion of those of us who might stand to benefit from critical theory in the most concrete ways: current and future teachers at the elementary and secondary levels; faculty and students at community colleges; and faculty and students in all departments at the thousands of liberal arts colleges responsible for the bulk of American education but whose members may not be on the "fast track" to academic stardom.

What are the concrete ways in which we can benefit from an understanding of critical theory? As I hope the following chapters will illustrate, theory can help us learn to see ourselves and our world in valuable new ways, ways that can influence how we educate our children, both as parents and teachers; how we view television, from the nightly news to situation comedies; how we behave as voters and consumers; how we react to others with whom we do not agree on social, religious, and political issues; and how we recognize and deal with our own motives, fears, and desires. And if we believe that human productions – not just literature but also, for example, film, music, art, science, technology, and architecture – are outgrowths of human experience and therefore reflect human desire, conflict, and potential, then we can learn to interpret those productions in order to learn something important about ourselves as a species. Critical theory, I think you will find, provides excellent tools for that endeavor, tools that not only can show us our world and ourselves through new and valuable lenses but also can strengthen our ability to think logically, creatively, and with a good deal of insight.

To that end, each chapter will explain the basic principles of the theory it addresses in order to enable you to read what the theorists themselves have written. Each chapter will focus on a critical theory that has had a significant impact on the practice of literary criticism today and will attempt to show the world through the lens of that theory. Think of each theory as a new pair of eyeglasses through which certain elements of our world are brought into focus while others, of course, fade into the background. Did that last idea give you pause, I hope? Why should some ideas have to fade into the background in order to focus on others? Doesn't this suggest that each theory can offer only an incomplete picture of the world?

It seems unavoidable, and part of the paradox of seeing and learning is that in order to understand some things clearly we must restrict our focus in a way that highlights certain elements and ignores others, just as the close-up camera crystallizes whatever it frames and renders the rest a blurred background. Perhaps this is why, for example, science and religion often seem so at odds, not just because they often offer conflicting explanations of the same phenomena but because they focus our vision on different dimensions of our own experience. This is why it seems to me so important that we study a number of theories in succession, not just to remind ourselves that multiple viewpoints are important if we are to see the whole picture but to grasp the very process of understanding that underlies human experience and to thereby increase our ability to see both the value and the limitations of every method of viewing the world. In fact, one of the most important things theory can show us is that methodologies are ways of seeing the world, whether we're talking about physics or sociology, literature or medicine.

Indeed, because they are ways of seeing the world, critical theories compete with one another for dominance in educational and cultural communities. Each theory offers itself as the most (or the only) accurate means of understanding human experience. Thus, competition among theories has always had a strong political dimension in at least two senses of the word *political*: (1) different theories offer very different interpretations of history and of current events, including interpretations of government policies, and (2) advocates of the most popular theories of the day usually receive the best jobs and the most funding for their projects.

Even within the ranks of any given critical theory there are countless disagreements among practitioners that result in the emergence of different schools of thought within a single theory. In fact, the history of every critical theory is, in effect, the history of an ongoing debate among its own advocates as well as an ongoing debate with the advocates of other theories. However, before you can understand an argument, you have to understand the language or languages in which the opponents express their ideas. By familiarizing you with the language each theory speaks — that is, with the key concepts on which each theory is grounded — this book will prepare you to understand the ongoing debates both within and among critical theories. Learning to use the different languages of theory offered here will also accustom you to "thinking theoretically," that is, to seeing the assumptions, whether stated or not, that underlie every viewpoint.

For example, as you read the following chapters, I hope it will become clear to you that even our "personal," "natural" interpretations of literature and of the world we live in – interpretations "unsullied" by theory – are based on assumptions, on ways of seeing the world, that are themselves theoretical and that we don't realize we've internalized. In other words, there is no such thing as a non-theoretical interpretation. We may not be aware of the theoretical assumptions that guide our thinking, but those assumptions are there nevertheless. For example, why do we assume that the proper way to interpret a story for an English class is to show how images and metaphors convey ideas and feelings or how the story illustrates a theme or reflects some aspect of history or communicates the author's viewpoint? Why isn't the proper response, instead, to do volunteer work at a shelter for the homeless, sculpt a statue, or throw a party? In other words, the interpretations of literature we produce before we study critical theory may seem completely personal or natural, but they are based on beliefs – beliefs about literature, about education, about language, about selfhood – that permeate our culture and that we therefore take for granted.

I hope you will also find, once you've become better acquainted with critical theory, that it increases rather than decreases your appreciation of literature. Think back to your junior high or high school experiences as a reader. Can you remember a story or two, or a novel or play, that you just loved or just hated, yet when you read it again a few years later your reaction had significantly changed? The more we experience in life, the more we are capable of experiencing in literature. So as you grow in your capacity to understand theory, to think more broadly and more deeply about human experience and the world of ideas, the more you will be capable of appreciating the rich density, the varied texture and shades of meaning, available in literary works. It's possible that an old favorite might fall by the wayside, but you'll have new favorites, and you'll have the capacity to see more and therefore appreciate more in everything you read.

In order to illustrate the various ways in which different critical theories interpret literature, each chapter will include, in addition to short examples drawn from different literary texts, a fully developed reading of the same work: F. Scott Fitzgerald's well-known novel *The Great Gatsby*, published in 1925.[1] The focus of the following chapters is primarily literary for two reasons: (1) I assume that most readers will approach critical theory as students or teachers of literature, and (2) literature, conceived as a "laboratory" of human life, provides examples of human experience presumably common to all readers.

Why *The Great Gatsby* and not some other literary work? I did not choose Fitzgerald's novel because I think you will find it necessarily a great work or even an enjoyable work, although many readers consider it both. I chose it because it lends itself well to the critical theories we are studying. Although, hypothetically at least, every literary work can be interpreted using every critical framework, most works lend themselves more readily to some frameworks than to others, and the attempt to read a text using an incompatible framework can be a relatively fruitless endeavor that risks distorting elements of the text, the theory, or both, as we try to make them fit each other. It's a judgment call, of course, and readers will differ as to which theories they are able to apply fruitfully to which literary works. Our task, then, is to know our own strengths and limitations as well as those of the theories we employ, even as we work to increase our ability to use theories.

Another fact to keep in mind as we apply critical theories to *The Great Gatsby* and as you begin to use them to read other literary works is that different theoretical interpretations of the same literary work can bring forth very different views of the work, focusing on different characters and different parts of the plot or generating opposing views of the same characters and events. Theories can also overlap a good deal with one another, producing very compatible, even similar, readings of the same work. Critical theories are not isolated entities, completely different from one another, separable into tidy bins, like the tubs of tulips, daffodils, and carnations we see at the florist. It would be more useful to think of theories, to continue the metaphor, as mixed bouquets, each of which can contain a few of the flowers that predominate in or that serve different purposes in other bouquets.

Thus, for example, while Marxism focuses on the socioeconomic considerations that underlie human behavior, it doesn't exclude the psychological domain of human experience; rather, when it addresses human psychology, it does so in order to demonstrate how psychological experience is produced by socioeconomic factors rather than by the causes usually posited by psychoanalysis. Similarly, while feminist analysis often draws on psychoanalytic and Marxist concepts, it uses them to illuminate feminist concerns: for example, to examine the ways in which women are psychologically and socioeconomically oppressed. And even when critics use the same theoretical tools to read the same literary work, they might produce very different interpretations of that work. Using the same theory doesn't necessarily mean reading the literary work in the same way. If you read other critics' interpretations of *The Great Gatsby*, you will probably find that they agree with my interpretations on some points and disagree on others even when we seem to be using the same critical tools.

At this point, a brief explanation of a few important concepts might be useful. I refer above to other "critics," and it's important to remind ourselves that the terms *critic* and *literary criticism* don't necessarily imply finding fault with literary works. Literary criticism, by and large, tries to explain the literary work to us: its production, its meaning, its design, its beauty. Critics tend to find flaws in one another's interpretations more than in literary works. Unlike movie critics and book reviewers, who tell us whether or not we should see the films or read the books they review, literary critics spend much more time explaining than evaluating, even when their official purpose, like that of the New Critics described in chapter 5, is to assess the aesthetic quality of the literary work. Of course, when we apply critical theories that involve a desire to change the world for the better – such as feminism, Marxism, African American criticism, lesbian/gay/queer criticism, and postcolonial criticism – we will sometimes find a literary work flawed in terms of its deliberate or inadvertent promotion of, for example, sexist, classist, racist, heterosexist, or colonialist values. But even in these cases, the flawed work has value because we can use it to understand how these repressive ideologies operate.

Critical theory (or *literary theory*), on the other hand, tries to explain the assumptions and values upon which various forms of literary criticism rest. Strictly speaking, when we interpret a literary text, we are doing literary criticism; when we examine the criteria upon which our interpretation rests, we are doing critical theory. Simply put, literary criticism is the application of critical theory to a literary text, whether or not a given critic is aware of the theoretical assumptions informing her or his interpretation. In fact, the widespread recognition that literary criticism cannot be separated from the theoretical assumptions on which it is based is one reason why the word criticism is often used as if it included the word *theory*.

Examples of critical theory include Jacques Derrida's essays on his deconstructive theory of language; Louise Rosenblatt's definitions of text, reader, and poem; and even my attempts in the following chapters to explain the operations of and relationships among theoretical concepts from various critical schools. Examples of literary criticism would include a deconstructive interpretation of Mary Shelley's *Frankenstein* (1818), a Marxist analysis of Toni Morrison's *The Bluest Eye* (1970), a gay reading of the imagery in Walt Whitman's "Song of Myself" (1855), and the various interpretations of *The Great Gatsby* offered in the following chapters.

Despite their tendency to interpret rather than to evaluate literature, literary critics have an enormous effect on the literary marketplace, not in terms of what they say about particular works but in terms of which works they choose to interpret and which works they ignore. And of course, critics tend to interpret works that lend themselves readily to the critical theory they employ. Thus, whenever a single critical theory dominates literary studies, those works that lend themselves well to that theory will be considered "great works" and will be taught in the college classroom, while other works will be ignored. Because most of us who become teachers tend to teach the works we were taught, a popular critical theory can result in the institutionalization, or canonization, of certain literary works: those works then are taught to successive generations of students as "great works" with "timeless" appeal.

The last concept I want to discuss with you, before explaining how this book is organized, might be called *reading "with the grain"* or *"against the grain"* of a literary work. When we read with the grain of a literary work, we interpret the work the way it seems to invite us to interpret it. For example, the Marxist interpretation of *The Great Gatsby* in Chapter 3 reads with the grain of the story to the extent that it clarifies the ways in which the text itself explicitly condemns the superficial values

that put social status above every other concern. In contrast, that same interpretation reads against the grain of the story when it seeks to show the ways in
which the novel, apparently unwittingly, actually promotes the values it clearly
wants to condemn. Thus, when we read against the grain, we analyze elements in
the text of which the text itself seems unaware. To give another example, because
The Great Gatsby explicitly shows that Tom, Daisy, and Myrtle are hardly ideal
spouses, our psychoanalytic interpretation of the novel in Chapter 2 reads with the
grain – interprets the novel the way it seems to invite us to interpret it – when
our interpretation suggests that these characters are not really in love with their
mates. However, because the novel presents Gatsby's love for Daisy in such a traditional romantic manner – Nick says that Gatsby "committed himself" to Daisy as
"to the following of a grail" (156; ch. 8), and Gatsby ends up sacrificing his life for
her – our psychoanalytic interpretation may be said to read against the grain when
it argues that his feelings for Daisy are as far from real love as those of the other
characters. This latter interpretation of Gatsby is one of which the novel seems
unaware, given the ways in which the work portrays Gatsby's devotion to Daisy in
contrast to the shallow relationships of the other characters.

Reading with the grain thus implies seeing what the author intended us to see,
while reading against the grain implies seeing something the author didn't intend,
something of which he or she was unaware. However, we generally talk about what
the text intends, rather than about what the author intended. As the New Critics
observed, we can't always know what the author intended, and even if authors say
what they intended, the literary work might fail to live up to that intention or
might go beyond it. Of course, some critics do choose to talk about the author's
intention, and they shoulder the burden of providing biographical arguments to try
to convince us that they're right. By the same token, talking about what the text
intends doesn't guarantee that our analysis is correct; we still must provide evidence from the text to support our view. In any event, any given theory can read
with or against the grain of any literary work at any given point in the text. It's
usually important to know whether we're reading with or against the grain so that
we don't, for example, condemn a literary work for its portrayal of sexist behavior
when that very portrayal is given in order to condemn sexism. Like many elements
of literary interpretation, this is a sticky one, and readers often disagree about
what a work invites us to see and what it does not.

While such issues are important, at this point in time they shouldn't concern you
too much. For now, just let them float around in the back of your mind as you read
through the chapters that follow. Indeed, I think this book will do its job best if
you read it for interest and enjoyment rather than in hopes of becoming a master
theoretician who understands everything. For one thing, reading this book won't
make you a master theoretician who understands everything. Of course, there's no
such creature. And the book you have in your hands is only an introduction to

critical theory, a first step into what I hope will be a long and enriching process. While this book will acquaint you with what many of us consider the most well-known and useful theories, there are many other theories not offered here. Having read this book, however, you should be ready to read about additional theories on your own if you're interested, and you should also be ready to read more about the theories covered here if you find you have a particular interest in some of them.

To help you attain that readiness, each chapter begins with an explanation of the theory in question in plain English, drawing on examples from everyday experience and well-known literary works to clarify key points. To help you look at literature the way a theorist might, each chapter also contains a list of general questions such theorists ask about literary works. Then, as a specific illustration, an interpretation of Fitzgerald's novel through the lens of the theory at hand follows. Next, you will find questions for further practice, which serve as guides to applying the theory under consideration to other literature. These questions (which also can function as paper topics) attempt to focus your attention on specific theoretical concepts illustrated in specific literary works. Most of these works are frequently anthologized and appear often on college syllabi, but you or your instructor might want to apply the questions to different pieces of literature. Finally, in case you would like to learn more about a particular theory, each chapter closes with a bibliography of theory and criticism, "For further reading" and "For advanced readers," that will serve as a useful follow-up to what you have just learned. Chapter 13, "Gaining an Overview," offers you a way to clarify and organize your thoughts about the critical theories discussed in this textbook by providing questions – one for each theory – that each represent the general focus, a kind of bird's-eye view, of each school of criticism. In addition, Chapter 13 attempts to explain how theories reflect the history and politics of the culture that produces them and how different theories can be used in conjunction to produce a single interpretation of a literary work.

It might also be helpful to know that the theories we will examine are presented in logical sequence rather than in strict chronological order.[2] We will begin with those theories I think you will find most accessible and most clearly related to our everyday world and then move on to others in terms of some logical connection among them, so that you can see theories as overlapping, competing, quarrelling visions of the world rather than as tidy categories. Thus, we will begin with a chapter on psychoanalytic criticism because most of us have been exposed to some psychoanalytic concepts in our daily lives, albeit as clichéd commonplaces, and because psychoanalysis draws on personal experiences to which most of us can very readily relate. A chapter on Marxist criticism immediately follows because Marxism both overlaps and argues with psychoanalysis. Feminism follows these theories because it both draws on and argues with psychoanalytic and Marxist concepts. And so on. Although historical categories will not provide our main organizing principle, historical relationships among theories (for example, how New Criticism was a reaction against traditional historicism or how deconstruction was a reaction against structuralism) will be explained because such relationships can clarify some of the theoretical concepts we're using and some of the ways in which, as noted earlier, the struggle for intellectual dominance is also a struggle for economic, social, and political dominance.

Let me close with a personal anecdote that you might find relevant to your initial encounter with critical theory. When I first read Jacques Derrida's "Structure, Sign and Play" – possibly the most widely reprinted introduction to his theory of deconstruction – I was sitting in my '64 Chevy, stuck in a parking lot during a violent thunderstorm. I was just beginning to learn about critical theory, and my reaction to the essay was a burst of tears, not because I was moved by the essay or by the sublime nature of the thunderstorm but because I couldn't understand what I'd just read. I'd thought, until then, that I was very intelligent: I'd studied philosophy diligently in college, and I was a great "decoder" of dense, difficult writing. "So why can't I understand this essay?" I wondered. "Am I a good deal less intelligent than I'd thought?" (Sound familiar?) I finally learned that my problem was not with the complexity of Derrida's ideas, though they are complex, but with their unfamiliarity. There seemed to be nothing in my experience up to that point to enable me to relate his ideas to anything I already knew. I had no road map. I was lost. I think this experience is common for students approaching any new theory (not just deconstruction). We simply don't know how to get there from here.

In a very real sense, then, what I'm offering you in the following chapters is a road map. And I think the journey metaphor is appropriate for our endeavor here. For knowledge isn't something we acquire: it's something we are or something we hope to become. Knowledge is what constitutes our relationship to ourselves and to our world, for it is the lens through which we view ourselves and our world. Change the lens and you change both the view and the viewer. This principle is what makes knowledge at once so frightening and so liberating, so painful and so utterly, utterly joyful. If this book can help you discover that the joy is worth the pain and that the pain itself is honorable – if it can help you value your initial fear and confusion as signs that you've taken your first big step into an unfamiliar territory worthy of the work required to explore it – then it will have accomplished something important.

Notes

1 References to *The Great Gatsby* are cited parenthetically throughout this textbook and refer to the 1992 edition of the novel published by Macmillan (with notes and preface by Matthew J. Bruccoli). Parenthetical references include chapter as well as page numbers to aid those readers using a different edition of the novel.

2 In studying critical theory, adherence to a strict chronological order would pose problems even if we wanted to achieve it. Perhaps the most pressing problem is that the chronological order in which theories appeared in academia differs from their chronological order if looked at from a

broader historical perspective. For example, if we wanted to use academic history as our principle of organization, this book probably would begin with New Criticism (Chapter 5), the academic origins of which can be found in the 1920s, although New Criticism's domination of academia didn't begin until after World War II. If we wanted to use history in the broader sense of the word as our principle of organization, then this book probably would begin with feminism (Chapter 4), which one could argue began with Mary Wollstonecraft's *Vindication of the Rights of Woman* (1792) or perhaps even earlier. While I do adhere to what I believe is a logical order in the presentation of chapters, please note that chronology is not abandoned, merely reconsidered. In addition to being foundational in nature, the first three theories presented – psychoanalysis, Marxism, and feminism – historically precede New Criticism, which is the next chapter offered. Chapters on the remaining theories follow in a chronological order based, for the most part, on the period during which each theory achieved an important, widespread presence in academia.

Works cited

Fitzgerald, F. Scott. *The Great Gatsby*. 1925. New York: Macmillan, 1992.

2 Psychoanalytic criticism

We're starting our study of critical theory with psychoanalytic criticism because, whether we realize it or not, psychoanalytic concepts have become part of our everyday lives, and therefore psychoanalytic thinking should have the advantage of familiarity. If you've ever told an angry friend "Don't take it out on me!" you were accusing that friend of displacement, which is the psychoanalytic name for transferring our anger with one person onto another person (usually one who won't fight back or can't hurt us as badly as the person with whom we are really angry). Psychoanalytic concepts such as sibling rivalry, inferiority complexes, and defense mechanisms are in such common use that most of us feel we know what they mean without ever having heard them defined. The disadvantage of such common usage, however, is that most of us have acquired a very simplistic idea of what these concepts mean, and in their clichéd form they seem rather superficial if not altogether meaningless. Couple this unfortunate fact with our fear that psychoanalysis wants to invade our most private being and reveal us to ourselves and to the world as somehow inadequate, even sick, and the result is very often a deep-seated mistrust of "psychobabble." Indeed, our common use of the word *psychobabble* illustrates our belief that psychoanalysis is both impossible to understand and meaningless. Thus, in a culture that uses psychoanalytic concepts in its everyday language we frequently see the wholesale rejection of psychoanalysis as a useful way of understanding human behavior.

I hope this chapter will show you that seeing the world psychoanalytically can be simple without being simplistic. If we take the time to understand some key concepts about human experience offered by psychoanalysis, we can begin to see the ways in which these concepts operate in our daily lives in profound rather than superficial ways, and we'll begin to understand human behaviors that until now may have seemed utterly baffling. And, of course, if psychoanalysis can help us better understand human behavior, then it must certainly be able to help us understand literary texts, which are about human behavior. The concepts we'll discuss below are based on the psychoanalytic principles established by Sigmund Freud (1856–1939),

Freud

whose theory of the psyche often is referred to today as *classical psychoanalysis*. We must remember that Freud evolved his ideas over a long period of time, and many of his ideas changed as he developed them. In addition, much of his thinking was, as he pointed out, speculative, and he hoped that others would continue to develop and even correct certain of his ideas over time. So the attempt in this chapter is to outline those areas of classical psychoanalytic theory that are particularly useful to literary criticism and to show how this view of human behavior is relevant to our experience of literature. Later in the chapter, we'll also take a brief look at the more recent work of nontraditional psychoanalytic theorist Jacques Lacan.[1]

The origins of the unconscious

When we look at the world through a psychoanalytic lens, we see that it is comprised of individual human beings, each with a psychological history that begins in childhood experiences in the family and each with patterns of adolescent and adult behavior that are the direct result of that early experience. Because the goal of psychoanalysis is to help us resolve our psychological problems, often called disorders or dysfunctions (and none of us is completely free of psychological problems), the focus is on patterns of behavior that are destructive in some way. I say patterns of behavior because our repetition of destructive behavior reveals the existence of some significant psychological difficulty that has probably been influencing us for some time without our knowing it. In fact, it is our not knowing about a problem – or, if we do know we have a problem, not realizing when it is influencing our behavior – that gives it so much control over us. For this reason, we must begin our discussion with the concept central to all psychoanalytic thinking: the existence of the unconscious.

Do you remember the song "You Can't Always Get What You Want" by the Rolling Stones? The idea expressed is "You can't always get what you want, but … you get what you need." This formulation, with the addition of two words, gives us the key to thinking psychoanalytically: "You can't always get what you *consciously* want, but you get what you *unconsciously* need." The notion that human beings are motivated, even driven, by desires, fears, needs, and conflicts of which they are unaware – that is, unconscious – was one of Sigmund Freud's most radical insights, and it still governs classical psychoanalysis today.

The unconscious is the storehouse of those painful experiences and emotions, those wounds, fears, guilty desires, and unresolved conflicts we do not want to know about because we feel we will be overwhelmed by them. The unconscious comes into being when we are very young through the repression, the expunging from consciousness, of these unhappy psychological events. However, repression doesn't eliminate our painful experiences and emotions. Rather, it gives them force by making them the organizers of our current experience: we unconsciously behave in ways that will allow us to "play out," without admitting it to ourselves, our conflicted feelings about the painful experiences and emotions we repress. Thus, for psychoanalysis, the unconscious isn't a passive reservoir of neutral data, though the word is sometimes used this way in other disciplines and in common parlance; rather, the unconscious is a dynamic entity that engages us at the deepest level of our being.

Until we find a way to know and acknowledge to ourselves the true cause(s) of our repressed wounds, fears, guilty desires, and unresolved conflicts, we hang onto them in disguised, distorted, and self-defeating ways. For example, if I don't realize that I still long for the love I never received from my long-dead, alcoholic father, I am very liable to select an alcoholic, aloof mate so that I can reenact my relationship with my father and "this time" make him love me. In fact, even when I do realize that I have this kind of psychological issue with my father, it is difficult to recognize when I am "acting it out" with another person. Indeed, I probably won't see the profound similarity between my father and my beloved: I'll focus instead on superficial differences (my father has dark hair and my beloved is blond). In other words, I will experience my longing for my neglectful father as longing for my current heartthrob. I will feel that I am in love with my current sweetheart, perhaps even desperately in love, and I will believe that what I really want is for my sweetheart to love me back.

I will not necessarily realize that what I really want in wanting this man is something I never received from my father. The evidence will lie in the similarities between his treatment of me and my father's treatment of me and in the fact that, should I succeed in gaining the kind of attention I want from my current "crush," either it will not be enough (he will never be able to convince me that he really loves me; I will think that my insecurity is proof of his indifference), or if he does convince me that he really loves me, I will lose interest in him because the attentive lover does not fulfill my need to re-experience the abandonment I suffered at the hands of my father. The point is that I want something I don't know I want and can't have: the love of my neglectful father. In fact, even if my father were still alive and had the kind of psychological rebirth that permitted him to give me his love, I would still have to heal the psychological wounds he inflicted over the course of my childhood – my feelings of inadequacy and abandonment, for example – before I could benefit from his love.

As you can see in the above example, the *family* is very important in psychoanalytic theory because we are each a product of the role we are given in the family-complex. In one sense, the "birth" of the unconscious lies in the way we perceive our place in the family and how we react to this self-definition: for example, "I'm the failure"; "I'm the perfect child"; "I must always 'come in second' to my brother"; "I'm unlovable"; or "I'm responsible for my parents' problems." The *oedipal* conflict (competition with the parent of the same gender for the attention and affection of the parent of the opposite gender) and all the commonplace ideas of old-style Freudian theory (for example, sibling rivalry, penis envy, castration anxiety) are merely descriptions of the dominant ways in which family conflicts can be lived. They give us merely starting points for understanding differences among individuals. For example, in some families, sibling rivalry (competition with siblings for the attention and affection of parents) can occur, in an important sense, between a parent and child. If I feel jealous of my mate's affection for our child, what may be going on is a reenactment of my unresolved childhood rivalry with a sibling I believed was more loved by my parents than I. That is, seeing my mate's affection for our child reawakens some or all of the hurt I felt when I saw my parents' affection for the sibling I believed they preferred. And so I now find myself competing with my child for the attention of my mate.

It is important to note that oedipal attachments, sibling rivalry, and the like are considered developmental stages. In other words, we all go through these experiences, and they are a natural and healthy part of maturing and establishing our own identities. It is when we fail to outgrow these conflicts that we have trouble. Here's an example common to many women. If I remain in competition with my mother for my father's love (a competition that can go on in my unconscious long after one or both parents are dead), I will probably be most attracted to men who already have girlfriends or wives because their attachment to another woman will allow me to replay my competition with my mother and "this time" win. Of course, I might not win the man this time, and even if I do, once I've won him I'll lose interest in him. Although I probably don't realize it consciously, his desirability lies in his attachment to someone else. Once he's mine, he's not so exciting anymore. On the other hand, if as a child I felt that I won my father's affection from my mother (which he may have given me as a way of punishing or avoiding my mother), then I may be attracted to men who already have girlfriends or wives (and who don't seem likely to leave them) because I feel I need to be punished for "stealing" Dad from my mother. Of course, another way to punish myself for stealing Dad from my mother (or for wanting to steal him or, if he sexually molested me, for feeling that it was somehow my fault) is to be unable to respond sexually to my mate.

A common way in which men replay unresolved oedipal attachments involves what is often called the "good-girl/bad-girl" attitude toward women. If I remain in competition (usually unconscious) with my father for my mother's love, I am very liable to deal with my guilt by categorizing women as either "like Mom" ("good girls") or "not like Mom" ("bad girls") and then by being able to enjoy sex only with women who are "not like Mom." In other words, because I unconsciously associate sexual desire with desire for my mother, sexual desire makes me feel guilty and dirty, and for this reason I can enjoy it only with "bad girls," who are themselves guilty and dirty and whom I don't associate with Mom. This view often creates a seduce-and-abandon pattern of behavior toward women. When I seduce a "bad girl," I must abandon her (sooner or later) because I cannot allow myself to be permanently attached to someone so unworthy of marriage, that is, unworthy of being classified with my mother. When I seduce a "good girl," two things happen: (1) she becomes a "bad girl" and, like other "bad girls," unworthy of my permanent commitment, and (2) I feel so guilty for "soiling" her (which is like "soiling" Mom) that I must abandon her to avoid my guilt. The point is that, for both women and men, only by recognizing the psychological motivations for our destructive behavior can we hope to begin to change that behavior.

The defenses, anxiety, and core issues

Our unconscious desires not to recognize or change our destructive behaviors — because we have formed our identities around them and because we are afraid of what we will find if we examine them too closely — are served by our *defenses.* Defenses are the processes by which the contents of our unconscious are kept in the unconscious. In other words, they are the processes by which we keep the repressed repressed in order to avoid knowing what we feel we can't handle knowing. Defenses include *selective perception* (hearing and seeing only what we feel we can handle), *selective memory* (modifying our memories so that we don't feel overwhelmed by them or forgetting painful events entirely), *denial* (believing that the problem doesn't exist or the unpleasant incident never happened), *avoidance* (staying away from people or situations that are liable to make us anxious by stirring up some unconscious — i.e., repressed — experience or emotion), *displacement* ("taking it out" on someone or something less threatening than the person who caused our fear, hurt, frustration, or anger), and *projection* (ascribing our fear, problem, or guilty desire to someone else and then condemning him or her for it, in order to deny that we have it ourselves).

Perhaps one of the most complex defenses is *regression*, the temporary return to a former psychological state, which is not just imagined but relived. Regression can involve a return either to a painful or a pleasant experience. It is a defense because it carries our thoughts away from some present difficulty (as when *Death of a Salesman*'s Willy Loman flashes back to his past in order to avoid the unpleasant realities of his present life). However, it differs from other defenses in that it carries with it the opportunity for *active reversal*, the acknowledgment and working through of repressed experiences and emotions, because we can alter the effects of a wound only when we relive the wounding experience. This is why regression is such a useful therapeutic tool.

Many psychological experiences can function as defenses, even when not formally defined as such. For example, *fear of intimacy* — fear of emotional involvement with another human being — is often an effective defense against learning about our own psychological wounds because it keeps us at an emotional distance in relationships most likely to bring those wounds to the surface: relationships with lovers, spouses, offspring, and best friends. By not permitting ourselves to get too close to significant others, we "protect" ourselves from the painful past experiences that intimate relationships inevitably dredge up. Having more than one romantic or sexual partner at a time, breaking off romances when they start to evolve past the infatuation stage, and keeping oneself too busy to spend much time with family and friends are just a few of the many ways we can maintain an emotional distance from loved ones without admitting to ourselves what we are doing.

Of course, sometimes our defenses momentarily break down, and this is when we experience *anxiety*, the disturbing, often overwhelming, feeling that something is wrong or that we are in danger. Anxiety can be an important experience because it can reveal our *core issues*, those deeply rooted, psychological problems that are the source of our self-destructive behavior. Let's begin our discussion of core issues and their relationship to anxiety with some examples of the more common core issues.

Fear of intimacy – the chronic and overpowering feeling that emotional closeness will seriously hurt or destroy us and that we can remain emotionally safe only by remaining at an emotional distance from others at all times. As we saw above, fear of intimacy can also function as a defense. If this particular defense occurs frequently or continually, then fear of intimacy is probably a core issue.

Fear of abandonment – the unshakable belief that our friends and loved ones are going to desert us (physical abandonment) or don't really care about us (emotional abandonment).

Fear of betrayal – the nagging feeling that our friends and loved ones can't be trusted, for example, can't be trusted not to lie to us, not to laugh at us behind our backs, or in the case of romantic partners, not to cheat on us by dating others.

Low self-esteem – the belief that we are less worthy than other people and, therefore, don't deserve attention, love, or any other of life's rewards. Indeed, we often believe that we deserve to be punished by life in some way.

Insecure or unstable sense of self – the inability to sustain a feeling of personal identity, to sustain a sense of knowing ourselves. This core issue makes us very vulnerable to the influence of other people, and we may find ourselves continually changing the way we look or behave as we become involved with different individuals or groups.

Oedipal fixation (or *oedipal complex*) – a dysfunctional bond with a parent of the opposite sex that we don't outgrow in adulthood and that doesn't allow us to develop mature relationships with our peers.

You may notice that some of the core issues listed above seem related. Just as fear of intimacy can function as both a defense and a core issue, a given core issue can result from another core issue or can cause the emergence of another core issue. For example, if fear of abandonment is my core issue, I am liable to develop fear of intimacy as a core issue as well. My conviction that I will eventually be abandoned by anyone for whom I care might lead me to chronically avoid emotional intimacy in the belief that, if I don't get too close to a loved one, I won't be hurt when that loved one inevitably abandons me. To use another example, if low self-esteem is my core issue, I might develop fear of abandonment as a core issue as well. My belief that I am unworthy of love might lead me to expect that I will be abandoned eventually by anyone I love. Or my low self-esteem might lead me to develop fear of intimacy. My belief that I am less worthy than other people might lead me to keep others at an emotional distance in the hope that they won't find out that I am unworthy of them. Of course, these are just some of the ways that core issues are connected to one another. I'm sure you can think of others.

The most important fact to remember is that core issues define our being in fundamental ways. They do not consist of occasional negative feelings, such as passing episodes of insecurity or low self-image. Having an occasional "bad-hair day," for instance, does not indicate the presence of a core issue. Rather, core issues stay with us throughout life and, unless effectively addressed, they determine our behavior in destructive ways of which we are usually unaware. In other words, anxiety can tell us a good deal about ourselves because we are anxious in situations in which our core issues are in play. For example, I become anxious when one of my friends goes to the movies with another friend because it makes me relive the abandonment I felt from a neglectful parent whether or not I see the connection between the two events. That is, I feel abandoned now because I was wounded by feeling abandoned as a child, and I am anxious because I don't want to admit to myself that, in some important way, I was abandoned by my parent. So I become hurt and angry with my friend without consciously knowing why. My unconscious knowledge of the reason why is what makes me anxious. In this way, anxiety always involves the return of the repressed: I am anxious because something I repressed – some painful or frightening or guilty experience – is resurfacing, and I want to keep it repressed. Psychoanalysis, as a form of therapy, is the controlled working in and with anxiety. Its goal (unlike that of ego psychology, which is a popular form of therapy today) isn't to strengthen our defenses or restore us to social adaptation but to break down our defenses in order to effect basic changes in the structures of our personality and the ways we act.

Under ordinary circumstances, however, our defenses keep us unaware of our unconscious experience, and our anxiety, even if it is somewhat prolonged or recurrent, doesn't succeed in breaking through our repression. How then, without the aid of psychotherapy, can we learn about the operations of our own unconscious? As I noted earlier, patterns in our behavior, if we can recognize them, provide clues, especially in the area of interpersonal relations and, within that domain, especially in our romantic or sexual relationships, because it is here that our initial unresolved conflicts within the family are reenacted. In addition, we have access to our unconscious, if we know how to use it, through our dreams and through any creative activities we engage in because both our dreams and our creativity, independent of our conscious will or desire, draw directly on the unconscious.

Dreams and dream symbols

When we sleep, it is believed that our defenses do not operate in the same manner as they do when we are awake. During sleep, the unconscious is free to express itself, and it does so in our dreams. However, even in our dreams there is some censorship, some protection against frightening insights into our repressed experiences and emotions, and that protection takes the form of dream distortion. The "message" our unconscious expresses in our dreams, which is the dream's underlying meaning, or *latent content*, is altered so that we don't readily recognize it through processes called displacement and condensation. *Dream displacement* occurs whenever we use a "safe" person, event, or object as a "stand-in" to represent a more threatening person, event, or object. For example, I may dream that an elementary school teacher is sexually molesting me in order to express (and at the same time avoid) my unconscious knowledge that one of my parents sexually molested me. *Condensation* occurs during a dream whenever we use a single dream image or event to represent more than one unconscious wound or conflict. For example, my dream that I'm battling a ferocious bear might represent psychological "battles" or conflicts both at home and at work. Or, to expand on the earlier example, my dream that I am being sexually molested by an elementary school teacher might represent my unconscious feeling that my self-esteem is under attack by any number of family members, friends, and colleagues. (A single dream event may thus be a product of both displacement and condensation.)

Because displacement and condensation occur while we dream, these processes are referred to collectively as *primary revision.* What we actually dream, once primary revision has disguised the unconscious message, or the dream's latent content, is the dream's *manifest content.* The dream images described above – images of an elementary school teacher molesting me and of myself battling a ferocious bear – are examples of manifest content. What these images actually mean is the dreams' latent content, and that is a matter of interpretation. Is the elementary school teacher a stand-in for one of my parents, or are the images of sexual molestation a stand-in for verbal attacks on my self-esteem? Does the bear represent a psychological conflict, and if so, what is that conflict? In interpreting our dreams then, our goal is to recall the manifest content and try to uncover the latent content. However, we must remember that, at this conscious stage as well, we're very liable to unconsciously change the dream in order to further protect ourselves from knowing what is too painful to know. For example, we might forget certain parts of the dream or remember those parts somewhat differently from how they actually occurred. This process, which takes place when we are awake, is called *secondary revision*.

It may be helpful to think of the dream's manifest content as a kind of dream symbolism that can be interpreted in much the same way we interpret symbols of any kind, if we keep in mind that there is no one-to-one correspondence between a given symbol and its meaning. That is, while there are some images that tend to have the same symbolic meaning from dreamer to dreamer, at least if those dreamers are members of the same culture, there are also important individual differences in the ways we represent our unconscious experience in our dreams. So to increase our chances of interpreting our dreams accurately, we must learn over time how we tend to represent certain ideas, feelings, and people in our dreams, and we must know the context in which a particular dream image occurred: what happened in the dream before, during, and after a particular dream image appeared?

Certain general principles of dream interpretation tend to apply in most cases, and they are as follows. Because dreamers create all the "characters" in their dreams, there is a real sense in which each person we dream about is really a part of our own psychological experience that we project during the dream onto a stand-in. If I dream that my sister gives birth to a stillborn child, for example, I might be dreaming either that *I* have given birth to a stillborn child (a failed relationship? a failed career? a failed artistic endeavor?) or that I *am* a stillborn child (am I feeling abandoned? helpless? depressed?). As this example makes evident, dreams about children almost always reveal something about our feelings toward ourselves or toward the child that is still within us and that is probably still wounded in some way.

Given that our sexuality is such an important reflection of our psychological being, our dreams about our gender roles or about our attitudes toward ourselves and others as sexual beings are also revealing. In order to interpret these dreams, we need to be aware of the male and female imagery that can occur in them. Male imagery, or *phallic symbols*, can include towers, rockets, guns, arrows, swords, and the like. In short, if it stands upright, goes off, or has a serpentine form, it might be functioning as a phallic symbol. For example, if I dream that I am holding my friend at gunpoint, I might be expressing unconscious sexual aggression toward that friend or toward someone else for whom that friend is a safe stand-in (such as my friend's mate or my mate). In addition, my sexual aggression might be interpreted in a number of ways: is the emphasis on the sexual, on the aggression, or on both? Do I desire my friend's mate, or am I jealous of my friend's mate? Do I want to become more assertive in my sexual relationship with my mate, or do I want to hurt my mate's sexual self-image as my mate has hurt mine? To decide which interpretation is correct requires more data in the form of other similar dreams, patterns in my waking behavior, and an honest analysis of my feelings about the dream and about the people involved. Analogously, if I dream that I am being held at gunpoint, I might be expressing an unconscious feeling that my sexuality, or my identity in general, is being exploited or endangered.

Female imagery can include caves, rooms, walled-in gardens (like the ones we see in paintings representing the Virgin Mary), cups, or enclosures and containers of any kind. If the image can be a stand-in for the womb, then it might be functioning as female imagery. Thus, if I dream I am trapped or lost in a small, dark room, I might be expressing an unconscious fear of my mother's control over me or an unconscious fear that I have never completely matured as a human being. Perhaps I'm expressing both, for these two problems are certainly related. Female imagery can also include milk, fruit, and other kinds of food as well as the containers in which food is delivered, such as bottles or cups (yes, there is an overlap here with womb imagery) – in other words, anything that can be a stand-in for the breast, which is itself a stand-in for emotional nurturing. So if I dream that I am trying to feed a litter of hungry kittens from a small and rapidly diminishing bottle of milk (a dream that either gender can have), I might be expressing an unconscious feeling that too much is being asked of me by my children or by my spouse or by my employer – or by all of them – or that I am putting too much pressure on myself to take care of others. Analogously, if I dream I am hungry or looking for food, I might be expressing an unconscious need for emotional nurturing.

To move to other kinds of symbols, if I dream about water – which is fluid, changeable, sometimes soothing, sometimes dangerous, and often deeper than it looks – chances are good that I'm dreaming about my sexuality or the realm of the emotions or the realm of the unconscious. So a dream that I'm about to be overwhelmed by a tidal wave probably indicates some fear of being overwhelmed by a repressed emotion that I fear is about to erupt. Of course, water is also related to our experience in the womb, so dreams that involve water, especially immersion in water, might also be about our relationships with our mothers. Dreams about buildings may refer to my relationship with myself, with the attic or the basement as the stand-in for the unconscious. Or dreams about buildings may refer to my relationship with some institution that the building represents for me, for example, the church, the school, the company for which I work, or the law (which, because it represents social rules and definitions, might be a stand-in for my superego). Although we might often dream about fears and wounds that we know we have – that are clearly part of our conscious experience – our dreams about these concerns probably indicate that we need to work further on them, that they bite into us in ways we aren't ready to admit. Of course, recurring dreams or recurring dream images are the most reliable indicators of our unconscious concerns.

Regardless of how frightening or disturbing our dreams are, they are relatively safe outlets for unconscious wounds, fears, guilty desires, and unresolved conflicts because, as we have seen, they come to us in disguised form, and we will interpret them only to whatever extent we are ready to do so. In addition, if a dream becomes too threatening, we will wake up, as we most often do during nightmares. However, if my nightmares begin to occur while I'm awake – that is, if the breakdown of my defenses is more than temporary, if my anxiety cannot be abated, if the truth hidden by repression comes out before my conscious self in a manner I can neither disguise nor handle – then I am in *crisis, or trauma.*

The meaning of death

Crisis brings into the spotlight wounds, fears, guilty desires, or unresolved conflicts that I have failed to deal with and that demand action. I am flooded by the past because I can now see what was really going on. This is how I can know myself through crisis. The word *trauma* is also used, of course, to refer to a painful experience that scars us psychologically. Thus, I might experience the childhood trauma of losing a sibling to illness, accidental death, or suicide and, in later life, experience the trauma, or crisis, of being flooded by all the guilt, denial, and conflict I've repressed concerning that death. And I might also see, for example, the ways in which my parents unconsciously encouraged my guilt in order to relieve their own.

In fact, our relationship to death, whether or not we are traumatized by it in childhood, is a principal organizer of our psychological experience. Before we examine how our relationship to death operates in this way, it is important to note that death is the subject that, it seems to me, has given psychoanalytic theorists the most trouble, probably because of its importance in their own, as well as everyone else's, psychological experience. There has been some tendency to treat death as an abstraction – that is, to theorize about it in ways that don't allow us to feel its force too intimately – presumably because its force is too frightening. So even when, or especially when, theorists have addressed the subject of death directly, they sometimes have done so in ways that tend to keep it at an emotional distance from themselves and, therefore, from us. I think this is the reason – to cite just one example – behind the theory, still held by many psychoanalytic theorists, that human beings have a "built-in" drive toward death, an inborn compulsion toward oblivion, commonly called the *death drive, or thanatos.*

In suggesting that human beings have a death drive, the attempt is to account for the alarming degree of self-destructive behavior we see both in individuals, who seem bent on destroying themselves psychologically if not physically, and in whole nations, whose constant wars and internal conflicts often seem much like a form of mass suicide. There must be something, then, in our makeup as a species to explain this *death work*, this psychological and physical self-destruction. Of course, when we conceptualize our death work as a drive, as something common to all of us and unavoidable, we are off the hook of having to probe too deeply into its workings or to try to change it; after all, nothing we do can alter an inborn human drive. This is why I call the concept of the death drive an abstraction, an idea that operates only on the conceptual level, with no connection to the concrete world of experience. Although death itself is, of course, a concrete reality, the concept of the death *drive* takes our thoughts and our feelings out of the everyday world of action and responsibility, just as abstractions do. And this is exactly why I think some theorists have found abstract explanations of death attractive. Such explanations take us out of the everyday world in which our acts of psychological and physical self-destruction occur.

A more useful, and I think more accurate, way of understanding our relationship to death is to examine it in relation to the rest of our psychological experience, of which it is an integral part. If we do this, we will see that death, in particular fear of death, is intimately connected to a number of other psychological realities. And we will see that individuals respond to death in various ways because of differences in their psychological makeup. In other words, while the processes I am about to describe probably occur in all of us, they will occur to different degrees and with different results in each individual.

First and foremost, for many of us, the thought of our own death keys into our fear of abandonment, our fear of being alone. Death is the ultimate abandonment: no matter how close we are to our loved ones, no matter how important we are in our communities, when we die we die alone. Even if we die in a plane crash with two hundred other people, we each die our own private death. Thus, one of the greatest comforts religious belief can offer is to assure us that we will not die alone and that after we die we will not be alone: God will be there for us and with us. He will not abandon us even when everyone else we know has done so.

Fear of abandonment also plays a role when we fear the death of others. When children lose a parent, when adults lose a spouse, the overwhelming feeling of loss is often a feeling of abandonment. How could you leave me? Don't you love me? What did I do wrong? Sometimes the bereaved feel abandoned even by God. In this context, whether we realize it or not, the death of a loved one pushes our guilt buttons: somehow I must have been inadequate; I must have done something wrong or I wouldn't be punished in this way. In fact, fear of such a loss, of such intense psychological pain, is probably the biggest reason why some of us are afraid to get too close to another person or are afraid to love too deeply. If I can hold something back, not give my whole self over to the loved one, then I will be better able to bear the loss when the beloved dies.

Fear of death is thus often responsible – along with other reasons, as we saw earlier – for fear of intimacy. This is one of the ways we can see how fear of death often results in fear of life. That is, our fear of death, of losing our life, can result in our fear of being intimately attached to life. "When you ain't got nothin', you got nothin' to lose," as so many blues and folk songs have pointed out. This fear of life can also be played out as a fear of risk. The ultimate loss, of which I am utterly terrified, is death. Therefore, I can't take any risk that might result in death. But life itself ultimately and inevitably results in death. Therefore, I can't risk living my life. I must somehow remove myself from it by doing as little as possible and by feeling as little as possible: I will try to be emotionally dead to avoid being hurt by death. Taken to its logical extreme, this relationship to death will result in suicide. My intense fear of losing my life makes living so painful and frightening that my only escape is death.

If we complicate matters by realizing that our fear of death is not merely fear of biological death but translates for most of us into fear of loss in general – loss of my mate's attention, loss of my children's love, loss of my health, loss of my job, loss of my looks, loss of my money – then we can see how death, emotional death if not biological death, is so attractive, at least on the unconscious level: if I don't feel anything, then I can't be hurt. And if we realize that our first experience of death is not biological at all, but the psychological "death" most of us suffered the first time we felt abandoned by a parent, then we can see the ways in which our early experiences of abandonment created our fear of death. This desire not to feel, this desire to insulate ourselves from life in order to insulate ourselves from pain, is probably the most common form of death work.

Is it any wonder then, given the enormous role that death plays in our lives, that we should be fascinated with it? In fact, I think it's reasonable to conclude that the greater our fear is, the greater our fascination becomes. Put another way, the greater the role that death work plays in our psychological being, the greater our attraction is, despite the horror that accompanies it, to death in all its forms: we can't see too many violent movies or docudramas about natural disasters; we can't keep our eyes off the roadside car wreck; we can't see too many news reports about child abuse, rape, and AIDS; we can't see too many made-for-television movies about people who kill their spouses or their lovers' spouses, or too many talk shows on which members of dysfunctional relationships display their dysfunctions apparently with no more self-awareness than children displaying their favorite toys. Our fascination with media representations of death and death work is another example of how we project our fears and problems onto people and events outside ourselves. This fascination thus operates as a defense: if I think about the child abuser on the other side of town (or from a different social class or ethnic background from mine) I divert my attention from the ways in which I've been abused or from my abuse of others.

The meaning of sexuality

Another area of psychological experience that has tended to elicit abstract explanations – and as we saw above, this points to its frightening power in our lives – is human sexuality. For some scientific thinkers, especially in the past, sexuality was a matter of a biological pressure that is discharged in the act of sexual intercourse. Freud, however, considered sexual desire an inborn life-affirming drive, or eros, and placed it in opposition to the death drive, or thanatos. And he didn't stop there. For one thing, Freud realized that our sexuality is part and parcel of our identity and thus relates to our capacity to feel pleasure in ways that are not generally considered sexual. This is why he believed that even infants are sexual beings who pass through stages – oral, anal, and genital – in which pleasure is focused in different parts of the body. (You can imagine the furor and the misunderstanding *that* caused in Victorian society!) Theorists have continued to build on Freud's insights, and psychoanalysis today sees a close connection between our sexuality and our identity because the origin of our sexual being is in the nature of the affirmation or disruption of our sense of self that occurs in childhood. Therefore, our sexuality is one of the clearest and most consistent barometers of our psychological state in general. For psychoanalysis, our sexuality is an inescapable human reality to which we must live a relationship. Our sexuality is not a matter of biological drive-discharge mechanisms but a matter of meanings. In analyzing sexual behavior then, the appropriate psychoanalytic question is "What conscious and unconscious meanings and purposes do I express or enact in my sexuality?" Do I use sex to "purchase" something I want from my mate? Do I withhold sex to punish my mate? Do I avoid sexual encounters altogether? Do I seek frequent sexual encounters with different people? It is interesting to note that these last two questions both suggest a fear of intimacy – if I get too close to someone I will lose myself or be emotionally harmed – because varying our sexual partners can protect us from getting close to any one person as effectively as avoiding sexual encounters completely.

Of course, sexual behavior is also a product of our culture because our culture sets down the rules of proper sexual conduct and the definitions of normal and abnormal sexual behavior. (For psychoanalysis, there is no meaningful difference between normal and abnormal, and the issue isn't one of moral versus immoral behavior; there are merely psychological differences among individuals, and the issue is one of nondestructive versus destructive behavior.) Society's rules and definitions concerning sexuality form a large part of our superego, or the social values and taboos that we internalize (consciously or unconsciously) and experience as our sense of right and wrong. Whereas the word conscience, as it is usually used, generally implies something good – as Disney's Jiminy Cricket says, "Let your conscience be your guide" – the word *superego* often implies feeling guilty when we shouldn't, feeling guilty only because we are socially programmed (usually through the family) to feel so, as when we feel guilty for taking a lower-paying job even when we know that it is a more satisfying or socially important one, or when we feel guilty, as many of us still do, for having sexual relations with our beloved prior to marriage.

The superego is in direct opposition to the *id*, the psychological reservoir of our repressed aggressive desires, and to our *libido*, or sexual energy. The id is devoted solely to the gratification of prohibited desires of all kinds – desire for power, for sex, for amusement, for food – without an eye to consequences. In other words, the id consists largely of those desires repressed by the ego because they are forbidden by social convention. Thus, the superego – or the internalization of cultural taboos – determines which desires the id will contain. The *ego* – the conscious self that experiences the external world through the senses and is the source of our self-image and feeling of stability – tries to play referee between the id and superego, and all three are defined by their relationships to one another: none acts independently of the others and a change in one always involves changes in the other two. In this way, the ego is, to a large degree, the product of conflicts between what society says we can't have and what we (therefore) want. For this reason, the relationships among ego, id, and superego tell us as much about our culture as they do about ourselves.

Indeed, it is an appreciation of the cultural context within which Freud worked that has helped us come to a more meaningful understanding of some of Freud's early concepts that seem to contradict our own sense of how the world works. For example, many women, whether they consider themselves feminists or not, have a difficult time believing that little girls, upon realizing that little boys have penises, suffer from *penis envy*, or the desire to have a penis, or that little boys, upon realizing that little girls don't have penises, suffer from *castration anxiety*, or the fear that they will lose their penises. The explanation for these two phenomena becomes clear, however, when we realize the cultural context within which Freud observed them: Victorian society's rigid definition of gender roles, which was used to oppress females of all ages and to elevate males to positions of dominance in all spheres of human activity. Is it any wonder that a little girl will want (at least unconsciously) to be a little boy when she realizes that little boys have rights and privileges she isn't supposed to even desire? In other words, when you see "penis envy" read "power envy." It's power and all that seems to go with it – self-esteem, fun, freedom, apparent safety from physical violation by the opposite sex – that little girls envy. And what little boy, upon realizing his social superiority to, and power over, little girls, isn't going to have some anxiety about losing it? "You're a girl, you sissy!" has the power to wound little boys (and big boys!) because it threatens them with just such a loss of power. Castration anxiety is thus perhaps best understood as fear of demotion to the powerless position occupied by females.

Lacanian psychoanalysis

While the classical psychoanalytic theory we've discussed so far in this chapter has long been the standard psychoanalytic approach to literature, there is a brand of nontraditional psychoanalytic theory that is beginning to make its way into the undergraduate English curriculum: that of French psychoanalyst Jacques Lacan (1901–81). Lacan's work is rather abstract, often ambiguous, and almost always difficult to understand. In fact, he claimed that writing about the unconscious should be ambiguous and difficult to understand because the unconscious is itself ambiguous (its manifestations in our dreams, our behavior, and our artistic production, for example, usually have multiple meanings), and the unconscious is difficult to understand. Furthermore, there is a good deal of disagreement among interpreters of Lacan concerning what he actually intended by many of his statements. Finally, Lacan sometimes changed the meanings of some of his key terms over time. Despite these challenges, however, I think we need at least to take an introductory look at some of the main concepts of Lacanian psychoanalysis because these concepts are beginning to show up in students' writing, and all too often they are being used incorrectly.

As you'll see shortly, for example, the word *symbolic* doesn't have the same meaning when Lacan uses it that it has when we generally use the term in our literary studies. Yet beginning students of theory often refer to Lacan's use of this term as if he intended it to mean what we commonly mean when we write about the symbols in a literary work, a usage of the word that could hardly be farther from Lacan's. I think perhaps one reason for this problem can be traced to some of the summaries of Lacanian psychoanalysis from which students frequently take their information, which are often too brief and almost as abstract as Lacan's own writing. Certainly, you won't emerge from reading the summary of Lacanian psychoanalysis offered here with a profound and thorough understanding of Lacan's work, but I hope you will have a better sense of what Lacan's ideas do not mean as well as a clearer grasp of what they do.

In order to understand the Lacanian concepts that are most relevant to literary interpretation, we need to begin at the beginning with Lacan's theory of the psychological development of the infant. In its early months, Lacan maintains, the infant experiences both itself and its environment as a random, fragmented, formless mass. Indeed, the infant doesn't even differentiate itself from its environment and doesn't know that parts of its own body are, in fact, parts of its own body because it doesn't have a sense of itself that is capable of such an understanding. For example, its own toes are objects to be explored, placed in the mouth, and so forth, just like its rattle or other objects in its environment. Between six and 18 months, however, what Lacan calls the *Mirror Stage* occurs. Whether the child sees itself in an actual mirror or sees itself "mirrored" back to itself in the reactions of its mother, the point is that the infant now develops during this stage a sense of itself as a whole rather than a formless and fragmented mass. In other words, the child develops a sense of itself as a whole *as if* it had identified with the whole image of itself that can be seen reflected in a mirror.

Of course, the child doesn't have words for these feelings, for it is still preverbal. Indeed, Lacan claims that the Mirror Stage initiates what he calls the *Imaginary Order*, by which he means the world of images. This is not the world of the imagination, but a world of perception. It's the world that the child experiences through images rather than through words. And it is a world of fullness, completeness, and delight because with the child's sense of itself as a whole comes the illusion of control over its environment, of which it still perceives itself as an inseparable part, and over its mother, with whom it feels it is in a union of mutual satisfaction: my mother is all I need and I am all my mother needs. Remember, the child's preverbal feeling of complete union with its mother and, therefore, complete control over its world is illusory, but it is nonetheless very satisfying and very powerful. Lacan refers to this experience as the *Desire of the Mother*, intending to imply the two-way desire just described, that is, the desire of the mother for the child and the child's desire of the mother. During this period, the child's feeling of connection with its mother is, for good or ill, its first and most important experience, and this primary dyad, or twosome, continues until the child acquires language, a change that, for Lacan, is of paramount importance.

For Lacan, the child's acquisition of language means a number of important things. He refers to the child's acquisition of language as its initiation into the *Symbolic Order*, for language is first and foremost a symbolic system of signification, that is, a symbolic system of meaning-making. Among the first meanings we make – or more correctly, that are made for us – are that I am a separate being ("I" am "me," not "you") and that I have a gender (I am a girl, not a boy, or vice versa). Our entrance into the Symbolic Order thus involves the experience of separation from others, and the biggest separation is the separation from the intimate union we experienced with our mother during our immersion in the Imaginary Order. For Lacan, this separation constitutes our most important experience of loss, and it is one that will haunt us all our lives. We will seek substitutes great and small for that lost union with our mother. We will spend our lives unconsciously pursuing it in the Symbolic Order – maybe I'll recapture that feeling of union if I find the perfect mate; if I acquire more money; if I convert to a different religion; if I become better looking; if I become more popular; or if I buy a flashier car, a bigger house, or whatever the Symbolic Order tells me I should want – but we will never be able to sustain a feeling of complete fulfillment. Why? Lacan explains that it's because the kind of fulfillment we seek, though we don't realize that we're seeking it, is that feeling of completeness, plenitude, and union with our mother/our world that disappeared from conscious experience when we entered the Symbolic Order, that is, when we acquired language.

Lacan refers to this lost object of desire as *objet petit a,* or "object small a," with the letter *a* standing for *autre*, the French word for *other*. Lacan scholars offer various reasons for Lacan's use of this particular piece of formulaic shorthand. One useful explanation might be that, in separating us from our preverbal world of idealized union with our mother, the Symbolic Order changed our mother into an other (someone separate from me) just as it changed everything else in our pre-verbal world of union into a world of people and things separate from ourselves. Why a small a (*autre: other*) instead of the capitalized *Other* Lacan uses, as we'll discuss shortly, to refer to a particular quality of the Symbolic Order? Perhaps it's because our relationship to our *objet petit a*, to our lost object of desire, feels so personal, so individual, so utterly private, whereas our experiences in the Symbolic Order do not. *Objet petit a* is the "little other" that belongs only to me, that influences only me. As we'll see, *Other* with a capital *O*, in contrast, influences everyone.

It is important to note that *objet petit a* also refers to anything that puts me in touch with my repressed desire for my lost object. For example, when the narrator of Marcel Proust's *Remembrance of Things Past* (1913) tastes for the first time since childhood a small teacake called a *madeleine*, he experiences a joyful regression to his early youth. He is flooded with unexpected and vivid memories. For him, the madeleine is *objet petit a*. For *The Great Gatsby*'s Jay Gatsby, perhaps the green light at the end of Daisy's dock is *objet petit a,* for one might argue that the light holds for Gatsby not just the promise of Daisy, but the promise of a return to his inno-cent youth, a return to a time before he was disappointed and corrupted by life. As these examples illustrate, although the lost object of desire is, literally, our preverbal fantasy union with our mother, there can be events or even whole peri-ods of time later in our youth that we unconsciously associate with that fantasy union, that are stand-ins for it, and that we therefore respond to as lost objects of desire.

The importance of loss and lack in Lacanian psychoanalysis cannot be stressed too strongly. The use of language in general, in fact, implies a loss, a lack, because I wouldn't need words as stand-ins for things if I still felt that I was an inseparable part of those things. For example, I need the word *blanket* as a stand-in for my blanket precisely because I no longer have my former experience of my blanket. If I felt that my blanket and myself were still in union, were still one and the same thing, I wouldn't need the word *blanket* to refer to it. Thus, the Symbolic Order, or the world known through language, ushers in the world of lack. I am no longer one with my blanket, my mother, my world. So I need words to represent my concepts of these things.

In addition, the Symbolic Order, as a result of the experience of lack just described, marks the split into conscious and unconscious mind. In fact, the unconscious is created by our initial repression of our desire for the union with our mother we felt we had prior to the advent of the Symbolic Order. For the lack we experienced was repressed – our overwhelming sense of loss, our frustrated desire, our guilt over having certain kinds of desire, and the fears that accompany a loss of such magnitude – and as we learned earlier in this chapter, it is repression that first creates the unconscious. Indeed, Lacan's famous statement that "the unconscious is structured like a language" (*Seminar, Bk. VII* 12) implies, among other things, the way in which unconscious desire is always seeking our lost object of desire, the fantasy mother of our preverbal experience, just as language is always seeking ways to put into words the world of objects we inhabit as adults, objects that didn't need words when we felt, as preverbal infants, one with them.

The unconscious is also structured like a language in another way that involves loss or lack. For Lacan argues that the operations of the unconscious resemble two very common processes of language that imply a kind of loss or lack: metaphor and metonymy. Now stay with me here. This argument is less dry and more clever than you might expect. Metaphors occur in language when one object is used as a stand-in for another, dissimilar object to which we want to nevertheless compare it. A *red rose*, for example, can be a metaphor for *my love* if I want to suggest that, despite their obvious dissimilarities, my love has the qualities of a red rose: striking beauty, softness to the touch, the ability to hurt me (a rose has thorns, after all), and so forth. Metonymy occurs in language when an object associated with or part of another object is used as a stand-in for the whole object. For instance, I might say, "I think the crown should be expected to behave better" to indicate that I do not approve of something the king has done, with *crown* as the metonym for *king* because it is associated with the latter. Note that both metaphor and metonymy involve an absence, a kind of loss or lack: they're both stand-ins for something being pushed aside, so to speak. The qualities of the rose and the function of the crown are momentarily foregrounded here: the metaphor and the metonym occupy the stage, not the individuals whom these figures of speech represent.

Metaphor, Lacan observes, is akin to the unconscious process called condensation because both processes bring dissimilar things together. As mentioned earlier in this chapter, in the section entitled "Dreams and Dream Symbols," condensation occurs when we substitute a person or object for several dissimilar persons or objects, which are thus "brought together." For example, I might dream I am being pursued by a hungry lion when it is actually my creditors, my disgruntled spouse, and my dissatisfied employer that are all upsetting me. Analogously, metonymy is akin to the unconscious process of displacement because both processes substitute a person or object for another person or object with which the first is, in some way, associated. As described in the previous sections entitled "The Defenses, Anxiety, and Core Issues" and "Dreams and Dream Symbols," displacement occurs when we substitute a less threatening person or object for the person or object that is actually distressing us. For instance, I might yell at my child (someone who is "under" me) when it is actually my employer (someone I am "under") with whom I'm angry.

In all of these examples of the ways in which the unconscious is structured like a language, note that the key ingredient is loss or lack. In our recent examples of metaphor and metonymy, one thing is always being substituted for another that gets pushed into the background. In our earlier example – of the use of words as a vain effort to reconnect with our pre-verbal feeling of union with our world – something lost is always being pursued but is never found. Thus, in entering the Symbolic Order – the world of language – we're entering a world of loss and lack. We've exited the Imaginary Order, the world in which we had the illusion of ful-fillment and control. We now inhabit a world in which others have needs, desires, and fears that limit the ways in which and the extent to which we can attend to our own needs, desires, and fears. There is no more illusion of sustained fulfillment here, no more comforting fantasy of complete control. This new world is one in which there are rules we must obey and restrictions by which we must abide.

The first rule, according to Lacan, is the rule that Mother belongs to Father and not to me. For little boys, at least, this initiation into the Symbolic Order is what Freud calls the oedipal prohibition. Junior must find substitutes for Mother because she is no longer his alone. In fact, because she is Father's, she is no longer Junior's at all. It should come as no surprise, then, that Lacan says the Symbolic Order marks the replacement of the Desire of the Mother with the Name-of-the-Father. For it is through language that we are socially programmed, that we learn the rules and prohibitions of our society, and those rules and prohibitions were and still are authored by the Father, that is, by men in authority past and present. Indeed, the phallus (the symbolic equivalent of the penis and therefore a metaphor for patri-archal power) ironically holds the promise of complete power yet is the sign of lack because it is the sign of the Symbolic Order. And Lacan's pun on the Name-of-the-Father (in French, the Name-of-the-Father is the *Nom-du-Père*, which is a pun on the *Non* – or *No* – *du Père:* the "No"-of-the-Father) underscores the restrictive dimension of the Symbolic Order.

So enormous is the role of the Symbolic Order in the formation of what we refer to as our "selves," in fact, that we are not the unique, independent individuals we think we are. Our desires, beliefs, biases, and so forth are constructed for us as a result of our immersion in the Symbolic Order, especially as that immersion is carried out by our parents and influenced by their own responses to the Symbolic Order. This is what Lacan means by his claim that "desire is always the desire of the Other" (*Seminar, Bk. XI* 235). We may think that what we want out of life, or even what we want at any given moment, is the result of our own unique person-alities, our own wills and judgments. However, what we desire is what we are taught to desire. If we were raised in a different culture – that is, in a different Symbolic Order – we would have different desires. In other words, the Symbolic Order consists of society's ideologies: its beliefs, values, and biases; its system of government, laws, educational practices, religious tenets, and the like. And it is our responses to our society's ideologies that make us who we are. This is what Lacan means when he capitalizes the word *other* when discussing the Symbolic Order. *Other* refers to anything that contributes to the creation of our subjectivity, or what we commonly refer to as our "selfhood": for example, the Symbolic Order, language, ideology – which are virtually synonymous – or any authority figure or accepted social practice.

It is important to note, however, that in repressing, in rendering unconscious, our desire for the world of our preverbal childhood – the world in which we had the illusion of fulfillment and control, the world in which we believed Mother lived for us alone – we are not repressing the Imaginary Order. Rather, the Imaginary Order continues to exist in the background of consciousness even as the Symbolic Order holds sway in the foreground. The Symbolic Order dominates human culture and social order, for to remain solely in the Imaginary Order is to render oneself incapable of functioning in society. Nevertheless, the Imaginary Order makes itself felt through experiences of the kind the Symbolic Order would classify as misinterpretations, misunderstandings, or errors of perception. That is, the Imaginary Order makes itself felt through any experience or viewpoint that does not conform adequately to the societal norms and expectations that constitute the Symbolic Order. Yet in this capacity, the Imaginary Order is also a fertile source of creativity without which we probably wouldn't recognize ourselves as fully human. One might even argue that the profound value of the Imaginary Order lies in the very fact of its *not* controlling our lives the way the Symbolic Order does. Ironically, it is this "lack" of control that probably offers us the only resistance we have to the ideological systems that constitute the Symbolic Order. Nevertheless, Lacan posits that both the Symbolic and the Imaginary Orders attempt to control or avoid what he calls the Real.

Lacan's notion of the Real is a very difficult concept that he had trouble explaining. One way to think of the Real is as that which is beyond all our meaning-making systems, that which lies outside the world created by the ideologies society uses to explain existence. That is, the Real is the uninterpretable dimension of existence; it is existence without the filters and buffers of our signifying, or meaning-making, systems. For example, the Real is that experience we have, perhaps on a daily basis even if it's only for a moment, when we feel that there is no purpose or meaning to life, when we suspect that the religious and secular values governing society are hoaxes or mistakes or the results of chance. In other words, we experience the Real when we have a moment in which we see through ideology, when we realize that it is ideology – and not some set of timeless values or eternal truths – that has made the world as we know it. We sense that ideology is like a curtain upon which our whole world is embroidered, and we know that behind that curtain is the Real. But we can't see behind the curtain. The Real is something we can know nothing about, except to have the anxious feeling from time to time that it's there. That's why Lacan calls this kind of experience the *trauma of the Real.* It terrifies us because it tells us that the meanings society has created for us are just that — the creations of society — but it gives us nothing in place of those meanings. The trauma of the Real gives us only the realization that the reality hidden beneath the ideologies society has created is a reality beyond our capacity to know and explain and therefore certainly beyond our capacity to control.

Okay, if you've hung on this far, you must be asking, "What does all this have to do with literary interpretation?" Given that Lacanian literary interpretation is quite different from the more standard, or classical, psychoanalytic approach to literature that we address in the rest of this chapter, it might be a good idea just to become generally acquainted with the kinds of literary analysis done by Lacanian literary critics. Our goal here is not to enable you to do a Lacanian analysis yourself but simply to familiarize you with this kind of interpretation so that you'll be more comfortable and knowledgeable when you read Lacanian literary interpretations and, when you're ready, try one yourself.

Perhaps the most reliable way to interpret a literary work through a Lacanian lens, especially when you first try the approach, is to explore the ways in which the text might be structured by some of the key Lacanian concepts we've just discussed and see what this exploration can reveal. For example, do any characters, events, or episodes in the narrative seem to embody the Imaginary Order, in which case they would involve some kind of private and either fantasy or delusional world? What parts of the text seem informed by the Symbolic Order? That is, where do we see ideology and social norms in control of characters' behavior and narrative events? How is the relationship between these two orders portrayed? What do we learn about characters if we can discover where they've invested their unconscious desire for *objet petit a*? In other words, where has a given character placed (or displaced, to be more precise) his or her unconscious desire for the haunting, idealized mother of infancy? Does any part of the text seem to operate as a representative of the Real, of that dimension of existence that remains so terrifyingly beyond our ability to comprehend it that our impulse is to flee it, to repress and deny it?

Let's look briefly at two literary examples. First, I'm sure many of you have read the frequently anthologized story by Charlotte Perkins Gilman entitled "The Yellow Wallpaper" (1892). In what way might we say that the story's unnamed narrator spends more and more time in the Imaginary Order until she, in effect, lives there entirely? How is her recourse to the Imaginary Order a rejection of the Symbolic Order, which is evidently embodied in her husband and brother? How might the wallpaper be seen as a representation of the Lacanian Real? How do the narrator's encounters with the wallpaper illustrate the trauma of the Real? Might we be justified in hypothesizing that "The Yellow Wallpaper" illustrates a situation in which a character finds herself caught between a Lacanian rock and a hard place, so to speak, in that she's caught between two unlivable alternatives: a Symbolic Order she finds too restrictive and the incomprehensible Real? The only position left her, to which she gradually becomes acclimated and which she finally inhabits entirely, is the Imaginary Order. Indeed, the story ends with the protagonist crawling around the room like a very young child, unable to function as a member of society, which Lacanian theory tells us is always the result of total immersion in the Imaginary Order.

For our second brief example, let's try Kate Chopin's frequently anthologized novella *The Awakening* (1899). Here again, we have a female protagonist, Edna Pontellier, who is drawn to the Imaginary Order: in her case, the world of art, music, sexual freedom, and unfettered romance. She is drawn to the Imaginary Order partly in response to the emotionally distant father and older sister who raised her and partly in response to her husband Léonce, who is so thoroughly bound to the Symbolic Order that he is practically its poster child. However, Edna is also drawn to the Imaginary Order in search of something she can't identify. She is haunted by a longing that can't be satisfied, not by her art, not by Mademoiselle Reisz's music, not by her own sexual freedom, and not by romance. A Lacanian reader might say that Edna remains unsatisfied because she doesn't realize that art, music, sexual freedom, and romance are just her substitutes for *objet petit a*, the fantasy union with her mother/her world she experienced in infancy and still unconsciously desires. Indeed, we might argue that it is the strength of this unconscious desire that finally draws her, as naked as the day she was born, into her fatal union with the sea, where her last experiences are sensory, not verbal, memories of her youth: she hears the barking of a dog, the clanging of spurs, the hum of bees, and she smells the odor of flowers. In terms of Edna's experience, then, we might be justified in hypothesizing that *The Awakening* is structured by the protagonist's unconscious search for *objet petit a*, a search that is necessarily unsuccessful, for *objet petit a* is always a lost object that can never be found.

Lacanian psychoanalysis employs many more concepts and is much more complex than a brief summary like this can convey. Nevertheless, even these few theoretical concepts and literary examples can allow us to begin to understand the unique perspective on human experience and the interesting insights into literature Lacan offers us.

Classical psychoanalysis and literature

Of course, there are also many more concepts in classical psychoanalysis than the ones discussed earlier. And as in every field, there is a good deal of disagreement among classical psychoanalytic theorists concerning, for example, the ways in which our personalities are formed and the best ways of treating dysfunctional behavior. Among psychoanalytic literary critics, there is much disagreement concerning how psychoanalytic concepts can best be applied to our study of literature. What role should an author's literary output play in our psychoanalysis of his or her life? To what extent is it legitimate to psychoanalyze literary characters as if they were real people? When doing so, which psychoanalytic theorists offer us the best insights? What role do readers play in "creating" the text they're reading by projecting their own desires and conflicts onto the work? As you'll see when you read Chapter 6 on reader-response criticism, psychoanalysis and reader-response theory overlap in many ways concerning their attention to the psychological experience of the reader. We'll also see in Chapters 3 and 4 some overlap of psychoanalysis with Marxism and feminism as well as some ways in which Marxism and feminism reject the psychoanalytic perspective. Our purpose at this point, however, is simply to cover the main ideas, the basic principles of psychoanalysis to which most other psychoanalytic concepts are in some way related in order to facilitate your reading of psychoanalytic theorists and literary critics with some understanding of the issues they raise.

It stands to reason that you won't find every psychoanalytic concept we've discussed represented in every literary work you read. Our job, when we read psychoanalytically, is to see which concepts are operating in the text in such a way as to enrich our understanding of the work and, if we plan to write a paper about it, to yield a meaningful, coherent psychoanalytic interpretation. From the perspective of classical psychoanalytic theory, which is our primary focus in this chapter, we might attend mainly to the work's representation of oedipal dynamics or of family dynamics in general; to what the work can tell us about human beings' psychological relationship to death or to sexuality; to the way the narrator's unconscious problems keep asserting themselves over the course of the story; or to any other psychoanalytic concepts that seem to produce a useful understanding of the text.

Some critics have objected to the use of psychoanalysis to understand the behavior of literary characters because literary characters are not real people and, therefore, do not have psyches that can be analyzed. However, psychoanalyzing the behavior of literary characters is probably the best way to learn how to use the theory. Furthermore, this practice has been defended by many psychoanalytic critics on two important grounds: (1) when we psychoanalyze literary characters, we are not suggesting that they are real people but that they represent the psychological experience of human beings in general; and (2) it is just as legitimate to psychoanalyze the behavior represented by literary characters as it is to analyze their behavior from a feminist, Marxist, or African American critical perspective, or from the perspective of any critical theory that analyzes literary representations as illustrations of real-life issues.

Let's look at a few specific examples to see the kinds of insights produced by using classical psychoanalysis to interpret the behavior represented by literary characters. A psychoanalytic reading of Arthur Miller's *Death of a Salesman* (1949) might examine the ways in which Willy Loman's flashbacks to the past are really regressive episodes brought on by his present psychological trauma: his own and his sons' lack of success in the business world, success Willy needed in order to assuage the massive insecurity he's suffered since his abandonment in childhood by his father and older brother. The play is thus structured by the return of the repressed, for Willy has spent his life repressing, through denial and avoidance, his psychological insecurity and the social inadequacy and business failure that have resulted. From a psychoanalytic perspective, then, *Death of a Salesman* might be read as an exploration of the psychological dynamics of the family: an exploration of the ways in which unresolved conflicts about our roles within the family are "played out" in the workplace and "passed down" to our children.

Similarly, a psychoanalytic reading of Toni Morrison's *The Bluest Eye* (1970) might analyze the ways in which the novel reveals the debilitating psychological effects of racism, especially when these effects are internalized by its victims, which we see in the belief of many of the black characters that their race has the negative qualities ascribed to it by white America. These psychological effects are evident, for example, in the Breedloves' conviction that they are ugly simply because they have African features; in Mrs. Breedlove's devotion to the white family for whom she works, while she neglects her own family; in the self-hatred of the young black boys who mercilessly pick on Pecola for having black skin; in the assumption by black characters as well as white that Maureen Peal, a light-skinned African American girl, is superior in every way to her darker-skinned classmates; and in Geraldine's inability to relax and enjoy her life or let herself love her husband and son because she fears that the slightest loss of control (whether it be the control of her emotions or of her hair's natural curl) will make her a "nigger," as she calls any black person who does not conform to her standard of dress and behavior. As these examples illustrate, the novel shows how internalized racism results in self-contempt on the part of the black characters and in a projection of that self-hatred onto other members of their race. We see particularly damaging forms of this projection in much of the black characters' treatment of Pecola, whose self-negating desire for blue eyes is the most striking illustration of the psychological destructiveness of racism. Or we might use psychoanalysis to understand the ways in which the Breedloves illustrate the dynamics of the dysfunctional family, the roots of which can be seen in Pauline and Cholly's youthful experiences of isolation, abandonment, and betrayal.

Finally, a psychoanalytic reading of Mary Shelley's *Frankenstein* (1818) might reveal the ways in which Victor's creation of a monster responsible for the deaths of his family and friends serves his unconscious need to punish his father and mother (for whom Elizabeth is an obvious surrogate) and play out the intense, unresolved sibling rivalry created by their adoption of Elizabeth, the "perfect" child, when Victor was five years old. The total absence of any normal childhood jealousy on Victor's part, coupled with his frequent protestations of love for the newcomer who dethroned him as the sole object of parental attention and affection, suggest the repression of feelings of abandonment that, because they are kept in the unconscious, are never resolved. We see numerous signs of these unresolved conflicts in Victor's adult life, for example, in his extremely prolonged absence from his beloved family, including Elizabeth, to whom he is betrothed; in the dream sequence that reveals his psychological merger of Elizabeth and his dead mother and foreshadows the former's death; in his fits of feverish disorientation, which read like dream sequences and include frequent expressions of fear that he is losing his mind or protestations that he is perfectly sane; and in the uncanny way he seems to always make exactly the right move to facilitate the monster's next murder. Furthermore, we might cautiously speculate on the relationship between the representation of psychological abandonment in the novel and the experiences of abandonment Mary Shelley apparently suffered in her own life: her mother died shortly after Mary was born; her father found single parenthood more than he could handle; and the woman her father subsequently wed neglected Mary in favor of her own daughter by a previous marriage.

This might be a good place to pause and answer a frequently asked question concerning psychoanalytic readings of literary works: if we find psychoanalytic concepts operating in a literary text, does it mean that the author has deliberately put them there, and how can an author put them there if he or she lived before Freud or never heard of him? The answer is simple: Freud didn't invent psychoanalytic principles; he discovered them operating in human beings. In other words, Freud named and explained principles of human behavior that were present long before he found them and that would be present even if he hadn't described them. So any literary text that accurately describes human behavior or that is the product of an author's unconscious (which we presume all creative works are to some extent) will include psychoanalytic principles whether or not the author had any awareness of those principles when writing the work. For psychoanalysis, literature, and indeed all art forms, are largely products of unconscious forces at work in the author, in the reader, or, for some contemporary psychoanalytic critics, in our society as a whole.

Our use of psychoanalytic concepts is not limited to one literary genre or to one artistic medium; we can use psychoanalytic criticism to read works of fiction, poetry, drama, folklore, and nonfiction, and we can use it to interpret paintings, sculptures, architecture, films, and music. Any human production that involves images, that seems to have narrative content (the way many paintings seem to tell a story), or that relates to the psychology of those who produce or use it (which means just about everything!) can be interpreted using psychoanalytic tools.

Some questions psychoanalytic critics ask about literary texts

The following questions are offered to summarize psychoanalytic approaches to literature. Whatever approach you use, it is customary to note that the psychoanalytic dimension of the text you examine helps drive the narrative (is responsible for a good deal of the plot). Question 7 offers a specifically Lacanian approach to literature.

1 How do the operations of repression structure or inform the work? That is, what unconscious motives are operating in the main character(s); what core issues are thereby illustrated; and how do these core issues structure or inform the piece? (Remember, the unconscious consists of repressed wounds, fears, unresolved conflicts, and guilty desires.)

2 Are there any oedipal dynamics – or any other family dynamics – at work here? That is, is it possible to relate a character's patterns of adult behavior to early experiences in the family as represented in the story? How do these patterns of behavior and family dynamics operate and what do they reveal?

3 How can characters' behavior, narrative events, and/or images be explained in terms of psychoanalytic concepts of any kind (for example, regression, crisis, projection, fear of or fascination with death, sexuality – which includes love and romance as well as sexual behavior – as a primary indicator of psychological identity, or the operations of ego-id-superego)?

4 In what ways can we view a literary work as analogous to a dream? That is, how might recurrent or striking dream symbols reveal the ways in which the narrator or speaker is projecting his or her unconscious desires, fears, wounds, or unresolved conflicts onto other characters, onto the setting, or onto the events portrayed? Symbols relevant to death, sexuality, and the unconscious are especially helpful. Indeed, the use of dream symbols can be very useful in interpreting literary works, or passages thereof, that seem unrealistic or fantastic, in other words, that seem dreamlike.

5 What does the work suggest about the psychological being of its author? Although this question is no longer the primary question asked by psychoanalytic critics, some critics still address it, especially those who write psychological biographies (psychobiographies). In these cases, the literary text is interpreted much as if it were the author's dream. Psychoanalyzing an author in this manner is a difficult undertaking, and our analysis must be carefully derived by examining the author's entire corpus as well as letters, diaries, and any other biographical material available. Certainly, a single literary work can provide but a very incomplete picture.

6 What might a given interpretation of a literary work suggest about the psychological motives of the reader? Or what might a critical trend suggest about the psychological motives of a group of readers (for example, the tendency of literary critics to see Willy Loman as a devoted family man and ignore or underplay his contribution to the family dysfunction)?

7 In what ways does the text seem to reveal characters' emotional investments in the Symbolic Order, the Imaginary Order, the Mirror Stage, or what Lacan calls

objet petit a? Does any part of the text seem to represent Lacan's notion of the Real? Do any Lacanian concepts account for so much of the text that we might say the text is structured by one or more of these concepts?

Depending on the literary work in question, we might ask one or any combination of these questions. Or we might come up with a useful question not listed here. These are just some starting points to get us thinking about literary works in productive psychoanalytic ways. It is important to keep in mind that not all psychoanalytic critics will interpret the same work in the same way, even if they focus on the same psychoanalytic concepts. As in every field, even expert practitioners disagree. Our goal is to use psychoanalysis to help enrich our reading of literary works, to help us see some important ideas they illustrate that we might not have seen so clearly or so deeply without psychoanalysis.

The following psychoanalytic reading of F. Scott Fitzgerald's *The Great Gatsby* is offered as an example of what a psychoanalytic interpretation of that novel might yield. I will argue that fear of intimacy forms a pattern of psychological behavior that is common to all of the novel's main characters and responsible for a good deal of the narrative progression. Through a psychoanalytic lens, then, *The Great Gatsby* is not the great love story that enthralls so many of its readers, but a psychological drama of dysfunctional love.

"What's Love Got to Do with It?": a psychoanalytic reading of *The Great Gatsby*

One area of human behavior explored in F. Scott Fitzgerald's *The Great Gatsby* (1925) that has important implications for psychoanalytic criticism is found in the romantic relationships portrayed in the novel. Indeed, even for readers not viewing the novel through a psychoanalytic lens, one of the most memorable qualities of the book is the force and endurance of Gatsby's love for Daisy, the emotional magnetism of which, for many fans, renders *The Great Gatsby* one of the great American love stories. For many nonpsychoanalytic literary critics, in fact, Jay Gatsby is a rather larger-than-life romantic hero,[2] quite different from the other characters portrayed in the novel. For a psychoanalytic reading, however, the interest created by the romance between Gatsby and Daisy lies not in its apparent uniqueness but in the ways in which it mirrors all of the less appealing romantic relationships depicted – those between Tom and Daisy, Tom and Myrtle, Myrtle and George, and Nick and Jordan – and thereby reveals a pattern of psychological behavior responsible for a good deal of the narrative progression. As we shall see, this pattern is grounded in the characters' fear of intimacy, the unconscious conviction that emotional ties to another human being will result in one's being emotionally devastated. This psychological problem is so pervasive in the novel that *The Great*

Gatsby's famous love story becomes, through a psychoanalytic lens, a drama of dysfunctional love. For the sake of clarity, let's begin by examining the relationship most obviously based on fear of intimacy: the marriage of Tom and Daisy Buchanan.

Perhaps the clearest indication of fear of intimacy in the novel lies in Tom Buchanan's chronic extramarital affairs, of which Jordan became aware three months after the couple's wedding. Jordan tells Nick,

> I saw [Tom and Daisy] in Santa Barbara when they came back [from their honeymoon]. ... A week after I left ... Tom ran into a wagon on the Ventura road one night and ripped a front wheel off his car. The girl who was with him got into the papers too because her arm was broken – she was one of the chambermaids in the Santa Barbara Hotel.
>
> (81–82; ch. 4)

When we meet Tom, he's engaged in his latest affair, this time with Myrtle Wilson. Dividing his interest, time, and energy between two women protects him from real intimacy with either. Indeed, Tom's relationships with women, including his wife, reveal his desire for ego gratification rather than for emotional intimacy. For Tom, Daisy represents social superiority: she's not the kind of woman who can be acquired by a "Mr. Nobody from Nowhere" (137; ch. 7) like Jay Gatsby. Tom's possession of Myrtle Wilson – whom Nick describes as a "sensu[ous]," "smouldering" woman with "an immediately perceptible vitality" (29–30; ch. 2) – reinforces Tom's sense of his own masculine power, which is why he brings her to fashionable restaurants where they are seen by his male acquaintances and why he introduces her to Nick so soon after their reunion at his East Egg home. In fact, Tom's interest in other women is so routine that Daisy has come to expect it. When Tom tells her he wants to eat supper with a group of strangers at Gatsby's party, rather than with her, because he finds one of the men amusing, she immediately realizes that her husband is pursuing another woman: she offers him her "little gold pencil" in case he wants to "take down any addresses," and "[s]he looked around after a moment and told [Nick] that the girl was 'common but pretty'" (112; ch. 6).

Daisy's fear of intimacy, though as intense as Tom's, is not quite as immediately apparent. Indeed, her marital fidelity, until her affair with Gatsby, and her distress over Tom's involvement with Myrtle might suggest to some readers that Daisy desires emotional intimacy with her husband. Jordan's description of Daisy after her honeymoon reinforces this interpretation:

> I'd never seen a girl so mad about her husband. If he left the room for a minute she'd look around uneasily and say "Where's Tom gone?" and wear the most abstracted expression until she saw him coming in the door. She used to

sit on the sand with his head in her lap by the hour, rubbing her fingers over his eyes and looking at him with unfathomable delight.

(81–82; ch. 4)

However, the history of Tom and Daisy's relationship suggests psychological motives that point to a different interpretation of Daisy's "delight" in her husband.

It is obvious that Daisy didn't love Tom when she married him: she tried to call off the wedding the evening before when she'd received an overseas letter from Gatsby. In fact, her behavior upon receiving his letter suggests that she married Tom to keep herself from loving Gatsby, to whom she had gotten too attached for her own comfort: she got drunk for the first time in her life, and "she cried and cried. ... [W]e ... got her into a cold bath. She wouldn't let go of [Gatsby's] letter. ... [A]nd [she] only let [Jordan] leave it in the soap dish when she saw that it was coming to pieces like snow" (81; ch. 4). Why else would she marry Tom, when she obviously preferred Gatsby, who she believed was "from much the same strata as herself ... [and] fully able to take care of her" (156; ch. 8)? Yet just three months after the wedding she seemed obsessively fond of her new husband. What happened in this short time to change Daisy's attitude so dramatically? Given Tom's compulsive pursuit of women, it is probable that by the time he and Daisy arrived in Santa Barbara, Daisy already suspected him of infidelity. This would explain why she seemed so distracted whenever Tom was out of sight. She had good reason to fear that, if he wasn't with her, he might be pursuing another woman, as she believes he was doing, for example, when she "woke up out of the ether with a totally abandoned feeling," after giving birth to Pammy, "and Tom was God knows where" (21; ch. 1). Rather than hate him for such mistreatment, however, Daisy fell head-over-heels in love with him. Although such a response may not seem to make sense, it can be explained psychologically.

In psychoanalytic terms, a woman who falls in love with a man suffering from severe fear of intimacy probably fears intimacy herself. If she fears intimacy, nothing can make her feel safer than a man who has no desire for it. Upon learning that Tom's interest did not focus exclusively on her, such a woman would have become very capable of loving him intensely because he posed no threat to her protective shell: he wouldn't have wanted to break through it even if he could have. And this is just what we see in Daisy's changed attitude toward Tom, though she certainly wouldn't use this language to describe her feelings, and it is very unlikely that she was even aware of her psychological motives.

As we learned earlier in this chapter, fear of intimacy with others is usually a product of fear of intimacy with oneself. Because close interpersonal relationships dredge up the psychological residue of earlier family conflicts and bring into play aspects of our identity we don't want to deal with or even know about, the best way to avoid painful psychological self-awareness is to avoid close interpersonal relationships, especially romantic relationships. Why not simply avoid romantic relationships altogether? Although this practice may be an effective form of avoid-ance for some people who fear intimacy, the psychological wounds responsible for that fear usually demand a stage on which to reenact, in disguised form, the ori-ginal wounding experience, and a romantic relationship provides an excellent stage. For example, if I was hurt by a parent who was neglectful or abusive, I will seek a mate who has these same characteristics, unconsciously hoping to fulfill whatever psychological needs were left unfulfilled by that parent. Ironically, choosing a mate who shares my parent's negative qualities almost guarantees that my unmet psy-chological needs will remain unmet. However, by this time in my life, due to the low self-esteem produced by my psychological wounds, I probably feel I don't deserve to have my needs met. Because the unconscious premise operating here – I wouldn't have these wounds if I were a good person – remains repressed, its illogic remains unchallenged, and I remain in its grasp.

For both Tom and Daisy, fear of intimacy is related to low self-esteem. If Tom were as emotionally secure as his wealth and size make him appear, he wouldn't work as hard as he does to impress others with his money and power, as he does, for example, when he brags about his house and stables to Nick, when he flaunts Myrtle before Nick and others, when he degrades those who don't belong to the "dominant race" (17; ch. l), and when he toys with George Wilson concerning whether or not he will sell George a car that the poor mechanic might be able to resell at a profit. Even Tom's choice of mistresses – all from the lower class – bespeaks his need to bolster an insecure psyche through power over others.

Daisy's low self-esteem, like her fear of intimacy, is indicated in large part by her relationship with Tom. Falling so much in love with a man who is openly unfaithful to her suggests an unconscious belief that she doesn't deserve better. Furthermore, Daisy's insecurity, like Tom's, frequently requires the ego reinforcement obtained by impressing others, attempts at which we see in her numerous affectations. Nick notes her artifice when she "assert[s] her membership in a rather distinguished secret society to which she and Tom belon[g]" (22; ch. 1):

> "I think everything's terrible anyhow. ... Everybody thinks so – the most advanced people. And I *know*. I've been everywhere and seen everything and done everything." Her eyes flashed around her in a defiant way, rather like Tom's, and she laughed with thrilling scorn. ... The instant her voice broke off ... I felt the basic insincerity of what she had said.
>
> (22; ch. 1)

We see Daisy's affected behavior almost every time we see her in a group, as the following examples illustrate. When Nick joins the Buchanans and Jordan Baker for the first time at Daisy's Long Island home, Daisy tells him, "'I'm p-paralyzed with happiness.' ... She laughed ... as if she said something very witty ... looking up into my face, promising that there was no one in the world she so much wanted to see. That was a way she had" (13; ch. 1). At Gatsby's party she tells Nick, "If you want to kiss me any time during the evening ... just let me know and I'll be glad to arrange it for you. Just mention my name. Or present a green card" (111; ch. 6). When Gatsby visits the Buchanans with Nick and Jordan, Daisy sends Tom out of the room, and then she "got up and went over to Gatsby, and pulled down his face kissing him on the mouth. ... 'I don't care!' cried Daisy and began to clog on the brick fireplace" (122–23; ch. 7). Affectation is often a sign of insecurity, of which Daisy clearly has a good deal.

Tom and Daisy's fear of intimacy is apparent in their relationships with others as well. Neither of them spends time with Pammy. Their daughter is being raised by her nurse, and Daisy's artificial behavior toward the child – "'Bles-sed pre-cious,' she crooned, holding out her arms. 'Come to your own mother that loves you'" (123; ch. 7) – bespeaks, as usual, an eye for the dramatic pose rather than maternal ardor. Neither Tom nor Daisy forms close ties with Nick or Jordan, although the former is Daisy's cousin and the latter, whom Daisy has known since childhood, spends a good deal of time living under their roof. In this light, the couple's frequent relocations – as Nick puts it, they "drifted here and there unrestfully" (10; ch. 1) – are not the cause of their lack of intimacy with others, but the result: they don't stay in one place for any length of time because they don't want to become close to anyone.

It is no surprise, therefore, that Tom's relationship with Myrtle lacks intimacy. He has no desire to be close to his mistress; she is merely the means by which he avoids being close to his wife. And his treatment of Myrtle certainly suggests no deep emotional investment. He calls for her when it suits him, lies to her about Daisy's religious opposition to divorce in order to keep her from becoming inconveniently demanding, and casually breaks her nose with "a short deft movement" (41; ch. 2) when she becomes so anyway. Tom's maudlin account of his final visit to the small apartment he kept for their rendezvous, where he "sat down and cried like a baby" (187; ch. 9), suggests sentimental self-indulgence, not love. The only counterweight to Tom's insensitivity to her is Myrtle's lack of real concern for him.

For Myrtle, Tom Buchanan represents a ticket out of George Wilson's garage. Through Tom, Myrtle hopes to acquire permanent membership in a world where she can display the "impressive hauteur" she enjoys exhibiting at the party in the couple's apartment, during which "[h]er laughter, her gestures, her assertions became more violently affected moment by moment" (35; ch. 2). While economic desperation, rather than fear of intimacy, is the only motive given in the novel for Myrtle's pursuit of Tom, her other relationships also suggest that she wants to avoid emotional closeness. She was apparently induced to marry George Wilson not by any personal feeling for him but by her mistaken impression that he was from a higher class than the one to which he belongs: she "thought he was a gentleman" who "knew something about breeding," and when she learned that the good suit in which he was married was borrowed, she "cried to beat the band all afternoon" (39; ch. 2). George's complete emotional dependence on Myrtle, like his belief that the billboard eyes of Doctor T. J. Eckleburg are the eyes of God, suggests psychological disorientation rather than emotional intimacy. With a man as lost in space as George, Myrtle need not fear his getting too close. And her artificial behavior toward her sister and the McKees, apparently her only friends, indicates that these relationships provide opportunities for social display, not for intimacy.

The romance between Nick and Jordan reveals that they, too, fear intimacy. Indeed, Nick is first attracted to Jordan by her self-containment, by the image of emotional distance she projects. He refers approvingly to Jordan's apparent "complete self sufficiency" (13; ch. 1) and describes her, along with Daisy, in terms that denote the appeal of their emotional aloofness:

> Sometimes [Daisy] and Miss Baker talked at once, unobtrusively and with a bantering inconsequence that was never quite chatter, that was as cool as their white dresses and their impersonal eyes in the absence of all desire.
>
> (16–17; ch. 1)

He frequently uses words such as *insolent*, *impersonal*, *cool*, and *contemptuous* to describe what he considers the "pleasing" (23; ch. 1) expression on Jordan's face. And he remains interested in her as long as she seems to belong to a faraway world, the world of "rotogravure pictures of the sporting life at Asheville and Hot Springs and Palm Beach" (23; ch. 1), a world seemingly untouched by emotional realities. However, once the household she shares with the Buchanans becomes too emotionally "untidy," Nick beats a hasty retreat. After returning with her from the scene of Myrtle Wilson's death, he declines Jordan's invitation to keep her company in the Buchanan home: "I'd be damned if I'd go in; I'd had enough of them for one day and suddenly that included Jordan too. She must have seen something of this in my expression for she turned abruptly away and ran up the porch steps into the house" (150; ch. 7).

Nick subsequently avoids Jordan and shortly thereafter ends the relationship in a manner that keeps him emotionally insulated. He represses the memory of breaking up with her on the telephone the day after Myrtle's death – "I don't know which of us hung up with a sharp click" (163; ch. 8) – although he did "throw [her] over" (186; ch. 9), as we learn when Jordan later reminds him of the event. And even when he meets with her to discuss what had happened between them, he admits that he "talked over and around" (185; ch. 9) their shared past, implying that there was a good deal of avoidance of painful issues during the conversation.

That Nick's fear of intimacy is not limited to his relationship with Jordan is suggested by his two previous romances. Although he claims that he "wasn't even vaguely engaged" to "an old friend" (24; ch. 1) back home in Minnesota,[3] he admits that he came east, in part, to escape local rumors to that effect. The only way he could have been, as he puts it, "rumored into marriage" (24; ch. 1) was if the young lady in question didn't consider herself just an "old friend." We learn that she was more than a friend when Nick decides that, before getting involved with Jordan, "first [he] had to get [him]self definitely out of that tangle back home" (64; ch. 3). Clearly, this relationship was more serious than he cares to acknowledge, and he wants out. Similarly, in New York City he "had a short affair with a girl ... who worked in the accounting department" at his place of business, "but her brother began throwing mean looks in [his] direction so when she went on her vacation in July [he] let it blow quietly away" (61; ch. 3). In other words, when the affair became somewhat serious, he dropped her, again in the manner most likely to avoid an emotional scene. In his relationships with women, Nick is a master of avoidance and denial.

As Jordan's "cool insolent smile" (63; ch. 3) suggests, she shares Nick's desire to remain emotionally insulated, and it is no coincidence that her career and the friends she chooses allow her to do so. Her sporting life provides a ready-made glossy image – "the bored haughty face that she turned to the world" (62; ch.3) – to shield her from intimacy with others. "[S]he was a golf champion and everyone knew her name" (62; ch. 3), but she made sure, through various "subterfuges" (63; ch. 3), that that's all they knew about her. Her choice of friends like the Buchanans, who prefer the world of social image to that of genuine emotional engagement, also protects her from intimacy. They don't want to be close any more than she does. And as Nick observes, Jordan "instinctively avoided clever shrewd men" (63; ch. 3) who might see through her charade. Surely, in choosing men like Nick, Jordan is safe from the threat of emotional ties.

Although the intense affair between Gatsby and Daisy seems to be offered as counterpoint to the Buchanans' marriage of psychological convenience, and to all the other emotionally distant relationships in the novel as well, Gatsby and Daisy's romance has striking similarities to the others. For example, Daisy has no more desire for intimacy with Gatsby than she has for intimacy with Tom. Her extra-marital affair, like her earlier romance with her lover, would not have occurred had she known that Gatsby does not belong to her social class. Whatever she feels for Gatsby requires the reinforcement of the same social status Tom provides. Indeed, Tom's revelation of Gatsby's social origin during their confrontation in the New York hotel room results in Daisy's immediate withdrawal:

[Gatsby] began to talk excitedly to Daisy, denying everything, defending his name against accusations that had not been made. But with every word she was drawing further and further into herself, so he gave that up and only the dead dream fought on as the afternoon slipped away ... struggling ... toward that lost voice across the room.

The voice begged again to go.

"*Please,* Tom! I can't stand this any more."

Her frightened eyes told that whatever intentions, whatever courage she had had, were definitely gone.

(142; ch. 7)

All the years of Gatsby's devotion, as well as Daisy's desire to be part of his life, disappear for her when she learns that Gatsby does not come from "the right side of the tracks." And Daisy herself disappears shortly thereafter, as she and Tom pack their bags and leave town directly after Gatsby's death the following day.

Daisy doesn't realize it, but Gatsby and Myrtle function in much the same capacity for the Buchanans: as psychological pawns in their relationship with each other. Just as Tom uses Myrtle to avoid the emotional problems in his marriage, so Daisy uses Gatsby. Gatsby came along again just in time to buffer Daisy from what seems to be a new development in Tom's extramarital activities. The insistent Myrtle intrudes herself, by means of repeated telephone calls, right into Daisy's home. Tom's flaunting Myrtle out of Daisy's sight does not invade his wife's territory as does his accepting his mistress's telephone calls at home. Just because a mate's behavior has psychological payoffs for us – as Tom's affairs do for Daisy – it does not mean that those behaviors do not also give us pain. That's why psychological problems are so often referred to as conflicts: we unconsciously desire a particular experience because it fulfills a psychological need, but because that need is the result of a psychological wound, the experience is often painful.

Daisy's marriage has become painful, and her affair with Gatsby provides a welcome distraction. If she has Gatsby, she can tell herself that she doesn't need Tom, that she doesn't even have to think about Tom (or, better yet, she can think about how her affair with Gatsby is an appropriate punishment for Tom), and she can therefore afford the blasé attitude toward Tom's womanizing that she exhibits at Gatsby's party. Daisy's affair thus functions as a psychological defense, and as such it underscores the psychological importance of her dysfunctional marriage: if her marriage weren't a powerful force in her life then she wouldn't have to defend against it. In fact, it is the continued unconscious importance of her marriage that finally makes Daisy feel safe enough to be with Gatsby again. As long as she remains psychologically involved with Tom, she need not fear that she will develop the kind of attachment she had to Gatsby before her marriage.

Given that Gatsby and Myrtle are psychological tokens in the Buchanans' marriage, it is symbolically significant that Tom and Daisy, in effect, kill each other's lover. Although it is apparently a genuine accident, Daisy is the driver who kills

Myrtle with Gatsby's car. Far less of an accident, surely, is Tom's sending George Wilson, armed and crazed, to Gatsby's house. Even if, from fear for his and Daisy's lives, Tom felt he had to tell Wilson that it was Gatsby who killed Myrtle (or so Tom thought), had Tom not hoped Wilson would kill his wife's lover he could have phoned Gatsby to warn him. That Daisy lets Gatsby take the blame for Myrtle's death, apparently without a second thought, indicates both her conception of him as an emotional buffer between her and the world and, once her knowledge of his social origin renders him useless as her lover, his expendability.

For many readers, perhaps the most difficult case to make for fear of intimacy is the case for Gatsby. How can we say that Gatsby fears intimacy when he is committed to Daisy as to "the following of a grail" (156; ch. 8), when he kept a scrapbook of all news items concerning her, when he remained faithful to her even during the long years of her married life, and when all the money he acquired during that time was acquired only to win Daisy back? We can make the case by examining what it is that Gatsby remains devoted to in remaining devoted to Daisy.

Although Gatsby believes that his ultimate goal is the possession of Daisy – a belief that many readers, as well as Nick, Jordan, Tom, and Daisy, seem to share – Daisy is merely the key to his goal rather than the goal itself. Gatsby had set his sights on the attainment of wealth and social status long before he knew Daisy. The boyhood "schedule" of Jimmy Gatz (Jay Gatsby's legal name) – in which the young man divided his day, in the self-improvement tradition of Ben Franklin, among physical exercise, the study of electricity, work, sports, the practice of elocution and poise, and the study of needed inventions – suggests that he'd long planned to live the "rags-to-riches" life associated with such self-made millionaires as John D. Rockefeller and Andrew Carnegie.

Gatsby's desire to move up in the world resulted from his unhappy life with his impoverished parents, "shiftless and unsuccessful farm people" (104; ch. 6). And, apparently, the unhappiness of his boyhood resulted from more than his family's poverty, as is hinted when Mr. Gatz tells Nick, "He told me I et like a hog once and I beat him for it" (182; ch. 9). Whatever psychological traumas Gatsby suffered in his youth, they were sufficient to make him completely reject his emotional relationship with his parents: "his imagination had never really accepted them as his parents at all" (104; ch. 6). Thus, from a psychoanalytic perspective, Gatsby's invented past is more than just a ploy to pass himself off as a member of the upper class; it's also a form of denial, a psychological defense to help him repress the memory of his real past. And his claim that his invented family "all died and [he] came into a good deal of money" (70; ch. 4) becomes, in this context, a metaphor for his desire to psychologically kill the parents whose wounding influence still inhabits his own psyche and, paradoxically, receive from those parents the psychological nourishment – the "money" – they'd never given him.

The financial achievements Gatsby planned for himself revealed their ultimate psychological payoff, however, only upon meeting Daisy. "She was the first 'nice' girl he had ever known. ... [H]e had come in contact with such people but always with indiscernible barbed wire between" (155; ch. 8). Through Daisy, he could imagine what it would feel like to be part of her world, to be, as he felt she was, "gleaming like silver, safe and proud above the hot struggles of the poor" (157; ch. 8), the struggles he experienced as a youth, which he can't help but associate with the psychological pain of that period of his life. Daisy is, for him, not a flesh-and-blood woman but an emblem of the emotional insulation he unconsciously desires: emotional insulation from himself, from James Gatz and the past to which he belongs. As we saw in the case of Tom and Daisy, the best way to achieve emotional insulation from oneself is to avoid intimacy with others. Gatsby's outrageous idealization of Daisy as the perfect woman – she can do no wrong; she can love no one but him; time cannot change her – is a sure sign that he seeks to avoid intimacy, for it is impossible to be intimate with an ideal. In fact, we can't even know a person we idealize because we substitute the ideal for the real human being, and that's all we see. Even during the years when his only access to her was through the news items he read in the society pages, Gatsby's obsession with Daisy protected him from intimacy with other women.

It is significant, then, that Fitzgerald could not imagine what went on emotionally between Gatsby and Daisy during their Long Island affair. As the author notes in a letter to Edmund Wilson, he "had no feeling about or knowledge of ... the emotional relations between Gatsby and Daisy from the time of their reunion to the catastrophe" (Letters 341–42). I think it is clear, from a psychoanalytic perspective, that Fitzgerald was unable to provide us with an account of their emotional relationship because there is none. I'm not suggesting that Gatsby and Daisy don't experience emotions, but that whatever they feel for each other is always a means of avoiding feeling the effects of something else, something profoundly disturbing that they want to keep repressed, for example, Gatsby's unhappy youth, Daisy's dysfunctional marriage, and both characters' fear of intimacy.

Clearly, a psychoanalytic lens reveals a much different love story than the one ordinarily associated with *The Great Gatsby*. As the novel illustrates, romantic love is the stage on which all of our unresolved psychological conflicts are dramatized, over and over. Indeed, it's the over-and-over, the repetition of destructive behavior, that tells us an unresolved psychological conflict is "pulling the strings" from the unconscious. All of the characters discussed above illustrate this principle, though its operations are, at once, most dramatic and most camouflaged – that is, most repressed – in Gatsby's obsession with Daisy. For Gatsby's repression of his psychological motives outstrips that of all the other characters put together. His famous words "Can't repeat the past? ... Why of course you can!" (116; ch. 6) are especially meaningful in this context because they betoken the implicit premise on which the psychoanalytic content of the novel is based: that our repression of psychological wounds condemns us to repeatedly incur them. Gatsby's lonely pursuit of Daisy replays the loneliness of his youth, and he seems to feel as much an outsider in the mansion he bought to receive her – the only room he uses or marks with a personal possession is his bedroom – as he must have felt in the home of his parents. Surely, Gatsby could not have been wounded more severely by his parents than he is by Daisy's abandonment of him, both when she married Tom and when he loses her again to his rival the night of Myrtle Wilson's death. Thus, whether it intends to do so or not, *The Great Gatsby* shows us how effectively romantic relationships can facilitate our repression of psychological wounds and thereby inevitably carry us, as the novel's closing line so aptly puts it, "ceaselessly into the past" (189; ch. 9).

Questions for further practice: psychoanalytic approaches to other literary works

The following questions are intended as models. They can help you use psychoanalytic criticism to interpret the literary works to which they refer or other texts of your choice. Question 5 offers a specifically Lacanian approach to literature.

1 How might an understanding of the return of the repressed help us understand the relationship of the reincarnated Beloved (who might be viewed as the embodiment of the former slaves' unbearable pasts) to Sethe, Paul D, and the black community in Toni Morrison's *Beloved* (1987)?

2 How might an understanding of the ways in which death work can be projected onto the environment help us interpret Marlow in Joseph Conrad's *Heart of Darkness* (1902)?

3 How might an understanding of denial and displacement (in this case, displacement of negative feelings for one's husband onto one's child) help us analyze the narrator's relationship to her troubled daughter in Tillie Olsen's "I Stand Here Ironing" (1956)?

4 How might we use an understanding of repression, the superego, and dream symbolism (especially water as a symbol of the emotions or of sexuality) to help us interpret Emily Dickinson's "I Started Early – Took My Dog" (1862)?

5 How might we argue that the experiences of Victor, the protagonist in Mary Shelley's *Frankenstein* (1818), result from his nostalgia for the Imaginary Order and his conflicted relationship to the Symbolic Order? How might we further argue that Victor's feelings for Elizabeth and Clerval, and even Victor's motive for creating the Monster, are all displacements of the desire for his *objet petit a?*

For further reading

Bettelheim, Bruno. *The Uses of Enchantment: The Meaning and Importance of Fairy Tales.* 1975. New York: Vintage Books, 2010. (See especially "Part Two: In Fairyland," 159–310.)

Bristow, Joseph. "Psychoanalytic Drives [Freud and Lacan]." *Sexuality.* 2nd ed. London and New York: Routledge, 2011. 57–89.

Davis, Walter A. "The Drama of the Psychoanalytic Subject." *Inwardness and Existence: Subjectivity in/ and Hegel, Heidegger, Marx, and Freud.* Madison: University of Wisconsin Press, 1989. (See especially "The Familial Genesis of the Psyche," 242–50; "Identity and Sexuality," 296–307; and "Love Stories," 307–13.)

———. *Get the Guests: Psychoanalysis, Modern American Drama, and the Audience.* Madison: University of Wisconsin Press, 1994.

Dor, Joël. *Introduction to the Reading of Lacan: The Unconscious Structured Like a Language.* New York: Other Press, 1998.

Easthope, Antony. *The Unconscious.* London and New York: Routledge, 1999.

Freud, Sigmund. *The Complete Introductory Lectures on Psychoanalysis.* Trans. James Strachey. New York: W. W. Norton, 1966.

———. *The Freud Reader.* Ed. Peter Gay. New York: W. W. Norton, 1989.

———. *The Interpretation of Dreams.* 1900. Rpt. in *The Basic Writings of Sigmund Freud.* Trans. Dr. A. A. Brill, ed. New York: Modern Library, 1938. 180–549.

Jung, Carl G. *The Archetypes and the Collective Unconscious.* Vol. 9, Part I of *Collected Works.* 2nd ed. Trans. R. F. C. Hull. Princeton, NJ: Princeton University Press, 1968.

Segal, Hanna. *Introduction to the Work of Melanie Klein.* 2nd ed. New York: Basic Books, 1974.

Tate, Claudia. *Psychoanalysis and Black Novels: Desire and the Protocols of Race.* New York and Oxford: Oxford University Press, 1998.

Thurschwell, Pamela. *Sigmund Freud.* 2nd ed. London and New York: Routledge, 2009.

Wright, Elizabeth. *Psychoanalytic Criticism: A Reappraisal.* 2nd ed. New York: Routledge, 1998.

For advanced readers

Ahad, Badia Sahar. *Freud Upside Down: African American Literature and Psychoanalytic Culture.* Urbana: University of Illinois Press, 2010.

Armstrong, Philip. *Shakespeare in Psychoanalysis.* London and New York: Routledge, 2001.

Campbell, Jan. *Arguing with the Phallus: Feminist, Queer, and Postcolonial Theory – A Psychoanalytic Contribution.* New York: Zed Books, 2000.

Ellmann, Maud, ed. *Psychoanalytic Literary Criticism.* New York: Longman, 1994.

Hinshelwood, R. D. *A Dictionary of Kleinian Thought.* 2nd ed. London: Free Association Books, 1991.

Homer, Sean. *Jacques Lacan.* London and New York: Routledge, 2005.

Klein, George S. *Psychoanalytic Theory: An Exploration of Essentials.* New York: International Universities Press, 1976.

Klein, Melanie. *"Envy and Gratitude" and Other Works, 1946–63.* New York: Delacorte, 1975.

———. *"Love, Guilt, and Reparation" and Other Works, 1921–1945.* New York: Delacorte, 1975.

Lacan, Jacques. *Écrits: A Selection.* Trans. Alan Sheridan. New York: W. W. Norton, 1977. (See especially "The Mirror Stage as Formative of the Function of the I," 1–7; "The Agency of the Letter in the Unconscious or Reason since Freud," 146–75; and "The Signification of the Phallus," 281–91.)

Sokol, B. J., ed. *The Undiscovered Country: New Essays on Psychoanalysis and Shakespeare.* London: Free Association Books, 1993.

Žižek, Slavoj. *Looking Awry: An Introduction to Jacques Lacan through Popular Culture.* Cambridge, MA: The MIT Press, 1991.

Notes

1 The psychological theories of Carl G. Jung (1875–1961) have generated a school of psychological literary criticism distinct from both the Freudian, or classical, and Lacanian psychoanalytic

criticism discussed in this chapter. Indeed, adequate coverage of Jungian criticism (sometimes called archetypal criticism or myth criticism) would require a chapter of its own. Jungian criticism is not covered in this textbook because its practice is not widespread enough at this time to warrant its inclusion. In any event, students who wish to study Jungian criticism will need to begin with a reasonably thorough understanding of classical psychoanalysis, to which this chapter offers an introduction. Jung's *Collected Works* is listed in "For Further Reading."

2 See, for example, Bewley, Burnam, Chase, Gallo, and Hart. For a darker view of Gatsby as a pathological narcissist, see Mitchell.

3 Many thanks to Professor James Postema and his students at Concordia College-Moorhead for their persuasive argument that Nick Carraway is from St. Paul, Minnesota, the home of the prominent families Nick mentions during a reminiscence about his childhood (184; ch. 9) and the birthplace of author F. Scott Fitzgerald, as well.

Works cited

Bewley, Marius. "Scott Fitzgerald's Criticism of America." *Sewanee Review* 62 (1954): 223–46. Rpt. in *Modern Critical Interpretations of F. Scott Fitzgerald's* The Great Gatsby. Ed. Harold Bloom. New York: Chelsea, 1986. 11–27.

Burnam, Tom. "The Eyes of Dr. Eckleburg: A Re-Examination of *The Great Gatsby.*" *College English* 13 (1952). Rpt. in *F. Scott Fitzgerald: A Collection of Critical Essays.* Ed. Arthur Mizener. Englewood Cliffs, NJ: Prentice Hall, 1963. 104–11.

Chase, Richard. *"The Great Gatsby." The American Novel and Its Traditions.* New York: Doubleday, 1957. Rpt. in The Great Gatsby: *A Study.* Ed. Frederick J. Hoffman. New York: Scribner's, 1962. 297–302.

Chopin, Kate. *The Awakening.* Chicago: H. S. Stone, 1899.

Fitzgerald, F. Scott. *The Great Gatsby.* 1925. New York: Macmillan, 1992.

Gallo, Rose Adrienne. *F. Scott Fitzgerald.* New York: Ungar, 1978.

Gilman, Charlotte Perkins. "The Yellow Wallpaper." *New England Magazine* 5 (January 1892).

Hart, Jeffrey. "'Out of it ere night': The WASP Gentleman as Cultural Ideal." *New Criterion* 7.5 (1989): 27–34.

Lacan, Jacques. *The Seminar. Book VII. The Ethics of Psychoanalysis, 1959–1960.* Trans. Dennis Porter. London: Routledge, 1992.

———. *The Seminar. Book XI. The Four Fundamental Concepts of Psychoanalysis.* 1964. Trans. Alan Sheridan. London: Hogarth Press and Institute of Psycho-Analysis, 1977.

Miller, Arthur. *Death of a Salesman.* New York: Viking, 1949.

Mitchell, Giles. "Gatsby Is a Pathological Narcissist." Excerpted from "The Great Narcissist: A Study of Fitzgerald's Gatsby." *American Journal of Psychoanalysis* 51.4 (1991): 587–96. Rpt. in *Readings on* The Great Gatsby. Ed. Katie de Koster. San Diego: Greenhaven Press, 1998. 61–67.

Morrison, Toni. *The Bluest Eye.* New York: Holt, Rinehart, and Winston, 1970.

Shelley, Mary. *Frankenstein.* London: Lackington, Hughes, Harding, Mavor, & Jones, 1818.

3   Marxist criticism

Students new to the study of critical theory often ask why we study Marxist criticism now that the Communist Bloc in Europe has failed, thereby proving that Marxism is not a viable theory. In addition to ignoring the existence of communist countries in other parts of the world, such a question overlooks two important facts. First, beyond some relatively small and relatively short-lived communes, there has never been a society completely in keeping with the principles developed by Karl Marx (1818–83), just as there has never been a democracy completely in keeping with its abstract definition. Second, even if all communist countries were true Marxist societies and even if all of them had failed, Marxist theory would still give us a meaningful way to understand history and current events. Indeed, one could use Marxist criticism to interpret the failure of a Marxist society. However, before we can attempt a Marxist interpretation of such political events, or of events of any kind, we must first, of course, understand Marxist theory.

The fundamental premises of Marxism

What exactly is Marxist theory? Let's begin to answer that question by answering another: what would Marxist critics say about the preceding chapter on psychoanalytic criticism? They would say that, by focusing our attention on the individual psyche and its roots in the family complex, psychoanalysis distracts our attention from the real forces that create human experience: the economic systems that structure human societies. Indeed, Marxist critics would have the same complaint, more or less, about all the other theories discussed in this book. If a theory does not foreground the economic realities of human culture, then it misunderstands human culture. For Marxism, getting and keeping economic power is the motive behind all social and political activities, including education, philosophy, religion, government, the arts, science, technology, the media, and so on. Thus, economics is the *base* on which the *superstructure* of social/political/ideological realities is built. Economic power therefore always includes social and political power as well, which is why many Marxists today refer to socioeconomic class, rather than economic class, when talking about the class structure.

In Marxist terminology, economic conditions are referred to as material circumstances, and the social/political/ideological atmosphere generated by material conditions is called the historical situation. For the Marxist critic, neither human events (in the political or personal domain) nor human productions (from nuclear submarines to television shows) can be understood without understanding the specific material/historical circumstances in which those events and productions occur. That is, all human events and productions have specific material/historical causes. An accurate picture of human affairs cannot be obtained by the search for abstract, timeless essences or principles but only by understanding concrete conditions in the world. Therefore, Marxist analysis of human events and productions focuses on relationships among socioeconomic classes, both within a society and among societies, and it explains all human activities in terms of the distribution and dynamics of economic power. And Marxist *praxis*, or methodology, dictates that theoretical ideas can be judged to have value only in terms of their concrete applications, that is, only in terms of their applicability to the real world.

From a Marxist perspective, differences in socioeconomic class divide people in ways that are much more significant than differences in religion, race, ethnicity, or gender. For the real battle lines are drawn, to put the matter simply, between the "haves" and the "have-nots," between the *bourgeoisie* – those who control the world's natural, economic, and human resources – and the *proletariat,* the majority of the global population who live in substandard conditions and who have always performed the manual labor – the mining, the factory work, the ditch digging, the railroad building – that fills the coffers of the rich. Unfortunately, those in the proletariat are often the last to recognize this fact; they usually permit differences in religion, race, ethnicity, or gender to separate them into warring factions that accomplish little or no social change. Few Marxists today believe, as Marx did, that the proletariat will one day spontaneously develop the class consciousness needed to rise up in violent revolution against their oppressors and create a classless society. However, were the proletariat of any given country to act as a group, regardless of their differences (for example, were they all to vote for the same political candidates, boycott the same companies, and go on strike until their needs were met), the current power structure would be radically altered.

The class system in America

It has become increasingly difficult in the United States to clearly place people either in the bourgeoisie or the proletariat. How do we classify, for example, the person who employs several workers in a small, family-owned business but whose yearly profits are less than the annual wages of a salesperson working for a big corporation?

In other words, in this country at least, some workers earn more than some owners. To complicate matters further, the words *bourgeoisie* (noun) and *bourgeois* (adjective) have come to refer in everyday speech to the middle class in general, with no distinction between owners and wage earners. At this point in history, therefore, it might be more useful to classify Americans according to socio-economic lifestyle, without reference to the manner in which their income is acquired. For the sake of clarity, let's take a moment to do so now by drawing a simplified sketch of the major socioeconomic divisions in contemporary America.

Whether or not we would agree on which individuals belong to the bourgeoisie and which to the proletariat, most of us can observe the striking difference in socioeconomic lifestyle among the following groups: the homeless, who have few, if any, material possessions and little hope of improvement; the poor, whose limited educational and career opportunities keep them struggling to support their families and living in fear of becoming homeless; the financially established, who own nice homes and cars and can usually afford to send their children to college; the well-to-do, who can afford two or more expensive homes, several cars, and luxury items; and the extremely wealthy, such as the owners of large, well-established corporations, for whom money (mansions, limousines, personal airplanes, yachts) is no problem whatsoever. We might loosely refer to these five groups as America's underclass, lower class, middle class, upper class, and "aristocracy."

Clearly, members of the underclass and the lower class are economically oppressed: they suffer the ills of economic privation, are hardest hit by economic recessions, and have limited means of improving their lot. In sharp contrast, members of the upper class and "aristocracy" are economically privileged: they enjoy luxurious lifestyles, are least affected by economic recessions, and have a great deal of financial security. But what about members of the middle class? Are they economically oppressed or economically privileged? Of course, the answer is prob-ably both. Their socioeconomic lifestyle is certainly better than that of the classes below them, but they'll probably never own a mansion; they have more financial stability than the lower classes, yet they are often hard hit by economic recessions and usually have good reason to worry about their financial future; they benefit from institutionalized forms of economic security, such as good medical insurance and pension plans, but they shoulder an enormous (and, many would argue, unfair) tax burden relative to their income.

Why don't the economically oppressed fight back? What keeps the lower classes "in their place" and at the mercy of the wealthy? At least for the poor and home-less in America today, the struggle to survive is certainly a factor in keeping them down. Who has the time to become politically active, or even politically aware, when one is struggling just to stay alive and feed one's children? Other elements oppressing them are the police and other government strong-arm agencies, who, under government orders, have mistreated the lower-class and underclass poor, who are perceived as a threat to the power structure, such as the striking workers who were arrested, beaten, or killed in the early days of American labor unions or the homeless who were routed from their cardboard boxes in New York's Central Park some years ago because their shanties, in effect, "ruined the view" from the windows of the wealthy living in posh apartments nearby. The poor are oppressed even more effectively, however, by ideology.

The role of ideology

For Marxism, an (ideology) is a belief system, and all belief systems are products of cultural conditioning. For example, capitalism, communism, Marxism, patriotism, religion, ethical systems, humanism, environmentalism, astrology, and karate are all ideologies. The critical theories we will study in this book are all ideologies. Even our assumption that nature behaves according to the laws of science is an ideology. However, although almost any experience or field of study we can think of has an ideological component, not all ideologies are equally productive or desirable. Undesirable ideologies promote repressive political agendas and, in order to ensure their acceptance among the citizenry, pass themselves off as natural ways of seeing the world instead of acknowledging themselves as ideologies. "It's natural for men to hold leadership positions because their biological superiority renders them more physically, intellectually, and emotionally capable than women" is a sexist ideology that sells itself as a function of nature, rather than as a product of cultural belief. "Every family wants to own its own home on its own land" is a capitalist ideology that sells itself as natural by pointing, for example, to the fact that almost all Americans want to own their own property, without acknowledging that this desire is created in us by the capitalist culture in which we live. Many Native American nations, in contrast, don't believe that land is something that can be owned. For them, it's like trying to own the air we breathe.

By posing as natural ways of seeing the world, repressive ideologies prevent us from understanding the material/historical conditions in which we live because they refuse to acknowledge that those conditions have any bearing on the way we see the world. Marxism, a nonrepressive ideology, acknowledges that it is an ideology. Marxism works to make us constantly aware of all the ways in which we are products of material/historical circumstances and of the repressive ideologies that serve to blind us to this fact in order to keep us subservient to the ruling power system. Although Marxist theorists differ in their estimation of the degree to which we are "programmed" by ideology, all agree that the most successful ideologies are not recognized as ideologies but are thought to be natural ways of seeing the world by the people who subscribe to them. Thus, although we could argue that the economic interests of middle-class America would best be served by a political alliance with the poor in order to attain a more equitable distribution of

America's enormous wealth among the middle and lower classes, in political matters the middle class generally sides with the wealthy against the poor.

To cite one simple example, the middle class tends to resent the poor because so much middle-class tax money goes to government programs to help the poor. However, the middle class fails to realize two important socioeconomic realities: (1) that it is the wealthy in positions of power who decide who pays the most taxes and how the money will be spent (in other words, it is the wealthy who make the middle class support the poor), and (2) that the poor receive but a small portion of the funds earmarked for them because so much of it goes, through kickbacks and "creative" bookkeeping, into the pockets of the wealthy who control our social services and the middle-class employees who administer them. What is the ideology that blinds the middle class to the socioeconomic inequities in contemporary America? In large part, the middle class is blinded by their belief in the American dream, which tells them that financial success is simply the product of initiative and hard work. Therefore, if some people are poor, it is because they are shiftless and lazy.

In this country, we believe that it is natural to want to "get ahead," to want to own a better house and wear better clothes. The key word here is *better*, which refers not only to "better than I had before" but also to "better than other people have." That is, embedded within the belief in "getting ahead" is the belief in competition as a natural or necessary mode of being. After all, haven't we learned from science that nature demands the "survival of the fittest"? And doesn't this view of human behavior fit perfectly with the belief in rugged individualism upon which America was founded and without which it would not have become the great nation it is today? For that matter, isn't all of the above – getting ahead, competition, and rugged individualism – part and parcel of the American dream, according to which we are all born equal and are free to advance as far as our own "get-up-and-go" will take us?

While this view of human endeavor may seem, to most Americans at least, quite natural and proper – and we can certainly point to the success of self-made men like Benjamin Franklin and Abraham Lincoln to underscore its apparent fairness – Marxist analysis reveals that the American dream is an ideology, a belief system, not an innate or natural way of seeing the world. And like all ideologies that support the socioeconomic inequities of capitalist countries like ours – that is, countries in which the means of production (natural, financial, and human resources) are privately owned and in which those who own them inevitably become the dominant class – the American dream blinds us to the enormities of its own failure, past and present: the genocide of Native Americans, the enslavement of Africans, the virtual enslavement of indentured servants, the abuses suffered by immigrant populations, the widening economic gulf between America's rich and poor, the growing ranks of the homeless and hungry, the enduring socioeconomic barriers against women and people of color, and the like. In other words, the success of the American dream – the acquisition of a wealthy lifestyle for a few – rests on the misery of the many. And it is the power of ideology, of our belief in the naturalness and fairness of this dream, that has blinded us to the harsh realities it masks.

Some of us might want to pause at this point to ask, "But isn't the American dream an ideal? Although our ideals may fail in practice, shouldn't we continue to aspire to them? Should we abandon, for example, the ideal that human life is sacred just because we sometimes fail to live up to it?" For Marxism, when an ideal functions to mask its own failure, it is a false ideal, or *false consciousness,* whose real purpose is to promote the interests of those in power. In the case of the American dream, then, the question for Marxist analysis is, "How does the American dream enlist the support of all Americans, even of those who fail to achieve it, in promoting the interests of those in power?"

The answer, at least in part, is that the American dream, much like the state lotteries or the big-bucks sweepstakes that are its latest incarnation, opens the possibility that anyone can win, and, like gambling addicts, we cling to that possibility. In fact, the less financial security we have, the more we need something to hope for. The American dream also tells us what we want to hear: that we are all "as good as" the wealthiest among us. It's not supposed to matter that the wealthy don't think I'm as good as they are as long as I believe it's true. And it's not supposed to matter that "as good as" doesn't mean entitled to the same health care, material comforts, or social privileges, including the privilege of hiring the best lawyers should the need arise. In my need to "feel good about myself," especially if my life is burdened with financial worries, I will cling to the ego gratification offered by the American dream. Analogously, if I want to avoid the guilt that accompanies my acquisition of a large fortune while so many of my fellow citizens can barely eke out a living, I will be comforted by the assurance I receive from the American dream that I deserve whatever wealth I have the initiative to amass. Indeed, the power of the American dream to mask material/historical reality is such that it can invoke an America for whom class doesn't matter and plunk that ideology down right in the middle of an America whose class system is too complex for me to map, beyond the rough outline provided earlier.

From a Marxist perspective, the role of ideology in maintaining those in power is so important that we should briefly examine a few more examples so that we can see how it works. *Classism,* for example, is an ideology that equates one's value as a human being with the social class to which one belongs: the higher one's social class, the better one is assumed to be because quality is "in the blood," that is, inborn. From a classist perspective, people at the top of the social scale are naturally superior to those below them: those at the top are more intelligent, more responsible, more trustworthy, more ethical, and so on. People at the bottom of the social scale, it follows, are naturally shiftless, lazy, and irresponsible. Therefore, it is only right and natural that those from the highest social class should hold all the positions of power and leadership because they are naturally suited to such roles and are the only ones who can be trusted to perform them properly. Classism thus inevitably promotes social, economic, and political discrimination against the poor.

Patriotism is an ideology that keeps poor people fighting wars against poor people from other countries (one way or another, sufficient money can generally keep one out of the armed forces during war time or, at least, out of the combat units) while the rich on both sides rake in the profits of war-time economy. Because patriotism leads the poor to see themselves as members of a nation, separate from other nations, rather than as members of a worldwide oppressed class opposed to all privileged classes including those from their own country, it prevents the poor from banding together to improve their condition globally.

Religion, which Karl Marx called "the opiate of the masses," is an ideology that helps to keep the faithful poor satisfied with their lot in life, or at least tolerant of it, much as a tranquilizer might do. The question of God's existence is not the fundamental issue for Marxist analysis; rather, what human beings do in God's name – organized religion – is the focus. For example, while many Christian religious groups work to feed, clothe, house, and even educate the world's poor, the religious tenets that are disseminated along with the food and clothing include the conviction that the poor, if they remain nonviolent, will find their reward in heaven. Obviously, the 10 percent (or less) of the world's population who own 90 percent (or more) of the world's wealth have a vested interest in promoting this aspect of Christian belief among the poor and historically have exploited Christianity for just this purpose. Indeed, the Bible has been used successfully to justify and promote the enslavement of Africans in America and the subordination of women and of lesbian, gay, bisexual, and transgender (LGBT) individuals.

Rugged individualism, which, as we have seen, is a cornerstone of the American dream, is an ideology that romanticizes the individual who strikes out alone in pursuit of a goal not easily achieved, a goal that often involves risk and one that most people would not readily undertake. In the past, such a goal would have been, for example, the rush for gold and silver on the American frontier, an attempt in which many individuals risked losing their lives. Today, such a goal might be the undertaking of a high-risk business, in which one risks losing all one's money. Although it may sound like an admirable character trait, Marxist thinkers consider rugged individualism an oppressive ideology because it puts self-interest above the needs – and even above the survival – of other people. By keeping the focus on "me" instead of on "us," rugged individualism works against the well-being of society as a whole and of underprivileged people in particular. Rugged individualism also gives us the illusion that we make our own decisions without being significantly influenced by ideology of any sort when, in fact, we're all influenced by various ideologies all the time, whether we realize it or not.

Consumerism, or shop-'til-you-drop-ism, is another cornerstone of the American dream. Consumerism is an ideology that says "I'm only as good as what I buy." Thus, it simultaneously fulfills two ideological purposes: it gives me the illusion that I can be "as good as" the wealthy if I can purchase what they purchase or a reasonable facsimile thereof (albeit on credit) and it fills the coffers of the wealthy who manufacture and sell the consumer products I buy and who reap the 15–20 percent interest on my credit-card bills.

Of course, there are many more capitalist ideologies we could analyze. These few are intended just to illustrate in general terms the Marxist view of repressive ideologies. Our goal as Marxist critics is to identify the ideology at work in cultural productions – literature, films, paintings, music, television programs, commercial advertisements, education, popular philosophy, religion, forms of entertainment, and so on – and to analyze how that ideology supports or undermines the socioeconomic system (the power structure) in which that cultural production plays a significant role. While Marxists believe that all social phenomena, from child-rearing practices to environmental concerns, are cultural productions – and that culture cannot be separated from the socioeconomic system that produced it – many Marxists are interested in cultural productions in the narrower sense of the word: for example, art, music, film, theater, literature, and television. For these critics, culture, in this narrower sense, is the primary bearer of ideology because it reaches so many people in what seems to be an innocent form: entertainment. When we are being entertained, our guard is down, so to speak, and we are especially vulnerable to ideological programming.

Consider, for example, a representation of a homeless man I saw on a situation comedy on television. The man sleeps every night in a bus station, where the sitcom is set. We see him in a public phone booth, talking on the phone, when he is interrupted by one of the workers, who gives him his mail. (Big laugh: the guy hangs around the station so much that the post office thinks it's his home!) He inspects his mail and makes a casual comment like, "I wish the post office would do something about all this junk mail!" (Another big laugh: instead of complaining about – or even noticing – the situation he's in, he's complaining about junk mail!) The scene may seem innocent enough, but a Marxist critic would see in it an implied message that serves the capitalist power structure in America: "Don't worry about the homeless; they're doing all right for themselves" or, worse, "The homeless like to live this way; it's as natural to them as our lifestyle is to us."

How does the American dream contribute to just such a view of the homeless? It does so by promoting the myth, which we discussed earlier, that financial success can be achieved in this country merely through initiative and hard work. Therefore, the poor must be shiftless and lazy. We are thus encouraged to forget, for example, that a homeless person can't get a job without an address and can't get an address without a job; that most homeless people become so due to economic circumstances wholly beyond their control; and that many people are homeless today because they were evicted from the mental health institutions closed during the Reagan administration and are, therefore, in need of increasingly expensive medication and/or therapy as well as homes.

Human behavior, the commodity, and the family

Although the later works of Karl Marx focus on economics, on the workings of society as a whole, rather than on the individual, it is important to remember that he began as a student of human behavior – we might even say a social psychologist – in his own right. For example, his concern over the rise of industrialism in the mid-nineteenth century was a concern for the effects of factory work on people who were forced to sell their labor to the industries that were replacing independent artisans and farmers. Because factory workers produced such large quantities of products, none of which bore their names or any other mark of their individual contributions, Marx observed that they became disassociated not only from the products they produced but from their own labor as well, and he noted the debilitating effects of what he called alienated labor on the laborer and on the society as a whole.

Similarly, Marx's concern over the rise of a capitalist economy was a concern for the effects of capitalism on human values. In a capitalist economic system, an object's value becomes impersonal. Its value is translated into a monetary "equivalent" – the word *capital* means money – and determined solely in terms of its relationship to a monetary market. The question becomes, how many people will buy the object, and how much money will they be willing to pay for it? Whether or not people really need the object in question and whether or not it is really worth its assigned price are irrelevant issues. In Anglo-European culture, capitalism replaced a barter economy in which labor or goods were exchanged for other labor or goods, depending on the abilities and needs of the individuals involved in the exchange. The focus of many later Marxists on the ways in which ideology is transmitted through popular culture and operates in our emotional lives is thus a natural extension of Marx's own interest in human behavior and experience.

Of course, many Marxist insights into human behavior involve the damaging effects of capitalism on human psychology, and those damaging effects often appear in our relationship to the *commodity*. For Marxism, a commodity's value lies not in what it can do (*use value*) but in the money or other commodities for which it can be traded (*exchange value*) or in the social status it confers on its owner (*sign-exchange value*). An object becomes a commodity only when it has exchange value or sign-exchange value, and both forms of value are determined by the society in which the object is exchanged. For example, if I read a book for pleasure or for information, or even if I use it to prop up a table leg, the book has use value. If I sell that same book, it has exchange value. If I leave that book out on my coffee table to impress my date, it has sign-exchange value. Commodification is the act of relating to objects or persons in terms of their exchange value or sign-exchange value. I commodify a work of art when I buy it as a financial investment, that is, with the intention of selling it for more money, or when I buy it to impress other people with my refined tastes. If I purchase and display costly goods or services excessively in order to impress people with my wealth, I am guilty of conspicuous consumption, as when I buy a full-length, white mink coat (or even a pair of $100 designer sunglasses), not just for the object's usefulness or beauty but in order to show the world how much money I have.

Finally, I commodify human beings when I structure my relations with them to promote my own advancement financially or socially. Most of us know what it means to treat a person like an object (for example, a sex object). An object becomes a commodity, however, only when it has exchange value or sign-exchange value. Do I choose my dates based on how much money I think they will spend on me (their exchange value) or on how much I think they will impress my friends (their sign-exchange value)? If so, then I'm commodifying them.

From a Marxist perspective, because the survival of capitalism, which is a market economy, depends on consumerism, it promotes sign-exchange value as our primary mode of relating to the world around us. What could be better for a capitalist economy than for its members to be unable to "feel good about them-selves" unless they acquire a fashionable "look" that can be maintained only by the continual purchase of new clothing, new cosmetic products, and new cosmetic services? In other words, in economic terms, it's in capitalism's best interests to promote whatever personal insecurities will motivate us to buy consumer goods. (Are my teeth not white enough? Should my hair be blonder? Should my muscles bulge more? Is my breath fresh enough?) And because the kinds of personal inse-curities that make us buy consumer products are produced by comparing ourselves with other people (Are my teeth as white as his? Is my hair as blond as hers?), competition is promoted not just among companies who want to sell products but among people who feel they must "sell" themselves in order to be popular or successful.

Capitalism's constant need for new markets in which to sell goods and for new sources of raw materials from which to make goods is also responsible for the spread of imperialism, the military, economic, and/or cultural domination of one nation by another for the financial benefit of the dominating nation with little or no concern for the welfare of the dominated. Spain's rule of Mexico, England's domination of India, Belgium's exploitation of the Congo region of Africa, and US efforts to subordinate native populations in North, Central, and South America are but a few examples of imperialist activities. When the imperialist nation establishes communities in an "underdeveloped" country, those communities are called colonies, as were the American Colonies before the American Revolution, and it uses those colonies to extend its economic interests. For the motive of all imperialist endeavor, no matter what positive influence the conquering nation claims to have on the local population, is economic gain for the "mother country."

Less clear cut, perhaps, but equally important for our understanding of capitalism today, is the way in which consciousness can be "colonized" by imperialist governments. To colonize the consciousness of subordinate peoples means to convince them to see their situation the way the imperialist nation wants them to see it, to convince them, for example, that they are mentally, spiritually, and culturally inferior to their conquerors and that their lot will be improved under the "guidance" and "protection" of their new leaders. Antebellum slave owners, for example, tried to convince African slaves that they were uncivilized, godless savages who would revert to cannibalism without the constant vigilance of their white masters. In reality, of course, African slaves came from ancient cultures that could boast many forms of art, music, religion, and ethics. This same attempt to colonize consciousness along racial lines continued into the twentieth century and endures today through, for example, stereotypes of black Americans in the media, the inadequate representation of African American experience in American history books, and the promotion of an Anglo-Saxon ideal of beauty. Thus, the attempt to colonize consciousness can be practiced against us by our own culture. Indeed, the promotion of consumerism discussed earlier is just such another example.

Clearly, Marxism's concern with human psychology overlaps with that of psychoanalysis: both disciplines study human behavior and motivation in psychological terms. However, while psychoanalysis focuses on the individual psyche and its formation within the family, Marxism focuses on the material/historical forces – the politics and ideologies of socioeconomic systems – that shape the psychological experience and behavior of individuals and groups. For Marxism, the family is not the source of the individual's psychological identity, for both the individual and the family are products of material/historical circumstances. The family unconsciously carries out the cultural "program" in raising its children, but that program is produced by the socioeconomic culture within which the family operates. While it is our parents who read us bedtime stories, take us to movies, and, in these and other ways, form our morals, it is our social system that provides the stories, movies, and morals, all of which ultimately serve the economic interests of those in control of that social system. Thus, while psychoanalytic critics examine the family conflicts and psychological wounds that determine individual behavior, Marxist critics examine that same behavior as a product of the ideological forces carried, for example, by film, fashion, art, music, education, and law. Indeed, the Marxist critic will show us the ways in which family dysfunctions are themselves products of the socioeconomic system and the ideologies it promotes.

Marxism and literature

Of course, the family is a recurrent theme in literature, so let's begin our discussion of Marxism and literature by contrasting Marxist and psychoanalytic readings of Arthur Miller's greatest familial play, *Death of a Salesman* (1949). A psychoanalytic reading of the play would focus on such elements as Willy's abandonment at a very young age by his father and older brother; Willy's insecurity and the massive denial of reality that results; Willy's projection of his personal needs onto his son Biff; Happy's sibling rivalry with Biff; the oedipal dimension at work in the family dynamic; and Linda's avoidance and displacement of her problems with Willy. The central scene for such an interpretation would be Biff's confrontation with Willy in the hotel, where he discovers his father with another woman. These aspects of the play would be of interest to psychoanalytic critics because they focus on the individual psyche as the product of the family.

A Marxist reading, in contrast, would focus on the ways in which the psychological problems listed above are produced by the material/historical realities within which the family operates: the ideology of the American dream that tells Willy his self-worth is earned only by economic success and that keeps him looking up to his predatory brother Ben; the rampant consumerism that keeps the Lomans buying on credit what they can't afford; the competitiveness of the business world that puts Willy back on straight commission work after 30 years of employment with the same firm; the exploitative potential of a socioeconomic system that doesn't require all companies to provide adequate pension coverage for their employees; and the ideology of "survival-of-the-fittest" capitalism that allows Howard to fire Willy with no concern for the latter's deteriorating mental condition. The central scene for such an interpretation would be that in which Howard (after displaying signs of his own economic success) fires Willy, telling him to turn to his sons for financial help.

Clearly, if a Marxist critic uses a psychoanalytic concept, it is used in service of a Marxist interpretation. For example, Willy's denial of reality, and the regressive hallucinations that accompany it, would be viewed as evidence of the American dream's debilitating ideological agenda: the American dream is certainly good for capitalist economics, but it sacrifices the well-being of the many individuals who don't achieve it. Similarly, as you read other Marxist interpretations of culture and cultural productions, you may notice that concepts from other theories we are studying will appear. For example, you may notice that by revealing the subtle but profound capitalist similarities between, say, Democratic, Republican, Socialist, and Fascist cultural and educational funding policies, a Marxist critic is engaged in a kind of structuralist enterprise. Or you may notice that, by revealing the ways in which a literary work covertly reinforces the capitalist values it criticizes, a Marxist critic is engaged in a deconstructive enterprise. Indeed, many Marxist critics are, among other things, feminists, deconstructors, social psychologists, and cultural anthropologists. In every case, however, you will see that concepts overlapping with or borrowed from other fields are put in service of Marxist goals.

Of course, the Marxist concepts discussed above do not exhaust the field; there are many others. And as in every field, there is a great deal of disagreement among Marxist theorists and literary critics concerning, for example, the formation and role of class solidarity among the proletariat, the role of the media in manipulating our political consciousness, the relationship between ideology and psychology, the compatibility of Marxism with other critical theories, and many other topics. However, the concepts provided in this chapter can be considered the basic principles, the main ideas you need to know in order to read Marxist theorists and literary critics with some understanding of the issues they raise. Before we extend these concepts to the realm of literary interpretation, let's take a look at Marxism's view of literature in general.

For Marxism, literature does not exist in some timeless, aesthetic realm as an object to be passively contemplated. Rather, like all cultural manifestations, it is a product of the socioeconomic and hence ideological conditions of the time and place in which it was written, whether or not the author intended it so. Because human beings are themselves products of their socioeconomic and ideological environment, it is assumed that authors cannot help but create works that embody ideology in some form.

The fact that literature grows out of and reflects real material/historical conditions creates at least two possibilities of interest to Marxist critics: (1) the literary work might tend to reinforce in the reader the ideologies it embodies, or (2) it might invite the reader to criticize the ideologies it represents. Many texts do both. And it is not merely the content of a literary work – the "action" or the theme – that carries ideology, but the form as well or, as most Marxists would argue, the form primarily. Realism, naturalism, surrealism, symbolism, romanticism, modernism, postmodernism, tragedy, comedy, satire, interior monologue, stream of consciousness, and other genres and literary devices are the means by which form is constituted. If content is the "what" of literature, then form is the "how."

Realism, for example, gives us characters and plot as if we were looking through a window onto an actual scene taking place before our eyes. Our attention is drawn not to the nature of the words on the page but to the action those words convey. Indeed, we frequently forget about the words we're reading and the way the narrative is structured as we "get lost" in the story. Part of the reason we don't notice the language and structure, the form, is because the action represented is ordered in a coherent sequence that invites us to relate to it much as we relate to the events in our own lives, and the characters it portrays are believable, much like people we might meet. So we get "pulled into" the story. In contrast, a good deal of postmodern literature (and nonrealistic, experimental literature of any kind) is written in a fragmented, surreal style that seems to defy our understanding and serves to distance or estrange us from the narrative and the characters it portrays.

For some Marxists, realism is the best form for Marxist purposes because it clearly and accurately represents the real world, with all its socioeconomic inequities and ideological contradictions, and encourages readers to see the unhappy truths about material/historical reality, for whether or not authors intend it they are bound to represent socioeconomic inequities and ideological contradictions if they accurately represent the real world. Marxist fans of realist fiction often have been inclined to reject nonrealistic, experimental fiction for being inaccessible to the majority of readers and for being too exclusively concerned with the inner workings of an individual mind rather than with the individual's relationship to society. However, many Marxists value nonrealistic, experimental fiction because the fragmentation of experience it represents and the estrangement the reader often experiences constitute a critique of the fragmented world and the alienated human beings produced by capitalism in today's world.

To see how form affects our understanding of content (or how form is a kind of content), let's take another brief look at *Death of a Salesman*. As we have seen, the play has a strong Marxist component in that it invites us to condemn the capitalist exploitation Willy suffers at the hands of his employer, and it shows us the contradictions inherent in capitalist ideology, which promotes the interests of big business at the expense of the "little man" who has "bought into" capitalist values. However, for many Marxists, this anticapitalist theme is severely undermined by the fact that the play is written in the form of a tragedy. You will recall that tragedy portrays the ruin of an individual human being due to some character flaw — usually hubris, or excessive pride — in that individual's personal makeup. The tragic form of *Death of a Salesman* thus encourages us to focus primarily on the character flaws in Willy as an individual rather than on the society that helped produce those flaws, and we are thus led to overlook the negative influence of the capitalist ideology that is, at bottom, responsible for all the action in the play.

Although Marxists have long disagreed about what kinds of works are most useful in promoting social awareness and positive political change, many today believe that even those literary works that reinforce capitalist, imperialist, or other classist values are useful in that they can show us how these ideologies work to seduce or coerce us into collusion with their repressive ideological agendas. Mary Shelley's *Frankenstein* (1818), for example, may be said to reinforce classist values to the extent that it portrays those born into the upper class — for example, Alphonse Frankenstein, Elizabeth Lavenza, and the DeLaceys — as morally and intellectually superior to those below them on the social scale. Characters at the bottom of the social ladder, on the other hand, are often depicted as rude, insensitive, and easily incensed to mob behavior. In contrast, Toni Morrison's *The Bluest Eye* (1970) undermines classist values by illustrating the injustices suffered under the class system imposed by American capitalism in the early 1940s. In addition, by revealing the ways in which religion and escapist movies harm the poor by encouraging them to ignore the harsh realities of their lives, rather than organize politically and fight collectively for their fair share of the pie, this novel can be said to have a Marxist agenda.

Some questions Marxist critics ask about literary texts

The following questions are offered to summarize Marxist approaches to literature.

1 Does the work reinforce (intentionally or not) capitalist, imperialist, or classist values? If so, then the work may be said to have a capitalist, imperialist, or classist agenda, and it is the critic's job to expose and condemn this aspect of the work.
2 How might the work be seen as a critique of capitalism, imperialism, or classism? That is, in what ways does the text reveal, and invite us to condemn, oppressive socioeconomic forces (including repressive ideologies)? If a work criticizes or invites us to criticize oppressive socioeconomic forces, then it may be said to have a Marxist agenda.
3 Does the work in some ways support a Marxist agenda but in other ways (perhaps unintentionally) support a capitalist, imperialist, or classist agenda? In other words, is the work ideologically conflicted?
4 How does the literary work reflect (intentionally or not) the socioeconomic conditions of the time in which it was written and/or the time in which it is set, and what do those conditions reveal about the history of class struggle?
5 How might the work be seen as a critique of organized religion? That is, how does religion function in the text to keep a character or characters from realizing and resisting socioeconomic oppression?

Depending on the literary work in question, we might ask one or any combination of these questions. Or we might come up with a useful question of our own not listed here. These are just some starting points to get us thinking about literary works in productive Marxist ways. Remember, not all Marxist critics will interpret the same work in the same way, even if they focus on the same Marxist concepts. As always, even expert practitioners disagree. Our goal is to use Marxist theory to help enrich our reading of literary works, to help us see some important ideas they illustrate that we might not have seen so clearly or so deeply without Marxist theory, and, if we use Marxist theory the way it is intended to be used, to help us see the ways in which ideology blinds us to our own participation in oppressive sociopolitical agendas.

The following Marxist reading of F. Scott Fitzgerald's *The Great Gatsby* is offered as an example of what a Marxist interpretation of that novel might yield. It focuses on what I will argue is the novel's critique of American capitalist ideology. In addition, I will try to show the ways in which the novel fails to push its critique far enough, becoming the unwitting prey of the capitalist ideology it attacks.

You are what you own: a Marxist reading of *The Great Gatsby*

Written and set during the post-World War I economic boom of the 1920s, F. Scott Fitzgerald's *The Great Gatsby* (1925) can be seen as a chronicle of the American dream at a point in this nation's history when capitalism's promise of economic opportunity for all seemed at its peak of fulfillment. "Get-rich-quick" schemes abounded, and many of them succeeded, for it was a time when stocks could be bought on a 10 percent margin, which means that a dollar's worth of stocks could be purchased, on credit, for ten cents. So even the "little man" could play the stock market and hope to make his fortune there. We see the tenor of the times in the feverish abandon of Gatsby's party guests – confident that their host's abundance of food and drink, like the nation's resources, will never be depleted – and in Gatsby himself, whose meteoric rise from being the son of "shiftless and unsuccessful farm people" (104; ch. 6) to the proprietor of a "colossal" Long Island mansion with "a marble swimming pool and over forty acres of lawn and garden" (9; ch. 1) seems to embody the infinite possibility offered by the American dream.

The Great Gatsby, however, does not celebrate the heady capitalist culture it portrays but, as a Marxist interpretation of the novel makes especially clear, reveals its dark underbelly instead. Through its unflattering characterization of those at the top of the economic heap and its trenchant examination of the ways in which the American dream not only fails to fulfill its promise but also contributes to the decay of personal values, Fitzgerald's novel stands as a scathing critique of American capitalist culture and the ideology that promotes it. In addition, we will see how a Marxist perspective shows us the ways in which the novel fails to push its critique of capitalism far enough, falling an unwitting prey to the very ideology it tries to undermine.

One of the most effective ways *The Great Gatsby* criticizes capitalist culture is by showing the debilitating effects of capitalist ideology even on those who are its most successful products, and it does so through its representation of commodification. As you may recall, a commodity, by definition, has value not in terms of what it can do (use value) but in terms of the money or other commodities for which it can be traded (exchange value) or in terms of the social status its ownership confers (sign-exchange value). An object becomes a commodity only when it has exchange value or sign-exchange value, and neither form of value is inherent in any object. Both are forms of social value: they are *assigned* to objects by human beings in a given social context. Commodification, then, is the act of relating to persons or things in terms of their exchange value or sign-exchange value to the exclusion of other considerations. Of course, commodification is a necessary function of buying and selling, and thus it is a necessary function of capitalism, which depends for its survival on buying and selling. However, as the novel illustrates, commodification, especially in the form of sign-exchange value, is not merely a marketplace activity that we can leave at the office when we go home at the end of the day. Rather, it is a psychological attitude that has invaded every domain of our existence.

Nowhere in *The Great Gatsby* is commodification so clearly embodied as in the character of Tom Buchanan. The wealthiest man in the novel, Tom relates to the world only through his money: for him, all things and all people are commodities. His marriage to Daisy Fay was certainly an exchange of Daisy's youth, beauty, and social standing for Tom's money and power and the image of strength and stability they imparted to him. Appropriately, the symbol of this "purchase" was the $350,000 string of pearls Tom gave his bride-to-be. Similarly, Tom uses his money and social rank to "purchase" Myrtle Wilson and the numerous other working-class women with whom he has affairs, such as the chambermaid with whom he was involved three months after his marriage to Daisy and the "common but pretty" (112; ch. 6) young woman he picks up at Gatsby's party. Tom's consistent choice of lower-class women can also be understood in terms of his commodified view of human interaction: he "markets" his socioeconomic status where it will put him at the greatest advantage – among women who are most desperate for and most easily awed by what he has to sell.

Of course, Tom's acts of commodification are not limited to his relationships with women. Because capitalism promotes the belief that "you are what you own" – that our value as human beings is only as great as the value of our possessions – much of Tom's pleasure in his expensive possessions is a product of their sign-exchange value, of the social status their ownership confers on him. "I've got a nice place here," he tells Nick, adding, "It belonged to Demaine, the oil man" (12; ch. 1), as if the house's "pedigree" could confer a pedigree on him. We see this same desire to flex his socioeconomic muscles, so to speak, when he toys with George Wilson concerning the mechanic's wish to buy Tom's car in order to sell it at a profit. Given that Tom was born into enormous wealth, apparently more than he could ever spend, why should he need the socioeconomic ego boost provided by such posturing?

One of the ironies of commodification is that it creates desire even as it fulfills it. Because the sense of self-worth it fosters in us is always derived from external standards, such as fashion trends, we can never rest secure in our possessions: something new and better is always being sold, and others may purchase something we don't have, in which case they will be "better" than we are. In Tom's case, this kind of insecurity is increased by his awareness of a type of social status he can never acquire: the status that comes from being born in the East. Although he inherited his wealth from an established Chicago family – so his money is not "new" in the sense of having been earned during his lifetime – an established Chicago family in the 1920s would not have been considered "old" in the East, where America's "bluebloods" had lived since their English and Dutch forebears' initial immigration. For Easterners, in the 1920s at least, one of the requirements of old money was that it be earned not only in the past but in the East. To be from the Midwest, regardless of the size or age of one's fortune, was to be a latecomer in the eyes of Easterners.

Having attended Yale, Tom must be, as Fitzgerald was at Princeton, painfully aware of the Eastern social requirement he can never by birth fulfill. Even if he and Daisy return to Europe or the Midwest, Tom carries the knowledge of his social inferiority inside himself. He therefore seeks a status other than the one he can't have, a status that would declare his indifference to the issue of old money versus new. Thus his vulgarity – his lack of discretion with Myrtle Wilson; his loud, aggressive behavior; his rudeness – can be seen as an attempt to reassure himself that his money and power are all that count, an attempt to show that his wealth insulates him from considerations of class or refinement. The pseudoscientific "intellectualism" Tom adopts in referring Nick to a book he'd read about white civilization – as well as the racism endorsed by his reading – might be seen in this same light. He doesn't need to belong to old money because he belongs to a larger and more important group: the Aryan race. As Tom puts it, "[W]e've produced all the things that go to make civilization – oh, science and art and all that" (18; ch. 1).

A corollary of Tom's commodification of people is his ability to manipulate them very cold-bloodedly to get what he wants, for commodification is, by definition, the treatment of objects *and people* as commodities, as *things* whose only importance lies in their benefit to ourselves. In order to get Myrtle Wilson's sexual favors, he lets her think that he may marry her someday, that his hesitation is due to Daisy's alleged Catholicism rather than to his own lack of desire. And in order to eliminate his rival for Daisy's affection, he sacrifices Gatsby to George Wilson, whom he deliberately sends, armed and crazed, to Gatsby's house without even telephoning Gatsby to warn him. In addition, Tom's sinister capabilities are hinted at through his familiarity with the underworld in the person of Walter Chase, who was involved in illegal activities with Gatsby.

While a character such as Tom Buchanan is likely to make us sympathize with anyone who is dependent upon him, Daisy is not merely an innocent victim of her husband's commodification. In the first place, Daisy's acceptance of the pearls – and of the marriage to Tom they represent – is, of course, an act of commodification: she wanted Tom's sign-exchange value as much as he wanted hers. And certainly, Daisy is capable, like Tom, of espousing an idea for the status she thinks it confers on her, as when she commodifies disaffection in order to impress Nick:

"You see I think everything's terrible anyhow," she went on in a convinced way. "Everybody thinks so — the most advanced people. And I *know*. I've been everywhere and seen everything and done everything." Her eyes flashed around her in a defiant way, rather like Tom's. ...

The instant her voice broke off ... I felt the basic insincerity of what she had said. ... [I]n a moment she looked at me with an absolute smirk on her lovely face as if she had asserted her membership in a rather distinguished secret society to which she and Tom belonged.

(21–22; ch. 1)

Even Daisy's extramarital affair with Gatsby, like her earlier romance with him, is based on a commodified view of life. She would never have become interested in him had she known that Gatsby was not from "much the same strata as herself ... [and] fully able to take care of her" (156; ch. 8), and when she learns the truth during the confrontation scene in the hotel suite, her interest in him quickly fades. The apparent ease with which she lets Gatsby take the blame for Myrtle's death, while she beats a hasty retreat with Tom, indicates that her commodification of people, like that of her husband, facilitates the cold-blooded sacrifice of others to her convenience.

The Buchanans' commodification of their world and the enormous wealth that makes it possible for them to "smas[h] up things and creatures and then retrea[t] back into their money" (187–88; ch. 9) are rendered especially objectionable by the socioeconomic contrast provided by the "valley of ashes" (27; ch. 2) near which George and Myrtle Wilson live. People like the Wilsons don't stand a chance in a world dominated by people like the Buchanans. The "valley of ashes" —

a fantastic farm where ashes grow like wheat into ridges and hills and grotesque gardens; where ashes take the forms of houses and chimneys and rising smoke and finally, with a transcendent effort, of men who move dimly and already crumbling through the powdery air

(27; ch. 2)

— is a powerfully chilling image of the life led by those who do not have the socioeconomic resources of the Buchanans. Ashes are what's left over after something is used up or wasted, and, indeed, the area is a literal "dumping ground" where "occasionally a line of grey [train] cars ... comes to rest, and immediately the ash-grey men swarm up with leaden spades and stir up an impenetrable cloud" (27; ch. 2) as they remove the refuse from the cars. It's obviously a human "dumping ground" as well: aside from the men who remove the trash from the train, there is only "a small block of yellow brick" (28; ch. 2) containing a shop for rent, "an all-night restaurant approached by a trail of ashes" (29;

ch. 2), and George Wilson's garage above which he and Myrtle occupy a small apartment.

It is precisely from settings such as this that the American dream is supposed to emerge, that a shaky but persistent business enterprise is supposed to lead to financial security for oneself and one's children. But the language used to describe this scene makes it clear that this is a land of hopelessness, not of dreams likely to be fulfilled: it is a "grey land," "impenetrable," with "spasms of bleak dust ... drift[ing] endlessly over it" and "bounded ... by a small foul river" (27–28; ch. 2). And there are no children here, no emblems of hope for a better future, except for the "grey, scrawny Italian child ... setting torpedoes [firecrackers] in a row along the railroad track" (30; ch. 2), hardly the embodiment of a promising tomorrow. The only way to survive this hell on earth is to let someone like Tom Buchanan exploit you, as George does when he tolerates Tom's humiliating banter in the hope of getting a good price on Tom's car and as Myrtle does when she accepts Tom's mistreatment in the hope of getting out of the valley of ashes for good. But the only way out of capitalism's "dumping ground," as George and Myrtle both finally learn, is in a coffin.

Even Jay Gatsby, the character who seems at first to embody the American dream and the hope capitalism thereby offers to all, reveals, upon closer inspection, the hollowness of that dream. In true rags-to-riches style, Gatsby has risen from extreme poverty to extreme wealth in a very few years. His boyhood "schedule," in which he divided his time, in the self-improvement tradition of Benjamin Franklin, among such pursuits as the practice of "elocution" and the study of "needed inventions" (181; ch. 9), resonates strongly with the American dream's image of the self-made man. And even his motive for amassing wealth seems pure: he did it to win the woman he loves. If Gatsby is the novel's representative of the American dream, however, the dream must be a corrupt one, for Gatsby achieves it only through criminal activities, a fact that severely deflates the image of the honest, hardworking man that the dream is supposed to foster. And although Gatsby is certainly more charming than Tom and Daisy, and more sympathetically portrayed by Nick, he commodifies his world just as they do. In fact, one might argue that he commodifies it more.

However much the Buchanans' possessions are important to them in terms of sign-exchange value, they also have use value: we see the couple reclining on their sofas and eating at their tables. In contrast, we are told that the only room Gatsby occupies in his magnificently furnished mansion is his simple bedroom, and during the only time we see him there his purpose is to show it to Daisy. He almost never uses his library, pool, or hydroplane himself; and he doesn't drink the alcohol or know most of the guests at his lavish parties. It seems that for Gatsby the sole function of material possessions is sign-exchange value: he wants the image their ownership confers on him and nothing more. Furthermore, Gatsby's commodity signs are almost all empty: his Gothic library filled with uncut (and, therefore, unopened) books, his "*imitation* ... Hôtel de Ville" with its "spanking new" tower "under a *thin beard* of raw ivy" (9; ch. 1, my italics), and his photo of himself at Oxford are all surfaces without interiors, all images without substance. It seems fitting, then, that he acquired them in order to acquire the ultimate image of sign-exchange value he wants to possess: Daisy.

Possession of Daisy would give Gatsby what he really wants: a permanent sign that he belongs to her socioeconomic class, to the same bright, spotless, airy, carefree world of the very rich that Daisy embodied for him when they first met. For Gatsby, her presence gave the house in which she lived a feeling of "breathless intensity,"

> a hint of bedrooms upstairs more beautiful and cool than other bedrooms, of gay and radiant activities taking place through its corridors, and of romances that were ... redolent of this year's shining motor cars and of dances whose flowers were scarcely withered.
>
> (155–56; ch. 8)

Possession of Daisy, the ultimate commodity sign, would, in Gatsby's eyes, "launder" his "new money" and make it "old," would make his "spanking new" imitation Hôtel de Ville an ancestral seat. Thus, in accumulating material goods in order to win Daisy, he accumulated one kind of commodity sign in order to acquire another.

Gatsby's commodification of his world is linked, like Tom's, to the cold-blooded aggression with which he pursues what he wants. The lap of luxury in which Gatsby lives does not exist in a vacuum. It is supported by a very dark and sinister world of corruption, crime, and death. The underworld activities from which his wealth derives include bootlegging and the selling of fraudulent bonds. This is the underworld of Meyer Wolfsheim, who has such unlimited criminal connections that he was able to "fix" the 1919 World Series. And this is the man who takes credit for giving Gatsby his start.

We get a glimpse of this world in the "villainous" looking servants (119; ch. 7) Wolfsheim sends to work for Gatsby and in the phone calls Gatsby receives (and which, after Gatsby's death, Nick receives by accident) from obvious criminal sources. This is a world of predators and prey in which illegal – and thus often imperfect – liquor is sold over the counter to anyone with the money to pay for it and in which fake bonds are passed in small towns to unsuspecting investors. Some of the people who buy the liquor may become ill from it; some may die. All of the small investors who buy the fraudulent bonds will lose money that they can't afford to lose. And when the inevitable mistakes are made and the law steps in, someone will have to be sacrificed as Gatsby sacrifices Walter Chase.

Even the protagonist's desire for Daisy is informed by an underworld perspective. When Gatsby first courted Daisy at her parents' home in Louisville, he "let her believe that he was a person from much the same strata as herself" when, in fact, "he had no comfortable family standing behind him and he was liable at the whim of an impersonal government to be blown anywhere about the world" (156; ch. 8):

> However glorious might be his future ... he was at present a penniless young [soldier] without a past, and at any moment the invisible cloak of his uniform might slip from his shoulders. So he made the most of his time. He took what he could get, ravenously and unscrupulously – eventually he took Daisy one still October night, took her because he had no real right to touch her hand.
>
> (156; ch. 8)

This language – "he took what he could get, ravenously and unscrupulously" – is hardly the language of love. Rather, it is the kind of language that would be used to describe a hoodlum, the kind of language that resonates strongly with Gatsby's dubious association with Dan Cody before meeting Daisy and with his criminal activities subsequent to their initial affair.

Thus, Gatsby is not exempt from the novel's unflattering portrait of the wealthy. Indeed, his characterization suggests that the American dream does not offer a moral alternative to the commodified world of the Buchanans but produces the same commodification of people and things as does Tom and Daisy's inherited wealth. *The Great Gatsby*'s representation of American culture, then, reveals the debilitating effects of capitalism on socioeconomic "winners" such as Tom, Daisy, and Gatsby, as well as on "losers" such as George and Myrtle.

Operating against *The Great Gatsby*'s powerful critique of capitalism is the novel's subtle reinforcement of capitalism's repressive ideology. This counter-movement operates in three ways. First, the unflattering portraits of George and Myrtle Wilson deflect our attention from their victimization by the capitalist system in which they both struggle to survive. Second, because Nick is seduced by the American dream Gatsby represents, his narrative romanticizes the protagonist, obscuring the ways in which Jimmy Gatz's investment in the dream produced the amoral Jay Gatsby. Third, the lush language used to describe the world of the wealthy makes it attractive despite the people like the Buchanans who populate it.

Perhaps *The Great Gatsby*'s most obvious flaw, from a Marxist perspective, is its unsympathetic rendering of George and Myrtle Wilson, the novel's representatives of the lower class. George and Myrtle try to improve their lot the only way they know how. George clings to his foundering business, and Myrtle, in a sense, tries to start one of her own by marketing the only commodity she has in stock: she "rents" her body to Tom Buchanan, hoping he'll want someday to "purchase" it by marrying her. They are victims of capitalism because the only way to succeed in a capitalist economy is to succeed in a market, and, as neither George nor Myrtle succeed in the only markets open to them, they are condemned to the "valley of ashes." Their characterizations, however, are so negative that it is easy to overlook the socio-economic realities that control their lives. Indeed, one might argue that the novel's portrayal of the Wilsons is a classist stereotype of a lower-class couple: George is not very bright; Myrtle is loud, obnoxious, and overtly sexual. We may feel sorry for George, but our sympathy is undercut by his personal failings. That is, instead of feeling sorry (or angry at the system) that he is a victim of class oppression, we feel sorry (or angry at him) that he doesn't have what it takes to "pull himself up by his bootstraps" and better himself, as the American dream tells us he should: we blame the victim instead of the system that victimizes him. Similarly, Myrtle's cruel rejection of George and brazen pursuit of Tom make her an easy target for our disapproval: our awareness of Myrtle's severely limited options is dimmed by the very fact that she does her best to use them.

In a more subtle manner, the novel is also flawed, from a Marxist perspective, by Nick's romanticization of Gatsby. Nick may like to think he disapproves of Jay Gatsby – because he knows he *should* disapprove of him for the same reasons he disapproves of the Buchanans – but it is clear from the beginning that the narrator is charmed by him. As Nick tells us, "There was something gorgeous about him, some heightened sensitivity to the promises of life. ... [I]t was an extraordinary gift for hope, a romantic readiness such as I have never found in any other person and which it is not likely I shall ever find again" (6; ch. 1).

This idealization is foregrounded in Nick's narrative through his focus on romantic images of Gatsby: the rebellious boy, the ambitious young roughneck, the idealistic dreamer, the devoted lover, the brave soldier, the lavish host. Gatsby's criminal connections are acknowledged, but because of Nick's response to them, they don't influence his opinion of the man. For example, Nick's manner of dis-cussing Gatsby's criminal life tends to deflect attention away from the moral implications of Gatsby's underworld activities, as when Nick reports the following conversation he overheard at one of Gatsby's parties: "'He's a bootlegger,' said the young ladies, moving somewhere between his cocktails and his flowers" (65; ch. 4). The rhetoric of this phrase is typical of Nick's defense of Gatsby against his detractors, even when those detractors are right: his statement focuses on Gatsby's generosity and on the willingness to abuse it of those who gossip about him, thereby sidestepping the fact that "his cocktails and his flowers" weren't rightfully his at all: they were purchased with funds obtained from his criminal activities.

Similarly, Nick influences our reaction to Gatsby by his own emotional investment in those events that show Gatsby in a good light. For example, when Gatsby, con-fronted by Tom, admits in front of everyone that his Oxford experience was pro-vided by a government arrangement for American soldiers who remained in Europe after World War I, Nick "wanted to get up and slap him on the back" (136; ch. 7). This small concession to reality on Gatsby's part elicits in Nick a renewal "of com-plete faith in him" (136; ch. 7). Despite what Nick knows about the underworld sources of Gatsby's wealth, despite the "unaffected scorn" Nick says he has for Gatsby's world, Gatsby himself is "exempt" from Nick's disapprobation: "Gatsby turned out all right at the end; it is what preyed on Gatsby, what foul dust floated in the wake of his dreams" (6; ch. 1) that elicits Nick's disaffection – and that of many readers. It is easy to be influenced by the warmth of Nick's feelings because these feelings so strongly inform the portrait he paints. Following Nick's lead, and typical of the response of many literary critics to the title character, Tom Burnam says that Gatsby "survives sound and whole in character, uncorrupted by the corruption which surrounded him" (105), and Rose Adrienne Gallo believes that Gatsby "maintained his innocence" to the end (43).[1]

Why should Nick deceive himself, and us, about Gatsby? Why should he foreground all the positive, likable qualities in Gatsby's personality and shift responsibility for the unpleasant ones onto others' shoulders? I think it is because the narrator is himself seduced by Gatsby's dream. At the age of 30, and still being financed by his father while he tries to figure out what he should do, it is not surprising that Nick wants to believe life still holds promise because he is afraid that it doesn't. He fears that all he has to look forward to is, as he puts it, "a thinning list of single men to know, a thinning brief-case of enthusiasm, thinning hair" (143; ch. 7). With his summer in New York – his latest in a series of adventures – having ended in disaster, he wants to believe in the possibility of hope. Nick believes in Gatsby because he wants to believe that Gatsby's dream can come true for himself: that a young man at loose ends can make the kind of outrageous financial success of himself that Gatsby has made, can find the woman of his dreams, and can be so optimistic about the future. Nick doesn't want to be reminded that Gatsby's glittering world rests on corruption because he wants that kind of hopeful world for himself. He is in collusion with Gatsby's desire, and his narrative can lead readers into collusion with that desire as well.

The appeal to readers of Gatsby's desire to belong to the magical world of the wealthy – as Andrew Dillon puts it, "Gatsby has possessed what the reader must also desire: the orgiastic present" (61) – is also a testimonial to the power of the commodity. Gatsby may not make the best use of his mansion, his hydroplane, his swimming pool, and his library, but many of us might feel that we certainly would. Thus another flaw in the novel, from a Marxist perspective, is the way in which the commodity's appeal is powerfully reinforced for the reader by the lush language used to describe this world of leisure and luxury. Consumer goods are invested with magic – with the capacity to transform reality – which suggests that the commodity is *itself* transcendent, beyond earthly limitation. Even the refreshments at Gatsby's parties, for example, seem enchanted: a "tray of cocktails *floated* at us through the twilight" (47; ch. 3, my italics), and on "buffet tables, garnished with glistening hors-d'oeuvre, spiced baked hams crowded against salads of *harlequin* designs and pastry pigs and turkeys *bewitched* to a dark gold" (44; ch. 3, my italics).

The commodity is especially compelling in the following description of the Buchanans' home on East Egg:

> Their house was ... a cheerful red and white Georgian Colonial mansion overlooking the bay. The lawn started at the beach and ran toward the front door for a quarter of a mile, jumping over sun-dials and brick walks and burning gardens – finally when it reached the house drifting up the side in bright vines as though from the momentum of its run. The front was broken by a line of French windows, glowing now with reflected gold, and wide open to the warm windy afternoon. ...
>
> [T]he front vista ... [included] in its sweep a sunken Italian garden, a half acre of deep pungent roses and a snub-nosed motor boat that bumped the tide off shore. ...
>
> We walked through a high hallway into a bright rosy-colored space, fragilely bound into the house by French windows at either end. ... A breeze blew through the room, blew curtains in at one end and out the other like pale flags, twisting them up toward the frosted wedding cake of the ceiling – and then rippled over the wine-colored rug, making a shadow on it as wind does on the sea.
>
> (11–12; ch. 1)

This passage is a delicious appeal to every one of the five senses, with language so sensual that the house seems to breathe with a life of its own. This setting thus has an existence independent of the characters who inhabit it: the estate doesn't need Tom and Daisy in order to be gorgeous; it was gorgeous before Tom bought it, and it will be gorgeous after the Buchanans are gone. In fact, we could easily, and happily, imagine this place without its occupants. That is, the setting is bigger than the Buchanans – it contains and exceeds them. They neither use it up nor exhaust its possibilities. And it is impervious to their corruption: we are not led to associate the place with the events that occur there. Therefore, it can exert a magnetic appeal on many readers. As much as Fitzgerald is the critic of capitalism, he is also its poet laureate, and his poetry can attract readers to the very thing that, on a more overt level, the novel condemns.

While *The Great Gatsby* offers a significant critique of capitalist ideology, it also repackages and markets that ideology anew. This double movement of the text gives the closing line a special irony: if we do "beat on, boats against the current, borne back ceaselessly into the past" (189; ch. 9), there is in this novel that which strengthens the backflow, bearing us ceaselessly back under capitalism's spell. In the end, Gatsby fails to realize the American dream, but because the novel falls prey to the capitalist ideology it condemns, many readers will continue to invest in it.

Questions for further practice: Marxist approaches to other literary works

The following questions are intended as models. They can help you use Marxist criticism to interpret the literary works to which they refer or other texts of your choice.

1   How is the rigid class structure evident in William Faulkner's "A Rose for Emily" (1931) responsible for much of the story's action and characterization? Would you say the story does or does not invite us to criticize the classism it represents?
2   What can we learn from Toni Cade Bambara's "The Lesson" (1972) about conspicuous consumption and commodification? How does the story use its representation of these capitalist realities to criticize class oppression?
3   How does John Steinbeck's *The Grapes of Wrath* (1939) qualify as a Marxist critique of American capitalism? How does the novel's form (realism) support that critique? How does the ending of the film version (which is flawed, from a Marxist perspective) undermine the more realistic ending of the novel?
4   Describe the class system operating in the lives of the characters in Kate Chopin's "The Storm" (1898). In what ways does the story fail to criticize, and fail to invite us to criticize, the classism it depicts?
5   How does Langston Hughes' "On the Road" (1952) qualify as a Marxist critique of organized religion?

For further reading

Day, Gary. *Class*. New York: Routledge, 2001.
Eagleton, Terry. *Marxism and Literary Criticism*. 1976. 2nd ed. London and New York: Routledge, 2002.
———. *Why Marx Was Right*. New Haven, CT and London: Yale University Press, 2011.
Haslett, Moyra. *Marxist Literary and Cultural Theories*. New York: St. Martin's, 2000.
hooks, bell. *Where We Stand: Class Matters*. New York: Routledge, 2000.
Horkheimer, Max, and Theodor Adorno. *Dialectic of Enlightenment*. 1944. Trans. John Cumming. New York: Continuum, 1982. (See especially "The Culture Industry," 120–67.)
Marx, Karl. *Capital: A Critique of Political Economy*. 1867. New York: International Publishers, 1967.
Tokarczyk, Michelle M. *Class Distinctions: On the Lives and Writings of Maxine Hong Kingston, Sandra Cisneros, and Dorothy Allison*. Selinsgrove, PA: Susquehanna University Press, 2008.
Veblen, Thorstein. *The Theory of the Leisure Class: An Economic Study of Institutions*. 1899. New York: Mentor-NAL, 1953.
Weber, Max. *The Protestant Ethic and the Spirit of Capitalism*. New York: Scribner's, 1958.
Williams, Raymond. *Marxism and Literature*. 1977. Rpt. New York: Oxford University Press, 2009.
Wright, Erik Olin. *Class Counts*. Student edition. New York: Cambridge University Press, 2000.

For advanced readers

Althusser, Louis. *Lenin and Philosophy and Other Essays*. Trans. Ben Brewster. New York: Monthly Review, 1971. (See especially "Ideology and Ideological State Apparatuses," 127–86.)

Baudrillard, Jean. *For a Critique of the Political Economy of the Sign.* 1972. Trans. Charles Levin. St. Louis, MO: Telos, 1981.

Benjamin, Walter. *Illuminations.* Trans. Harry Zohn. Ed. Hannah Arendt. New York: Harcourt, Brace and World, 1955.

Bennett, Tony. *Formalism and Marxism.* 1979. 2nd ed. London and New York: Routledge, 2003.

Camara, Babacar. *Marxist Theory, Black/African Specificities, and Lacan.* Lanham, MD: Lexington Books, 2008.

Eagleton, Terry. *Myths of Power: A Marxist Study of the Brontës.* 1975. Anniversary edition. Basingstoke and New York: Palgrave Macmillan, 2005.

Jameson, Fredric. *The Political Unconscious: Narrative as a Socially Symbolic Act.* 1981. 2nd ed. London and New York: Routledge, 2002.

Lukács, Georg. *History and Class Consciousness.* 1923. Trans. Rodney Livingstone. Cambridge, MA: The MIT Press, 1971.

Macherey, Pierre. *A Theory of Literary Production.* Trans. G. Wall. London: Routledge and Kegan Paul, 1978.

Sinfield, Alan. *Shakespeare, Authority, Sexuality: Unfinished Business in Cultural Materialism.* London and New York: Routledge, 2006.

Wood, Allen W. *Karl Marx.* 2nd ed. London and New York: Routledge, 2004.

Žižek, Slavoj. *The Sublime Object of Ideology.* London: Verso, 1989.

Note

1 For similar views of Gatsby, see, for example, Bewley, Cartwright, Chase, Dillon, Hart, Le Vot, Moore, Nash, Stern, and Trilling. For views of Gatsby's sinister side see, for example, Pauly and Rowe.

Works cited

Bewley, Marius. "Scott Fitzgerald's Criticism of America." Sewanee Review 62 (1954): 223–46. Rpt. in *Modern Critical Interpretations: F. Scott Fitzgerald's* The Great Gatsby. Ed. Harold Bloom. New York: Chelsea, 1986. 11–27.

Burnam, Tom. "The Eyes of Dr. Eckleburg: A Re-Examination of *The Great Gatsby.*" *College English* 13 (1952). Rpt. in *F. Scott Fitzgerald: A Collection of Critical Essays.* Ed. Arthur Mizener. Englewood Cliffs, NJ: Prentice Hall, 1963. 104–11.

Cartwright, Kent. "Nick Carraway as Unreliable Narrator." *Papers on Language and Literature* 20.2 (1984): 218–32.

Chase, Richard. *"The Great Gatsby."* *The American Novel and Its Traditions.* New York: Doubleday, 1957. 162–67. Rpt. in The Great Gatsby: A Study. Ed. Frederick J. Hoffman. New York: Scribner's, 1962. 297–302.

Dillon, Andrew. *"The Great Gatsby:* The Vitality of Illusion." *Arizona Quarterly* 44.1 (1988): 49–61.

Fitzgerald, F. Scott. *The Great Gatsby.* 1925. New York: Macmillan, 1992.

Gallo, Rose Adrienne. *F. Scott Fitzgerald.* New York: Ungar, 1978.

Hart, Jeffrey. "'Out of it ere night': The WASP Gentleman as Cultural Ideal." *New Criterion* 7.5 (1989): 27–34.

Le Vot, André. *F. Scott Fitzgerald: A Biography.* Trans. William Byron. Garden City, NY: Doubleday, 1983.

Miller, Arthur. *Death of a Salesman.* New York: Viking, 1949.

Moore, Benita A. *Escape into a Labyrinth: F. Scott Fitzgerald, Catholic Sensibility, and the American Way.* New York: Garland, 1988.

Morrison, Toni. *The Bluest Eye.* New York: Holt, Rinehart, and Winston, 1970.

Nash, Charles C. "From West Egg to Short Hills: The Decline of the Pastoral Ideal from *The Great Gatsby* to Philip Roth's *Goodbye, Columbus.*" *Philological Association* 13 (1988): 22–27.

Pauly, Thomas H. "Gatsby Is a Sinister Gangster." Excerpted from "Gatsby as Gangster." *Studies in American Fiction* 21.2 (Autumn 1995). Rpt. in *Readings on* The Great Gatsby. San Diego: Greenhaven Press, 1998. 41–51.

Rowe, Joyce A. "Delusions of American Idealism." Excerpted from *Equivocal Endings in Classic American Novels.* Cambridge: Cambridge University Press, 1988. Rpt. in *Readings on* The Great Gatsby. San Diego: Greenhaven Press, 1998. 87–95.

Shelley, Mary. *Frankenstein.* London: Lackington, Hughes, Harding, Mavor, & Jones, 1818.

Stern, Milton R. *The Golden Moment: The Novels of F. Scott Fitzgerald.* Urbana: University of Illinois Press, 1970.

Trilling, Lionel. "F. Scott Fitzgerald." *The Liberal Imagination.* New York: Viking, 1950. 243–54. Rpt. in The Great Gatsby: *A Study.* Ed. Frederick J. Hoffman. New York: Scribner's, 1962. 232–43.

4   Feminist criticism

"I'm not a feminist – I like men!"
"I'm not a feminist – I think women should be able to stay at home and raise children if they want to!"
"I'm not a feminist – I wear a bra!"

Contrary to the opinions of many students new to the study of feminist literary criticism, many feminists like men, think that women should be able to stay at home and raise children if they want to do so, and wear bras. Broadly defined, feminist criticism examines the ways in which literature (and other cultural productions) reinforces or undermines the economic, political, social, and psychological oppression of women. However, just as the practitioners of all critical theories do, feminist critics hold many different opinions on all of the issues their discipline examines. In fact, some feminists call their field *feminisms* in order to underscore the multiplicity of points of view of its adherents and offer ways of thinking that oppose the traditional tendency to believe there is a single best point of view. Yet many of us who are new to the study of feminist theory, both male and female, have decided ahead of time that we are not feminists because we don't share whatever feminist point of view we have found the most objectionable. In other words, before we even come to the theory classroom, many of us have reduced feminism to whatever we consider its most objectionable element and, on that basis, have rejected it. This attitude reveals, I think, the oversimplified, negative view of feminism that persists in American culture today. For it is from the culture at large – the home, the workplace, the media, and so on – that we have gathered the antifeminist bias we sometimes bring into the classroom.

To see how this negative oversimplification works to blind us to the seriousness of the issues feminism raises, let's briefly examine one of the most maligned feminist claims: that we should not use the masculine pronoun *he* to represent both men and women. For many people, this claim suggests what they see as the trivial, even infantile, nature of feminist demands. What possible difference could it make if we continue to use the "inclusive *he*" to refer to members of both sexes? We know what we mean when we do it: it's simply a convention of language that includes both males and females. Such people believe that feminists should just concentrate on getting women an equal crack at the dough and forget all this nonsense about pronouns! For many feminists, however, the use of the pronoun *he* to refer to members of both sexes reflects and perpetuates a "habit of seeing," a way of looking at life, that uses male experience as the standard by which the experience of both sexes is evaluated. In other words, although the "inclusive he" claims to represent both men and women, in reality it is part of a deeply rooted cultural attitude that ignores women's experiences and women's points of view. The damaging effects of this attitude can be seen in a number of areas.

For example, before the centuries-old struggle for women's equality finally emerged in literary studies in the late 1960s, the literary works of (white) male authors describing experience from a (white) male point of view were considered the standard of universality – that is, representative of the experience of all readers – and universality was considered a major criterion of greatness. Because the works of (white) female authors (and of all authors of color) do not describe experience from a (white) male point of view, they were not considered universal and hence did not become part of the literary canon. It is interesting to note that popularity was not necessarily considered evidence of universality, for many women writers who enjoyed widespread fame during their lives were not "canonized" in literary histories, which focused primarily on male writers. Of course, those holding up this standard of greatness did not believe they were being unfairly discriminatory; they simply believed that they were rejecting literary texts that were not universal, that were not great. Even when (white) women authors began to appear more frequently in the canon and on college syllabi in the mid-1970s, they were not represented on an equal basis with (white) male authors.

Even today, unless the critical or historical point of view is feminist, there is a tendency to underrepresent the contribution of women writers. For example, in Matthew J. Bruccoli's preface to recent editions of *The Great Gatsby*, he notes that the 1920s was "an age of achievement ... in American literature" (x) and lists the names of 12 authors to support his claim. Only one of those authors – Willa Cather – is a woman. What about Ellen Glasgow, Susan Glaspell, Nella Larsen, Edna St. Vincent Millay, Rolla Lynn Riggs, Gertrude Stein, Djuna Barnes, Elizabeth Maddox Roberts, H. D. (Hilda Doolittle), or Marianne Moore? That many students probably recognize only a few of these names illustrates the marginalization of many women writers by literary history, though not necessarily by the reading public at the time these women wrote. Similarly, in most Hollywood films, even today, the camera eye (the point of view from which the film is shot) is male: the female characters, not male, are the objects gazed on by the camera and often eroticized as if a male eye were viewing them, as if the point of view of the "universal" moviegoer were male.

Perhaps the most chilling example of the damaging effects of this "habit of seeing" is found in the world of modern medicine, where drugs prescribed for both sexes often have been tested on male subjects only. In other words, in laboratory tests to determine the safety of prescription drugs before marketing them, men's responses frequently have been used to gather statistical data on the medications' effectiveness and possible side effects. As a result, women may experience unexpected side effects while male users are unaffected. How could medical scientists not have anticipated this problem? Surely, the cultural habit of seeing male experience as universal played a role.

Traditional gender roles

I offer the above examples up front because I think they show some of the ways in which all of us have been programmed to see (or to be blind), myself included. I consider myself a recovering patriarchal woman. By *patriarchal woman* I mean, of course, a woman who has internalized the norms and values of *patriarchy*, which can be defined, in short, as any culture that privileges men by promoting traditional gender roles. *Traditional gender roles* cast men as rational, strong, protective, and decisive; they cast women as emotional (irrational), weak, nurturing, and submissive. These gender roles have been used very successfully to justify inequities, which still occur today, such as excluding women from equal access to leadership and decision-making positions (in the family as well as in politics, academia, and the corporate world), paying men higher wages than women for doing the same job (if women are even able to obtain the job), and convincing women that they are not fit for careers in such areas as mathematics and engineering. Many people today believe such inequities are a thing of the past because, over time, antidiscriminatory laws have been passed in an effort to guarantee women equal pay for equal work. However, these laws can be readily undermined, if not completely sidestepped. For example, an employer can pay a woman less for performing the same work as a man (or for doing more work than a man) simply by giving her a different job title. So women working in the United States, for instance, still are paid, on average, between 55 and 77 cents – depending on their ethnicity, age, and geographic location – for every dollar earned by men. In countries where such laws don't exist at all, women workers, of course, generally suffer even greater disparity.[1]

Patriarchy is thus, by definition, *sexist*, which means it promotes the belief that women are innately inferior to men. This belief in the inborn inferiority of women is a form of what is called *biological essentialism* because it is based on biological differences between the sexes that are considered part of our unchanging essence as men and women. A striking illustration is the word *hysteria*, which derives from the Greek word for womb (*hystera*) and refers to psychological disorders deemed peculiar to women and characterized by overemotional, extremely irrational behavior. Feminists don't deny the biological differences between men and women; in fact, many feminists celebrate those differences. But they don't agree that such differences as physical size, shape, and body chemistry make men naturally superior to women: for example, more intelligent, more logical, more courageous, or better leaders. Much Anglo-American feminism therefore distinguishes between the word sex, which refers to our biological constitution as female or male, and the word gender, which refers to our cultural programming as feminine or mas-culine. In other words, women are not born feminine, and men are not born masculine. Rather, these gender categories are constructed by society, which is why this view of gender is an example of what has come to be called social constructionism.

The belief that men are superior to women has been used, feminists have observed, to justify and maintain the male monopoly of positions of economic, political, and social power, in other words, to keep women powerless by denying them the educational and occupational means of acquiring economic, political, and social power. That is, the inferior position long occupied by women in patriarchal society has been culturally, not biologically, produced. For example, it is a patri-archal assumption, rather than a fact, that more women than men suffer from hysteria. But because it has been defined as a female problem, hysterical behavior in men won't be diagnosed as such. Instead, it will be ignored or given another, less damaging name, for example, shortness of temper. Of course, not all men accept patriarchal ideology, and those who don't — those who don't believe, for example, that because men generally have been endowed by nature with stronger muscles, they have been endowed with any other natural superiority — are often derided, by both patriarchal men and women, as weak and unmanly, as if the only way to be a man were to be a patriarchal man.

I call myself a patriarchal woman because I was socially programmed, as are most women and men, not to see the ways in which women are oppressed by traditional gender roles. I say that I'm recovering because I learned to recognize and resist that programming. For me, such recognition and resistance will always require effort — I'm recovering rather than recovered — not just because I internalized patriarchal programming years ago but because that program continues to assert itself in my world: in movies, television shows, books, magazines, and advertisements as well as in the attitudes of salespeople who think I can't learn to operate a simple machine, repair technicians who assume I won't know if they've done a shoddy job, and male drivers who believe I'm flattered by sexual offers shouted from passing cars (or, worse, who don't give a moment's thought to how I might feel or, worse yet, who hope I feel intimidated so that they can feel powerful). The point here is fairly simple: patriarchy continually exerts forces that undermine women's self-confidence and assertiveness, then points to the absence of these qualities as proof that women are naturally, and therefore correctly, self-effacing and submissive.

To cite a similar example of patriarchal programming, little girls have been (and some still are) told early in their educational careers that they can't do math. If not told so explicitly in words (by parents, teachers, or friends), they are told so by the body language, tone of voice, and facial expression of adults and peers. Because it is often assumed that little girls can't do math and, furthermore, that this deficiency doesn't really matter because most of them won't need math in later life, girls are not called on by the teacher as frequently as boys to perform mathematical operations. In fact, girls are often "rewarded" for failing at math: they receive ready sympathy, coddling, and other debilitating though enticing payoffs for being feminine. If girls manage to do well in math despite these obstacles, they are considered exceptions to the rule (which, from a child's point of view, usually means they are considered "freaks"). In short, girls are programmed to fail. Then the patriarchal mind-set points to girls' lower test scores in math and their failure to become math majors as proof that they are biologically ill-suited to mathematical studies, which, given the close relationship between math and logic, suggests that females are less logical than males. In other words, patriarchy creates the failure that it then uses to justify its assumptions about women.

Because I'm a recovering patriarchal woman, I am also very aware of the ways in which patriarchal gender roles are destructive for men as well as for women. For example, because traditional gender roles dictate that men are supposed to be strong (physically powerful and emotionally stoic), they are not supposed to cry because crying is considered a sign of weakness, a sign that one has been overpowered by one's emotions. For similar reasons, it is considered unmanly for men to show fear or pain or to express their sympathy for other men. Expressing sympathy (or any loving feeling) for other men is especially taboo because patriarchy assumes that only the most mute and stoic (or boisterous and boyish) forms of male bonding are free of homosexual overtones. In addition, men are not permitted to fail at anything they try because failure in any domain implies failure in one's manhood.

Failure to provide adequate economic support for one's family is considered the most humiliating failure a man can experience because it means that he has failed at what is considered his biological role as provider. The imperative for men to succeed economically has become an extremely pressurized situation in contemporary America because the degree of success men are expected to achieve keeps increasing: to be a "real" man in this day and age one must have a more expensive house and car than one's father, siblings, and friends, and one must send one's children to a more expensive school. If men can't achieve the unrealistic economic goals set for them in contemporary America, then they must increase the signs of their manhood in some other area: they must be the most sexually active (or make others believe that they are) or be able to hold the most liquor or display the most anger. It is not surprising, in this context, that anger and other violent emotions are the only emotions permitted, even encouraged, in men, for anger is a very effective means of blocking out fear and pain, which are not permitted, and anger usually produces the kind of aggressive behaviors associated with patriarchal manhood.

I refer to male programming, at this point, for two reasons, both of which reflect my personal feminist biases. I want the men reading this chapter to see in feminism the potential for learning a good deal about themselves as well as about women. And I want readers of both sexes to see that, even when we think we're talking about men, we're also talking about women because, in a patriarchy, everything that concerns men usually implies something (usually negative) about women. For example, it is important to note that all the behaviors described in the preceding two paragraphs – behaviors forbidden to men – are considered "womanish," that is, inferior, beneath the dignity of manhood. Men, and even little boys, who cry are called "sissies." *Sissy* sounds very much like *sister*, and it means "cowardly" or "feminine," two words that, in this context, are synonyms. Clearly, one of the most devastating verbal attacks to which a man can be subjected is to be compared to a woman. Thus, being a "real" man in patriarchal culture requires that one hold feminine qualities in contempt. Homosexuality is included on the list of "feminine" behaviors, at least for American men, because despite the plentiful example of very masculine homosexual men, the American stereotype of the homosexual male is an extremely feminine one. This phenomenon implies that whenever patriarchy wants to undermine a behavior, it portrays that behavior as feminine. It is important to note, too, that the patriarchal concept of femininity – which is linked to frailty, modesty, and timidity – disempowers women in the real world: it is not feminine to succeed in business, to be extremely intelligent, to earn big bucks, to have strong opinions, to have a healthy appetite (for anything), or to assert one's rights.

To briefly illustrate the debilitating effects of patriarchal gender roles on both women and men, consider the story of "Cinderella." Feminists have long been aware that the role of Cinderella, which patriarchy imposes on the imagination of young girls, is a destructive role because it equates femininity with submission, encouraging women to tolerate familial abuse, wait patiently to be rescued by a man, and view marriage as the only desirable reward for "right" conduct. By the same token, however, the role of Prince Charming – which requires men to be wealthy rescuers responsible for making their women happy "ever after" – is a destructive role for men because it promotes the belief that men must be unflagging superproviders without emotional needs.

Unfortunately, the notion of a feminist critique of fairy tales has been the target of mockery by social commentators who offer absurdly humorous and what they claim are politically correct versions of classic fairy tales in order to show us the allegedly ridiculous extremes to which feminists and other "malcontents" would lead us. However, feminist readings of fairy tales can, in fact, provide a wonderful means for illustrating the ways in which patriarchal ideology informs what appear to be even the most innocent of our activities. Consider, for example, the similarities among the ever popular "Snow White and the Seven Dwarfs," "Sleeping Beauty," and, of course, "Cinderella." In all three tales, a beautiful, sweet young girl (for females must be beautiful, sweet, and young if they are to be worthy of romantic admiration) is rescued (for she is incapable of rescuing herself) from a dire situation by a dashing young man who carries her off to marry him and live happily ever after. The plot thus implies that marriage to the right man is a guarantee of happiness and the proper reward for a right-minded young woman. In all three tales, the main female characters are stereotyped as either "good girls" (gentle, submissive, virginal, angelic) or "bad girls" (violent, aggressive, worldly, monstrous). These characterizations imply that if a woman does not accept her patriarchal gender role, then the only role left her is that of a monster. In all three tales, the "bad girls" – the wicked queen in "Snow White," the wicked fairy in "Sleeping Beauty," and the wicked stepmother and stepsisters in "Cinderella" – are also vain, petty, and jealous, infuriated because they are not as beautiful as the main character or, in the case of the wicked fairy, because she wasn't invited to a royal celebration. Such motivations imply that even when women are evil, their concerns are trivial. In two of the stories, the young maiden is awakened from a deathlike slumber by the potent (after all, it brings her to life) kiss of the would-be lover. This ending implies that the proper patriarchal young woman is sexually dormant until "awakened" by the man who claims her. We could analyze these tales further, and we could analyze additional tales, but the point here is to see how pervasive patriarchal ideology is and how it can program us without our knowledge or consent.

I refer in the above paragraph to "good girls" and "bad girls," and this concept deserves more attention because it's another way in which sexist ideology continues to influence us. As we saw above, patriarchal ideology suggests that there are only two identities a woman can have. If she accepts her traditional gender role and obeys the patriarchal rules, she's a "good girl"; if she doesn't, she's a "bad girl." These two roles – also referred to as "madonna" and "whore" or "angel" and "bitch" – view women only in terms of how they relate to the patriarchal order. Of course, how "good girls" and "bad girls" are specifically defined will alter somewhat according to the time and place in which they live. But it is patriarchy that will do the defining because both roles are projections of patriarchal male desire: for example, the desire to own "valuable" women suited to be wives and mothers, the desire to control women's sexuality so that men's sexuality cannot be threatened in any way, and the desire to dominate in all financial matters. This last desire is well served by the patriarchal ideology that deems certain kinds of work improper for "good girls," an ideology that forced many women writers in Victorian England to publish their work under male pseudonyms and that required women writers on both sides of the Atlantic to accommodate their art to patriarchal expectations or face the consequences (as Kate Chopin did at the turn of the twentieth century when her work was buried due to its feminist content, not to be reprinted until it was rediscovered by feminists in the late 1960s).

According to a patriarchal ideology in full force through the 1950s, versions of which are still with us today, "bad girls" violate patriarchal sexual norms in some way: they're sexually forward in appearance or behavior, or they have multiple sexual partners. Men sleep with "bad girls," but they don't marry them. "Bad girls" are used and then discarded because they don't deserve better, and they probably don't even expect better. They're not good enough to bear a man's name or his legitimate children. That role is appropriate only for a properly submissive "good girl." The "good girl" is rewarded for her behavior by being placed on a pedestal by patriarchal culture. To her are attributed all the virtues associated with patriarchal femininity and domesticity: she's modest, unassuming, self-sacrificing, and nurturing. She has no needs of her own, for she is completely satisfied by serving her family. At times, she may be sad about the problems of others, and she frequently worries about those in her care – but she is never angry. In Victorian culture in England she was the "angel in the house." She made the home a safe haven for her husband, where he could spiritually fortify himself before resuming the daily struggles of the workplace, and for her children, where they could receive the moral guidance needed to eventually assume their own traditional roles in the adult world.

What's wrong with being placed on a pedestal? For one thing, pedestals are small and leave a woman very little room to do anything but fulfill the prescribed role. For example, to remain on her Victorian pedestal, the "good girl" had to remain uninterested in sexual activity, except for the purpose of legitimate procreation, because it was believed unnatural for women to have sexual desire. In fact, "good" women were expected to find sex frightening or disgusting. For another thing, pedestals are shaky. One can easily fall off a pedestal, and when a woman does, she is often punished. At best, she suffers self-recrimination for her inadequacy or "unnaturalness." At worst, she suffers physical punishment from the community or from her husband, which until relatively recently was encouraged by law and custom and which is still too often tacitly condoned by an ineffectual or complicit justice system. It is interesting to note, in this context, that patriarchy *objectifies* both "bad girls" and "good girls." That is, patriarchy treats women, whatever their role, like objects: like objects, women exist, according to patriarchy, to be used without consideration of their own perspectives, feelings, or opinions. After all, from a patriarchal standpoint, women's perspectives, feelings, and opinions don't count unless they conform to those of patriarchy.

In upwardly mobile, middle-class American culture today, the woman on the pedestal is the woman who successfully juggles a career and a family, which means she looks great at the office and over the breakfast table, and she's never too tired after work to fix dinner, clean house, attend to all her children's needs, and please her husband in bed. In other words, patriarchal gender roles have not been eliminated by modern women's entrance into the male-dominated workplace, even if some of those women now hold what used to be traditionally male jobs. For many of those same women are still bound by patriarchal gender roles in the home, which they must now fulfill in addition to their career goals.

Furthermore, the persistence of repressive attitudes toward women's sexuality is still visible in our language today. For example, we use the negative word *slut* to describe a woman who sleeps with a number of men while we use the positive word *stud* to describe a man who sleeps with a number of women. And though women's fashions have radically changed since the nineteenth century, the most "feminine" clothing still promotes patriarchal ideology. For example, the extremely tight corsets worn by nineteenth-century women prevented them from getting enough oxygen to be physically active or to experience emotion without getting "the vapors": shortness of breath or slight fits of fainting, which were considered very feminine and proved that women were too fragile and emotional to participate in a man's world. Analogously, one of the most "feminine" styles of clothing for today's woman is the tight skirt and high heels, which create a kind of "feminine" walk (while precluding running) symbolically akin both to the restrained physical capability imposed by nineteenth-century women's clothing and to the male sexual access to women's bodies such attire allows.

A summary of feminist premises

So far, we've examined how patriarchal ideology works to keep women and men in traditional gender roles and thereby maintain male dominance. That patriarchal ideology functions in this way is a belief shared by all feminists even if they disagree about other issues. In fact, most feminists share several important assumptions, which might be summarized as follows.

1 Women are oppressed by patriarchy economically, politically, socially, and psychologically; patriarchal ideology is the primary means by which they are kept so.
2 In every domain where patriarchy reigns, woman is *other:* she is objectified and marginalized, defined only by her difference from male norms and values, defined by what she (allegedly) lacks and that men (allegedly) have.
3 All of Western (Anglo-European) civilization is deeply rooted in patriarchal ideology, as we see, for example, in the numerous patriarchal women and female monsters of Greek and Roman literature and mythology; the patriarchal interpretation of the biblical Eve as the origin of sin and death in the world; the representation of woman as a nonrational creature by traditional Western philosophy; and the reliance on *phallogocentric* thinking (thinking that is male

oriented in its vocabulary, rules of logic, and criteria for what is considered objective knowledge) by educational, political, legal, and business institutions. As we saw earlier, even the development of the Western canon of great literature, including traditional fairy tales, was a product of patriarchal ideology.

4   While biology determines our sex (male or female), culture determines our gender (masculine or feminine). That is, at least for most English-speaking feminists, the word gender refers not to our anatomy but to our behavior as socially programmed men and women. I behave "like a woman" (for example, submissively) not because it is natural for me to do so but because I was taught to do so. In fact, all the traits we associate with masculine and feminine behavior are learned, not inborn.

5   All feminist activity, including feminist theory and literary criticism, has as its ultimate goal to change the world by promoting women's equality. Thus, all feminist activity can be seen as a form of *activism*, although the word is usually applied to feminist activity that directly promotes social change through political activity such as public demonstrations, boycotts, voter education and registration, the provision of hotlines for rape victims and shelters for abused women, and the like. Although frequently falsely portrayed in opposition to "family values," feminists continue to lead the struggle for better family policies such as nutrition and health care for mothers and children; parental leave; and high-quality, affordable day care.

6   Gender issues play a part in every aspect of human production and experience, including the production and experience of literature, whether we are consciously aware of these issues or not.

Of course, the assumptions listed above are related, overlapping ideas, and, together, they imply that patriarchal ideology has a pervasive, deeply rooted influence on the way we think, speak, see ourselves, and view the world in which we live. The pervasiveness of patriarchal ideology raises some important questions for feminist theory. For example, if patriarchal ideology influences our identity and experience so strongly, how can we ever get beyond it? If our modes of thinking and our language are patriarchal, how can we ever think or speak differently? In other words, if the fabric of our existence is patriarchal, how can we ever become nonpatriarchal?

Getting beyond patriarchy

Feminists have long puzzled over the problem of getting beyond patriarchal programming and have offered many different solutions. For example, one way to deal with our apparent entrapment within patriarchal ideology is to consider the possibility that no ideology succeeds in fully programming all of the people all of the time. Every ideology has points of self-contradiction, of illogic, that permit us to understand its operations and decrease its influence, for instance, as Mary Woll-stonecraft resisted patriarchal ideology in 1792 when she wrote *A Vindication of the Rights of Woman*, as Virginia Woolf resisted patriarchal ideology in 1929 when she wrote *A Room of One's Own*, as Simone de Beauvoir resisted patriarchal ideology in 1949 when she wrote *The Second Sex*, and as feminist theorists continue to resist it today. Perhaps the difficulty in theorizing our way out of patriarchal ideology arises when we think of our immersion in it as an all-or-nothing situation: if we're not completely beyond patriarchy, then we must be completely programmed by it. I think it might be more useful to look at our relationship to patriarchal ideology as a dynamic situation: we must constantly struggle to understand and resist the various ways in which patriarchy dictates our lives, although we can't always see all the ways in which it does so. Individually and collectively, we will move forward in some areas even as we remain static or backslide in others, but we must continue to move forward – to understand and resist patriarchal ideology – wherever and whenever we can.

Given the difficulties involved in resisting patriarchal programming, many feminist theorists and literary critics believe we should be especially cautious about using frameworks that are themselves patriarchal, such as psychoanalysis and Marxism. Such frameworks are considered patriarchal because they embody various elements of patriarchal ideology. For example, because he used male experience as the standard against which he measured female experience, Freud believed that women suffer from what he called "penis envy" and that they tend to see their first-born sons as "penis substitutes" to make up for their own lack. Despite Marx's insights into the ways in which economic forces determine the lives of both sexes, he failed to realize the ways in which women have been oppressed by men despite their economic class.

Nevertheless, many feminists draw on elements of psychoanalytic and Marxist theory as well as other critical theories because they find them useful in examining issues relevant to women's experience. For example, psychoanalysis can be used to help us understand the psychological effects of patriarchal ideology as well as how and why women and men internalize it. Marxism can be used to help us understand how economic forces have been manipulated by patriarchal law and custom to keep women economically, politically, and socially oppressed as an underclass. Structuralist principles can be used to study underlying similarities among the experiences and productions of women from various cultures as well as underlying similarities in the ways they are oppressed. And deconstruction can be used to find the ways in which a literary work covertly reinforces the patriarchal ideology it criticizes, which some feminist literary critics were doing in America before the theory of deconstruction reached American shores.

Deconstruction, which is discussed in Chapter 8, helps us see, among other things, when our thinking is based on false oppositions, that is, on the belief that two ideas, qualities, or categories are polar opposites – for example, love/hate or good/evil – when, in fact, they are not. So deconstruction is also useful to feminists in helping us see the ways in which patriarchal ideology is often based on false oppositions. For instance, in refuting the sexist belief that men are naturally rational while women are naturally emotional, a feminist might do more than argue, for example, that women have been programmed to be more emotional or that both categories apply equally to both genders. Using deconstructive principles, she might argue that we are mistaken to separate the rational and the emotional into such diametrically opposed categories. Aren't our rational reasons for subscribing to a particular philosophical view or theoretical framework based, consciously or unconsciously, on how that viewpoint or framework makes us feel? Don't the rational and the emotional, properly understood, often work in tandem in our lives?

To my mind, one of feminism's strengths is the freedom with which it borrows ideas from other theories and adapts them to its own rapidly evolving needs. This is one reason why I believe that feminist theory will never become stale: it constantly incorporates new ideas from other fields and finds new ways to use old ideas. This is also why feminism can be seen as an interdisciplinary theory that can help us learn to make connections among seemingly divergent schools of thought. While all of the theories addressed in this book overlap with one another in various ways, few acknowledge that fact or use it to broaden or deepen their theoretical explorations to the extent that feminism does.

Of course, the question of how we can get beyond any ideology that dominates the way we think is a question relevant to any theory that purports to be new, which means it's a question relevant to all theories, though few directly address it. In fact, many of the unsolvable theoretical problems that feminist thinkers continue to engage are unsolvable problems for every theory, though these problems either remain unacknowledged by practitioners in those fields or are considered solved by earlier thinkers. For example, related to the problem of the possibility (or impossibility) of getting beyond any ideology that dominates the way we think is the problem of one's own *subjectivity*: one's own selfhood, the way one views oneself and others, which develops from one's own individual experiences. Given that we can't be aware of all the ways in which our own subjectivity determines how we interpret the world, how can we ever know that our speculations about human experience, or about anything else for that matter, are anything but expressions of our own subjectivity?

As we'll see in subsequent chapters, deconstruction and new historicism engage this problem, but most of the other theories do not directly address it. For feminism, as for deconstruction and new historicism, all perceptions, therefore all acts of interpretation, are unavoidably subjective. We cannot leave ourselves out of the picture when describing what we see because what we see is a product of who we are: our gender, our politics, our religion, our race, our socioeconomic class, our sexual orientation, our education, our family background, our problems, our strengths, our weaknesses, our theoretical framework, and so on. To claim that we are objective, as patriarchy encourages men to do, is merely to blind ourselves to the ways in which we are not so.

From a feminist perspective, when we interpret texts or anything else, the way to deal with our subjectivity is not to try to avoid it but to be as aware of it as possible, to include it in our interpretation as fully as possible, so that others will be able to take it into account when evaluating our viewpoints. This is why it's especially appropriate that I refer in this chapter, as you may have noticed, to my own experience and biases. My experience as a middle-aged, middle-class, hetero-sexual, white American woman with a Ph.D. in English and a lovingly dysfunctional family is bound to affect my interpretation of feminism as well as the feminist reading of *The Great Gatsby* I offer at the end of this chapter. Unavoidably, I'll see some things differently from other theorists and literary critics, and many of those differences can probably be accounted for by differences in the personal data I listed above. By knowing a little bit about me, it is hoped that my readers will be on the lookout for the ways in which my point of view is just that: what I see from where I'm standing.

French feminism

Additional strategies for getting beyond patriarchy have been offered by French feminists. Like American feminism, French feminism is diverse: it consists of many different points of view. Also like American feminism, French feminism believes in the importance of social and political activism in order to ensure equal opportunity and equal access to justice for women. We're taking a brief look at French feminism as a separate category, however, because French feminists have tended to focus more strongly on the philosophical dimension of women's issues than have British and American feminists, although French feminist theory has become, over time, an increasingly visible presence in Anglo-American feminism.

Generally speaking, the focus of French feminism has taken two different forms: *materialist feminism* and *psychoanalytic feminism*. The first form is interested in the social and economic oppression of women while the second form, as you might expect, concentrates on women's psychological experience. Although these two approaches to analyzing women's experience in patriarchal culture often contrast significantly, French feminists are also concerned with the ways in which women's social/economic and psychological experience are connected. For now, however, let's look at these two forms separately. I think that if we can gain a fairly clear idea of each, we will readily see the ways in which they compliment as well as contrast with each other.

French materialist feminism examines the patriarchal traditions and institutions that control the material (physical) and economic conditions by which society oppresses women, for example, patriarchal beliefs about the difference between men and women and the laws and customs that govern marriage and motherhood. Although Simone de Beauvoir didn't refer to herself as a materialist feminist, her groundbreaking *The Second Sex* (1949) created a theoretical basis for materialist feminists for decades to come. In a patriarchal society, Beauvoir observes, men are considered essential subjects (independent selves with free will), while women are considered contingent beings (dependent beings controlled by circumstances). Men can act upon the world, change it, give it meaning, while women have meaning only in relation to men. Thus, women are defined not just in terms of their difference from men, but in terms of their inadequacy in comparison to men. The word *woman*, therefore, has the same implications as the word *other*. A woman is not a person in her own right. She is man's Other: she is less than a man; she is a kind of alien in a man's world; she is not a fully developed human being the way a man is.

The first to argue that women are not born feminine but rather conditioned to be feminine by patriarchy, Beauvoir articulated an idea that is now called, as we saw earlier in this chapter, social constructionism in her now-famous words, "One is not born a woman; one becomes one" (cited in Moi 92). Indeed, Beauvoir argues that, despite patriarchy's assumptions to the contrary, women are not even born with a maternal instinct. An instinct is something all members of a species have as part of their natural biological makeup, whereas not all women want to have children or feel comfortable being mothers. Yet patriarchy tells them that they are unfulfilled as women if they don't have children, and there is a great deal of pressure brought to bear upon women in order to recruit them for motherhood. Clearly, how can we know what "woman" is "by nature," given that we never see her outside the social conditioning of patriarchy?

Beauvoir maintains that women should not be content with investing the meaning of their lives in their husbands and sons, as patriarchy encourages them to do. As Jennifer Hansen observes, "Beauvoir strongly believed that marriage ... trapped and stunted women's intellectual growth and freedom" (2). In investing themselves so thoroughly in the accomplishments of their husbands and sons, Beauvoir claims, women are trying to escape their own freedom to fulfill their own potential in the world, a freedom that they often try to avoid because it is frightening: it demands personal responsibility while offering no guarantee of success or even of well-being. "If woman seems to be the inessential [being] which never becomes the essential," Beauvoir suggests, "it is because she herself fails to bring about this change" (10).

Why is it so difficult for women to recognize their own subjugation, let alone do something about it? Beauvoir points out that, unlike other oppressed groups – for example, oppressed classes and oppressed racial and religious minorities – there is no historical record of women's shared culture, shared traditions, or shared oppression. They have been, in this sense, "written out" of history, not considered a topic worth covering. Furthermore, she observes that women

> lack a concrete means for organizing themselves into a unit. ... They have no [collective recorded] past ... no religion of their own. ... They live dispersed among the males, attached through residence, housework, economic condition, and social standing to certain men – fathers or husbands – more firmly than they are to other women.
>
> (11)

In other words, women's allegiance to men from their own social class, race, or religion always supersedes their allegiance to women from different classes, races, or religions. In fact, women's allegiance to men also supersedes their allegiance to women from their *own* class, race, or religion.

One of many thinkers influenced by Beauvoir, Christine Delphy offers a feminist critique of patriarchy based on Marxist principles. Delphy, who coined the phrase *materialist feminism* in the early 1970s, focuses her analysis on the family as economic unit. Just as the lower classes are oppressed by the upper classes in society as a whole, she explains, women are the subordinates within families. As such, women constitute a separate oppressed class, based on their oppression as women, regardless of the socioeconomic class to which they belong. For Delphy, marriage is a labor contract that ties women to unpaid domestic labor, commonly trivialized as "housework," not considered important enough to be seriously analyzed as a topic, or a problem, in its own right. An understanding of the implications of this situation is central, she notes, to an understanding of women's oppression. Delphy points out that

> [a]ll contemporary "developed" societies ... depend on the unpaid labour of women for domestic services and child-rearing. These services are furnished within the framework of a particular relationship to an individual (the husband). They are excluded from the realm of exchange [i.e., these services are not treated like the jobs people do for money outside their own home] and consequently have no *value*. They are unpaid. Whatever women receive in return is independent of the work which they perform because it is not handed out in exchange for that work (i.e., as a wage to which their work entitles them), but rather as a gift. The husband's only obligation, which is obviously in his own interest, is to provide for his wife's basic needs, in other words he maintains her labour power.
>
> (60)

In addition, Delphy contends that women's domestic work in their own homes is unpaid not because their work is unimportant or involves less time or labor than the paid work performed by men outside the home, but because <u>patriarchy defines</u> <u>women in their domestic roles as nonworkers</u>. And nonworkers, of course, should not expect to be paid. Ironically, "all the anthropological and sociological evidence reveals," Delphy notes, "that the dominant classes make the classes in their power do the productive work – that the pre-eminent sex does less work" (61). In other words, in a patriarchy women do the domestic labor at home that men don't want to do, and their work day is 24 hours long. So when you add it all up, women work longer hours than men, though women's work in the home isn't recognized as real labor deserving of pay. It should not be surprising, then, that in order to understand anything about sexuality or gender we must first understand, Delphy argues, that all relationships between men and women are based on power: patriarchal men want to keep all of it; nonpatriarchal women want power to be equally distributed. As more and more American wives take jobs outside the home, while they still perform the lion's share of domestic labor and child-rearing tasks, Delphy's analysis seems especially relevant to the lives of American women today.

For our final example of French materialist feminism let's take a look at the work of Colette Guillaumin. Guillaumin observes that men are defined primarily and referred to primarily in terms of what they do, according to their value in society as participants in the workforce, as decision-makers, and so forth. Women are defined primarily and referred to primarily in terms of their sex. As Guillaumin notes, from phrases she collected within a single 48-hour period, a "group meeting to give their opinion on some matter" was said to consist of a "company director, a lathe-operator, a croupier [a person who runs a gambling table at a casino] and a woman" (73). Similarly, Guillaumin reports, a world leader, discussing a repressive regime to which he was opposed, said, "They killed tens of thousands of workers, students, and women" (73). In other words, Guillaumin observes, in terms of their function in society, "female human beings ... [are] ... primarily and fundamentally women" (73). And for Guillaumin, this means they are primarily and fundamentally property, for example, property to be "exchanged" or "given away" (depending on the culture to which they belong) in marriage.

The primary form of women's oppression, Guillaumin argues, which also reveals their function as property, is appropriation. As she explains, it is not merely the case that women are exploited, as everyone knows, in the labor market (for example, paid less than men for the same work) and in the home, where they are generally not paid at all for their labor. Women are also oppressed by what Guil- laumin calls "direct physical appropriation," by which she means "the reduction of women to the state of material objects" (74) and which she compares to slavery and serfdom. In the case of women, Guillaumin calls this appropriation *sexage.* Sexage occurs, she believes, in four main forms: (1) the appropriation of women's time, (2) the appropriation of the products of women's bodies, (3) women's sexual obligation, and (4) women's obligation to care for whichever members of the family can't care for themselves as well as for healthy male family members.

Let's take a brief look at each of these forms of sexage. As Guillaumin observes, (1) the marriage contract puts no limits on the time wives (and any other women living in the family, such as daughters, aunts, and grandmothers) will have to work and specifies no holidays on which they won't have to work. (2) In some cultures, women's hair and even their milk are sold by male members of the family; the number of children a couple will have is decided by the male; and children are still the legal property of the husband. (3) Women's sexual obligation to men occurs both in marriage and in prostitution. For Guillaumin, the primary difference between the two is that time limits are placed on a man's use of prostitutes, and he must pay for the specific acts he wants. (4) Although the caretaking of babies, children, the elderly, and the sick is sometimes carried out by paid workers (who are usually women), the overwhelming majority of it is done by unpaid female family members or, in some cultures, by unpaid female religious workers, such as nuns. The overall effect of all four areas of appropriation is to deprive women of a sense of their individuality as well as of their independence and autonomy. In short, women are, as Guillaumin puts it, "the social tool assigned to those tasks" (79) that men don't want to do.

In contrast to materialist feminism, French feminist psychoanalytic theory is interested in patriarchy's influence on women's psychological experience and creativity. Its focus is on the individual psyche, not on group experience. For the oppression of women is not limited to the economic, political, and social domains; it includes women's psychological repression at the level of the unconscious as well. And it is here, in each woman's personal psychology, that she must learn to liberate herself if women's materialist liberation is going to have any lasting foundation. For a woman can't be liberated in any meaningful way if she doesn't know that she needs to be liberated. And for many French psychoanalytic feminists, the possibilities for women's psychological liberation must be investigated at the site at which most, if not all, of their psychological subjugation occurs – language – because it is within language that detrimental patriarchal notions of *sexual difference* (what patriarchy believes are the essential, or inborn, differences between women and men) have been defined and continue to exert their repressive influence.

For instance, Hélène Cixous argues that language reveals what she calls *patriarchal binary thought*, which might be defined as seeing the world in terms of polar opposites, one of which is considered superior to the other. Examples include such hierarchical binary oppositions as head/heart, father/mother, culture/nature, intelligible/palpable (that which can be understood by the mind versus that which can be felt by the body), sun/moon, and activity/passivity. Oppositions like these organize the way we think, and for each opposition Cixous asks, "Where is [the woman]?" (91). That is, which side of each opposition is assumed to define some aspect of the female? Clearly, according to patriarchal thinking, the woman occupies the right side of each of these oppositions, the side that patriarchy considers inferior – heart, mother, nature, palpable, moon, and passivity – while it is assumed that the male is defined by the left side of each opposition, the side that patriarchy considers superior: head, father, culture, intelligible, sun, and activity. "Traditionally," Cixous notes, "the question of sexual difference is treated by coupling it with the opposition activity/passivity" (92). In other words, patriarchal thinking believes that women are born to be passive while men are born to be active because it is natural for the sexes to be different in this way. Thus, if a woman is not passive, she is not really a woman. Of course, it follows that women are naturally submissive to men, that men are natural leaders, and so forth.

For Cixous, women will not learn to resist patriarchal thinking by becoming part of the patriarchal power structure, that is, by obtaining equal status and equal opportunity in current patriarchal society. For women's acquisition of power within the existing sociopolitical system would not adequately change the system. Indeed, the result would be that women would become more like patriarchal men because they would learn to think as patriarchal men have been trained to think. Instead, she argues that, as the source of life, women are themselves the source of power, of energy. We therefore need a new, feminine language that undermines or eliminates the patriarchal binary thinking that oppresses and silences women. This kind of language, which Cixous believes best expresses itself in writing, is called *écriture féminine* (feminine writing). It is fluidly organized and freely associative. It resists patriarchal modes of thinking and writing, which generally require prescribed, "correct" methods of organization, rationalist rules of logic (logic that stays "above the neck," relying on narrow definitions of cognitive experience and discrediting many kinds of emotional and intuitive experience), and linear reasoning (x precedes y, which precedes z).

Although women's prolonged bonds with their mothers, with their original source of power and energy, have given them a privileged relationship to *écriture féminine*, a man who can get in touch with his early bond with his mother can also produce it. As examples of such writing, Cixous names the work of French writers Marguerite Duras, Colette, and Jean (John) Genet as well as that of Brazilian writer Clarice Lispector. I think we can speculate that literary works such as Toni Morrison's *Beloved*, Virginia Woolf's *Mrs. Dalloway*, James Joyce's *Finnegan's Wake*, and William Faulkner's *Absalom, Absalom!* might also serve as examples. Cixous sees this kind of writing as a way to spontaneously connect (or reconnect) to the unfettered, joyous vitality of the female body, which as we saw earlier, she emphasizes as the source of life. Thus, for her, writing can be an enactment of liberation. The abandonment of patriarchal thinking envisioned here may indeed seem utopian, but as Toril Moi observes, "[u]topian thought has always been a source of inspiration for feminists" (121).

Similarly, Luce Irigaray suggests that, in a patriarchal culture, much of women's subjugation occurs in the form of psychological repression enacted through the medium of language. In other words, women live in a world in which virtually all meaning has been defined by patriarchal language. Therefore, though they may not realize it, women don't speak as active originators of their own thoughts. Rather, they passively imitate previously spoken ideas. This state of affairs is not as surprising as it initially may seem when we consider the history of Western patriarchal thought. As Irigaray observes, for Western philosophers the woman is just a mirror of their own masculinity. That is, men have defined femininity in terms of their own needs, fears, and desires. For example, she points out that Freud – although she finds his theories useful, even groundbreaking – was projecting the masculine fear of castration onto women when he hypothesized that women suffer from penis envy, that they feel they have been castrated. Clearly, such a viewpoint assumes that women want the same things men want, that women do not have feelings or desires that are theirs alone. Caught within patriarchy, Irigaray posits, women have only two choices: (1) to keep quiet (for anything a woman says that does not fit within the logic of patriarchy will be seen as incomprehensible, meaningless), or (2) to imitate patriarchy's representation of herself as it wants to see her (that is, to play the inferior role given her by patriarchy's definition of sexual difference, which foregrounds men's superiority). Obviously, this is hardly a real choice.

Patriarchal power is also evident, for Irigaray, in what many thinkers refer to as the male gaze: the man looks; the woman is looked at. And it is the one who looks who is in control, who holds the power to name things, the power to explain the world and so to rule the world. The one looked at – the woman – is merely an object to be seen. Thus, in a patriarchy, women are merely tokens, markers, commodities in a male economy. In other words, women function to display men's relations to other men. To cite the simplest example, a patriarchal man who feels he must have a beautiful woman on his arm in order to impress other people isn't interested in impressing other people. He's interested in impressing other men. In short, patriarchy is a man's world: men invent the rules of the game, they play it only with one another, and women are merely to be found among the prizes.

Like Cixous, Irigaray argues that the way to get beyond patriarchy is by means of the same vehicle that programmed us within patriarchy: language. And she believes that women-only groups are necessary for the development of nonpatriarchal ways of thinking and speaking. Irigaray calls her notion of woman's language womanspeak, and she finds its source in the female body, specifically in what she sees as the contrast between female and male sexual pleasure. For her, female sexual pleasure is "far more diversified, more multiple in its differences, more complex, more subtle, than is commonly imagined" (28). And so is womanspeak more diversified, more multiple in its meanings, more complex, and more subtle than patriarchal language. As Irigaray puts it, when a woman dares speak in her own way, "'she' sets off in all directions leaving 'him' [the patriarchal man] unable to discern the coherence of any meaning. Hers are contradictory words, somewhat mad from the standpoint of reason, inaudible for whoever listens to them with ready-made grids, with a fully elaborated code in hand" (29). For some feminist thinkers, Irigaray's definition of womanspeak is particularly controversial because, among other things, it seems to reinforce patriarchal stereotypes of women as illogical or even irrational. One productive way to view womanspeak, however, might be to consider what seems to me, at least, to be the very strong possibility that Irigaray is not saying that women speak incoherently but that this is how it seems to patriarchal people, programmed to attribute meaning only to language that conforms to patriarchal rules of logic, that is, to linear, thesis-oriented language.

In contrast, Julia Kristeva, another French psychoanalytic feminist, doesn't believe in *écriture féminine* or womanspeak because she believes that any theory that *essentializes* women (that is, that posits essential – inborn, biological – characteristics for women) misrepresents their infinite diversity and leaves them vulnerable to the patriarchal essentialization of women as naturally submissive, overly emotional, and so forth. Indeed, for Kristeva, *the feminine* can't be defined because there are as many definitions of *the feminine* as there are women. We can, however, know this about femininity, Kristeva asserts: it is marginalized, oppressed, just as the working class is marginalized and oppressed.

Furthermore, what have been generally accepted by many feminists as the bio-logical differences that make women female and men male (as opposed to the dif-ferences socially imposed by patriarchy that define us as feminine or masculine) are seen by Kristeva as social differences rather than biological differences because of their concrete effects on women in the real world. As she puts it, the "sexual, biological, physiological, and reproductive difference [between women and men] reflects a difference in ... the social contract" ("Woman's Time" 188). In other words, if one is born with the biology of a female, one's place in society is accorded fewer rights – particularly the right to own and control one's body sexually, both in terms of the kind and number of sexual relationships one will have and in terms of abortion and contraceptive rights – than if one is born with the biology of a male. In the final analysis, the issue is not how biological difference should be defined; rather the issue is that whatever meaning biological difference may have is instantly consumed, overshadowed, displaced by the social (patriarchal) meaning that accompanies it. And it is the social meaning given to sexual difference that oppresses women. Thus for Kristeva, as for most French feminists – including materialist feminists like the ones discussed earlier – the difference between sex and gender posited by Anglo-American feminists does not exist. Patriarchy defines and controls the way we relate to sex (female) and gender (feminine) as if they were the same thing. Indeed, there is no word in French for *gender* as we use the word in English.

Instead of embracing *écriture féminine* and womanspeak as a means to take us beyond patriarchal oppression, Kristeva maintains that women and men can get beyond patriarchal language and patriarchal thinking by seeking access to what she calls the semiotic dimension of language (not to be confused with the field of study called *semiotics*, which is the analysis of cultural sign systems). For Kristeva, language consists of two dimensions: the symbolic and the semiotic. The symbolic dimension is the domain in which words operate and meanings are attributed to them. What she calls the semiotic dimension of language is that part of language that, in contrast, consists of such elements as intonation (sound, tone of voice, volume, and for lack of a better word, musicality); rhythm; and the body language that occurs as we speak, which reveals our feelings and bodily drives (for example, bodily drives that relate to the sexual, to survival, and so forth). Perhaps we can say, then, that the semiotic consists of the way we speak, for instance the emotions that come across in our voice and body language as we talk. So it is not unexpected that, as Kristeva notes, "Scientific discourse, for example ... tends to reduce as much as possible the semiotic component. On the contrary ... [in] poetic language ... the semiotic ... tends to gain the upper hand" (*Desire in Language* 134).

Indeed, the semiotic is the first "speech" infants have available to them – the vocal sounds and bodily movements they produce – before they acquire language. And they learn this "speech" through their contact with the gestures, rhythms, and other nonverbal forms of communication associated with the mother's body. Thus it is through the semiotic aspect of language that we remain, though unconsciously, in continual contact with our precognitive, preverbal experience: with our instinctual drives and with our earliest connections to our mothers. It is noteworthy, Kristeva observes, that both our instinctual drives and our earliest connections to our mothers are repressed by our entrance into language. For language is the dominion of patriarchy, which controls its symbolic, or meaning-making, dimension. The semiotic, however, remains beyond patriarchal programming, and whatever patriarchy can't control outright, it represses. Of course, Kristeva is not suggesting that we can or should return to the semiotic state of the infant but that we can and should access that part of our unconscious where the semiotic resides, for example, through such creative means as art and literature. For these are the vehicles that allow us a new way to relate to language and to thereby overcome the stranglehold patriarchy has on the way women and men think.

Before we leave this section, I think it's important to address an issue of which you may or may not be aware. Often, when the phrase *French feminism* is used, we think of the kinds of topics that fall within the realm of French psychoanalytic feminism. For many Americans, the work done by French materialist feminists doesn't come readily to mind because that work – with the exception of the writing of Simone de Beauvoir – hasn't received as much press, so to speak, in mainstream academia as has psychoanalytic feminism. Certainly, there are a variety of reasons for this imbalance. Surely, one reason is the fact that the branch of American academia that has had the most influence over the dissemination of critical theory is more accustomed to the kind of abstract theorizing we find in French psychoanalytic feminism and therefore has welcomed it more readily. In addition, however, I can't help but notice that French psychoanalytic feminism's tendency toward abstraction has the double pay-off of (1) being difficult for novices to understand, thereby securing the position of those professors, theorists, and literary critics already holding academic power in the field of critical theory, and (2) rendering French feminism vulnerable to ridicule and dismissal, which is rather ironic given that the work of many leading American theorists is often rather abstract. Unfortunately, the desire to ignore or dismiss French feminism has been a desire of long standing in much of American academia, including among some feminists as well as nonfeminists.

It's true that much French psychoanalytic feminism does seem to have been written primarily for people who have the educational background to comprehend it. Among other factors, most of it draws on, extends, or quarrels with the work of two French thinkers whose work is quite difficult for the uninitiated to understand: Jacques Derrida, who came up with the interpretive approach called deconstruction, and Jacques Lacan, who offers us an interpretation of Freudian psychoanalysis the logic of which, if we are to reap its full benefit, requires, I think, an understanding of both structuralism and deconstruction. (If you wish, you can read about Lacanian psychoanalysis in Chapter 2 and about structuralism and deconstruction in Chapters 7 and 8, respectively.) In fact, most French feminists, though their work may be less abstract than that of the psychoanalytic feminists discussed above, write within a philosophical tradition with which students of literature in America might not be acquainted. So don't be put off when you first read the work of French feminists for yourself. Whatever their philosophical orientation may be, they're not trying to exclude you. Like the philosophers upon whom they draw and with whom they often disagree, they're trying to break new ground and open up new ways of thinking. And I hope you'll agree that learning to think in new ways is a task that, though difficult, is well worth our effort.

Multicultural feminism

Awareness of one's own subjectivity, which as we noted earlier is a feminist goal, has become especially important as white, middle-class, heterosexual feminists, who have always held the most visible positions of leadership in women's movements in the United States, are finally recognizing the ways in which their policies and practices have reflected their own experiences while ignoring the experiences of women of color, lesbians, and poor, undereducated women both in America and throughout the world. While all women are subject to patriarchal oppression, each woman's specific needs, desires, and problems are greatly shaped by her race, socioeconomic class, sexual orientation, educational experience, religion, nationality, and geographic location.

For one thing, patriarchy operates differently in different countries: there are significant differences between patriarchy in the United States and patriarchy in, say, India, Mexico, or Iran. Furthermore, even within the borders of a single country, cultural differences affect women's experience of patriarchy. In the United States, for example, the experience of patriarchy for women of color is inseparable from their experience of racism (see Chapter 11); lesbians' experience of patriarchy is inseparable from their experience of heterosexism (see Chapter 10); poor women's experience of patriarchy is inseparable from their experience of classism (see Chapter 3); and so forth. And you can imagine the complex operations of oppression in the lives of women who belong to three or more of these categories. Therefore, the promotion of sisterhood – psychological and political bonding among women based on the recognition of common experiences and goals – must include respect for and attention to individual differences among women as well as an equitable distribution of power among various cultural groups within feminist leadership.

African American feminists have been especially helpful in revealing the political and theoretical limitations inherent in white mainstream feminists' neglect of cultural experiences different from their own. For example, black feminists have analyzed the ways in which gender oppression cannot be understood apart from racial oppression. A black woman is oppressed by patriarchy, black feminists observe, not just because she's a woman but because she's a black woman, a category that has been defined historically in America as less valuable than the category of white woman. The white Victorian ideal of the "true woman" as submissive, fragile, and sexually pure, which still influences patriarchal thinking today, excluded by definition black women and poor women of all races whose survival demanded hard physical labor and who were vulnerable to rape and to sexual exploitation in the workplace. The logic was circular and deadly: a woman whose economic situation forced her into hard labor outside the home and made her the victim of sexual predators was defined as unwomanly and therefore unworthy of protection from those who exploited her. This view was widely held by men, both white and black, and by white women as well. Black women, therefore, were in a double bind. They could expect neither gender solidarity from white women nor racial solidarity from black men, the two groups on whom they should have been able to count for help.

Unfortunately, this dilemma persists today. White mainstream feminism, while it has tended to marginalize black women because of their race, nevertheless encourages them to prioritize gender issues over racial issues, arguing that black women are oppressed more by sexism than by racism. At the same time, the black male community, while it has tended to marginalize black women because of their gender, nevertheless encourages them to prioritize racial issues over gender issues, arguing that black women are oppressed more by racism than by sexism. As Lorraine Bethel observes, an understanding of this double oppression forms the basis of African American feminist criticism:

> Black feminist literary criticism offers a framework for identifying the common socio-aesthetic problems of authors who attempt to fashion a literature of cultural identity in the midst of racial/sexual oppression. It incorporates a political analysis that enables us to comprehend and appreciate the incredible achievements Black women ... made in establishing artistic and literary traditions of any sort, and to understand their qualities and sensibilities. Such understanding requires a consciousness of the oppression these artists faced daily in a society full of institutionalized and violent hatred for both their Black skins and their female bodies. Developing and maintaining this consciousness is a basic tenet of Black feminism.
>
> (178)

On the other hand, some black women feel that feminism is a divisive force in the black community. As a result, some have either abandoned feminism or sought ways to reconcile it with the concerns of the black community, as Alice Walker did when she called herself a "womanist" (xi) because she works for the survival and wholeness of her people, men and women both, and for the promotion of dialogue and community as well as for the valorization of women and of all the varieties of work women perform. Similarly, as Carolyn Denard points out, many African American women "advocate what may be called ethnic cultural feminism" (172), which is "concerned more with the particular female cultural values of their own ethnic group rather than with those of women in general" (171). Drawing on the novels of Toni Morrison to illustrate this approach, Denard explains that ethnic cultural feminism acknowledges the damaging effects of sexism on women of color, both inside and outside their ethnic community, but it "does not advocate as a solution to their oppression [a] ... political feminism that alienates black women from their ethnic group" (172). Furthermore, ethnic cultural feminism "celebrat[es] the unique feminine cultural values that black women have developed in spite of and often because of their oppression" (172).

Whatever theoretical preferences black feminist critics bring to their analyses of literature, their interpretations often demonstrate the importance of understanding gender issues in cultural context. Given that some cultural groups have their own categories of literary criticism and that some women may find their concerns addressed in more than one category, it might be useful to pause here and note what some of those categories are.

Depending on its theoretical orientation, literary criticism that addresses women's issues may fall under one or more different headings. Among them are feminist criticism, African American criticism (which studies, among other things, works by African Americans within the context of African American experience, history, and literary traditions), lesbian criticism, Marxist criticism, and postcolonial criticism (which studies, among other things, works that have emerged from cultures that developed in response to colonial domination, for example, works by writers from India, which was controlled by Britain until 1947). Of course, women's issues will also be addressed in any literary criticism that focuses on women writers from a particular ethnic group: for example, to name a few we haven't mentioned, Chicanas, Latinas, Native American women, and Asian American women. Although all of these categories may address women's experience, generally speaking it is only when a feminist perspective helps guide the interpretation that a piece of criticism is referred to as feminist. Clearly, these categories easily overlap, and it is not unusual to find literary critics who consider themselves hybrids of a sort, for example, Marxist-feminist or lesbian-feminist-Chicana critics.

Gender studies and feminism

As we have seen throughout this chapter, feminist analysis focuses a good deal on the enormous role played by gender – that is, by a society's definitions of femininity and masculinity – in our daily lives. For example, our gender plays a key role in forming our individual identity: both our self-perception and the way we relate to others. And our gender strongly influences how we are treated by others and by society as a whole as it is embodied in such institutions as the medical profession, the law, the educational system, and our culture's hiring and employment practices. In addition, queer theory, which you can read about in Chapter 10 ("Lesbian, gay, and queer criticism"), has brought a good deal of attention to gender issues over the last several years by raising questions concerning our society's heterosexual assumptions about sexuality and gender, for example, its assumption that males are "naturally masculine" and that females are "naturally feminine." It seems logical, then, that gender has emerged as a field of study in its own right devoted to these and to all topics pertaining to gender. Indeed, you may already have taken a course called Gender Studies or Women and Gender Studies: the latter title is often given to courses about gender when their primary focus is the relationship between gender and the patriarchal oppression of women.

For our purposes, an understanding of some of the major issues addressed by gender studies is a useful and perhaps indispensable part of our understanding of the ways in which feminist concerns are continuing to evolve and expand. Among other issues that figure prominently in gender studies are the following overlapping topics: (1) patriarchal assumptions about gender and gender roles that continue to oppress women, (2) alternatives to the current way we conceptualize gender as either feminine or masculine, (3) the relationship between sex and gender (between the ways our bodies are biologically constructed and the genders to which we are assigned), and (4) the relationship between sexuality and gender (between our sexual orientation and the ways in which we are viewed in terms of gender). Of course, we've discussed throughout this chapter many of the ways in which patriarchal assumptions about gender and gender roles continue to oppress women, so let's take a look now at each of the three remaining areas.

To begin, we need alternatives to the current way we think about gender because the current way we think about gender includes so many inaccuracies. Although research findings about gender, just like research findings in every field, often can be complex and contradictory, they can nevertheless alert us to the ways in which we've taken as facts too many widely held but unsubstantiated opinions and myths about gender. Let me cite just two striking examples, starting with a belief that I think most of us share about the biological operations of testosterone, or the "male hormone."

We've often said or heard it said about a male exhibiting overly or inappropriately aggressive behavior, "Oh, he just has too much testosterone." That is, aggressive behavior in males is generally considered an instinct rather than a product of such social factors as upbringing, psychological dynamics in the home, exposure to a dangerous environment outside the home, and the like. And once a behavior is considered instinctual and linked to gender, it is difficult for many of us to see it in any other light. Robert M. Sapolsky points out, however, that studies of testosterone levels in males have been limited to showing merely that increased testosterone levels *accompany* increased aggression. That is, there is no research indicating that increased testosterone levels *cause* aggression; it is merely assumed that they do so. Sapolsky's research indicates that, in fact, testosterone does not elevate aggression. Rather, "aggression elevates testosterone secretion" (16). Sapolsky observes that "[s]ome testosterone" is necessary for "normal aggressive behavior" (17), but the range of what is necessary is very wide. "[A]nywhere from roughly 20 percent of normal to twice normal" (17) produces roughly the same amount of normal aggressive behavior in males. So even if we know the testosterone level for each individual in a given group of males, we will not be able to predict their aggression because the range of what is considered a normal amount of testosterone is so wide. Excessive amounts of testosterone, Sapolsky notes, can "*exaggerat[e]*" the aggression that's already there" (17, Sapolsky's italics), but it doesn't cause aggression. In other words, testosterone permits aggression to occur only if that aggression is elicited by "the social factors and environment in which [aggression] occurs" (Sapolsky 19).

Just as unsubstantiated opinion has been widely accepted as fact concerning the role of testosterone in male aggression – a role that is also associated, for many of us, with the male "instinct" to be the breadwinner and to protect the home – so has unsubstantiated opinion been widely accepted as fact concerning the role of the maternal instinct in females. Again, because caregiving, especially caregiving to infants and young children, has been labeled a female instinct, it is difficult for many of us to consider it in any other light. As Linda Brannon notes, however, "research on ... emotion has revealed that there may be few gender differences in the inner experience of emotion. Gender differences appear in how and when emotion is displayed" (213), she observes, rather than in how and when emotion is felt. Specifically, Brannon finds that "[r]esearch on gender differences in responsiveness to babies has shown differences in self-reports, but not in physiological measures, of responses to babies" (214). Thus, "girls and women show more responsiveness to babies because they believe they should, and ... boys and men show less responsiveness for the same reasons" (214).

Of course, women are still much more involved in childcare than men, and women who take care of children report that they experience both a great deal of pleasure and a great deal of irritation in caring for them. It is interesting to note, however, that men who spend a great deal of time caring for children often report similar responses (Brannon 214). Indeed, most of us have seen the growing trend in fathers' increased involvement in the lives of their children. Moreover, Brannon points out, "research indicates that ... the concept of maternal instinct has no support as a biologically based explanation for caregiving, and both men and women have similar emotions related to nurturing" (214). While no one is trying to say that women are not good caregivers to children, a more accurate statement is that many women *and* men are good caregivers to children and enjoy that role a great deal; at the same time, however, many women and men wouldn't choose that role as their primary function in the household if they had a choice. In short, nurturing is not a role biologically linked to sex although many people long have believed it to be.

Both of the examples just given suggest that gender is socially constructed rather than a matter of biology: women and men usually behave in ways associated with their assigned gender because they are socially programmed to do so, not because it is natural for them to do so. However, if there is one dimension of gender studies that is perhaps even more capable of making us rethink our conventional way of viewing gender, it is cross-cultural studies in gender. For as Joan Z. Spade and Catherine G. Valentine point out, "The variations and fluidity in the definitions and expressions of gender across cultures illustrate that the American gender system is not universal" (5).

The American gender system is referred to as a binary system because it consists of two genders, masculine and feminine, that are based on two sexes, male and female, and because those two genders are considered polar opposites. There is no in-between: you're either masculine or feminine because you're either male or female, and if you're not one or the other of these two genders, then there must by something wrong with you. In numerous other cultures, however, there are gender systems that are not binary. Among the many that have existed in the past and those that still exist today, let's take a brief look at a few interesting examples. Specifically, let's take a look at two Southeast Asian cultures in which men and women are considered more alike than different – so much so that they are not considered different genders in our sense of the term – and at Native American cultures in which there are more than two genders.

Christine Helliwell, for instance, observes that there are many societies in Southeast Asia that emphasize the similarities between men and women rather than their differences. As one example, she points to the Gerai people of Indonesia, where

> there is no sense of a dichotomized [separated into two polar opposites] mas-
> culinity and femininity. Rather, men and women are seen to have the same
> kinds of capacities and proclivities [inclinations, especially toward objectionable
> behavior]. ... [I]n terms of the central quality of nurturance (perhaps the most
> valued quality in Gerai) ... Gerai people see no difference between men and
> women.
>
> (126)

In fact, even the sexual organs of Gerai men and women are "explicitly con-
ceptualized as the same. ... [T]hey have the same ... conical shape, narrower at the
base and wider at the top"; the difference is simply that women's sexual organs are
"inside the body" while men's are "outside the body" (Helliwell 127). In case you
have difficulty visualizing this similarity, you might imagine the penis as analogous to the birth canal and the testicles as analogous to the ovaries: the overall,
bird's-eye-view formation is roughly the same; it's just the location that's different.

Another useful illustration of the similarities between women and men – this
time in terms of the power dynamics that can be found in some cultures – is
offered by Maria Alexandra Lepowsky's example of the people of Vanatinai, a small
island near New Guinea, where "[i]deologies of male superiority or right of
authority over women are notably absent, and ideologies of gender equivalence are
clearly articulated" (150). Men and women in this culture have equal rights over
their own labor and the products of their labor, equal access to the accumulation of
material wealth, and equal access to the acquisition of prestige in the community.
"Women are not characterized as weak or inferior. Women and men are valorized
for the same qualities of strength, wisdom, and generosity" (Lepowsky 158). As
both the cultures of the Gerai and of the Vanatinai Islanders illustrate, we can't
claim that male dominance is natural or universal – although many Americans do
claim just that – and therefore we can't claim that dominant behavior in human
beings is biologically linked to sex.

In other cultures, gender systems are neither binary, like the gender system in
force in the United States today, nor what might be called unitary – that is, without significant gender differentiation – like the two gender systems described

above. In contrast, some cultures see gender as a system of multiple possibilities. As one example among many, consider the hundred or more North American Indian societies that had multiple gender systems, that is, systems consisting of more than two genders, especially prior to the takeover of the Americas by European colonizers. Native North American societies tended to define gender in ways specific to their own cultures, differing in what aspects of social life were considered primary in their conceptions of gender. Yet most Native North American cultures included three or four of the following genders: (1) women; (2) female variants, or variant gender roles adopted by biological females; (3) men; and (4) male variants, or variant gender roles adopted by biological males (Nanda 66).

In determining a person's gender, neither biological sex nor sexual orientation was generally the primary factor in Native North American societies. Rather, occupational interests and pursuits were of central importance. Clothing sometimes played a role, although persons adopting variant gender roles might have worn, depending on the culture to which they belonged, any combination of men's and women's clothes. In some North American Indian cultures, gender variants played valued roles in the community, such as healers or performers of sacred ritual functions, because gender variance was associated, as it is in many cultures, with sacred power. Whatever the case, however, members of many communities could choose, irrespective of biological makeup, the gender to which they wished to belong (Nanda 66).

In addition to exploring alternatives to our current binary conception of gender, gender theorists are also interested in the relationship between sex and gender: between the ways in which our bodies are biologically constructed and the genders to which we are assigned. As Judith Lorber puts it, despite common belief,

> [n]either sex nor gender are pure [separate, autonomous, discrete] categories. Combinations of incongruous genes, genitalia, and hormonal input are ignored in sex categorization [as male or female], just as combinations of incongruous physiology, identity, sexuality, appearance, and behavior are ignored in the social construction of gender statuses [masculine or feminine].
>
> (14)

In short, the whole idea that there are only two genders is based on the idea that there are only two sexes. However, researchers from a variety of fields have revealed that such is not the case: biological sex does not fit neatly into two separate, opposite categories. It would be more accurate to say that, following the European model, American society has imposed the two-sex system despite the fact that this system does not fit a significant portion of the population. In other words, biological sex categories have not imposed the two-gender system on Americans; rather, Americans have imposed the two-gender system on biological sex categories.

According to Anne Fausto-Sterling, although complete frequency data is difficult to find, a reasonable estimate based on numerous available records indicates that approximately 1.7 percent of all children born each year are *intersexual* (51), or as various gender theorists refer to them, intersexed or intersex. That is, intersex individuals have some combination of male and female reproductive organs, genitals, chromosomal and/or hormonal makeup. Fausto-Sterling observes,

> Even if we've overestimated by a factor of two, that still means a lot of inter-sexual children are born each year. At the rate of 1.7 percent, for example, a city of 300,000 people would have 5,100 people with varying degrees of intersexual development. Compare this with albinism [an albino has no pigmentation and therefore has white hair, white skin, and red eyes], another relatively uncommon human trait [in the United States] but one that most readers can probably recall having seen.

(51)

The reason we don't "see" the numerous intersex individuals to whom Fausto-Sterling refers is not simply because the parts of the body involved are usually inside the body or hidden under clothing. Rather, as Sharon Preeves notes, so embedded is our belief that there are only two sexes and two corresponding genders, that intersex infants have been routinely, quickly, and often without their parents' knowledge or consent, surgically altered to physically resemble either a male or a female (32).

The decisions on how to "sex" the infant are usually based on cosmetic factors (will the child look "normal"?) and social factors (if the child is sexed as a boy, will he be able to urinate standing up and will his penis be large enough as an adult to perform sexually?) rather than on the possibility that the child may be in every other respect – chemically, hormonally, genetically – a different sex or a combination of both sexes. For example, an intersex infant may have a male genetic makeup (xy), but if the penis part of its genitals is considered too small by the medical team in charge, unlikely to pass as "normal" when the child matures, and probably unable to urinate from a standing position (for example, because the urethra opens at the base of the penis instead of at the tip), the infant is most likely to be surgically and hormonally reconstructed as a female. This practice has continued despite studies showing that the size of an infant's penis or clitoris is unrelated to the size of its adult genitals (Preeves 33).

As recently as the 1990s, Preeves reports, transgender activists (a transgender person's gender doesn't match his or her biological sex) have argued that intersex individuals should not be seen as abnormalities but as normal people belonging to a different sex category. Some activists have, in fact, suggested that there are really five sexes that occur naturally: (1) female, (2) female intersex (an intersex person with more prominent or functional female sex organs), (3) true intersex (an intersex person with equally prominent or functional male and female sex organs), (4) male intersex (an intersex person with more prominent or functional male sex organs), and (5) male (Preeves 37).

Perhaps the most striking point to consider here is not the frequency of intersex births, though their frequency will certainly come as a surprise to many of us, but the reaction of the medical profession to the situation. Unless there were a health consideration at stake (for example, a nonfunctioning urethra), does there have to be such a rush to surgery? Why isn't it more common to first offer parents educational materials so they can have the opportunity to learn about the many ramifications of their child's sexual makeup? Why aren't parents immediately put in touch with an organization of parents with intersex children, or, more to the point, why do such organizations not – or not enough of them – exist? Why doesn't the child, as it matures, have the option to learn about his or her intersexuality and, if a surgical change is an option, why can't the child make the choice at a later point in time?

Surely the reasons why include what might be called the tyranny of the two-sex/ two-gender system. And I think it's reasonable to suspect that, at least to some extent, society practices the same two-sex/two-gender tyranny on the medical profession that the medical profession practices on society. "What's wrong with my child?" "Can't the doctor fix it?" Surely these questions leap to the minds of many parents who are told that their newborns are intersex because we're all socially programmed to think within the confines of our binary sex/gender system. For many gender theorists, however, the problem is that parents too often are not told that their infants are intersex. Rather, they're generally told that their infants have a genital birth defect and that the doctors need to discover and restore the newborn's "true sex" (Fausto-Sterling 30). What kind of choice can that language possibly offer parents?

The good news is that attitudes are changing in the medical profession. Doctors and scientists have begun to realize that genital altering surgery should not be performed on infants. Many believe that it is best to wait, for example, until the child self-identifies as a boy or a girl or until parents and intersex children have time to learn about their options. For once a surgery is performed, it may be difficult or impossible to undo it.[2]

Finally, many gender theorists are interested in the relationship between sexuality and gender, that is, between our sexual orientation and the ways in which we are viewed in terms of gender. For one thing, much of the cruel and unfair treatment many lesbian, gay, bisexual, and transgender (LGBT) individuals endure is due largely to the fact that they often don't conform to traditional gender behavior or appearance. In fact, many gender theorists agree that while "binaristic understandings of femininity and masculinity shape the ways we perceive gender ... the assumption of heterosexuality determines the ways we constitute that femininity and masculinity" (Cranny-Francis *et al.* ix). In other words, gendering a child (raising a child to conform to his or her traditional gender role both socially and psychologically) is always heterosexual gendering. Thus, "the sex/gender system establishes not only the sex of bodies but also the kinds of desire they can have" (Cranny-Francis *et al.* 6).

It's interesting to consider, in this context, a noteworthy piece of history revealed in old medical and theological writings of some Western European cultures. These writings indicate, Sharon Preeves reports, that in centuries past some Western European cultures considered intersex people members of a third sex, sometimes viewed as normal, sometimes viewed as abnormal, but nevertheless acknowledged as belonging to a unique sex (34). In addition, intersex people were usually allowed to choose their sex, gender, and sexuality. Sounds good, but here's where things really get interesting. Consider it: intersex people were acknowledged as members of a third sex – not male or female – but they nevertheless had to choose to identify themselves as either male or female. And once they made their choice, they were not allowed to change their minds. So not only was this system controlled by the binary sex/gender mind-set that still controls our culture today, but it was also controlled by the homophobia that continues to plague us. For as Preeves points out, this pick-one-sex-and-stick-to-it attitude, which was enforced legally, was based on the fear that, without this law, an intersex person could choose to be a woman (use her female genitals only), marry a man, then change her mind and choose to be a man (use her male genitals), in which case a married couple would consist of two men (36).

Before we leave this topic, it's important to remember that, in talking about sex and gender, we're talking about people and how they live their daily lives. So let's give some thought to the experience of people who don't feel they fit neatly into a traditional heterosexual binary sex/gender system like ours. For despite the progress made in such fields as feminism, gender studies, and queer theory, our society persists in thinking that the words sex and gender mean basically the same thing and that the only people worth thinking about are the straight people who fit the traditional masculine-male/feminine-female categories. This state of affairs ignores the theoretical progress that has given us, for example, such concepts as gender identity, androgyny, and the category of sex/gender identification called *questioning*. Consider the enormous contribution that these three examples alone offer us in terms of our ability to understand the complexity of the concept of gender. The term *gender identity* implies that one's gender may not match one's biological sex – indeed, may not match either primary biological sex – for if it always did, we wouldn't need the term *gender identity*. *Androgyny* tells us that, regardless of one's sex, one's gender identity may consist of some combination of feminine and masculine behaviors. Finally, *questioning* opens the door both for people who feel unsure

of their sexual orientation and for people whose "sex and gender identification …
may not [have] an existing label" (Perry and Ballard-Reisch 30).

Unfortunately, gender discrimination exists today in myriad forms, yet too often
the only people aware of it are those who must suffer it themselves or whose loved
ones must suffer it. Linda A. M. Perry and Deborah Ballard-Reisch report three
examples of sex and gender discrimination that I think you will find both instruc-
tive and thought-provoking. Let me just list them here briefly to give you an idea of
the range of gender identification available to human beings and of the oppression
with which anything deemed different is so often met.

In the first example offered by Perry and Ballard-Reisch, a heterosexual man
who is married, a father, and also at times a *cross-dresser* — one who adopts the
attire of the opposite sex but who behaves in a manner associated with one's biological sex — has been verbally and physically abused by both straight and gay
people. As a heterosexual cross-dresser he doesn't fit the stereotype of the gay
cross-dresser with which both communities are familiar, and he has therefore
experienced rejection from both (21–22). In another example, Perry and Ballard-
Reisch describe a gay *transvestite* (one who adopts both the attire and the behavior
of the opposite sex, usually in an exaggerated manner) who repeatedly has
experienced rejection by members of the gay community wanting to advance gay
political visibility — to give gay people a stronger voice in social and political
issues — and fearing to offend straight people. The irony is self-evident and painful:
a group that advocates diversity, that has been rejected because of its own diversity,
rejects one of its members for being diverse (22–23). In Perry and Ballard-Reisch's
final example, we meet a man who has had a biological sex change from female to
male in order to have a body that matches his gender identity, which has always been
masculine. Before his sex-change procedure, he had been a masculine lesbian. Now,
as a man, he is still sexually attracted to women, so, of course, he is now a heterosexual
male. His problem, it seems, should be solved. However, he is still unable to find
acceptance because of his sex/gender history. He has spent his life trying to explain
his sexual and gender identities and being harassed and battered due to his difference.
As a biological female, he didn't feel he fit into society because his gender identity
was that of a masculine male attracted to women. After his sex change, he did not
feel he fit into society because his family and friends would not accept his physical
transformation. Nevertheless, he persists in being open about his sex/gender history
because he believes that being "out" is necessary in order for society to recognize that
a large number of people do not fit the heterosexual standard of "normality" (24).

Clearly, feminism and gender studies are intimately related. They share some of
the same subject matter as well as a desire for justice and a belief in the power of
education to change our society for the better. For centuries feminism has worked
for gender equality: for a dissolution of the patriarchal gender roles that, even
today, continue to short-circuit efforts to achieve complete equality between

women and men. And gender studies is working to broaden our understanding of how complex the concept of gender really is.

Of course, there are many more feminist issues than the ones discussed in this chapter. And as in every field, there is a great deal of disagreement among feminist theorists and literary critics concerning, for example, how (and how much) women are programmed by patriarchal ideology; whether or not there is a distinctive way of writing that might be called feminine; whether or not the work of women writers should be interpreted along different lines than writing by men; the ways in which various cultural factors intersect with sex and gender in creating women's experience; and as we have just seen, the new horizons offered by the efforts of gender theorists to enlarge and problematize our conception of gender. Our purpose here is merely to introduce you to the main ideas and the general principles you need to know in order to read feminist theorists and literary critics with some understanding of the issues they raise.

Feminism and literature

Naturally, some literary works will lend themselves more readily than others to feminist analysis or at least to certain kinds of feminist analyses. For students new to the field, I think it useful to examine the ways in which literary texts reinforce patriarchy because the ability to see when and how patriarchal ideology operates is crucial to our ability to resist it in our own lives. This approach, applied to literary works in the male canon, was the dominant mode of feminist literary analysis in America during the 1970s, and it usually requires reading "against the grain" of the text's apparent intention, for patriarchal literature is usually unconscious of the sexist ideology it promotes, or perhaps more precisely, patriarchal literature sees nothing wrong with its own sexism.

A feminist analysis of the patriarchal ideology operating in Arthur Miller's *Death of a Salesman* (1949), for example, might examine three related areas: (1) the ways in which the female characters (Biff's and Happy's various "conquests," the woman Willy meets in the Boston hotel room, and Linda Loman) function as tokens of male status; (2) the ways in which the "good-girl"/"bad-girl" view of women validates the Loman men's sexism; and (3) the ways in which Linda Loman has internalized patriarchal ideology. A feminist reading would also note that the play reinforces patriarchal ideology through its sympathetic portrayal of Willy and apparent approval of Linda's support for his patriarchal attitude. Such a reading would also relate the play's patriarchal ideology to the period in which it was written and is set: post-World War II America. This was a time when American patriarchy attempted to counteract the war-time freedom of women who took on the jobs and family responsibilities of their absent men by reestablishing the belief that "the (good) woman's place is in the home."

Of course, it is also important to be able to recognize when a literary work depicts patriarchal ideology in order to criticize it or invite us to criticize it. For example, a feminist reading of Toni Morrison's *The Bluest Eye* (1970) might examine the ways in which the novel invites us to criticize the sexist behaviors and attitudes it portrays. A striking illustration of the novel's insight into patriarchal psychology is its depiction of women as the site upon which men's pain and anger are displaced, a memorable example of which we see in the young Cholly's hatred of Darlene, upon whom he displaces his hatred of the white hunters who humiliate them. In addition, the novel's feminist agenda is revealed in its appreciation of strong women – such as Aunt Jimmy, M'Dear, and Mrs. MacTeer – and of the importance of sisterhood to women's survival. *The Bluest Eye* also shows us how gender issues intersect with race, for Cholly's hatred of Darlene is a direct result of the black youngster's powerlessness in the face of the white hunters' racism, and the importance of sisterhood to women's survival becomes especially acute when the women are victims of the combined forces of sexism and racism.

Finally, many literary works have a conflicted response to patriarchal ideology, as we see, for example, in Mary Shelley's *Frankenstein* (1818). On the one hand, the text undermines patriarchy's belief in female weakness through its portrayal of women's strength: Caroline is the sole financial and moral support of her ruined father; Justine bears up bravely and nobly under the community's unjust condemnation of her, which includes the penalty of death; and Safie defies her patriarchal father and successfully undertakes a dangerous journey in pursuit of her own goals. The monster, too, can be read as an indirect advocate for women's rights. In many ways, the monster occupies the woman's position in eighteenth-century European society: it is considered inferior to men and therefore denied the rights and comforts men enjoy. Nevertheless, it acquires an education on its own, is clearly very intelligent and articulate, and wants only to be accepted as an equal member of the human family, to which it will willingly contribute its share (as we see it do when it anonymously helps the De Lacey family).

On the other hand, the novel reinforces patriarchal ideology through its admiration of the ways in which Caroline, Justine, Elizabeth, and Agatha conform to traditional gender roles. Three of these "madonnas" devote themselves to nurturing others to the point, whether they realize it or not, of sacrificing their lives for them. Caroline dies as a dutiful mother, tending Elizabeth; Justine dies as a dutiful servant and surrogate mother, when it should be Victor who dies; and Elizabeth dies as a dutiful wife and surrogate mother, trusting her husband's judgment and catering to his needs, when, again, it should be Victor who dies. Even Safie's independent behavior is in the service of the traditional woman's desire to secure herself a husband. In addition, the novel does not seem to invite us to criticize the *misogyny* (hatred of women) or *gynophobia* (fear and loathing of women as sexual and reproductive beings) clearly evident in Victor's murderous rage against the female monster and more subtly suggested by his prolonged avoidance of Elizabeth. This reading of *Frankenstein* might also examine the ways in which the novel's conflicted response to patriarchal ideology is reflected in Mary Shelley's own conflicts concerning her personal experience of patriarchy: for example, she was an ardent admirer of the antipatriarchal essays of her late mother, Mary Wollstonecraft; she violated patriarchal values when she eloped with a married man, Percy Shelley; yet she seemed extremely dependent on, even submissive to, her husband.

Because feminist issues range so widely across cultural, social, political, and psychological categories, feminist literary criticism is wide ranging, too. Whatever kind of analysis is undertaken, however, the ultimate goal of feminist criticism is to increase our understanding of women's experience, both in the past and present, and promote our appreciation of women's value in the world.

Some questions feminist critics ask about literary texts

The questions that follow are offered to summarize feminist approaches to literature. Approaches that attempt to develop a specifically female framework for the analysis of women's writing (such as questions 6, 7, and 8) are often referred to as *gynocriticism.*

1 What does the work reveal about the operations (economically, politically, socially, or psychologically) of patriarchy? How are women portrayed? How do these portrayals relate to the gender issues of the period in which the novel was written or is set? In other words, does the work reinforce or undermine patriarchal ideology? (In the first case, we might say that the text has a patriarchal agenda. In the second case, we might say that the text has a feminist agenda. Texts that seem to both reinforce and undermine patriarchal ideology might be said to be ideologically conflicted.)

2 What does the work suggest about the ways in which race, class, and/or other cultural factors intersect with gender in producing women's experience?

3 How is the work "gendered"? That is, how does it seem to define femininity and masculinity? Does the characters' behavior always conform to their assigned genders? Does the work suggest that there are genders other than feminine and masculine? What seems to be the work's attitude toward the gender(s) it portrays? For example, does the work seem to accept, question, or reject the traditional view of gender?

4 What does the work imply about the possibilities of sisterhood as a mode of resisting patriarchy and/or about the ways in which women's situations in the world – economic, political, social, or psychological – might be improved?

5 What does the history of the work's reception by the public and by the critics tell us about the operations of patriarchy? Has the literary work been ignored

or neglected in the past? Why? Or, if recognized in the past, is the work ignored or neglected now? Why?

6   What does the work suggest about women's creativity? In order to answer this question, biographical data about the author and historical data about the culture in which she lived will be required.

7   What might an examination of the author's style contribute to the ongoing efforts to delineate a specifically feminine form of writing (for example, *écriture féminine*)?

8   What role does the work play in terms of women's literary history and literary tradition?

Depending on the literary work in question, we might ask one or any combination of these questions. Or we might come up with a useful question not listed here. These are just some starting points to get us thinking about literary works in productive feminist ways. Keep in mind that not all feminist critics will interpret the same work in the same way even if they focus on the same feminist concepts. As in every field, even expert practitioners disagree. Our goal is to use feminist theory to help enrich our reading of literary works; to help us see some important ideas they illustrate that we might not have seen so clearly or so deeply without feminist theory; and to help us see the ways in which patriarchal ideology blinds us to our own participation in, or at least complicity with, sexist agendas.

The following feminist reading of F. Scott Fitzgerald's *The Great Gatsby* is offered as an example of what a feminist interpretation of that novel might yield. It focuses on what I will argue is the novel's sexist agenda as revealed through the text's characterizations of women, the ideological content of which should be fairly easy for you to see at this point. In addition, I will situate the novel's patriarchal ideology in terms of the changing role of American women during the 1920s because most feminists have come to realize the importance of seeing how specific historical circumstances foster particular ideologies. The historical component of my argument is not complex, however, but rather draws on historical information with which most of you are probably somewhat familiar.

" … next they'll throw everything overboard … ": a feminist reading of *The Great Gatsby*

In a sudden panic over his discovery that his wife has taken a lover, Tom Buchanan, from F. Scott Fitzgerald's *The Great Gatsby* (1925), exclaims, "Nowadays people begin by sneering at family life and family institutions and next they'll throw everything overboard and have intermarriage between black and white" (137; ch. 7). In addition to Tom's double standard for his own and his wife's behavior (as well as his racism), this statement reveals Tom's assumptions that the moral structure of society rests on the stability of the patriarchal family and that the stability of the patriarchal family rests on the conformity of women to patriarchal gender roles. Of course, through the vehicle of Nick Carraway's narration, the novel clearly ridicules Tom's position: "Flushed with his impassioned gibberish," Nick observes, "[Tom] saw himself standing alone on the last barrier of civilization" (137; ch. 7). Nevertheless, I think it can be shown that *The Great Gatsby* also shares Tom's view of patriarchal gender roles.

The novel was written and is set in the decade following World War I, which ended in November 1918. The Roaring Twenties, or the Jazz Age, a term coined by Fitzgerald, was a period of enormous social change in America, especially in the area of women's rights. Before World War I, American women did not enjoy universal suffrage. In 1920, two years after the end of the war (and after 72 years of organized political agitation), they were finally given the vote. Before the war, standard dress for women included long skirts, tightly laced corsets, high-buttoned shoes, and long hair demurely swept up onto the head. A few years after the war, skirts became shorter (in some cases, much shorter), laced corsets began to disappear (indeed, the most bold and unconventional young women wore few, if any, restraining undergarments), modern footwear frequently replaced high-buttoned shoes, and "bobbed" hair (cut short and worn loosely) became the fashion for young women.

Perhaps most alarming for proponents of the old ways, women's behavior began to change. Women could now be seen smoking and drinking (despite Prohibition), often in the company of men and without chaperones. They could also be seen enjoying the sometimes raucous nightlife offered at nightclubs and private parties. Even the new dances of the era, which seemed wild and overtly sexual to many, bespoke an attitude of free self-expression and unrestrained enjoyment. In other words, as we often see during times of social change, a "New Woman" emerged in the 1920s. And, again as usual, her appearance on the scene evoked a good deal of negative reaction from conservative members of society, both male and female, who felt, as they generally do at these times, that women's rejection of any aspect of their traditional role inevitably results in the destruction of the family and the moral decline of society as a whole.

This view of women as the standard-bearers of traditional values, whose presence as nonwage-earning supervisors of hearth and home was deemed necessary to maintain the moral structure of society, became the dominant patriarchal ideology of the industrialized nineteenth century as the home ceased to be the place where the family worked together to earn their living and men went off to earn the family bread at various occupations in the towns. That is, as woman's economic role in the home disappeared, a spiritualized domestic role was created for her in order to keep her, among other things, from competing with men on the job market. Thus, although most Americans believed the survival of America's moral structure depended on traditional gender roles, it was really the nation's economic structure, which gave economic dominance to men, that depended upon the axiom "a woman's place is in the home." Of course, another advantage of keeping women at home, modestly dressed and quietly behaved, was that it reaffirmed men's ownership of women's sexual and reproductive capacities. The threat posed by the New Woman of the 1920s, then, had repercussions on many levels of public consciousness.

Literary works often reflect the ideological conflicts of their culture, whether or not it is their intention to do so, because, like the rest of us, authors are influenced by the ideological tenor of the times. Even a writer like F. Scott Fitzgerald, who cut a dashing figure among the avant-garde social set of the 1920s and who was himself married to a New Woman, was subject to the ideological conflicts that character-ized his age. One might speculate that it was precisely his experience of "life in the fast lane" that created some (conscious or unconscious) misgivings about the changes occurring in America during the 1920s. Or one might speculate that he was able to accept the New Woman only as long as he could view her as psycho-logically troubled and in need of his help, a situation illustrated in his semi-auto-biographical novel *Tender Is the Night* (1934), as well as in his turbulent life with his wife, Zelda. However, it's not my intention to examine Fitzgerald's life but to examine the ways in which *The Great Gatsby*, his most enduring work, embodies its culture's discomfort with the post-World War I New Woman.

We see this discomfort in the novel's representation of its minor female char-acters, and we see it in more complex ways in the novel's characterizations of main characters Daisy Buchanan, Jordan Baker, and Myrtle Wilson, who, despite their numerous differences, are all versions of the New Woman. We can assume that Nick's descriptions of these characters represent the novel's ideological biases, and not merely his own, because the text portrays Nick sympathetically, unlike Tom Buchanan. In addition to the sympathy Nick evokes by the author's use of first-person narration – because we see the narrative events through Nick's eyes, we are able to more or less "walk in his shoes" – Nick also gains our sympathy because he tells his story in a sensitive and engaging manner, sharing with the reader his per-sonal feelings: his desires, dislikes, fears, doubts, and affections. Finally, as the only character who is consistently aware of ethical considerations, Nick functions as the moral center of the novel. It is therefore reasonable to conclude that, whether or not Fitzgerald intended Carraway as a reliable narrator, many readers will be strongly influenced by Nick's perspective.

The novel abounds in minor female characters whose dress and activities identify them as incarnations of the New Woman, and they are portrayed as clones of a single, negative character type: shallow, exhibitionist, revolting, and deceitful. For example, at Gatsby's parties we see insincere, "enthusiastic meetings between women who never knew each other's names" (44; ch. 3), as well as numerous narcissistic attention-seekers in various stages of drunken hysteria. We meet, for example, a young woman who "dumps" down a cocktail "for courage" and "dances out alone on the canvas platform" (45; ch. 3); "a rowdy little girl who gave way upon the slightest provocation to uncontrollable laughter" (51; ch. 3); a drunken woman who "was not only singing, she was weeping too," her face lined with "black rivulets" created when her "tears ... came into contact with her heavily beaded eyelashes" (55–56; ch. 3); a drunken young girl who has her "head stuck in a pool" (113; ch. 6) to stop her from screaming; and two drunken young wives who refuse to leave the party until their husbands, tired of the women's verbal abuse, "lifted [them] kicking into the night" (57; ch. 3). Then there are Benny McClenahan's "four girls":

> They were never quite the same ones in physical person, but they were so identical one with another that it inevitably seemed they had been there before. I have forgotten their names – Jaqueline, I think, or else Consuela, or Gloria or Judy or June, and their last names were either the melodious names of flowers and months or the sterner ones of the great American capitalists whose cousins, if pressed, they would confess themselves to be.
>
> (67; ch. 4)

In other words, all of these lookalike women who accompanied McClenahan to Gatsby's parties invented names and biographies for themselves to impress their new acquaintances. We should not be too surprised, then, to hear Nick say, "Dishonesty in a woman is a thing you never blame deeply" (63; ch. 3), implying that women don't seem able to help it: perhaps it's just a natural failing, like so many other feminine weaknesses.

The only minor female characters we get to know a little better, both of whom fit the category of the New Woman, are Mrs. McKee – who is described as "shrill, languid, handsome, and horrible" (34; ch. 2) – and Myrtle's sister, Catherine, who perfectly fits the negative stereotype outlined above. The novel gives Catherine a good deal of attention for such a minor character, perhaps because she has been chosen to represent the physical unattractiveness of her type, which is only hinted at in the descriptions of the other minor female characters.

> The sister ... was a slender, worldly girl of about thirty with a solid sticky bob of red hair and a complexion powdered milky white. Her eyebrows had been plucked and then drawn on again at a more rakish angle but the efforts of nature toward the restoration of the old alignment gave a blurred air to her face. When she moved about there was an incessant clicking as innumerable pottery bracelets jingled up and down upon her arms. She came in with such proprietary haste and looked around so possessively at the furniture that I

wondered if she lived here. But when I asked her she laughed immoderately, repeated my question aloud, and told me she lived with a girl friend at a hotel.

(34; ch. 2)

This is the description of a rather revolting, loud, vulgar young woman whose opening words to Nick are an obvious lie. And Catherine fulfills the expectations such a description raises by the vulgar nature of her conversation with Nick concerning Myrtle and her "sweetie" (39; ch. 2) and by her claim that she doesn't drink, which we learn is a lie when she turns up drunk at George Wilson's garage the night of Myrtle's death. Her vulgarity, as well as her foolishness, is further revealed in her description of her and her girlfriend's experience in Monte Carlo:

We had over twelve hundred dollars when we started but we got gypped out of it all in two days in the private rooms. We had an awful time getting back, I can tell you. God, how I hated that town!

(38; ch. 2)

One could argue that the novel's bias here is not sexist, but classist, for all the women described above belong to the lower socioeconomic strata of society. However, there are several male characters from these same strata who are described sympathetically. For example, George Wilson is portrayed as a simple, hardworking man who, despite his other limitations, is devoted to his wife. Mr. Michaelis, who owns a coffee shop in the "valley of ashes" (27; ch.2), is kind to George and tries to take care of him after Myrtle's death. And even the two party-going husbands mentioned earlier, themselves sober, tolerate their wives' drunken abuse with admirable patience. Thus it is these women's violation of patriarchal gender roles, not their socioeconomic class, that elicits the novel's condemnation.

The novel's discomfort with the New Woman becomes evident, in a more complex fashion, in the characterizations of main characters Daisy Buchanan, Jordan Baker, and Myrtle Wilson. Despite their striking differences in class, occupation, marital status, personal appearance, and personality traits, these three characters are all versions of the New Woman. Like the minor female characters who embody the New Woman in appearance and social freedom, Daisy, Jordan, and Myrtle look and act the part. Their hair and clothing are very modern, and they don't feel, as their mothers and grandmothers surely did, that they must behave modestly in public by avoiding hard liquor, cigarettes, and immodest dancing. In addition, all three women display a good deal of modern independence. Only two are married, and they don't keep their marital unhappiness a secret, although secrecy about such matters is one of the cardinal rules of patriarchal marriage. Jordan has a career of her own and, on top of that, it's in the male-dominated field of professional golf. They all prefer the excitement of nightlife to the more traditional employments of hearth and home. There is only one child among them, Daisy's daughter, Pammy, and while Pammy is well looked after by her nurse and affectionately treated by her mother, Daisy's life does not revolve exclusively around her maternal role. Finally, all three women violate patriarchal sexual taboos: Jordan engages in premarital sex, and Daisy and Myrtle are engaged in extramarital affairs.

That the novel finds this freedom unacceptable in women is evident in its unsympathetic portrayals of those who exercise it. Daisy Buchanan is characterized as a spoiled brat and a remorseless killer. She is so used to being the center of attention that she can think of no one's needs but her own. Although Myrtle's death is accidental, Daisy doesn't stop the car and try to help the injured woman. On the contrary, she speeds off and lets Gatsby take the blame. (One can't help but wonder if some readers, at least in decades past, have said to themselves, "See what happens when you let a woman get behind the wheel of a car?") Once she learns that Gatsby doesn't come from the same social stratum as herself, she retreats behind the protection of Tom's wealth and power, abandoning her lover to whatever fate awaits him. Indeed, much of our condemnation of Daisy issues from her failure to deserve Gatsby's devotion. Although she lets Gatsby believe she will leave her husband for him, Nick observes during the confrontation scene in the New York hotel room that "[h]er eyes fell on Jordan and me with a sort of appeal, as though she ... had never, all along, intended doing anything at all" (139; ch. 7). Even her way of speaking is frequently so affected – "I'm p-paralyzed with happiness" (13; ch. 1); "You remind me of a – of a rose, an absolute rose" (19; ch. 1); and "Bles-sed precious. ... Come to your own mother that loves you" (123; ch. 7) – as to make it difficult to take anything she says seriously. Thus, on top of all her other sins, she's a phony.

Jordan Baker is characterized as a liar and a cheat. Nick catches her lying about having left a borrowed car out in the rain with its top down, and apparently she was caught cheating during a golf tournament, though she managed to get away with it under circumstances that imply the use of bribery or coercion: "The thing approached the proportions of a scandal – then died away. A caddy retracted his statement and the only other witness admitted that he might have been mistaken" (62–63; ch. 3). Like Daisy, Jordan exhibits a lack of concern for others that manifests itself in a refusal to take responsibility for herself, as we see when Nick reports that she drove her car "so close to some workmen that our fender flicked a button on one man's coat" (63; ch. 3). Her response to Nick's admonition that she should drive more carefully or not drive at all is a careless remark that "They'll [other people will] keep out of my way. ... It takes two to make an accident" (63; ch. 3). When Nick says, "Suppose you met somebody just as careless as yourself" (63; ch. 3), Jordan's manipulativeness is revealed in her response: "I hope I never will. ... I hate careless people. That's why I like you" (63; ch. 3). And her manipulation works: "for a moment I thought I loved her," Nick admits (63; ch. 3). Of course, the fact that Jordan must cheat to succeed at golf also implies that women can't succeed in a man's field purely on their own ability. And her physical description completes the stereotype that women who invade the male domain are rather masculine: "She was a slender, small-breasted girl with an erect carriage which she accentuated by throwing her body backward at the shoulders like a young cadet" (15; ch. 1). The word most frequently used to describe her appearance is jaunty. In other words, Jordan looks like a boy.

Surely, the most unsympathetic characterization of the three is that of Myrtle Wilson. She's loud, obnoxious, and phony, as we see in her "violently affected" (35; ch. 2) behavior at the party in the small flat Tom keeps for their rendezvous. She cheats on George, who is devoted to her – so she doesn't even have the excuse Daisy has of an unfaithful husband – and she bullies and humiliates him as well. She has neither the youth nor the beauty of Daisy and Jordan: "She was in the middle thirties, and faintly stout. ... Her face ... contained no facet or gleam of beauty" (29–30; ch. 2). And unlike the other two women, she is overtly sexual: "[S]he carried her surplus flesh sensuously" (29; ch. 2), and "there was an immediately perceptible vitality about her as if the nerves of her body were continually smouldering" (30; ch. 2). In addition, she's much more sexually aggressive than Daisy or Jordan. When Tom and Nick show up unexpectedly at Wilson's Garage,

> [s]he smiled slowly and, walking through her husband as if he were a ghost, shook hands with Tom, looking him flush in the eye. Then she wet her lips and without turning around spoke to her husband in a soft, coarse voice:
> "Get some chairs, why don't you, so somebody can sit down."
> "Oh sure," agreed Wilson. ... A white ashen dust veiled his dark suit and his pale hair as it veiled everything in the vicinity – except his wife, who moved close to Tom.
>
> (30; ch. 2)

In fact, Myrtle is the only woman in the novel we "see" having sex: when Nick returns to their flat after his errand to buy cigarettes, she and Tom have disappeared into the bedroom and emerge only as the rest of their company begins to arrive. Furthermore, Myrtle's interest in Tom is clearly mercenary. She was first attracted to him by the expensive quality of his clothing, she begins spending his money the instant they meet in town, and she wants him to divorce Daisy and marry her so that she can move out of the garage apartment she's shared with George for the past eleven years.

It is important to note that, in addition to being negatively portrayed (few if any readers find Daisy, Jordan, or Myrtle likeable), in all three cases, these transgressive women are punished by the progression of narrative events. That Daisy gets stuck with Tom in a loveless marriage seems, at that point in the narrative, only right and proper: she doesn't deserve any better, and we can be relatively certain, given Tom's desire for extramarital affairs, that her punishment will fit her crime. Tom will continue to be unfaithful to her just as she has been unfaithful to him and, more important, unfaithful to Gatsby. Jordan is punished when Nick "throw[s] [her] over" (186; ch. 9) during a telephone conversation just before Gatsby's murder. Later, at the end of Nick's farewell visit to Jordan, he says, "[S]he told me without comment that she was engaged to another man. I doubted that though there were several she could have married at a nod of her head" (185–86; ch. 9). Jordan also tells Nick, during that visit, "I don't give a damn about you now but [being rejected] was a new experience for me and I felt a little dizzy for a while" (186; ch. 9). The way in which Jordan insists she doesn't care merely underscores the fact that she is finally "brought down a peg or two."

The most severe punishment, however, is meted out to the woman who threatens patriarchy the most: Myrtle Wilson. I say she threatens patriarchy the most because she violates patriarchal gender roles so unabashedly and because, despite the powerlessness of her situation as a woman from the lower strata of society, her sexual vitality is portrayed as a form of aggressiveness, a personal power much greater than that of Daisy or Jordan. Her husband all but disappears in her presence, and her "intense vitality" (35; ch. 2) makes her the only thing in the garage to stand out from the "cement color of the walls" into which her husband "mingl[es] immediately" (30; ch. 2). Even as Nick speeds past Wilson's garage on his way to town with Gatsby, he can't help but notice "Mrs. Wilson straining at the garage pump with panting vitality" (72; ch. 4). As Michaelis observes, "Wilson was his wife's man and not his own" (144; ch. 7). Indeed, Michaelis believes "there was not enough of him for his wife" (167; ch. 8). Myrtle even stands up to Tom, insisting that she has a right to "mention Daisy's name": "'Daisy! Daisy! Daisy!' shouted Mrs. Wilson. 'I'll say it whenever I want to!'" (41; ch. 2).

Her punishment for saying Daisy's name is swift and merciless: "Making a short deft movement, Tom Buchanan broke her nose with his open hand" (41; ch. 2). But Nick quickly trivializes the incident, effectively forestalling any sympathy we might feel for Myrtle. "Then there were bloody towels upon the bathroom floor and women's voices scolding" (41; ch. 2), he reports. Mr. McKee is so unimpressed by the event that he slowly rambles out the door, and Nick follows him, leaving Mrs. McKee "and Catherine scolding and consoling as they stumbled here and there among the crowded furniture with articles of aid" (41–42; ch. 2). In other words, the breaking of Myrtle's nose is no big deal, just another mess for women to clean up, nothing important enough to concern men, and what's more, Myrtle had it coming.

Of course, Tom's abuse of Myrtle is slight in comparison to the novel's punishment of her: as Myrtle flees her husband and attempts to flag down the car she believes carries her lover, she is hit by that car and killed. It is important to note that her death includes sexual mutilation – "when they had torn open her shirt-waist still damp with perspiration they saw that her left breast was swinging loose like a flap" (145; ch. 7) – which underscores the notion that Myrtle's sexual vitality, that is, her aggressiveness, was her real crime. Indeed, the description of her death closes with a reference to her vitality: "The mouth was wide open and ripped at the corners as though she had choked a little in giving up the tremendous vitality she had stored so long" (145; ch. 7). Thus, although Myrtle's misconduct is much less serious than that of Daisy or Jordan – she doesn't, like Daisy, commit vehicular homicide and then let her lover take the blame; and she is not, like Jordan, fundamentally dishonest – her punishment is by far the most severe. Obviously, the novel finds aggressiveness, especially sexual aggressiveness, the most unattractive and unforgivable quality a woman can have. Daisy and Jordan may be "bad girls" from time to time, but Myrtle's sexual aggressiveness makes her a "bad girl" all the time.

The Great Gatsby's discomfort with the post-World War I New Woman, which, I have argued, is responsible for its negative characterizations and punitive treatment of the modern women it portrays, persists in some of the patriarchal ideology still operating in American culture today. Certainly, women are no longer generally condemned for wearing their hair or their skirts short, for dancing wild dances, or for frequenting raucous nightclubs (unless violence is perpetrated against them under these circumstances, in which case they may be blamed for "bringing it on themselves"). But women are still often looked at askance for other violations of patriarchal gender roles, such as opting to have children out of wedlock and raise them on their own, being sexually assertive, being "too" success-oriented on the job, or putting career before marriage and family: all of these behaviors are frequently considered "too aggressive" for women and are often satirized by the television and movie industries. Like Myrtle Wilson, American women today are often punished for what is perceived as their aggressiveness. Indeed, some Americans want to blame women's increased aggressiveness, or at least what is perceived as such, for the increase in crimes of violence against women in this country. At the same time, however, the public doesn't want to admit that women's gender is a factor in the crimes of violence committed against them.

Although, finally, laws have been passed to protect women from sexual harassment on the job, to protect them from sexual abuse and other forms of domestic violence in the home, and to censure rape as a crime of violence rather than tacitly condone it as a crime of passion, public awareness and willingness to support the victims of such mistreatment still lag far behind the legislation. For example, there is the lingering belief that the victim must somehow be responsible: "How low-cut was her dress?" "Did she aggravate her husband before he beat her?" This is called blaming the victim: we want to believe that it is women's aggressive or inappropriate or foolish behavior, not their gender, that can get them into trouble. Even the United States Federal Bureau of Investigation (FBI) overlooks the role of gender in its definition of a hate crime, which the Bureau describes as "a criminal offence against a person or property motivated in whole or in part by an offender's bias against a race, religion, disability, ethnic origin or sexual orientation."

Yet when the women engineering students were lined up against a classroom wall at a Canadian university several years ago and shot by a male intruder, wasn't that a hate crime against women? And when, shortly thereafter, women engineering students at an American university began to receive anonymous threatening letters, wasn't that a hate crime against women? Aren't rape, sexual harassment, and wife-beating hate crimes against women? Yes, of course they are, but they are still not generally recognized as such. In other words, the patriarchal ideology responsible for the oppression of women can't be effectively addressed until there is public as well as legal recognition that it still exists.

I can understand very well the difficulty involved in recognizing patriarchal ideology because I've had difficulty learning to recognize it myself, even when I've been its victim. In the white, working-class household in which I was raised, the emphasis was on economic survival, on issues of class rather than gender. My parents taught me to see the ways in which political leaders, and our social system as a whole, favored the rich and penalized the middle classes, especially the middle-middle and lower-middle classes. While I was very strongly encouraged to go to college and not to feel that marriage was an inevitable goal, my parents nevertheless believed that it would be to my best advantage to be trained as a schoolteacher because the hours and the nature of the work would not interfere with my future duties as a wife and mother should I choose to marry. Perhaps the absence of a focus on gender issues, combined with a very strong focus on other political issues, helped blind me to the operations of patriarchy.

I'm sure, however, that I was also blinded by my own desire to avoid pain: I didn't want to know all the ways in which I was oppressed because I didn't think there was anything I could do about it. So when I was fired from a job after twice turning down a date with my married boss, I simply thought he had no more use for my services. When I didn't receive a job offer from the man whose hand I removed from my left breast during the job interview, I simply felt sorry for whatever poor woman might end up working for him. And when I noticed that one of my professors seemed extremely uncomfortable whenever I approached him and would quickly leave whatever group he was talking with when I came near, it didn't occur to me that it might have something to do with my being the only woman in the graduate program in philosophy at that time or with my being a head taller than he was.

It should come as no surprise, therefore, that when I first read *The Great Gatsby* in my early twenties and found the female characters – especially Myrtle – heartless, amoral, and unsympathetic, it didn't occur to me that the novel had a patriarchal agenda. I didn't see any connections between the novel's portrayals of women and the countless sexist portrayals of women I'd seen in the other male-authored works I loved (works I still value highly for different reasons today) because I didn't see how sexist these portrayals really are. The process of "opening my eyes" has been a long and painful one, and it's still in progress. I know from talking with numerous students, friends, and colleagues that my experience has been shared by many women and by some men as well.

Clearly, there is an important connection between our ability to recognize patriarchal ideology and our willingness to experience the pain such knowledge is liable to cause us. Perhaps this is one reason why feminism is still regarded so suspiciously by many women and men today: it holds a mirror not just to our public lives but to our private lives as well, and it asks us to reassess our most personal experiences and our most entrenched and comfortable assumptions. For this reason, works like *The Great Gatsby* can be very helpful to new students of feminist criticism. By helping us learn to see how patriarchal ideology operates in literature, such works can prepare us to direct our feminist vision where we must eventually learn to focus it most clearly: on ourselves.

Questions for further practice: feminist approaches to other literary works

The following questions are intended as models. They can help you use feminist criticism to interpret the literary works to which they refer or other texts of your choice.

1 How does Charlotte Perkins Gilman's "The Yellow Wallpaper" (1892) critique patriarchal ideology, specifically as it manifested itself in nineteenth-century marriage and medical practices?
2 How does Joseph Conrad's *Heart of Darkness* (1902) reflect patriarchal ideology through Marlow's comments about and attitude toward women and through his sexist representations of the numerous minor female characters that populate the novel (including his aunt, Kurtz's intended, the "savage" woman, the native laundress, and the women in black at company headquarters in Europe)? Does the novel invite us to accept or criticize Marlow's sexism? Is the novel even aware of his sexism?
3 How does Toni Morrison's *Beloved* (1987) reveal the ways in which race inter-sects with gender in creating women's experience? How does the work under-score the importance of sisterhood, of women's community? How might we argue that the novel offers us an example of *écriture féminine*?
4 When Kate Chopin's "The Storm" was written in 1898, it was generally con-sidered unnatural for women to have sexual desire. How does Chopin's story

critique this patriarchal belief? What other patriarchal ideology does the story critique? What does the story suggest about the intersection of patriarchy, religion, and socioeconomic class?

5   In what ways might we say that William Faulkner's "A Rose for Emily" (1931) plays with traditional gender categories, revealing the biases and limitations of traditional definitions of gender?

For further reading

Christian, Barbara. *New Black Feminist Criticism, 1985–2000*. Eds. Gloria Bowles, M. Gieilia Fabi, and Arlene R. Keizer. Chicago: University of Illinois Press, 2007.

de Beauvoir, Simone. "Introduction." *The Second Sex*. Rpt. in *French Feminism Reader*. Ed. Kelly Oliver. New York: Rowman & Littlefield, 2000. 6–20.

Frye, Marilyn. *Willful Virgin: Essays in Feminism*. Freedom, CA: Crossing, 1992.

Gilbert, Sandra M., and Susan Gubar. *Madwoman in the Attic: The Woman Writer and the Nineteenth-Century Literary Imagination*. New Haven, CT: Yale University Press, 1979.

Guy-Sheftall, Beverly. *Words of Fire: An Anthology of African-American Feminist Thought [1831–1993]*. New York: New Press, 1995.

hooks, bell. *Ain't I a Woman: Black Women and Feminism*. Boston: South End Press, 1981.

Ikard, David. *Breaking the Silence: Toward a Black Male Feminist Critique*. Baton Rouge: Louisiana State University Press, 2007.

McCann, Carole R., and Seung-Kyung Kim, eds. *Feminist Theory Reader: Local and Global Perspectives*. 2nd ed. New York and London: Routledge, 2010.

Moi, Toril. *Sexual/Textual Politics: Feminist Literary Theory*. 2nd ed. New York: Routledge, 2000.

Moraga, Cherríe, L., and Gloria Anzaldúa, eds. *This Bridge Called My Back: Writings by Radical Women of Color*. 3rd ed. Berkeley, CA: Third Woman Press, 2002.

Oliver, Kelly, ed. *The French Feminism Reader*. New York: Rowman & Littlefield, 2000.

Rackin, Phyllis. *Shakespeare and Women*. Oxford and New York: Oxford University Press, 2005.

Showalter, Elaine. *A Literature of Their Own: British Women Novelists from Brontë to Lessing*. Princeton, NJ: Princeton University Press, 1977.

For advanced readers

Allen, Paula Gunn. *The Sacred Hoop: Recovering the Feminine in American Indian Traditions*. Boston: Beacon Press, 1986.

Cixous, Hélène. *The Hélène Cixous Reader*. Ed. Susan Sellers. London and New York: Routledge, 1994.

Collins, Patricia Hill. *Black Feminist Thought: Knowledge, Consciousness, and the Politics of Empowerment*. 1990. London and New York: Routledge, 2008.

Cooper, Katherine, and Emina Short, eds. *The Female Figure in Contemporary Historical Fiction*. Basingstoke and New York: Palgrave Macmillan, 2012.

Irigaray, Luce. *The Irigaray Reader*. Ed. Margaret Whitford. Cambridge, MA: Basil Blackwell, 1991.

James, Joy, and T. Denean Sharply-Whiting, eds. *The Black Feminist Reader*. Malden, MA: Blackwell, 2000.

Kristeva, Julia. *The Kristeva Reader*. Ed. Toril Moi. Oxford: Blackwell, 1986.

Leonard, Diana, and Lisa Adkins, eds. *Sex in Question: French Materialist Feminism*. London: Taylor & Francis, 1996.

Mitchell, Juliet. *Psychoanalysis and Feminism: A Radical Reassessment of Freudian Psychoanalysis*. 1974. New ed. New York: Basic Books, 2000.

Mohanty, Chandra Talpade. *Feminism without Borders: Decolonizing Theory, Practicing Solidarity*. Durham, NC and London: Duke University Press, 2003.

Warhol-Down, Robyn, and Diane Price Herndl, eds. *Feminisms Redux*. New Brunswick, NJ: Rutgers University Press, 2009.

Zinn, Maxine Baca, Pierrette Hondagneu-Sotelo, and Michael A. Messner, eds. *Gender Through the Prism of Difference*. New York: Oxford University Press USA, 2010.

Notes

1 For economic, social, and political information concerning the worldwide gender gap, see the World Economic Forum's annual *Global Gender Gap Report*, available online at www.weforum.org/reports/global-gender-gap-report.

2 For information on current issues concerning intersexuality, you can go online to the Organization Intersex International (OII) website at www.oiiinternational.com; the Intersex Society of North America (ISNA) website at www.isna.org; and the United Kingdom Intersex Association (UKIA) website at www.ukia.co.uk.

Works cited

Bethel, Lorraine. "'This Infinity of Conscious Pain': Zora Neale Hurston and the Black Female Literary Tradition." *All the Women Are White, All the Blacks Are Men, but Some of Us Are Brave*. Eds. Gloria T. Hull, Patricia Bell Scott, and Barbara Smith. Old Westbury, NY: Feminist Press, 1982. 176–88.

Brannon, Linda. *Gender: Psychological Perspectives*. 4th ed. Boston: Pearson/Allyn & Bacon, 2005.

Bruccoli, Matthew J. "Preface." *The Great Gatsby*. F. Scott Fitzgerald. New York: Macmillan, 1992. vii–xvi.

Cixous, Hélène. "Sorties: Out and Out: Attacks/Ways Out/Forays." Rpt. in *The Feminist Reader*. 2nd ed. Eds. Catherine Belsey and Jane Moore. Malden, MA: Blackwell, 1997. 91–103.

Cranny-Francis, Anne, Wendy Waring, Pam Stavropoulos, and Joan Kirkby. *Gender Studies: Terms and Debates*. New York: Palgrave Macmillan, 2003.

de Beauvoir, Simone. "Introduction." *The Second Sex*. Rpt. in *French Feminism Reader*. Ed. Kelly Oliver. New York: Rowman & Littlefield, 2000. 6–20.

Delphy, Christine. *Close to Home: A Materialist Analysis of Women's Oppression*. Trans. Diana Leonard. London: Hutchinson, 1984.

Denard, Carolyn. "The Convergence of Feminism and Ethnicity in the Fiction of Toni Morrison." *Critical Essays on Toni Morrison*. Ed. Nellie Y. McKay. Boston: G. K. Hall, 1988. 171–78.

Fausto-Sterling, Anne. *Sexing the Body: Gender Politics and the Construction of Sexuality*. New York: Basic Books, 2000.

Fitzgerald, F. Scott. *The Great Gatsby*. 1925. New York: Macmillan, 1992.

——. *Tender Is the Night*. New York: Scribner's, 1934.

Guillaumin, Colette. "The Practice of Power and Belief in Nature." *Sex in Question: French Materialist Feminism*. Eds. Diana Leonard and Lisa Adkins. London: Taylor & Francis, 1996. 72–108.

Hansen, Jennifer. "One Is Not Born a Woman." *French Feminism Reader*. Ed. Kelly Oliver. New York: Rowman & Littlefield, 2000. 1–6.

Helliwell, Christine. "'It's Only a Penis': Rape, Feminism, and Difference." *Signs: Journal of Women in Culture and Society* 25.3 (2000): 789–816. Rpt. in *The Kaleidoscope of Gender: Prisms, Patterns, and Possibilities*. Eds. Joan Z. Spade and Catherine G. Valentine. Belmont, CA: Thomson/Wadsworth, 2004. 122–36.

Irigaray, Luce. *This Sex Which Is Not One*. Trans. Catherine Porter. Ithaca, NY: Cornell University Press, 1985.

Kristeva, Julia. *Desire in Language: A Semiotic Approach to Literature and Art*. Ed. Leon S. Roudiez. New York: Columbia University Press, 1980.

———. "Woman's Time." Trans. Alice Jardine and Harry Blache. *Signs* 7 (1981): 13–35. Rpt. in *French Feminism Reader*. Ed. Kelly Oliver. New York: Rowman & Littlefield, 2000. 181–200.

Lepowsky, Maria Alexandra. "Gender and Power." *Fruit of the Motherland*. New York: Columbia University Press, 1993. Rpt. in *The Kaleidoscope of Gender: Prisms, Patterns, and Possibilities*. Eds. Joan Z. Spade and Catherine G. Valentine. Belmont, CA: Thomson/Wadsworth, 2004. 150–59.

Lorber, Judith. "Believing Is Seeing: Biology as Ideology." *Gender and Society* 7.4 (December 1993): 568–81. Rpt. in *Through the Prism of Difference: Readings on Sex and Gender*. Eds. Maxine Baca Zinn, Pierrette Hondagneu-Sotelo, and Michael A. Messner. Boston: Allyn & Bacon, 1997. 13–22.

Miller, Arthur. *Death of a Salesman*. New York: Viking, 1949.

Moi, Toril. *Sexual/Textual Politics: Feminist Literary Theory*. New York: Methuen, 1985.

Morrison, Toni. *The Bluest Eye*. New York: Holt, Rinehart, and Winston, 1970.

Nanda, Serena. "Multiple Genders among North American Indians." *Gender Diversity: Crosscultural Variations*. Prospect Heights, IL: Waveland, 2001. Rpt. in *The Kaleidoscope of Gender: Prisms, Patterns, and Possibilities*. Eds. Joan Z. Spade and Catherine G. Valentine. Belmont, CA: Thomson/Wadsworth, 2004. 64–70.

Perry, Linda A. M., and Deborah Ballard-Reisch. "There's a Rainbow in the Closet: On the Importance of Developing a Common Language for 'Sex' and 'Gender.'" *Readings in Gender Communication*. Eds. Philip M. Backlund and Mary Rose Williams. Belmont, CA: Thomson/Wadsworth, 2004. 17–34.

Preeves, Sharon E. "Sexing the Intersexed: An Analysis of Sociocultural Responses to Intersexuality." *The Kaleidoscope of Gender: Prisms, Patterns, and Possibilities*. Eds. Joan Z. Spade and Catherine G. Valentine. Belmont, CA: Thomson/Wadsworth, 2004. 31–45. Based on "Sexing the Intersexed." *Signs: Journal of Women in Culture and Society* 27.2 (2001): 523–26.

Sapolsky, Robert M. "The Trouble with Testosterone: Will Boys Just Be Boys?" *The Trouble with Testosterone*. New York: Scribner's/Simon & Schuster, 1997. Rpt. in *The Gendered Society Reader*. Ed. Michael S. Kimmel. New York: Oxford University Press, 2000. 14–20.

Shelley, Mary. *Frankenstein*. London: Lackington, Hughes, Harding, Mavor, & Jones, 1818.

Spade, Joan Z., and Catherine G. Valentine. "Introduction." *The Kaleidoscope of Gender: Prisms, Patterns, and Possibilities*. Eds. Joan Z. Spade and Catherine G. Valentine. Belmont, CA: Thomson/Wadsworth, 2004. 1–13.

United States Federal Bureau of Investigation. "Hate Crimes Overview." Available online at www.fbi.gov/about-us/investigate/civilrights/hate_crimes/overview. (accessed April 2, 2014)

Walker, Alice. *In Search of Our Mothers' Gardens*. San Diego: Harcourt Brace Jovanovich, 1984.

Wollstonecraft, Mary. *A Vindication of the Rights of Woman: With Strictures on Political and Moral Subjects*. London: J. Johnson, 1792.

5   New Criticism

New Criticism occupies an unusual position, both in this textbook and in the field of literary studies today. On the one hand, it's the only theory covered in this book that is no longer practiced by literary critics, so it can't really be called a contemporary theory. On the other hand, New Criticism, which dominated literary studies from the 1940s through the 1960s, has left a lasting imprint on the way we read and write about literature. Some of its most important concepts concerning the nature and importance of textual evidence – the use of concrete, specific examples from the text itself to validate our interpretations – have been incorporated into the way most literary critics today, regardless of their theoretical persuasion, support their readings of literature. In fact, if you're an English major, you probably take for granted the need for thorough textual support for your literary interpretations because this practice, which the New Critics introduced to America and called "close reading," has been a standard method of high school and college instruction in literary studies for the past several decades. So in this sense, New Criticism is still a real presence among us and probably will remain so for some time to come.

Few students today, however, are aware of New Criticism's contribution to literary studies or of the theoretical framework that underlies the classroom instruction it has fostered. For this reason, I think we should give New Criticism the same kind of attention we give to the other theories in this textbook. In addition, we need to understand New Criticism in order to understand those theories that have developed in reaction against it. As we'll see in subsequent chapters, reader-response criticism opposes New Criticism's definition of the literary text and method of interpreting it, and structuralism rejects New Criticism's focus on the individual literary work in isolation from other literature and from other cultural productions. In addition, deconstruction's theory of language and new historicism's view of objective evidence are directly opposed to New Critical assumptions about language and objectivity.

"The text itself"

To fully appreciate New Criticism's contribution to literary studies today, we need to remember the form of criticism it replaced: the biographical-historical criticism that dominated literary studies in the nineteenth century and the early decades of the twentieth. At that time, it was common practice to interpret a literary text by studying the author's life and times to determine *authorial intention*, that is, the meaning the author intended the text to have. The author's letters, diaries, and essays were combed for evidence of authorial intention as were autobiographies, biographies, and history books. In its most extreme form, biographical-historical criticism seemed, to some, to examine the text's biographical-historical context instead of examining the text. As one of my former professors described the situation, students attending a lecture on Wordsworth's "Elegiac Stanzas" (1805) could expect to hear a description of the poet's personal and intellectual life: his family, friends, enemies, lovers, habits, education, beliefs, and experiences. "Now you understand the meaning of 'Elegiac Stanzas,'" they would be told, without anyone in the room, including the lecturer, having opened the book to look at the poem itself. Or, in a similar manner, scholars viewed the literary text merely as an adjunct to history, as an illustration of the "spirit of the age" in which it was written, not as an art object worthy of study for its own sake. For New Critics, however, the poem itself was all that mattered.

"The *text itself*" became the battle cry of the New Critical effort to focus our attention on the literary work as the sole source of evidence for interpreting it. The life and times of the author and the spirit of the age in which he or she lived are certainly of interest to the literary historian, New Critics argued, but they do not provide the literary critic with information that can be used to analyze the text itself. In the first place, they pointed out, sure knowledge of the author's intended meaning is usually unavailable. We can't telephone William Shakespeare and ask him how he intended us to interpret Hamlet's hesitation in carrying out the instructions of his father's ghost, and Shakespeare left no written explanation of his intention. More important, even if Shakespeare had left a record of his intention, as some authors have, all we can know from that record is what he wanted to accomplish, not what he did accomplish. Sometimes a literary text doesn't live up to the author's intention. Sometimes it is even more meaningful, rich, and complex than the author realized. And sometimes the text's meaning is simply different from the meaning the author wanted it to have. Knowing an author's intention, therefore, tells us nothing about the text itself, which is why New Critics coined the term *intentional fallacy* to refer to the mistaken belief that the author's intention is the same as the text's meaning.

Just as we cannot look to the author's intention to find the meaning of a literary text, neither can we look to the reader's personal response to find it. Any given reader may or may not respond to what is actually provided by the text itself. Readers' feelings or opinions about a text may be produced by some personal association from past experience rather than by the text. I may, for example, respond to Hamlet's mother based solely on my feelings about my own mother and nevertheless conclude that I have correctly interpreted the literary character. Such a conclusion would be an example of what New Critics called the *affective fallacy.* While the intentional fallacy confuses the text with its origins, the affective fallacy confuses the text with its affects, that is, with the emotions it produces. The affective fallacy leads to impressionistic responses (if a reader doesn't like a character, then that character must be evil) and relativism (the text means whatever any reader thinks it means). The final outcome of such a practice is chaos: we have no standards for interpreting or evaluating literature, which is therefore reduced to the status of the ink-blot on which psychiatric patients project their own meanings.

Although the author's intention or the reader's response is sometimes mentioned in New Critical readings of literary texts, neither one is the focus of analysis. For the only way we can know if a given author's intention or a given reader's interpretation actually represents the text's meaning is to carefully examine, or "closely read," all the evidence provided by the language of the text itself: its images, symbols, metaphors, rhyme, meter, point of view, setting, characterization, plot, and so forth, which, because they form, or shape, the literary work are called its *formal elements.* But before we discuss how this method of close reading operates, we need to understand just what New Critics meant by "the text itself" because their definition of the literary work is directly related to their beliefs concerning the proper way to interpret it.

For New Criticism, a literary work is a *timeless, autonomous* (self-sufficient) *verbal object.* Readers and readings may change, but the literary text stays the same. Its meaning is as objective as its physical existence on the page, for it is constructed of words placed in a specific relationship to one another – specific words placed in a specific order – and this one-of-a-kind relationship creates a complex of meaning that cannot be reproduced by any other combination of words. A New Critical reading of Robert Hayden's "Middle Passage" (1966) can help us appreciate the poem by explaining how the poem's complex of meaning works, but it cannot replace that complex of meaning: only "Middle Passage" is "Middle Passage," and it will always be "Middle Passage." This is why New Criticism asserted that the meaning of a poem could not be explained simply by paraphrasing it, or translating it into everyday language, a practice New Critics referred to as the *heresy of paraphrase.* Change one line, one image, one word of the poem, they argued, and you will have a different poem.

Literary language and organic unity

The importance of the formal elements of a literary text is a product of the nature of *literary language,* which, for New Criticism, is very different from scientific language and from everyday language. Scientific language, and a good deal of everyday language, depends on denotation, the one-to-one correspondence between words and the objects or ideas they represent. Scientific language doesn't draw attention to itself, doesn't try to be beautiful or emotionally evocative. Its job is to point not to itself but to the physical world beyond it, which it attempts to describe and explain. Literary language, in contrast, depends on connotation: on the implication, association, suggestion, and evocation of meanings and of shades of meaning. (For example, while the word *father* denotes *male parent*, it connotes *authority, protection,* and *responsibility*.) In addition, literary language is expressive: it communicates tone, attitude, and feeling. While everyday language is often connotative and expressive, too, in general it is not deliberately or systematically so, for its chief purpose is practical. Everyday language wants to get things done. Literary language, however, organizes linguistic resources into a special arrangement, a complex unity, to create an aesthetic experience, a world of its own.

Unlike scientific and everyday language, therefore, the form of literary language — the word choice and arrangement that create the aesthetic experience — is inseparable from its content, its meaning. Put more simply, *how* a literary text means is inseparable from *what* it means. For the form and meaning of a literary work, at least of a great literary work, develop together, like a complex living organism whose parts cannot be separated from the whole. And indeed, the work's *organic unity* — the working together of all the parts to make an inseparable whole — is the criterion by which New Critics judged the quality of a literary work. If a text has an organic unity, then all of its formal elements work together to establish its theme, or the meaning of the work as a whole. Through its organic unity, the text provides both the *complexity* that a literary work must have, if it is to adequately represent the complexity of human life, and the *order* that human beings, by nature, seek. For New Criticism, then, the explanation of literary meaning and the evaluation of literary greatness became one and the same act, for when New Critics explained a text's organic unity they were also establishing its claim to greatness. Let's take a closer look at each of the criteria of literary value embodied in organic unity: complexity and order.

For New Criticism, the complexity of a text is created by the multiple and often conflicting meanings woven through it. And these meanings are a product primarily of four kinds of linguistic devices: paradox, irony, ambiguity, and tension. Briefly, *paradox* is a statement that seems self-contradictory but represents the actual way things are. For example, it is a biblical paradox that you must lose your life in order to gain it. On the surface, that phrase seems self-contradictory: how can you gain an object by losing it? However, the phrase means that by giving up one kind of life, the transitory life of the flesh, you gain another, more important kind of life: the eternal life of the soul. Similarly, a paradox of everyday experience can be seen in the old saying Joni Mitchell uses so effectively in her song "Big Yellow Taxi": "You don't know what you've got 'till it's gone." Not unlike the biblical reference above, this old adage tells us that you have to lose something (physically) before you can find it (spiritually). Many of life's spiritual and psychological realities are paradoxical in nature, New Critics observed, and paradox is thus responsible for much of the complexity of human experience and of the literature that portrays it.

Irony, in its simple form, means a statement or event undermined by the context in which it occurs. The following description of a wealthy husband's sense of moral rectitude, from Edith Wharton's *House of Mirth* (1905), is an example of an ironic statement.

> Once in the winter the rector would come to dine, and her husband would beg her to go over the list and see that no divorcées were included, except those who had showed signs of penitence by being remarried to the very wealthy.
>
> (57)

Part of the ironic implication of this passage is that the husband is a hypocrite: he condemns divorce only if it is not followed by the acquisition of equal or greater wealth, so what he really condemns, under the guise of moral principles, is financial decline. An example of an ironic event can be seen in Toni Morrison's *The Bluest Eye* (1970) when Pecola finally receives the blue eyes she has wished for so desperately. Her wish has been "fulfilled" only because she has lost touch with reality so completely that she believes her brown eyes are blue.

New Criticism, however, primarily valued irony in a broader sense of the term, to indicate a text's inclusion of varying perspectives on the same characters or events. We see this kind of irony, for example, when Jane Austen's *Sense and Sensibility* (1811) offers us perspectives from which we may utterly condemn Willoughby for his treachery to Marianne; forgive him because his behavior resulted from a combination of love, financial desperation, and a weakness of character which he himself laments; sympathize with him for the severity of the punishment his behavior has brought upon him; and see the ways in which Marianne's willful foolishness contributed to her own heartbreak. Such a variety of possible viewpoints is considered a form of irony because the credibility of each viewpoint undermines to some extent the credibility of the others. The result is a complexity of meaning that mirrors the complexity of human experience and increases the text's believability. In contrast, had Willoughby been portrayed as purely and uncomplicatedly evil, Marianne would have been idealized as a completely innocent victim, and the text would have become vulnerable to the reader's skepticism, which would put the reader at an ironic distance from the text. Thus the text's own internal irony, or awareness of multiple viewpoints, protects it from the external irony of the reader's disbelief.

Ambiguity occurs when a word, image, or event generates two or more different meanings. For example, in Toni Morrison's *Beloved* (1987), the image of the tree produced by the scar tissue on Sethe's back implies, among other things, suffering (the "tree" resulted from a brutal whipping, which is emblematic of all the hardships experienced under slavery), endurance (trees can live for hundreds of years, and the scar tissue itself testifies to Sethe's remarkable ability to survive the most traumatic experiences), and renewal (like the trees that lose their leaves in the fall and are "reborn" every spring, Sethe is offered, at the novel's close, the chance to make a new life). In scientific or everyday language, ambiguity is usually considered a flaw because it's equated with a lack of clarity and precision. In literary language, however, ambiguity is considered a source of richness, depth, and complexity that adds to the text's value.

Finally, the complexity of a literary text is created by its *tension*, which, broadly defined, means the linking together of opposites. In its simplest form, tension is created by the integration of the abstract and the concrete, of general ideas embodied in specific images. For example, in Arthur Miller's *Death of a Salesman* (1949), the concrete image of Willy's tiny house, bathed in blue light and surrounded by enormous apartment buildings that emanate an angry orange glow, embodies the general idea of the underdog, the victim of forces larger and more numerous than itself. Similarly, the concrete image of Linda Loman singing Willy to sleep embodies the general idea of the devoted wife, the caretaker, the nurturer. Such *concrete universals* – or images and fictional characters that are meaningful on both the concrete level, where their meaning is literal and specific, and on the symbolic level, where they have universal significance – are considered a form of tension because they hold together the opposing realms of physical reality and symbolic reality in a way characteristic of literary language. In other words, the Loman home and the character of Linda Loman represent both themselves and something larger than themselves.

Tension is also created by the dynamic interplay among the text's opposing tendencies, that is, among its paradoxes, ironies, and ambiguities. For example, we might say that the action of *Death of a Salesman* is structured by the tension between reality and illusion: between the harsh reality of Willy Loman's life and the self-delusion into which he keeps trying to escape. Ideally, the text's opposing tendencies are held in equilibrium by working together to make a stable and coherent meaning. For example, the tension between harsh reality and self-delusion in *Death of a Salesman* is held in equilibrium by the following meaning: so great is Willy's desire to succeed as a salesman and a father that his only defense against the common man's inevitable failures in a dog-eat-dog world is self-delusion, but that self-delusion only increases his failure. Thus, the play shows us how harsh reality and self-delusion feed off each other until the only escape is death.

As noted earlier, the complexity of the text, to which all of these linguistic devices contribute, must be complemented by a sense of order if a literary work is to achieve greatness. Therefore, all of the multiple and conflicting meanings produced by the text's paradoxes, ironies, ambiguities, and tensions must be resolved, or harmonized, by their shared contribution to the theme. The text's *theme*, or complete meaning, is not the same thing as its topic. Rather, the theme is what the text does with its topic. For example, adultery is the topic of both Kate Chopin's "The Storm" (1898) and Alberto Moravia's "The Chase" (1967), but the meaning of adultery – its moral and psychological implications – is quite different in each story. In Chopin's tale, a single, spontaneous act of adultery seems to improve the emotional health and marriages of the two participants. The theme of "The Storm," we might say, is that individual circumstances, not abstract rules, determine what is right and wrong, healthy and unhealthy. In Moravia's story, in contrast, the young wife's extramarital affair seems to both result from and contribute to the emotional distance between her husband and herself. The theme of "The Chase," it might be argued, is that adultery is a form of emotional distance, and, as such, it signals the end of emotional intimacy in a marriage. Thus, the theme is an interpretation of human experience, and if the text is a great one, the theme serves as a commentary on human values, human nature, or the human condition. In other words, great literary works have themes of universal human (moral and/or emotional) significance.[1] They tell us something important about what it means to be human. We may not like or agree with the theme a story offers, but we can still see what that theme is and, most important for New Criticism, we can judge whether or not that theme is established by the text's formal elements in a way that produces an organic unity.

Close reading, the scrupulous examination of the complex relationship between a text's formal elements and its theme, is how the text's organic unity was established by the New Critic. Because of New Criticism's belief that the literary text can be understood primarily by understanding its form (which is why you'll sometimes hear it referred to as a type of *formalism*), a clear understanding of the definitions of specific formal elements is important. In addition to the formal elements discussed above – the linguistic devices of paradox, irony, ambiguity, and tension – we should also take a moment to briefly define a few of the most frequently used kinds of figurative language: images, symbols, metaphors, and similes.

Figurative language is language that has more than, or other than, a strictly literal meaning. For instance, "It's raining cats and dogs" is a figurative expression used to indicate that it's raining very heavily. If it were taken literally, then the phrase would mean, of course, that actual cats and dogs were falling from the sky. Broadly defined, an *image* as illustrated by our use of the word earlier, consists of a word or words that refer to an object perceived by the senses or to sense perceptions themselves: colors, shapes, lighting, sounds, tastes, smells, textures, temperatures, and so on. More narrowly defined, and most common in the practice of analyzing literary texts, imagery is visual, consisting of descriptions of objects, characters, or settings as they are seen by the eye. Although images always have literal meaning – a description of clouds means that the weather is cloudy – they can evoke an emotional atmosphere as well: for example, a description of clouds can be used to evoke sadness.

If an image occurs repeatedly in a text, it probably has symbolic significance. A *symbol* is an image that has both literal and figurative meaning, a concrete universal, such as the swamp in Ernest Hemingway's "Big, Two-Hearted River" (1925). The swamp is a literal swamp – it's wet, it contains fish and other forms of aquatic life, one needs boots and special equipment to fish in it – but it also "stands for," or "figures," something else: the emotional problems the protagonist does not feel quite ready to face. Public symbols are usually easy to spot. For example, spring is usually a symbol of rebirth or youth; autumn is usually a symbol of death or dying; a river is usually a symbol of life or of a journey. Thus, a symbol has properties similar to those of the abstract idea it stands for. For example, a river can symbolize life because both a river and life are fluid and forward moving; both have a source and an endpoint. In addition, a river literally nurtures life: some life forms live in it; others drink from it.

The context provided by the text also helps us figure out a symbol's meaning. To use the example of Hemingway's swamp again, in addition to the similarities between a swamp and emotional problems – both are difficult to deal with because both involve unknown pitfalls that may be dangerous and are certainly challenging – the protagonist manifests the same attitude toward the swamp that he manifests toward his emotional problems: he avoids them. And this similarity tips us off to the swamp's symbolic content. Sometimes, the context provided by the text is all we have to go on because some symbols are private, or meaningful only to the author, and therefore more difficult to figure out. We may suspect, for example, that the image of a purple felt hat has symbolic significance in a story because it recurs frequently or plays a role that seems to reverberate with some abstract quality such as love or loneliness or strength, but we'll have to figure out what that symbolic significance is by studying how the hat operates within the overall meaning of the text. Of course, how something operates within the overall meaning of the text was always the bottom line for New Criticism, so it does not matter whether or not our analysis of the text's private symbolism matches the author's intention. What matters is that our analysis of the text's private symbolism, like our analysis of all its formal elements, supports what we claim is the text's theme.

In contrast with the double dimension of the symbol – its inclusion of both literal and figurative meaning – a *metaphor* has only figurative meaning. A metaphor is a comparison of two dissimilar objects in which the properties of one are ascribed to the other. For example, the phrase "my brother is a gem" is a metaphor. Obviously, it has no literal meaning. If it did, it would mean that my mother gave birth to a crystalline stone, for which feat she'd be on the cover of every tabloid in the nation. The figurative meaning of the phrase, which is the only meaning it has, is that my brother shares certain properties with a gem: for example, he is of great worth. Thus, "he's a gem" is generally used to mean "he's a great guy." To get from metaphor to *simile* requires one small step: add *like* or *as*. "My brother is like a gem" or "my brother is as valuable as a gem" are similes that make the same comparison as the metaphor from which I derived them, though one might argue that the simile is softer because the connection between the idea of "brother" and the idea of "gem" is less direct or less forceful.

I think it's time we put these New Critical tools to work in order to see the New Critical method in action. So let's do a close reading of Lucille Clifton's "There Is a Girl Inside" (1977).

A New Critical reading of "There Is a Girl Inside"

There Is a Girl Inside

there is a girl inside.
she is randy as a wolf.
she will not walk away
and leave these bones
to an old woman.

she is a green tree
in a forest of kindling.
she is a green girl
in a used poet.

she has waited
patient as a nun
for the second coming,
when she can break through gray hairs
into blossom

and her lovers will harvest
honey and thyme
and the woods will be wild
with the damn wonder of it.

The poem's title, "There Is a Girl Inside," which also serves as the opening line, and the final two lines of the first stanza, which refer to "these bones" of an "old woman," suggest immediately that the speaker is an old woman who still feels young and vital inside. Is this initial observation supported by any additional textual evidence? Well, there's the fact that the speaker refers to the "girl inside" in the third person, as "she," as someone other and younger than herself. In addition, at the end of the second stanza the speaker refers to herself as "a used poet," which also implies age. So we know that the central tension in the poem is probably the tension between youth and age, between what the speaker feels like on the inside and what she looks like on the outside. This tension structures the poem as a whole through the alternation of the language of youthful vitality ("girl," "randy" – which suggests sexual attraction or arousal – "green tree," "green girl," and "blossom") with the language of aging and decay ("bones," "old woman," "kindling" – which is old, dried-up wood used for starting fires – "used poet," and "gray hairs"). In addition, the narrative dimension of the poem, or the "story" the poem tells, reveals an old woman dreaming about the miraculous rejuvenation, the "second coming" of youth, that she feels awaits the "girl inside" herself, the girl that she is still, despite her "bones" and "gray hairs." Thus we might hypothesize, at this point, that the theme of the poem probably involves the paradox of timeless youth. (Timeless youth is a paradox because, on the literal level of biology, time and youth are mutually exclusive: the passage of time inevitably results in aging.) To discover the specific nature of the theme, and to understand how the poem establishes it, we need to closely examine more of the poem's formal elements.

The first thing we might notice, looking at the poem as a whole, is that the alternation of images of youth with images of age ends with the fourth line of the third stanza. The final five lines of the poem, which include the entire last stanza, consist of images of youth, fertility, and sexuality, and they evoke the youthfulness the speaker believes can overpower age: "blossom," "lovers," "harvest," "honey and thyme," "woods," "wild," and "wonder." Does anything else in the poem reinforce this emphasis on the triumph of youth over age? Still looking at the poem as a whole, note the decrease in punctuation as the poem progresses, which is literally a decrease in stops and pauses. There are a total of five periods (full stops) in the first two stanzas, but there is only one comma (pause) in the third stanza and no punctuation at all in the final stanza until we get to the period that ends the poem. In fact, counting from the comma in stanza three, there is no punctuation in the final six lines of the poem. This dramatic decrease in punctuation, or decrease in stops and pauses, suggests acceleration, excitement, and power, thus reinforcing the emphasis on the triumph of youth in the final stanza.

As we are already engaged in examining the poem's punctuation, let's take a look at the parts of speech it employs. For example, let's see what its use of verbs can tell us. First, we might note the speaker's use of powerful verbs in the active voice: the girl inside "will not walk away," she "can break through," and "her lovers will harvest." These powerful, active verbs reinforce the idea that this girl is powerful and active, strong enough to get what she wants. I think the use of "has waited" in the third stanza reinforces the idea that the girl inside is ready to emerge. The line does not read "she is waiting," which would imply that the waiting will go on for an indeterminate length of time, but "she has waited," which suggests that her waiting is over or should be over soon. In this context, we should also mention the simile "she is randy as a wolf," for a wolf is a powerful animal that fights for what it wants and usually gets what it fights for. ("Randy as a rabbit," for example, would certainly not carry the same implication.)

Are there any other images associated with the girl inside, and if so, do they contribute to the theme we're trying to formulate? The metaphor "she is a green tree" is useful for our purposes because it invokes the growing seasons, spring and summer, the seasons of rebirth and plenitude. And because "green tree" is a nature image, it carries with it the inevitability of rejuvenation. The tree that has been a mere skeleton all winter, like the old woman's "bones," and as dead looking as "kindling," has blossomed. The rejuvenating power of the "green tree" inside the winter tree is thus linked to the rejuvenating power of the "green girl" two lines down. If the green tree can "break through ... / into blossom," then so can the green girl who waits inside the old woman.

Of course, "green girl" also implies that the girl is inexperienced, naive, unused to the world. And this aspect of the image fits nicely with the simile in the second line of the next stanza: "patient as a nun." As you may know, nuns belonging to most religious orders renounce the world of selfish pleasures, the world of the flesh, as we see, for example, in the vows of chastity, poverty, and obedience taken by Roman Catholic nuns. The image of the nun thus forms a bridge between the inexperienced girl and the old woman, for all three are cut off, in one way or another, from the world of the flesh. And just as a nun waits patiently for her reward – the second coming of Christ – so the old woman and the girl inside have both waited patiently for theirs: the second coming of youth.

Is there anything else in the poem that reinforces the link between the aging speaker and the young girl inside? Let's look again at the language of the final stanza, where youth, which has "blossom[ed]" at the end of the previous stanza, will be "harvest[ed]." Closing lines are always very important, and these seem to have especially rich images. We said earlier that this is the stanza where youth triumphs over age, and indeed it does, for this is the stanza in which the speaker imagines the newly emerged girl consummating her sexual desire in the woods. However, the words "harvest," "honey," and "thyme" have an ambiguity that also reinforces the bond between youth and age. For in addition to their connotations of youthful sexual vitality, "harvest," "honey," and "thyme" can refer to activities associated with autumn and therefore with the old woman.

A harvest occurs in the fall at the end of the growing season, when the plants are fully mature, not when they are "green," or young, like the "green girl" inside. Honey and thyme, in that they are crops that are harvested, carry the same meaning. For honey is the product bees make from flower pollen after the pollen is harvested; beekeepers, in turn, harvest the honey from the hive after it is made.

And thyme, a fragrant herb used to season food, is used primarily after it has dried up. Metaphorically, then, the stanza implies a merger of age and youth. The word "kindling" in the second stanza has an ambiguity that is useful in this context, too. As noted earlier, "kindling" refers to old, dried-up wood used to start fires. But the very fact that kindling catches fire so easily associates it with the quality of passion, which also "catches fire" easily. In this sense, we might say that, in passion, youth and age are one.

Let's see what we can learn about the relationship between youth and age from the poem's *tone,* which it might be helpful to think of as the speaker's tone of voice, for it expresses the speaker's attitude toward what he or she is saying and toward the reader. We know that the speaker is an old woman. Is her tone somber or lighthearted? Weary or energetic? Formal or informal? How would we characterize it? Right away, her use of slang – "randy" to indicate sexual hunger in the second line of the poem and "damn" in the final stanza – tells us that the tone is somewhat playful and irreverent, a tone often associated with youth. And so is her play on words in the third stanza: the "second coming" for which the "nun" has waited can refer to both the second coming of Christ and the speaker's second "coming," or the second time in her life when she can experience sexual desire, sexual vitality, sexual climax.

The informality created by the speaker's use of slang and humor is reinforced by the poem's short lines, which make it seem as if she were speaking to us conversationally, and by the absence of traditional features such as capital letters, rhyme, and meter. We might say, then, that in the playful irreverence and informality of the speaker's tone, we have the merger of youth and age: the young person who disdains formality and the old woman who has grown beyond it. Or to put it another way, we know that the girl inside the speaker is an important presence in her life because we can hear her youthful voice in the voice of the old woman. And surely the tone of voice in the last line is the voice of both girl and woman, the voice through which we can almost see them raise their hands to their hips as they refer to "the damn wonder of it."

Perhaps, then, we can formulate our theme in the following manner. The theme of "There Is a Girl Inside" is not merely a restatement of the old adage "Hope springs eternal in the human breast," but a transformation of that adage into a new one of equally universal importance: youth springs eternal in the human breast. For the poem suggests that age brings with it a special "harvest" of its own, which is the capacity to appreciate the gifts of youth that remain within us as seeds remain within a ripened fruit and, as a result, to feel young even when we are old. Thus the theme of the poem brings together, or resolves, the tension between youth and age that structures it. And we can conclude that the poem has an organic unity because, as we have seen, its theme is carried by all of its formal elements; that is, its form and content are inseparable. Furthermore, although the poem appears to be charmingly, and disarmingly, simple, our analysis of its organic unity reveals a surprising complexity in the operations of its formal elements. We would be justified in arguing, then, that from a New Critical perspective, "There Is a Girl Inside" is a finely wrought literary text, a unified, complex art object the theme of which has universal human significance.

New Criticism as intrinsic, objective criticism

As I hope the reading of Clifton's poem illustrates, New Criticism asked us to look closely at the formal elements of the text to help us discover the poem's theme and to explain the ways in which those formal elements establish it. For New Critics believed that this was the only way to determine the text's value. By staying within the poem in this manner, New Critics believed they allowed the literary work itself to provide the context within which we interpret and evaluate it. To use an obvious example, in analyzing Clifton's poem my discussion of the word randy focused only on the slang meaning of the term because only that meaning makes sense in terms of the context of the poem as a whole. Other meanings of the word found in *Webster's New Universal Unabridged Dictionary* include "crude" or "vulgar," "a quarrelsome woman," and "a threatening beggar." Had any of these meanings enriched our reading of the poem by bringing another dimension to the theme, I would have analyzed it as part of the word's ambiguity. But because none of these meanings seemed appropriate in terms of the poem's theme, I ignored them. Thus, although most words can be found to have more than one dictionary definition, a word's ambiguity is determined not by the dictionary but by the context of the poem as a whole, in terms of which alone the word's meaning or meanings must be judged.

Similarly, I did not mention that Clifton is an African American poet, and there is nothing in my reading that would indicate the author's race. Although an African American critic would most probably include some mention of the ways in which the poem participates in the African American literary tradition, from a New Critical perspective such information, while of historical interest, is irrelevant to our evaluation of the poem's organic unity and universal significance. (See Chapters 11 and 12, "African American criticism" and "Postcolonial criticism," for a discussion of the discriminatory properties of the concept of "universalism.")

Finally, I did not try to analyze the speaker's psychological state – though a psychoanalytic reading might have analyzed "wolf," "bones," "kindling," "used," "break," and "wild" in order to argue that a fear of violence and self-destruction lies beneath the poem's sexual imagery – because there doesn't seem to be anything in the poem itself to warrant such an analysis. The speaker's psychology is not involved in the theme of the poem, and it is not relevant to our understanding of the theme of the poem. Sometimes New Critics did believe that the text warranted a discussion of its psychological, sociological, or philosophical elements because those elements were obviously integral to the work's characterization or plot, as we might find psychological elements integral to characterization or plot in William Faulkner's "A Rose for Emily" (1931) or Edgar Allan Poe's "The Tell-Tale Heart" (1843). In such cases, New Critics addressed these elements, but they did so for the purpose of examining how such elements operate to establish the text's theme (or to undermine it, if the text is flawed). In other words, New Critics didn't ignore the obvious psychological, sociological, or philosophical dimensions of the text; they aestheticized them. That is, they treated psychological, sociological, and philosophical content the same way they treated the text's formal elements: to learn what these elements contribute to the aesthetic experience created by the work's organic unity. In this way, New Critics claimed, their interpretation stayed within the context created by the text itself.

Because New Critics believed their interpretations were based solely on the context created by the text and the language provided by the text, they called their critical practice *intrinsic criticism*, to denote that New Criticism stayed within the confines of the text itself. In contrast, forms of criticism that employ psychological, sociological, or philosophical frameworks – in other words, all criticism other than their own – they called *extrinsic criticism* because it goes outside the literary text for the tools needed to interpret it. New Critics also called their approach *objective criticism* because their focus on each text's own formal elements ensured, they claimed, that each text – each object being interpreted – would itself dictate how it would be interpreted.

The single best interpretation

Given that the text was thus seen as an independent entity with a stable meaning of its own, New Critics believed that a single best, or most accurate, interpretation of each text could be discovered that best represents the text itself: that best explains what the text means and *how* the text produces that meaning, in other words, that best explains its organic unity. This is why, during New Criticism's heyday, essays interpreting a literary text frequently began with a survey of other critics' interpretations of the same text in order to show that everyone else's reading fell short – that important scenes or images were unaccounted for, that tensions structuring the text were not resolved – often because a proper understanding of the text's theme was lacking. In other words, in order to establish that yours was the best reading of a literary work, you would have to begin by establishing that all former readings were in some way inadequate.

In light of the scrupulous attention paid to textual details by the New Critics, it is understandable that their method worked best on short poems and stories because the shorter the text, the more of its formal elements could be analyzed. When longer works were examined, such as long poems, novels, and plays, New Critical readings usually confined themselves to the analysis of some aspect (or aspects) of the work, for example, its imagery (or perhaps just one kind of imagery, such as nature imagery), the role of the narrator or of the minor characters, the function of time in the work, the pattern of light and dark created by settings, or some other formal element. Of course, whatever formal element was analyzed, it had to be shown to play an important role in the text's advancement of its theme and thus contribute to the unity of the work as a whole.

Through your own familiarity or unfamiliarity with the New Critical principles discussed in this chapter, you can probably form some idea of New Criticism's lasting contribution to literary studies. Some of its principles and terminology seem to have fallen by the wayside. For example, few literary critics today assert that a literary text is independent of the history and culture that produced it or that it has a single, objective meaning. And almost no one uses the word *tension* to refer to the symbol's integration of concrete images and abstract ideas. Nevertheless, New Criticism's success in focusing our attention on the formal elements of the text and on their relationship to the meaning of the text is evident in the way we study literature today, regardless of our theoretical perspective. For whatever theoretical framework we use to interpret a text, we always support our interpretation with concrete evidence from the text that usually includes attention to formal elements, and, with the notable exception of some deconstructive and reader-response interpretations, we usually try to produce an interpretation that conveys some sense of the text as a unified whole.

It's rather ironic, then, that New Criticism's gift to critical theory – its focus on the text itself – was responsible for its downfall. New Criticism was eclipsed in the late 1960s by the growing interest, among almost all other schools of critical theory, in the ideological content of literary texts and the ways in which that content both reflects and influences society, an interest that could not be served by the New Critical insistence on analyzing the text as an isolated aesthetic object with a single meaning.

The question New Critics asked about literary texts

Given New Criticism's focus on the single meaning of the text and its single method of establishing that meaning, it should not be surprising that our list of questions New Critics asked about literary texts should consist of only one complex question:

1 What single interpretation of the text best establishes its organic unity? In other words, how do the text's formal elements, and the multiple meanings those elements produce, all work together to support the theme, or overall meaning, of the work? Remember, a great work will have a theme of universal human significance. (If the text is too long to account for all of its formal elements,

apply this question to some aspect or aspects of its form, such as imagery, point of view, setting, or the like.)

Regardless of the literary text at hand, this is the question we ask in order to produce a New Critical interpretation. It is interesting to note that, despite their belief in the text's single, objective meaning, New Critics rarely agreed about what that meaning was or how the text worked to produce it. Instead, different inter-pretations of the same texts abounded. As in every field, even expert New Critical practitioners disagreed about the meaning of specific works. Our goal is to use New Criticism to help enrich our reading of literary texts, to help us see and appreciate in new ways the complex operations of their formal elements and how those elements function to create meaning.

The following interpretation of F. Scott Fitzgerald's *The Great Gatsby* is offered as an example of what a New Critical reading might yield. I discovered what I believe is the novel's topic – human longing – by analyzing the text's imagery, the beauty and emotional force of which make it the most memorable and revealing dimension of the novel. Then I examined other formal elements in the text – specifically, characterization, setting, and elements of style – to determine what I claim is the novel's theme: that unfulfilled longing is an inescapable part of the human condition. As a practitioner of New Criticism, I was interested in the historical time and place described in the novel only as they manifest a theme that transcends historical time and place, a theme that has universal human significance.

The "deathless song" of longing: a New Critical reading of *The Great Gatsby*

Few readers of F. Scott Fitzgerald's *The Great Gatsby* (1925) will fail to notice the breathtaking beauty of its imagery. Indeed, the haunting, wistful quality of the novel's images evokes the melancholy lyricism of the author's favorite poet, John Keats. Yet there has been little analysis of how the imagery in Fitzgerald's powerfully poetic novel structures the meaning of the text as a whole.

It might be argued that this oversight has resulted from the critical focus on *The Great Gatsby* as the chronicle of the Jazz Age – as a social commentary on a specific period in America's past – which has diverted attention onto historical issues and away from the text's formal elements. Most critics agree that Fitzgerald's novel offers a scathing critique of American values in the 1920s, the corruption of which is represented by Wolfsheim's exploitativeness, Daisy's duplicity, Tom's treachery, Jordan's dishonesty, Myrtle's vulgarity, and the shallowness of an American popu-lace – embodied in Gatsby's parasitical party guests – whose moral fiber had declined with each passing year. This is a world run by men like Tom Buchanan and Meyer Wolfsheim, and despite their positions on opposite sides of the law, both characters are predators consumed by self-interest, capable of rationalizing their way around any ethical obstacle to get what they want. It's an empty world where selfishness, drunkenness, and vulgarity abound, where the graceful social art of dancing has become "old men pushing young girls backward in eternal graceless circles" and "superior couples holding each other tortuously, fashionably, and keeping in the corners" (51; ch. 3). And it's a world of impermanence and instability. The Buchanans are forever "drift[ing] here and there unrestfully wherever people played polo and were rich together" (10; ch.1). Jordan is always on the move among hotels, clubs, and other people's homes. And even George Wilson, with the scant means he has at his disposal, thinks he can solve his problems by pulling up stakes and moving west. Anonymity and isolation are the rule rather than the exception, and superficial values put the pursuit of social status and good times above every other consideration. Indeed, one could say that the "valley of ashes" (27; ch. 2) – the name Nick gives to the dumping ground near which George and Myrtle Wilson live – is a metaphor for the spiritual poverty of this world:

> a fantastic farm where ashes grow like wheat into ridges and hills and grotesque gardens, where ashes take the forms of houses and chimneys and rising smoke and finally ... of men who move dimly and already crumbling through the powdery air.
>
> (27; ch. 2)

Because Jay Gatsby is clearly portrayed as a romantic figure of rather mythic proportions, a good deal of critical attention has been given to the narrative tension between the corrupt world of the novel and its title character. And for most critics, Gatsby's capacity to dream and to devote himself to the woman who embodies that dream, including his blindness to the fact that she doesn't deserve his devotion, give him an "innocence" that he "maintain[s]" to the end (Gallo 43). Indeed, there is considerable critical consensus with Marius Bewley's opinion that Gatsby represents "the energy of the spirit's resistance" and "immunity to the final contamination" of "cheapness and vulgarity" (13). As Tom Burnam puts it, Gatsby "survives sound and whole in character, uncorrupted by the corruption which surrounded him" (105).[2] For these critics, the protagonist's innocence serves to indict further the society that destroys him.

This critical focus, however, overlooks a more central tension in the novel than that between Gatsby and the world in which he lives. For we cannot ignore the obvious textual evidence, even if we want to contrast Gatsby with the society he inhabits, that he shares at least some of its corruption: for example, he was Wolfsheim's protégé and has made his fortune by selling bootlegged liquor and fake bonds.[3] It seems to me that the text's central tension is, instead, that between the world of corrupt, vulgar materialism portrayed in the novel and the lyric imagery –

the wistful beauty and emotional force of which make it the most memorable and revealing dimension of the novel – so frequently used to describe that world. This tension structures the narrative regardless of how we measure the relative innocence or corruption of any particular character, and it is resolved by a theme of universal human significance that transcends the historical period in which the novel is set: the theme that unfulfilled longing is part of the human condition, common to all and inescapable. As we'll see, the imagery of unfulfilled longing is used to describe characters and settings regardless of the wealth or poverty, refinement or vulgarity, corruption or innocence they represent. In addition, the imagery of unfulfilled longing is often linked with nature imagery, which suggests that unfulfilled longing is as inevitable as, for example, the change of the seasons. Finally, the imagery of unfulfilled longing often has a static, timeless quality in the novel, which underscores both its universality and its inevitability: unfulfilled longing has always been and will always be a part of the human condition.

Let's begin by examining how the imagery of unfulfilled longing weaves a common thread through characters who represent very different elements of society. To accomplish this task, we'll analyze Fitzgerald's lyric imagery in terms of the three ways in which it informs characterization in the novel: (1) as nostalgia for a lost past; (2) as dreams of future fulfillment; and (3) as vague, undefined longing that has no specific goal.

We see the imagery of longing for a lost past in the idyllic description of Daisy and Jordan's "beautiful white ... girlhood" (24; ch. 1) in Louisville, where Jordan "first learned to walk upon golf courses on clean, crisp mornings" (55; ch. 3). This is a romantic past where, Jordan recalls, she walked on "soft ground" in her "new plaid skirt ... that blew a little in the wind" and where Daisy

> dressed in white and had a little white roadster, and all day long the telephone rang in her house and excited young officers from Camp Taylor demanded the privilege of monopolizing her that night. "Anyways for an hour!"
>
> (79; ch. 4)

This is a world of virginal romance: "clean, crisp mornings," "soft ground," new skirts, white dresses, white roadsters, ringing telephones, and handsome young officers. Even the dust on the ground has a magical glow: "a hundred pairs of golden and silver slippers shuffled the *shining* dust" (158; ch. 8, my italics).

Similarly, Nick's description of the Midwest of his youth is filled with nostalgic images of an idyllic past. Remembering his Christmas train rides back home from boarding school and college, he says,

> When we pulled out into the winter night and the real snow, our snow, began to stretch out beside us and twinkle against the windows, and the dim lights of

small Wisconsin stations moved by, a sharp wild brace came suddenly into the air. We drew in deep breaths of it ... unutterably aware of our identity with this country. ...

That's my middle-west ... the thrilling, returning trains of my youth and the street lamps and sleigh bells in the frosty dark and the shadows of holly wreaths thrown by lighted windows on the snow.

(184; ch. 9)

Like the "clean, crisp mornings," "soft ground," and "shining dust" of Daisy and Jordan's girlhood, the nature imagery in this passage evokes a fresh, clean, virginal past, untouched by the corrupt world. Phrases such as "the real snow, our snow, began to stretch out beside us and twinkle" and "a sharp wild brace came suddenly into the air" evoke open spaces – clean, white, and shining – that invigorate not just the body but the spirit as well. "[T]he real snow" refers, of course, to the enormous quantity of clean, white snow that falls in the upper Midwest and lasts all winter, as contrasted with the sooty snow that becomes slush under the wheels of New York City traffic. But the phrase "real snow" also suggests that life in the Midwest of Nick's youth was more real, more genuine, than the artificial atmosphere he associates with his adult life. This idea is underscored by the homey images of street lamps, sleigh bells, holly wreaths, and lighted windows, whose festive, inviting quality evokes the security and stability of a happy childhood.

In *The Great Gatsby*, even brief images of longing for the past carry emotional force. For example, the images of the young Gatsby revisiting Louisville after Daisy's departure, "stretch[ing] out his hand desperately as if to snatch only a wisp of air, to save a fragment of the spot that she had made lovely for him" (160; ch. 8), and of Tom Buchanan, "drift[ing] on forever seeking a little wistfully for the dramatic turbulence of some irrecoverable football game" (10; ch. 1), are haunting and painful because they bespeak an emptiness that can never be filled. Like the imagery used to describe the youth of Daisy, Jordan, and Nick, these images of Gatsby and Tom evoke a world that is forever lost because it is forever past. We can never be young again, and the world of the past, as Gatsby finally learns, inevitably changes with time.

Perhaps the most powerfully nostalgic images of an idyllic past forever vanished are those that close the novel. As Nick sits on the beach the evening before his return to Minnesota, he muses on

the old island here that flowered once for Dutch sailors' eyes – a fresh green breast of the new world. Its vanished trees, the trees that had made way for Gatsby's house, had once pandered in whispers to the last and greatest of all human dreams; for a transitory enchanted moment man must have held his breath in the presence of this continent, compelled into an aesthetic contemplation he neither understood nor desired, face to face for the last time in history with something commensurate to his capacity for wonder.

(189; ch. 9)

In this passage, Nick's nostalgic longing is universalized in global historical proportions: all of our individual longing for the dreams of lost youth and lost love – which, just like America, "flowered once," "fresh" and "green," while we "held [our] breath" – is absorbed in and expressed by a longing for the "enchanted ... wonder" of a pristine American continent forever gone. And the repetition of words associated with this loss – "once," "vanished," "once," "last," "transitory," and "for the last time in history" – underscore its utter, heartbreaking finality.

The imagery of unfulfilled longing also weaves a common thread through characterization in the form of dreams of future fulfillment. Early in the novel, for example, Nick dreams about his successful future in the bond business, embodied in the books he bought on banking and investments, the description of which is immediately preceded by, and wedded to, nature imagery:

And so with the sunshine and the great bursts of leaves growing on the trees ... I had that familiar conviction that life was beginning over again with the summer.

There was so much to read, for one thing, and so much fine health to be pulled down out of the young breath-giving air. I bought a dozen volumes on banking and credit and investment securities and they stood on my shelf in red and gold like new money from the mint, promising to unfold the shining secrets that only Midas and Morgan and Maecenas knew.

(8; ch. 1)

The language used to describe the books – "new," "promising to unfold," and "shining" – links Nick's longing for success with the longing for new life awakened in the spring by the "sunshine," "great bursts of leaves," and "breath-giving air." Furthermore, the inclusion of financier J. P. Morgan's name with the names of mythical figures Midas and Maecenas imbues the passage with an ambience of myth, of fantasy, reinforcing the idea that Nick's success is not guaranteed but dreamed of, longed for with a visionary hopefulness that merges with, and is as natural as, the aching beauty of spring.

Though certainly developed on a less grand scale, the imagery of unfulfilled longing nevertheless ties the depictions of Myrtle and George Wilson to those of the other characters who dream of future fulfillment. As Nick and Gatsby head to New York City for their lunch appointment, they drive through the "valley of ashes":

We passed Port Roosevelt, where there was a glimpse of red-belted ocean-going ships, and sped along a cobbled slum lined with the dark, undeserted

saloons of the faded gilt nineteen-hundreds. Then the valley of ashes opened
out on both sides of us, and I had a glimpse of Mrs. Wilson straining at the
garage pump with panting vitality as we went by.

(72; ch. 4)

We are prepared for our glimpse of the "valley of ashes" by the two neighborhoods – neither of them wealthy residential areas – that precede it. The first
contains wharves; the second is a slum. Yet in both we see images of unfulfilled
longing. In Port Roosevelt we see "red-belted ocean-going ships," which evoke the
possibility of future adventure, enjoyment, profit, or at least change. In the slum we
see "undeserted saloons of the faded gilt nineteen-hundreds," which evoke past
glamour and excitement. Then we see Myrtle Wilson, whose posture at this
moment, "straining at the garage pump," embodies longing for future fulfillment,
presumably in the form of marriage to Tom Buchanan, who will rescue her from
the "valley of ashes" and deliver her into a world of, from her perspective, paradisal
happiness. That she is "panting with vitality" underscores her connection with life,
with springtime, with nature, in direct opposition to the "desolate area of land"
(27; ch. 2) in which she lives, where people and objects alike appear "ash-grey" in
the "powdery air" (27; ch. 2).

Although George Wilson is one of those "ash-grey" people, who "mingl[es] …
with the cement color" (30; ch. 2) of his garage, even he is energized by longing
for future fulfillment: when he sees Tom and Nick pull into his garage, "a damp
gleam of hope spr[ings] into his light blue eyes" (29; ch. 2). This is the only time a
lively verb is used to describe George, and it's the only time that color, or at least a
healthy color, is associated with him. Notably, it's the color the novel frequently
associates with Gatsby's hopefulness: the mansion he bought in order to be near
Daisy has "blue gardens" (43; ch. 3) and a "blue lawn" (189; ch. 9); his trees have
"blue leaves" (159; ch. 8); and when he and Daisy reunite, "a damp streak of hair
lay like a dash of blue paint across her cheek" (90; ch. 5). In addition, the "*damp
gleam* of hope" in George's eyes resonates with the "*wet light*" with which the moon
"soaked" young Gatsby's "tangled clothes upon the floor" (105; ch. 6, my italics) as
he dreamed of the future in his bed at night.

Of course, the imagery of unfulfilled longing finds some of its most poetic
expression when it evokes Gatsby's dreams of the future. For example, the young
protagonist, in love with Daisy Fay and longing to possess her, is fascinated by
everything about her, including the house in which she and her family live.

[W]hat gave [her house] an air of breathless intensity was that Daisy lived
there. … There was a ripe mystery about it, a hint of bedrooms upstairs more
beautiful and cool than other bedrooms, of gay and radiant activities taking
place through its corridors, and of romances that were not musty and laid

away already in lavender, but fresh and breathing and redolent of this year's shining motor cars and of dances whose flowers were scarcely withered.

(155–56; ch. 8)

Because, in this passage, Gatsby dreams of a lifestyle that is largely unknown to him and seems unattainable, he idealizes it just as Daisy, Jordan, Nick, and Tom idealize their irretrievable youth. The phrases "breathless intensity," "ripe mystery," and "hint of bedrooms" create simultaneously an air of sensuality and a feeling that Gatsby is a little boy with his face pressed against the window of a candy store, longing for the sweets he sees displayed inside, which is, metaphorically, precisely what he is doing. The imagery here also creates a sense of fecundity, of a fruition so longed for that it seems about to happen, as we see in the words "ripe," "radiant," "fresh and breathing and redolent," and "flowers." In fact, such is the power of Gatsby's longing that it can turn "motor cars" into natural objects: the romances that occur in Daisy's house are "redolent" – that is, sweet-smelling, usually of flowers – of "this year's shining motor cars." It should be no surprise, then, that such a longing as this can disconnect itself from its human source and live on its own, as it does when Daisy withdraws from Gatsby during his confrontation with Tom in the New York hotel room: "only the dead dream fought on as the afternoon slipped away, trying to touch what was no longer tangible, struggling unhappily, undespairingly, toward that lost voice across the room" (142; ch. 7).

One of the more frequently noted images of Gatsby's longing for future fulfillment is that of the protagonist standing alone on the beach before his Long Island mansion, "trembling" (26; ch. 1) under the "silver pepper of the stars" (25; ch. 1) with his arms outstretched toward the "single green light, minute and far away" (26; ch. 1) at the end of Daisy's dock. This image recalls one discussed earlier: that of Gatsby in Louisville after Daisy's departure, his hand outstretched toward his lost past. But this time, the image of Gatsby's outstretched arms merges longing for the past with longing for the future, which, for him, have become one and the same: the fulfillment of his love for Daisy that he has come to Long Island to gain. The light at the end of her dock is green, carrying with it the hope of new beginnings that the green verdure of spring brings with it. And though the green light seems "minute and far away," Gatsby is, paradoxically, geographically and financially closer to Daisy than he has been since he lost her.

Perhaps the densest imagery used to describe Gatsby's longing for future fulfillment occurs in the description of the young protagonist walking down a Louisville street with Daisy, dreaming of greatness to come:

Now it was a cool night with that mysterious excitement in it which comes at the two changes of the year. The quiet lights in the houses were humming out into the darkness and there was a stir and bustle among the stars. Out of the corner of his eye Gatsby saw that the blocks of the side-walks really formed a ladder and mounted to a secret place above the trees – he could climb to it, if he climbed alone, and once there he could suck on the pap of life, gulp down the incomparable milk of wonder.

His heart beat faster and faster as Daisy's white face came up to his own. He knew that when he kissed this girl, and forever wed his unutterable visions to her perishable breath, his mind would never romp again like the mind of God. So he waited, listening for a moment longer to the tuning fork that had been struck upon a star. Then he kissed her. At his lips' touch she blossomed for him like a flower and the incarnation was complete.

(117; ch. 6)

In this remarkable passage, the imagery of unfulfilled longing performs at least two important functions. First, as we saw in the case of Nick's longing for future success, the imagery here links human dreams to the concerns of nature: the "stir and bustle among the stars" seem in sympathy with the "mysterious excitement" the characters feel because of the change of seasons, which is linked, in turn, to the threshold of the future at which they stand and which Gatsby longs to cross. In other words, the imagery suggests that human longing is as natural and inevitable as the seasons. Second, the imagery weds the cosmic quality of Gatsby's longing – his "unutterable visions" of the future in which his mind "romp[s] ... like the mind of God" and he dreams of "gulp[ing] down the incomparable milk of wonder" – to the mortal "incarnation" of that longing: Daisy. In other words, even when human longing is attached to something as specific and ordinary as the desire for a woman, it is really the incarnation of a cosmic force larger than we are.

To put the matter in slightly different terms, even when we think we long for a specific person, event, or object, our longing is fed by something greater than our individual selves, by something inherent in the condition of being human. Indeed, the most frequent images of unfulfilled longing used to depict characters are those in which the longing is vague and undefined, not attached to any specific goal. For example, the vague quality of Nick's longing is expressed in his comment upon crossing from Long Island into New York City: "The city seen from the Queensboro Bridge is always the city seen for the first time, in its first wild promise of all the mystery and the beauty in the world" (73; ch. 4). We're not told what kind of mystery and beauty are promised because Nick doesn't know. His longing is non-specific. All he knows is that he wants something new and fresh ("seen for the first time"), exciting ("first wild promise"), and extravagant ("all the mystery and the beauty in the world").

We see the same kind of vague longing in the novel's numerous images of people looking through windows. For example, on Nick's frequent evening walks along Fifth Avenue he gazes in the windows of throbbing taxi cabs, bound for the theatre district. ... Forms leaned together in the taxis as they waited, and voices sang, and there was laughter from unheard jokes, and lighted cigarettes outlined unintelligible gestures inside.

(62; ch. 3)

Of course, Nick longs to be a part of what he sees, to belong, to share in the excitement visible through the cab windows. But he experiences the same kind of longing when he is one of the people inside the window, looking out. As he looks from the window of Tom and Myrtle's apartment during their party, he muses,

high over the city our line of yellow windows must have contributed their share of human secrecy to the casual watcher in the darkening streets, and I was him too, looking up and wondering. I was within and without, simultaneously enchanted and repelled by the inexhaustible variety of life.

(40; ch. 2)

I'm not suggesting that the gathering at Tom and Myrtle's apartment should satisfy Nick or make him feel less lonely. As this passage indicates, it makes him feel, yet again, that he is on the outside looking in. My point is simply that, in his 30 years of life, Nick has yet to meet people for whom he can sustain the desire to belong. His longing is a form of loneliness, but he doesn't quite know what it is he's lonely for. He knows only that he is like the young clerks in one of the novel's most touching images of vague, unfulfilled longing: "poor young clerks who loitered in front of windows waiting until it was time for a solitary restaurant dinner – young clerks in the dusk, wasting the most poignant moments of night and life" (62; ch. 3). Furthermore, the image of Nick looking out of Tom and Myrtle's apartment window, imagining that he is "the casual watcher in the darkening streets ... looking up" at its yellow light, universalizes the image. Nick is not merely describing his own vague, unfulfilled longing, but the vague, unfulfilled longing of an "Everyman" figure, as well – the "casual watcher" – thus evoking the vague, unfulfilled longing experienced by us all.

It is interesting to note that the image of outstretched arms, which, as we have seen, embodies the longing for both past and future, occurs a third time as an image of nonspecific longing at the end of the novel.

Gatsby believed in the green light, the orgastic future that year by year recedes before us. It eluded us then, but that's no matter – to-morrow we will run faster, stretch out our arms farther. ... And one fine morning –

So we beat on, boats against the current, borne back ceaselessly into the past.

(189; ch. 9)

Here the novel insists on the universal nature of Gatsby's longing. Gatsby's green light and outstretched arms become ours: The future "recedes before *us*," "eluded *us*," but "*we* will run faster" and "stretch out *our* arms farther." And in becoming universal, Gatsby's longing also becomes nonspecific: for the protagonist, the green light represents Daisy; for us, it could represent anything. But whatever it represents, we will pursue it despite the fact that our longing will never be fulfilled. Although we're longing toward the future, with the prow of our boat facing forward, we are, in fact, like Gatsby, "borne back ceaselessly into the past." For in the timelessness of human longing, past and future are one, and our own unfulfilled longing is the "current" against which we "beat on" in vain. Thus, while few of the characters in *The Great Gatsby* are sympathetically portrayed, their unfulfilled longing – the experience they have in common with one another and, as this final passage underscores, with us – is portrayed with great poignancy.

The imagery of unfulfilled longing is also pervasive in the novel's evocation of setting, and here, too, it weaves a common thread through disparate social strata. The first notable example occurs in the description of Gatsby's mansion, "a colossal affair by any standard – it was a factual imitation of some Hôtel de Ville in Normandy, with a tower on one side, spanking new under a thin beard of raw ivy" (9; ch. 1). Before we even meet Gatsby, the setting in which he lives suggests the unfulfilled longing that is at the core of his existence. Like Gatsby, the mansion is larger than life, "a colossal affair," that is trying to be something it's not, something it can only imitate – a Hôtel de Ville in Normandy – just as the "thin beard of raw ivy" evokes the image of an adolescent boy trying to be a man. The tower, reaching toward the sky, also suggests a yearning for something beyond the immediately available. Furthermore, the mansion looks out over the bay, again as if yearning for something beyond itself, and as we saw earlier, it faces the green light at the end of Daisy's dock, the novel's icon of unfulfilled longing.

More frequently, an atmosphere of unfulfilled longing is created in the novel by settings that evoke a romantic ambience opposite that experienced by the characters who populate those settings. For example, in the midst of the tension and strife at the Buchanans' home during Nick's first visit there – Tom and Daisy have obviously been fighting, insistent phone calls from Myrtle intrude during dinner, Jordan shamelessly tries to overhear the Buchanans' quarrel in the next room, Tom pontificates about his racist views – the setting is described with keen appreciation for the idyllic fulfillment promised, though not delivered, by the setting.

> We walked through a high hallway into a bright rosy-colored space, fragilely bound into the house by French windows at either end. The windows were ajar and gleaming white against the fresh grass outside that seemed to grow a little way into the house. A breeze blew through the room, blew curtains in at one end and out the other like pale flags, twisting them up toward the frosted

wedding cake of the ceiling, and then rippled over the wine-colored rug, making a shadow on it as wind does on the sea.

(12; ch. 1)

Everything about this setting suggests newness, hopefulness, and fulfillment. The space Nick enters is "rosy-colored," the traditional ambience of romantic fulfillment. The "gleaming white" open windows, the "fresh grass," and the description of the ceiling as a "frosted wedding cake" evoke the hopefulness of new beginnings: virginity, springtime, weddings. In addition, the references to wedding cake and wine suggest celebration and the fulfillment of hopes. The net result of the dissonance between the fulfillment promised by the setting and the dissatisfaction experienced by the characters within that setting is an atmosphere of unfulfilled longing, such as Coleridge's Ancient Mariner describes, though far less romantically, on his becalmed boat: "Water, water every where, / Nor any drop to drink" (ll. 121–22).

Settings described with images of harmony, refinement, and plenitude imbue even the most vulgar scenes with a sense of unfulfilled longing that yearns toward a paradisal beauty ironically at odds with the current action. For example, the apartment Tom keeps for his adulterous trysts with Myrtle, where the couple also entertain Myrtle's noisy, vulgar, hard-drinking friends, is in a "long white cake of apartment houses" (32; ch. 2) and filled with tapestried furniture displaying "scenes of ladies swinging in the gardens of Versailles" (33; ch. 2). When Nick accompanies Tom and Myrtle to their apartment, he notes that Fifth Avenue looks "so warm and soft, almost pastoral, on the summer Sunday afternoon that I wouldn't have been surprised to see a great flock of white sheep turn the corner" (32; ch. 2). "[L]ong white cake," "ladies" on swings, "gardens," "Versailles," "warm and soft," "pastoral," "summer Sunday afternoon," "great flock of white sheep" – this is an idyllic language, a language of plenitude, fulfillment, pleasure, and harmony. Again, the dissonance between the drunken, violent vulgarity of the party scene – guests stumble about; Myrtle and Mrs. McKee make anti-Semitic, elitist, and obscene remarks; Tom and Myrtle quarrel; Tom breaks Myrtle's nose – and the pastoral plenitude of the descriptive language noted above creates an ambience of unfulfilled longing for life the way it should be, life the way we want it to be, life the way it isn't.

The sense of unfulfilled longing created by the dissonance between vulgar characters and a setting that bespeaks harmony, refinement, and plenitude is especially interesting in the description of Gatsby's parties. Like the money with which he bought his mansion, the money that pays for Gatsby's extravagant parties comes from criminal activities associated with Meyer Wolfsheim, the novel's most sinister and one of its most vulgar characters. And as Nick points out, Gatsby's guests "conducted themselves" in extremely vulgar fashion, "according to the rules of behavior associated with amusement parks" (45; ch.3). Almost everyone is rude and obnoxious. They gossip mercilessly about their host, whom few have met or care to meet. And the crowd, itself in varying degrees of drunken hysteria, is frequently treated to a drunken display by one or another of its members. There is, for example, a young woman who "dumps" down a cocktail "for courage" and "dances out alone on the canvas platform" (45; ch. 3); "a rowdy little girl who gave way upon the slightest provocation to uncontrollable laughter" (51; ch. 3); a driver so drunk that, when his car winds up in a ditch beside the driveway, "violently shorn of one wheel" (58; ch. 3), he doesn't realize it has stopped moving; and a drunken young girl who has to have her "head stuck in a pool" (113; ch. 6) to stop her from screaming.

The setting is described, however, in an intensely romantic fashion: "There was music from my neighbor's house through the summer nights. In his blue gardens men and girls came and went like moths among the whisperings and the champagne and the stars" (43; ch. 3). The "premature moon" is "produced like the supper, no doubt, out of a caterer's basket" (47; ch. 3), and even the refreshments seem enchanted: a "tray of cocktails floated at us through the twilight" (47; ch. 3), and on "buffet tables garnished with glistening hors-d'oeuvre, spiced baked hams crowded against salads of harlequin designs and pastry pigs and turkeys bewitched to a dark gold" (44; ch. 3). The setting is thus described as if it were a quiet pastoral scene — "blue gardens," "whisperings," "stars" — in a mythical kingdom where the moon is somehow magically produced "premature[ly]"; where cocktails "floa[t]" toward those who desire them; and where food is "bewitched."

Of course, we must remember that Nick is our narrator. We see the settings in the novel through his eyes. Therefore, it would not be unreasonable to conclude that, in those scenes in which setting and action are at odds, the unfulfilled longing evoked is Nick's. He yearns for a world of pastoral beauty, like the world he knew as a youth in Minnesota, but that world is gone. The combined effects of adulthood, World War I, and his own lack of purpose have wiped it out for him. But opulence creates romantic possibilities. What Nick said of Gatsby is also true of himself: he "was overwhelmingly aware of the youth and mystery that wealth imprisons and preserves" (157; ch. 8). Nick longs for the romantic possibilities he sees in the world of the wealthy although most of the people who inhabit that world seem blind to, or take for granted, its idyllic quality.

As these examples illustrate, *The Great Gatsby*'s haunting imagery tells us that unfulfilled longing is universal and inevitable. No matter who we are or what we have, we cannot be long content: we will inevitably long for something else. We may attach that longing to an object and believe that we are longing for something, whether that something lies in our past or in our future. Or we may not attach that longing to an object, in which case we will experience it as a vague restlessness, the kind of restlessness that sends Melville's Ishmael to sea "whenever it is a damp, drizzly November in [his] soul" (21). But unfulfilled longing, in one form or another, is inescapable. Even on that afternoon when Gatsby finally reunites with Daisy and "glow[s]" with "well-being" (94; ch. 5) because he has learned that she still loves him, "there must have been moments … when Daisy tumbled short of his dreams – not through her own fault but because … [n]o amount of fire or freshness can challenge what a man will store up in his ghostly heart" (101; ch. 5).

This sense of inescapability, this feeling that unfulfilled longing is inherent in the human condition, is reinforced in the novel by the static quality of its imagery of unfulfilled longing. Each of the images we've analyzed – indeed, most of the imagery in the novel – seems to exist in a timeless present, a fixed tableau, frozen forever like the lovers carved on the Grecian urn in Keats' famous ode: "Bold Lover, never, never canst thou kiss, / Though winning near the goal – yet, do not grieve; / She cannot fade, though thou hast not thy bliss, / For ever wilt thou love, and she be fair!" (ll. 17–20). For just as wealth "imprisons and preserves" forever "youth and mystery" (157; ch. 8), unfulfilled longing imprisons and preserves forever that for which it longs. Let's take a look at two images of unfulfilled longing that illustrate this quality of timelessness with particular clarity.

When Tom and Daisy finally attend one of Gatsby's parties, Daisy is attracted, at the beginning of the evening, by the sight of a "celebrity of the movies," a "gorgeous, scarcely human orchid of a woman who sat in state under a white plum tree" with her director "bending over her" (111; ch. 6). At the end of the evening, Nick notices that "the moving picture director and his Star" are "still under the white plum tree … their faces … touching except for a pale thin ray of moonlight between" (113; ch. 6). He says, "It occurred to me that he had been very slowly bending toward her all evening to attain this proximity" (113; ch.6). This is an image of longing – literally, a physical leaning toward the object of desire – that seems to exist in a dimension beyond time, like the moment frozen forever on Keats' urn. The characters seem barely to move over the course of an entire evening, and the timeless quality of the image is increased by the otherworldliness of the pictorial details: the woman is a "scarcely human orchid," the only vegetation in sight is a "white plum tree," and the only light is a "pale thin ray of moonlight."

A similar tableau of unfulfilled longing is presented when Tom, Nick, and Gatsby, waiting outside the Buchanans' house to drive Daisy and Jordan to New York City, see a single sailboat in the distance.

> On the green Sound, stagnant in the heat, one small sail crawled slowly toward the fresher sea. … Our eyes lifted over the rosebeds and the hot lawn and the weedy refuse of the dog days alongshore. Slowly the white wings of the boat moved against the blue cool limit of the sky. Ahead lay the scalloped ocean and the abounding blessed isles.
>
> (124; ch. 6)

The unfulfilled longing represented here is the longing for paradisal fulfillment, the longing to escape the real world. The extremely slow movement of the boat, insisted on twice in this short passage (it "crawled slowly" and "[s]lowly the white wings of the boat moved"), the great distance the boat seems to be from land (from where the characters stand, it looks like "one small sail"), and the classic colors of the seascape (white sails against blue sky) freeze this image as it would be frozen by paint on canvas. The sense of timelessness this image evokes is increased by its mythical quality: the "fres[h]," "cool" world in which the boat sails is contrasted sharply with the real world in which Tom, Nick, and Gatsby stand, with its "stagnant ... heat," "hot lawn," and "weedy refuse of the dog days alongshore"; the boat's sail turns into "white wings"; and its destination is some mythical never-never land, "the abounding blessed isles."

It is interesting to note in this context that time seems almost literally to stand still at the very center of the novel, when Gatsby and Daisy, whose relationship embodies unfulfilled longing, reunite. The clock on Nick's mantlepiece – which Gatsby leans his head against, knocks over, and catches in his hands – is "defunct" (91; ch. 5): time has stopped. As the scene progresses, Gatsby's existence in time stops, too: he "run[s] down like an overwound clock" (97; ch. 5). And as he and Daisy sit silently together in the gathering dusk, "remot[e]" (102; ch. 5) from the real world in which time passes, the timeless dimension they inhabit is foregrounded by its sharp contrast with the bustle of the real world outside: "Outside the wind was loud and ... [a]ll the lights were going on in West Egg now; the electric trains, men-carrying, were plunging home" (101; ch. 5).

It is the universal theme of unfulfilled longing, so powerfully carried by the novel's magnificent imagery, that has made *The Great Gatsby* the enduring masterpiece it is. As publisher Charles Scribner III said of the novel in 1992, "to the present day its place at the top of Scribner bestsell[ing paperbacks] has never been challenged" (205). *The Great Gatsby* doesn't have this kind of enduring value because of its social commentary on the Jazz Age, though an excellent social commentary it surely is. The novel has maintained its "hallowed place in American literature" (Scribner 205) because it speaks to something deep in the heart of human experience: the unfulfilled longing that is at the core of the human condition. Like Daisy's voice, which "held [Gatsby] most with its fluctuating, feverish warmth because it couldn't be over-dreamed," the lyric melancholy of unfulfilled longing is a "deathless song" (101; ch. 5), and Fitzgerald's superb novel has captured that song as no other novel has.

Questions for further practice: New Critical approaches to other literary works

The following questions are intended as models. They can help you use New Criticism to interpret the literary works to which they refer or other texts of your choice.

1   In Kate Chopin's "The Storm" (1898), how do nature imagery and point of view support the theme that individual circumstances, not abstract rules, determine what is right and wrong, healthy and unhealthy?

2   In Alberto Moravia's "The Chase" (1967), how does the characterization of the narrator, the story's opening and closing scenes, and the use of nature imagery support the theme that adultery is a form of emotional distance that signals the end of intimacy in a marriage?

3   How does Langston Hughes' "The Negro Speaks of Rivers" (1926) use geographical, historical, and biblical allusion, as well as nature imagery, to forward his theme about the negro race? How would you state that theme?

4   In Arthur Miller's *Death of a Salesman* (1949), how does setting work to create sympathy for Willy as the victim of forces beyond his control, thus contributing to the theme that the needs of the individual are often sacrificed to the demands of society?

5   In Toni Cade Bambara's "The Lesson" (1972), how is the topic of initiation suggested by the point of view from which the story is told, the narrator's tone of voice and use of slang, and the imagery used to describe the toy store and the children's response to it? What theme do you think is implied by your analysis of these formal elements? Is that theme borne out by the story's characterization of the narrator? How? (If not, try to find a theme that is supported by all of these formal elements.)

For further reading

Brooks, Cleanth. *The Well-Wrought Urn: Studies in the Structure of Poetry.* New York: Reynal & Hitchcock, 1947. (See especially "Gray's Storied Urn," 96–113; "Keats' Sylvan Historian: History without Footnotes," 139–52; and "The Heresy of Paraphrase," 176–96.)

———. *Community, Religion, and Literature.* Columbia and London: University of Mississippi Press, 1995. (See especially "The Primacy of the Linguistic Medium," 16–31; "The New Criticism," 80–97; "The Primacy of the Author," 170–83; and "The Primacy of the Reader," 244–58.)

Brooks, Cleanth, and Robert Penn Warren. *Understanding Fiction.* 1943. 2nd ed. New York: Appleton-Century-Crofts, 1959. (See especially "Letter to the Teacher," xi–xx; and "What Theme Reveals," 272–78.)

———. *Understanding Poetry.* 1938. 4th ed. New York: Holt, Rinehart and Winston, 1976. (See especially "Poetry as a Way of Saying," 1–16; "Tone," 112–15; and "Theme, Meaning, and Dramatic Structure," 266–70.)

Davis, Todd F., and Kenneth Womack. *Formalist Criticism and Reader-Response Theory.* New York: Palgrave, 2002.

Litz, A. Walton, Louis Menand, and Lawrence Rainey, eds. *Modernism and the New Criticism.* Vol. 7. *The Cambridge History of Literary Criticism.* New York: Cambridge University Press, 2000.

Spurlin, William J., and Michael Fischer, eds. *The New Criticism and Contemporary Literary Theory: Connections and Continuities.* New York: Garland, 1995.

Wellek, René. *"The Attack on Literature" and Other Essays.* Chapel Hill: The University of North Carolina Press, 1982. (See especially "Criticism as Evaluation," 48–63, and "The New Criticism: Pro and Contra," 87–103.)

Wellek, René, and Austin Warren. *Theory of Literature*. 1949. 2nd ed. New York: Harcourt, Brace and World, 1956. (See especially "Image, Metaphor, Symbol, Myth," 175–201.)

Wimsatt Jr., W. K. *The Verbal Icon: Studies in the Meaning of Poetry*. Lexington: University of Kentucky Press, 1954. (See especially "The Intentional Fallacy," 3–18; "The Affective Fallacy," 21–39; "The Structure of Romantic Nature Imagery," 103–16; and "Explication as Criticism," 235–51.)

For advanced readers

Blackmur, R. P. *The Lion and the Honeycomb: Essays in Solicitude and Critique*. New York: Harcourt Brace, 1955.

Bogel, Fredric V. *New Formalist Criticism: Theory and Practice*. Basingstoke and New York: Palgrave Macmillan, 2013.

Davis, Garrick, ed. *Praising It New: The Best of the New Criticism*. Athens, OH: Swallow Press/Ohio University Press, 2008. (See especially Davis' "The Golden Age of Poetry Criticism," xxi–xxvii; Brooks' "The Formalist Critics," 84–91; Jarrell's "Texts from Housman," 161–69; and Winters' "The Morality of Poetry," 233–43.)

Eliot, T. S. *Selected Prose of T. S. Eliot*. Ed. Frank Kermode. New York: Harcourt Brace Jovanovich, 1975. (See especially "Tradition and the Individual Talent," 37–44; and "Hamlet," 45–49.)

Empson, William. *Seven Types of Ambiguity*. New York: Noonday, 1955.

Hickman, Miranda B. and John D. McIntyre, eds. *Rereading the New Criticism*. Columbus: The Ohio State University Press, 2012.

Jancovich, Mark. *The Cultural Politics of the New Criticism*. New York: Cambridge University Press, 1993.

Krieger, Murray. *The New Apologists for Poetry*. Minneapolis: University of Minnesota Press, 1956.

Ransom, John Crowe. *The New Criticism*. New York: New Directions, 1941.

Richards, I. A. *Coleridge on Imagination*. New York: W. W. Norton, 1950.

Wimsatt Jr., W. K., ed. *Explication as Criticism: Selected Papers from the English Institute, 1941–52*. New York: Columbia University Press, 1963. (See especially Brooks' "Literary Criticism: Marvell's 'Horatian Ode,'" 100–30; Bush's "John Milton," 131–45; and Trilling's "Wordsworth's 'Ode': Intimations of Immortality," 175–202.)

Notes

1 Most literary critics today, regardless of their theoretical orientation, acknowledge that New Criticism's concept of "universal significance" was bogus, even harmful, because a text's "universality" was determined by, and thus too often limited to, white male American experience.

2 For similar arguments, see, for example, Cartwright, Chase, Dillon, Gross, Hart, Le Vot, Moore, Nash, Stern, and Trilling.

3 The view that Gatsby shares the corruption of his world is held, for example, by Bruccoli, Dyson, and Fussell.

Works cited

Austen, Jane. *Sense and Sensibility*. 1811. New York: Alfred A. Knopf, 1992.

Bewley, Marius. "Scott Fitzgerald's Criticism of America." *Sewanee Review* 62 (1954): 223–46. Rpt. in *Modern Critical Interpretations: F. Scott Fitzgerald's* The Great Gatsby. Ed. Harold Bloom. New York: Chelsea, 1986. 11–27.

Bruccoli, Matthew J. *Some Sort of Epic Grandeur: The Life of F. Scott Fitzgerald*. New York: Harcourt, 1981.

Burnam, Tom. "The Eyes of Dr. Eckleburg: A Re-Examination of *The Great Gatsby.*" *College English* 13 (1952). Rpt. in *F. Scott Fitzgerald: A Collection of Critical Essays.* Ed. Arthur Mizener. Englewood Cliffs, NJ: Prentice Hall, 1963. 104–11.

Cartwright, Kent. "Nick Carraway as Unreliable Narrator." *Papers on Language and Literature* 20.2 (1984): 218–32.

Chase, Richard. *"The Great Gatsby." The American Novel and Its Traditions.* New York: Doubleday, 1957. Rpt. in The Great Gatsby: A Study. Ed. Frederick J. Hoffman. New York: Scribner's, 1962. 297–302.

Chopin, Kate. "The Storm." 1898. *The Complete Works of Kate Chopin.* Ed. Per Seyersted. Baton Rouge: Louisiana State University, 1970.

Clifton, Lucille. "There Is a Girl Inside." 1977. *Good Woman: Poems and a Memoir, 1969–1980.* Rochester, NY: BOA Editions, 1987. 170.

Coleridge, Samuel Taylor. "The Rime of the Ancient Mariner." 1797. *Romantic and Victorian Poetry.* 2nd ed. Ed. William Frost. Englewood Cliffs, NJ: Prentice Hall, 1961. 122–39.

Dillon, Andrew. "*The Great Gatsby:* The Vitality of Illusion." *Arizona Quarterly* 44.1 (1988): 49–61.

Dyson, A. E. "*The Great Gatsby*: Thirty-Six Years After." *Modern Fiction Studies* 7.1 (1961): 37ff. Rpt. in *F. Scott Fitzgerald: A Collection of Essays.* Ed. Arthur Mizener. Englewood Cliffs, NJ: Prentice Hall, 1963. 112–24.

Fitzgerald, F. Scott. *The Great Gatsby.* 1925. New York: Macmillan, 1992.

Fussell, Edwin. "Fitzgerald's Brave New World." *ELH, Journal of English Literary History* 19 (1952). Rpt. in *F. Scott Fitzgerald: A Collection of Critical Essays.* Ed. Arthur Mizener. Englewood Cliffs, NJ: Prentice Hall, 1963. 43–56.

Gallo, Rose Adrienne. *F. Scott Fitzgerald.* New York: Ungar, 1978.

Gross, Barry Edward. "Jay Gatsby and Myrtle Wilson: A Kinship." *Tennessee Studies in Literature* 8 (1963): 57–60. Excerpted in *Gatsby.* Ed. Harold Bloom. New York: Chelsea House, 1991. 23–25.

Hart, Jeffrey. "'Out of it ere night': The WASP Gentleman as Cultural Ideal." *New Criterion* 7.5 (1989): 27–34.

Hemingway, Ernest. "Big Two-Hearted River." 1925. *The Short Stories.* New York: Scribner's, 1997.

Keats, John. "Ode on a Grecian Urn." 1820. *Romantic and Victorian Poetry.* 2nd ed. Ed. William Frost. Englewood Cliffs, NJ: Prentice Hall, 1961. 236–37.

Le Vot, André. *F. Scott Fitzgerald: A Biography.* Trans. William Byron. Garden City, NY: Doubleday, 1983.

Melville, Herman. *Moby Dick.* 1851. New York: Signet, 1980.

Miller, Arthur. *Death of a Salesman.* New York: Viking, 1949.

Moore, Benita A. *Escape into a Labyrinth: F. Scott Fitzgerald, Catholic Sensibility, and the American Way.* New York: Garland, 1988.

Moravia, Alberto. "The Chase." 1967. *Literature: The Human Experience.* 6th ed. Eds. Richard Abcarian and Marvin Klotz. New York: St. Martin's, 1966. 492–95.

Morrison, Toni. *The Bluest Eye.* New York: Holt, Rinehart, and Winston, 1970.

———. *Beloved.* New York: Alfred A. Knopf, 1987.

Nash, Charles C. "From West Egg to Short Hills: The Decline of the Pastoral Ideal from *The Great Gatsby* to Philip Roth's *Goodbye, Columbus.*" *Philological Association* 13 (1988): 22–27.

Scribner, Charles, III. "Publisher's Afterword." *The Great Gatsby.* 1925. F. Scott Fitzgerald. New York: Simon & Schuster, 1995. 195–205.

Stern, Milton R. *The Golden Moment: The Novels of F. Scott Fitzgerald.* Urbana: University of Illinois Press, 1970.

Trilling, Lionel. "F. Scott Fitzgerald." *The Liberal Imagination.* New York: Viking, 1950. 243–54. Rpt. in The Great Gatsby: A Study. Ed. Frederick J. Hoffman. New York: Scribner's, 1962. 232–43.

Wharton, Edith. *The House of Mirth.* 1905. New York: Scribner's, 1969.

6   Reader-response criticism

As its name implies, reader-response criticism focuses on readers' responses to literary texts. Many new students of critical theory are relieved and happy when they get to the unit on reader-response criticism, perhaps because they enjoy the idea that their responses are important enough to become the focus of literary interpretation. Or perhaps they assume that reader-response criticism means "I can't be wrong because any way I interpret the text is my response, so the professor can't reject it." Let me break the bad news to you up front. Depending on the kind of reader-response theory we're talking about, your response to a literary text can be judged insufficient or less sufficient than others. And even when a given reader-response theory does assert that there is no such thing as an insufficient (or inaccurate or inappropriate) response, your job as a practitioner of that theory isn't merely to respond but to analyze your response, or the responses of others, and that analysis can be found wanting.

The good news, however, is that reader-response criticism is a broad, exciting, evolving domain of literary studies that can help us learn about our own reading processes and how they relate to, among other things, specific elements in the texts we read, our life experiences, and the intellectual community of which we are members. In addition, for those of you who plan on teaching or are already doing so, reader-response theory offers ideas that can help you in the classroom, whether that classroom is in an elementary school or on a college campus.

If you're getting the feeling that reader-response criticism covers a good deal of diverse ground, you're right. In fact, any time an essay analyzes the act of reading or readers' responses, one could classify that essay as reader-response criticism. For example, psychoanalytic criticism, when it investigates the psychological motives for certain kinds of interpretations of a literary text, is also a form of reader-response criticism. Feminist criticism, when it analyzes how patriarchy teaches us to interpret texts in a sexist manner, is also a form of reader-response criticism. Structuralist criticism, when it examines the literary conventions a reader must have consciously or unconsciously internalized in order to be able to read a particular literary text, is also considered a form of reader-response criticism.[1] And lesbian and gay criticism, when it studies how our homophobic culture suppresses our ability to see homoeroticism in literary texts, is also a form of reader-response criticism.

Attention to the reading process emerged during the 1930s as a reaction against the growing tendency to reject the reader's role in creating meaning, a tendency that became a formal principle of the New Criticism that dominated critical practice in the 1940s and 1950s. As we saw in Chapter 5, the New Critics believed that the timeless meaning of the text – what the text *is* – is contained in the text alone. Its meaning is not a product of the author's intention and does not change with the reader's response. As you may remember, New Critics claimed that attention to the reader's response confuses what the text *is* with what the text *does*. Reader-response theory, which didn't receive much attention until the 1970s, maintains that what a text is cannot be separated from what it does. For despite their divergent views of the reading process, which we'll examine a little later, reader-response theorists share two beliefs: (1) that the role of the reader cannot be omitted from our understanding of literature, and (2) that readers do not passively consume the meaning presented to them by an objective literary text; rather they actively make the meaning they find in literature.

This second belief, that readers actively make meaning, suggests, of course, that different readers may read the same text quite differently. In fact, reader-response theorists believe that even the same reader reading the same text on two different occasions will probably produce different meanings because so many variables contribute to our experience of the text. Knowledge we've acquired between our first and second reading of a text, personal experiences that have occurred in the interim, a change in mood between our two encounters with the text, or a change in the purpose for which we're reading it can all contribute to our production of different meanings for the same text.

To get a clear idea of just how much the nature of the reader's involvement with a text can alter its meaning, let's look at the following passage. As you read it, imagine that you're a home buyer and circle any detail, positive or negative, that you think would be important if you were considering buying the house described in the passage.

The house passage[2]

> The two boys ran until they came to the driveway. "See, I told you today was good for skipping school," said Mark. "Mom is never home on Thursday," he added. Tall hedges hid the house from the road so the pair strolled across the finely landscaped yard. "I never knew your place was so big," said Pete. "Yeah, but it's nicer now than it used to be since Dad had the new stone siding put on and added the fireplace."

There were front and back doors and a side door which led to the garage, which was empty except for three parked 10-speed bikes. They went in the side door, Mark explaining that it was always open in case his younger sisters got home earlier than their mother.

Pete wanted to see the house so Mark started with the living room. It, like the rest of the downstairs, was newly painted. Mark turned on the stereo, the noise of which worried Pete. "Don't worry, the nearest house is a quarter of a mile away," Mark shouted. Pete felt more comfortable observing that no houses could be seen in any direction beyond the huge yard.

The dining room, with all the china, silver, and cut glass, was no place to play so the boys moved into the kitchen, where they made sandwiches. Mark said they wouldn't go to the basement because it had been damp and musty ever since the new plumbing had been installed.

"This is where my Dad keeps his famous paintings and his coin collection," Mark said as they peered into the den. Mark bragged that he could get spending money whenever he needed it since he'd discovered that his Dad kept a lot in the desk drawer.

There were three upstairs bedrooms. Mark showed Pete his mother's closet, which was filled with furs and the locked box which held her jewels. His sisters' room was uninteresting except for the color TV, which Mark carried to his room. Mark bragged that the bathroom in the hall was his since one had been added to his sisters' room for their use. The big highlight in his room, though, was a leak in the ceiling where the old roof had finally rotted.

Many readers probably would produce a list of positive and negative qualities something like the following:

Positive qualities	Negative qualities
tall hedges (privacy)	damp, musty basement
finely landscaped yard	new plumbing amiss
stone siding	rotting roof
fireplace	leak in bedroom ceiling
garage	
newly painted downstairs	
nearest house 1/4 mi. away (privacy)	
den	
3 upstairs bedrooms	
new bathroom added to bedroom	

Now reread the passage and underline any detail, positive or negative, that you think would be important if you were casing the house in order to rob it. Many readers probably would produce a list of positive and negative qualities something like the following:

Positive qualities   **Negative qualities**

tall hedges (safe from observation)
no one home on Thursdays
finely landscaped yard (these folks have money)
three 10-speed bikes in garage
side door always left open
nearest house 1/4 mi. away (safe from
observation)
many portable goods: stereo, china, silver, cut
glass, paintings, coin collection, furs, box of
jewels, TV set, cash kept in desk drawer

During our second reading of this passage, because we're thinking of robbing the house, we focus on very different details, and even when we focus on the same details, they have a very different meaning for us. For example, the privacy that is an asset for many home buyers becomes a liability in terms of the home's vulnerability to burglars. Merely changing the purpose for which we read a passage can radically alter the passage we read. Of course, some home-buying readers might immediately see the negative aspect of the home's privacy because their experience has made them more aware of crime, illustrating reader-response theory's assertion that readers draw on their personal experiences to create meaning.

As the above exercise illustrates, a written text is not an object, despite its physical existence, but an event that occurs within the reader, whose response is of primary importance in creating the text. Theorists disagree, however, about how our responses are formed and what role, if any, the text plays in creating them. Opinions range from the belief that the literary text is as active as the reader in creating meaning to the belief that the text doesn't exist at all except as it is created by readers.

Let's take a look at a representative sample of this range of approaches, which may be loosely organized under five headings: transactional reader-response theory, affective stylistics, subjective reader-response theory, psychological reader-response theory, and social reader-response theory. It is important to remember that these categories are somewhat artificial: the dividing lines are often fluid and indistinct because practitioners in different schools will hold some ideas in common while practitioners within each school will differ on some points. In addition, as we saw earlier, any attempt to classify reader-response approaches will inevitably include some theories whose practitioners may not call themselves reader-response critics and omit some theories that a different system of classification would include. However, it is precisely because the fabric of reader-response theory is woven of so many diverse and controversial threads that some method of classification is necessary, at least at this stage of the game. The method I've chosen is the one I think will give you the clearest sense of the reader-response enterprise in general and prepare you to read the work of theorists in this field.

Transactional reader-response theory

Often associated with the work of Louise Rosenblatt, who formulated many of its premises, transactional reader-response theory analyzes the transaction between text and reader. Rosenblatt doesn't reject the importance of the text in favor of the reader; rather she claims that both are necessary in the production of meaning. She differentiates among the terms *text*, which refers to the printed words on the page; *reader*; and *poem*, which refers to the literary work produced by the text and the reader together.

How does this transaction take place? As we read a text, it acts as a *stimulus* to which we respond in our own personal way. Feelings, associations, and memories occur as we read, and these responses influence the way in which we make sense of the text as we move through it. Literature we've encountered prior to this reading, the sum total of our accumulated knowledge, and even our current physical condition and mood will influence us as well. At various points while we read, however, the text acts as a *blueprint* that we can use to correct our interpretation when we realize it has traveled too far afield of what is written on the page. This process of correcting our interpretation as we move through the text usually results in our going back to reread earlier sections in light of some new development in the text. Thus, the text guides our self-corrective process as we read and will continue to do so after the reading is finished if we go back and reread portions, or the entire text, in order to develop or complete our interpretation. Thus the creation of the poem, the literary work, is a product of the transaction between text and reader, both of which are equally important to the process.

In order for this transaction between text and reader to occur, however, our approach to the text must be, in Rosenblatt's words, aesthetic rather than efferent. When we read in the *efferent* mode, we focus just on the information contained in the text, as if it were a storehouse of facts and ideas that we could carry away with us. "Arthur Miller's *Death of a Salesman* (1949) is a play about a traveling salesman who kills himself so that his son will receive his life-insurance money" is an example of an efferent stance toward the text. In contrast, when we read in the *aesthetic* mode, we experience a personal relationship to the text that focuses our attention on the emotional subtleties of its language and encourages us to make judgments. "In *Death of a Salesman*, Willy Loman's plight is powerfully evoked by the contrast between his small house, bathed in soft blue light, and the large, orange-colored apartment buildings that surround it" is an example of an aesthetic stance toward the text. Without the aesthetic approach, there could be no transaction between text and reader to analyze.

Followers of Wolfgang Iser[3] might explain what Rosenblatt refers to as the blueprint and stimulus functions of the text in terms of two kinds of meaning every text offers: determinate and indeterminate meaning. *Determinate meaning* refers to what might be called the facts of the text, certain events in the plot or physical descriptions clearly provided by the words on the page. In contrast, *indeterminate meaning*, or *indeterminacy*, refers to "gaps" in the text – such as actions that are not clearly explained or that seem to have multiple explanations – which allow or even invite readers to create their own interpretations. (Thus, Rosenblatt's efferent approach depends entirely on determinate meaning, while her aesthetic approach depends on both determinate and indeterminate meaning.) In *Death of a Salesman* we might say, for example, that the text's determinate meaning includes the fact that Willy habitually lies to Linda about his success on the job, about how well liked he is, and about how important his role in the company has been. The play's indeterminacy includes issues such as how much (or how little) of the truth Linda knows about her husband's career, at what point she realizes the truth (if she ever does), and why she doesn't let Willy tell her the truth about his shortcomings when he tries to do so. Of course, the burden is on us to support our claim that a given textual meaning is determinate or indeterminate.

The interplay between determinate and indeterminate meanings, as we read, results in a number of ongoing experiences for the reader: retrospection, or thinking back to what we've read earlier in the text; anticipation of what will come next; fulfillment or disappointment of our anticipation; revision of our under-standing of characters and events; and so on. For what at one point in the work appears to be determinate meaning will often, at a later point in the work, appear to be indeterminate, as our point of view shifts among the various perspectives provided by, for example, the narrator, the characters, and the events of an unfolding plot. Thus, for Iser, though the reader projects meaning onto the text, the reading activities through which we construct that meaning are prestructured by, or built into, the text. In other words, Iser believes that the text itself guides us through the processes involved in interpreting (projecting meaning onto) it.

According to transactional theorists, different readers come up with different acceptable interpretations because the text allows for a range of acceptable mean-ings, that is, a range of meanings for which textual support is available. However, because there is a real text involved in this process to which we must refer to justify or modify our responses, not all readings are acceptable and some are more so than others. Even authors' stated intentions in writing their texts, as well as any interpretations they may offer afterward, are but additional readings of the text, which must be submitted for evaluation to the text-as-blueprint just as all other readings are. Thus, transactional analysis relies a good deal on the authority of the text, insisted on by the New Critics, while also bringing the reader's response into the limelight. In addition, transactional analysis accounts for the range of successful readings produced even by the New Critics themselves, despite their belief that every text authorizes a single best reading.[4]

Affective stylistics

Affective stylistics is derived from analyzing further the notion that a literary text is an event that occurs in time – that comes into being as it is read – rather than an object that exists in space. The text is examined closely, often line by line or even word by word, in order to understand *how* (stylistics) it *affects* (affective) the reader in the process of reading. Although there is thus a great deal of focus on the text, which is why some theorists consider this approach transactional in nature, many practitioners of affective stylistics do not consider the text an objective, autonomous entity – it does not have a fixed meaning independent of readers – because the text consists of the results it produces, and those results occur within the reader. For example, when Stanley Fish describes how a text is structured, the structure he describes is the structure of the reader's response as it occurs from moment to moment, not the structure of the text as we might assemble it – like puzzle pieces all spread out at once before us – after we've finished reading. Nevertheless, affective stylistics is not a description of the reader's impressionistic responses but a cognitive analysis of the mental processes produced by specific elements in the text. Indeed, it is the "slow-motion," phrase-by-phrase analysis of how the text structures the reader's response for which affective stylistics is perhaps best known.

Some of the finest examples of this procedure have been produced by Fish. To see how this approach works, let's take a look at his analysis of the following sentence.

> That Judas perished by hanging himself, there is no certainty in Scripture: though in one place it seems to affirm it, and by a doubtful word hath given occasion to translate it; yet in another place, in a more punctual description, it maketh it improbable, and seems to overthrow it.
>
> ("Literature" 71)

According to Fish, the question "What does this sentence mean?" or "What does this sentence say?" yields little because the sentence provides us with no facts with which we could answer the question. Even if we notice that the sentence does say something – it says that Scripture gives us no clear indication of whether or not Judas hanged himself – his point is that the sentence tells us only that it is unable to tell us anything. In contrast, he notes, the question "What does the sentence do to the reader?" or "How does the reader of this sentence make meaning?" yields something quite useful.

What this passage about Judas *does*, Fish notes, is move the reader from certainty to uncertainty. The first clause, "that Judas perished by hanging himself" (which, as most of us know, is a kind of shorthand for "the fact that Judas perished by hanging himself"), is an assertion we accept as a statement of fact. We thus begin with a feeling of certainty that leads us, without our being quite conscious of it, to anticipate a number of possible ways the sentence might end, all of which would confirm our certainty that Judas hanged himself. Fish offers these three examples of the kinds of endings the first clause leads us to expect.

1 That Judas perished by hanging himself *is* (an example for us all).
2 That Judas perished by hanging himself *shows* (how conscious he was of the enormity of his sin).
3 That Judas perished by hanging himself *should* (give us pause).

("Literature" 71)

These expectations narrow the possible meanings of the next three words in the passage: "there is no." At this point, the reader expects to see "there is no doubt," but is given instead "there is no certainty." Now the fact of Judas' hanging himself, upon which our understanding of the sentence has rested, becomes uncertain. Now the reader is involved in a completely different kind of activity. As Fish puts it, "Rather than following an argument along a well-lighted path (a light, after all, has gone out), [the reader] is now looking for one" ("Literature" 71). In such a situation, the reader will tend to read on in hopes of finding clarification. But as we continue to read the passage, our uncertainty only increases as we move back and forth between words that seem to promise clarity – "place," "affirm," "place," "punctual," "overthrow" – and words that seem to withdraw that promise: "though," "doubtful," "yet," "improbable," "seems." Uncertainty is further increased by the excessive use of the pronoun *it* because, as the sentence progresses, the reader has more and more difficulty figuring out what *it* refers to.

Such analyses are performed by reader-response critics in order to map the pattern by which a text structures the reader's response while reading. This response is then used to show that the meaning of the text does not consist of the final conclusion we draw about what the text *says*; rather, the meaning of the text consists of our experience of what the text *does* to us as we read it. For a text is an event that occurs in time: it acts on us as we read each word and phrase. As we just saw, Fish's passage first reinforces a belief about Judas the reader probably already holds and then takes that reinforcement away, leading the reader on in hopes of finding an answer that is never provided. If the kind of experience created in this passage is repeated throughout the text from which the passage is taken, then a reader-response critic might say that the text teaches us, through a pattern of raised expectations disappointed, how to read that text and, perhaps, how to read the world: we must expect to have our expectation of acquiring sure knowledge raised and disappointed. We desire sure knowledge. We pursue it, and we expect to get it. But this text teaches us that we cannot be certain of anything. In other words, for a reader-response critic, this text isn't primarily about Judas or Scripture but about the experience of reading.

In addition to an analysis of the reading activities that structure the reader's response, other kinds of evidence are usually gathered to further support the claim that the text is about the experience of reading. For example, most practitioners of affective stylistics will cite the responses of other readers – of other literary critics, for example – to show that their own analyses of the reading activities provided by a particular text are valid for readers other than just themselves. A critic might even cite an extreme divergence of critical opinion about the text to support, for example, the contention that the text provides an unsettling, decentering, or confusing reading experience. This wouldn't mean that the text is flawed but that by unsettling the reader it demonstrates, say, the fact that interpretation of written texts, and perhaps of the world, is a problematic endeavor from which we should not expect to achieve certainty.

Thematic evidence from the text itself is also usually provided to show that the text is about the experience of reading. For example, the reader-response critic shows how the experiences of characters and descriptions of settings mirror the reader's experience reading the text. If I were to claim that Joseph Conrad's *Heart of Darkness* (1902) provides a reading experience that keeps the reader off balance, unsure of how to interpret the characters and events unfolded by the plot, I would start, as we've just seen, by analyzing the reading activities that produce the uncertainty. Then I would show that the reader's experience of uncertainty is mirrored in Marlow's uncertainty – his inability to interpret Kurtz – and in the recurring references to darkness and obscurity (which are metaphors for uncertainty) that occur in the descriptions of the jungle, the company headquarters in Europe, and the deck of the ship on which Marlow tells his story. I would also look for images described in the text that serve as emblems of the reading experience I've described. Of course, reading materials or acts of reading described in the story work especially well for this purpose. For example, the tattered book that Marlow finds abandoned in the jungle, which he is unable to read, is emblematic of his, and our, inability to decipher what we see before us. Marlow doesn't even know what language the book is written in: he thinks it's some form of code language; he later learns that it's written in Russian.

As noted above, the textual evidence at this point is thematic: the critic shows that the theme of the text is a particular kind of reading experience, such as the difficulties involved in reading, the processes involved in making sense of the text, or the inevitability of misreading. Although many practitioners of affective stylistics believe that the text, as an independent object, disappears in their analysis and becomes what it really is – an experience that occurs within the reader – their use of thematic evidence, as we've just seen, underscores the important role played by the text in establishing what the reader's experience is.

Subjective reader-response theory

In stark contrast to affective stylistics and to all forms of transactional reader-response theory, subjective reader-response theory does not call for the analysis of textual cues. For subjective reader-response critics, led by the work of David

Bleich, readers' responses are the text, both in the sense that there is no literary text beyond the meanings created by readers' interpretations and in the sense that the text the critic analyzes is not the literary work but the written responses of readers. Let's look at each of these two claims more closely.

To understand how there is no literary text beyond the meanings created by readers' interpretations, we need to understand how Bleich defines the literary text. Like many other reader-response critics, he differentiates between what he calls *real objects* and *symbolic objects*. Real objects are physical objects, such as tables, chairs, cars, books, and the like. The printed pages of a literary text are real objects. However, the experience created when someone reads those printed pages, like language itself, is a symbolic object because it occurs not in the physical world but in the conceptual world, that is, in the mind of the reader. This is why Bleich calls reading – the feelings, associations, and memories that occur as we react subjectively to the printed words on the page – *symbolization*: our perception and identification of our reading experience create a conceptual, or symbolic, world in our mind as we read. Therefore, when we interpret the meaning of the text, we are actually interpreting the meaning of our own symbolization: we are interpreting the meaning of the conceptual experience we created in response to the text. He thus calls the act of interpretation *resymbolization*. Resymbolization occurs when our experience of the text produces in us a desire for explanation. Our evaluation of the text's quality is also an act of resymbolization: we don't like or dislike a text; we like or dislike our symbolization of it. Thus, the text we talk about isn't really the text on the page: it's the text in our mind.

Because the only text is the text in the mind of the reader, this is the text analyzed by subjective reader-response critics, for whom the text is equated with the written responses of readers. Bleich, whose primary interest is pedagogical, offers us a method for teaching students how to use their responses to learn about literature or, more accurately, to learn about literary response. For contrary to popular opinion, subjective criticism isn't an anything-goes free-for-all. It's a coherent, purposeful methodology for helping our students and ourselves produce knowledge about the experience of reading.

Before we look at the specific steps in that methodology, we need to understand what Bleich means by *producing* knowledge. Subjective criticism and what he calls the subjective classroom are based on the belief that all knowledge is subjective – the perceived can't be separated from the perceiver – which is a belief held today by many scientists and historians as well as by many critical theorists. What is called "objective" knowledge is simply whatever a given community believes to be objectively true. For example, Western science once accepted the "objective" knowledge that the earth is flat and the sun revolves around it. Since that time, Western science has accepted several different versions of "objective" knowledge about the earth and the sun. The most recent scientific thinking suggests that what we take to be objective knowledge is actually produced by the questions we ask and the instruments we use to find the answers. In other words, "truth" isn't an "objective" reality waiting to be discovered; it's constructed by communities of people to fulfill specific needs produced by specific historical, sociological, and psychological situations.

Treating the classroom as a community, Bleich's method helps students learn how communities produce knowledge and how the individual member of the community can function as a part of that process. To summarize Bleich's procedure, students are asked to respond to a literary text by writing a response statement and then by writing an analysis of their own response statement, both of which tasks are performed as efforts to contribute to the class's production of knowledge about reading experiences. Let's look at each of these two steps individually.

Although Bleich believes that, hypothetically, every *response statement* is valid within the context of some group of readers for whose purpose it is useful, he stresses that, in order to be useful to the classroom community, a response statement must be *negotiable* into knowledge about reading experiences. By this he means that it must contribute to the group's production of knowledge about the experience of reading a specific literary text, not about the reader or the reality outside the reader. Response statements that are *reader oriented* substitute talk about oneself for talk about one's reading experience. They are confined largely to comments about the reader's memories, interests, personal experiences, and the like, with little or no reference to the relationship between these comments and the experience of reading the text. Reader-oriented response statements lead to group discussions of personalities and personal problems that may be useful in a psychologist's office but, for Bleich, do not contribute to the group's understanding of the reading experience at hand.

Analogously, response statements that are *reality oriented* substitute talk about issues in the world for talk about one's reading experience. They are confined largely to the expression of one's opinions about politics, religion, gender issues, and the like, with little or no reference to the relationship between these opinions and the experience of reading the text. Reality-oriented response statements lead to group discussions of moral or social issues, which members claim the text is about, but such response statements do not contribute to the group's understanding of the reading experience at hand.

In contrast, the response statements Bleich promotes are *experience oriented*. They discuss the reader's reactions to the text, describing exactly how specific passages made the reader feel, think, or associate. Such response statements include judgments about specific characters, events, passages, and even words in the text. The personal associations and memories of personal relationships that are woven throughout these judgments allow others to see what aspects of the text affected the reader in what ways and for what reasons. Bleich cites one student's description of the ways in which particular characters and events in a text reminded her of her sexuality as a young girl. Her response statement moved back and forth between her reactions to specific scenes in the text and the specific experiences they recalled in her adolescence.

A group discussion produced by this student's subjective response could go in any number of directions, some of them quite traditional. For example, the group might discuss whether or not one's opinion of this particular text depends on feelings one has left over from one's adolescent experiences. Or the group might discuss whether or not the text is an expression of the author's adolescent feelings or of the repressive sexual mores of the culture in which the author lived. Even in the case of these last two examples, for which students would have to seek bio-graphical and historical data, the questions themselves would have been raised by a reader's response and by the group's reaction to that response, so there probably would be a higher degree of personal engagement than would occur ordinarily for students on whom such an assignment had been imposed. The point is that response statements are used within a context determined by the group. The group decides, based on the issues that emerge from experience-oriented response statements, what questions they want answered and what topics they want to pursue.

In addition, the experience-oriented response statement is analyzed by the reader in a response-analysis statement. Here the reader (1) characterizes his or her response to the text as a whole; (2) identifies the various responses prompted by different aspects of the text, which, of course, ultimately led to the student's response to the text as a whole; and (3) determines why these responses occurred. Responses may be characterized, for example, as enjoyment, discomfort, fascina-tion, disappointment, relief, or satisfaction, and may involve any number of emo-tions, such as fear, joy, and anger. A student's response-analysis statement might reveal that certain responses resulted, for example, from identification with a par-ticular character, from the vicarious fulfillment of a desire, from the relief of (or increase of) a guilty feeling, or the like. The goal here is for students to understand their responses, not merely report them or make excuses for them. Thus, a response-analysis statement is a thorough, detailed explanation of the relationship among specific textual elements, specific personal responses, and the meaning the text has for the student as a result of his or her personal encounter with it.

It is interesting to note that, as Bleich points out, students using the subjective approach probably focus on the same elements of the text they would select if they were writing a traditional "objective" essay. To test this hypothesis, Bleich had his students respond to a literary text, not by writing a response statement and a response-analysis statement but by writing a meaning statement and a response statement. The meaning statement explained what the student thought was the meaning of the text, without reference to the student's personal responses. In contrast, the response statement, just like the one discussed above, recorded how the text produced specific personal reactions and memories of personal relationships and experiences. Bleich found that students' response statements clearly revealed the personal sources of their meaning statements, whether or not students were aware of the relationship between the two. In other words, even when we think we're writing traditional "objective" interpretations of literary texts, the sources of those interpretations lie in the personal responses evoked by the text. One of the virtues of the subjective approach is that it allows students to understand why they choose to focus on the elements they do and to take responsibility for their choices.

In addition, by writing detailed response statements, students often learn that more was going on for them during their reading experience than they realized. Some students discover that they benefited from a reading experience that they would have considered unpleasant or worthless had they not put forth the effort to think carefully and write down their responses. Students can also learn, by comparing their response statements to those of classmates or by contrasting their current response to a text with a response they remember having at an earlier age, how diverse and variable people's perceptions are, how various motives influence our likes and dislikes, and how adult reading preferences are shaped by childhood reading experiences.

From group discussions of response statements and from their own response-analysis statements, students can also learn how their own tastes and the tastes of others operate. As Bleich notes, one's announcement that one likes or dislikes a text, character, or passage is not enough to articulate taste. Rather, students must analyze the psychological pay-offs or costs the text creates for them and describe how these factors create their likes and dislikes. There's a big difference between knowing what you like and understanding your taste, and it is the latter goal that is, for Bleich, the appropriate goal for the classroom. Indeed, he believes that the organized examination of taste promoted in the subjective classroom is a natural place for students to begin their study of language and literature. The focus on self-understanding is extremely motivating for most students, and Bleich's subjective method fosters a kind of critical thinking that should prove useful to students throughout their lives because it shows that knowledge is created collaboratively, not just "handed down," and that its creation is motivated by personal and group concerns.

Psychological reader-response theory

Psychoanalytic critic Norman Holland also believes that readers' motives strongly influence how they read. Despite his claim, at least in his early work, that an objective text exists (indeed, he calls his method *transactive* analysis because he believes that reading involves a transaction between the reader and a real text),

Holland focuses on what readers' interpretations reveal about themselves, not about the text. Given his analyses of the subjective experiences of readers, he is sometimes referred to as a subjective reader-response critic. However, because Holland employs psychoanalytic concepts and focuses on the psychological responses of readers, many theorists think of him as a psychological reader-response critic, which is probably the most useful way for us to think of him, too.

Holland believes that we react to literary texts with the same psychological responses we bring to events in our daily lives. The situations that cause my defenses to emerge in my interpersonal life will cause my defenses to emerge when I read. To use a simple example, if I am quick to dislike new acquaintances who remind me of my alcoholic father, then I probably will be quick to dislike any fictional character who reminds me of him. Or if my overriding psychological trait is my need to control my world, then I probably will be threatened by literary texts that undermine my sense of control, for example, texts in which I can't find a powerful character with whom I can identify or in which I can't find the kind of orderly, logical world in which I feel comfortable. My defense in these situations might be to dislike the text, misunderstand it, or stop reading it altogether. Given that virtually all literary texts will in some way arouse my defenses by tapping some unconscious fear or forbidden desire, I must have a way to cope with texts if I am going to read them at all. According to Holland, that coping process is interpretation.

The immediate goal of interpretation, like the immediate psychological goal of our daily lives, is to fulfill our psychological needs and desires. When we perceive a textual threat to our psychological equilibrium, we must interpret the text in some way that will restore that equilibrium. Imagine, for example, two readers who, at some point in their lives, have felt victimized – perhaps "picked on" by siblings, rejected by peers, or neglected by a parent – for reasons beyond their control. These readers' defenses probably would be raised by the character of Pecola in Toni Morrison's *The Bluest Eye* (1970) because they would perceive her as a victim as they themselves had been. In other words, reading about Pecola would probably remind them of their own painful childhood isolation. The first reader might cope with this textual threat by interpreting the novel in a way that condemns Pecola instead of the characters who torment her: for example, Pecola instigates her own victimization by behaving in such a passive manner and refusing to stand up for herself. In this way, the reader identifies with the aggressor, rather than with the victim, and temporarily relieves his own psychological pain. The second reader for whom victimized characters threaten to stimulate painful childhood memories might cope with Pecola by minimizing the character's suffering, focusing instead on some positive quality Pecola retains intact: for example, Pecola is the only character in the novel who never hurts anyone, and she will remain forever in a state of childlike innocence. This reader denies Pecola's psychological pain in order to deny her own. Other readers upon whom victim figures have a personal psychological impact would have to cope with Pecola, too, and they would do so in the same ways they cope with their relationships to victimization in their own lives.

Holland calls the pattern of our psychological conflicts and coping strategies our *identity theme*. He believes that in our daily lives we project that identity theme onto every situation we encounter and thus perceive the world through the lens of our psychological experience. Analogously, when we read literature, we project our identity theme, or variations of it, onto the text. That is, in various ways we unconsciously recreate in the text the world that exists in our own mind. Our interpretations, then, are products of the fears, defenses, needs, and desires we project onto the text. Interpretation is thus primarily a psychological process rather than an intellectual one. A literary interpretation may or may not reveal the meaning of the text, but to a discerning eye it always reveals the psychology of the reader.

The reason why the psychological dimension of our interpretations is not readily apparent to ourselves and others is that we unconsciously couch it in aesthetic, intellectual, social, or moral abstractions to relieve the anxiety and guilt our projections arouse in us. For example, the two hypothetical readers who react to Pecola as described above might interpret the character – respectively, as the representative of self-destructive human frailty, like the biblical Eve, or in contrast as the representative of spiritual innocence – without realizing that their interpretations emerged from their own unconscious psychological conflicts.

Holland's definition of interpretation can thus be summarized as a process consisting of three stages or modes that occur and recur as we read. First, in the *defense mode*, our psychological defenses are raised by the text (for example, we find Pecola threatening because she reminds us of our own experience of victimization). Second, in the *fantasy mode*, we find a way to interpret the text that will tranquilize those defenses and thus fulfill our desire to be protected from threats to our psychological equilibrium (for example, we minimize Pecola's pain by focusing on the childlike innocence that will remain forever hers). Third, in the *transformation mode*, we transform the first two steps into an abstract interpretation so that we can get the psychological satisfaction we desire without acknowledging to ourselves the anxiety-producing defenses and guilt-producing fantasies that underlie our assessment of the text (for example, we decide that Pecola represents spiritual innocence). Thus, in the transformation mode, we focus on an intellectual interpretation of the text in order to avoid our own emotional response to it, and we ignore the fact that our intellectual interpretation grew out of our emotional response.

Of course, the possible value of Holland's method seems evident for facilitating therapeutic psychological self-knowledge. But with adequate training, one might also use it as a biographical tool for the study of an author. Holland provides an example of such an application in a brief analysis of Robert Frost. Holland doesn't analyze Frost the writer, but Frost the reader. That is, the focus of analysis is Frost as a person reading the world in which he lives, reacting to and interpreting it. Holland studied the poet's informal remarks; his letters; his tastes in literature; his personality traits; and his expressed attitudes toward science, politics, his own poetry, and himself in order to discover Frost's identity theme. According to Holland, Frost related to himself and to the world in terms of his need to "manage" the "huge unknown forces of sex and aggression" through the means of "smaller symbols: words or familiar objects" (127). Once this identity theme was established, Holland notes, it could be traced as well in Frost's poetry, which might itself be taken as the poet's interpretation of his world.

For Holland, the purpose of such an analysis is an empathic merger with the author. Whether we're analyzing a person or a literary text, every act of interpretation takes place within the context of the interpreter's identity theme, which, as we have seen, sets up defenses against as well as desire for such a merger. It is therefore the interpreter's task to break through the psychological barriers that separate self from other. Understanding an author's identity theme, Holland believes, allows us to fully experience, as a "mingling of self and other" (132), the gift the artist offers us.

Social reader-response theory

While the individual reader's subjective response to the literary text plays the crucial role in subjective reader-response theory, for social reader-response theory, usually associated with the later work of Stanley Fish, there is no purely individual subjective response. According to Fish, what we take to be our individual subjective responses to literature are really products of the *interpretive community* to which we belong. By interpretive community, Fish means those who share the interpretive strategies we bring to texts when we read, whether or not we realize we're using interpretive strategies and whether or not we are aware that other people share them. These interpretive strategies always result from various sorts of institutionalized assumptions (assumptions established, for example, in high schools, churches, and colleges by prevailing cultural attitudes and philosophies) about what makes a text a piece of literature – instead of a letter or a legal document or a church sermon – and what meanings we are supposed to find in it.

An interpretive community can be as sophisticated and aware of its critical enterprise as the community produced by the followers of a specific Marxist critical theorist. Or an interpretive community can be as unsophisticated and unaware of its interpretive strategies as the community produced by a high school teacher who instructs his students that it is natural to read literature in search of static symbols that tell us the "hidden meaning" of the story. Of course, interpretive communities aren't static; they evolve over time. And readers can belong, consciously or unconsciously, to more than one community at the same time, or they can change from one community to another at different times in their lives.

In any case, all readers come to the text already predisposed to interpret it in a certain way based on whatever interpretive strategies are operating for them at the time they read. Thus, while Bleich believes his students produce communal authority through a negotiation that occurs after they've read the text, Fish claims that a multiplicity of communal authorities, based on the multiplicity of interpretive communities to which students already belong, determines how students read the text in the first place.

In other words, for Fish, readers do not interpret poems; they create them. He demonstrated this point rather dramatically when he taught two college courses back to back. At the end of his first class he wrote an assignment on the board that consisted of the following list of linguists' names his students were studying. (The question mark after the final name was to indicate Fish's uncertainty about the spelling.)

Jacobs–Rosenbaum
    Levin
    Thorne
    Hayes
    Ohman (?)

(*Is There a Text?* 323)

When his second class entered the room, he told them that the writing on the board was a seventeenth-century religious poem like the ones they'd been studying and asked them to analyze it.

In the discussion that ensued, his students concluded that the poem celebrated God's love and mercy in giving his only begotten son for our redemption. Their interpretation accounted beautifully for every word in the poem, including, among other evidence, the following points: the poem is in the shape of a cross or an altar; "Jacobs" suggests Jacob's ladder, a reference to the Christian ascent into heaven; "Rosenbaum" literally means rose tree and refers to the Virgin Mary, the rose without thorns, whose son Jesus is the means by which human beings can climb to heaven; "Thorne" thus refers to Jesus' crown of thorns, a symbol of the sacrifice he made to redeem us; and the letters that occur most frequently in the poem are S, O, N (*Is There a Text?* 322–29).

I don't need to recount the students' argument in its entirety for you to see Fish's point: every literary judgment we make, including the judgment that a particular piece of writing is a poem, results from the interpretive strategies we bring with us when we read the text. A list of linguists' names, or anything else, can become a poem if a reader or group of readers uses the interpretive strategies required to make it one. That is, the qualities that make a poem a poem do not reside in the text but in the interpretive strategies we've learned, consciously or unconsciously, before we ever encountered the text.

Social reader-response theory doesn't offer us a new way to read texts. Nor does it promote any form of literary criticism that already exists. After all, its point is that no interpretation, and therefore no form of literary criticism, can claim to reveal what's *in* a text. Each interpretation will simply find whatever its interpretive strategies put there. This doesn't mean, however, that we are left with the anarchy of unconstrained interpretation. As Fish notes, interpretations will always be controlled by the relatively limited repertoire of interpretive strategies available at any given point in history. By understanding the principles of social reader-response theory, however, we can become more aware of what it is we're doing when we interpret a text and more aware of what our peers and students are doing as well. Such awareness could be especially useful to teachers by helping them analyze their students' interpretive strategies; helping them decide if and when to try to replace those strategies with others; and helping them take responsibility for the strategies they choose to teach instead of hiding behind the belief that certain ways of reading are natural or inherently right because they represent what's in the text.

Defining readers

Before we turn to the uses of reader-response theory in literary criticism, there's one final concept we need to discuss that relates to all the approaches discussed above. You may have noticed that some reader-response theorists refer to "readers" while others refer to "the reader." When theorists discuss actual readers whose responses they analyze, as Norman Holland and David Bleich do, for example, they refer to them as "readers" or "students" or call them by some other name that denotes real people. Many theorists, however, analyze the reading experience of a hypothetical ideal reader encountering a specific text, as we saw, for example, in our examination of affective stylistics. In these cases, references to "the reader" are really references to the critic analyzing his or her own carefully documented reading experience of a specific text according to specific reader-response principles. Because the experience of hypothetical readers may or may not correspond to the experience of actual readers, some hypothetical readers have been given names that describe the reading activity they represent. Thus, in Fish's practice of affective stylistics, he refers to the *informed reader*: the reader who has attained the *literary competency* necessary to experience the text as Fish himself does, in the fullness of its linguistic and literary complexity, and who conscientiously tries to suppress the personal or idiosyncratic dimension of his or her response. Of course, there is a variety of informed readers because the informed reader of, say, Emily Dickinson's poetry may or may not be the informed reader of Richard Wright's fiction. Other terms you may run across that refer to similar hypothetical readers include the *educated reader,* the *ideal reader,* and the *optimal reader.*

Analogously, Wolfgang Iser uses the term *implied reader,* by which he means the reader that the text seems to be addressing, whose characteristics we can deduce by studying the style in which the text is written and the apparent "attitude" of the narrative toward the reader. Thus, the implied reader of a Harlequin romance is quite different from the implied reader of a philosophical novel like Thomas Mann's *Doctor Faustus* (1947) or the implied reader of a psychologically intense, historical novel like Toni Morrison's *Beloved* (1987). Other terms you may encounter that refer to readers implied by the text include the *intended reader* and the *narratee.* The point here is that critics who use hypothetical readers are trying to show us what particular texts require of readers or how particular texts work to position readers in order to guide their interpretations. Whether or not readers accept that guidance or are even aware of it is another matter.

Of course, there are many more reader-response concepts than the ones discussed above. Our purpose here is merely to introduce you to the main ideas, the general principles you need to know in order to read reader-response theorists and literary critics with some understanding of the issues they raise. Naturally, some literary works will seem to lend themselves more readily than others to reader-response analysis or at least to certain kinds of reader-response analysis. And unlike many other theories addressed in this textbook, a reader-response analysis of a literary text is often an analysis not of the text itself but of the responses of actual readers.

Mary Lowe-Evans, for example, analyzed the oral and written responses of college juniors and seniors in her literature class in order to learn how students today form attitudes toward a specific literary text and how those attitudes determine their interpretation of it. The text she used was Mary Shelley's *Frankenstein* (1818), and she mapped the ways in which the following factors influenced students' interpretations of the novel: film versions of the novel (which created students' preconceptions of the text), her own interpretive prompts (whose story is this? what does the novel mean? is the narrator reliable?), and the determinate and indeterminate meanings in the text itself. Among other findings, Lowe-Evans confirmed the reader-response notion that interpretation is an ongoing process that evolves as readers use different interpretive strategies to actively work their way through a text. She also learned that preconceptions created by film versions of the novel, in which the monster is very different from Shelley's monster, facilitated certain interpretations of the story while frustrating others. Analogously, particular textual elements, such as the formal style of the tale's "Preface" and the epistolary format that opens the narrative (the story is presented as a series of letters from the narrator to his sister), counteracted the students' expectations of a superficial, entertaining monster story.

Whatever kind of analysis is undertaken, however, the ultimate goal of reader-response criticism is to increase our understanding of the reading process by investigating the activities in which readers engage and the effects of those activities on their interpretations.

Some questions reader-response critics ask about literary texts

The questions that follow are offered to summarize reader-response approaches to literature or, more accurately, to the reading of literature. Question 1 draws on transactional reader-response theory. Question 2 relates to affective stylistics. Question 3 concerns subjective reader-response theory. Question 4 draws on psychological reader-response theory. Question 5 relates to social reader-response theory. Question 6 draws on elements of both transactional reader-response theory and affective stylistics in the course of establishing a parallel between the theme of a given text and the reader's experience while reading it.

1   How does the interaction of text and reader create meaning? How, exactly, does the text's indeterminacy function as a stimulus to interpretation? (For example, what events are omitted or unexplained? What descriptions are omitted or incomplete? What images might have multiple associations?) And how exactly does the text lead us to correct our interpretation as we read?

2   What does a phrase-by-phrase analysis of a short literary text, or of key portions of a longer text, tell us about the reading experience prestructured by (built into) that text? How does this analysis of what the text does to the reader differ from what the text "says" or "means"? In other words, how might the omission of the temporal experience of reading this text result in an incomplete idea of the text's meaning?

3   If you have the resources to do it, what can you learn about the role of readers' interpretive strategies or expectations, about the reading experience produced by a particular text, or about any other reading activity by conducting your own study using a group of real readers (for example, your students, classmates, or fellow book-club members)? For instance, can you devise a study to test Bleich's belief that students' personal responses to literary texts are the source of their formal interpretations?

4   Drawing on a broad spectrum of thoroughly documented biographical data, what seems to be a given author's identity theme, and how does that theme express itself in the sum of his or her literary output? Or, using your own interpretation of a literary work to which you respond strongly, see if you can identify what might be your own identity theme.

5   What does the body of criticism published about a literary text during a given time period suggest about the social assumptions of the critics who interpreted that text? In other words, what social beliefs – about morality, about women,

about children, about religion, and about the purpose and value of literature – seem to have influenced the ways in which the literary critics of the time responded to a particular literary text?

6 How might we interpret a literary text to show that the reader's response is, or is analogous to, the topic of the story? In other words, how is the text really about readers reading, and what exactly does it tell us about this topic? To simplify further, how is a particular kind of reading experience an important theme in the text? Of course, we must first establish what reading experience is created by the text (see Questions 1 and 2) in order to show that the theme of the story is analogous to it. Then we must cite textual evidence – for example, references to reading materials, to characters reading texts, and to characters interpreting other characters or events – to show that what happens in the world of the narrative mirrors the reader's situation decoding it.

Depending on the literary work in question, we might ask one or any combination of these questions. Or we might come up with a useful question not listed here. These are just some starting points to get us thinking about literature in productive reader-response ways. Keep in mind that not all reader-response critics will interpret the same text, or even the same readers' responses, in the same way, even if they focus on the same reader-response concepts. As in every field, even expert practitioners disagree. Our goal is to use reader-response theory to help enrich our reading of literary works, to help us see some important ideas they illustrate that we might not have seen so clearly or so deeply otherwise, and to help us understand the complexities and varieties of the reading experience.

The following reader-response analysis of F. Scott Fitzgerald's *The Great Gatsby* is offered as an example of what a reader-response interpretation of that novel might yield. Using the principles of affective stylistics, Iser's notion of indeterminacy, and Holland's notion of projection, I will examine the way the novel continually problematizes our evolving perception of Jay Gatsby as we read, creating an indeterminacy that invites us to project our own beliefs and desires onto the protagonist. In addition, I will show how the novel's thematic content (what the novel "is about") mirrors the reader's experience reading it, that is, how the theme of the novel is the impossibility of establishing determinate meaning.

Projecting the reader: a reader-response analysis of *The Great Gatsby*

"Somebody told me they thought he killed a man once."

A thrill passed over all of us. The three Mr. Mumbles bent forward and listened eagerly.

"I don't think it's so much that," argued Lucille skeptically; "it's more that he was a German spy during the war."

One of the men nodded in confirmation.

"I heard that from a man who knew all about him, grew up with him in Germany," he assured us positively.

"Oh no," said the first girl, "it couldn't be that, because he was in the American army during the war." As our credulity switched back to her she leaned forward with enthusiasm. "You look at him sometimes when he thinks nobody's looking at him. I'll bet he killed a man."

(48; ch. 3)

The speculation Jay Gatsby inspires in his gossip-hungry party guests, who have an obvious desire to be shocked, is, in two important ways, a prototype of the speculation he inspires in the reader of F. Scott Fitzgerald's *The Great Gatsby* (1925). Our credulity, like that of Gatsby's party guests, is continually "switched" in different directions as we make our way through Nick Carraway's narration, and the final outcome of our speculation – our interpretation of Gatsby and therefore of the meaning of the novel as a whole – is largely a product of our own beliefs and desires, which the tale's indeterminacy invites us to project. In other words, *The Great Gatsby* dramatizes reader-response theory's concept of reading as the making of meaning, and the novel reproduces within the action of the story the reader's experience while reading it.

With Jay Gatsby as the "text" they decode, the characters in the novel model a reading experience that could be described by the following formula: projection + data gathered = confirmation of projection. In other words, the data that interpreters gather from the environment have one primary function: to validate for them the interpretation they've already projected or are in the process of projecting. For example, as we just saw, Gatsby's party guests perform all three steps of the formula in a single conversation. Although the outlandish rumors they rely on are inaccurate, rumors are the only data available, and they are hardly more shocking than the truth about Gatsby's criminal activities. More important, outlandish rumors fulfill the desire for scandal that prompts them to interpret Gatsby in the first place: it hardly matters, in terms of their enjoyment of the "text" that is Gatsby, which of the rumors they believe, as long as the rumor is sufficiently outrageous or provokes further shocking speculations. In other words, the party guests interpret Gatsby in order to be shocked, and their interpretations fulfill their desire.

Analogously, Tom Buchanan wants to believe that Gatsby is a crook with no respectable family background, and he hires private investigators to provide him with the evidence he needs to prove it. Daisy wants to believe Gatsby is her upper-class knight in shining armor, so she conveniently doesn't see through his veneer of wealth and status, which is as thin as the "thin beard of raw ivy" (9; ch. 1) covering the tower of his mansion. Wolfsheim wants to believe that Gatsby is "a man of fine breeding" (76; ch. 4) so he can "use him good" (179; ch. 9) in his underworld activities, and therefore he doesn't see the contradiction in a finely bred man, "an Oggsford," being "so hard up he had to keep on wearing his uniform because he couldn't buy some regular clothes" (179; ch. 9). George Wilson wants to believe that Gatsby seduced and murdered his wife because this belief will permit Wilson to avenge Myrtle's seduction and death and achieve the emotional closure he needs. So Wilson readily believes the first story he hears: he asks no questions and has no doubts about Tom's explanation despite having seen Tom himself driving the "death" car earlier that day and despite Tom's unfulfilled promises to Wilson in the recent past. Finally, Mr. Gatz wants to believe that his son "had a big future before him": "If he'd of lived he'd of been a great man. A man like [railroad tycoon] James J. Hill. He'd of helped build up the country" (176; ch. 9). Mr. Gatz therefore interprets his son's boyhood "schedule" as proof that "Jimmy was bound to get ahead" (182; ch. 9), having swallowed completely whatever improbable lies Gatsby surely told him about the source of his wealth.

I'm not suggesting that these characters have the ability or the opportunity to acquire more accurate information about Gatsby. My point is simply that the eagerness with which they embrace the information they acquire and the readiness with which they use it to construct what they choose to regard as the complete picture of Gatsby are products of the degree to which the information fulfills their own desires concerning the man.

It might be reasonable to conclude that the amount of inaccuracy produced by this sort of interpretation teaches the reader to try another method, that the novel discredits the subjective, self-serving interpretation represented by these characters. However, as we shall see, Nick Carraway – whose first-person narration guides us through the morally ambiguous world of the novel – interprets Gatsby through the lens of his own projections as well. Furthermore, he does so because, in the inde-terminate world of the novel, there is no other way to interpret Gatsby. As we follow Nick through his "now-I-like-Gatsby; now-I-don't" narration, we are thrust, along with him, back and forth between opposing perceptions of the protagonist. Nick's opening evaluation of the character – in which he says that Gatsby "repre-sents everything ... [Nick] ... scorn[s]" and yet is "exempt from [Nick's negative] reaction" (6; ch. 1) to his Long Island friends – announces the paradoxical experience of Gatsby he will share with us as his narrative unfolds.

Nick's narrative creates an intricate pattern of reader sympathy for and criticism of Gatsby that would require an essay of its own to trace in detail, but a rough sketch of its contours should demonstrate the sense of indeterminacy this pattern promotes. After the paradoxical evaluation of Gatsby with which Nick introduces us to the character, noted above, the narrator takes us back to the beginning of his tale, or before the beginning, to a description of his own "prominent, well-to-do" (7; ch. 1) family in Minnesota and his decision to go to New York and learn the bond business. Throughout the rest of chapter 1 the only feeling about Gatsby Nick shares with us is his curiosity about the man, which is revealed through his description of "Gatsby's mansion. Or rather, as [Nick] didn't know Mr. Gatsby, it was a mansion inhabited by a gentleman of that name" (9; ch. 1). In other words, we travel back in time with Nick and experience events as he experienced them unfolding in time. The "Gatsby" introduced on page 6 has become "Mr. Gatsby" on page 9 because Nick has taken us back to a point in time when he hadn't yet met the protagonist.

Our curiosity is raised when Jordan mentions Gatsby, a man she met at West Egg, and Daisy demands, "Gatsby? ... What Gatsby?" (15; ch. 1), but Nick and the reader don't meet Gatsby until the middle of chapter 3, when the narrator attends one of Gatsby's parties. Having excited our curiosity, and revealed his own, by his minute observations of what he can see of Gatsby's parties from the porch of his cottage, Nick's initial meeting with his neighbor initiates the pattern of conflicting interpretations of Gatsby that will characterize his experience, and ours, throughout the novel. Gatsby introduces himself to Nick, then smiles, and the narrator is charmed. Nick says,

> It was one of those rare smiles with a quality of eternal reassurance in it. ... [I]t had precisely the impression of you that, at your best, you hoped to convey. Precisely at that point it vanished – and I was looking at an elegant young rough-neck ... whose elaborate formality of speech just missed being absurd.
>
> (53; ch. 3)

In other words, Nick's positive impression that Gatsby is a charming gentleman is immediately followed by a negative impression that Gatsby is a phony.

This pattern is repeated until Nick leaves the party at the end of the evening. The narrator, catching a glimpse of Gatsby "standing alone on the marble steps," says, "I could see nothing sinister about him" (54; ch. 3). But in the very next sentence Nick wonders if Gatsby's innocent appearance is an illusion produced by "the fact that [Gatsby] was [the only one] not drinking ... for it seemed to me that he grew more correct as the fraternal hilarity increased" (54; ch. 3). Again, as Nick bids Gatsby goodnight he implies that his host is insincere. Gatsby calls Nick "old sport," but "[t]he familiar expression held no more familiarity than the hand which reassuringly brushed my shoulder" (57; ch. 3). Then a few seconds later Gatsby smiles, and Nick likes him again – "suddenly there seemed to be a pleasant significance in having been among the last to go, as if he had desired it so all the time" (58; ch. 3) – and Gatsby's "Good night, old sport. ... Good night" (58; ch. 3) feels warm and sincere. Finally, as Nick glances back at Gatsby from across the lawn as he heads home, he describes the protagonist in a way that underscores the ambiguity of his own response to him: "A sudden *emptiness* seemed to flow now from the windows and the great doors, endowing with complete *isolation* the figure of the host who stood on the porch, his hand up in a *formal gesture* of farewell" (60; ch. 3, my italics). Does this language emphasize Gatsby's coldness, which would decrease our sympathy for him, or his loneliness, which would increase it? Nick doesn't clarify his own attitude – perhaps he's not sure – so the reader is left, after a series of conflicting responses to Gatsby, to project his or her personal experience onto the protagonist.

Our next encounter with Gatsby occurs at the beginning of chapter 4, when the protagonist drives Nick to New York. During this scene, our attitude toward Gatsby is again shifted back and forth between positive and negative poles. Nick starts us off with the following account of his change in attitude toward Gatsby prior to their drive to New York, based on the half-dozen conversations he'd had with his neighbor during the month since they'd met:

> [T]o my disappointment ... he had little to say. So my first impression, that he was a person of some undefined consequence, had gradually faded and he had become simply the proprietor of an elaborate road-house next door.
>
> (69; ch. 4)

Then, as Nick puts it, "came that disconcerting ride" (69; ch. 4). As Gatsby tells Nick the story about his wealthy family, "all dead now" (69; ch. 4), and his Oxford education, Nick says,

> He looked at me sideways. ... [And] [h]e hurried the phrase "educated at Oxford." ... And with this doubt his whole statement fell to pieces and I wondered if there wasn't something a little sinister about him after all.
>
> (69; ch. 4)

Of course, Nick now believes nothing Gatsby says about his jewel collecting, "chiefly rubies" (70; ch. 4), big-game hunting, and painting, and only "[w]ith an effort" does Nick "manag[e] to restrain [his] incredulous laughter" (70; ch. 4). Gatsby's war story, which he tells next, sounds just as exaggerated as the rest of his tale, and Nick feels as though he is "skimming hastily through a dozen magazines" (71; ch. 4). However, Gatsby then shows Nick a war medal with his name on it, and "[t]o [Nick's] astonishment the thing had an authentic look" (71; ch. 4). When Gatsby produces a snapshot of himself with a group of fellow students at Oxford, Nick concludes, "Then it was all true" (71; ch. 4).

Nick's belief in Gatsby is quickly submerged under his annoyance, however, when Gatsby says that Jordan Baker is going to make a request of Nick on Gatsby's behalf: "I was sure the request would be something utterly fantastic and for a moment I was sorry I'd ever set foot upon his overpopulated lawn" (72; ch. 4). When Nick notes that Gatsby's "correctness grew on him as we neared the city"

(72; ch. 4), he seems to be implying again that Gatsby is a phony. Yet the scene ends with an incident that seems to leave Nick's sympathies, and ours, again mired in ambiguity. When Gatsby is pulled over for speeding, he produces a piece of paper that not only gets him out of a ticket but also causes the officer who pulled him over to apologize. Gatsby explains, "I was able to do the commissioner a favor once, and he sends me a Christmas card every year" (73; ch. 4). While this incident certainly underscores Gatsby's importance and therefore supports the story he just told Nick, how should we feel about the touch of corruption hinted at here? Nick's response doesn't help – "Even Gatsby could happen [in a place like New York] without any particular wonder" (73; ch. 4) – so we're once more left on our own.

An analysis of the scenes that shape the reader's evolving view of Gatsby through the rest of the novel reveals a similar pattern of opposing influences, as we see in the following summary of those scenes.

1 *Nick, Gatsby, and Wolfsheim have lunch* (73–79; ch. 4) – Our impression of Gatsby is shaped *negatively* due to Nick's description of Gatsby's close association with Wolfsheim, who is very negatively portrayed, and Nick's suspicious comments about Gatsby.

2 *Jordan tells Nick about Gatsby and Daisy* (79–85; ch. 4) – Our impression of Gatsby is shaped *positively* due to Gatsby's faithful devotion to Daisy, his fear of offending Jordan and Nick, and Nick's sympathetic response to Gatsby's plight.

3 *Nick and Gatsby arrange Gatsby's reunion with Daisy* (86–88; ch. 5) – Our impression of Gatsby is shaped *negatively* due to Nick's consistently cool responses to Gatsby's attempts at friendliness, especially after Gatsby "obviously and tactlessly" (88; ch. 5) offers him a chance to make some easy money in exchange for arranging the reunion with Daisy.

4 *Gatsby and Daisy reunite* (88–94; ch. 5) – Our sympathy for Gatsby is shaped *positively* by Nick's description of the protagonist's total emotional investment in Daisy – his nervous apprehension before the meeting, his intense anxiety during the initial awkwardness with Daisy, and his overwhelming joy when he realizes she still loves him – and by Nick's vicarious experience of the protagonist's embarrassment and happiness.

5 *Nick and Gatsby wait for Daisy on Nick's lawn* (95; ch. 5) – Our impression of Gatsby is shaped *negatively* by Nick's catching Gatsby in an apparent lie about where he got the money to buy his house and by Gatsby's rude and defensive reply – "That's my affair" (95; ch. 5) – when Nick asks him what business he's in.

6 *Gatsby shows his house to Daisy and Nick* (96–102; ch. 5) – Our response to Gatsby is moved between *positive and negative* poles as Nick's sympathetic description of Gatsby's devotion to Daisy is interrupted in the middle by an ominous phone call that hints strongly at Gatsby's hidden criminal life.

7 *Nick relates the real story of Gatsby's youth* (104–7; ch. 6) – Our response to Gatsby is moved between *positive* and *negative* poles as Nick's sympathetic description of Gatsby's impoverished youth, boyhood dreams, hard work, and sobriety is interrupted twice by Nick's observations that Gatsby's dreams were in "the service of a vast, vulgar and meretricious beauty" (104; ch. 6) and that they inhabited a "universe of ineffable gaudiness" (105; ch. 6). At the end of the scene Nick says, "[Gatsby] told me all this very much later ... when I had reached the point of believing everything and nothing about him" (107; ch. 6), thus reinforcing our uncertainty for some time to come.

8 *Tom and friends on horseback stop at Gatsby's house* (107–10; ch. 6) – Our response to Gatsby is moved between *positive* and *negative* poles as Nick's sympathetic description of Gatsby's politeness in the face of his visitors' rudeness is interrupted by his description of Gatsby's "almost aggressiv[e]" attempts to push Tom into talking in order to learn more about him.

9 *Nick, Tom, and Daisy attend Gatsby's party* (110–18; ch. 6) – Our response to Gatsby is shaped *positively* by Nick's sympathetic descriptions of Gatsby's attentions to Daisy, by his angry defense of Gatsby against Tom's insinuations, and by his extremely poetic rendition of Gatsby's account of his early days with Daisy, though that rendition is somewhat undercut by Nick's *negative* reference to Gatsby's "appalling sentimentality" (118; ch. 6).

10 *Nick learns about Gatsby's new servants* (119–20; ch. 7) – Our response to Gatsby is *negatively* shaped by Nick's description of Gatsby's association with Wolfsheim's people and the protagonist's apparent failure to notice their sinister quality.

11 *Nick and Gatsby lunch with the Buchanans and Jordan* (121–28; ch. 7) – Our response to Gatsby is shaped *positively* by Nick's description of Gatsby's quiet good manners in the face of Tom's aggressiveness and Daisy's open displays of affection for her lover. This response is undercut somewhat at the end of the scene by Nick's *negative* observation, which hints at the protagonist's dark side, that "an undefinable expression ... passed over Gatsby's face" (127) when Tom makes a veiled reference to Gatsby's criminal activities.

12 *Tom confronts Gatsby in the New York hotel suite* (133–42; ch. 7) – Our sympathy for Gatsby is shaped *positively* by Nick's description of Gatsby's honesty about his Oxford experience and his description of Gatsby's desperate and pathetic attempt to hold Daisy in the face of Tom's ruthlessness and her withdrawal.

13 *Nick meets Gatsby outside the Buchanans' house after Myrtle's death* (150–53; ch. 7) – Our response to Gatsby is moved from the *negative* to the *positive* by the change in Nick's behavior toward Gatsby after he learns that Daisy, not Gatsby, drove the hit-and-run car and Gatsby is taking the blame for her.

14 *Nick and Gatsby talk at Gatsby's house the morning after Myrtle's death* (154–62; ch. 8) – Our response to Gatsby is moved between *positive* and *negative* poles as Nick's sympathetic description of Gatsby's devotion to Daisy is interrupted by

his statement that Gatsby "took" Daisy, "ravenously and unscrupulously" (156), under false pretenses.

15 *Nick makes Gatsby's funeral arrangements* (171–83; ch. 9) – Our response to Gatsby is moved several times between *positive* and *negative* poles as Nick's "feeling of … scornful solidarity" with Gatsby "against them all" (173) is repeatedly interrupted by reminders of the protagonist's criminal activities.

16 *Nick walks on Gatsby's beach the night before he heads back to Minnesota* (189; ch. 9) – Our sympathy for Gatsby is *positively* shaped by Nick's poetic comparison of Gatsby's "wonder when he first picked out the green light at the end of Daisy's dock" (189) with the wonder inspired by the virgin American continent, the "fresh, green breast of the new world" (189).

Thus, while the text actively shapes the reader's response to Gatsby in each of these scenes, as we move through the tale we experience a significant degree of indeterminacy. For we gradually learn that the text will support two opposing interpretations of Gatsby: (1) Gatsby the criminal, who will hurt anyone and do anything to get what he wants, and (2) Gatsby the romantic hero, who has pulled himself out of poverty and devoted his life to Daisy as "to the following of a grail" (156; ch. 8). In other words, the novel gives us a protagonist who uses wholly corrupt means, including bootlegging and fraudulent bonds, to achieve pure ends – Gatsby's "incorruptible dream" (162; ch. 8) of winning Daisy and living the good life – and then asks us to decide if the ends justify the means. But the novel doesn't provide the kind of unequivocal evidence we need to answer the question.

A simple "no," the obvious "right" answer from an abstract moral perspective, does not adequately respond to the complexities of the question, given the wretched poverty of Gatsby's childhood and the novel's portrayal of the dumping ground Nick refers to as the "valley of ashes" (27; ch. 2) as the only alternative to the life lived by the rich and famous. Our perception of the contrast between wealth and poverty is reinforced throughout the novel by alternating descriptions of, on the one hand, the exciting world of Nick and his crowd and, on the other hand, the dreary world of the Wilsons, the McKees, Myrtle's sister Catherine, and such random characters as Gatsby's freeloading, vulgar party guests and the "poor young clerks who loitered in front of windows … in the dusk, wasting the most poignant moments of night and life" (62; ch. 3).

The simple conclusion that Gatsby's ends do not justify his means does not work for Nick either. But neither does the narrator simply conclude that Gatsby's ends do justify his means. As we have seen, it's through Nick that we learn about Gatsby's dark side: his criminal activities, his deception of Daisy, his invented identity, his association with Wolfsheim, and his insensitivity to the welfare of anyone but Daisy and himself. Yet it's Nick who is also Gatsby's chief defender, who experiences, for example, one of many "renewals of complete faith in him" (136; ch. 7) simply because Gatsby makes a small concession to reality by admitting that his Oxford experience was provided by a government arrangement for American soldiers after World War I. And it's Nick who concludes that Gatsby is "worth the whole damn bunch [of Nick's crowd] put together" (162; ch. 8). In fact, Nick's warm and frequent defense of the protagonist should, on the whole, tend to elicit our sympathy for Gatsby, even while the dark side of his characterization reminds us that Gatsby is not one of the good guys in the white hats. That is, without answering the question the novel poses, without suggesting that Gatsby's ends justify his means, Nick nevertheless sees Gatsby as the only person he met in the East who "turned out all right at the end" (6; ch. 1).

Why should Nick finally interpret Gatsby in such a one-sided manner, given the knowledge he has of him? The enthusiastic tone of Nick's frequent "renewals of complete faith" (136; ch. 7) in Gatsby suggests that, like so many other characters in the novel, Nick projects his own desires onto Gatsby. At the age of 30, and still being financed by his father while he tries to figure out what he should do with himself, it is not surprising that Nick wants to believe life still holds promise because he is afraid that it doesn't. He fears that all he has to look forward to is, as he puts it, "a thinning list of single men to know, a thinning briefcase of enthusiasm, thinning hair" (143; ch. 7). With one failed romance back home and one in New York, Nick wants to believe that the possibility of romance still exists. With his summer in New York – his latest in a series of adventures – having ended in disaster, he wants to believe in the possibility of fulfilled hope he sees in Gatsby: hope that a young man at loose ends can make the kind of outrageous financial success of himself that Gatsby has made, can fall so completely in love with a woman, and can feel so optimistic about the future. Indeed, as we see throughout the second half of the novel, Nick is so emotionally invested in Gatsby that, without hesitation and despite his own conservative upbringing, he facilitates Gatsby's adulterous affair with Daisy, Nick's own relative.

Nick's tendency to project his own desire into his interpretation of Gatsby seems unavoidable and feels natural given that his, and our, experience of the protagonist develops within a setting that is itself full of unanswered questions, contradictions, and multiple possible interpretations. The affective thrust of the novel as a whole thus invites us to project, like Nick, our own meanings onto the world of the novel in order to interpret it at all.

Even the briefest list of the text's indeterminacies would include the following unanswered questions, which my students frequently find disturbing. Why does Daisy marry Tom after receiving Gatsby's letter from Europe? As Gatsby returned to Louisville within three months of Daisy's wedding, didn't his letter tell her that she could expect him soon? Why is Daisy "so mad about her husband" (81; ch. 4) after only three months of marriage, given that she didn't want to marry him the night before the wedding? Given Tom's chronic infidelity, the couple's frequent relocations, and their apparent dissatisfaction with the marriage, what keeps Tom and Daisy together? What is Gatsby and Daisy's relationship like after their reunion? (Fitzgerald wrote that he, himself, "had no feeling about or knowledge of ... the emotional relations between Gatsby and Daisy from the time of their reunion to the catastrophe" [*Letters* 341–42].) What's the real story of Nick's relationship with the young woman he left behind in his hometown? How do Nick and Jordan really feel about each other? What kind of person is Jordan? Given the novel's obvious rejection of Tom's sexist and racist attitudes, what are we to make of Nick's sexist and racist remarks, which the text offers without comment and seems to invite us to accept? (See, for example, Nick's remark in chapter 3, page 63, that "[d]ishonesty in a woman is a thing you never blame deeply" and his reference in chapter 4, page 73, to three black characters in a limousine as "two bucks and a girl" at whom he "laughed aloud as the yolks of their eyeballs rolled toward [Gatsby and him] in haughty rivalry.") Given the text's unflattering portraits of the poor as well as the rich, is the novel anti-elitist or merely misanthropic? What are the "grotesque and fantastic conceits" that "haunted [Gatsby] in his bed at night" (105; ch. 6)? (Nick doesn't tell us.) And which definition of *conceits* is operating here and elsewhere: "concepts," "visions," "affectations of style or speech," or "self-flattering opinions"? What are we to make of the eyes of Doctor T. J. Eckleburg, which hold such a prominent position in the novel's imagery but could be taken to represent so many different ideas?

The eyes of Doctor T. J. Eckleburg are, in fact, only one of many ambiguous images in a novel dense with vague, evocative descriptions that encourage readers to project their own meanings in interpreting them. For example, what is a "pale gold odor" or a "sparkling odor" (96; ch. 5)? What does it mean that a "gleam of hope" is "damp" (29; ch. 2)? What should we make of Gatsby's "blue gardens" (43; ch. 3) or the hair that lies across Daisy's cheek "like a dash of blue paint" (90; ch. 5)? How can Daisy's voice, "struggl[ing] through the heat," "moul[d] its senselessness into forms" (125; ch. 7), and what forms are thus produced? In addition, Nick's descriptions often acknowledge their own inability to provide concrete, specific details by their frequent use of the words *indefinable, uncommunicable, unutterable, ineffable,* and *inexplicable,* an evocative diction that reaches the height of its ambiguity in such phrases as "[t]hat unfamiliar yet recognizable look was back again in Gatsby's face" (141; ch. 7). If Nick can't define, communicate, utter, or explain what he has in mind, then readers must imagine for themselves what he means, and such gaps in the text invite us to project our own experience and desires in order to make meaning.

That *The Great Gatsby* easily supports the many different theoretical readings contained in this textbook is a testimony to the novel's indeterminacy. In short, there is so little determinate meaning in the novel that if we don't project our own beliefs and desires onto the text, the only interpretation left us would be that *The*

Great Gatsby portrays the indeterminacy of meaning in a morally ambiguous world. While I think that's a useful interpretation of the novel, most readers, including myself, desire more closure than such an interpretation provides. It is interesting to note, in this context, a trend in critical response to Jay Gatsby. Despite the novel's two-sided characterization of the title character, a significant proportion of critical response casts Gatsby as a romantic hero, as we see in the following examples. According to Marius Bewley, Gatsby is "all aspiration and goodness" (25); he's "an heroic personification of the American romantic hero" (14) who represents "the energy of the spirit's resistance" and "immunity to the final contamination" of "cheapness and vulgarity" (13). Jeffrey Hart agrees that Gatsby is "a representative American hero" (34), and Charles C. Nash claims that "Emerson's 'Infinitude of the Private Man'" is "best represented by Jay Gatsby, for whom all things are possible" (23). Andrew Dillon believes Gatsby is imbued with a "sacred energy" (61), and Kent Cartwright says that Gatsby's "dream ... ennobles him" (229). For Tom Burnam, Gatsby "survives sound and whole in character, uncorrupted by the corruption which surrounded him" (105). Similarly, Rose Adrienne Gallo believes that Gatsby "maintained his innocence" to the end (43), or, as André Le Vot puts it, Gatsby never loses his "fundamental integrity, his spiritual intactness" (144). Even when the protagonist's darker side is acknowledged, it is excused. As Cartwright argues, "Gatsby can be both criminal and romantic hero because the book creates for him a visionary moral standard that transcends the conventional and that his life affirms" (232). Or as Andrew Dillon sums up what he sees as the protagonist's merger of worldliness and spirituality, Gatsby is "a sensual saint" (50).[5]

Of course, Nick's defense of Gatsby encourages readers to respond sympathetically to the protagonist. However, given the amount and kind of negative data about Gatsby that Nick himself provides, some additional factors probably influenced the response of those critics who see only the good in Gatsby. In other words, although Nick clearly wants us to exempt Gatsby, as he does, from our condemnation of Gatsby's world, the narrator nevertheless provides us with more than enough data to problematize the sympathetic judgment of the protagonist he promotes. In fact, the critical controversy over whether or not Nick is a reliable narrator underscores this dimension of the novel's indeterminacy.[6]

One possible explanation for a critical trend that ignores so much material in the novel, focusing only on the admirable elements in Gatsby's characterization, is that the protagonist taps some personal belief or desire that many readers have in common and that encourages them to see Gatsby in a wholly positive light. And indeed, I found that most of the critics who idealize Gatsby also idealize what they see as America's uncorrupted past, which they believe Gatsby represents. For these readers, Gatsby stands for a pristine America that was destroyed, as they believe he was, by the selfishness and vulgarity of people like Meyer Wolfsheim and Tom Buchanan.

Richard Chase, for example, sees Gatsby as part of "an earlier pastoral ideal," in that he shares, with Natty Bumppo, Huck Finn, and Ishmael, an "ideal of innocence, escape, and the purely personal code of conduct" (301). Similarly, Marius Bewley argues that the "young dandy of the frontier, dreaming in the dawn and singing to the morning," such as that described by Davy Crockett in 1836, "is a progenitor of Gatsby. It is because of such a traditional American ancestry that Gatsby's romanticism transcends the limiting glamor of the Jazz Age" (128). Thus, Gatsby is seen as "the true heir of the American dream" (Bewley 128) before that dream was corrupted by the influence of the moral wasteland that continues to extend its borders farther into the core of American society. Indeed, one might argue that the American ideology of the "rugged individual" – variations of which include, among other types, the loner, the nonconformist, and the maverick – predispose many readers to see only the admirable side of Gatsby's characterization.

Most of those critics who do not contrast the Jazz Age world of the novel with an earlier, pristine period of American history interpret Gatsby in nonidealized terms. Edwin Fussell, for example, believes that the novel represents Fitzgerald's deliberate and scathing criticism of the American dream and of Jay Gatsby, the representative American. Neither Matthew Bruccoli nor A. E. Dyson idealizes Gatsby, and, like Fussell, they recognize that the protagonist does not transcend the corruption of the world he lives in: rather, he shares it. In other words, many critics seem to interpret Gatsby largely according to their own assumptions about America's past. Perhaps the belief that America was once uncorrupted contributes to the vision of Gatsby as the representative of that pristine past, now gone forever. In any case, the degree to which the critics who idealize Gatsby completely ignore or actively excuse Gatsby's darker side suggests that the projection of our own beliefs and desires, at least when powerfully invited by the text, is stronger than the correctives to interpretation the text provides.

The resistance of many critics to the correctives provided by the novel – the negative data about Gatsby – is mirrored in the text's numerous references to reading materials that don't accomplish anything, that remain unread or unfinished, that fail to impose their reality on their readers. For example, the books in Gatsby's library are uncut, revealing that no one ever has read them. The magazine story Jordan reads to Tom Buchanan is unfinished, "to be continued in our very next issue" (22; ch. l), and apparently doesn't succeed in entertaining her as it is supposed to do, for she reads it in a "murmurous and uninflected" tone (22; ch. 1). The popular novel Nick reads while waiting for Tom and Myrtle to emerge from the bedroom of their apartment "didn't make any sense" to him (34; ch. 2). Gatsby's letter to Daisy from overseas, which was intended to prevent her marriage to Tom, fails its mission entirely and crumbles in her bath. Neither does Nick's letter to Wolfsheim, entreating him to attend Gatsby's funeral, achieve its purpose.

Gatsby has a whole collection of newspaper clippings about the Buchanans despite which "he doesn't know very much about Tom" (84; ch. 4). Nick has bought a whole set of books on banking to help him learn the bond business, but they do him no good: he admits to Gatsby that he's not making much money (87; ch. 5), and he winds up quitting his job when he returns to Minnesota at the end of the summer. Gatsby's boyhood "schedule" for self-improvement, which he wrote at the back of his book on Hopalong Cassidy, a Western icon of the American "good guy," implies a future dedicated to hard work and clean living, yet Gatsby grew up to be a criminal. And ironically, the only text that does the job for which it is intended doesn't have any job to do: Tom is a bigot long before he reads *The Rise of the Coloured Empires*, so the book merely confirms the racist attitude he already has.

As these examples illustrate, the novel shows us what little power texts have to achieve their intended purposes. Even if texts do have meaning independent of readers, that meaning often cannot compete with the meanings we project. In a novel with the degree of indeterminacy we experience in *The Great Gatsby*, the power of readers' projections in the creation of meaning is especially foregrounded, both in the novel's thematic content and in the active reading experience the text promotes. Thus, Fitzgerald's novel illustrates a theory of reading-as-projection as it simultaneously invites us to project our beliefs and desires onto the text. And as a good deal of critical response to the novel suggests, this theory of reading, at least in terms of *The Great Gatsby*, seems quite accurate.

Questions for further practice: reader-response approaches to other literary works

The following questions are intended as models. They can help you use reader-response criticism to interpret the literary works to which they refer or other texts of your choice.

1 As the reader moves through each of the five sections of Kate Chopin's "The Storm" (1898), what reading experience is produced by the story's indeterminacy (for example, actions, characters, and images that are not clearly explained or that could have multiple meanings)? How is this reading experience reflected in the story's thematic content (for example, characters "reading," or decoding, other characters or situations)?

2 What does a line-by-line analysis of Robert Hayden's "Those Winter Sundays" (1975), or any other poem you would like to use, reveal about the ways in which the poem structures the reader's response as an event that occurs in time?

3 What does the history of critical response to Joseph Conrad's *Heart of Darkness* (1902) reveal about the interpretive communities that have analyzed the novel?

You might, for example, differentiate and analyze interpretive communities by determining the interpretive strategies used, the assumptions on which those strategies were based, and the readings that were thereby produced.

4 Using a narrative with a strong focus on issues of gender, race, and/or socio-economic class – for example, Toni Morrison's *The Bluest Eye* (1970) – collect a series of brief response statements from your students (or classmates or book-club members). Response statements should focus on sections of the narrative (selected by you) in which these issues are clearly foregrounded. Use these written responses and what you learn from group discussions to analyze the possible relationships between one's own gender, race, and/or socioeconomic back-ground and one's responses to the narrative's representations of gender, race, and/or socioeconomic background. Although this exercise is speculative rather than scientific, what inferences can you derive from it that might be worth putting into experimental practice in the teaching of literature?

5 Select a text you loved (or hated) as a youngster but that you haven't reread in years. Relying on memory and on any diary entries, letters, or the like that you may have available, summarize the story as you remember it, and write a thor-ough response statement from the perspective of your initial encounter with the book, including the personal experiences and relationships that helped you relate to the book at the time. Now read the book again, and write a current response statement. What does a response-analysis statement, comparing and contrasting your two encounters with the text, reveal about the role of subjective factors and interpretive strategies in the way readers make meaning? How might you apply what you've learned to improve the way literature is taught?

For further reading

Beach, Richard. *A Teacher's Introduction to Reader-Response Theories.* Urbana, IL: NCTE, 1993.

Bleich, David. *Readings and Feelings: An Introduction to Subjective Criticism.* Urbana, IL: NCTE, 1975.

Davis, Todd F., and Kenneth Womack. *Formalist Criticism and Reader-Response Theory.* New York: Palgrave, 2002.

Fish, Stanley. *Is There a Text in This Class? The Authority of Interpretive Communities.* Cambridge, MA: Harvard University Press, 1980. (See especially "Literature in the Reader: Affective Stylistics," 21–67, and "Is There a Text in This Class?" 303–21.)

Holland, Norman. "Hamlet – My Greatest Creation." *Journal of the American Academy of Psychoanalysis* 3 (1975): 419–27. Rpt. in *Contexts for Criticism.* Ed. Donald Keesey. 2nd ed. Mountain View, CA: Mayfield, 1994. 160–65.

——. "Unity Identity Text Self." *PMLA* 90 (1975): 813–22. Rpt. in *Reader-Response Criticism: From Formalism to Post-Structuralism.* Ed. Jane P. Tompkins. Baltimore, MD: The Johns Hopkins University Press, 1980. 118–33.

Mailloux, Steven J. *Interpretive Conventions: The Reader in the Study of American Fiction.* Ithaca, NY: Cornell University Press, 1982.

Phelan, James. *Narrative as Rhetoric: Technique, Audiences, Ethics, Ideology.* Columbus: Ohio State University Press, 1996.

Probst, Robert E. *Response Analysis: Teaching Literature in Secondary School.* 2nd ed. Portsmouth, NH: Heinemann, 2004.

Rabkin, Norman, ed. *Reinterpretations of Elizabethan Drama.* New York and London: Columbia University Press. 1969. (See especially Rabkin's "Forward," v–x; Hapgood's "Shakespeare and the Included Spectator," 117–36; and Booth's "On the Value of *Hamlet*," 137–76.)

Rosenblatt, Louise. *The Reader, the Text, the Poem: The Transactional Theory of the Literary Work.* Carbondale: Southern Illinois University Press, 1978.

Tompkins, Jane P. "An Introduction to Reader-Response Criticism." *Reader-Response Criticism: From Formalism to Post-Structuralism.* Ed. Jane P. Tompkins. Baltimore, MD: The Johns Hopkins University Press, 1980. ix–xxvi.

For advanced readers

Bleich, David. *Subjective Criticism.* Baltimore, MD: The Johns Hopkins University Press, 1978.

Booth, Stephen. *An Essay on Shakespeare's Sonnets.* New Haven, CT: Yale University Press, 1969.

Fish, Stanley. *Surprised by Sin: The Reader in Paradise Lost.* New York: St. Martin's, 1967.

——. *The Stanley Fish Reader.* Ed. Aram H. Veeser. Malden, MA and Oxford: Blackwell, 1999.

Halsey, Katie. *Jane Austen and Her Readers, 1786–1945.* London and New York: Anthem, 2012.

Holland, Norman. *5 Readers Reading.* New Haven, CT: Yale University Press, 1975.

Iser, Wolfgang. *The Implied Reader: Patterns of Communication in Prose Fiction from Bunyan to Beckett.* Baltimore, MD: The Johns Hopkins University Press, 1974.

——. *The Act of Reading: A Theory of Aesthetic Response.* Baltimore, MD: The Johns Hopkins University Press, 1978.

Richards, I. A. *Practical Criticism: A Study of Literary Judgement.* 1929. New York: Harcourt Brace, 1935.

Rosenblatt, Louise. *Making Meaning with Texts: Selected Essays.* Portsmouth, NH: Heinemann, 2005.

Tompkins, Jane, ed. *Reader-Response Criticism: From Formalism to Post-Structuralism.* Baltimore, MD: The Johns Hopkins University Press, 1980.

Notes

1 For example, reader-response anthologies often include an essay from Jonathan Culler's *Structuralist Poetics: Structuralism, Linguistics and the Study of Literature* because of Culler's interest in the way readers use interpretive strategies to make meaning. However, Culler's goal is to map the structures that underlie the interpretive strategies we use, just as structural linguistics seeks to map the structures that underlie the languages we speak. For Culler, underlying structures, not readers, are the ultimate objects of analysis, which is why we'll examine his work in Chapter 7, "Structuralist criticism."

2 This passage, and the hypothesis that the reader's purpose in reading it will influence his or her perception of the passage, is taken from a psychological study conducted by J. A. Pichert and R. C. Anderson. My thanks to Brian White, my colleague at Grand Valley State University, for showing me how it can be used to teach reader-response theory.

3 Although Iser is generally classified as a phenomenological critic (one who studies the activity of reading as an interaction between the author's consciousness and the reader's), his work has a good deal in common with that of Rosenblatt.

4 Rhetorical reader-response criticism, aptly named by James Phelan, might be seen as a more nuanced, linguistically attentive form of transactional reader-response theory. As its name implies, rhetorical reader-response criticism analyzes the rhetorical devices (specific writing strategies) authors use that create particular responses in their readers. In addition to Phelan's *Narrative as Rhetoric*, key

texts include Wayne Booth's *The Rhetoric of Fiction* and Peter Rabinowitz's *Before Reading*. (You will also see these texts elsewhere categorized as examples of rhetorical criticism or narratology.)

5 For similar readings of Gatsby, see, for example, Chase, Gross, Moore, Stern, and Trilling.

6 Critics who believe Nick's viewpoint is trustworthy include, for example, Baxter, Dillon, and Nash. Critics who believe the narrator's perceptions cannot be trusted include, for example, Cartwright, Chambers, and Scrimgeour.

Works cited

Baxter, Charles. "De-faced America: *The Great Gatsby* and *The Crying of Lot 49*." *Pynchon Notes* 7 (1981): 22–37.

Bewley, Marius. "Scott Fitzgerald's Criticism of America." *Sewanee Review* 62 (1954): 223–46. Rpt. in *Modern Critical Interpretations: F. Scott Fitzgerald's* The Great Gatsby. Ed. Harold Bloom. New York: Chelsea, 1986. 11–27.

Bleich, David. *Subjective Criticism*. Baltimore, MD: The Johns Hopkins University Press, 1978.

Booth, Wayne C. *The Rhetoric of Fiction*. Chicago: University of Chicago Press, 1961.

Bruccoli, Matthew J. "*The Great Gatsby* (April 1925)." *Some Sort of Epic Grandeur: The Life of F. Scott Fitzgerald*. New York: Harcourt Brace Jovanovich, 1981. 220–24.

———. "Preface." *The Great Gatsby*. 1925. New York: Macmillan, 1992. vii–xvi.

Burnam, Tom. "The Eyes of Dr. Eckleburg: A Re-Examination of *The Great Gatsby*." *College English* 13 (1952). Rpt. in *F. Scott Fitzgerald: A Collection of Critical Essays*. Ed. Arthur Mizener. Englewood Cliffs, NJ: Prentice Hall, 1963. 104–11.

Cartwright, Kent. "Nick Carraway as an Unreliable Narrator." *Papers on Language and Literature* 20.2 (1984): 218–32.

Chambers, John B. "*The Great Gatsby*." *The Novels of F. Scott Fitzgerald*. London: Macmillan, 1989. 91–126.

Chase, Richard. "*The Great Gatsby*." *The American Novel and Its Traditions*. New York: Doubleday, 1957. 162–67. Rpt. in The Great Gatsby: A Study. Ed. Frederick J. Hoffman. New York: Scribner's, 1962. 297–302.

Conrad, Joseph. *Heart of Darkness*. 1902. New York: Norton, 1988.

Culler, Jonathan. *Structuralist Poetics: Structuralism, Linguistics, and the Study of Literature*. Ithaca, NY: Cornell University Press, 1975.

Dillon, Andrew. "*The Great Gatsby*: The Vitality of Illusion." *Arizona Quarterly* 44.1 (1988): 49–61.

Dyson, A. E. "*The Great Gatsby*. Thirty-Six Years After." *Modern Fiction Studies* 7.1 (1961). Rpt. in *F. Scott Fitzgerald: A Collection of Critical Essays*. Ed. Arthur Mizener. Englewood Cliffs, NJ: Prentice Hall, 1963. 112–24.

Fish, Stanley. "Literature in the Reader: Affective Stylistics." *New Literary History* 2.1 (1970): 123–62. Rpt. in *Reader-Response Criticism: From Formalism to Post-Structuralism*. Ed. Jane P. Tompkins. Baltimore, MD: The Johns Hopkins University Press, 1980. 70–100.

———. *Is There a Text in This Class? The Authority of Interpretive Communities*. Cambridge, MA: Harvard University Press, 1980.

Fitzgerald, F. Scott. *The Great Gatsby*. 1925. New York: Simon & Schuster, 1995.

———. *The Letters of F. Scott Fitzgerald*. Ed. Andrew Turnbull. New York: Scribner's, 1963.

Fussell, Edwin. "Fitzgerald's Brave New World." *ELH, Journal of English Literary History* 19 (1952). Rpt. in *F. Scott Fitzgerald: A Collection of Critical Essays*. Ed. Arthur Mizener. Englewood Cliffs, NJ: Prentice Hall, 1963. 43–56.

Gallo, Rose Adrienne. *F. Scott Fitzgerald*. New York: Ungar, 1978.

Gross, Barry Edward. "Jay Gatsby and Myrtle Wilson: A Kinship." Excerpted in *Gatsby*. Ed. Harold Bloom. New York: Chelsea House, 1991. 23–25.

Hart, Jeffrey. "'Out of it ere night': The WASP Gentleman as Cultural Ideal." *New Criterion* 7.5 (1989): 27–34.

Holland, Norman. "Unity Identity Text Self." *PMLA* 90 (1975): 813–22. Rpt. in *Reader-Response Criticism: From Formalism to Post-Structuralism*. Ed. Jane P. Tompkins. Baltimore, MD: The Johns Hopkins University Press, 1980. 118–33.

Iser, Wolfgang. *The Act of Reading: A Theory of Aesthetic Response*. Baltimore, MD: The Johns Hopkins University Press, 1978.

Le Vot, André. *F. Scott Fitzgerald: A Biography*. Trans. William Byron. Garden City, NY: Doubleday, 1983.

Lowe-Evans, Mary. "Reading with a 'Nicer Eye': Responding to *Frankenstein*." *Case Studies in Contemporary Criticism. Mary Shelley's* Frankenstein. Ed. Johanna M. Smith. Boston, MA: Bedford, 1992. 215–29.

Miller, Arthur. *Death of a Salesman*. New York: Viking, 1949.

Moore, Benita A. *Escape into a Labyrinth: F. Scott Fitzgerald, Catholic Sensibility, and the American Way*. New York: Garland, 1988.

Morrison, Toni. *The Bluest Eye*. New York: Holt, Rinehart, and Winston, 1970.

Nash, Charles C. "From West Egg to Short Hills: The Decline of the Pastoral Ideal from *The Great Gatsby* to Philip Roth's *Goodbye, Columbus*." *Philological Association* 13 (1988): 22–27.

Phelan, James. *Narrative as Rhetoric: Technique, Audiences, Ethics, Ideology*. Columbus: Ohio State University Press, 1996.

Pichert, J. A., and R. C. Anderson. "Taking Different Perspectives on a Story." *Journal of Educational Psychology* 69.4 (1977): 309–15.

Rabinowitz, Peter J. *Before Reading: Narrative Conventions and the Politics of Interpretation*. Ithaca, NY: Cornell University Press, 1987.

Rosenblatt, Louise. *The Reader, the Text, the Poem: The Transactional Theory of the Literary Work*. Carbondale: Southern Illinois University Press, 1978.

Scrimgeour, Gary J. "Against *The Great Gatsby*." *Criticism* 8 (1966): 75–86. Rpt. in *Twentieth-Century Interpretations of* The Great Gatsby. Ed. Ernest Lockridge. Englewood Cliffs, NJ: Prentice Hall, 1968. 70–81.

Shelley, Mary. *Frankenstein*. London: Lackington, Hughes, Harding, Mavor, & Jones, 1818.

Stern, Milton R. *The Golden Moment: The Novels of F. Scott Fitzgerald*. Urbana: University of Illinois Press, 1970.

Trilling, Lionel. "F. Scott Fitzgerald." *The Liberal Imagination*. New York: Viking, 1950. 243–54. Rpt. in The Great Gatsby: A Study. Ed. Frederick J. Hoffman. New York: Scribner's, 1962. 232–43.

7 Structuralist criticism

The first thing you have to get used to when you begin to study structuralism is that common uses of the word *structure* do not necessarily imply structuralist activity. For example, you are not engaged in structuralist activity if you examine the physical structure of a building to discover if it is physically stable or aesthetically pleasing. However, you are engaged in structuralist activity if you examine the physical structures of all the buildings built in urban America in 1850 to discover the underlying principles that govern their composition, for example, principles of mechanical construction or of artistic form. You are also engaged in structuralist activity if you examine the structure of a single building to discover how its composition demonstrates the underlying principles of a given structural system. In the first example of structuralist activity, you're generating a structural system of classification; in the second, you're demonstrating that an individual item belongs to a particular structural class.

In terms of literary study, the same model of structuralist activity holds true. You are not engaged in structuralist activity if you describe the structure of a short story to interpret what the work means or evaluate whether or not it's good literature. However, you are engaged in structuralist activity if you examine the structure of a large number of short stories to discover the underlying principles that govern their composition, for example, principles of narrative progression (the order in which plot events occur) or of characterization (the functions each character performs in relation to the narrative as a whole). You are also engaged in structuralist activity if you describe the structure of a single literary work to discover how its composition demonstrates the underlying principles of a given structural system.

In other words, structuralists are not interested in individual buildings or individual literary works (or individual phenomena of any kind) except in terms of what those individual items can tell us about the structures that underlie and organize all items of that kind. For structuralism sees itself as a human science whose effort is to understand, in a systematic way, the fundamental structures that underlie all human experience and, therefore, all human behavior and production. For this reason, structuralism shouldn't be thought of as a field of study. Rather, it's a method of systematizing human experience that is used in many different fields of study: for example, linguistics, anthropology, sociology, psychology, and literary studies.

For structuralism, the world as we know it consists of two fundamental levels – one visible, the other invisible. The visible world consists of what might be called surface phenomena: all the countless objects, activities, and behaviors we observe, participate in, and interact with every day. The invisible world consists of the structures that underlie and organize all of these phenomena so that we can make sense of them. For example, the English language consists of over a million words, each of which can be pronounced in any number of different ways by different speakers, resulting in millions of different utterances of individual words. How is it possible that native speakers of English master enough of this overwhelming collection of linguistic items to communicate effectively with one another at a rather advanced level of sophistication and at a rather early age?

The answer is fairly simple: while there are millions of individual linguistic surface phenomena (individual words and all the different ways people pronounce them), there is a relatively simple structure underlying all these words, and it is that structure we master. The structure of English vocabulary consists of approximately 31 phonemes (fundamental units of sound recognized as meaningful by native speakers of a language) and the rules of their combination. Most of us are not aware of these phonemes and could not describe the rules of their combination, but our ability to use English vocabulary demonstrates that we have unconsciously internalized these structures. Similarly, our ability to construct simple sentences depends on our internalization, whether or not we are aware of it, of the grammatical structure subject-verb-object. Without a structural system to govern communication, we would have no language at all. Analogously, without the structuring principles that allow us to organize and understand the natural world, the data provided by our five senses would be overwhelming and meaningless. Structuring principles, whether or not we are aware of them, allow us, for example, to differentiate vegetables (they grow in soil; they reproduce; they're edible) from stones (they don't grow; they don't reproduce; they're not edible) and from all other kinds of physical matter. Structuring principles also allow us to differentiate among groups within a given domain, for example, we might differentiate plant life with medicinal properties from plant life with harmful properties from plant life with neutral properties.

As these examples illustrate, the world we live in consists of innumerable events and objects, that is, innumerable surface phenomena. However, the structures that underlie and organize these phenomena are relatively few. Without these structures our world would be chaos.

Where do these structures come from? Structuralists believe they are generated by the human mind, which is thought of as a structuring mechanism. This is an important and radical idea because it means that the order we see in the world is the order we impose on it. Our understanding of the world does not result from our perception of structures that exist in the world. The structures we think we perceive in the world are actually innate (inborn) structures of human consciousness, which we project onto the world in order to be able to deal with the world. It's not that there is no factual reality; it's that there are too many facts to be perceived without conceptual systems to limit and organize them. And those conceptual systems originate within human consciousness. Thus, structuralism sees itself as a science of humankind, for its efforts to discover the structures that underlie the world's surface phenomena – whether we place those phenomena, for example, in the domain of mathematics, biology, linguistics, religion, psychology, or literature – imply an effort to discover something about the innate structures of human consciousness.

Before we go any further, we should take a moment to consider how structuralism defines the word structure. First of all, as we noted earlier, structures aren't physical entities; they're conceptual frameworks that we use to organize and understand physical entities. A structure is any conceptual system that has the following three properties: (1) wholeness, (2) transformation, and (3) self-regulation. Wholeness simply means that the system functions as a unit; it's not merely a collection of independent items. The whole is different from the sum of its parts because the parts working together create something new. To use a physical example, water is a whole that is different from its component parts (hydrogen and oxygen). Transformation means that the system is not static; it's dynamic, capable of change. The system is not merely a structure (a noun); it also structures (a verb). In other words, new material is always being structured by the system. For example, language, a structural system, is capable of transforming its basic components (phonemes) into new utterances (words and sentences). Self-regulation means that the transformations of which a structure is capable never lead beyond its own structural system. The elements engendered by transformations (for example, new linguistic utterances) always belong to the system and obey its laws.

Structuralism assumes that all surface phenomena belong to some structural system, whether or not we are consciously aware of what that system is. The relationship of surface phenomena to structure might be illustrated by the following simplified diagram.

Surface phenomena:

	dog	runs	happily
	tree	appears	green
(words)	Susan	is	tall
	clouds	roll	ominously
	wisdom	comes	slowly

Structure:

(parts of speech)	Noun	Verb	Descriptor

| (rules of combination) | Subject | + | Predicate |

If you read the rows of surface phenomena from left to right, you have a list of individual utterances, such as "dog runs happily" and "tree appears green." However, if you read the columns of the whole diagram from top to bottom, you can see that the surface phenomena, which consist of 15 different items but could consist of many more, are governed by a structure that consists, in this case, of only three parts of speech and two rules of combination. Thus, the utterance "dog runs happily" (or any utterance that follows the same grammatical pattern) is a surface phenomenon governed by the following structure:

Subject (Noun) + *Predicate* (Verb + Descriptor)

The components of a structure (in this example, parts of speech and rules of combination) are always fewer in number than the surface phenomena they underlie because their purpose is to organize, classify, and simplify.

So far, most of my examples have come from language. This is not surprising because language is considered the most fundamental structure of humankind and the one on which most other structures depend. In fact, the field of structural linguistics is the source of most of structuralism's terminology. So let's take a brief look at that field now.

Structural linguistics

Structural linguistics was developed by Ferdinand de Saussure between 1913 and 1915, although his work wasn't translated into English and popularized until the late 1950s. Before Saussure, language was studied in terms of the history of changes in individual words over time, or *diachronically,* and it was assumed that words somehow imitated the objects for which they stood. Saussure realized that we need to understand language not as a collection of individual words with individual histories but as a structural system of relationships among words as they are used at a given point in time, or *synchronically.* This is the structuralist focus. Structuralism doesn't look for the causes or origins of language (or of any other phenomenon). It looks for the rules that underlie language and govern how it functions: it looks for the structure.

In order to differentiate between the structure that governs language and the millions of individual utterances that are its surface phenomena, Saussure called the structure of language *langue* (the French word for *language*), and he called the individual utterances that occur when we speak *parole* (the French word for *speech*). For the structuralist, of course, *langue* is the proper object of study; *parole* is of interest only in that it reveals *langue*. And these terms are used, as well, by structuralists who study literature: as we'll see later, structuralist critics look for the *langue* that structures individual literary works and that structures the system of literature as a whole.

As we saw above, the components of a structure are not merely a collection of independent items: they form a working unit because they exist in relation to one another. They interact. And we are able to perceive those components, as Saussure noted in terms of the structure of language, only because we perceive their difference from one another. *Difference* simply means that our ability to identify an entity (such as an object, a concept, or a sound) is based on the difference we perceive between it and all other entities. For example, if we believed that all objects were the same color, we wouldn't need the word *red* (or *blue* or *green*) at all. Red is red only because we perceive it to be different from blue and green. According to structuralism, the human mind perceives difference most readily in terms of opposites, which structuralists call *binary oppositions:* two ideas, directly opposed, each of which we understand by means of its opposition to the other. For example, we understand up as the opposite of down, female as the opposite of male, good as the opposite of evil, black as the opposite of white, and so on.

Furthermore, unlike his predecessors, Saussure argued that words do not simply refer to objects in the world for which they stand. Instead, a word is a linguistic *sign* consisting, like the two sides of a coin, of two inseparable parts: signifier + signified. A *signifier* is a "sound-image" (a mental imprint of a linguistic sound); the *signified* is the concept to which the signifier refers. Thus, a word is not merely a sound-image (signifier), nor is it merely a concept (signified). A sound-image becomes a word only when it is linked with a concept. Furthermore, the relationship between signifier and signified, Saussure observed, is arbitrary: there is no necessary connection between a given sound-image and the concept to which it refers. There is no reason why the concept of a tree should be represented by the sound-image "tree" instead of by the sound-image "arbre"; the concept of a book is just as well represented by the sound-image "livre" as the sound-image "book." The relationship between signifier and signified is merely a matter of social convention: it's whatever the community using it says it is.

The idea that signifiers, or linguistic sound-images, do not refer to things in the world but to concepts in our mind is crucial for structuralism. As we noted earlier, structuralists believe that our perceptions of the world result from the conceptual framework that is an innate feature of human consciousness. We don't discover the world; we "create" it according to innate structures within the human mind. Given that language is the most fundamental of these structures, and the one through which our beliefs are passed on from one generation to the next, it makes sense that it is through language that we learn to conceive and perceive the world the way we do. This is why learning a new language carries with it the potential to learn to see the world in new ways.

If native speakers of English learn to speak an Eskimo language, for example, they may learn to see snow quite differently, for they will learn that there are many different words for what English calls *snow,* depending on the size and texture of the flake, the density of the snowfall, the angle at which it falls, the direction from which the storm originates, and so on. Similarly, if native speakers of English learn to speak Spanish, they may learn a new way to view the idea of human existence, for they will learn that Spanish has two different verbs for the English verb *to be*: *ser* and *estar*. *Ser* means "to be" in the sense of what one permanently considers oneself. One uses ser to say "I am a human being," "I am a woman," "I am Mexican," and the like. One uses estar to make statements about one's changeable state of being, such as "I am at the supermarket" or "I am a cab driver." And one uses neither *ser* nor *estar* to say "I am hungry" or "I am sleepy," for in Spanish these are not considered states of being. In Spanish one *has* hunger or sleepiness — *tengo hambre* or *tengo sueño* — but these are not states of being. Thus, when speaking a particular language, our attention is drawn to particular aspects of our experience, or, more precisely, particular experiences are generated by that language. In other words, our language *mediates* our experience of our world and ourselves: it determines what we see when we look around us and when we look at ourselves.

The belief in the primacy of language in structuring human experience is of great interest to many students of human culture. Before we examine structuralist approaches to literature, let's take a brief look at two related areas of cultural study in which structuralist thought plays an important role: structural anthropology, which is the comparative study of human cultures, and semiotics, which is the study of sign systems, especially as they apply to the analysis of popular culture. Examples of structuralist activity in both these areas can help us grasp the structuralist enterprise as a whole and prepare us to better understand its applications to literature.

Structural anthropology

Structural anthropology, created by Claude Lévi-Strauss in the late 1950s, seeks the underlying common denominators, the structures, that link all human beings regardless of the differences among the surface phenomena of the cultures to which they belong. Despite the very different ritual forms in which different cultures express important aspects of community life, it seems that all human cultures have some codified process of, for example, mate selection, kinship ties, and initiation into adulthood. While trial by ordeal (for example, being expected to survive on one's own in the wilderness for a specified period of time without the provision of food, clothing, or weapons) certainly appears different from, say, a twenty-first birthday party at a college dormitory, structural anthropologists would argue that the differences are only at the level of surface phenomena or, as structural linguists would put it, at the level of *parole*. For as rites of initiation, both cultural practices have the same underlying structures, the same *langue*. Both involve some sort of ritual ceremony: being bathed by members of the community upon one's return from the wilderness or blowing out candles and being toasted by assembled friends. Both involve some special form of personal decoration: special markings painted on the body or party hats. And both involve eating some sort of special food at the end of the ritual: perhaps the heart of a powerful animal or birthday cake and beer.

The existence of structural similarities among seemingly different myths of different cultures was one of Lévi-Strauss' particular areas of interest. His goal was to discover when "different" myths are actually different versions of the same myth in order to show that human beings from very different cultures share structures of consciousness that project themselves in the formation of structurally similar myths. These structural similarities, he claimed, reveal that certain human concerns cross cultural boundaries, and they include such practical questions as how to define kinship ties (in order to determine rights of inheritance and incest taboos) and such philosophical questions as how to account for the origin of the human race. An illustration of the latter question occurs in Lévi-Strauss' analysis of the Oedipus myth, which he believed embodies the conflict between our knowledge that we are born of sexual union and the persistent belief among many cultures that we are born of the earth, as the Spartoi spring from the soil in the Oedipus myth (or, we might add, as Adam is fashioned from clay in the Bible). Lévi-Strauss argued that there is no "true" or "original" version of any myth. Each version of a given myth is equally valid because each embodies the attempt of all structures to make sense out of an otherwise chaotic world.

When examined from a structuralist perspective, he found that the enormous number of myths from various cultures reduces itself to a rather limited number of what he called *mythemes*, the fundamental units of myths. A mytheme is analogous to a sentence in that it represents a relationship between two or more concepts, often in the form of a subject–verb relationship. A hero killing a monster is an example of a mytheme, as is a hero violating a moral law. Lévi-Strauss defines mythemes as "bundles" of relations because a mytheme consists of all its variants. For example, the mytheme "the hero kills a monster" includes a variety of different kinds of heroes (rich, poor, orphaned, of good family) killing different kinds of monsters (male, female, half-human, sedentary, mobile, land-bound, seafaring, articulate, mute) for different reasons (to win a wife, to save a community, to prove himself). The point is that a structural approach to myth shows us that there is a relatively limited, knowable *langue* (underlying structure) by means of which we can order and understand the otherwise overwhelming number of different myths produced all over the world.

Of course, myths are forms of narrative, and mythemes are therefore narrative structures. So the structural analysis of myths has obvious implications for the structural study of literature. Indeed, as we'll see later in this chapter, in the section entitled "The Structure of Literary Genres," some literary critics believe that all literature consists of the retelling, in various guises, of the same myths.

Semiotics

Just as structural anthropology applies structuralist insights to the comparative study of human cultures, semiotics applies structuralist insights to the study of what it calls sign systems. A *sign system* is a linguistic or nonlinguistic object or behavior (or collection of objects or behaviors) that can be analyzed as if it were a specialized language. In other words, semiotics examines the ways linguistic and nonlinguistic objects and behaviors operate symbolically to "tell" us something. In terms of literary analysis, semiotics is interested in literary conventions: the rules, literary devices, and formal elements that constitute literary structures. We'll examine this topic at some length in the following section, "Structuralism and Literature." So let's concentrate here on the nonlinguistic uses of semiotics, which I think you'll find rather interesting.

For example, the picture of the reclining blond beauty in the skin-tight, black velvet dress on the billboard advertising a particular brand of whiskey, when examined semiotically, "tells" us that those who drink this whiskey (presumably men) will be attractive to seductive, beautiful women like the one on display. As this example illustrates, semiotics is especially useful in analyzing popular culture. Other examples of the kinds of pop-culture sign systems semioticians often examine might include pictorial ads in magazines, popular dances, Disneyland, roller derby, Barbie dolls, automobiles, and, to use two examples analyzed by the famous semiotician Roland Barthes, professional wrestling and the striptease.

Here's a simplified summary of Barthes' semiotic analysis of professional wrestling. He argues that professional wrestling (the brand of wrestling in which the contestants use pseudonyms like Gladiator or The Barbarian, dress in costume, and orchestrate the match in advance) can be viewed as a sign system. It can be interpreted as a language with a very specific purpose: to provide the audience with the cathartic satisfaction of watching justice triumph in a situation that (unlike life) makes it very clear who is good and who is evil. This purpose is revealed in the structural similarities of the matches, regardless of who the contestants are: for example, (1) each wrestler is a clear type (clean-cut All-American, mean-tempered slob, barbarous evildoer, and so on); (2) each match contains contestants who – by their type, their behavior during a particular match, or both – can be clearly identified as the "good guy" and the "bad guy"; and (3) each match ends with the triumph of goodness over evil.

The match, Barthes further observes, greatly resembles the spectacle of ancient Greek theater, as the wrestlers act out their pain, despair, or triumph with exaggerated gestures and grimaces. The exhibition of suffering, defeat, and justice is thus the purpose of the spectacle. The signs we read in order to come to this conclusion include the names, physiques, and costumes of the contestants; their body language in the ring (strutting, cowering, swaggering, menacing, placating, and the like); and their facial expressions (smug, outraged, proud, horrified, triumphant, defeated, and so on). It doesn't matter that the contest is rigged because its purpose is not to determine who is the better wrestler but to enact the kind of spectacle different versions of which have for centuries provided the public with the vicarious release of anger, fear, and frustration.

Now let's take a look at some of the theoretical concepts underlying semiotic analyses like the one just summarized. Semiotics recognizes language as the most fundamental and important sign system. As we saw in our discussion of structural linguistics, a linguistic sign is defined as a union of signifier (sound-image) and signified (concept to which the signifier refers). For semiotics, too, *sign* = signifier + signified. However, as we just saw, semiotics expands the signifier to include objects, gestures, activities, sounds, images – in short, anything that can be perceived by the senses. Clearly, semiotics gives the signifier a wide range of possibilities. However, of the three recognized classes of signs – index, icon, and symbol – semiotics limits its study to signs that function as symbols. Let's pause briefly to examine why this is the case.

An *index* is a sign in which the signifier has a concrete, causal relationship to the signified. For example, smoke signifies fire; a knock on the door signifies that someone is there. An *icon* is a sign in which the signifier physically resembles the signified. For example, a painting is an icon to the extent that the picture resembles the subject it represents. A realistic painting of President Kennedy is an icon. A *symbol* is a sign in which the relationship between signifier and signified is neither natural nor necessary but arbitrary, that is, decided on by the conventions of a community or by the agreement of some group.

As we saw earlier, language is an example of a symbolic sign system. The sound-image "tree" refers to the idea of a tree only because speakers of English have agreed to use it that way. While smoke is an index of fire, and a realistic painting of fire is an icon of fire, the word *fire* is a symbol of fire. There is no quality of fire inherent in the word *fire*. Any other sound-image agreed upon by a group could be used to represent fire. Let's consider a different example. Ice crystals on your living room window are an index of winter. A photograph of a frozen landscape is an icon of winter. However, that same photograph of a frozen landscape or a written description of it in a story (such as Jack London's "To Build a Fire") would function for most English majors as a symbol of death.

Thus, of the three kinds of signs, only the symbol is a matter of interpretation. A group of people doesn't decide that fire produces smoke (an index). It is simply the case that fire produces smoke. A group of people doesn't decide that a realistic portrait of President Kennedy (an icon) will have the same color hair, eyes, skin, and other physical features that the late president had. If the portrait didn't have these physical features, it wouldn't be an icon. But a group of people does have to decide that the color white symbolizes virginity, that the color red symbolizes sexuality, that horns and a pitchfork symbolize Satan, and that the cross symbolizes Christianity.

It is the business of semiotics, then, to isolate and analyze the symbolic function of sign systems, although the objects or behaviors under investigation will often have other functions as well. For example, food and clothing have obvious biological functions (they keep us nourished and protected from the elements) and economic functions (fluctuations in the price of food and clothing influence a society's standard of living). But a semiotician will be interested in food and clothing only to the extent to which they function as sign systems, only to the extent to which they have symbolic content. Furthermore, as a structuralist enterprise, semiotics will analyze a sign system by focusing on a group of similar objects (for example, billboards or pictorial magazine ads or restaurant menus) synchronically (at a given moment in time). To analyze the semiotics of food as it is expressed in restaurant menus, for example, one would not examine menus from a single restaurant as they have changed over time (diachronically). Instead, one would examine a large number of menus produced by different restaurants at the same point in time (synchronically) in order to discover their *semiotic codes*, the underlying structural components that carry a nonverbal cultural message of some sort.

What might a semiotic analysis of restaurant menus reveal? In other words, besides the concrete data about the five food groups communicated by the words on the menu, what nonlinguistic messages are these menus sending? By examining such signs as the menus' color, size, decoration, type of print, size of margins, amount and distribution of blank space, prices, names of dishes (not words like *steak* or *baked potato*, but "tags" like *à la Parisienne* or *Pioneer's*), and the predominance or absence of foods that carry symbolic value (such as hamburgers or caviar), we would probably be able to discover a "fashion industry" of food in which, for example, messages about patrons' self-images are communicated. The semiotics of some menus will send the message, "If you're a well-bred, well-educated person of distinction with an extremely discriminating palate and the wallet to back it up, you will slip into your Guccis, slide into your BMW, and dine with us." Other menus will send the message, "If you're a down-to-earth nonphony who doesn't want to waste time or hard-earned dough on sissified showing off, come on in." Still other menus will send the message, "If you're a patriotic American who still believes in God and Grandma's apple pie, you'll celebrate your family values by eating here."

If you're a movie fan, you might be interested in trying to map out a semiotics of the musical comedy, the murder mystery, or the love story. Similarly, you might want to see if you can discover a semiotics of daytime drama, or "soap operas." For semioticians, anything can be a sign. The whole world of human culture is a "text" waiting to be "read," and structuralism provides the theoretical framework to do it.

Structuralism and literature

For students of literature, structuralism has very important implications. After all, literature is a verbal art: it is composed of language. So its relation to the "master" structure, language, is very direct. In addition, structuralists believe that the structuring mechanisms of the human mind are the means by which we make sense out of chaos, and literature is a fundamental means by which human beings explain the world to themselves, that is, make sense out of chaos. So there seems to be a rather powerful parallel between literature as a field of study and structuralism as a method of analysis.

Our discussion of structuralist approaches to literature will focus on the narrative dimension of literary texts because structuralist criticism deals mainly with narrative. This focus is not as narrow as it may seem at first glance, however, if we remember that narrative includes a long history and broad range of texts, from the simple myths and folk tales of the ancient oral tradition to the complex mélange of written forms found in the postmodern novel. In addition, most drama and a good deal of poetry, though not classified as narrative, nevertheless have a narrative dimension in that they tell a story of some sort. In any event, as we'll see, narratives provide fertile ground for structuralist criticism because, despite their range of forms, narratives share certain structural features, such as plot, setting, and character.

We must keep in mind, however, that structuralism does not attempt to interpret what individual texts mean or even whether or not a given text is good literature. Issues of interpretation and literary quality are in the domain of surface phenomena, the domain of *parole*. Structuralism seeks instead the *langue* of literary texts, the structure that allows texts to make meaning, often referred to as a *grammar* because it governs the rules by which fundamental literary elements are identified (for example, the hero, the damsel in distress, and the villain) and combined (for example, the hero tries to save the damsel in distress from the villain). In short, structuralism isn't interested in what a text means, but in *how* a text means what it means. Thus, *The Great Gatsby*'s Jay Gatsby, Daisy Buchanan, and Tom Buchanan are surface phenomena that draw their meaning from the ways in which they relate to the structures underlying them: respectively, hero, damsel in distress, and villain.

As you may remember from Chapter 6, reader-response critics also focus on how a text means rather than what it means. Indeed, there is some overlap between the two disciplines, for structuralists and reader-response critics would agree that there is a relationship between the underlying structure of the text and the reader's response to it. After all, structuralism believes that the structures we perceive in literature, as in everything else, are projections of the structures of human consciousness. However, you'll recall that the final goal of reader-response criticism is to understand the reader's experience, which structuralists would call a surface phenomenon. In contrast, the final goal of structuralism is to understand the underlying structure of human experience, which exists at the level of *langue*, whether we are examining the structures of literature or speculating on the relationship between the structures of literature and the structures of human consciousness. In other words, reader-response criticism does not seek a universal science that would link innate structures of human consciousness to all human experience, behavior, and production. Structuralism seeks precisely that.

Structuralist approaches to literature have tended to focus on three specific areas of literary studies: the classification of literary genres, the description of narrative operations, and the analysis of literary interpretation. For the sake of clarity, we'll discuss these three areas separately.

The structure of literary genres

Let's begin our discussion of structuralist approaches to genre with a simplified summary of one of its most complex and sweeping examples: what Northrop Frye calls his *theory of myths,* which is a theory of genres that seeks the structural principles underlying the Western literary tradition.[1] *Mythoi* (plural of *mythos*) is a term Frye uses to refer to the four narrative patterns that, he argues, structure myth. These mythoi, he claims, reveal the structural principles underlying literary genres: specifically, comedy, romance, tragedy, and irony/satire.

According to Frye, human beings project their narrative imaginations in two fundamental ways: in representations of an ideal world and in representations of the real world. The ideal world, which is better than the real world, is the world of innocence, plenitude, and fulfillment. Frye calls it the *mythos of summer,* and he associates it with the genre of romance. This is the world of adventure, of successful quests in which brave, virtuous heroes and beautiful maidens overcome villainous threats to the achievement of their goals. Examples of romance you may be familiar with include the chivalrous adventures in Sir Thomas Malory's *Le Morte d'Arthur* (1470), Edmund Spenser's *The Faerie Queene* (1596), John Bunyan's *The Pilgrim's Progress* (1678), and "Sleeping Beauty."

In contrast, the real world is the world of experience, uncertainty, and failure. Frye calls it the *mythos of winter,* and he associates it with the double genre of irony/satire. Irony is the real world seen through a tragic lens, a world in which protagonists are defeated by the puzzling complexities of life. They may try to be heroic, but they never achieve heroic stature. They may dream of happiness, but they never attain it. They're human, like us, and so they suffer. Examples of ironic texts you may have read include Shakespeare's *The Tempest* (1611), Edith Wharton's *The Age of Innocence* (1920), Richard Wright's *Native Son* (1940), and John Steinbeck's *Of Mice and Men* (1937).

Analogously, satire is the real world seen through a comic lens, a world of human folly, excess, and incongruity. In the world of satire, human frailty is mocked, sometimes with biting, merciless humor. Examples of satire you may be acquainted with include Jonathan Swift's *Gulliver's Travels* (1726), George Orwell's *Animal Farm* (1946), the episodes satirizing the abuses of the antebellum American South in Mark

Twain's *Adventures of Huckleberry Finn* (1885), and the passages satirizing conservative complacency and leftist self-delusion in Ralph Ellison's *Invisible Man* (1952).

While romance occurs within an ideal world and irony/satire occurs within the real world, the remaining two mythoi involve a movement from one of these worlds to the other. Tragedy involves a movement from the ideal world to the real world, from innocence to experience, from the mythos of summer to the mythos of winter, and therefore Frye calls tragedy the *mythos of autumn.* In tragedy, a hero with the potential to be superior, like a romantic hero, falls from his romantic height into the real world, the world of loss and defeat, from which he can never rise. Well-known examples of tragedy include Sophocles' *Oedipus the King* (fifth century BC), Shakespeare's *Hamlet* (1601) and *Othello* (1604), and Mary Shelley's *Frankenstein* (1818).

In contrast, comedy involves a movement from the real world to the ideal, from experience to innocence, from the mythos of winter to the mythos of summer, and therefore Frye calls comedy the *mythos of spring.* In comedy, a protagonist caught in a web of threatening, real-world difficulties manages, through various twists in the plot, to overcome the circumstances that have thwarted him and attain happiness. Unlike the villains who obstruct romantic heroes, those who obstruct the protagonists of comedy are absurd and humorous. And in the end, the protagonist moves, usually with his or her beloved, from the cold, troublesome real world to a happier, kinder, gentler fictional space. Examples of comedy you may be familiar with include Shakespeare's *Comedy of Errors* (1590) and *A Midsummer Night's Dream* (1595), William Wycherley's *The Country Wife* (1675), and Henry Fielding's *Tom Jones* (1749).

This description of Frye's framework is merely a skeletal map of his detailed analysis of each mythos and the genre to which it is related. He argues that each genre identifies itself with a particular repertoire of themes, character types, moods, kinds of action, and versions of the plot formulas summarized above. Taken together, the four genres form a kind of master plot, or key to understanding narrative as a whole. And for Frye, that master plot is the structure of the quest, of which each mythos represents one leg.

Frye notes that the traditional quest has four structural components: conflict, catastrophe, disorder and confusion, and triumph. Conflict, he observes, is the basis of romance, which consists of a series of fantastic adventures in which superheroes encounter obstacles. Catastrophe is the basis of tragedy, which consists of the hero's downfall. Disorder and confusion are the basis of irony and satire, which require that confusion and anarchy reign supreme and that effective action be impossible. And triumph is the basis of comedy, in which the protagonist and his or her beloved become the centerpiece of some sort of improved social order. Taken together, then, the genres of romance, tragedy, irony/satire, and comedy – in that order – spell out the structure of what Frye calls a "total quest-myth." Thus, for

Frye, all narrative is structurally related because it's all some version of some part of the quest formula.

Frye calls this method of classification archetypal criticism because it deals with the recurrence of certain narrative patterns throughout the history of Western literature. The word archetype refers to any recurring image, character type, plot formula, or pattern of action. An archetype, then, is a kind of supertype, or model, different versions of which recur throughout the history of human production: in our myths, literature, dreams, religions, and rituals of social behavior. Frye's method thus seeks the structural principles that underlie the Western literary tradition. Indeed, archetypes are themselves structural in nature: in order to be an archetype, an image, character type, or other narrative element must serve as a structural model that generates numerous different versions of itself, that is, numerous different surface phenomena with the same underlying structure. So while the specific content of particular romances, tragedies, ironic/satiric narratives, and comedies is different – that is, their surface phenomena are different – the structure of each genre remains the same.[2]

Another method with which Frye seeks the structural principles that govern genres in the Western literary tradition he calls his theory of modes. His classification of fiction into modes is based on the protagonist's power to take action as it compares to the power of other men and to the power of their environment (nature and/or society). Frye's modes are also determined according to whether the protagonist is superior in kind to others (of a type beyond the reach of ordinary people, like gods or demigods) or merely superior in degree (having the same positive attributes that all humans are capable of but having them to a greater degree). Perhaps a chart will help clarify Frye's system.

Protagonist's power	Fictional mode	Character type
1. Superior in kind to both men and their environment	Myth	Divine beings
2. Superior in degree to both	Romance	Heroes
3. Superior in degree to men but not to their environment	High mimesis (imitation of life, like that found in epic and tragedy)	Leaders
4. Superior in no way	Low mimesis (imitation of life, like that found in comedy and realism)	Common people
5. Inferior	Irony	Antiheroes

Frye notes that, for the most part, myths, though early forms of narrative, fall outside the usual literary categories. For this reason, and because it seems somewhat odd to include comedy and realism under the same heading, Robert Scholes offers a different version of Frye's modes, one he believes will provide a more clear and useful basis of differentiation among genres by eliminating the nonliterary mode of myth and inserting a new category in order to account for the difference between comedy and realism. Here's a chart outlining Scholes' system of classification.

Protagonist's power	Fictional mode	Character type
1. Superior in kind to both men and their environment	Romance	Heroes
2. Superior in degree to men but not to their environment	High mimesis (imitation of life, like that found in epic and tragedy)	Leaders
3. Equal in degree to men and their environment	Middle mimesis (imitation of life, like that found in realism)	Ordinary people like ourselves
4. Inferior in degree to men and their environment	Low mimesis (imitation of life, like that found in comedy)	Comic and pathetic figures
5. Inferior in kind	Irony	Antiheroes

As these two charts indicate, different structuralists can have different ways of categorizing the same material. And there are many more structuralist theories of genre than those outlined here. This kind of structural analysis is an ongoing attempt to classify and thereby understand the relationships among literary texts by finding the most useful way to represent the structural system governing literature as a whole.

The structure of narrative (structuralist narratology)

Structuralist analyses of narrative examine in minute detail the inner "workings" of literary texts in order to discover the fundamental structural units (such as units of narrative progression) or functions (such as character functions) that govern texts' narrative operations. A good deal of literary criticism that today goes under the name *narratology* bears a strong family resemblance to this kind of structuralist approach. We'll limit ourselves to three examples that are representative of the field in general and that I think you'll find most useful at this stage in your understanding of structuralism: the work of A. J. Greimas, Tzvetan Todorov, and Gérard Genette.

Greimas observes that human beings make meaning by structuring the world in terms of two kinds of opposed pairs: "A is the opposite of B" and "-A (the negation of A) is the opposite of -B (the negation of B)." In other words, we perceive every entity as having two aspects: its opposite (the opposite of love is hate) and its negation (the negation of love is the absence of love). He believes that this fundamental structure of binary oppositions, consisting of four components arranged in two pairs, shapes our language, our experience, and the narratives through which we articulate our experience.

In our narratives, this structure is embodied in the form of plot formulas, such as conflict and resolution, struggle and reconciliation, and separation and union. These plot formulas are carried out by means of *actants*, or character functions, which are slots filled by the actual characters (surface phenomena) in a given story. For example, in *The Great Gatsby*, we might argue that Jay Gatsby functions as the quester hero, Daisy Fay Buchanan as the object of the hero's quest, Nick Carraway as the hero's helper, and Tom Buchanan as the hero's opponent.

For Greimas, the forwarding of the plot – the movement from conflict to resolution, struggle to reconciliation, separation to union, and so forth – involves the transfer of some entity (such as an object or a quality) from one actant to another. For example, Daisy is transferred from Tom to Gatsby or, more precisely, from Gatsby to Tom to Gatsby then back to Tom. And, to consider a more subtle example, Gatsby's overwhelming loss – of Daisy, of his dream of happiness, of his life – is transferred to Nick in the form of the latter's profound disillusionment at the end of his sojourn in New York. Thus, the fundamental structure of narrative is the same as the fundamental structure of language: subject-verb-object. This basic narrative grammar generates the following three patterns of plots by aligning what Greimas sees as the six fundamental actants into three pairs of oppositions.

Actants	Plot types
Subject–Object	Stories of Quest/Desire (a subject, or hero, searches for an object: a person, thing, or state of being)
Sender–Receiver	Stories of Communication (a sender – a person, god, or institution – sends the subject in search of the object, which the receiver ultimately receives)
Helper–Opponent	Subplots of Stories of Quest/Desire or Communication (a helper aids the subject in the quest; an opponent tries to hinder the subject)

Finally, in order to account for various possible narrative sequences, Greimas suggests the following structures, which he derived from his study of folk tales.

1 *Contractual structures* involve the making/breaking of agreements or the establishment/violation of prohibitions and the alienation or reconciliation that follows.
2 *Performative structures* involve the performance of tasks, trials, struggles, and the like.
3 *Disjunctive structures* involve travel, movement, arrivals, and departures.

We might explore, for instance, the ways in which *The Great Gatsby* conforms to Greimas' notion of contractual structures, including both agreements made and broken (such as those between Gatsby and Daisy, Tom and Daisy, Nick and Jordan, and Myrtle and George) and the numerous violations of prohibitions occurring in the novel that are followed by alienation.

Greimas uses his system to analyze the works of twentieth-century French author Georges Bernanos, concluding that the novelist creates a world in which all conflicts reduce to the fundamental symbolic conflict between life and death. Furthermore, this key conflict expresses itself, Greimas suggests, in the following

Available experiences	Possible transformations	Ideological choices
1. joy/pain	Truth: revolt + acceptance	Life: joy + pain
2. boredom/disgust	Lie: refusal + resignation	Death: boredom + disgust

structure (which I have simplified) that governs the author's fictional universe. The grammar of Bernanos' novels thus structures a world in which we can avoid feeling pain only if we are willing to give up joy as well, for the two are linked: our capacity to feel joy makes us vulnerable to pain. Thus, we must either accept the truth that life is a double-edged sword of joy and pain (though we tend, initially, to revolt against that truth), or we must refuse the truth and resign ourselves to the only alternative: boredom and disgust, which are a kind of emotional death we choose in order to protect ourselves from the emotional risks of life.

In a manner similar to that of Greimas, Todorov draws an analogy between the structural units of narrative – such as elements of characterization and plot – and the structural units of language: parts of speech and their arrangement in sentences and paragraphs.

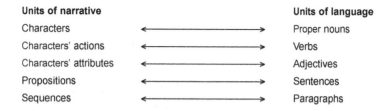

Units of narrative		Units of language
Characters	←————————————→	Proper nouns
Characters' actions	←————————————→	Verbs
Characters' attributes	←————————————→	Adjectives
Propositions	←————————————→	Sentences
Sequences	←————————————→	Paragraphs

A *proposition* is formed by combining a character with an irreducible action (for example, "X kills Y" or "X arrives in town") or irreducible attribute (for example, "X is evil" or "X is queen"), that is, an action or attribute in its most basic form. A *sequence* is a string of propositions that can stand on its own as a story. The structure of the most basic sequence is (1) attribution, (2) action, (3) attribution: the protagonist starts out with an attribute (for example, he is unloved), and by means of an action (he seeks love) that attribute is transformed (he is loved or, at least, has learned something important as a result of his quest). A story must contain at least one sequence, though it may contain many sequences. Todorov further subdivides his structural system into such categories as *negation* (the absence of an action or attribute), *comparison* (the presence of an action or attribute to different degrees), and *modes* (the qualification of an action or attribute, such as occurs when an action or attribute is desired, feared, expected, done unwillingly, and the like).

This "grammar" of narrative allows Todorov to analyze texts in terms of what he sees as their fundamental narrative properties. Once a text's propositions are discovered – by combining each character (noun) with an action (verb) or attribute (adjective) – the kinds of actions and attributes that recur in a text can be categorized as can the kinds of propositions and the relations between propositions. For example, in his analysis of the stories in Boccaccio's *The Decameron* (1350), Todorov finds, among other things, that all attributes can be reduced to three categories of adjectives: *states* (unstable attributes, such as happiness and unhappiness), *qualities* (more stable attributes, such as good and evil), and *conditions* (the most stable attributes, such as one's sex, religion, or social position).

Especially significant, I think, is his claim that all actions in *The Decameron* can be reduced to three verbs: to modify, to transgress, and to punish. For this discovery led to his observation of a significant pattern of recurrence in the tales: changes are continually made, and sins continually go unpunished. This pattern, and his knowledge of history, led Todorov to speculate that there is a connection between the values operating in Boccaccio's stories and those of the culture in which he lived. Todorov suggests that, in both *The Decameron* and Boccaccio's world, a new system of values was emerging, one that appreciated the personal daring and initiative associated with the free-enterprise system of capitalism, which was beginning to replace the older, more restrictive system of commerce.

It is important to note that both Greimas and Todorov derive their frameworks from and apply them to a large body of materials — Greimas uses all the works of a single author, and Todorov uses a long work that consists of a collection of tales — because they want to produce a structural system useful for understanding narrative in general. Similarly, Genette develops his narrative theory by means of a detailed study of Marcel Proust's seven-volume work, *Remembrance of Things Past* (1927).

Genette begins by differentiating among three levels of narrative that generally have been included under the umbrella of the term *narrative*: story, narrative, and narration.

Story consists of the succession of events being narrated. The story thus provides the content of the tale in the order in which events "actually happened" to the characters, an order that does not always coincide with the order in which they are presented in the narrative.

Narrative refers to the actual words on the page, the discourse, the text itself, from which the reader constructs both story and narration. The narrative is produced by the narrator in the act of narration.

Narration refers to the act of telling the story to some audience and thereby producing the narrative. However, just as the narrator almost never corresponds exactly to the author, the audience (*narratee*) almost never corresponds exactly to the reader.

For example, in *The Great Gatsby*, Nick describes his summer in New York to some audience (narration). In doing so, he presents a verbal discourse, which we see as the words on the page (narrative). And that discourse represents the events in which Nick appears as a character (story).

Genette's work focuses on narrative, the words on the page, but he notes that all three levels work together. That is, for the purposes of analysis, he separates aspects of a text that don't operate separately, but he does so in order to see how they interact. And he observes that story, narrative, and narration interact by means of three qualities, which he calls tense, mood, and voice.

1 *Tense* is the arrangement of events in the narrative with respect to time. That arrangement involves the notions of order, duration, and frequency.
   a *Order* refers to the relationship between the chronology of the story (the order in which the events of the story occur in the fictional world) and the chronology of the narrative (the order in which the narrative presents those events). For example, Jay Gatsby's story consists, in part, of the following facts in the following order: he was born to poor farmers, ran away from home, worked for Dan Cody, courted Daisy, went to war, returned, and set about acquiring a fortune and reclaiming Daisy. However, the narrative presents these events in a different order. For example, we don't learn about his boyhood until chapter 6.
   b *Duration* refers to the relationship between the length of time over which a given event occurs in the story and the number of pages of narrative devoted to describing it. A character's trip to Europe may last five years in the story, but the narrative may describe it in five lines. Conversely, a conversation between lovers may take five minutes in the story, but the narrative may describe it in five pages. Thus, duration is what produces the sense of narrative speed.
   c *Frequency* involves the relationship between the ways in which events may be repeated in the story (the same event may occur more than once) and in the narrative (a single event may be described more than once).
2 *Mood* is the atmosphere of the narrative created by distance and perspective.
   a *Distance* is created when the narrator is one of the characters in the narrative, a "go-between" through whose consciousness the story is filtered. The more intrusive the narrator, the greater the distance between narration and story. Conversely, the least distance is created when we are unaware of the narrator's presence, when a tale seems to "tell itself." Distance is also created by the absence of descriptive detail. The less detail given, the less the effect of reality is created, and the greater the sense of distance between narration and story. The more detail given, the less distance exists. Thus, the least distance, or the greatest imitation of life, is produced by maximum information and minimum presence of the narrator.
   b *Perspective* refers to point of view, or the eyes through which we see any given part of the narrative. Although the narrator may be speaking, the point of view may be that of one of the other characters, and the feelings of a point-of-view character may be different from those of the narrator telling that character's story.

3 *Voice* refers to the voice of the narrator. The voice we hear (the narrator's) may not be the same as the eyes we see through (the perspective). When we analyze voice, we analyze the relationship of the narrator (the act of narration) to the story being told and to the narrative (the way the story is being told). Voice helps us determine the narrator's attitude toward the story and reliability.

It is interesting to note that tense, mood, and voice are all aspects of verbs. For in Genette's opinion, all fiction functions like an expanded verb: all narrative reduces to action. Although his definitions may seem "cut and dried," he generates his categories, in large part, to be able to show when a literary text creates its effects by "violating" those categories. In his study of *Remembrance of Things Past*, for example, Genette shows how Proust creates an effect of intense immediacy, of great intimacy between narration and story, by combining maximum information with maximum presence of narrator, an effect that is traditionally produced by combining maximum information with minimum presence of narrator. Thus, Genette underscores the notion that systems of classification should be used to help us illuminate the complexity of literary works, not obscure that complexity through oversimplification.

Of course, the work of Greimas, Todorov, and Genette is far more complex than this summary implies. Our purpose here is simply to understand the kinds of analyses made possible by structuralist narratology. It might be helpful to think of this approach as looking at narrative through a microscope in order to identify its smallest units and see how they work. Structuralist narratology thus offers us a way of seeing the details of narrative operations and a vocabulary with which to describe them.

It is important to note, however, that Greimas, Todorov, and Genette, once they identify the formula that structures a narrative or group of narratives, use that formula to address larger questions about literary meaning and its relationship to human life. That is, once we identify the formula of a given narrative or group of narratives, we must then ask ourselves, "How does this formula reveal a pattern in narrative in general, and what does this pattern imply about human experience or the structures of human consciousness?" In other words, what does a given narrative pattern contribute to our knowledge of the relatively small number of stories human beings have been telling themselves for thousands of years (though the stories may take hundreds of different forms, they are still, structurally, the same stories) in order to help themselves cope with life? For at the heart of structuralist analysis of any kind is the desire to understand what it means to be human.

The structure of literary interpretation

According to Jonathan Culler, the structural system that governs both the writing and interpretation of literary texts is the system of rules and codes, which we have consciously or unconsciously internalized, that tell us how to make meaning when we read literature. Some of these rules and codes are taken for granted by the public at large (for example, that a fairy tale is a fictional story not to be taken literally), but many of them are learned in the classroom (for example, that the use of nature imagery reveals a good deal about a work's theme).

In America, this system of rules and codes is part of the Western literary tradition as it has been passed on by our universities, and our individual *literary competence* is determined by how much of the system we have internalized. The point is not that any two competent readers would necessarily agree in their interpretations of a particular work but that both interpretations would be guided by the same structural system of interpretive rules and codes. Culler thus believes that what we refer to as the structure of literature is really the structure of the system of interpretation we bring to it. His effort is to unearth this structural system and show us how it operates. Perhaps the best way to acquaint you with the structural system Culler has identified is simply to describe some of its major components, which he has named as follows: the convention of distance and impersonality, naturalization, the rule of significance, the rule of metaphorical coherence, and the rule of thematic unity.

The convention of distance and impersonality is an assumption we make as soon as we see that we are reading a literary work, even if that work is in the form of nonliterary writing, such as a letter (like Barthelme's story "The Sandman," 1972) or a journal (like Doris Lessing's *Memoirs of a Survivor*, 1974). As soon as we know we're reading a piece of fiction or poetry rather than a letter or journal, we read it differently than we would read a real letter or journal: we know we're entering a fictional world, and this creates a fictional distance, so to speak, that carries with it a kind of impersonality that would not be present if we knew we were reading a factual account of a human being's personal experience. The convention of distance and impersonality is the code that enables all the following codes to come into play.

Naturalization is the process by which we transform the text so that the strangeness of its literary form, which we don't see in everyday writing – for example, rhyme; meter; divisions into stanzas, acts, or chapters; and interior monologues – makes sense in terms of the world we live in. When we read, for example, "My darling is a ripening pear," we don't think the narrator is in love with a piece of fruit; we assume he is speaking metaphorically. And we appreciate the beauty and strangeness of the literary language even as we translate it into an idea we understand. Furthermore, we generally assume we are hearing the voice of a narrator, rather than that of the author, and it is to the narrator's point of view that we ascribe any inconsistencies or biases in the narration. Other ways in which we naturalize the text include recognizing the codes that tell us how to interpret such literary elements as characters and symbols. For example, in real life we don't believe that a person with fine, clear skin necessarily has a fine, clear soul, but we would accept this correlation in certain kinds of fiction.

The rule of significance is the assumption that the literary work expresses a significant attitude about some important problem, and so we pay attention to what it says in ways that we wouldn't do with other kinds of writing. If our spouse left us a note saying "I've gone to the antique store in search of a lamp," we'd probably take the message at face value: our spouse wants to buy an antique lamp. If this same sentence were broken into a four-line poem, however, the words "I've gone," "in search," "antique," and "lamp" would suddenly take on greater resonance. We might conclude, for example, that the poem represents the desire to escape some unsatisfactory situation in the present in order to return to the past and find some kind of enlightenment that can't be found in the here and now.

The rule of metaphorical coherence is the requirement that the two components of a metaphor (the vehicle, or metaphorical term, and the tenor, or subject to which the metaphor is applied) have a consistent relationship within the context of the work. Imagine, for example, a story about the plight of a penniless, aging, Native American drifter who, at the close of the tale, falls asleep forever under a freezing sky. In this context, the description of a pale, winter sunset could be a metaphor for the death of the character and perhaps for the end of an era, but it couldn't very well be a metaphor for the restful sleep that precedes the hopeful beginning of a bright new life.

The rule of thematic unity is the chief reason why there is a rule of metaphorical coherence, for the rule of thematic unity is our expectation that the literary work has a unified, coherent theme, or main point. In fact, it is because we expect a literary work to have thematic unity that we almost always manage to find it or, more precisely, construct it when we interpret the text. We tend to create thematic unity, Culler observes, by means of certain procedures, which include, among others, (1) theme as a binary opposition (good versus evil), (2) theme as the resolution of a binary opposition (good conquers evil), and (3) theme as the displacement of a binary opposition by a third term (good-versus-evil is absorbed by an all-encompassing Nature, as we see in Whitman's "Song of Myself," 1855).

It's not difficult to see why Culler's structuralist approach is of interest to reader-response theorists. Like the social reader-response theory of Stanley Fish discussed in Chapter 6, Culler's approach asserts that our understanding of literature is based on the interpretive strategies we bring to the text. As we noted earlier, structuralists believe that we "create" the world we see by projecting onto it our structures of consciousness. Apply this belief to literature, and the result is the same as the reader-response notion that we "create" the literary text as we read it. But the structuralist move Culler makes is his question, "What is the structure that underlies the surface phenomena of our interpretations?" And to find the answer, he examines interpretation as a structural system. Unlike reader-response theorists,

Culler examines the *langue*, the structural system of rules and codes, that operate (consciously or unconsciously) when authors write and readers interpret within the Western literary tradition.

Even the small sampling of approaches offered here illustrates the wide range of structuralist methodologies, both in terms of the kinds of theoretical frameworks structuralists use and the kinds of texts, literary and otherwise, they analyze.

Some questions structuralist critics ask about literary texts

The following questions are offered to summarize structuralist approaches to literature. Keep in mind that structuralists don't try to determine whether or not a literary text constitutes great literature. Their focus is on the structural systems that underlie and generate literary meaning.

1 Using a specific structuralist framework (such as the ones we examined by Frye and Scholes), how should the text be classified in terms of its genre?
2 Using a specific structuralist framework (such as that of Greimas, Todorov, or Genette), analyze the text's narrative operations. Can you speculate about the relationship between the text's "grammar" and that of similar texts? Can you speculate about the relationship between the text's grammar and the culture from which the text emerged?
3 Using Culler's theory of literary competence, what rules or codes of interpretation must be internalized in order to "make sense" of the text? Depending on the text in question, it might be necessary to identify codes in addition to those specified by Culler. (In other words, what does a given text contribute to our knowledge of literary competence?)
4 What are the semiotics of a given category of cultural phenomena, or "texts," such as high school football games, television and/or magazine ads for a particular brand of perfume (or any other consumer product), or even media coverage of a historical event, such as Operation Desert Storm, an important legal case, or a presidential election campaign? In other words, analyze the nonverbal messages sent by the "texts" in question, as well as the semiotic implications of such verbal "tags" as "Desert Storm" or "White Diamonds" (a brand of perfume). What is being communicated, and how exactly is it being communicated?

Depending on the literary text or texts in question, we might ask one or any combination of these questions. Or we might come up with a useful question not listed here. These are just starting points to get us thinking about productive ways to approach literature from a structuralist perspective. Remember that not all structuralists will interpret the same texts in the same way, even if they use the same approach. As in every field, even expert practitioners disagree. Our goal is to use structuralism to help us see some fundamental connections among the structures of literary texts, between the structure of literature and that of language, and among the structures of cultural phenomena of every sort, including, for example, literature, mythology, art, social rituals, sports, forms of entertainment, and advertising. The construction of a systematic, universal terminology to describe the fundamental structures of literature offers us the opportunity to make clearer and more rigorous comparisons as we try to increase our understanding of the processes at work in literary production and literary history.

The following structuralist reading of F. Scott Fitzgerald's *The Great Gatsby* is offered as an example of what a structuralist analysis of that novel might yield. Drawing on Todorov's notion of narrative "grammar," I will argue that all of the action in the novel can be reduced to three verbs: to seek, to find, and to lose, which grammar can be interpreted, I think, as the modern novel's rejection of the traditional seek-and-find quest formula. In addition, I will suggest that *The Great Gatsby's* seek-find-lose grammar offers us an interesting way to use Frye's theory of mythoi to analyze the relationship between the novel's two principal plot-lines, those concerning Jay Gatsby and Nick Carraway.

"Seek and ye shall find" … and then lose: a structuralist reading of *The Great Gatsby*

In many ways, F. Scott Fitzgerald's *The Great Gatsby* (1925) is so carefully organized that the novel's structure seems to draw attention to itself. A brief description of the text's structural symmetry should illustrate this point. The narrative revolves around Jay Gatsby's pursuit, attainment, and loss of Daisy Fay Buchanan. As we learn in flashback, this failed quest is a replay of the same pursuit, attainment, and loss of the same beloved that occurred in Gatsby's youth, before the novel opens. Each failed quest occurs during the compressed period of a few months, and in both instances Gatsby disguises his true origins, so there is a kind of narrative symmetry between the structure of fictional past and fictional present. Another kind of structural symmetry is produced when Gatsby is reunited with Daisy in chapter 5, which is at the physical center of the novel's nine chapters and at the temporal center of the narrative action: it is late July, the midpoint between Nick's first visit to the Buchanans' new home in early June, when "the history of the summer really begins" (10; ch. 1), and Gatsby's death in early September.

In addition, the narrative unfolds in a pattern of similarly structured triads, bounded at the beginning and end of the novel by narrator Nick Carraway's meditative reflections on the events he recounts:

Opening: Narrator's opening meditation (ch. 1)

   I: The world of wealth described (ch. 1)

II: The world of poverty described (ch. 2)

III: Intersection of I and II – rich and poor mingle at Gatsby's party (ch. 3)

I: Nick hears story of Gatsby's past (ch. 4)

II: Nick hears story of Daisy's past (ch. 4)

III: Intersection of I and II – Gatsby and Daisy reunite at Nick's house (ch. 5)

I: The eternal triangle appears – Tom, Daisy, and Gatsby at Gatsby's party (ch. 6)

II: The eternal triangle explodes – the confrontation scene in the New York hotel room (ch. 7)

III: Intersection of I and II – three disasters result

    A. Myrtle Wilson's death (ch. 7)

    B. Gatsby's death (ch. 8)

    C. George Wilson's death (ch. 8)

Closing: Narrator's closing meditation (ch. 9)

Of course, any of these narrative patterns could serve as a starting point for a structural analysis of *The Great Gatsby*. The particular structure I want to focus on, however, is the one I believe is at the foundation of all the others: the novel's narrative "grammar," which is illuminated, I think, by the use of Tzvetan Todorov's schema of propositions. As you'll recall, according to this framework we try to discover how the text is structured by the pattern of relations among recurring actions (which are analogous to verbs) and attributes (which are analogous to adjectives) associated with particular characters (which are analogous to nouns). In other words, we try to discover how the text is structured by the repetition of the same grammar, the same formula, the same "sentence," so to speak.

In the case of *The Great Gatsby*, I think all the action can be reduced to three verbs: "to seek," "to find," and "to lose." These three verbs produce, in turn, the repetition of two related "sentences," or narrative patterns: (1) "X seeks, finds, and then loses Y," or simply (2) "X seeks but doesn't find Y." (X = the character in question; Y = a desired person, object, state, or condition.) In both cases, of course, the overall narrative formula is the same:

1   Attribute: X lacks Y
2   Action: X seeks Y
3   Attribute: X lacks Y
    (either because X doesn't find Y or because X finds but then loses Y)

I'd like to begin my analysis of the novel by revealing how this formula structures the text as a whole by structuring the narratives of the main characters. Then I will suggest that the seek-find-lose grammar can be seen as the modern novel's rejection of the traditional seek-and-find quest formula. Finally, I will argue that this narrative grammar offers us an interesting application of Northrop Frye's theory of mythoi. For in *The Great Gatsby*, this grammar produces a narrative that embeds the mythos of summer (Gatsby's story, the genre of romance) within the mythos of winter (Nick's story, the genre of irony). And although the mythos of summer is eventually overridden by the mythos of winter, the latter structure remains "haunted" by the former.

Of course, the "master plot" of the novel's seek-find-lose formula is the story of its title character, Jay Gatsby. As we noted above, he seeks, finds, and loses Daisy twice: once in his youth, before the novel begins, and again during the summer that Nick lives next door to him on West Egg. In addition, the narrative of Gatsby's pursuit, attainment, and loss of Daisy is accompanied by the narrative of his pursuit, attainment, and loss of the new life he sought when he changed his name from James Gatz to Jay Gatsby. His seek-find-lose story is thus repeated not merely in two different time periods but in terms of two different goals: love and social status. Both are lost to him, of course, when he dies. Furthermore, Gatsby's narrative provides the framework on which the narratives of the other characters are "strung," so to speak: it is in the unfolding of Gatsby's story by Nick that the other stories are told.

Daisy's story mirrors not only the seek-find-lose pattern of Gatsby's narrative but its repetitive quality as well. As we learn in flashback, the young Daisy Fay sought excitement, found it in the form of her love for Lieutenant Jay Gatsby, then lost him to the war. Next she sought emotional security, found it in the form of marriage to Tom Buchanan, then lost it when she soon discovered that he was chronically unfaithful to her. Finally, she craves the attention that she isn't getting from Tom, finds it in Gatsby, and loses it when he dies (or, perhaps more precisely, when Tom reveals that Gatsby isn't the man Daisy thought he was).

Similar seek-find-lose grammars structure the narratives of Tom Buchanan, Myrtle Wilson, and her husband George. As a young man, Tom sought ego gratification, found it in his career as a college football hero, then lost it when he graduated from college. As a married man, Tom seeks a similar kind of ego gratification – the adoration of "inferiors" – by seducing a series of working-class women, the latest incarnation of which is Myrtle Wilson. In each case, however, the ego gratification lasts only as long as the affair, so Tom continually returns to the position of the unfulfilled seeker.

Analogously, Myrtle Wilson seeks escape from the boredom and economic poverty of her marriage, finds it in Tom Buchanan, then loses it when she is killed in the hit-and-run accident. Of course, even if she had lived she would not have succeeded in marrying Tom. His intention to avoid a permanent commitment to Myrtle is evident in his lie to her that Daisy's Catholicism would never permit her to divorce him. Operating as a shadow behind Myrtle's seek-find-lose narrative is that of George Wilson, who sought love, found it in his marriage to Myrtle, and lost it when she became unfaithful to him with Tom (or, perhaps more precisely, when she learned that George didn't own the suit in which he was married).

As a backdrop to these seek-find-lose grammars is a subset of seek-find-lose: seek-but-don't-find. We see this pattern operating in George's pursuit of financial security, which is an impossible dream, and in Jordan's pursuit of social and financial security, which seem ever to elude her grasp just as the winning putt remains, of late, just beyond her reach. The grammar of seek-but-don't-find also structures the setting in the form of the numerous minor characters who populate it. Mr. McKee seeks but doesn't find success as a photographer. Myrtle's sister Catherine seems a permanently dissatisfied seeker: her trip to Monte Carlo was a financial disaster; her "solid sticky bob of red hair," "complexion powdered milky white," and "rakish" painted eyebrows "blurred" by the plucked hairs growing back (34; ch. 2) are a fashion disaster; and her search for a good time seems merely to take her from one scene of drunken chaos to another. Even Gatsby's innumerable party guests have the air of dissatisfied wanderers, coming to his mansion from parts unknown, seeking something new in the latest dances, and seeking excitement, or perhaps just escape from their dissatisfaction, at the bottom of a bottle.

Certainly the most well-developed seek-but-don't-find narrative in the novel is that of Nick Carraway. Nick's summer in New York is just the latest in a series of unsuccessful pursuits. His experience in World War I apparently involved the pursuit of excitement from which he returned more empty-handed than when he left: "I enjoyed [World War I] so thoroughly that I came back restless. Instead of being the warm center of the world the Middle West now seemed like the ragged edge of the universe – so I decided to go East and learn the bond business" (7; ch. 1). As his narrative reveals, of course, his venture in the bond business, and in the East in general, also follows the seek-but-don't-find pattern: he abandons both within a few months of his arrival in New York. Neither is his search for the right woman successful. He leaves his hometown, in part, to escape a woman he was feeling pressured to marry. He apparently cares so little about the woman at work with whom he has an affair that he allows her brother's "mean looks in [his] direction" (61; ch. 3) to drive him off. And his relationship with Jordan Baker is rather clearly an infatuation with no staying power: he tires of her as soon as he tires of the Buchanans.

Nick's most important seek-but-don't-find pattern, however, seems to be his unfulfilled search for a purpose in life. Throughout his narrative, Nick seems "at loose ends." At the age of 30 he is still without a stable career, without a serious love interest, and without a home of his own. And he feels their lack acutely: "Thirty – the promise of a decade of loneliness, a thinning list of single men to know, a thinning briefcase of enthusiasm, thinning hair" (143; ch. 7). In fact, he's still being supported by his wealthy father, who "agreed to finance [him] for a year" (7; ch. 1) while he learned the bond business. It's no wonder he seems so fascinated by Gatsby, for Gatsby has, to an extreme degree, the quality Nick lacks most, the quality he is unable to acquire despite his best efforts: purpose.

It might be interesting to think of the seek-find-lose grammar of *The Great Gatsby* as the modern novel's rejection of the traditional quest formula. The traditional quest is structured by a seek-and-find grammar. Even if the hero dies achieving the goal of his quest, or attempting to achieve it, the world is transformed in some way by his effort: something important is found. Thus, the basic plot formula Todorov isolated consists of an attribute transformed by an action: (1) attribute (for example, the protagonist is unsuccessful), (2) action (he seeks success), (3) attribute (he is successful or, at least, has learned something important as a result of his quest). The traditional quest is thus redemptive in some way.

As we have seen, in Fitzgerald's novel, the characters' attributes are not transformed by the hero's action nor by their own actions. At the novel's end the characters have the same attribute – the same lack – with which they began, and apparently nothing is learned in the process. Gatsby is dead, presumably without having admitted to himself that Daisy has abandoned him and without living long enough to benefit from that insight had it occurred. Myrtle and George are dead, without having learned anything from their experience. The last time we see Jordan, she's putting up her usual false front, lying to Nick that she is unmoved by his withdrawal from their relationship and is engaged to someone else. Finally, Tom and Daisy, true to form, flee the chaos they helped create, "retreat[ing] back into their money or their vast carelessness or whatever it was that kept them together" (188; ch. 9).

The only exception to this rule is Nick, who is transformed by his experience in New York. As the narrative opens, he is very optimistic, feeling that "life was beginning over again with the summer" (8; ch. 1). He's excited by his new job and his new life in New York. By the end of the summer he is utterly disillusioned, abandoning his plans for a new career and a new life in the East: "When I came back from the East last autumn I felt that I wanted the world to be in uniform and at a sort of moral attention forever; I wanted no more riotous excursions with privileged glimpses into the human heart" (6; ch. 1). However, Nick's transformation is not redemptive. Although he certainly learns something important about human nature over the course of that summer, the lesson produces in him a dark vision of human life. His attitude, as the novel closes, is hopeless and despairing: "So we beat on, boats against the current, borne back ceaselessly into the past" (189; ch. 9).

If the traditional quest formula – seek-and-find (or seek-and-be-transformed) – can be associated with a worldview that includes the possibility of redemption, then perhaps the seek-find-lose (or seek-but-don't-find) grammar can be associated with a worldview in which redemption is impossible or highly unlikely. This more pessimistic, or some would say realistic, vision of human experience is the vision

associated with the modernist worldview, which dominated Anglo-European literature from the beginning of World War I (1914) to the end of World War II
(1945) and which *The Great Gatsby* epitomizes. We can certainly find numerous
examples of this grammar in modern novels, for example, D. H. Lawrence's *Sons
and Lovers* (1913) and *Women in Love* (1920), Virginia Woolf's *To the Lighthouse*
(1927), and Richard Wright's *Native Son* (1940). Presumably, the readers of these
works, rather than the characters that populate them, are supposed to undergo
whatever transformation is possible, but the texts do not offer a worldview that
could be called redemptive. (Analogously, we might characterize the grammar of
the postmodern novel as don't-bother-to-seek. Certainly, it might be argued that
novels such as Thomas Pynchon's *The Crying of Lot 49* [1966], Joan Didion's *Play It
as It Lays* [1970], Joseph Heller's *Something Happened* [1974], and Don DeLillo's
White Noise [1985] are structured by such a grammar.)

My speculation that *The Great Gatsby*'s seek-find-lose grammar reflects the
modern novel's rejection of the traditional quest formula is compatible with the
way in which I think Fitzgerald's novel requires us to apply Northrop Frye's theory
of mythoi. For according to Frye's framework, *The Great Gatsby* embeds the structure of romance (Gatsby's narrative, the mythos of summer, the quest) within the
structure of irony (Nick's narrative, the mythos of winter, realism), and the second
structure offers a kind of running commentary on the first, which, by the novel's close,
forces Nick to realize that the structure of romance (Gatsby's narrative) is no longer
possible in the modern world. That is, in Fitzgerald's novel, the structure of irony
contains and eventually overrides the structure of romance.

Gatsby is, of course, the hero of the romantic quest. Although all the other
characters have "quests" of their own, only Gatsby's occurs within the mode of
romance. In *Anatomy of Criticism* Frye notes, "[t]he romance is nearest of all literary
forms to the wish-fulfillment dream, and for that reason ... [i]n every age the
ruling social or intellectual class tends to project its ideals in some form of
romance" (186). For the get-rich-quick Jazz Age of the American 1920s, the kind
of meteoric financial rise Jay Gatsby achieved was emblematic of the American
dream, which clearly was and still is a romantic dream of wish fulfillment. Typical
of romance, too, is Gatsby's persistent search for a past Golden Age, which, for
him, was his courtship of Daisy Fay in Louisville before he was sent to war. Upon
his return to America after the war, he devoted himself to amassing a fortune and
following her social activities in the newspapers. When he was able, finally, to buy a
mansion across the bay from hers, he arranged to meet her again so that he could
"fix everything just the way it was before" (17; ch. 1), so that he could return to
the Golden Age.

In fact, all of Gatsby's activities between the time he met Dan Cody to the
moment at which he is reunited with Daisy at Nick's cottage constitute the series
of minor adventures the romantic hero must undertake before the major

adventure – reclaiming Daisy for his own – occurs. His adventures with Cody taught him the skills he needed to succeed in life, including the perseverance and temperance that mark the romantic hero. His military achievements resulted in his rapid ascendancy through the ranks from lieutenant to major and covered him with medals for his valor on the battlefield. Then with similar rapidity, he ascended the ranks of Wolfsheim's organization, gaining a fortune to rival that of Tom Buchanan.

Gatsby's major adventure (his quest to regain Daisy) is also typical of the romantic quest to obtain a bride. Like the hero of the traditional quest, who is often separated from his love by a barrier of water, Gatsby is separated from Daisy by the bay between his mansion on West Egg and her home on East Egg. And, again typically, he can see the "promised land" – the green light at the end of the Buchanans' dock – from his side of the gulf that separates them. Furthermore, his quest for Daisy pits Gatsby against an antagonist with whom the reader can have little sympathy. Indeed, Tom fills the role of the usurper, from whose selfish machinations Daisy must be rescued.

The climactic struggle of the romantic conflict between hero and antagonist occurs, for Gatsby, during the confrontation scene with Tom in the New York hotel room. Although the hero sometimes dies as a result of this battle, his will-ingness to sacrifice himself for his quest proves him a hero. And, indeed, Gatsby does die, both symbolically – "'Jay Gatsby' had broken up like glass against Tom's hard malice" (155; ch. 8) – and literally, when Tom sends George Wilson, armed and crazed, to Gatsby's house. In fact, Gatsby's willingness to sacrifice himself for Daisy becomes the dominant motif as the narrative moves toward his death.

In a subtler fashion, Gatsby's quest also resembles that of another incarnation of the romantic hero: the quester-hero who saves the kingdom from the ravages of a monster. As Frye puts it, "the quest-romance is the victory of fertility over the waste land" (193): the monster to be defeated is the sterile, fallen world that waits to be redeemed by some sort of messiah. For the modern wasteland embodied in the novel's setting – including both the "valley of ashes" (27; ch.2) and the empty pleasures of the idle rich – Gatsby represents the renewal of life and vitality. In Nick's words, Gatsby has a "heightened sensitivity to the promises of life," an "extraordinary gift for hope, a romantic readiness such as I have never found in any other person and which it is not likely I shall ever find again" (6; ch. 1). Gatsby has, in short, what the modern world desperately needs to save it from the hopelessness of its own sterility. Like a messiah-figure, he represents renewed hope.

Although Gatsby may seem, on one level, part of the sterile modern world – he engages in criminal activities and throws parties that inevitably turn into drunken revels – he is symbolically separate from it. Like the quester-hero who saves the imperiled kingdom, he is isolated from the world he inhabits. He lives alone and is close to no one but Daisy. He knows none of the people at his parties, which he throws only in the hope that Daisy will "wander i[n] ... some night" (84; ch. 4).

And he is pictured, most frequently, alone in a tableau that bespeaks his romantic isolation. For example, one evening Nick observes that Gatsby "emerged from the shadow of [his] mansion" and "stretched out his arms toward the dark water" (25; ch. 1), "trembling" toward the "single green light, minute and far away" (26; ch. 1) at the end of Daisy's dock. The night Myrtle Wilson is killed, he stands guard alone, in a "sacre[d] … vigil" (153; ch. 7) outside Daisy's house, in case Tom "tries to bother her" (151; ch. 7) about their affair. Even at his riotous parties, Gatsby is pictured in romantic isolation: "A sudden emptiness seemed to flow now from the windows and the great doors, endowing with complete isolation the figure of the host who stood on the porch, his hand up in a formal gesture of farewell" (60; ch. 3). In a world of corruption, Gatsby is incorruptible because he has an "incorruptible dream" (162; ch. 8).

Gatsby's early life, too, fits that of the quester-hero who saves the fallen world. His origins are mysterious, and even when he reveals who his parents are we learn that "his imagination had never really accepted them as his parents at all. The truth was that Jay Gatsby … sprang from his Platonic conception of himself. He was a son of God. … [A]nd to this conception he was faithful to the end" (104; ch. 6). Gatsby even goes through a kind of baptism by water, typical of the messiah figure. "It was James Gatz who had been loafing along the beach that afternoon" (104; ch. 6), but by the time he rowed out to Cody's yacht anchored off the shore of Lake Superior, "it was … Jay Gatsby" (104; ch. 6) who emerged from the water to accept a job as Cody's steward. And like the sun god who, Frye tells us, "is represented as sailing in a boat on the surface of our world" (192), Gatsby sailed with Cody for five years. Indeed, just as the quester-hero is often "a third son, or the third to undertake the quest, or successful on his third attempt" (Frye 187), Gatsby's travels by boat took him "three times around the Continent" (106; ch. 6) before he "landed" in the modern world.

The narrative of Gatsby's romantic quest is embedded within a very different kind of narrative: that of Nick's summer in New York. We learn about Gatsby because Nick's relationship with him forms a large part of the narrator's own experience. However, Nick's narrative is structured by a genre that is the polar opposite of romance: the genre of irony, which, Frye says, "is consistent … with complete realism of content" (224). Irony, Frye argues, derives from the mythos of winter. In contrast to the idealized world of romance, Frye observes, the mythos of winter "attempts to give form to the shifting ambiguities and complexities of un-idealized existence" (223). This "unidealized existence" is not a world of heroes but of everyday, flawed human beings. It's a world in which human misery is the result not of fate or of some kind of cosmic intervention but of sociological and psychological causes. In other words, this is the real world, warts and all.

In the real world, in which Nick and all the other nonheroic characters live, it isn't easy to amass a fortune or find your one true love. Sometimes it isn't even easy to find a satisfying career, as Nick knows, or survive financially, as George Wilson knows. In this world, people don't look "gorgeous" in their "pink rag of a suit" (162; ch. 8) or throw lavish parties in the hope that their lost love will appear, as Gatsby does. Instead, like Gatsby's guests, they go to parties to sponge off a host they've never met and get obnoxiously drunk on his liquor. Their clothing "stretch[es] tight over ... rather wide hips" (31; ch. 2), like Myrtle's, and they have "sticky bob[s] of red hair" (34; ch. 2), as Myrtle's sister Catherine has. In the real world, "grey, scrawny Italian child[ren]" (30; ch. 2) live in places like the "valley of ashes," and people enjoy standing around the scene of an accident to watch human misery.

In the real world, furthermore, a woman doesn't always wait for her knight in shining armor, even when she knows who he is. Sometimes she marries Tom Buchanan instead. Even when she has a second chance at happiness, because her knight is faithful to her to the end, a small bend in the road to true love might send her scurrying home, as Daisy scurries back to her selfish, brutish, unfaithful husband. And when her knight dies protecting her from a charge of hit-and-run homicide, she might leave town before the minister arrives for the funeral.

In the real world, a man doesn't always remain faithful to his woman, even when he's married to her. Sometimes he has frequent extramarital affairs and parades them in public places, as Tom does with Myrtle, and sometimes he breaks his mistress's nose. Here, "bad guys" like Tom Buchanan and Meyer Wolfsheim call the shots. A simple, honest man like George Wilson is deceived by his wife and manipulated by her lover into killing an innocent man. And a "great sportswom[an]" like Jordan Baker, who Gatsby believes would "never do anything that wasn't all right" (76; ch. 4), cheats at golf, lies about damaging a borrowed car, and "deal[s] in subterfuges ... in order to keep that cool, insolent smile turned to the world and yet satisfy the demands of her hard, jaunty body" (63; ch. 3).

Perhaps most important, in the real world the death of a romantic hero is not a martyrdom that saves humanity. It's a sign that humanity is beyond saving, beyond hope. And once that sign is given, Nick knows there is nothing to do but go back home: forget his plans for the future, give up his optimism, cut his losses, and get out. In this way, Nick's narrative, grounded in the structure of irony, closes the door, so to speak, on the romantic tale it tells, that is, on the structure of romance. In other words, in *The Great Gatsby*, the ironic structure associated with the modern novel overrides the structure of romance as if to say that romance is no longer possible.

This process finds its symbolic expression in the confrontation scene between Gatsby and Tom in the New York hotel. According to the romantic formula, it is here that the hero wins his bride and reveals his true origins, which are royal or associated with some kind of important parentage. Instead, Gatsby reveals, with Tom's help, that his true origins are far beneath those of his beloved, and the result is that she abandons him. Thus, from the perspective of Frye's theory of mythoi, the romantic formula "jumps the track," ceases to function, and the void is filled by the only structure left in the narrative: that of irony.

The structure of irony does not succeed, however, in eradicating the structure of romance. Instead, the structure of irony is "haunted" by the very structure it overrides. Perhaps because he knows that romance is no longer possible, Nick's narrative is marked by an intense nostalgia for a lost past, for the lost world of romance that Gatsby represents. We see this longing in his lyric descriptions of a virginal, idyllic past: descriptions of Daisy and Jordan's "beautiful white ... girlhood" (24; ch. 1) in Louisville and of Christmas in the Midwest of his youth, with its "street lamps and sleigh bells in the frosty dark and the shadows of holly wreaths thrown by lighted windows on the snow" (184; ch. 9).

This nostalgia for a lost innocence, a lost paradise, for the mythos of summer, the genre of romance, reaches its climax in Nick's closing description of a literal paradise forever gone. As Nick sits on the beach the evening before his return to Minnesota, he muses on

> the old island here that flowered once for Dutch sailors' eyes – a fresh, green breast of the new world. Its vanished trees, the trees that had made way for Gatsby's house, had once pandered in whispers to the last and greatest of all human dreams; for a transitory enchanted moment man must have held his breath in the presence of this continent, compelled into an aesthetic contemplation he neither understood nor desired, face to face for the last time in history with something commensurate to his capacity for wonder.
>
> (189; ch. 9)

This passage is emblematic of the structural process that occurs over the course of the novel: the mythos of summer (romance, the successful quest) is overridden by the mythos of winter (irony, the complexities of reality), which remains haunted by the loss of the structure it has overcome.

In *The Great Gatsby,* then, we see the operations of quite a complex structure. We see a narrative grammar consisting of seek-find-lose and its subset, seek-but-don't-find. This grammar, I have suggested, reflects a worldview associated with the modernist period and with the modern novel's rejection of the traditional seek-and-find quest. Analogously, the text is structured by a struggle for dominance between two very different literary genres: romance (the mythos of summer and the genre to which Gatsby's narrative belongs) and irony (the mythos of winter and the genre to which Nick's narrative belongs). I have argued that the genre of romance is overcome by that of irony in the novel, although, throughout the text, the former "haunts" the latter in the form of the narrator's lyric descriptions of a lost past, a romantic, paradisal youth.

This analysis has thus attempted to illustrate two aspects of structuralism that sometimes seem in conflict: its reliance on formulaic description, which derives from its commitment to the kind of objectivity associated with mathematics, and its philosophical grounding as a science of humanity, which requires us to speculate on the relationship between the structural formulas we describe and the world in which we live. Although this second aspect is often forgotten in the practice of structuralist criticism, it is the dual nature of structuralism that, for many of us, makes it exciting.

Questions for further practice: structuralist approaches to other literary works

The following questions are intended as models. They can help you use structuralist criticism to interpret the literary works to which they refer or other texts of your choice.

1 How might you use Frye's theory of mythoi to analyze Joseph Conrad's *Heart of Darkness* (1902)? What kind of hero is Kurtz? How would you classify Marlow? In what sense might the novel be called a tragedy? In what sense does it belong to the genre of irony? What might our difficulties (or disagreements) in classifying this text suggest about Conrad's novel or about our system of classification?

2 Toni Morrison's *Beloved* (1987) is structured by the interweaving of several narratives, each the story of a particular character. There are, among others, narratives associated with Sethe, Denver, Beloved, Baby Suggs, Paul D, and Stamp Paid. Identify all the narratives present in the novel and analyze them structurally, as if they were a collection of stories (which, in a sense, they are). Is there a narrative grammar that informs all the "stories," or does a structural analysis reveal that they belong to different structural groups? What does your analysis suggest about the way in which Morrison's novel and similar texts make meaning?

3 William Faulkner's story "A Rose for Emily" (1931) has a complex structure that lends itself well to Genette's theoretical framework. Using Genette's categories, analyze the text in terms of the relationship among story, narrative, and narration. Be sure to discuss the functions of tense (order, duration, and frequency), mood (distance and perspective), and voice. How does your analysis help you understand the narrative effects Faulkner achieves in this story? Do your findings apply to other Faulkner works?

4 Although their content is quite different, Katherine Anne Porter's "The Jilting of Granny Weatherall" (1930) and Tillie Olsen's "I Stand Here Ironing" (1956) are short stories with a number of structural similarities. For example, both consist largely of interior monologues; both are narrated by a character within the story who has a very limited, subjective point of view; and both are structured by a

series of flashbacks. What other structural similarities can you find? Draw on the structural narratologist(s) whose work you find most helpful in illuminating these two pieces. Are structural similarities (or dissimilarities) related to similarities (or dissimilarities) in theme?

5   John Steinbeck's political novel *The Grapes of Wrath* (1939) was produced as a Hollywood film. For the most part, the film is very faithful to the novel's structure, characterization, and theme (the capitalist exploitation of tenant farmers who fled the Dust Bowl to become migrant laborers in California). However, the film's ending is triumphantly optimistic, in direct contrast to the ending of the novel. Analyze the novel's genre using Frye's theory of myths, Frye's theory of modes, and Scholes' theory of modes. Then analyze the ways in which the film's ending calls for a modification of your classification of the novel. What do your findings suggest about the conflict between political novels (to which category the genre of naturalism belongs) and the Hollywood tradition of "the happy ending"?

For further reading

Barthes, Roland. *Mythologies*. 1957. Complete ed. Trans. Richard Howard and Annette Lavers. New York: Hill and Wang, 2012.

Bouissac, Paul. *Saussure: A Guide for the Perplexed*. London and New York: Continuum, 2010. (See especially "Linguistics as a Science: Saussure's Distinction between *Langue* (Language as System) and *Parole* (Language in Use)," 72–89; "Signs, Signification, Semiology," 90–103; and "Synchrony and Dischrony," 104–14.)

Chandler, Daniel. *Semiotics: The Basics*. New York: Routledge, 2002.

Culler, Jonathan. "Literary Competence." *Structuralist Poetics: Structuralism, Linguistics, and the Study of Literature*. 1975. London and New York: Routledge, 2002. 131–52.

Davis, Todd F., and Kenneth Womack. "Charlotte Brontë and Frye's *Secular Scripture*: The Structure of Romance in *Jane Eyre*." *Formalist Criticism and Reader-Response Theory*. New York: Palgrave, 2002. 107–22.

Fludernik, Monika. *An Introduction to Narratology*. London and New York: Routledge, 2009.

Frye, Northrop. *Anatomy of Criticism: Four Essays*. Princeton, NJ: Princeton University Press, 1957.

Hawkes, Terence. *Structuralism and Semiotics*. 2nd ed. London and New York: Routledge, 2003.

Lévi-Strauss, Claude. *Tristes Tropiques*. Trans. John and Doreen Weighman. New York: Atheneum, 1974.

Pratt, Annis, *et al. Archetypal Patterns in Women's Fiction*. Bloomington: Indiana University Press, 1981.

Rowe, John Carlos. "Structure." *Critical Terms for Literary Study*. 2nd ed. Eds. Frank Lentricchia and Thomas McLaughlin. Chicago: University of Chicago Press, 1995. 23–38.

Scholes, Robert. *Structuralism in Literature: An Introduction*. New Haven, CT: Yale University Press, 1974.

For advanced readers

Barthes, Roland. *Image, Music, Text*. Trans. Stephen Heath. New York: Hill and Wang, 1977. (See especially "Introduction to the Structural Analysis of Narratives," 79–124, and "The Struggle with the Angel," 125–41.)

Culler, Jonathan. *Structural Poetics: Structuralism, Linguistics, and the Study of Literature.* 2nd ed. London and New York: Routledge, 2002.

Davis, Todd F., and Kenneth Womack. "Reader-Response Theory, Narratology, and the Structuralist Imperative." *Formalist Criticism and Reader-Response Theory.* New York: Palgrave, 2002. 57–63.

Genette, Gérard. *Narrative Discourse.* Trans. Jane Lewin. Ithaca, NY: Cornell University Press, 1980.

Greimas, A. J. *On Meaning: Selected Writings in Semiotic Theory.* 1970. Trans. Paul Perron and Frank Collins. Minneapolis: University of Minnesota Press, 1987.

Herman, David, ed. *Narratologies: New Perspectives on Narrative Analysis.* Columbus: Ohio State University Press, 1999.

Jakobson, Roman. "Linguistics and Poetics." *Style in Language.* Ed. T. Sebeok. Cambridge, MA: The MIT Press, 1960. 350–77.

Lévi-Strauss, Claude. *The Raw and the Cooked.* 1964. Trans. John and Doreen Weighman. New York: Harper, 1975.

Propp, Vladimir. *The Morphology of the Folktale.* 1928. Trans. Laurence Scott. Austin: University of Texas Press, 1968.

Saussure, Ferdinand de. *Course in General Linguistics.* 1916. Trans. Wade Baskin. New York: McGraw-Hill, 1966.

Segal, Robert A., ed. *Structuralism in Myth: Lévi-Strauss, Barthes, Dumézil, and Propp.* New York and London: Garland: 1996.

Todorov, Tzvetan. *The Poetics of Prose.* Trans. Richard Howard. Ithaca, NY: Cornell University Press, 1977.

Notes

1 Frye's *Anatomy of Criticism: Four Essays* attempts to systematize literature in four different ways. He calls these approaches his (1) theory of modes, or historical criticism (tragic, comic, and thematic); (2) theory of symbols, or ethical criticism (literal/descriptive, formal, mythical, and anagogic); (3) theory of myths, or archetypal criticism (comedy, romance, tragedy, irony/satire); and (4) theory of genres, or rhetorical criticism (epos, prose, drama, lyric). Although there has been some debate concerning whether or not Frye's work falls within the category of structuralism, it seems rather clear that all four of the approaches offered in *Anatomy of Criticism* are structuralist theories of genre because all seek the structural principles – such as plot formulas and character functions – that underlie genres in the Western literary tradition.

2 Not all archetypal criticism relates the mythic motifs found in literature to literary genres. Many archetypal critics, or myth critics – most of whom have been influenced by the work of Carl G. Jung – analyze literary works in order to identify the specific myths on which they draw. See, for example, Bodkin, Campbell, and Jung.

Works cited

Barthes, Roland. "The World of Wrestling." *Mythologies.* 1957. Trans. Annette Lavers. New York: Hill and Wang, 1972. 15–25.

Bodkin, Maud. *Archetypal Patterns in Poetry: Psychological Studies of Imagination.* 1934. New York: Random House, 1958.

Campbell, Joseph. *The Hero with a Thousand Faces.* Rev. ed. Princeton, NJ: Princeton University Press, 1968.

Culler, Jonathan. *Structuralist Poetics: Structuralism, Linguistics, and the Study of Literature.* Ithaca, NY: Cornell University Press, 1975.

Fitzgerald, F. Scott. *The Great Gatsby.* 1925. New York: Macmillan, 1992.

Frye, Northrop. *Anatomy of Criticism: Four Essays.* Princeton, NJ: Princeton University Press, 1957.

Genette, Gérard. *Narrative Discourse*. Trans. Jane Lewin. Ithaca, NY: Cornell University Press, 1980.

Greimas, A. J. *Structural Semantics*. 1966. Trans. Daniele McDowell, Ronald Schleifer, and Alan Velie. Lincoln: University of Nebraska Press, 1983.

Jung, Carl G., ed. *Man and His Symbols*. Garden City, NY: Doubleday, 1964.

——. *The Archetypes and the Collective Unconscious*. Vol. 9, Part I of *Collected Works*. 2nd ed. Trans. R. F. C. Hull. Princeton, NJ: Princeton University Press, 1968.

Lévi-Strauss, Claude. "The Structural Study of Myth." *Structural Anthropology*. 1958. Trans. Claire Jacobson and Brooke Schoepf. New York: Basic, 1963. 206–32.

Saussure, Ferdinand de. *Course in General Linguistics*. 1916. Trans. Wade Baskin. New York: McGraw-Hill, 1966.

Scholes, Robert. *Structuralism in Literature: An Introduction*. New Haven, CT: Yale University Press, 1974.

Todorov, Tzvetan. *Grammaire du Décaméron*. The Hague: Mouton, 1969.

8   Deconstructive criticism

For many of us who consider ourselves lovers of literature, phrases such as "the random play of signifiers" and "the transcendental signified" evoke the kind of fear and loathing the Crusaders must have felt when they learned that the infidels had taken the Holy City. Although deconstruction is no longer a new phenomenon on the academic scene – the theory was inaugurated by Jacques Derrida in the late 1960s and became a major influence on literary studies during the late 1970s – many students and faculty alike continue to misperceive deconstruction as a superficial analysis of wordplay that destroys our appreciation of literature and our ability to interpret it meaningfully. Perhaps one reason deconstruction is frequently misunderstood is that the writing by some of the biggest names in the field – Jacques Derrida, Luce Irigaray, Geoffrey Hartman – as well as the explanations offered by those who attempt to summarize the work of these thinkers, frequently employ such unusual language and organizational principles that they seem to defy our understanding and acceptance.

Nevertheless, deconstruction has a good deal to offer us: it can improve our ability to think critically and to see more readily the ways in which our experience is determined by ideologies of which we are unaware because they are "built into" our language. And because deconstruction offers these advantages, it can be a very useful tool for Marxism, feminism, and other theories that attempt to make us aware of the oppressive role ideology can play in our lives. In order to understand how deconstruction reveals the hidden work of ideology in our daily experience of ourselves and our world, we must first understand deconstruction's view of language because, according to Derrida, language is not the reliable tool of communication we believe it to be, but rather a fluid, ambiguous domain of complex experience in which ideologies program us without our being aware of them.

Deconstructing language

In our daily lives, most of us take language for granted, assuming that it communicates what we want it to, and if it doesn't, we assume that the fault is in ourselves, not in language. A phrase such as "Mary, please hand John the book" usually results in the desired action, and even when it doesn't we assume that the fault lies not in language but in Mary's or John's failure to understand the request or refusal to act on it. Because we are so used to the everyday patterns and rituals in which language seems to work the way we want it to, we assume that it is by nature a stable and reliable means of communicating our thoughts, feelings, and wishes. Deconstruction's theory of language, in contrast, is based on the belief that language is much more slippery and ambiguous than we realize.

Consider, for example, the following sentence: *Time flies like an arrow.* Most of us are familiar with this old saying, and we know it means that time passes quickly:

Time	*flies*	*like an arrow*	=	Times passes quickly.
(noun)	(verb)	(adv. clause)		

If I asked you to suggest additional meanings, you might say that the sentence could also mean that time moves in one direction, or straight ahead, because that's how arrows fly. But what would happen if we thought of the first word of the sentence as a verb in the imperative mode – telling us to do something – and the second word as if it represented a kind of insect? Then the sentence would be giving us an order:

Time	*flies*	*like an arrow*	=	Get out your stopwatch
(verb)	(obj.)	(adv. clause)		and time the speed of flies
				as you'd time an arrow's flight.

And what would happen if we thought of the first two words of the sentence as if they represented a kind of insect – time flies (think of fruit flies) – and the third word as if it were a form of the verb *to like?* Then the sentence would tell us something about the emotional life of a certain kind of insect:

Time flies	*like*	*an arrow*	=	Time flies are fond of arrows
(noun)	(verb)	(obj.)		(or at least of one particular
				arrow).

This exercise shows how, without changing a word, a single sentence can have several meanings.

Changes in tone of voice and emphasis can further reveal the slippery quality of language. Imagine, for example, that a newscaster were given the following line to read: *President Reagan says the Marines do not have to go to El Salvador.*

Now note how the meaning of the sentence changes dramatically, depending on which word is emphasized:

1 President Reagan *says* the Marines do not have to go to El Salvador (implying that he's lying).
2 President Reagan says the Marines do *not* have to go to El Salvador (implying that he's correcting a false rumor).
3 President Reagan says the *Marines* do not have to go to El Salvador (implying that some other group has to go).
4 *President Reagan* says the Marines do not have to go to El Salvador (implying that another important person had said that the marines have to go to El Salvador).
5 President Reagan says the Marines do not *have* to go to El Salvador (implying that they can go if they want to).
6 President Reagan says the Marines do not have to go to *El Salvador* (implying that they have to go somewhere else).

These two exercises should help you begin to see that language isn't as stable and reliable as we generally assume it is. Let's examine this idea further. As we saw in Chapter 7, structuralists and semioticians use the word *sign* to denote a basic element of communication, and they define *sign* by the following formula.

$$\text{sign} \quad = \quad \text{signifier} \quad + \quad \text{signified}$$

| (sound, image, | (concept to which |
| gesture, etc.) | the signifier refers) |

A word is a linguistic sign. For example, if the sign is the word *rose*, then the signifier is the group of letters written or pronounced as a unit ("rose"), and the signified is the rose you picture in your mind. If the signifier (or, in this case, pair of signifiers) is "red rose," then the signified is the red rose you picture in your mind. Of course, in response to the signifier "rose," different people will probably picture different kinds of roses. And for some people, both of the above signifiers – "rose" and "red rose" – will produce the same signified because these people always picture roses as red roses unless prompted to do otherwise.

To avoid this kind of vagueness and ambiguity, let's look at a very simple, concrete phrase uttered in a context so specific that the signifiers should produce a very clear and unambiguous signified. Picture a person standing in an open field pointing to the only tree in sight. In this context, a phrase consisting of the signifiers "This tree is big" seems to imply a single, clear signified: there is only one tree in question, and we know that a claim is being made about its size.

Deconstruction, however, asks us to look at the sentence's ambiguities, even when the sentence seems, at first glance, as clear and specific as this one does. When the speaker says, "This tree is big," is she comparing the tree to herself? To another tree? What other tree? Is she surprised by the size of the tree? Or is she merely informing us that the tree is big? Is she informing us so that we will know something about the tree or so that we will understand something about the word *big*? What must she think of us if she believes we need such information? Does she think we are just learning to speak English? Or is she being sarcastic? If so, why? This string of questions may seem to push the point a bit far, but it does illustrate that human utterances are rarely, if ever, as clear and simple as the structuralist formula *signifier + signified* seems to imply. As we have seen, any given signifier can refer to any number of signifieds at any given moment. And although context often helps us to limit the range of possible signifieds for some signifiers, it simultaneously increases the range of possible signifieds for others. This is why communication is such a complicated and uncertain thing.

If we stopped at this point, we could rewrite the structuralist formula as *sign = signifier + signified ... + signified*. That is, we could try to explain communication as a sliding accumulation of signifieds. But what does the term *signified* mean? If the signifier is "tree," then the signified must be the tree in our imagination that we can picture. But what do we understand by this imagined tree? Of what does our concept consist? Our concept of the tree consists of all the chains of signifiers we have come to associate with it over the course of our lives, in my own case, for example, "shade," "picnics," "climbing," "broken collarbone," "hiking," "Hocking Hills, Ohio," "vertigo," "autumn leaves," "raking," "planting Douglas firs," "pine-needle scale," "lime sulfur," and so on. What structuralism calls the signified is really always a chain of signifiers.

According to deconstruction, then, the word *tree* never reaches the point when it refers to a concept, a signified. The signifier I utter refers to chains of signifiers in my mind and evokes chains of signifiers in the mind of the person who hears my utterance. And each signifier in those chains is itself constituted by another chain of signifiers, and so on. So for deconstruction, language does not consist of the union of signifiers and signifieds; it consists only of chains of signifiers. As we saw in Chapter 7, structuralism says that language is *nonreferential* because it doesn't refer to things in the world but only to our concepts of things in the world. Deconstruction takes that idea a big step further by claiming that language is nonreferential because it refers neither to things in the world nor to our concepts of things but only to the play of signifiers of which language itself consists.

Deconstruction thus offers us a radical vision of the activity of thinking. Our mental life consists not of concepts – not of solid, stable meanings – but of a fleeting, continually changing play of signifiers. These signifiers may seem to be stable concepts – they look stable enough when we hear them spoken or see them written down! – but they don't operate in a stable manner in our mind. As we saw earlier, every signifier consists of and produces more signifiers in a never-ending *deferral*, or postponement, of meaning: we seek meaning that is solid and stable, but we can never really find it because we can never get beyond the play of signifiers that is language. In Derrida's words, what we take to be meaning is really only the mental *trace* left behind by the play of signifiers. And that trace consists of the differences by which we define a word. Let me explain.

Meaning seems to reside in words (or in things) only when we distinguish their *difference* from other words (or things). For example, if we believed that all objects were the same color, we wouldn't need the word *red* (or *blue* or *green*) at all. Red is red only because we believe it to be different from blue and green (and because we believe color to be different from shape). So the word *red* carries with it the trace of all the signifiers it is not (for it is in contrast to other signifiers that we define it).

To sum up, Derrida argues that language has two important characteristics: (1) its play of signifiers continually defers, or postpones, meaning, and (2) the meaning it seems to have is the result of the differences by which we distinguish one signifier from another. In French, the word *différer* means either "to defer" or "to differ." So Derrida coined a word intended to suggest both meanings – to defer and to differ – at the same time: *différance*, which is his name for the only "meaning" language can have.[1] At this point, you may wonder, why use language at all if it seems to refer to a kind of stable meaning that doesn't really exist? We must use language, Derrida explains, because we must use the tool at our disposal if we don't have another. But even while we use this tool, we can be aware that it doesn't have the solidity and stability we have assumed it has, and we can therefore improvise with it, stretch it to fit new modes of thinking (an activity called *bricolage*). Derrida does this stretching activity when he puts a word *under erasure*, as he calls it, by writing it and then crossing it out with a large X (for example, as I'm doing here with the word ~~meaning~~) to indicate that he's using an old word in a new way.

It seems rather important that we stretch language in new ways, given deconstruction's belief that language is what forms us and there is no way to get beyond it. There is no getting beyond language, beyond the play of signifiers, because we exist – we think, we perceive, we feel – within the language into which we were born. How we perceive and understand ourselves and the world is thus governed by the language with which we are taught to perceive them. That is, language *mediates* our experience of ourselves and the world. And for deconstruction, language is wholly ideological: it consists entirely of the numerous conflicting, dynamic *ideologies* – or systems of beliefs and values – operating at any given point in time in any given culture. For example, our use of the word *slut* for a woman who sleeps with many men and the word *stud* for a man who sleeps with many women reveals and perpetuates the cultural belief that sexual relations with multiple partners should be a source of shame for women and a source of pride for men.

To cite an extended example of the ideological quality of language, let me pass on a story my high school biology teacher told us about the attempt to introduce the rhythm method of birth control in a technologically underdeveloped country many years ago. Each woman in the program was given an abacus-like device, consisting of red and white beads arranged to represent her fertility cycle. Each bead represented one day and, if a given day's bead was red, she was not to have sexual intercourse; a white bead meant that sex on that day was safe. After several months passed, statistics showed that the pregnancy rate among women in the program had not changed at all, and social workers were at a loss to understand the problem. They finally discovered that women who wanted to have sex on red-bead days would simply push the beads over until a white one appeared: they assumed the beads were a kind of magic. Thus the program initially failed because both clients and social workers were able to view the project only in terms of their own cultural, or ideological, perspectives. Clients and social workers thought they understood each other's language, but they didn't because they didn't understand the ideologies of which each other's language was composed.

To explore the specific ways in which our language determines our experience, Derrida borrowed and transformed structuralism's idea that we tend to conceptualize our experience in terms of polar opposites – each of which we understand by means of its opposition to the other – called *binary oppositions*. For example, according to structuralism, we understand the word *good* by contrasting it with the word *evil*. Similarly, we understand *reason* as the opposite of *emotion*, *masculine* as the opposite of *feminine*, *civilized* as the opposite of *primitive*, and so on. However, Derrida noted that these binary oppositions are also little hierarchies. That is, one term in the pair is always *privileged*, or considered superior to the other. (In the binary oppositions listed above, the first term in each pair is, in Western culture, the privileged term.) Therefore, by finding the binary oppositions at work in a cultural production (such as a novel, a film, a conversation, a classroom, or a courtroom trial), and by identifying which member of the opposition is privileged, one can discover something about the ideology promoted by that production.

In order to discover the limitations of the ideology one thus has uncovered, Derrida observed, one must examine the ways in which the two members of the opposition are not completely opposite, the ways in which they overlap or share some things in common. For example, consider the binary opposition in American culture between the words *objective* and *subjective*. We tend to identify the objective with the impersonal, the rational (which implies the intelligent), and the scientific dimensions of human experience and therefore consider objectivity a necessary criterion of reliability. In sharp contrast, we tend to identify the subjective with the personal, the emotional (which implies the unintelligent), and even the irrational dimensions of human experience and therefore consider it unreliable. We can see this privileging of the objective over the subjective in our culture's praise of "objective" news reporting, in its acceptance of "objective" historical data, and in its reliance on "objective" scientific experimentation. For us, the objective is the source of knowledge; the subjective is merely the source of opinion.

To deconstruct this binary opposition and learn something about the limitations of the ideology it supports, let's consider the ways in which the objective and the subjective are not really opposites. For example, when reporters, historians, and scientists gather "objective" data, on what basis do they decide which data to use and which to discard? Even if they are following specific guidelines for data collection, how can we be sure those guidelines are "objective," and, in any case, how can we be sure that the guidelines are "objectively" interpreted and applied to each piece of data collected or discarded? That is, aren't reporters, historians, and scientists human beings with subjective needs, fears, and desires (including career motivations) that might influence them with or without their knowledge? Can one totally escape one's own viewpoints, feelings, and biases? Surely, to claim that one has done so is to claim the impossible. Isn't objectivity, then, really a lie we tell ourselves and others about our subjectivity? Isn't objectivity, therefore, subjectivity in disguise?

Looked at from a different perspective, isn't the privileging of the objective over the subjective a product of the privileging of reason over emotion? After all, subjectivity is discredited because it is "contaminated" by emotion, which we believe clouds our thinking and undermines our ability to be objective, that is, to be rational. However, is it really rational to lump all emotions in the category of the irrational? Aren't some emotions sometimes the most "rational" response one can have to a given situation, that is, the response that produces the most accurate, useful, and reliable insights? And isn't the insistence on the rational sometimes an emotional response produced by fear of one's own feelings? The point here is that language – the meanings of words, the linguistic categories by which we organize our experience – doesn't operate in the tidy fashion we like to think it does. Language is constantly overflowing with implications, associations, and contradictions that reflect the implications, associations, and contradictions of the ideologies of which it is formed.

Deconstructing our world

Because it is through language that a culture's ideologies are passed on, it is not unreasonable to say that it is through language that we come to conceive and perceive our world and ourselves. To put the matter in philosophical terms, for deconstruction, language is our "ground of being," or the foundation from which our experience and knowledge of the world are generated. But, as we shall see, language, from a deconstructive perspective, is a very different ground of being from those generally associated with traditional Western philosophies.

In the history of Western thought since Plato, every philosophical system has had its ground of being. That is, all systems of Western philosophy derive from and are organized around one grounding principle from which we believe we can figure out the meaning of existence. For some thinkers, the ground of being is some cosmic principle of order or harmony, as illustrated, for example, by Plato's idea of perfect Forms that exist in an abstract, timeless dimension of thought. For others, that grounding principle is rational thought engaged in the act of self-reflection, as illustrated by Descartes' famous statement, "I think, therefore I am" (*Cogito ergo sum*). For others still, the grounding principle is some innate (inborn and permanent) quality in human beings as illustrated by structuralism's belief that human language and experience are generated by innate structures of human consciousness.

While these grounding concepts produce our understanding of the dynamic, evolving world around us – and of our dynamic, evolving selves as well – the concepts themselves remain stable. Unlike everything they explain, they are not dynamic and evolving. They are "out of play," as Derrida would put it. This type of philosophy – in short, all Western philosophy – Derrida calls *logocentric* because it places at the center (*centric*) of its understanding of the world a concept (*logos*) that organizes and explains the world for us while remaining outside of the world it organizes and explains. But for Derrida, this is Western philosophy's greatest illusion. Given that each grounding concept – Plato's Forms, Descartes' *cogito*, structuralism's innate structures of human consciousness, and so on – is itself a human concept and therefore a product of human language, how can it be outside the ambiguities of language? That is, how can any concept be outside the dynamic, evolving, ideologically saturated operations of the language that produced it?

For Derrida, the answer is that no concept is beyond the dynamic instability of language, which *disseminates* (as a flower scatters its seeds on the wind) an infinite number of possible meanings with each written or spoken utterance. For deconstruction, then, language is the ground of being, but that ground is *not* out of play: it is itself as dynamic, evolving, problematical, and ideologically saturated as the worldviews it produces. For this reason, there is no center to our understanding of existence. There are, instead, an innumerable number of vantage points from which to view it, and each of these vantage points has a language of its own, which deconstruction calls its *discourse*. For example, there is the discourse of modern physics, the discourse of Christian fundamentalism, the discourse of liberal arts education in the opening decades of the twenty-first century, the discourse of nineteenth-century British medicine, and so on. In other words, Derrida *decentered* Western philosophy just as Copernicus decentered the earth in the 1600s by asserting that the universe does not revolve around it.

The theory that our view of the world is constructed by language performs a key role in the decentering of Western philosophy because language is no longer seen as a product of our experience (first we see an enormous hole in the ground; then we call it the Grand Canyon) but rather as the conceptual framework that creates our experience. For example, when the early Spanish explorers first saw what non-Native Americans now call the Grand Canyon, there was nothing in their conceptual repertoire – in their language – to enable them to perceive its dimensions accurately. For instance, they thought the Colorado River, at the bottom of the canyon, was only a few hundred feet away. As a result, foot soldiers in full armor were ordered to reconnoiter the area – to run down and have a look around – and to the surprise of their countrymen, they never returned. This example illustrates how conception (what we think) precedes perception (what we experience through our senses) and how our expectations, beliefs, and values – all of which are carried by language – determine the way we experience our world. While structuralists were among the first to argue that our view of the world is constructed by the language we speak, they believe that language is generated by stable, innate structures of human consciousness. Thus, deconstruction is called a *poststructuralist* theory, not only because it emerged in the wake of structuralism's popularity but also because it constitutes a reaction against structuralism's orderly vision of language and human experience.

Deconstructing human identity

For deconstruction, if language is the ground of being, then the world is infinite *text*, that is, infinite chains of signifiers always in play. Because human beings are constituted by language, they, too, are texts. In other words, deconstruction's theory of language has implications for *subjectivity*, for what it means to be a human being.

As we have seen, deconstruction asserts that our experience of ourselves and our world is produced by the language we speak, and because all language is an unstable, ambiguous force-field of competing ideologies, we are, ourselves, unstable and ambiguous force-fields of competing ideologies. The self-image of a stable identity that many of us have is really just a comforting self-delusion, which we produce in collusion with our culture, for culture, too, wants to see itself as stable and coherent when in reality it is highly unstable and fragmented. We don't really have an identity because the word *identity* implies that we consist of one, singular self, but in fact we are multiple and fragmented, consisting at any moment of any number of conflicting beliefs, desires, fears, anxieties, and intentions. However, as we grow up, we internalize through language the ideological conflicts and contradictions of our culture, each finding a way to "fit in" by finding a way to deny, both to ourselves and others, the fragmented experience of ourselves produced by the fragmented, ambiguous language within which we live.

Does all this sound rather grim, if not completely confusing? Well, don't jump ship yet. Let's consider first some of the interesting vantage points on human experience deconstruction opens up for us. First of all, doesn't the idea of a fragmented self explain a good deal of our day-to-day experience? Aren't most of us very different people on the job, at the store, on a date, or alone in front of the television set? And even if we confine our investigation to our experience of ourselves on the job, for example, doesn't that experience change from day to day, sometimes from hour to hour or minute to minute, as we encounter different people or as various thoughts, memories, and emotions occur? In other words, isn't each of us really a kaleidoscope of selves? In fact, don't we sometimes have the feeling that we don't know who we really are, especially when we contrast ourselves to other people who (because we view them from the outside) seem so consistent in their self-image? Similarly, if we've invented our "identity," then we can reinvent it. Isn't that exactly what many people do when they join Alcoholics Anonymous or have a "change of heart" as a result of psychological counseling or religious conversion? Finally, doesn't the ambiguous, ideological nature of language explain many of the difficulties we encounter in communicating with others, especially with others from backgrounds different from our own? Perhaps an understanding of deconstruction's theory of language can help us see when and how such ideological differences are operating.

Deconstructing literature

Now let's take a moment to summarize the three main points we've discussed so far in this chapter. For deconstruction, (1) language is dynamic, ambiguous, and unstable, continually disseminating possible meanings; (2) existence has no center, no stable meaning, no fixed ground; and (3) human beings are fragmented battlefields for competing ideologies whose only "identities" are the ones we invent and choose to believe. As you may have noticed, the key word here is *unstable*. It should come as no surprise, then, to learn that, for deconstruction, literature is as dynamic, ambiguous, and unstable as the language of which it is composed.

Meaning is not a stable element residing in the text for us to uncover or passively consume. Meaning is created by the reader in the act of reading. Or, more precisely, meaning is produced by the play of language through the vehicle of the reader, though we generally refer to this process as "the reader." Furthermore, the meaning that is created is not a stable element capable of producing closure; that is, no interpretation has the final word. Rather, literary texts, like all texts, consist of a multiplicity of overlapping, conflicting meanings in dynamic, fluid relation to one another and to us. What have been considered the "obvious" or "commonsense" interpretations of a given text are really ideological readings – interpretations produced by a culture's values and beliefs – with which we are so familiar that we consider them "natural." In short, we create the meaning and value we "find" in the text. Just as authors can't help but draw on the assumptions of their cultural milieux when they construct their texts, readers can't help but draw on the assumptions of theirs when they construct their readings. Therefore, both literary and critical texts can be deconstructed.

There are generally two main purposes in deconstructing a literary text, and we may see either or both at work in any given deconstructive reading: (1) to reveal the text's *undecidability* and/or (2) to reveal the complex operations and limitations of the ideologies of which the text is constructed. At this stage in your relationship to deconstruction, I think you'll find the second procedure more meaningful and useful, so I'll provide only a brief summary of the first approach and then describe the second more fully.

To reveal a text's undecidability is to show that the "meaning" of the text is really an indefinite, undecidable, plural, conflicting array of possible meanings and that the text, therefore, has no meaning, in the traditional sense of the word, at all. One way to pursue this goal is outlined, in brief, below. This outline is offered, not in the expectation that you will perform a textual analysis along these lines, but to help increase your sense of what it means to say that texts are, ultimately, undecidable.

1 Work conscientiously to discover as many examples as you can of the various interpretations – interpretations of the text as a whole as well as interpretations of particular characters, plot events, images, and so on – the text seems to offer.
2 Find as many examples as you can of the ways in which specific aspects of these interpretations conflict with one another.
3 Explain how these conflicts are either irreconcilable – they can't operate together to produce a single, meaningful interpretation of the text – or how attempts to resolve these conflicts through additional interpretation uncover additional conflicting meanings in the text.
4 Use steps 1, 2, and 3 to argue for the text's undecidability.

Undecidability does not mean that the reader is unable to choose among possible interpretations. And it does not mean that the text cannot "make up its mind" as to what it wants to say. Rather, undecidability means that reader and text alike are inextricably bound within language's dissemination of meanings. That is, reader and text are interwoven threads in the perpetually working loom of language. Specific meanings are just "moments" of meaning that give way, inevitably, to more meanings. Thus, the literary text is used to illustrate the indefinite, plural, conflicting possible meanings that constitute all texts, literary and otherwise, because all texts are made of language. This is a useful and interesting endeavor because such readings serve as helpful reminders that language and all of its products, including ourselves, are rich, exciting, sometimes alarming but always interesting, proliferations of meanings.

The other purpose in deconstructing a literary text, which we'll discuss at greater length, is to see what the text can show us about the ideologies of which it is constructed. This endeavor usually shows us something about the ways in which ideologies operate in our own view of the world as well. For these reasons, I think it is an extremely useful exercise whatever your theoretical preferences are. To understand how this kind of deconstruction works, let's contrast it with the New Critical approach discussed in Chapter 5 because enough New Critical principles are still taught in the classroom to make that approach fairly familiar to most of us and because a New Critical reading often can serve as the first step in the deconstruction of a text.

As you may recall, New Criticism seeks to reveal how the text works as a unified whole by showing how its main theme, or overall meaning or message, is established by the text's formal, or stylistic, elements: imagery, symbolism, tone, rhyme, meter, plot, characterization, setting, point of view, and so forth. First, the New Critic identifies the central tension operating in the text, for example, the struggle between good and evil, the protagonist's evolution from innocence to experience, the conflict between science and religion, or some other tension that is emotionally or morally compelling. Then the New Critic shows how that tension is resolved in the text's advancement of its main theme – for example, that good and evil exist in all of us; that the evolution from innocence to experience, though necessary, can be costly as well as rewarding; that science becomes dangerous when it becomes a religion; or some other theme that has human significance – to which all the formal elements in the text contribute. While New Critics especially appreciate tension, irony, ambiguity, and paradox in a literary text, all of these qualities must serve the unifying purpose of supporting the text's main theme. Any conflicting meanings that seem to appear in the text must be shown to serve some function for the main theme so that the whole text can be seen to achieve its artistic purpose smoothly, seamlessly, and completely.

For deconstruction, this means that the New Critic is in collusion with the text to hide the self-contradictions that reveal the limitations of its ideological framework. To find that ideological framework and understand its limitations, a deconstructive critic looks for meanings in the text that conflict with its main theme, focusing on self-contradictions of which the text seems unaware. The best way to grasp this procedure is to try it. Let's do so with Robert Frost's wonderful poem "Mending Wall" (1914).

A deconstructive reading of Robert Frost's "Mending Wall"

Mending Wall

Something there is that doesn't love a wall,
That sends the frozen-ground-swell under it,
And spills the upper boulders in the sun,
And makes gaps even two can pass abreast.

The work of hunters is another thing:
I have come after them and made repair
Where they have left not one stone on a stone,
But they would have the rabbit out of hiding,
To please the yelping dogs. The gaps I mean,
No one has seen them made or heard them made,
But at spring mending-time we find them there.
I let my neighbor know beyond the hill;
And on a day we meet to walk the line
And set the wall between us once again.
We keep the wall between us as we go.
To each the boulders that have fallen to each.
And some are loaves and some so nearly balls
We have to use a spell to make them balance:
"Stay where you are until our backs are turned!"
We wear our fingers rough with handling them.
Oh, just another kind of outdoor game,
One on a side. It comes to little more:
There where it is we do not need the wall:
He is all pine and I am apple orchard.
My apple trees will never get across
And eat the cones under his pines, I tell him.
He only says, "Good fences make good neighbors."
Spring is the mischief in me, and I wonder
If I could put a notion in his head:
"*Why* do they make good neighbors? Isn't it
Where there are cows? But here there are no cows.
Before I built a wall I'd ask to know
What I was walling in or walling out,
And to whom I was like to give offense.
Something there is that doesn't love a wall,
That wants it down." I could say "Elves" to him,
But it's not elves exactly, and I'd rather
He said it for himself. I see him there,
Bringing a stone grasped firmly by the top
In each hand, like an old-stone savage armed.
He moves in darkness as it seems to me,
Not of woods only and the shade of trees.
He will not go behind his father's saying,
And he likes having thought of it so well
He says again, "Good fences make good neighbors."

A New Critical reading of the text – What is the central tension at work in this poem, and how is it resolved in the poem's unified advancement of its main theme? – is often a useful first step in deconstructing a literary work because such readings can almost always be found to rest on a binary opposition in which one member of the pair is privileged over the other. The member of the pair – the "side" of the binary opposition – the text supports usually reveals the ideology (or at least one of the ideologies) the text embraces. Once a New Critical reading is formulated, the binary opposition on which it rests can be deconstructed: that is, it can be examined to find the ways in which the opposing elements in the text overlap or aren't really opposed. And this is how we can learn something about the limitations of the ideology the text (consciously or unconsciously) promotes.

In the case of "Mending Wall," it seems rather clear that the binary opposition structuring the text can be found in the disagreement between the speaker and his neighbor. The speaker advocates nonconformity when the tradition one has followed no longer fits the circumstances in which one finds oneself. The neighbor, without even thinking about what he is doing, advocates conformity to the way things have always been done in the past. Thus the binary opposition structuring the poem is that between nonconformity and conformity. Because we see the situation from the speaker's point of view and our sympathies therefore lie with him, it is safe to say that nonconformity is the privileged term. The main theme, from a New Critical perspective – or, in deconstructive terms, the poem's *overt ideological project* – might be stated as follows: the poem criticizes mindless conformity to obsolete traditions for which the wall is a metaphor.

To be sure that we have identified the poem's ideological project and not just set up an easy target that we can then proceed to shoot down, we must find, in New Critical fashion, all the evidence the poem offers in support of the theme we've identified. For example, we accept the speaker's negative views of his neighbor and of obsolete traditions because he clearly shows that the wall has outlived its purpose – "My apple trees will never get across / And eat the cones under his pines" (ll. 25– 26) – and because the speaker associates himself with nature ("Spring [a natural event] is the mischief in me": l. 28), which is generally presumed good. Indeed, our faith in nature's wisdom promotes our initial acceptance of the speaker's viewpoint in the poem's opening four lines, which put nature in opposition to the wall: it is nature that "sends the frozen-ground-swell" to spill "the upper boulders in the sun" (ll. 2–3).

This theme is reinforced when the men "have to use a spell" to make the unwilling boulders, natural objects, stay in place (ll. 18–19) and when it is implied that the boulders will fall as soon as the men turn their backs (l. 19). Nature's "children" – the hunters in lines 5–7 and the elves in line 36 – also support the speaker's attitude toward the wall. In addition, we often associate the word *wall* with barriers to communication or emotional exchange, and this function is insisted upon in lines 13–15, thereby reinforcing our rejection of the wall and of the obsolete tradition that keeps it in place: "And on a day we meet ... / And set the wall *between* us once again. / We keep the wall *between* us as we go" (my italics). Finally, the neighbor is compared to an "old-stone savage" who "moves in darkness ... / Not of woods only and the shade of trees" (ll. 40–42), that is, who is unenlightened. Thus, the neighbor is contrasted sharply with the enlightened speaker, who knows that obsolete traditions should be abandoned.

So far we've located the binary opposition that thematically structures the poem: nonconformity/conformity. And we've determined which member of the opposition is privileged in the poem: nonconformity. The next step is to deconstruct this opposition by finding everything in the poem that conflicts with or undermines this hierarchy. That is, we must find textual evidence that contradicts the evidence we have just gathered in support of our New Critical reading of the poem's main theme. This contradictory evidence is the kind that tends to be overlooked when one is searching for a unified meaning in a literary text, as the New Critics did. Our goal now is to show that, once we begin to focus on the poem's internal contradictions instead of its unity, the poem reveals that neither side of the binary opposition supporting the main theme can be privileged over the other. In other words, though most readers have not been trained to see it, we will show how the poem deconstructs itself.

In the first place, a number of conflicts revolve around the poem's privileging of the speaker's nonconformity over the unthinking conformity of his neighbor, a difference represented by their attitudes toward the wall that separates their property. Siding with the speaker, nature – against tradition (that is, against conformity) – wants the wall down, but so do the hunters, who function not only as emblems of nature but of tradition as well. Because they hunt for sport (they want "the rabbit out of hiding," not necessarily for food, but to "please the yelping dogs": ll. 8–9), the hunters evoke a sporting tradition that has its roots in the traditional hunt of the British landed gentry. Analogously, while magic, in the form of elves, wants the wall down (l. 36), magic, in the form of the magic "spell" in lines 18–19, is invoked to keep the wall up. Furthermore, because elves are mischievous creatures who, according to legend, delight in making trouble for human beings, their desire to have the wall down can just as easily undermine our trust in the project rather than promote it. In fact, the speaker's use of such an ambiguous term as elves, and his difficulty in finding the right word ("it's not elves exactly": l. 37), imply his own unconscious ambivalence toward the wall and toward the tradition it represents. This ambivalence is reinforced by the speaker's having repaired the wall on his own in the past and by his having called on his neighbor to do so now. These behaviors certainly seem to contradict his nonconformist attitude toward the wall.

Finally, the main idea the poem criticizes – good fences make good neighbors – is actually valid within the action of the poem: it is the activity of mending the wall that brings the men together, presumably inspiring the poem's creation, and lets them be neighbors through the bonding activity of shared work. Evidently, this is the only time the two men meet at all. Even the poem's title suggests this idea if we read *mending* as an adjective rather than a verb: "Mending Wall" then becomes a wall that mends (for example, that mends relationships) rather than a wall that is mended.

Now that we've shown how the poem quietly collapses the binary opposition supporting its own main theme, the final step of our deconstruction is to consider the implications of this collapse. It would seem, for example, that the meaning, importance, and power of conformity and the meaning, importance, and power of nonconformity are not as easily placed in opposition as "Mending Wall" initially appears to suggest. The poem calls for a rational abandonment of a seemingly empty tradition, an attitude easily associated with the scientific and technological progress that occurred during the five decades preceding the poem's publication in 1914. Yet the value of that tradition, and the dubious nature of the attempt to abandon it, form a powerful counterweight against that call. Perhaps this conflict in the text suggests that much of the power of tradition lies in its ability to influence our attitudes without our being aware of its presence.

One reason the unresolvable conflict between nonconformity and conformity occurs in the poem is that some of the terms used to evoke their difference — especially the terms *nature* and *primitive* — themselves evoke mixed feelings in our culture. For example, we associate nature with goodness — innocence, purity, simplicity, health, intuitive wisdom — yet nature usually stands in the way of the scientific and technological progress we value so highly. Mountains are blown up to build our roads; forests are destroyed to foster our business enterprises; and air, soil, and water are polluted to promote our industries. Similarly, Western culture associates the primitive with the goodness of nature, yet it also associates the primitive with ignorance, the unknown, and the sinister, and this association evokes fear and contempt. And as we have seen, conflicting associations are also evoked by the words *magic*, *elves*, and *hunters*. Perhaps, then, our deconstruction of "Mending Wall" should make us reconsider other binary oppositions that inform our culture, such as masculine/feminine, individual/group, and objective/subjective.

As this reading of "Mending Wall" illustrates, deconstruction does not try to resolve the thematic tensions in literary texts into some stable, unified interpretation, but rather tries to sustain those tensions in order to learn from them. That a literary work has conflicting ideological projects that are not absorbed in some overarching purpose or theme is not considered a flaw, as it was for New Criticism, but a necessary product of the instability and ideological conflict inherent in language, and it is a product that can enrich our experience of the text. This is a vision of art as a seething cauldron of meanings in flux. As a dynamic entity tied to both the culture that produced it and the culture that interprets it, art becomes a vehicle for understanding our culture, our history, our language, and ourselves.

It is important to remember that all writing (or, more broadly, all communication), including our deconstruction of a literary text, continually deconstructs itself, continually disseminates meanings. In other words, strictly speaking, we do not deconstruct a text; we show how the text deconstructs itself. The process just outlined, then, helps us to observe how "Mending Wall" deconstructs itself and to use our observations to learn about the ideological operations of language. But we must remember that the meanings we derived from our analysis of the poem constitute only a "moment" in the text's dissemination of meanings, which it will continue to disseminate as long as the poem is read.

Some questions deconstructive critics ask about literary texts

The following two questions summarize the two deconstructive approaches discussed above.

1 How can we use the various conflicting interpretations a text produces (the "play of meanings") or find the various ways in which the text doesn't answer the questions it seems to answer, to demonstrate the instability of language and the undecidability of meaning? (Remember that deconstruction uses the word *undecidability* in a special way.)
2 What ideology does the text seem to promote? That is, what is the text's overt ideological project (its main theme, or overall meaning or message)? And how does conflicting evidence in the text show the limitations of that ideology? We can usually discover a text's overt ideological project by finding the binary opposition that structures the text's main theme.

Depending on the literary text in question, we might ask one or both of these questions. Or we might come up with a useful way of deconstructing the text not listed here. These are just two starting points to get us thinking about literary texts in productive deconstructive ways. Keep in mind that not all deconstructive critics will interpret the same work in the same way, even if they focus on the same ideological projects in the text. As in every field, even expert practitioners disagree. Our goal is to use deconstruction to help enrich our reading of literary texts, to help us see some important ideas they illustrate that we might not have seen so clearly or so deeply without deconstruction, and to help us see the ways in which language blinds us to the ideologies it embodies.

The following deconstructive reading of F. Scott Fitzgerald's *The Great Gatsby* is offered as an example of what a deconstruction of that novel might yield. It is important to note that a brief deconstructive reading of the novel has already been presented in the chapter on Marxist criticism. The Marxist reading of *The Great Gatsby*, you may recall, had two components. First, it showed the ways in which the text offers a powerful critique of capitalist ideology; then it showed the ways in which that critique is undermined by the text's own fascination with the capitalist world it condemns. The second component of this reading is a deconstruction of the first because it draws on elements in the novel to show the limitations of the text's own anticapitalist ideology. Thus, as we noted earlier, because deconstruction helps us understand the hidden operations of ideology, it can be a useful tool for any critic interested in examining the oppressive role ideology can play in our lives. In fact, Marxist and feminist critics had often used deconstructive principles in their analyses of literature and culture before those principles were developed as part of a theory of language and called *deconstruction*, and they still use them today.

In the deconstruction of *The Great Gatsby* that follows, I will argue that the novel's overt ideological project – the condemnation of American decadence in the 1920s, which replaced forever the wholesome innocence of a simpler time – is undermined by the text's own ambivalence toward the binary oppositions on which that ideological project rests: past/present, innocence/decadence, and West/East. This ambivalence finds its most conflicted expression in the characterization of Jay Gatsby, the romantic embodiment of the novel's covert fascination with the modern world it condemns. Although this deconstructive reading of the novel is much broader than the Marxist deconstruction described above, their shared focus on American decadence gives them, as we shall see, some elements in common.

" ... the thrilling, returning trains of my youth ... ": a deconstructive reading of *The Great Gatsby*

Toward the end of F. Scott Fitzgerald's *The Great Gatsby* (1925), narrator Nick Carraway, thoroughly disillusioned by his experience in the East, reminisces about his youth in Minnesota:

> One of my most vivid memories is of coming back west from prep school and later from college at Christmas time. Those who went farther than Chicago would gather in the old dim Union Station at six o'clock of a December evening ...
>
> When we pulled out into the winter night and the real snow, our snow, began to stretch out beside us and twinkle against the windows, and the dim lights of small Wisconsin stations moved by, a sharp wild brace came suddenly into the air. We drew in deep breaths of it ... unutterably aware of our identity with this country ...
>
> That's my middle-west ... the thrilling, returning trains of my youth and the street lamps and sleigh bells in the frosty dark and the shadows of holly wreaths thrown by lighted windows on the snow. I am part of that, a little solemn with the feel of those long winters, a little complacent from growing

up in the Carraway house in a city where dwellings are still called through
decades by a family's name.

(184; ch. 9)

Such nostalgia for the past emerges in various ways throughout the novel and lends
emotional force to what I will argue is the text's most pervasive and overt ideological project: the condemnation of American decadence in the 1920s, which
replaced forever the wholesome innocence of a simpler time. The grotesque portrayal of the modern world, the painful disillusionment of two hopeful young
men – Nick Carraway and Jay Gatsby – as they are initiated into the harsh realities
of that world, and the nostalgic representations of an idealized past create a novel
that deeply mourns the passing of America's innocence during the decade following
the end of World War I. As we shall see, however, this belief in an idealized past
corrupted by the decadence of the present is, in *The Great Gatsby*, an unstable
ideological project. For it is deconstructed by the text's own ambivalence toward
the binary oppositions on which that project rests – past/present, innocence/
decadence, and West/East – an ambivalence that finds its most conflicted expression in the characterization of Jay Gatsby, the romantic embodiment of the novel's
covert fascination with the modern world it condemns.

There is little to redeem the modern world portrayed in *The Great Gatsby*. It's a
world run by men like Tom Buchanan and Meyer Wolfsheim, and despite their
positions on opposite sides of the law, both characters are predators consumed by
self-interest, capable of rationalizing their way around any ethical obstacle to get
what they want. It's an empty world where selfishness, drunkenness, and vulgarity
abound, where the graceful social art of dancing has become "old men pushing
young girls backward in eternal graceless circles" and "superior couples holding
each other tortuously, fashionably, and keeping in the corners" (51; ch. 3). Unlike
life in the Minnesota of Nick's youth, there is no sense of permanence or stability.
The Buchanans are forever "drift[ing] here and there unrestfully wherever people
played polo and were rich together" (10; ch. 1). Jordan is always on the move
among hotels, clubs, and other people's homes. And even George Wilson, with the scant
means he has at his disposal, thinks he can solve his problems by pulling up stakes
and moving to the West. Anonymity and isolation are the rule rather than the
exception. None of the characters has close, lasting friendships, and the alienation
of humanity seems to be summed up in the "poor young clerks" Nick sees on the
streets of New York City, "who loitered in front of windows waiting until it was
time for a solitary restaurant dinner – young clerks in the dusk, wasting the most
poignant moments of night and life" (62; ch. 3).

Furthermore, the superficial values that put the pursuit of social status and good
times above every other consideration are found among every group portrayed in
the novel, regardless of the class, gender, or race of its members. The middle-class

and working-class characters – such as the McKees, Myrtle Wilson, Myrtle's sister Catherine, and Gatsby's menagerie of party guests – are as concerned with social status and as hungry for amusement as the wealthy Buchanans. The female characters who attend Gatsby's soirées are as shallow, selfish, and drunken as the male partygoers, if not more so. And the black characters Nick sees one day on his way to New York are as superficial and status-conscious as the white characters: from the back seat of their chauffeured limousine, they roll their eyes "in haughty rivalry" (73; ch. 4) toward the luxury car carrying Gatsby and Nick. The only characters who don't seem to exhibit these behaviors, George Wilson and Michaelis, the man who owns the restaurant next to Wilson's garage, are apparently too busy or too poor for such concerns: their energy is devoted to surviving the hopeless poverty of the "valley of ashes" (27; ch. 2), a location that is itself an indictment of the culture that produced it. Indeed, one could say that the "valley of ashes" is a metaphor for the spiritual poverty of the modern world:

> a fantastic farm where ashes grow like wheat into ridges and hills and grotesque gardens; where ashes take the forms of houses and chimneys and rising smoke and finally ... of men who move dimly and already crumbling through the powdery air.
>
> (27; ch. 2)

Nick Carraway, the narrator and apparent moral center of the novel, enters this corrupt world with all the innocent blindness that youthful vitality and optimism can create, oblivious, at first, to the "foul dust" (6; ch. 1) and "abortive sorrows" (7; ch. 1) that are the inevitable products of such a world. In the world in which Nick grew up, fathers gave sons advice about "the fundamental decencies" (6; ch. 1); sons graduated from Yale just as their fathers had before them; young men were considered engaged to be married if they had been seen in the company of the same young woman too often; and no one could have imagined that "one man" could fix the World Series, as Meyer Wolfsheim did, "with the single-mindedness of a burglar blowing a safe" (78; ch. 4). It is early summer in 1922 as Nick arrives at his rented cottage in West Egg to begin a new career and a new life, and we see his enthusiasm in his description of his new neighborhood, with its "great bursts of leaves growing on the trees ... and so much fine health to be pulled down out of the young breath-giving air" (8; ch. 1). Even New York City, where Nick works as a bond salesman, seems young and virginal to his eager eyes: "The city seen from the Queensboro Bridge is always the city seen for the *first* time, in its *first* wild *promise* of all the *mystery* and *beauty* in the world" (73; ch. 4, my italics).

By the end of the summer, however, Nick has turned 30 and feels he has nothing to look forward to but "a decade of loneliness, a thinning list of single men to know, a thinning briefcase of enthusiasm, thinning hair" (143; ch. 7). He has discovered that the Buchanans and their lot are "a rotten crowd" (162), and he has "had enough of all of them" (150; ch. 7). Thus, after spending a single summer in the East, Nick prepares, as the novel closes, to return once again to the Midwest, longing for the order and predictability of the life he knew there, sick of the spiritual bankruptcy of life in the modern world. As he tells us at the beginning of the novel, in a retrospective prologue to his narrative, "When I came back from the East last autumn I felt that I wanted the world to be in uniform and at a sort of moral attention forever; I wanted no more riotous excursions with privileged glimpses into the human heart" (6; ch. 1). And to complete the progression from Nick's youthful optimism to disillusionment, the novel ends in the autumn of that same year, "when the blue smoke of brittle leaves was in the air and the wind blew the wet laundry stiff on the line" (185; ch. 9): the time of year when nature's decay underscores the spiritual exhaustion that results from Nick's sojourn in the East.

Of course, Gatsby is part of the corrupt world Nick enters when he moves East, but "Gatsby ... was exempt from [Nick's] reaction" because, as the narrator observes, "Gatsby turned out all right at the end; it is what preyed on Gatsby, what foul dust floated in the wake of his dreams" that elicits Nick's "unaffected scorn" (6; ch. 1). It is Gatsby's quality as a romantic dreamer – his "heightened sensitivity to the promises of life" and his "romantic readiness" (6; ch. 1) – that insulates him from the corrupt world in which he lives and, therefore, from Nick's censure. Indeed, Gatsby has all the makings of a romantic hero, American style. His rags-to-riches success evokes the American romantic ideal of the self-made man, and even his boyhood "schedule" at the back of his Hopalong Cassidy book recalls the self-improvement maxims of Benjamin Franklin, an icon of America's romantic past. Gatsby's status as a war hero increases his value as a romantic symbol as does the fact that his meteoric financial rise was accomplished to win the woman of his dreams. His boyish good looks, his quiet, gentlemanly manners, and his flawless grooming accentuate his youth and innocence. Finally, his absolute devotion to Daisy, epitomized in the idealized image of the young lover "stretch[ing] out his arms" (25; ch. 1) toward the green light at the end of Daisy's dock, "trembling" (26; ch. 1), completes the romantic incarnation.

Unfortunately, Gatsby's unique romantic qualities, which echo the chivalry of ages past, ill suit him to survive the shallow vulgarity of the time in which he lives. Indeed, it is the empty values of the modern world, embodied in Tom and Daisy Buchanan, that crush Gatsby: when Daisy abandons him during his confrontation with Tom at the hotel in New York, "drawing further and further into herself" (142; ch. 7), Gatsby "br[eaks] like glass against Tom's hard malice" (155; ch. 8). With his death, which is the direct result of his chivalrously taking the blame for Daisy's hit-and-run killing of Myrtle, the modern world loses forever the gift that Gatsby had brought to it: "an extraordinary gift for hope ... such as [Nick] ha[s] never found in any other person and which it is not likely [he] shall find again" (6;

ch. 1). Indeed, that Gatsby's "romantic readiness" and "gift for hope" can't survive in the modern world depicted in the novel is one of the text's severest indictments of that world.

Juxtaposed against the fast-paced, shallow decadence of the American 1920s are passages that evoke an idyllic past, passages that serve to remind us of what it is America has lost. One of the most effective is the passage quoted at the opening of this essay, the passage in which Nick reminisces about his youth in Minnesota. Phrases such as "the real snow, our snow, began to stretch out beside us and twinkle" and "a sharp wild brace came suddenly into the air" (184; ch. 9) evoke open spaces – clean, white, and shining – that invigorate not just the body but the spirit as well. "[T]he real snow" refers, of course, to the enormous quantity of clean, white snow that falls in the upper Midwest and lasts all winter, as contrasted with the sooty snow that becomes slush under the wheels of New York traffic. But the phrase also reinforces the notion that life in the Midwest of Nick's youth was more real, more genuine, than the artificial atmosphere he associates with his adult life in the East. Certainly, life in the Minnesota of Nick's youth was more stable and secure as well. For as this same passage indicates, "dwellings are still called through decades by a family's name" (184; ch. 9), which suggests a sense of permanence and personal connection among residents of the community that Nick doesn't find in the East.

This contrast between past and present, between innocence and decadence, between West and East, is heightened by the narrator's description of his dreams about the East, which immediately follows his recollection of Minnesota winters:

> Even when the East excited me most … it had always for me a quality of distortion. West Egg especially still figures in my more fantastic dreams. I see it as a night scene by El Greco: a hundred houses, at once conventional and grotesque, crouching under a sullen, overhanging sky and a lustreless moon. In the foreground four solemn men in dress suits are walking along the sidewalk with a stretcher on which lies a drunken woman in a white evening dress. Her hand, which dangles over the side, sparkles cold with jewels. Gravely the men turn in at a house – the wrong house. But no one knows the woman's name, and no one cares.
>
> (184–85; ch. 9)

The images of human alienation here – the hundred grotesque houses, the drunken woman, the men who deliver her to the wrong house because they don't know her name and don't care to know it – are reinforced by images of an alienated, exhausted nature that contrast sharply with Nick's description of the Midwest of his youth: unlike the clean, bracing, Minnesota sky, the Eastern sky is "sullen" and "overhanging," and even the woman's cold jewels have more "sparkle" than the "lustreless" Eastern moon.

Other references to an idyllic past revolve around Daisy and Jordan's beautiful "white girlhood" (24; ch. 1) in Louisville, where, Nick imagines, Jordan "first learned to walk upon golf courses on clean, crisp mornings" (55; ch. 3). This is a romantic past where, Jordan recalls, she walked on "soft ground" in her "new plaid skirt ... that blew a little in the wind" (79; ch. 4) and where Daisy was

> by far the most popular of all the young girls. ... She dressed in white and had a little white roadster, and all day long the telephone rang in her house and excited young officers from Camp Taylor demanded the privilege of monopolizing her that night. "Anyways for an hour!"
>
> (79; ch. 4)

This is a world in which young girls made bandages for the Red Cross and a handsome young officer named Jay Gatsby "looked at Daisy ... in a way that every young girl wants to be looked at sometime" (80; ch. 4). This is a world of virginal romance: "clean, crisp mornings," "soft ground," new skirts, white dresses, white roadsters, ringing telephones, and handsome young officers. And the young Jay Gatsby was not immune to its charms:

> There was a ripe mystery about [Daisy's house], a hint of bedrooms upstairs more beautiful and cool than other bedrooms, of gay and radiant activities taking place through its corridors, and of romances that were not musty and laid away already in lavender, but fresh and breathing and redolent of this year's shining motor cars and of dances whose flowers were scarcely withered.
>
> (156; ch. 8)

Only such an idyllic past could produce the deed worthy of its romantic ambience: Gatsby's committing himself to Daisy as "to the following of a grail" (156; ch. 8).

Perhaps the most powerful passage that evokes an idyllic past forever vanished is the one that closes the novel. As Nick sits on the beach the evening before his return to Minnesota, he muses on

> the old island here that flowered once for Dutch sailors' eyes — a fresh, green breast of the new world. Its vanished trees, the trees that had made way for Gatsby's house, had once pandered in whispers to the last and greatest of all human dreams; for a transitory enchanted moment man must have held his breath in the presence of this continent, compelled into an aesthetic contemplation he neither understood nor desired, face to face for the last time in history with something commensurate to his capacity for wonder.
>
> (189; ch. 9)

In this passage, all the losses represented in the novel – the loss of values in modern America, the loss of a nation's innocence and vitality, the loss of Gatsby's dream – are associated with a loss of global historical magnitude: the original loss of a pristine American continent that was exploited, polluted, and destroyed by Europe's lust for more colonies and greater wealth.

Clearly, *The Great Gatsby* paints a grim picture of America in the 1920s. However, the novel's representation of this culture's decadence is undermined by the text's own ambivalence toward the binary oppositions on which this representation rests. As we have seen, the novel associates America's innocence, now vanished, with the youthful vitality of the past, especially as it is invoked by the text's descriptions of the West. In contrast, America's decadence is associated with the present-day setting of the novel – the modern world of the 1920s – and with the East, where Nick gets his first taste of the selfishness and superficiality that mark the decline in national values. If we examine the instability of these oppositions – past/present, innocence/decadence, and West/East – we will be able to see how the novel deconstructs its own ideological project.

The novel's evocation of an idyllic past in order to underscore, by contrast, the spiritual emptiness of modern America creates an unstable opposition between past and present because it undermines the text's own awareness that the past was not idyllic for everyone. Certainly, Jay Gatsby's past was not so. "His parents were shiftless and unsuccessful farm people" (104; ch. 6), and his father tells Nick, "He told me I et like a hog once and I beat him for it" (182; ch. 9). In fact, Gatsby found his past so unacceptable that he reinvented it: he left home, changed his name from Jimmy Gatz, and "invented just the sort of Jay Gatsby that a seventeen-year-old boy would be likely to invent, and to this conception he was faithful to the end" (104; ch. 6). As a penniless young lieutenant "he let [Daisy] believe that he was a person from much the same strata as herself" (156; ch. 8), and he tells Nick, "My family all died and I came into a good deal of money. ... After that I lived like a young rajah in all the capitals of Europe ... collecting jewels ... hunting big game, painting a little" (70; ch. 4). In this context, even Gatsby's singular determination to "repeat the past" (116; ch. 6) is really a determination to escape the past. For the past he wants to repeat is his initial liaison with Daisy, which was built on an invented past. Thus, for the character who embodies the novel's notion of the romantic past, the romantic past is, in reality, a tissue of lies.

Another problem with the opposition between past and present in *The Great Gatsby* is its link to the novel's opposition of innocence and decadence, which is itself an unstable opposition. For example, although Nick is the novel's chief spokesperson against the decadence of the age, he is very much attracted by it. Nick says,

> I began to like New York, the racy adventurous feel of it at night and the
> satisfaction that the constant flicker of men and women and machines gives to

the restless eye. I liked to walk up Fifth Avenue and pick out romantic women from the crowd and imagine that *in a few minutes I was going to enter into their lives, and no one would ever know or disapprove.* Sometimes, in my mind, I followed them to their apartments on the corners of hidden streets, and they turned and smiled back at me before they faded through a door into warm darkness.

(61; ch. 3, my italics)

Although Nick doesn't complete the thought, the italicized portion of the passage makes it clear that he imagines himself following these women into the "warm darkness"; their smiles are smiles of invitation. In other words, the "racy adventurous feel" of the city is produced, for him, by the infinity of illicit sexual possibilities it offers. This is not the Minnesota of Nick's youth, with its "interminable inquisitions which spared only the children and the very old" (185; ch. 9), and he's very glad it isn't.

A similar attraction to the decadence the novel condemns is revealed in the narrator's attraction to Jordan Baker. For she is not the "great sportswoman" who would "never do anything that wasn't all right" (76; ch. 4), as Gatsby believes. She's a cheat and a liar, and Nick knows it. Although he dismisses her dishonest behavior as if it were not a serious flaw — "Dishonesty in a woman is a thing you never blame deeply" (63; ch. 3) — it's her dishonesty that, in fact, attracts him because he believes it serves to mask a secret, illicit sexuality that he wants to experience: "I suppose she had begun dealing in subterfuges when she was very young in order to keep that cool, insolent smile turned to the world and yet satisfy the demands of her hard, jaunty body" (63; ch. 3).

It's interesting to note in this context that Nick seems to have great difficulty leaving the scenes that epitomize the superficial values he condemns. For example, he's among the very last to leave both of the parties he attends at Gatsby's house. Even more puzzling, he doesn't seem to be able to extract himself from the drunken revel at Tom and Myrtle's apartment:

I wanted to get out and walk eastward toward the park through the soft twilight, but each time I tried to go I became entangled in some wild strident argument which pulled me back, as if with ropes, into my chair.

(40; ch. 2)

Nick says that it's the "inexhaustible variety of life" that "simultaneously enchant[s] and repel[s]" him (40; ch. 2), but it seems to be the inexhaustible vulgarity of the modern world that, beneath his overt revulsion, fascinates him. And so we see him at the novel's close, once again the last to leave, lingering on the beach at West Egg long after Tom, Daisy, Jordan, and Gatsby are gone.

Another problem with *The Great Gatsby*'s opposition of innocence and decadence is the concept of innocence itself. As the above discussion of Nick implies, he is fascinated by decadence because he is innocent – that is, inexperienced – and therefore hungry for knowledge of the world. Analogously, Nick falls prey, at least for a time, to the decadence he condemns because he is innocent – that is, ignorant – and doesn't understand the kind of moral danger that is confronting him. In other words, the concept of innocence, because it includes the concepts of inexperience and ignorance, has built into it, so to speak, a vulnerability to decadence that is almost sure to result in a fall. Thus, it is not unreasonable to say that innocence leads to decadence; in fact, it creates decadence where before there was none.

A particularly revealing problem with the novel's opposition of innocence and decadence is seen in the characterization of George Wilson. In many ways, he is the only truly innocent character in the story. He harms no one, he trusts everyone, and he is rather childlike in his simplicity. Unlike Nick, who is fascinated by his first encounter with decadence, George's first experience of it – in the form of his wife's infidelity – literally makes him ill: "He had discovered that Myrtle had some sort of life apart from him in another world, and the shock had made him physically sick" (130; ch. 7). Yet George's innocence is portrayed not as a positive quality in its own right but as an absence of qualities of any kind. Wilson has almost no personality at all. As Michaelis notices, "when [George] wasn't working, he sat on a chair in the doorway and stared at the people and the cars that passed along the road. When anyone spoke to him he invariably laughed in an agreeable, colorless way" (144; ch. 7). He didn't even have a friend, Michaelis learns without surprise: there wasn't even "enough of him for his wife" (167; ch. 8). Thus, in a novel that mourns the loss of innocence, innocence is portrayed as ignorance, as the absence of qualities, as a kind of nothingness. And although decadence is overtly condemned by the narrator and by the novel's unsympathetic portrayals of decadent characters, the text seems to find decadence infinitely more interesting than innocence. Innocence is boring; decadence is not.

The thematic structure supported by the binary oppositions past/present and innocence/decadence is tied to a geographic structure that opposes West and East. As we have seen, the innocence of the past is associated with Nick's Minnesota and the Louisville in which Daisy and Jordan grew up. And though Gatsby's youth in North Dakota and Minnesota was an unhappy time in his life, the novel nevertheless associates the West with the innocent dreams of 17-year-old Jimmy Gatz, who "loaf[ed] along the beach [of Lake Superior] ... in a torn green jersey and a pair of canvas pants" (104; ch. 6) before he ever met Dan Cody or heard of Meyer Wolfsheim. In contrast, the decadence of the present is associated with the East, specifically with New York in the 1920s. However, the opposition between West and East in *The Great Gatsby* isn't entirely a matter of geography. For example, Chicago and Detroit are in the Midwest, yet the novel indicates that they share the decadence of New York. Neither is the opposition between West and East entirely that between countryside and city, for Nick's innocent youth, as well as the girlhoods of Daisy and Jordan, were passed in Midwestern cities.

The real distinction between West and East in the novel is the distinction between pristine nature – the "real snow" of Nick's Minnesota and the "old island that flowered once for Dutch sailors" – and the corrupting effects of civilization. That is, regardless of the geography involved, the word *West* invokes, for Americans, untouched, uncorrupted nature. The word *East*, in contrast, is associated with old, corrupt societies. Therefore, the "old island" Nick refers to, though it is New York's Long Island, is associated with the word *West* not only because it is west of the European civilization that colonized it, but because when the Dutch sailors first arrived there, it was pristine.

In *The Great Gatsby,* however, nature, even at its most youthful, energetic, and magical, is inextricably bound to the corrupt civilization of modern America, and this tie between the two further deconstructs the opposition between West and East. Nick associates nature with civilization, for example, in his opening description of early summer in West Egg. He compares the "great bursts of leaves growing on the trees" to the way "things grow in fast movies" (8; ch. 1). And in the very next sentence after he describes the "fine health to be pulled down out of the young breath-giving air," he speaks, in the same exalted tone, of the "shining secrets" he will learn about making his fortune from the "dozen volumes on banking and credit and investment securities" he bought, which "stood on [his] shelf in red and gold like new money from the mint" (8; ch. 1). Similarly, the text can't separate the beauty and vitality of nature from the corrupt power of the wealthy who "own" it, as we see in the following description of the Buchanans' home:

> The lawn started at the beach and ran toward the front door for a quarter of a mile, jumping over sun-dials and brick walks and burning gardens – finally when it reached the house drifting up the side in bright vines as though from the momentum of its run.
>
> (11; ch. 1)

Although the estate is on the edge of the sea, one of the most powerful natural forces on earth, nature, in this passage, is utterly domesticated. The wild grasses that normally border the ocean have been replaced by a lawn that "jump[s] over" objects like a trained dog, while vines adorn the house like jewelry. Yet the sensuous beauty of the lengthy description of the Buchanans' home, of which this passage is but a small part, suggests that the text is unaware of how images such as "the fresh grass outside ... seemed to grow a little way into the house" (12; ch. 1) use the purity of nature to validate the decadent civilization it decorates. Indeed, the beauties of nature are often referred to as if they were manufactured by civilization, as when Nick, attending one of Gatsby's parties, says that "the premature moon [was] produced like the supper, no doubt, out of a caterer's basket" (47; ch. 3). And the blending of nature and civilization is complete when the products of civilization are described as if they were products of nature, as when we're told that "two windows" on the second floor of the Buchanans' house "*bloomed* with light among the vines" (149; ch. 7, my italics).

We see the instability of all three oppositions – past/present, innocence/decadence, and West/East – in the person of Dan Cody, "a product of the Nevada silver fields, of the Yukon, of every rush for metal since Seventy-five" (105; ch. 6), a "florid man with a hard empty face – the pioneer debauchee who during one phase of American life brought back to the eastern seaboard the savage violence of the frontier brothel and saloon" (106). In the person of Dan Cody, and the historical period he represents, we see the past, not the present, associated with decadence, and we see the West corrupting the East.

The most pervasive source of the novel's ambivalence toward its own ideological project, however, is its characterization of Jay Gatsby. As we have seen, Gatsby is portrayed as a romantic hero: a rebellious boy, an ambitious young roughneck, an idealistic dreamer, a devoted lover, a brave soldier, a lavish host. The physical descriptions of his person also generate an ambience of innocence, vitality, and beauty: "[T]here was something gorgeous about him" (6; ch. 1), with his "gorgeous pink rag of a suit" (162; ch. 8), "his tanned skin … drawn attractively tight on his face" (54; ch. 3), and his "rare smil[e] … with a quality of eternal reassurance in it" (52; ch. 3). He is like a romantic knight of ages past somehow displaced in history, lost, with his "incorruptible dream" (162; ch. 8), in a time too superficial to appreciate him. Yet he is also the romantic embodiment of the modern world the novel condemns. That is, by romanticizing Gatsby, the novel also romanticizes the corruption that produced him, the corruption in which he willingly and successfully participates.

"I raised him up out of nothing, right out of the gutter" (179; ch. 9), says Meyer Wolfsheim, the man who fixed the 1919 World Series and the most sinister representative of the criminal world the novel offers. And through bootlegged liquor and fraudulent bonds, Gatsby made his extraordinary fortune in record time. Like the characters the novel condemns, Gatsby succeeds in a world of predators and prey. His illegal, and thus often imperfect, liquor is sold over the counter to anyone with the money to pay for it, and his false bonds are passed in small towns to unsuspecting investors. Some of the people who buy the liquor may become ill from it; some may die. All of the small investors who buy the fraudulent bonds will lose money that they probably can't afford to lose. And when the inevitable mistakes are made and the law steps in, someone will have to be sacrificed, as Gatsby does when he sacrifices Walter Chase.

Even the protagonist's desire for Daisy – which creates, for many readers, the most romantic image of him – is not free from the taint of his underworld view of life: when Gatsby first courted Daisy at her parents' home in Louisville, "[h]e took what he could get, ravenously and unscrupulously – eventually he took Daisy" (156; ch. 8). Gatsby did not just make love to Daisy; he "took" her "ravenously and unscrupulously." This language resonates strongly with his dubious association with Dan Cody before meeting Daisy and with his criminal activities subsequent to their initial affair. Gatsby's "incorruptible dream" (162; ch. 8) is thus mired in the corruption he participated in to fulfill it.

The novel's confusion of the opposing worlds Gatsby represents is largely responsible for the problematic nature of the closing passage we discussed earlier. Let's look at it again. As Nick stands on the beach at West Egg for the last time, he tells us that he

> became aware of the old island here that flowered once for Dutch sailors' eyes – a fresh, green breast of the new world. Its vanished trees, the trees that had made way for Gatsby's house, had once pandered in whispers to the last and greatest of all human dreams; for a transitory enchanted moment man must have held his breath in the presence of this continent, compelled into an aesthetic contemplation he neither understood nor desired, face to face for the last time in history with something commensurate to his capacity for wonder.
>
> (189; ch. 9)

Although Nick reminds us that the "fresh, green breast of the new world," that setting "commensurate to [our] capacity for wonder," "vanished" to make "way for Gatsby's house" – that is, was obliterated by civilization – Nick also associates this "enchanted" dream of the Dutch sailors with Gatsby's dream, which Gatsby attempted to fulfill through the criminal means of the corrupt civilization of which he was a part. For Nick says, "[A]s I sat there brooding on the old, unknown world, I thought of Gatsby's wonder when he first picked out the green light at the end of Daisy's dock" (189; ch. 9). In other words, the text associates the "fresh, green breast of the new world" with the "green light at the end of Daisy's dock," thus tying the romantic sublime of pristine nature to the corrupt civilization that replaced it – in the form of Gatsby – in a way that makes the two, emotionally if not logically, almost impossible to untangle. Furthermore, the "vanished trees," the pristine past, "*pandered* in whispers" (my italics). To *pander* resonates strongly with words like *to pimp*, that is, with soliciting or accommodating the indulgence of another's immoral desires. Thus, pristine nature, the innocent past, cannot be separated in this passage from the civilization that exploits it, just as Jay Gatsby cannot be separated from the corrupt world that exploits and is exploited by him.

The Great Gatsby condemns the modern decadence that, the novel suggests, replaced the innocent America of the past, an America associated with the unspoiled West. But this ideological project is undermined by the inseparability in the text itself of past and present, innocence and decadence, and West and East. Nevertheless, the novel's nostalgia for a lost past, an innocent past, a happier past, is a nostalgia shared, at least according to Western literature of the last several hundred years, by people from every age. Although our deconstructive reading of *The Great Gatsby* surely will not eliminate an emotional investment of such long standing, it can help us understand the ideological limitations of that investment. In addition, our analysis of Fitzgerald's novel illustrates the validity of deconstruction's view of fiction. According to deconstruction, fiction, because it is made of language, embodies the ideologies of the culture that produces it. Fiction can therefore show us the various ways in which our ideologies operate to create our perceptions of the world. In other words, as our deconstructive reading of *The Great Gatsby* demonstrates, fiction doesn't represent the world as it really is; it represents the world as we perceive it to be. And for deconstruction, the world as we perceive it to be is the only world we know.

Questions for further practice: deconstructive approaches to other literary works

The following questions are intended as models. They can help you use deconstructive criticism to interpret the literary works to which they refer or other texts of your choice.

1 The overt ideological project of Luis Valdez's "Los Vendidos" (1967) seems to be to ridicule the ethnic stereotypes that have been imposed on Mexican Americans. First, show how this one-act play accomplishes this ideological project. Then, show how the text deconstructs its own project by inadvertently reasserting, at the end of the play, some of the same stereotypes it has worked to undermine. What does this ideological conflict suggest about the difficulties involved in the attempt to avoid stereotypes or about the difficulty any oppressed group might have asserting its own identity in the face of prejudice?
2 How does Kate Chopin's "The Storm" (1898) forward its theme of the importance of sexual fulfillment for women, which seems to be the story's overt ideological project? How does the text's use of nature imagery and the standard fairy-tale happy ending both promote and undermine this project? What does this ideological conflict imply about the story's attempt to transcend the nineteenth-century social values of the culture it represents?
3 Robert Frost's "The Road Not Taken" (1916) has become an American icon of the value of nonconformity: "I took the one less traveled by, / And that has

made all the difference." Deconstruct this assumed ideological project by finding all the evidence in the poem that seems to undermine the value of non-conformity, for example, the ways in which the two roads are the same and the speaker's own apparent conformity at various points in the poem. You may find that there is, in fact, not as much support in the poem as you expected for the ideology of nonconformity. How might we account for the apparent failure of the American public to recognize this very different reading of the poem?

4 Mary Shelley's *Frankenstein* (1818), which was produced during England's romantic period by an author who associated with some of the leading romantic poets of her day, frequently represents nature as romantic sublime: the contemplation of nature's awesome grandeur – great mountains, storms at sea, huge trees blasted by lightning, and the like – can produce in human beings lofty, noble thoughts and feelings that take them beyond the finite boundaries of mundane experience. Find textual evidence to support this claim. Then show how the novel deconstructs this ideological project by finding, in the text, the ways in which nature does not live up to this definition. Speculate on the reasons why this ideological conflict is present in this text.

5 How might William Blake's "The Little Black Boy" (1789) provide an example of deconstruction's notion of undecidability? Specifically, how does the poem seem to promote the mutually exclusive themes of racial equality, the superiority of white people to black people, and the superiority of black people to white people? What are the implications of this apparent ideological conflict?

For further reading

Atkins, G. Douglas. *Reading Deconstruction: Deconstructive Reading.* Lexington: University of Kentucky Press, 1983.

Belsey, Catherine. *Critical Practice.* 2nd ed. London and New York: Routledge, 2002. (See especially "The Work of Reading," 95–113, and "Deconstruction and the Différance It Makes," 114–25.)

Crowley, Sharon. *A Teacher's Introduction to Deconstruction.* Urbana, IL: NCTE, 1989.

Derrida, Jacques. *Basic Writings.* Ed. Barry Stocker. London and New York: Routledge, 2007.

Deutscher, Penelope. *How to Read Derrida.* New York and London: W.W. Norton, 2005.

Esch, Deborah. "Deconstruction." *Redrawing the Boundaries: The Transformation of English and American Literary Studies.* Eds. Stephen Greenblatt and Giles Gunn. New York: Modern Language Association, 1992. 374–91.

Fink, Thomas. "Reading Deconstructively in the Two-Year College Introductory Literature Classroom." *Practicing Theory in Introductory College Literature Courses.* Eds. James M. Cahalan and David B. Downing. Urbana, IL: NCTE, 1991. 239–47.

Leitch, Vincent B. *Deconstructive Criticism: An Advanced Introduction.* New York: Columbia University Press, 1983.

Norris, Christopher. *Deconstruction: Theory and Practice.* 3rd ed. New York: Routledge, 2002.

Sarup, Madan. *An Introductory Guide to Post-Structuralism and Postmodernism.* 2nd ed. Athens: University of Georgia Press, 1993.

For advanced readers

Abel, Elizabeth. *Writing and Sexual Difference*. Chicago: University of Chicago Press, 1982.

Barthes, Roland. *S/Z*. 1970. Trans. Richard Miller. New York: Hill and Wang, 1975.

Bloom, Harold, *et al*. *Deconstruction and Criticism*. New York: Seabury, 1979.

Culler, Jonathan. *On Deconstruction: Theory and Criticism after Structuralism*. 1982. 25th anniversary ed. Ithaca, NY: Cornell University Press, 2007.

de Man, Paul. *Allegories of Reading: Figural Language in Rousseau, Nietzche, Rilke, and Proust*. New Haven, CT: Yale University Press, 1979.

——. *Blindness and Insight*. 2nd ed. Minneapolis: University of Minnesota Press, 1983.

Derrida, Jacques. "Structure, Sign, and Play in the Discourse of the Human Sciences." 1966. *The Languages of Criticism and the Sciences of Man*. Eds. Richard Macksey and Eugenio Donato. Baltimore, MD: The Johns Hopkins University Press, 1970. 247–65.

——. *Of Grammatology*. 1967. Trans. Gayatri Chakravorty Spivak. Baltimore, MD: The Johns Hopkins University Press, 1976.

Gasché, Rodolphe. *The Tain of the Mirror: Derrida and the Philosophy of Reflection*. Cambridge, MA: Harvard University Press, 1976.

Naas, Michael. *Taking on the Tradition: Jacques Derrida and the Legacies of Deconstruction*. Stanford, CA: Stanford University Press, 2003.

Royle, Nicholas, ed. *Deconstructions: A User's Guide*. New York: Palgrave, 2000.

——. *Jacques Derrida*. New York: Routledge, 2003.

Note

1 My thanks to Johnny Wink, Professor of English and Latin at Ouachita Baptist University in Arkadelphia, Arkansas, for pointing out a needed correction in my explanation of *différance*.

Works cited

Fitzgerald, F. Scott. *The Great Gatsby*. 1925. New York: Macmillan, 1992.

Frost, Robert. "Mending Wall." 1914. *The Poetry of Robert Frost*. Ed. Edward Connery Lathem. New York: Holt, Rinehart and Winston, 1969.

9 New historical and cultural criticism

As we've seen in previous chapters, critical theories can overlap with one another in a number of ways. Marxists can draw on psychoanalytic concepts to help them analyze the debilitating psychological effects of capitalism. Feminists can draw on Marxist concepts to examine the socioeconomic oppression of women. Essays analyzing the conventions of American literary interpretation can be included both in structuralist anthologies and in reader-response anthologies. And so forth.

Despite such overlap, however, most critical theories remain distinct from one another in terms of their purpose. Let's look, for example, at the very different goals of the critical theories just mentioned. Marxism attempts to reveal the ways in which our socioeconomic system is the ultimate source of our experience. Feminism attempts to reveal the ways in which patriarchal gender roles are the ultimate source of our experience. Psychoanalysis attempts to reveal the ways in which repressed psychological conflicts are the ultimate source of our experience. Structuralism attempts to reveal the simple structural systems that make possible our understanding of an otherwise chaotic world. And reader-response theory attempts to reveal the operations whereby readers create the texts they read.

Sometimes critical theories overlap so much, however, that it is difficult to determine the ways in which they are different, especially when practitioners disagree about what those differences are. Such is the case with new historicism and cultural criticism. As we'll see, these two fields share so much common theoretical ground that their approaches to literary interpretation are often quite similar. For the sake of clarity, however, and in order to fully appreciate the differences that do exist between new historicism and cultural criticism, we will begin by discussing the two fields separately. And because new historicists have articulated their theoretical premises more thoroughly than have cultural critics, we'll start with new historicism. Once you have a fairly clear idea of the new historical enterprise, it will be easier to see the ways in which cultural criticism compares and contrasts with it.

New historicism

Most of us raised to think about history in the traditional way would read an account of a Revolutionary War battle written by an American historian in 1944 and ask, if we asked anything at all, "Is this account accurate?" or "What does this battle tell us about the 'spirit of the age' in which it was fought?" In contrast, a new historicist would read the same account of that battle and ask, "What does this account tell us about the political agendas and ideological conflicts of the culture that produced and read the account in 1944?" New historical interest in the battle itself would produce such questions as, "At the time in which it was fought, how was this battle represented (in newspapers, magazines, tracts, government documents, stories, speeches, drawings, and photographs) by the American colonies or by Britain (or by European countries), and what do these representations tell us about how the American Revolution shaped and was shaped by the cultures that represented it?"

As you can see, the questions asked by traditional historians and by new historicists are quite different, and that's because these two approaches to history are based on very different views of what history is and how we can know it. Traditional historians ask, "What happened?" and "What does the event tell us about a particular time and place in history?" In contrast, new historicists ask, "How has the event been interpreted?" and "What do the interpretations tell us about the ideological forces in play for the interpreters?"

For most traditional historians, history is a series of events that have a *linear, causal* relationship: event A caused event B, event B caused event C, and so on. Furthermore, they believe we are perfectly capable, through *objective* analysis, of uncovering the facts about historical events, and those facts can sometimes reveal the spirit of the age, that is, the worldview held by the culture to which those facts refer. Indeed, some of the most popular traditional historical accounts have offered a key concept that would explain the worldview of a given historical population, such as the Renaissance notion of the Great Chain of Being – the cosmic hierarchy of creation, with God at the top of the ladder, human beings at the middle, and the lowliest creatures at the bottom – which has been used to argue that the guiding spirit of Elizabethan culture was a belief in the importance of order in all domains of human life.[1] You can see this aspect of the traditional approach in history classes that study past events in terms of the spirit of an age, such as the Age of Reason or the Age of Enlightenment, and you can see it in literature classes that study literary works in terms of historical periods, such as the neoclassical, romantic, or modernist periods. Finally, traditional historians generally believe that history is *progressive*, that the human species is improving over the course of time, advancing in its moral, cultural, and technological accomplishments.

New historicists, in contrast, don't believe we have clear access to any but the most basic facts of history. We can know, for example, that George Washington was the first American president and that Napoleon was defeated at Waterloo. But our understanding of what such facts mean, of how they fit within the complex web of competing ideologies and conflicting social, political, and cultural agendas of the time and place in which they occurred is, for new historicists, strictly a matter of interpretation, not fact. Even when traditional historians believe they are sticking to the facts, the way they contextualize those facts (including which facts are deemed important enough to report and which are left out) determines what story those facts will tell. From this perspective, there is no such thing as a presentation of facts; there is only interpretation. Furthermore, new historicists argue that reliable interpretations are, for a number of reasons, difficult to produce.

The first and most important reason for this difficulty, new historicists believe, is the impossibility of objective analysis. Like all human beings, historians live in a particular time and place, and their views of both current and past events are influenced in innumerable conscious and unconscious ways by their own experience within their own culture. Historians may believe they're being objective, but their own views of what is right and wrong, what is civilized and uncivilized, what is important and unimportant, and the like, will strongly influence the ways in which they interpret events. For example, the traditional view that history is progressive is based on the belief, held in the past by many Anglo-European historians, that the "primitive" cultures of native peoples are less evolved than, and therefore inferior to, the "civilized" Anglo-European cultures. As a result, ancient cultures with highly developed art forms, ethical codes, and spiritual philosophies, such as the tribal cultures of Native Americans, Africans, and Aboriginal Australians were often misrepresented as lawless, superstitious, and savage.

Another reason for the difficulty in producing reliable interpretations of history is its complexity. For new historicists, history cannot be understood simply as a linear progression of events. At any given point in history, any given culture may be progressing in some areas and regressing in others. And any two historians may disagree about what constitutes progress and what doesn't, for these terms are matters of definition. That is, history isn't an orderly parade into a continually improving future, as many traditional historians have believed. It's more like an improvised dance consisting of an infinite variety of steps, following any new route at any given moment, and having no particular goal or destination. Individuals and groups of people may have goals, but human history does not.

Similarly, while events certainly have causes, new historicists argue that those causes are usually multiple, complex, and difficult to analyze. One cannot make simple causal statements with any certainty. In addition, causality is not a one-way street from cause to effect. Any given event – whether it be a political election or a children's cartoon show – is a product of its culture, but it also affects that culture in return. In other words, all events – including everything from the creation of an art work, to a televised murder trial, to the persistence of or change in the condition of the poor – *are shaped by and shape* the culture in which they emerge.

In a similar manner, our subjectivity, or selfhood, is shaped by and shapes the culture into which we were born. For most new historicists, our individual identity is not merely a product of society. Neither is it merely a product of our own individual will and desire. Instead, individual identity and its cultural milieu inhabit, reflect, and define each other. Their relationship is mutually constitutive (they create each other) and dynamically unstable. Thus, the old argument between determinism and free will can't be settled because it rests on the wrong question: "Is human identity socially determined or are human beings free agents?" For new historicism, this question cannot be answered because it involves a choice between two entities that are not wholly separate. Rather, the proper question is, "What are the processes by which individual identity and social formations – such as political, educational, legal, and religious institutions and ideologies – create, promote, or change each other?" For every society constrains individual thought and action within a network of cultural limitations while it simultaneously enables individuals to think and act. Our subjectivity, then, is a lifelong *process* of negotiating our way, consciously and unconsciously, among the constraints and freedoms offered at any given moment in time by the society in which we live.

Thus, according to new historicists, power does not emanate only from the top of the political and socioeconomic structure. According to French philosopher and historian Michel Foucault (1926–84), whose ideas have strongly influenced the development of new historicism, power circulates in all directions, to and from all social levels, at all times. And the vehicle by which power circulates is a never-ending proliferation of exchange: (1) the exchange of material goods through such practices as buying and selling, bartering, gambling, taxation, charity, and various forms of theft; (2) the exchange of people through such institutions as marriage, adoption, kidnapping, and slavery; and (3) the exchange of ideas through the various discourses a culture produces.

A discourse is a social language created by particular cultural conditions at a particular time and place, and it expresses a particular way of understanding human experience. For example, you may be familiar with the discourse of modern science, the discourse of liberal humanism, the discourse of white supremacy, the discourse of ecological awareness, the discourse of Christian fundamentalism, and the like. And as you read the chapters of this textbook, you will become familiar with the discourses of psychoanalytic criticism, Marxist criticism, feminist criticism, and so on. Although the word *discourse* has roughly the same meaning as the word *ideology*, and the two terms are often used interchangeably, the word *discourse* draws attention to the role of language as the vehicle of ideology.

From a new historical perspective, no discourse by itself can adequately explain the complex cultural dynamics of social power. For there is no monolithic (single, unified, universal) spirit of an age, and there is no adequate totalizing explanation of history (an explanation that provides a single key to all aspects of a given culture). There is, instead, a dynamic, unstable interplay among discourses: they are always in a state of flux, overlapping and competing with one another (or, to use new historical terminology, negotiating exchanges of power) in any number of ways at any given point in time. Furthermore, no discourse is permanent. Discourses wield power for those in charge, but they also stimulate opposition to that power. This is one reason why new historicists believe that the relationship between individual identity and society is mutually constitutive: on the whole, human beings are never merely victims of an oppressive society, for they can find various ways to oppose authority in their personal and public lives.

For new historicism, even the dictator of a small country doesn't wield absolute power on his own. To maintain dominance, his power must circulate in numerous discourses, for example, in the discourse of religion (which can promote belief in the "divine right" of kings or in God's love of hierarchical society), in the discourse of science (which can support the reigning elite in terms of a theory of Darwinian "survival of the fittest"), in the discourse of fashion (which can promote the popularity of leaders by promoting copycat attire, as we saw when Nehru jackets were popular and when the fashion world copied the style of First Lady Jacqueline Kennedy), in the discourse of the law (which can make it a treasonous offense to disagree with a ruler's decisions), and so on.

As these examples suggest, what is "right," "natural," and "normal" are matters of definition. Thus, in different cultures at different points in history, homosexuality has been deemed abnormal, normal, criminal, or admirable. The same can be said of incest, cannibalism, and women's desire for political equality. In fact, Michel Foucault has suggested that all definitions of "insanity," "crime," and sexual "perversion" are social constructs by means of which ruling powers maintain their control. We accept these definitions as "natural" only because they are so ingrained in our culture.

Just as definitions of social and antisocial behavior promote the power of certain individuals and groups, so do particular versions of historical events. Certainly, the whitewashing of General Custer's now-infamous military campaigns against Native Americans served the desire of the white American power structure of his day to obliterate Native American peoples so that the government could seize their lands. And that same whitewashing continued to serve the white American power structure for many a decade beyond Custer's time, for even those who had knowledge of Custer's misdeeds deemed it unwise to air America's dirty historical laundry, even in front of Americans. Analogously, had the Nazis won World War II, we would all be reading a very different account of the war, and of the genocide of millions of Jews, than the accounts we read in American history books today. Thus, new historicism views historical accounts as narratives, as stories, that are inevitably biased according to the point of view, conscious or unconscious, of those who write them. The more unaware historians are of their biases – that is, the more "objective" they think they are – the more those biases are able to control their narratives.

So far, we've seen new historicism's claims about what historical analysis *cannot* do. Historical analysis (1) cannot be objective, (2) cannot adequately demonstrate that a particular spirit of the times or worldview accounts for the complexities of any given culture, and (3) cannot adequately demonstrate that history is linear, causal, or progressive. We can't understand a historical event, object, or person in isolation from the web of discourses in which it was represented because we can't understand it in isolation from the meanings it carried at that time. The more we isolate it, the more we will tend to view it through the meanings of our own time and place and, perhaps, our own desire to believe that the human race is improving with the passage of time.

Given these limitations, what *can* historical analysis accomplish? What approaches to historical understanding can be developed, and, most important for our purposes, what kinds of analyses can new historical literary critics attempt? If you've read Chapter 8, "Deconstructive Criticism," you're in a good position to understand the answer to these questions because a good deal of new historical practice incorporates deconstructive insights about human language and experience. For example, we might say that new historicism deconstructs the traditional opposition between history (traditionally thought of as factual) and literature (traditionally thought of as fictional). For new historicism considers history a text that can be interpreted the same way literary critics interpret literary texts, and conversely, it considers literary texts cultural artifacts that can tell us something about the interplay of discourses, the web of social meanings, operating in the time and place in which those texts were written. Let's take a closer look at each of these claims by discussing, first, the key elements of new historical practice and, then, the implications of new historicism for literary criticism.

By and large, we know history only in its textual form, that is, in the form of the documents, written statistics, legal codes, diaries, letters, speeches, tracts, news articles, and the like in which are recorded the attitudes, policies, procedures, and events that occurred in a given time and place. That is, even when historians base their findings on the kinds of "primary sources" listed above, rather than on the interpretations of other historians (secondary sources), those primary sources are almost always in the form of some sort of writing. As such, they require the same kinds of analyses literary critics perform on literary texts. For example, historical documents can be studied in terms of their rhetorical strategies (the stylistic devices by which texts try to achieve their purposes); they can be deconstructed to reveal the limitations of their own ideological assumptions; and they can be examined for the purpose of revealing their explicit and implicit patriarchal, racist, and homophobic agendas. In addition, historical accounts – secondary sources, written during the period in question or at a later date – can be analyzed in the same manner.

In other words, new historicists consider both primary and secondary sources of historical information forms of narrative. Both tell some kind of story, and therefore those stories can be analyzed using the tools of literary criticism. Indeed, we might say that in bringing to the foreground the suppressed historical narratives of marginalized groups – such as women, people of color, the poor, the working class, gay men and lesbians, prisoners, the inhabitants of mental institutions, and so on – new historicism has deconstructed the white, male, Anglo-European historical narrative to reveal its disturbing, hidden subtext: the experiences of those peoples it has oppressed in order to maintain the dominance that allowed it to control what most Americans know about history.

In fact, a focus on the historical narratives of marginalized peoples has been such an important feature of new historicism that some theorists have asked how new historicists can accept narratives from oppressed peoples any more readily than they have accepted narratives from the patriarchal Anglo-European power structure. One answer to this question is that a plurality of voices, including an equal representation of historical narratives from all groups, helps ensure that a master narrative – a narrative told from a single cultural point of view that, nevertheless, presumes to offer the only accurate version of history – will no longer control our historical understanding. At this point in time, we still do not have an equal representation of historical narratives from all groups. And even as the historical narratives of some groups are becoming more and more numerous, such as those of women and of people of color, those narratives generally do not receive the same kind of attention as patriarchal Anglo-European narratives do in the classroom, where most of us learn about history. Therefore, new historicism tries to promote the development of and gain attention for the histories of marginalized peoples.

A plurality of historical voices also tends to raise issues that new historicism considers important, such as how ideology operates in the formation of personal and group identity, how a culture's perception of itself (for example, Americans' belief that they are rugged individualists) influences its political, legal, and social policies and customs, and how power circulates in a given culture. We can see how a plurality of historical voices tends to raise these kinds of issues if we imagine the differences among the following hypothetical college courses on the American Revolution: (1) a course that studies traditional American accounts of the war; (2) a course that contrasts traditional American accounts of the war with traditional British, French, Dutch, and Spanish accounts of the war, countries for whom the American Revolution was but a moment in their struggle for colonial power, primarily in the Caribbean; (3) and a course that contrasts the above accounts with Native American accounts of the war recorded from the oral histories of tribes that were affected by it.

As we move, in our imagination, from the first course to the second and then to the third, our focus moves farther away from the "factual" content of historical accounts and foregrounds, instead, the ways in which history is a text that is interpreted by different cultures to fit the ideological needs of their own power structures, which is a new historical concern. In this context, new historicism might be defined as the history of stories cultures tell themselves about themselves. Or, as a corrective to some traditional historical accounts, new historicism might be defined as the history of lies cultures tell themselves. Thus, there is no history, in the traditional sense of the term. There are only representations of history.

In addition to its focus on marginalized historical narratives, new historical analysis involves what is called *thick description*, a term borrowed from anthropology. Thick description attempts, through close, detailed examination of a given cultural production – such as birthing practices, ritual ceremonies, games, penal codes, works of art, copyright laws, and the like – to discover the meanings that particular cultural production had for the people in whose community it occurred and to reveal the social conventions, cultural codes, and ways of seeing the world that gave that production those meanings. Thus, thick description is not a search for facts but a search for meanings, and as the examples of cultural productions listed above illustrate, thick description focuses on the personal side of history – the history of family dynamics, of leisure activities, of sexual practices, of childrearing customs – as much as or more than on such traditional historical topics as military campaigns and the passage of laws. Indeed, because traditional historicism tended to ignore or marginalize private life as subjective and irrelevant, new historicism tries to compensate for this omission by bringing issues concerned with private life into the foreground of historical inquiry.

Let me summarize an example of thick description offered by anthropologist Clifford Geertz in *The Interpretation of Cultures*. Imagine a young man winking at someone across a crowded room. A "thin description" of the event would describe it as a rapid contraction of the right eyelid – period. A thick description would attempt to find out what the wink *meant* in the context in which it occurred. First, was it a wink – that is, a public gesture intended to communicate a message – or just an involuntary twitch? If it was a wink, was it a wink performing its usual activity of imparting a conspiratorial signal? Or was it a fake wink, intended to make others believe a conspiracy was underway when, in fact, it was not? In this case, the wink would not mean conspiracy but deception. Or was it a parody of the fake wink just described, intended to satirize the person who winked in order to deceive? In this case, the wink would mean neither conspiracy nor deception, but ridicule. Now suppose that, in this last example, the would-be satirist is unsure of his ability: he doesn't want to be mistaken for someone merely twitching or winking; he wants his friends to know that he's mocking someone. So to be sure he can do it properly, he practices his satirical wink in front of a mirror. In this case, the wink would have a complicated meaning: it would be the rehearsal of a parody of a friend faking a wink to deceive others that a conspiracy is underway. Although this example of thick description may push the point a bit far, it illustrates the new historical notion that history is a matter of interpretations, not facts, and that interpretations always occur within a framework of social conventions.

Finally, new historicism's claim that historical analysis is unavoidably subjective is not an attempt to legitimize a self-indulgent, "anything goes" attitude toward the writing of history. Rather, the inevitability of personal bias makes it imperative that new historicists be as aware of and as forthright as possible about their own psychological and ideological positions relative to the material they analyze so that their readers can have some idea of the human "lens" through which they are viewing the historical issues at hand. This practice is called *self-positioning*.

For example, near the end of Louis Montrose's new historical essay, "Professing the Renaissance: The Poetics and Politics of Culture," he announces his own biases, which include those produced by his role as a Renaissance scholar and professor. He tells us that he has a personal investment in those representations of the Renaissance in texts for which he feels a particular affinity, such as those of Shakespeare and Spenser. Furthermore, he acknowledges that, in analyzing these texts, he writes about issues that are socially relevant today because he wants to participate not only in the current rethinking of Elizabethan culture but in the current rethinking of our own culture. Finally, Montrose admits that although his writing works to undermine traditional historical approaches to literary scholarship – such as the traditional demarcation of a finite period called the Renaissance to which specific cultural qualities are attributed – he has, as a professor and Renaissance scholar, "a complex and substantial stake in sustaining and reproducing the very institutions whose operations [he] wish[es] to call into question" (30).

Before we discuss the implications of new historicism for literary criticism, let's pause for a moment to review its key concepts.

1   The writing of history is a matter of interpretations, not facts. Thus, all historical accounts are narratives and can be analyzed using many of the tools used by literary critics to analyze narrative.
2   History is neither linear (it does not proceed neatly from cause A to effect B and from cause B to effect C) nor progressive (the human species is not steadily improving over the course of time).

3   Power is never wholly confined to a single person or a single level of society. Rather, power circulates in a culture through exchanges of material goods, exchanges of human beings, and, most important for literary critics as we'll see below, exchanges of ideas through the various discourses a culture produces.
4   There is no monolithic (single, unified, universal) spirit of an age, and there is no adequate totalizing explanation of history (an explanation that provides a single key to all aspects of a given culture). There is only a dynamic, unstable interplay among discourses, the meanings of which the historian can try to analyze, though that analysis will always be incomplete, accounting for only a part of the historical picture.
5   Personal identity – like historical events, texts, and artifacts – is shaped by and shapes the culture in which it emerges. Thus, cultural categories such as normal

and abnormal, sane and insane, are matters of definition. Put another way, our individual identity consists of the narratives we tell ourselves about ourselves, and we draw the material for our narratives from the circulation of discourses that constitutes our culture.

6 All historical analysis is unavoidably subjective. Historians must therefore reveal the ways in which they know they have been positioned, by their own cultural experience, to interpret history.

New historicism and literature

How, specifically, do new historical concepts operate in the domain of literary criticism? Although new historical literary criticism embeds our study of literary texts in the study of history, the study of history, as we've just seen, isn't what it used to be. Therefore, new historical criticism has little in common with traditional historical criticism. The latter, which dominated literary studies in the nineteenth century and the early decades of the twentieth, confined itself largely to studies of the author's life, in order to discover his or her intentions in writing the work, or to studies of the historical period in which the work was written, in order to reveal the spirit of the age, which the text was then shown to embody. For traditional literary historians, literature existed in a purely subjective realm, unlike history, which consisted of objectively discernible facts. Therefore, literature could never be interpreted to mean anything that history didn't authorize it to mean.

As you may recall from Chapter 5, "New Criticism," which dethroned traditional historical criticism and controlled literary studies from the 1940s to the 1960s, rejected traditional historicism's approach to literature. For the New Critics, the only thing literary historians could offer was interesting background material about literary works. The understanding of a text's meaning, however, has nothing whatsoever to do with history, the New Critics argued, because great literary works are timeless, autonomous (self-sufficient) art objects that exist in a realm beyond history. As a result of New Critical dominance, the historical study of literature faded into the background and tried to content itself with the tasks New Criticism deemed its proper work: for example, providing background material on authors' lives and times – which would not, however, be used to interpret their works – and preserving, through the provision of accurate editions of revered works, the canon of great literature.

New historicism, which emerged in academia in the late 1970s, rejects both traditional historicism's marginalization of literature and New Criticism's enshrinement of the literary text in a timeless dimension beyond history. For new historical critics, a literary text doesn't embody the author's intention or illustrate the spirit of the age that produced it, as traditional literary historians asserted. Nor are literary texts self-sufficient art objects that transcend the time and place in which they were written, as New Critics believed. Rather, literary texts are cultural artifacts that can tell us something about the interplay of discourses, the web of social meanings, operating in the time and place in which the text was written. And they can do so because the literary text is itself part of the interplay of discourses, a thread in the dynamic web of social meaning. For new historicism, the literary text and the historical situation from which it emerged are equally important because text (the literary work) and context (the historical conditions that produced it) are mutually constitutive: they create each other. Like the dynamic interplay between individual identity and society, literary texts shape and are shaped by their historical contexts.

Perhaps we can best see how new historical critics differ from their traditional counterparts by noting some of the ways in which new historical readings of specific literary works might contrast with traditional historical readings of those same works. We'll look at two well-known texts: Joseph Conrad's *Heart of Darkness* (1902) and Toni Morrison's *Beloved* (1987). It's interesting to note that, in our first example, the author wrote about a situation – Europe's commercial exploitation of Africa – produced by his own society and one that he'd experienced firsthand. In our second example, the author wrote about a population – former slaves struggling to survive both their own memories of the past and the harsh realities of daily life in antebellum Ohio – that had lived over 100 years before the publication of her novel. However, neither Conrad's firsthand experience with his subject matter nor Morrison's temporal distance from hers means that either narrative is necessarily more "accurate" than the other. For traditional historical criticism, the historical accuracy of both texts must be judged by comparisons with historical accounts of the populations represented. And for new historicism, historical "accuracy" is never a certainty: *Heart of Darkness* and *Beloved* offer us the authors' interpretations of the populations they depict, which may or may not provide us with new ways to view the historical experience portrayed but which will certainly give us insight into the circulation of discourses within which Conrad and Morrison wrote these novels.

A traditional historical reading of *Heart of Darkness* might analyze, based on historical accounts of European activities in the Congo during the nineteenth century, how faithful the novel is to the historical realities of European exploitation of human and natural resources in its quest for ivory. Was the waste of human life as flagrant as Conrad portrays it? What were the politics involved in the division of African territories among various European powers and in the administration of those territories? Or a traditional literary historian might examine biographical materials in order to determine what parts of the novel are drawn from Conrad's actual experience during his own trip up the Congo River as a steamship captain for a Belgian company. To what extent are Marlow's experiences actually those of Conrad? To what extent does the novel depict events that Conrad saw or heard about himself? Finally, a traditional historical critic might analyze biographical materials in order to learn about Conrad's creative imagination. What was the influence on Conrad's writing of his early interest in the great explorers of the nineteenth century? Did he keep extensive journals of his experiences as a sailor, or did he write largely from memory? How did his experience in the Congo, including the permanent impairment of his health that resulted therefrom, affect his artistic production?

Similarly, a traditional historical reading of *Beloved* might analyze – based on historical accounts of nineteenth-century American slaves, slaveholders, and former slaves – whether or not Morrison's depiction of this aspect of American experience is faithful to historical reality. Do her portraits of the Garners, their neighbors, Schoolteacher, and the Bodwins accurately represent the range of values held by slave owners and abolitionists at that time? Did Morrison capture the conflicting viewpoints that delineate the spirit of that troubled age? Or a traditional historical reading might investigate the circumstances of the novel's composition in order to find the historical sources of her characters, setting, and plot. For example, to what extent was Sethe's story modeled on that of runaway slave Margaret Garner, who, like Sethe, killed her baby daughter to save her from being returned to her master's plantation? What other characters and events in the novel are based on actual historical figures and events? What specific historical sources – newspaper accounts, slave narratives, legal documents, records of the Middle Passage, history books, and the like – did Morrison draw on? Finally, a traditional historical critic might analyze the author's reading habits in order to find evidence of the influence of other literary works on her own artistic technique. What African American literature, historical fiction, or Southern fiction did she read, and can their influence be perceived in the novel's plot, characterization, or style?

In contrast to these traditional historical concerns, a new historical analysis of *Heart of Darkness* might examine the ways in which Conrad's narrative embodies two conflicting discourses present in his own culture: anticolonialism and Eurocentrism. The novel's anticolonialist theme, which seems to be a primary focus of the text, can be seen in its representation of the evils of Europe's subordination and exploitation of African peoples. However, as Chinua Achebe observes, the novel nevertheless speaks from an (apparently unconscious) Eurocentric perspective: Marlow's harrowing insight into the European character consists of his realization that Europeans are, beneath their veneer of civilization, as "savage" as the African peoples they intend to subdue, which means that African tribal culture is held to epitomize "savagery." Or, despite the novel's Eurocentric bias, a new historical critic might analyze the text as a kind of prototype, or early embodiment, of new historical analysis. As Brook Thomas points out, Conrad's novel debunks the traditional historicist belief that history is progressive, that the human species improves over time; and its narrative structure, which obscures plot events behind a hazy veil of subjective description, implies that we do not have access to a clear, unbiased view of the past. Finally, a new historical analysis of *Heart of Darkness* might examine the history of the novel's reception by critics and the reading public to discover how the novel shaped and was shaped by discourses circulating at its point of origin (the time and place in which the book was written and published) and over the passage of time, including speculations about its relationship to possible future audiences. For example, how might the novel's reception over time reveal the ways in which interpretations of the text shaped and have been shaped by the discourses of historical progressivism, social Darwinism, white supremacy, Afrocentrism, multiculturalism, new historicism, and so on?

Similarly, a new historical analysis of *Beloved* might examine how the novel's departures from the historical accounts on which it is based constitute a revision of those accounts, that is, an interpretation of the history it represents. For example, to what extent do the transformations of Denver and Paul D, as they come to understand Sethe's experience, function as a guide for our own understanding of Sethe's historical situation? Or a new historical critic might examine how *Beloved* was shaped by and has shaped the modern debate between two conflicting views of slavery: (1) that slaves were, for the most part, reduced to a childlike dependency on their masters, and (2) that slaves managed, much more thoroughly and consistently than has been reported by traditional white historians, to build a coherent system of resistance through the creation of their own coded forms of communication, the establishment of their own communal ties, and the strategic use of personae (such as the "happy slave" or the "dim-witted slave") as camouflage for their opinions, intentions, and subversive activities. Finally, a new historical reading might investigate the circulation of mid-nineteenth-century discourses with which specific elements of the plot interact. For example, how do the various views of Sethe depicted in the novel – such as those of Schoolteacher, Mrs. Garner, Amy Denver, Mr. Bodwin, Stamp Paid, Ella, Beloved, and Paul D – reinforce or undermine the mid-nineteenth-century discourses of white supremacy, abolitionism, male supremacy, and motherly love?

As you may have noticed, in all of the above examples of traditional historical criticism, history – the historical situation represented in the text, the population portrayed, the author's life and times – is an objective reality that can be known and against which the subjective literary work is interpreted or measured. In contrast, in the new historical examples, the focus is on how the literary text itself functions as a historical discourse interacting with other historical discourses: those circulating at the time and place in which the text is set, at the time the text was published, or at later points in the history of the text's reception. For new historicism is concerned not with historical events as events, but with the ways in which events are interpreted, with historical discourses, with ways of seeing the world and modes of meaning. Indeed, as we saw earlier, historical events are viewed by new historicists not as facts to be documented but as "texts" to be "read" in order to help us speculate about how human cultures, at various historical "moments," have made sense of themselves and their world. We can't really know exactly what happened at any given point in history, but we can know what the people involved believed happened – we can know from their own accounts the various ways in which they interpreted their experience – and we can interpret those interpretations.

For new historical literary critics, then, the literary text, through its representation of human experience at a given time and place, is an interpretation of history. As such, the literary text maps the discourses circulating at the time it was written and is itself one of those discourses. That is, the literary text shaped and was shaped by the discourses circulating in the culture in which it was produced. Likewise, our interpretations of literature shape and are shaped by the culture in which we live.

Cultural criticism

If you've just read the sections on new historicism, you're already acquainted with many of the theoretical premises of cultural criticism, for the two fields share a good deal of the same theoretical ground. In fact, there are more similarities between them than there are differences. For example, cultural criticism shares with new historicism the view that human history and culture constitute a complex arena of dynamic forces of which we can construct only a partial, subjective picture. Both fields share the belief that individual human subjectivity (selfhood) develops in a give-and-take relationship with its cultural milieu: while we are constrained within the limits set for us by our culture, we may struggle against those limits or transform them. And both fields are interdisciplinary or, perhaps more accurately, antidisciplinary, for both argue that human experience, which is the stuff of human history and culture, cannot be adequately understood by means of academic disciplines that carve it up into such artificially separated categories as sociology, psychology, literature, and so forth. Indeed, both cultural criticism and new historicism draw heavily on the same philosophical sources, in particular the work of French philosopher and historian Michel Foucault, and in practice, cultural criticism is not always readily distinguishable from new historicism.

In addition to its similarity to new historicism, cultural criticism can pose an initial problem for beginners in the way the term is often used, in its broadest sense, to refer to any kind of analysis of any aspect of culture. For example, the readings of *The Great Gatsby* offered in this textbook in the chapters on Marxist criticism, feminist criticism, lesbian/gay/queer criticism, and African American criticism, and postcolonial criticism could all be considered examples of cultural criticism, in its broadest sense, because all of these interpretations use the novel to explore some aspect of American culture. Even my psychoanalytic reading of Fitzgerald's novel — which suggests that the story illustrates the psychology of dysfunctional love — could be revised to function as a cultural critique if I were to argue that the kind of dysfunctional love illustrated in *The Great Gatsby* is a form of cultural malaise produced by the cultural values that came to the fore during the American 1920s. And herein lies one important difference between cultural criticism and new historicism. Cultural criticism often draws on such political theories as those listed above because it tends to be much more politically oriented than new historicism.

Originally an outgrowth of Marxist criticism, then organized as an analytical approach in its own right during the mid 1960s, cultural criticism, in the narrower definition of the term, argues that working-class culture has been misunderstood and undervalued. The dominant class dictates what forms of art are to be considered "high" (superior) culture, such as the ballet, the opera, and the other "fine" arts. Forms of popular culture, on the other hand — such as television situation comedies, popular music, and pulp fiction — have been relegated to the status of "low" (inferior) culture. For cultural critics, however, there is no meaningful distinction between "high" and "low" forms of culture. For all cultural productions can be analyzed to reveal the *cultural work* they perform — that is, the ways in which they shape our experience by transmitting or transforming ideologies — which means, of course, the role of cultural productions in the circulation of power.

Indeed, cultural critics believe that the dominant class defines "high" and "low" culture in order to reinforce its own image of superiority and thus its own power. Nevertheless, cultural critics argue, subordinate populations produce forms of art that not only transform their own experience but affect the whole culture as well. The AIDS quilt might be considered an example of such a cultural production. Clearly, many cultural critics draw on Marxist, feminist, or other political theories in performing their analyses because those analyses often have political agendas, such as analyzing (and valorizing) the cultural productions of an oppressed group or exploring the power relations at work in the categorization of specific art forms as examples of "high" or "low" culture. As we saw earlier, many new historians, in contrast, believe that any single critical theory, political or otherwise, is too narrowly focused to adequately examine the complex operations of human culture.

So far, I've used the word *culture* without actually defining what cultural criticism means by the term. For cultural critics, culture is a process, not a product; it is a lived experience, not a fixed definition. More precisely, a culture is a collection of interactive cultures, each of which is growing and changing, each of which is constituted at any given moment in time by the intersection of gender, race, ethnicity, sexual orientation, socioeconomic class, occupation, and similar factors that contribute to the experience of its members.

To sum up, then, cultural criticism shares new historicism's theoretical premises except in the following three instances:

1 Cultural criticism tends to be more overtly political in its support of oppressed groups.
2 Because of its political orientation, cultural criticism often draws on Marxist, feminist, and other political theories in performing its analyses.
3 Cultural criticism, in the narrower sense of the term, is especially interested in popular culture.

It is important to remember, however, that even when cultural criticism analyzes the operations of oppression, it does not view oppressed peoples as helpless victims. Rather, like new historicism, cultural criticism views oppressed peoples as both victimized by the dominant power structure and as capable of resisting or transforming that power structure.

Cultural criticism and literature

For cultural critics, a literary text, or any other kind of cultural production, performs cultural work to the extent to which it shapes the cultural experience of those who encounter it, that is, to the extent to which it shapes our experience as members of a cultural group. According to Stephen Greenblatt, whose work is primarily responsible for the development of new historicism and cultural criticism during the 1980s, the following questions can help us begin to examine the kinds of cultural work performed by a literary text:

1 What kinds of behavior, what models of practice, does this work seem to enforce?
2 Why might readers at a particular time and place find this work compelling?
3 Are there differences between my values and the values implicit in the work I am reading?
4 Upon what social understandings does the work depend?
5 Whose freedom of thought or movement might be constrained implicitly or explicitly by this work?
6 What are the larger social structures with which these particular acts of praise or blame (that is, the text's apparent ethical orientation) might be connected? (226)

In Greenblatt's words, it might "appear that the analysis of culture is the servant of literary study, but in a liberal education broadly conceived it is literary study that is the servant of cultural understanding" (227). Thus, all of the above questions ask us to make connections between the literary text, the culture in which it emerged, and the cultures in which it is interpreted.

Perhaps it would help at this point to consider some specific applications of cultural criticism to literary works. Let's start by describing what a cultural critic might do with Joseph Conrad's *Heart of Darkness* and Toni Morrison's *Beloved*, the two texts we used earlier to illustrate the differences between traditional and new historical approaches to literature. As I mentioned before, many new historical readings could be considered forms of cultural criticism, broadly conceived. So all of the examples of new historical interpretations of Conrad's and Morrison's novels discussed earlier could be considered examples of cultural criticism to the extent that these interpretations examine the kind of cultural work performed by the literary text.

Let's look, however, at what kinds of readings might distinguish cultural critiques of *Heart of Darkness* and *Beloved* from new historical interpretations of these works. Given that both novels have been canonized as works of "high" culture, a cultural critic, in the narrower sense of the term, might choose to analyze popular representations of these novels, rather than just the novels themselves. For example, a cultural critic might study Francis Ford Coppola's *Apocalypse Now* (1978), which, as most film fans know, is based on Conrad's novel, or the made-for-television version of *Heart of Darkness* starring John Malkovich (1993). Similarly, a cultural critic might examine the film version of *Beloved* starring Oprah Winfrey (1998) or a television miniseries that might someday be produced based on Morrison's novel.

In analyzing these popular forms of canonized works, a cultural critic might try to determine the ways in which the popular versions transmit and/or transform the ideological content of the novels. For example, does the film version seem to have a darker vision of human nature than the novel? Or, in contrast, does the film provide a more optimistic view of the human condition that the novel does not offer? How does the film's representation of race, class, gender, sexual orientation, or any other cultural phenomenon resemble or differ from the novel's representation thereof? How does the film version handle narrative ambiguities, such as Marlow's reliability in *Heart of Darkness* or the meaning of the baby ghost in *Beloved*? Most important, what do the differences, if any, between the film version and the novel suggest about the popular imagination – that is, about the psychological desires and ideological assumptions of the viewing public – or about the entertainment industry's conception of the viewing public? And what does this contrast suggest about the ideological differences between the public for whom the film was produced and the public for whom the novel was written?

Cultural critics are often interested in productions of popular culture for which there are no corresponding versions in "high" culture: for example, the television situation comedies, popular music, and pulp fiction mentioned earlier, as well as such productions of pop culture as, for instance, print, radio, and television advertisements; toys and games; print and television cartoons; professional sports; urban legends and fairy tales; and beauty contests. For a cultural production may or may not take the form of a literal text, but for a cultural critic it always has some sort of ideological "story" to tell.

To appeal to the greatest possible number of critical-theory enthusiasts, let's take for our example video games. In one format common to many games, players try to accumulate some form of wealth or social rank by destroying as many as possible of the enemy figures that appear on the screen. Questions like the following might help us discover the cultural work being done – that is, the ideologies being transmitted or transformed – by such games. Why are the accumulation of great wealth and the acquisition of high social rank such motivating rewards? Why is competition against other players often an important part of the game? What do the enemy figures look like? Do their physical features or apparel make them look less than or other than human? What traditional masculine and/or feminine qualities does a player need in order to play the game successfully? What traditional masculine and/or feminine qualities seem to be valued in the world created by the game? What personal qualities are devalued or seem to be irrelevant? Are female figures present in the game? What do they look like, and how are they dressed? What kinds of behavior do they exhibit? How do male and female figures relate to figures of the opposite sex? How do they relate to figures of the same sex?

People who are not interested in cultural criticism probably would respond to these questions by saying, "It's human nature to dehumanize our enemies, to be strongly motivated by the prospect of accumulating great wealth and acquiring high social rank, and to enjoy competition" or "It's natural for traditional masculine traits to be valorized in a game that is, in one form or another, a game of physical combat." If you are interested in cultural criticism, however, you will want to examine what connections might exist between the values governing the world created in a given video game and the values supporting the culture that creates and plays that game. For example, how does the high value placed on competition for the acquisition of some form of wealth and status reinforce capitalist ideologies? How are masculinity and/or femininity defined in this game, and how are those definitions in keeping or not in keeping with the gender definitions in circulation – and, especially, in power – in the culture that creates and plays that game? The issue here isn't whether or not we play any particular kind of video game or whether we approve or disapprove of any particular kind of video game. Rather, the issue here is our ability to notice and interpret the messages we receive every day from video games and from all the other modes of popular entertainment and information that are so much a part of our culture that we may not give them a second thought.[2]

A cultural critic would also be inclined to take into account the ways in which a cultural production might not be perceived or used the way those who produced it intended it to be perceived or used. For example, as John Fiske observes,

> [h]omeless Native Americans ... chose to watch old westerns on the VCR in their shelter, but they selected only the first half of them, and switched off the

movie at the point when the wagon train had been successfully attacked, the fort captured – they chose not to watch the reassertion of white empire. Aboriginal people watching the Rambo movies in Australia chose to ignore the conflict between the free west and the communist east and focused instead on the conflict between Rambo, whom they saw, by a selection of physical and behavioral characteristics, as a member of the third world like them, and the white officer class that systematically and mistakenly underestimated his abilities.

(327)

So whether examining popular culture, "high" culture, or both, cultural critics try to map the changing ideological functions that a given cultural production performs at the hands of those who respond to it.

Some questions new historical and cultural critics ask about literary texts

The following questions are intended to summarize approaches to literary analysis employed by new historicists and cultural critics. In the terminology of cultural criticism, these questions offer us ways to examine the cultural work performed by literary texts. As you read these questions and imagine the ways in which a new historical or cultural critic might address them, keep in mind that, for such critics, no historical event, artifact, or ideology can be completely understood in isolation from the innumerable historical events, artifacts, and ideologies among which it circulates, and our own cultural experience inevitably influences our perceptions, making true objectivity impossible. For we can use new historical and cultural criticism properly only if we keep clearly in mind that our analysis is always incomplete, partial, and our perspective is always subjective. We can't stand outside our own culture and analyze texts from an objective vantage point. We can write only from within our own historical moment.

1   How does the literary text function as part of a continuum with other historical and cultural texts from the same period, for example, penal codes, birthing practices, educational priorities, the treatment of children under the law, other art forms (including popular art forms), attitudes toward sexuality, and the like? That is, taken as part of a "thick description" of a given culture at a given point in history, what does this literary work add to our tentative understanding of human experience in that particular time and place, including the ways in which individual identity shapes and is shaped by cultural institutions?

2   How can we use a literary work to "map" the interplay of both traditional and subversive discourses circulating in the culture in which that work emerged

and/or the cultures in which the work has been interpreted? Put another way, how does the text promote ideologies that support and/or undermine the prevailing power structures of the time and place in which it was written and/or interpreted?

3 Using rhetorical analysis (analysis of a text's purpose and the stylistic means by which it tries to achieve that purpose), what does the literary text add to our understanding of the ways in which literary and nonliterary discourses (such as political, scientific, economic, and educational theories) have influenced, overlapped with, and competed with one another at specific historical moments?

4 What does the literary work suggest about the experience of groups of people who have been ignored, underrepresented, or misrepresented by traditional history (for example, laborers, prisoners, women, people of color, lesbians and gay men, children, the insane, and so on)? Keep in mind that new historical and cultural criticism usually include attention to the intersection of the literary work with nonliterary discourses prevalent in the culture in which the work emerged and/or in the cultures in which it has been interpreted and often focus on such issues as the circulation of power and the dynamics of personal and group identity.

5 How has the work's reception by literary critics and the reading public – including the reception at its point of origin, changing responses to the work over time, and its possible future relationship with its audience – been shaped by and shaped by the culture in which that reception occurred?

Depending on the literary text in question, we might ask one or any combination of these questions. Or we might come up with a useful question not listed here. These are just some starting points to get us thinking about literary texts as new historical and cultural critics do. Keep in mind that not all new historical or cultural critics will interpret the same work in the same way even if they focus on the same theoretical concepts and have the same purpose. As in every field, even expert practitioners disagree. Our goal is to use new historicism and cultural criticism to help enrich our reading of literature by helping us see how literary texts participate in the circulation of discourses, shaping and shaped by the culture in which they emerge and by the cultures in which they are interpreted; by helping us see the ways in which the circulation of discourses *is* the circulation of political/social/intellectual/economic power; and by helping us see the ways in which our own cultural positioning influences our interpretations of literary and nonliterary texts.

The following reading of F. Scott Fitzgerald's *The Great Gatsby* is offered as an example of what a new historical interpretation of that novel might yield. In the terminology of cultural criticism, it analyzes the cultural work performed by the novel. I call my interpretation of Fitzgerald's novel a new historical reading, however, because it doesn't have the kind of overt political agenda often associated with cultural criticism and because I rely rather heavily on terminology associated with new historicism. However, the overlap between the two fields is such that my interpretation could also be called, quite legitimately, a cultural analysis, especially because my argument makes no distinction between Fitzgerald's canonized "classic" and various forms of popular culture informed by the same ideology.

Specifically, I argue that the novel circulates one of the dominant discourses of the period in which it was written: the discourse of the self-made man, which held that any poor boy in America, if he had the right personal qualities, could rise to the top of the financial world. In addition, I examine the ways in which *The Great Gatsby* embodies one of the central contradictions of the discourse of the self-made man: although this discourse claims to open the annals of American history to all those who have the ambition and perseverance required to "make their mark," the discourse is permeated by the desire to "escape" history, to transcend the historical realities of time, place, and human limitation.

The discourse of the self-made man: a new historical reading of *The Great Gatsby*

F. Scott Fitzgerald's *The Great Gatsby* (1925) was published during one of America's greatest periods of economic growth. As the nation expanded its borders and developed its industries between the end of the Civil War in 1865 and the stock-market crash in 1929, many private fortunes were made. Everyone in America knew the success stories of millionaires like John D. Rockefeller, Jay Gould, Jim Fisk, Andrew Carnegie, J. P. Morgan, Philip Armour, and James J. Hill. Even Gatsby's father, an uneducated and unsuccessful farmer, is aware of these stories. He says of his son, "If he'd of lived he'd of been a great man. A man like James J. Hill. He'd of helped build up the country" (176; ch. 9). With the exception of J. P. Morgan, the son of a wealthy banker, all of these millionaires were self-made men: from very humble beginnings they rose to their position at the top of the financial world. And popular belief held that any poor boy in America with the right personal qualities could do the same.

Thus, a dominant discourse of the period was the discourse of the self-made man, which circulated in the "success manuals" of the period; in the self-improvement speeches and essays composed by the self-made millionaires of that era; in the Horatio Alger novels; in the McGuffey Readers, which were used throughout the nation to teach young children to read; and in the biographies of famous self-made men. Fitzgerald's novel participates in the circulation of this discourse, I think, in at least two significant ways. It reflects the major tenets of the discourse and, I would argue, it embodies one of its central contradictions: the discourse of the self-made man, while it claims to open the annals of American history to all those who have the ambition and perseverance required to "make their mark," is permeated by the desire to "escape" history and to transcend the historical realities of time, place, and human limitation.

Let's begin by examining the ways in which *The Great Gatsby* reflects the major tenets of the discourse of the self-made man. Of course, readers frequently notice the similarities between Gatsby's boyhood "schedule" – in which the young man divided his day among physical exercise, the study of electricity, work, sports, the practice of elocution and poise, and the study of needed inventions – and the self-improvement ideology found in the autobiography of Benjamin Franklin, America's original self-made man. Obviously, Gatsby hoped, indeed planned, to live the "rags-to-riches" life associated with the self-made millionaires of his day. However, the characterization of Gatsby draws on the self-improvement tradition more thoroughly than some readers today may realize.

During the period in which Gatsby lived (1890–1922) – roughly the same historical period from which the novel emerged, for Fitzgerald was born in 1896 and *The Great Gatsby* was published in 1925 – books that explained how poor boys could rise to heights of great wealth, called "success manuals," flourished. In Austin Bierbower's *How to Succeed* (1900), a representative example of the genre, the following advice is given to the prospective self-made man: work hard, have a clear purpose, be prepared for opportunity, don't procrastinate, persevere, keep in good physical condition, and avoid drink. Poor boys have an advantage over rich boys, Bierbower notes, because they are introduced to hard work at a young age and motivated by financial need to apply themselves. In contrast, many wealthy youth, the author points out, avoid hard work and focus instead on insubstantial goals like fashion and etiquette, thereby sometimes failing to increase or even maintain the fortunes they inherited. The virtues extolled in similar publications include, in addition, the importance of saving money and of avoiding such slothful behaviors as smoking, using slang, and keeping bad company. In short, rising young men were advised to avoid any behavior that wasted time, cost money, or was injurious to health or reputation.

Making himself useful to his parents was also considered a good way for a young boy to develop the traits of industry and initiative, which would serve him well later in life. And for similar reasons, it was generally accepted that a rural upbringing, preferably on a farm, was superior to a boyhood spent in the city.[3]

Jay Gatsby fits this profile in a number of ways. He was born to poor "farm people" (104; ch. 6) and spent his youth in rural Minnesota. His boyhood list of "General Resolves," found in his copy of *Hopalong Cassidy* just below his Franklinesque daily schedule of activities, reads like a mini-success manual:

No wasting time at Shafters or [a name, indecipherable]
No more smokeing or chewing
Bath every other day

Read one improving book or magazine per week

Save $5.00 [crossed out] $3.00 per week

Be better to parents

(181–82; ch. 9)

Gatsby's physical fitness, a frequently mentioned self-improvement virtue, is evident in Nick's description of his "balancing himself on the dashboard of his car with that resourcefulness of movement that is so peculiarly American – that comes ... with the formless grace of our nervous, sporadic games" (68; ch. 4). Gatsby's "elaborate formality of speech," which gives Nick the impression that he is "picking his words with care" (53; ch. 3), illustrates the self-improvement virtue of avoiding slang, and we see another behavior recommended by success manuals in Gatsby's strict avoidance of alcohol, even at his own parties.

Unlike Tom Buchanan and Nick Carraway, Gatsby was motivated by the financial need to apply himself: he made his fortune during his first three years with Wolfsheim. Even Gatsby's outstanding war record marked him as a young man certain to get ahead in the world, while Nick's military experience seems singularly undistinguished, and we hear no mention of Tom's at all. Indeed, the characterization of Tom and Nick exemplify the dictum of the self-improvement tradition that inherited wealth is a handicap to self-improvement: Tom does nothing with his life but find more and more extravagant ways to spend his inherited fortune, while Nick, 30 years old and still being supported by his father while he learns the bond business, feels he has no clear direction in life. Finally, George Wilson's rather pathetic failure to adequately support himself and his wife serves as an implicit warning about the fate of poor men who, unlike Gatsby, lack the fortitude and drive to "pull themselves up by their bootstraps."

We see the same kind of success ideology at work in the speeches and essays in which many self-made millionaires revealed the secrets of their success, as Andrew Carnegie often did. In "The Road to Business Success" (1885), for example, Carnegie tells the would-be self-made man to aim high, save his money, and avoid liquor. To rise in the business world, Carnegie notes, a young man must be able to think for himself: "There never was a great character who did not sometimes smash the routine regulations and make new ones for himself" (8). In "How to Win Fortune" (1890), Carnegie argues that, given the competitive nature of the business world, it is unwise for the prospective self-made man to waste precious time acquiring a college education, even if he were able to somehow work his way through, because the time he spends in college will put him behind the young man who apprentices himself to a captain of industry at an early age. A "college education," Carnegie says, "seems almost fatal to [the] success" (91) of the self-made man.

As we saw above, Gatsby believed, even as a teenager, in the importance of saving money, and "he formed the habit of letting liquor alone" (107; ch. 6) early in life as well. In contrast to Tom and Nick, who both graduated from Yale, Gatsby refused to waste time attending college: led by an "instinct toward his future glory," he quit after two weeks at "the small Lutheran college of St. Olaf" (105; ch. 6). Perhaps the most interesting similarity between Carnegie's advice and Gatsby's behavior, however, is seen in Gatsby's consistent tendency to aim high and "smash the routine regulations" in order to "make new ones for himself" (Carnegie, "The Road" 8). Gatsby rose quickly in the esteem of Dan Cody, who "repos[ed] more and more trust in [him]" (106; ch. 6), just as he rose quickly to the rank of army major during World War I, just as he rose quickly in the organization of Meyer Wolfsheim. By the time we meet him, Gatsby clearly occupies an executive position, either in Wolfsheim's organization or in one of his own: he receives phone calls, at all hours and from various parts of the country, during which he makes decisions and gives orders to his underlings. And though Carnegie certainly didn't intend his advice to be taken in quite this way, Gatsby's disregard for routine regulations is obvious, of course, in his choice of a criminal career: he made his fortune in the management of bootlegging operations and the sale of fraudulent bonds.

Other texts that circulated the discourse of the self-made man were the novels of Horatio Alger, which were immensely popular during the late nineteenth and early twentieth centuries. In these tales, the hero is always a poor young boy who is hardworking, honest, neat, self-reliant, persevering, modest, kind, generous, and lucky. Luck, for Alger, included being ready to seize an opportunity when it occurs, which requires both imagination and nerve. In all of Alger's novels, the hero has obstacles to overcome, including a villain who cheats him in some way; there is a lesser hero in the story who helps him in some way; and there are one or more father figures in the form of successful, benevolent businessmen. The hero's outstanding qualities always end up bringing him some sort of financial success, and the stories thus extol the same virtues of the self-made man we see in the success manuals.

The Great Gatsby shares many important features with the Horatio Alger formula novel. Jay Gatsby's well-groomed appearance and quiet amiability, which is noted several times by Nick, give him much of the same appeal as the Alger hero, even if he doesn't share the latter's ethics. More striking, however, is the similarity in structure between Fitzgerald's novel and those of Alger. Like the Alger hero, Gatsby is of humble origins, willing to work hard to make his way in the world, and had more than enough imagination and nerve at his disposal when opportunity unexpectedly knocked in the form of Dan Cody:

> It was James Gatz who had been loafing along the beach that afternoon ... but it was already Jay Gatsby who borrowed a row-boat, pulled out to the Tuolomee, and informed Cody that a wind might catch him and break him up in half an hour.
>
> (104; ch. 6)

After working for Cody for five years and learning the ways of the world, Gatsby is cheated, again like the Alger hero, of his rightful reward: "a legacy of twenty-five thousand dollars" (107; ch. 6), promised to the 23-year-old Gatsby in Cody's will, went instead, through some "legal device that was used against him" (107; ch. 6), to Cody's companion, Ella Kaye. Gatsby is also, in a sense, cheated out of Daisy Fay when Tom marries her while Gatsby is still overseas after World War I. Fitzgerald's hero perseveres, however, in his pursuit both of fortune and of Daisy, and before the novel closes he attains both goals. Finally, the role of the lesser hero who helps the Alger hero in some way is played by Nick Carraway, and the role of the businessman-father figure is played by Dan Cody, as we saw above, and by Meyer Wolfsheim, who "raised him up out of nothing" (179; ch. 9) when Gatsby returned penniless from the war.

Perhaps the most pervasive vehicles for the ideology of the self-made man were the McGuffey Readers, a series of elementary school books used to teach reading, which were a dominant force in American education from the mid-nineteenth century to the early 1920s. The stories and poems contained in the Readers extol the same virtues promoted by the success manuals of the period: honesty, hard work, kindness, and the avoidance of alcohol and bad company. In addition, like the success manuals, Horatio Alger novels, and other texts that circulated the discourse of the self-made man, the Readers illustrated the belief that success is a product of good character. For example, a poor boy receives a job because the old man he has kindly helped cross the street turns out to own his own business. Or an orphan boy is adopted by a wealthy man because he has resisted the temptation to steal the man's gold watch.

As we have seen, Gatsby has many traits in common with the self-made hero, of which McGuffey's protagonists are just another version. And the job Gatsby receives from Dan Cody, which serves as his introduction to the world of financial success to which he has always aspired, is the product of the good deed he performed in rowing out to Cody's yacht to warn him of an impending storm, just as the success of McGuffey's boys is a product of their good character.

Finally, there is a startling resemblance between Gatsby's early life and the formative years of America's most famous self-made millionaires, the oft-told stories of which were another way in which the discourse of the self-made man circulated. In *The Robber Barons* (1934), Matthew Josephson details many of the common experiences shared by such self-made millionaires of the late nineteenth century as Jay Gould, Jim Fisk, Philip Armour, Andrew Carnegie, James Hill, John Rockefeller, and Jay Cooke. Although Josephson is not interested in literary analysis and makes no comparisons with *The Great Gatsby*, the similarities between the life stories Josephson narrates and the biography of Jay Gatsby are too striking to be ignored.

Born into poverty, "most of these young men," Josephson notes, "left the paternal shelter early in youth, to wander alone and make their own way. ... [T]hey showed promising signs of shiftiness and self-reliance in boyhood" (33). Although their companions often drank and gambled, these young men did not. Cool under pressure, "violence [did] not shake [them]" (35). Indeed, they often made their fortunes in the rush for gold or for the monopoly of natural resources, railroad lines, or stocks, all of which pursuits were not merely financially dangerous but physically dangerous as well: as fortunes were quickly made and lost, one's companions on the frontier, or even a group of stockholders one had defrauded on Wall Street, could turn into an angry, vengeful mob. And "[a]t the center of the stirring, shifting drama of material progress toward new railroads or gold fields," Josephson observes, "was the notion of individual fortune and change of station" (37).

In other words, much like Jay Gatsby, the self-made men of whom Josephson writes were driven by a desire to become rich and rise up out of the class into which they were born. And much like these self-made men, Gatsby left his parents' home as a teenager, wandered alone, and made his own way. Like them, he did not adopt the debilitating personal habits of his companions, and he made his fortune according to the dangerous rules of a violent subculture.

Clearly, *The Great Gatsby* reflects the discourse of the self-made man circulating in so many of the texts that both shaped and were shaped by American culture during the final decades of the nineteenth century and the early decades of the twentieth. For ideology does not observe boundaries between "high" and "popular" culture: a discourse circulating in such practical and mundane texts as success manuals, children's readers, and didactic formula-novels can also saturate the pages of one of the era's most sophisticated artistic productions.

However, the novel also serves as a comment on the discourse of the self-made man to the extent that it reveals one of its central contradictions, which concerns the relationship of that discourse to history. Although the discourse of the self-made man claims to open the annals of American history to all those who have the ambition and perseverance required to "make their mark" on its pages, the discourse is permeated by the desire to escape history, to transcend the historical realities of time, place, and human limitation.

This contradiction appears in many of the autobiographical stories of the self-made millionaires mentioned above. Although self-made men often spoke of the harsh historical realities they experienced as children, particularly of their poverty, they did so only to celebrate how far they had come. And the form that celebration took, I would argue, constitutes a denial of historical reality because it was a way of reinventing the suffering self-made men saw in their youth as nothing but a prelude to their success. Looking back on their lives, they saw their boyhood selves as "future millionaires in training," so to speak, being honed in the workshop of "hard knocks" and fired in the kiln of poverty. Such an ideology didn't permit them to see the debilitating effects of the poverty they escaped on those who didn't manage to do the same.

Among the general population of America's impoverished, relatively few, in any generation, have become millionaires. According to the discourse of the self-made man, those who didn't rise to the top had only themselves to blame, which implies, of course, that poverty and the degrading influence of tenement life (not to mention the almost insurmountable obstacles raised against business opportunities for women and people of color) are no excuse for the failure to rise in the business world. Such failure was defined as a failure of one's character, pure and simple. This is why many self-made millionaires refused to give money to charity, confining their philanthropy to endowing libraries, museums, and universities, which could, they reasoned, help only those who were willing to help themselves and not encourage the slothful behavior that charity would, they believed, encourage.[4]

For example, in his autobiography, Andrew Carnegie describes the happy family life he enjoyed as a child of poor immigrant parents. He notes, in addition to his family's economic hardship, how politically active his relatives were, how education was valued by his parents, and how he was trained by his home environment to engage in rigorous debate on the issues of the day. Indeed, Carnegie observes that the economic poverty he suffered in childhood was richly compensated by the training and support he received in the bosom of a strong family. Yet he was apparently unable to realize that many other poor youngsters in his own neighborhood – for example, the sons of parents who did not understand the value of education or the sons of drunken, abusive parents – did not have the same advantages he had and therefore could not be expected to raise themselves up as readily as he did. That is, in Carnegie's desire to focus on his own transcendence of historical reality, he ignores those aspects of history that cannot be overcome so readily.

The Great Gatsby reflects this same desire to transcend history in Gatsby's efforts to deny his true origins. Gatsby's "parents were shiftless and unsuccessful farm people," but "his imagination had never really accepted them as his parents at all" (104; ch. 6). Instead, Gatsby invented a family, an Oxford education, and an inheritance in order to convince himself and others that he was born to wealth and social position. That is, Gatsby wants to deny the historical realities of socio-economic class to which he had been subjected all his life. As Nick puts it, "Jay Gatsby ... sprang from his Platonic conception of himself" (104; ch. 6). A Platonic conception is one that, by definition, is outside history: it exists in a timeless dimension untouched by daily occurrences in the material world. And this is the dimension in which Gatsby wants to live.

Gatsby's claim that Daisy's love for Tom "was just personal" (160; ch. 8), a statement that confuses Nick as well as many readers, makes sense in this context. In Gatsby's eyes, Daisy's love for Tom exists within history, within the domain of the personal, and is thus no competition for the love she and Gatsby share, which exists in a timeless dimension beyond history. Similarly, Gatsby's belief in our power over the past makes sense only if he conceives of his own life outside the bounds of historical reality. His conviction that the three years Daisy has spent married to Tom can be "obliterated" by her telling Tom that she never loved him, and that they can "repeat the past" by "go[ing] back to Louisville and be[ing] married from her house – just as if it were five years ago" (116; ch. 6) is a conviction one can hold only from a place outside history, a place where the past is repeatable because it is timelessly preserved, forever accessible.

The discourse of the self-made man also "erases history" in choosing to ignore or marginalize the enormous character flaws of many famous self-made men while simultaneously defining self-made success as a product of one's character rather than of one's environment. The success manuals from this period offered very little, if any, practical advice about business matters. All of their advice focused, instead, on attributes of character – from honesty and integrity in the workplace to frugality and sobriety in the home – because it was believed that success comes from within the man. Therefore, character, rather than education or business acumen, was considered the foundation of the self-made man. Yet some of the moral failings of self-made millionaires were the very factors that enabled them to rise to the top by enabling them to ruthlessly and often unethically destroy their business rivals. Of course, this aspect of historical reality was absent from the proliferation of texts that extolled the virtues of the self-made man, or it was recast, in the popular imagination, as a capitalist virtue: competitiveness, aggressiveness, toughness.

It is interesting to note in this context that since the publication of *The Great Gatsby*, the majority of critical response to the novel's title character has romanticized him much as American culture has romanticized the self-made man, by idealizing his desire to succeed and ignoring or marginalizing the means by which he fulfilled that desire. What an early reviewer said of Gatsby in 1925 has continued to represent the feeling of a good many readers over the course of the novel's reception: Gatsby's "is a vitality ... the inner fire [of] which comes from living with an incorruptible dream, even if extraordinary material corruption has been practised in its realization" (E. K. 426). In 1945, William Troy describes Gatsby as the "projected wish fulfillment" of the "consciousness of a race" (21). And Tom Burnam argues in 1952 that Gatsby "survives sound and whole in character, uncorrupted by the corruption which surrounded him" (105). In 1954, Marius Bewley writes that Gatsby is "all aspiration and goodness" (25): "an heroic personification of the American romantic hero" (14), who represents "the energy of the spirit's resistance" and "immunity to the final contamination" of "cheapness and vulgarity" (13). And Barry Edward Gross suggests in 1963 that "Gatsby's dream is essentially 'incorruptible'" because it "is essentially immaterial," which is why "he turns 'out all right at the end'" (57). Similarly, in 1978 Rose Adrienne Gallo argues that Gatsby "maintained his innocence" to the end (43), or as André Le Vot puts it in 1983, Gatsby never loses his "fundamental integrity, his spiritual intactness" (144). Even when the protagonist's darker side is acknowledged, it is excused. As Kent Cartwright argues in 1984, "Gatsby can be both criminal and romantic hero because the book creates for him a visionary moral standard that transcends the conventional and that his life affirms" (232). Or as Andrew Dillon sums up, in 1988, what he sees as the protagonist's merger of worldliness and spirituality, Gatsby is "a sensual saint" (50).[5]

Finally, the connection between the discourse of the self-made man and the desire to transcend history can be seen in the McGuffey Readers. In the self-improvement discourse that informs the bulk of the material in the Readers there is a striking absence of reference to historical reality. Even during the period directly after the Civil War, when poems and songs about the war abounded, the only "historical" piece included isn't historical at all: it's a sentimental poem called "The Blue and the Gray" (1867) in which soldiers from both sides are glorified in terms such that they could be soldiers from almost any war fought during almost any historical period. In other words, the poem creates a timeless world that remains untouched by historical events. As Henry Steele Commager puts it,

> [t]hough the original volumes of the Readers appeared when men could still remember the Revolutionary War and the War of 1812 – McGuffey himself lived through that war, and on the Ohio frontier, too – there is no ardent hostility to Britain, no execration of George III, no atrocity story about the Indians. And though new Readers, and revisions of old Readers, poured from the presses all through the era of the Mexican War, of Manifest Destiny, and of Young America, the Readers reflect none of this: even the Oregon Trail and the gold rush to California were not allowed to ruffle the serenity of their pages. Even more startling is the fact that those who later revised the Readers … managed to avoid the Civil War! Aside from Francis Finch's "The Blue and the Gray" – a masterpiece of impartiality – the war might never have happened, as far as the Readers are concerned.
>
> (xiii)

History is also transcended in the McGuffey Readers through the sentimentalization of experience. The Readers are full of sentimental descriptions of injured animals, of virtuous children rewarded for their unselfishness by some monetary windfall, of the peaceful deaths of angelic children, and of heroic deeds. When experience is depicted in sentimental terms, that experience becomes general rather than specific, "larger than life" in the same way that fairy tales are larger than life: they exist in some timeless dimension beyond the daily course of human events, beyond history. As Stanley W. Lindberg observes about one of McGuffey's war poems, it is "safely sentimental" (320), by which he means, of course, outside the fray of the political and social issues of the day, that is, outside history.

There is a striking similarity between the overblown sentimentality of the McGuffey Readers and the "appalling sentimentality" (118; ch. 6) of the autobiographical narrative Gatsby offers Nick, a sentimentality that removes Gatsby's life, just as it removed the McGuffey Readers, from the realities of history. Gatsby tells Nick,

> My family all died and I came into a good deal of money. ... After that I lived like a young rajah in all the capitals of Europe ... collecting jewels, chiefly rubies, hunting big game, painting a little ... and trying to forget something very sad that had happened to me long ago.
>
> (70; ch. 4)

Gatsby's autobiographical sketch sounds more like an outline for a staged Victorian melodrama than a narrative about an actual life. As Nick puts it, "The very phrases were worn so threadbare that they evoked no image except that of a turbaned 'character' leaking sawdust at every pore" (70; ch. 4). But it is this sentimental "translation" of his life – which he offers, Nick says, in a "solemn" voice, "as if the memory ... still haunted him" (70) – that allows Gatsby to escape historical reality into a "larger-than-life" fairy tale.

Of course, the discourse of the self-made man retains much of its vitality today. On an episode of the American television series *Matlock*, for example, a son attempts to recuperate his murdered father's reputation as a ruthless, unethical business executive by saying that his father was a self-made man. Thus, the phrase still has the power to suggest that men capable of achieving such an important and respected goal should not be judged too harshly for their ruthless, unethical behavior because it requires "toughness" to make it as a self-made man. Similarly, the television series *America's Castles*, which offers guided tours of America's great mansions and of the lives of the men who built them, relies heavily on the discourse of the self-made man, even quoting uncritically the self-serving statements of nineteenth- and early-twentieth-century self-made millionaires concerning their own hard work and integrity.

Furthermore, Jay Gatsby remains the icon of America's romanticization of the self-made man. That actors Robert Redford and Leonardo DiCaprio, both known for their boyish good looks and often cast as romantic heroes, were chosen to play Gatsby in the movie versions of Fitzgerald's novel (released, respectively, in 1974 and 2013), reveals the persistence of a romantic view of Gatsby in the Western popular imagination. Indeed, during a discussion of self-made, Oklahoma oil millionaire E. W. Marland on an episode of *America's Castles*, the narrator notes Fitzgerald's belief that the story of a hero is always a tragic story while the well-known cover art of *The Great Gatsby* is superimposed over a photo of Marland's mansion. In other words this television biography attempts to romanticize Marland by associating him with Jay Gatsby.

Clearly, *The Great Gatsby*'s embodiment of the complexities and contradictions of the discourse of the self-made man reveals the complexities and contradictions that informed the attitude of Fitzgerald's America toward the achievement of financial success. Without the discourse of the self-made man, Fitzgerald's best-known novel would not be possible. For the character of Jay Gatsby would simply be the "cheap sharper" (159; ch. 8) – just another criminal – he fears people will see in him. It is this discourse, as much as his devotion to Daisy and his boyish optimism, that makes it possible for Gatsby to remain the romantic figure he is today.

Fitzgerald's novel also shows us how the circulation of discourses has very personal implications for all of us. For it illustrates the ways in which cultural discourses are the raw materials from which we fashion our individual identities. Nick Carraway may think that Gatsby "sprang from his Platonic" ahistorical "conception of himself" (104; ch. 6), a belief Gatsby clearly shares, but Gatsby's personal identity did not so originate. As we have seen, James Gatz's creation of Jay Gatsby drew heavily on the discourse of the self-made man, one of the dominant discourses circulating in the culture in which he lived. And like Jay Gatsby, all of us do the same. We each may draw on different discourses, and we each may draw on them in different ways, but it is through the discourses circulating in our culture that our individual identities are formed, are linked to one another, and are linked to the culture that both shapes and is shaped by each of us.

Questions for further practice: new historical and cultural criticism of other literary works

The following questions are intended as models. They can help you use new historical and cultural criticism to interpret the literary works to which they refer or to other texts of your choice. Your purpose in addressing these questions, the way in which you focus your essay, and your own self-identified critical orientation will determine whether your essay is considered an example of new historical or cultural criticism.

1 What is the relationship between Hawthorne's depiction of Hester Prynne's transgression, in thought and deed, of repressive Puritan values in *The Scarlet Letter* (1850) and such revolutionary nineteenth-century activities as the abolitionist movement and the women's movement? In other words, how does the story of Hester Prynne (a colonial Puritan) embody and/or criticize these nineteenth-century ideologies as they were circulated in pamphlets, popular stories, political activities, and other cultural texts?

2 Toni Morrison's *The Bluest Eye* (1970) was published at a time when conservative American ideologies concerning race, class, gender, and social justice were being called into question in almost every domain of American life. What

does the history of this novel's reception suggest about the circulation of conservative and liberal discourses addressing these pressing social issues since the time of the novel's publication to the present?

3   How was John Steinbeck's *The Grapes of Wrath* (1939) shaped by, and how did it shape, debates about the rights and responsibilities of workers circulating at the time the novel was published, for example, debates concerning the appropriate relationship among American business, government agencies, labor unions, and the individual citizen? In other words, what kinds of cultural work did the novel perform at the time of its publication?

4   In what ways does Kate Chopin's *The Awakening* (1899) interact with (reproduce, comment on, question) debates about women's rights and responsibilities circulating at the time the novel was written, for example, debates concerning women's suffrage, economic independence, marriage, and motherhood?

5   What is the relationship between William Blake's "The Little Black Boy" (1789) and discourses circulating in England during the second half of the eighteenth century concerning race, slavery, and the dark-skinned peoples inhabiting any part of the British Empire?

For further reading

Brannigan, John. *New Historicism and Cultural Materialism.* New York: St. Martin's, 1998.

Bristow, Joseph. "Discursive Desires [Foucault]." *Sexuality.* 2nd ed. London and New York: Routledge, 2011. 151–69.

Cox, Jeffrey N., and Larry J. Reynolds, eds. *New Historical Literary Study: Essays on Reproducing Texts, Representing History.* Princeton, NJ: Princeton University Press, 1993.

Fiske, John. "Popular Culture." *Critical Terms for Literary Study.* 2nd ed. Eds. Frank Lentricchia and Thomas McLaughlin. Chicago: University of Chicago Press, 1995. 321–35.

Greenblatt, Stephen. "The Circulation of Social Energy." *Shakespearean Negotiations: The Circulation of Social Energy in Renaissance England.* Berkeley: University of California Press, 1988. 1–20.

——. "Culture." *Critical Terms for Literary Study.* 2nd ed. Eds. Frank Lentricchia and Thomas McLaughlin. Chicago: University of Chicago Press, 1995. 225–32.

——. *Will in the World: How Shakespeare Became Shakespeare.* New York: W. W. Norton, 2004.

——. *The Swerve: How the World Became Modern.* New York and London: W.W. Norton, 2011.

Gutting, Gary. *Foucault: A Very Short Introduction.* New York: Oxford University Press, 2005.

Patterson, Lee. "Literary History." *Critical Terms for Literary Study.* 2nd ed. Eds. Frank Lentricchia and Thomas McLaughlin. Chicago: University of Chicago Press, 1995. 250–62.

Veeser, H. Aram, ed. *The New Historicism.* New York: Routledge, 1989. (See especially Veeser, "Introduction," ix–xvi; Greenblatt, "Towards a Poetics of Culture," 1–14; Montrose, "Professing the Renaissance: The Poetics and Politics of Culture," 15–36; and Gallagher, "Marxism and the New Historicism," 37–48.)

For advanced readers

Foucault, Michel. *The Order of Things.* New York: Pantheon, 1972.

——. *Discipline and Punish: The Birth of the Prison.* Trans. Alan Sheridan. New York: Vintage, 1979.

——. *The Foucault Reader.* Ed. Paul Rabinow. New York: Pantheon, 1984.

Gallagher, Catherine, and Stephen Greenblatt. *Practicing New Historicism.* Chicago: University of Chicago Press, 2000.

Geertz, Clifford. *The Interpretation of Cultures: Selected Essays.* New York: Basic Books, 1973.

Greenblatt, Stephen. *Shakespearean Negotiations: The Circulation of Social Energy in Renaissance England.* Berkeley: University of California Press, 1988.

——. *Learning to Curse: Essays in Early Modern Culture.* New York: Routledge, 1991.

——. *Renaissance Self-Fashioning: From More to Shakespeare.* 1980. Chicago: University of Chicago Press, 2005.

Grossberg, Lawrence, Cary Nelson, and Paula Treichler, eds. *Cultural Studies.* New York: Routledge, 1992.

Hens-Piazza, Gina. *The New Historicism.* Guides to Biblical Scholarship, Old Testament Series. Minneapolis, MN: Fortress Press, 2002.

Montrose, Louis. "New Historicisms." *Redrawing the Boundaries: The Transformation of English and American Literary Studies.* Eds. Stephen Greenblatt and Giles Gunn. New York: Modern Language Association, 1992. 392–418.

Pieters, Jürgen. *Moments of Negotiation: The New Historicism of Stephen Greenblatt.* Amsterdam: Amsterdam University Press, 2001.

Notes

1 Tillyard's *Elizabethan World Picture* makes this argument and is a frequently cited example of traditional literary history. Another oft-cited example of the traditional historical approach is Taine's *History of English Literature.*
2 This discussion of video games is based on a discussion of the same topic that appears in my *Using Critical Theory: How to Read and Write about Literature* (7–9).
3 Very much the same advice is offered in all the success manuals of the period. See, for example, those by Fowler and Marden.
4 Andrew Carnegie makes this argument in "The Gospel of Wealth."
5 For similar views of Gatsby, see Chase, Hart, Moore, Nash, Stern, and Trilling.

Works cited

Achebe, Chinua. "An Image of Africa: Racism in Conrad's *Heart of Darkness.*" *Massachusetts Review* 18 (1977): 782–94. Rpt. in *Hopes and Impediments, Selected Essays.* New York: Anchor, 1989. 1–20.

Bewley, Marius. "Scott Fitzgerald's Criticism of America." *Sewanee Review* 62 (1954): 223–46. Rpt. in *Modern Critical Interpretations: F. Scott Fitzgerald's* The Great Gatsby. Ed. Harold Bloom. New York: Chelsea House, 1986. 11–27.

Bierbower, Austin. *How to Succeed.* New York: R. F. Fenno, 1900.

Burnam, Tom. "The Eyes of Dr. Eckleburg: A Re-Examination of *The Great Gatsby.*" *College English* 13 (1952). Rpt. in *F. Scott Fitzgerald: A Collection of Critical Essays.* Ed. Arthur Mizener. Englewood Cliffs, NJ: Prentice Hall, 1963. 104–11.

Carnegie, Andrew. "The Road to Business Success: A Talk to Young Men." 1885. From *The Empire of Business.* Garden City, NY: Doubleday, Doran, 1933. 1–13.

——. "The Gospel of Wealth." *North American Review* CXLVIII (June 1889): 653–64 and CXLIX (December 1889): 682–98. Rpt. in *The Gospel of Wealth, and Other Timely Essays.* Ed. Edward C. Kirkland. Cambridge, MA: Belknap Press of Harvard University Press, 1962. 14–49.

——. "How to Win Fortune." 1890. From *The Empire of Business.* Garden City, NY: Doubleday, Doran, 1933. 85–101.

———. *The Autobiography of Andrew Carnegie*. New York, 1920.

Cartwright, Kent. "Nick Carraway as Unreliable Narrator." *Papers on Language and Literature* 20.2 (1984): 218–32.

Chase, Richard. "*The Great Gatsby.*" *The American Novel and Its Traditions*. New York: Doubleday, 1957. 162–67. Rpt. in The Great Gatsby: *A Study*. Ed. Frederick J. Hoffman. New York: Scribner's, 1962. 297–302.

Commager, Henry Steele. "Foreword." *McGuffey's Sixth Eclectic Reader* (1879 edition). New York: Signet, 1963. vii–xvi.

Conrad, Joseph. *Heart of Darkness*. 1902. New York: Norton, 1988.

Dillon, Andrew. "*The Great Gatsby*: The Vitality of Illusion." *Arizona Quarterly* 44.1 (1988): 49–61.

E. K. "Review of *The Great Gatsby.*" *Literary Digest International Book Review* (May 1925): 426–27. Excerpted in *Gatsby*. Ed. Harold Bloom. New York: Chelsea House, 1991. 7.

Fiske, John. "Popular Culture." *Critical Terms for Literary Study*. 2nd ed. Eds. Frank Lentricchia and Thomas McLaughlin. Chicago: University of Chicago Press, 1995. 321–35.

Fitzgerald, F. Scott. *The Great Gatsby*. 1925. New York: Macmillan, 1992.

Fowler, Jr., Nathaniel C. *Beginning Right: How to Succeed*. New York: George Sully, 1916.

Gallo, Rose Adrienne. *F. Scott Fitzgerald*. New York: Ungar, 1978.

Geertz, Clifford. "Thick Description: Toward an Interpretive Theory of Culture." *The Interpretation of Cultures: Selected Essays by Clifford Geertz*. New York: Basic Books, 1973. 3–30.

Greenblatt, Stephen. "Culture." *Critical Terms for Literary Study*. 2nd ed. Eds. Frank Lentricchia and Thomas McLaughlin. Chicago: University of Chicago Press, 1995. 225–32.

Gross, Barry Edward. "Jay Gatsby and Myrtle Wilson: A Kinship." *Tennessee Studies in Literature* 8 (1963): 57–60. Excerpted in *Gatsby*. Ed. Harold Bloom. New York: Chelsea House, 1991. 23–25.

Hart, Jeffrey. "'Out of it ere night': The WASP Gentleman as Cultural Ideal." *New Criterion* 7.5 (1989): 27–34.

Josephson, Matthew. *The Robber Barons: The Great American Capitalists, 1861–1901*. 1934. New York: Harvest, 1962.

Le Vot, André. *F. Scott Fitzgerald: A Biography*. Trans. William Byron. Garden City, NY: Doubleday, 1983.

Lindberg, Stanley W. *The Annotated McGuffey: Selections from the McGuffey Eclectic Readers, 1836–1920*. New York: Van Nostrand Reinhold, 1976.

Marden, Orison Swett. *How to Succeed; Or, Stepping-Stones to Fame and Fortune*. New York: The Christian Herald, 1896.

Montrose, Louis. "Professing the Renaissance: The Poetics and Politics of Culture." *The New Historicism*. Ed. H. Aram Veeser. New York: Routledge, 1989. 15–36.

Moore, Benita A. *Escape into a Labyrinth: F. Scott Fitzgerald, Catholic Sensibility, and the American Way*. New York: Garland, 1988.

Morrison, Toni. *Beloved*. New York: Norton, 1987.

Nash, Charles C. "From West Egg to Short Hills: The Decline of the Pastoral Ideal from *The Great Gatsby* to Philip Roth's *Goodbye, Columbus.*" *Philological Association* 13 (1988): 22–27.

Stern, Milton R. *The Golden Moment: The Novels of F. Scott Fitzgerald*. Urbana: University of Illinois Press, 1970.

Taine, Hippolyte. *History of English Literature*. 1864. Trans. H. Van Laun. London: Chatto and Windus, 1897.

Thomas, Brook. "Preserving and Keeping Order by Killing Time in *Heart of Darkness.*" *Heart of Darkness: A Case Study in Contemporary Criticism*. Ed. Ross C. Murfin. New York: Bedford, 1989. 237–55.

Tillyard, E. M. W. *Elizabethan World Picture*. New York: Macmillan, 1944.

Trilling, Lionel. "F. Scott Fitzgerald." *The Liberal Imagination*. New York: Viking, 1950. 243–54. Rpt. in *The Great Gatsby: A Study*. Ed. Frederick J. Hoffman. New York: Scribner's, 1962. 232–43.

Troy, William. "Scott Fitzgerald – The Authority of Failure." *Accent* 6 (1945). Rpt. in *F. Scott Fitzgerald: A Collection of Critical Essays*. Ed. Arthur Mizener. Englewood Cliffs, NJ: Prentice Hall, 1963. 20–24.

Tyson, Lois. *Using Critical Theory: How to Read and Write about Literature*, 2nd ed. London and New York: Routledge, 2011.

10 Lesbian, gay, and queer criticism

In the critical-theory survey course I teach, I sometimes open the unit on lesbian, gay, and queer criticism by reading the class a list of frequently anthologized British and American writers: for example, Oscar Wilde, Tennessee Williams, Willa Cather, James Baldwin, Adrienne Rich, Walt Whitman, Virginia Woolf, Elizabeth Bishop, Langston Hughes, Edward Albee, Gertrude Stein, Allen Ginsberg, W. H. Auden, William Shakespeare, Carson McCullers, Somerset Maugham, T. S. Eliot, James Merrill, H.D., Sarah Orne Jewett, Hart Crane, William S. Burroughs, and Amy Lowell. Then I ask my students if they are aware that these writers are gay, lesbian, or bisexual. Sometimes that question is met by an initial reticence to respond, a difficulty not encountered in our opening discussions of other theories.

Of course, I know that, unfortunately, the stigma attached to being thought gay or lesbian is still quite strong in America today, and some students may be unwilling to express anything on the subject until they see how the rest of the group responds. As one student told me, after signing out a number of books on lesbian and gay theory from the university library for a paper she was writing for my class, she thought perhaps the student who waited on her at the circulation desk wondered about her sexual orientation, and to her embarrassment she found herself wanting to shout, "Hey, wait a minute; I'm not a lesbian!"

Another reason for my students' difficulty, however, is their lack of knowledge. The work of gay and lesbian writers forms a major part of the literary canon and is therefore included in most literature courses, but many undergraduate students assume that these writers are heterosexual. And their assumptions are not always corrected. Of course, our anthologies of English and American literature usually include biographical introductions to the writers whose works they contain, and professors frequently offer additional information about authors' personal lives. We may be told, for example, that Charlotte Perkins Gilman suffered a deep depression after the birth of her only child; that, as a young man, Langston Hughes' difficult relationship with his father almost drove him to suicide; or that Robert Frost's dying wife refused to admit him to her room. But often we are given little biographical information about a writer's lesbian or gay sexual orientation, let alone information concerning how that orientation affected her or his life and literary production.

If personal information about writers' heterosexual lives is relevant to our appreciation of their work, why is personal information about writers' LGBTQ (lesbian, gay, bisexual, transgender, and queer)[+] lives often excluded from the realm of pertinent historical data? If the experience of gender and/or racial discrimination is an important factor in writers' lives, then why isn't it important to know about the oppression suffered by LGBTQ writers? Clearly, in many of our college classrooms today, LGBTQ sexuality is still considered an uncomfortable topic of discussion. Some literature professors simply avoid addressing LGBTQ issues in undergraduate courses not specifically devoted to LGBTQ writers. And at many colleges, although courses on LGBTQ writers can be offered as "special topics" courses, they do not always occur as regular course offerings in undergraduate English departments, despite the progress made by gay studies programs since the 1970s and the emergence of lesbian, gay, and queer theory as an important force in academia in the early 1990s.

In other words, my students' uncertainty concerning the sexual orientation of the writers they read reflects the silence of some of their professors on that subject, including the silence of some professors who compile anthologies. Furthermore, I would argue that the silence of some English faculty on the subject of LGBTQ writers reflects, in turn, the longstanding silence of many literary critics who have minimized or ignored the sexual identities of LGBTQ writers and distorted or overlooked the representations of LGBTQ characters in literary works.

The marginalization of LGBTQ people

Consider, for example, the critical response, analyzed by Lillian Faderman, to Henry James' *The Bostonians* (1885). As Faderman explains, James' novel, by his own testimony, describes a "Boston marriage," a term used in late-nineteenth-century New England to refer to a monogamous relationship of long standing between two single women who lived together; who were usually financially independent; and who often shared interests in culture, feminist issues, the betterment of society, and professional careers. Such relationships were not that uncommon, and although it's impossible to know how many of them included sexual relations, it is clear that the women involved shared a strong emotional tie and focused their time, attention, and energy on each other and on their women friends.

In James' novel, such a relationship exists between Olive and Verena, who are active in the women's movement of their day. Their relationship is broken up by Basil, whose overpowering determination finally convinces Verena, almost by the sheer force of his will, to abandon Olive and marry him. Although, as Faderman points out, James does not portray Olive heroically, and indeed satirizes her and her women companions, it is obvious the author has no sympathy for Basil either, whom he depicts as a selfish, brutish, competitive manipulator who is infuriated by the women's movement and sure to give Verena an unhappy life. In contrast, Verena's life with Olive is happy and productive. Yet, Faderman observes, critics have argued that Basil rescues Verena from what they see as her unnatural relationship with Olive and restores her to what they assume is the true love a woman can find only in the arms of a "real" man.

How can these critics ignore the very positive aspects of Verena's relationship with Olive and completely distort James' portrayal of Basil? Clearly, their interpretation rests on, and imposes on the novel, a view of heterosexual love as the only kind of normal, healthy love there is. Any other kind of love is presumed abnormal, unhealthy, and to be avoided. As a result, these critics are unable to recognize Basil's obvious and serious character flaws. Because he is heterosexual and takes Verena away from Olive, he is often viewed in a very positive, even heroic, light.

This kind of interpretation is an example of a *homophobic* reading, that is, a reading informed by the fear and loathing of homosexuality. Thus, it is part of a larger cultural context in which homophobia has long played a major role. Although LGBTQ individuals are no longer placed in mental institutions for "treatment" – which sometimes included aversion therapy, electric shock treatment, and even lobotomies – it wasn't until 1974 that such practices officially ended, when the category of homosexuality was removed from the American Psychiatric Association's list of psychological disorders. Moreover, it wasn't until 1990 that the 1952 immigration policy restricting homosexual immigration into the United States was lifted. And homophobia is evident in many forms of discrimination against the LGBTQ community still practiced today, despite the enormous social and political gains achieved by activist groups since the Gay Liberation Movement began in 1969, after the LGBTQ patrons of Greenwich Village's Stonewall Inn bar finally responded to police brutality by fighting back, two thousand strong, during two nights of rioting. This momentous event, referred to as *Stonewall*, has great symbolic significance because it marks the turning point when LGBTQ people renounced their victim status and stood up collectively for their rights as American citizens.

Today, although LGBTQ people in America have achieved significant gains toward equal treatment in the military, they still face discrimination in obtaining jobs and housing; in using public facilities, such as hotels and taverns; in areas of family law such as the right to marry, retain custody of their children, adopt children, or provide foster care; as victims of police harassment and violent hate crimes; and in AIDS-related discrimination.[2] Certainly the most alarming, and damaging, form of discrimination against LGBTQ individuals is the bullying of LGBTQ adolescents and young adults that continues to occur in and out of school and that remains too often under-addressed. The physical and emotional violence committed against young people who do not conform to conventional gender or sexual norms has greatly increased the school drop-out and suicide rates among these teens.[3] Finally, LGBTQ individuals who are members of racial minorities in America face a complex system of discrimination. In addition to the oppression they suffer in white heterosexist culture, LGBTQ African Americans, Asian Americans, Chicanos/as, and Latinos/as are sometimes heavily stigmatized in their own communities.

Part and parcel of the discrimination practiced against LGBTQ people are the negative myths that used to be generally accepted as truth and that still exert some influence today. These include the myth that LGBTQ people are sick, evil, or both and that it is therefore in their "nature" to be insatiable sexual predators, to molest children, and to corrupt youths by "recruiting" them to become LGBTQ. Another myth portrays the LGBTQ community as a very small population of deviants, when, in fact, it is estimated that LGBTQ people comprise at least 10 percent of the US population. Other common misconceptions include the belief that children raised by LGBTQ people will grow up to be LGBTQ, that unchecked LGBTQ behavior will result in the extinction of the human race, and that LGBTQ people are responsible for declines in US foreign power.

This might be a good place to pause and define some terms, many of which are related to discrimination against LGBTQ people. These are terms that you may encounter when you read lesbian, gay, and queer literary criticism. While the word *homophobia* is generally used to refer to an individual's pathological dread of same-sex love, I used the term above to refer to institutionalized discrimination (discrimination that is built into a culture's laws and customs) against LGBTQ people because I think we would be hard pressed to argue that such discrimination is based on anything other than the collective, if sometimes unconscious, homophobia promoted by patriarchy, or what many LGBTQ theorists call *heteropatriarchy*. (The word *heteropatriarchy* draws our attention to the fact that patriarchy, because it is biased in favor of traditional gender roles, is always biased in favor of hetero-sexuality.) *Internalized homophobia* refers to the self-hatred some LGBTQ people experience because, in their growth through adolescence to adulthood, they've internalized the homophobia pressed on them by heterosexual America.

The word more commonly used to refer to institutionalized discrimination against LGBTQ people, and the privileging of heterosexuality that accompanies it, is *heterosexism*. For example, a heterosexist culture enforces *compulsory heterosexuality*, a term used by Adrienne Rich, among others, to describe the enormous pressure to be heterosexual placed on young people by their families, schools, the church, the medical professions, and all forms of the media. Today, *heteronormative* is the more commonly used term for the social attitudes and assumptions that pressure everyone to be what is conventionally defined as sexually "normal."

Heterocentrism, a more subtle form of prejudice against LGBTQ individuals, is the assumption, often unconscious, that heterosexuality is universal, for instance that everyone in the room – unless someone makes a point of being otherwise – is heterosexual. Heterocentrism takes it for granted that everyone's experience can be understood within a heterosexual framework. Heterocentrism thus renders the experience of LGBTQ people invisible, making it possible in decades past, for example, for fans of Walt Whitman to be unaware of the homoerotic dimension of his poetry.

Don't be too concerned, right now, if the words *homophobia*, *heterosexism*, and *heterocentrism* seem a bit overlapping and, therefore, a bit confusing. Indeed, you'll sometimes hear them used interchangeably, perhaps because all three terms assume the inborn superiority of heterosexuals. And if you think about it for a minute, you'll probably realize that all three biases – homophobia, heterosexism, and heterocentrism – are heteronormative: they are all forms of compulsory heterosexuality. The difference among the three terms is apparently one of degree: *homophobia* suggests the most virulent anti-LGBTQ sentiment, *heterocentrism* the least virulent, though all three, of course, refer to extremely damaging forms of prejudice.

By focusing our attention on the LGBTQ community as an oppressed group, the words *homophobia*, *heterosexism*, *heterocentrism*, and *heteronormative* tend to spotlight the ways in which LGBTQ people constitute a political minority. As a minority they deserve, of course, the same protection under the law afforded to racial, ethnic, and religious minorities in America. Another concept that emphasizes the minority status of LGBTQ people is *biological essentialism*, the idea that a fixed segment of the population is naturally LGBTQ, just as the rest of the population is naturally heterosexual. Conversely, some theorists argue that, although LGBTQ people constitute an oppressed political minority in America, all human beings have the potential for same-sex desire or for sexual activity that does not fit a heterosexual framework. According to this view, which is called *social constructionism*, LGBTQ sexuality and heterosexuality are products of social, not biological, forces. Ways of understanding LGBTQ experience that focus on their minority status are called *minoritizing views*. Ways of understanding LGBTQ experience that focus on the homosexual potential in all people are called *universalizing views*.[4]

Interestingly, both essentialist (minoritizing) and constructionist (universalizing) views have been used to attack LGBTQ individuals: for example, (1) LGBTQ people are born sick (or evil); (2) LGBTQ people are sick (or evil) products of a sick (or evil) environment. By the same token, both essentialist and constructionist views have been used to defend or celebrate the LGBTQ community: for example, (1) it is biologically natural for some people to be LGBTQ, no matter what environment they're born into, and therefore they should be accepted as natural; (2) LGBTQ orientation is a normal response to particular environmental factors, and therefore LGBTQ people should be accepted as normal.

Finally, two oft-used words that refer to same-sex relationships are *homoerotic*, which I used earlier to describe Whitman's poetry, and *homosocial*. Homoerotic denotes erotic (though not necessarily overtly sexual) depictions that imply same-sex attraction or that might appeal sexually to a same-sex reader, for example, a sensually evocative description of women in the process of helping each other undress or of nude men bathing in a pond. Such depictions can occur in any medium, such as film, painting, sculpture, photography, and, of course, literature. The word *homosocial* denotes same-sex friendship of the kind seen in female- or male-bonding activities. For example, the relationship among the three prostitutes – China, Poland, and Miss Marie – in Toni Morrison's *The Bluest Eye* (1970) is homosocial, as is the relationship between Huck and Jim in Mark Twain's *Adventures of Huckleberry Finn* (1885) and between Edna Pontellier and Adèle Ratignolle in Kate Chopin's *The Awakening* (1899). Furthermore, in the descriptions of Edna's sensual response to Adèle's voluptuous beauty, the relationship between these two characters is homoerotic as well.

Why include the term *homosocial* here when homosocial activity is not unique to LGBTQ people? For example, "girls' night out" and "boys' night out" have long been an important part of many heterosexual cultures. I think we could argue that there are at least two reasons to include the term in this chapter. First, the very fact that homosocial bonding plays an important role in both heterosexual and LGBTQ cultures offers us an opportunity to appreciate a significant area of social and emotional experience shared by LGBTQ and straight people alike. Second, although homosocial bonding is generally considered vital to the emotional growth of children and the emotional health of adults, regardless of their sexual orientation, many individuals are apprehensive about some forms of same-sex bonding due to their own homophobia or for fear of a homophobic response from others. For instance, might a straight woman think twice before going to a "wine-and-white-tablecloth" restaurant for dinner with a female friend on a Saturday night? Yes? No? What about two straight male friends? What about two same-sex LGBTQ friends? When might a heterosexual parent become unduly concerned about the natural homosocial activities of a son or daughter? In short, the complex issues often associated with homosocial bonding sheds a strong light on the pervasiveness of homophobia's destructive impact on everyone's well being.

So far, I have discussed LGBTQ people as a group. Indeed, even the inclusion of gay, lesbian, and queer criticism in the same chapter implies that they constitute some sort of homogenous collectivity. Certainly, they share in common the political, economic, social, and psychological oppression they suffer as members of a sexual minority. And for many thinkers, the enormity of this shared experience, and the potential for political power generated when LGBTQ people act as a group, is sufficient to support the claim that they should be considered in this light.

Many lesbians and gay men, however, argue that oppression is one of the few experiences, if not the only one, they have in common and that, in most other ways, gay men and lesbians are polar opposites. For example, many gay men and lesbians have their most significant social, political, and personal experiences, if not all of their experiences, in same-sex groups. In addition, many lesbians identify exclusively with women, while many gay men identify exclusively with men. Furthermore, lesbians, even if "closeted" (posing as heterosexuals), have experienced the gender oppression that all women, straight or gay, have experienced, while closeted gay men have had the opportunity to enjoy the patriarchal privileges extended to straight men. And whether closeted or not, gay male writers have enjoyed an incomparably greater representation in literary history than lesbians (or heterosexual women) because, until recently, works by male authors were much more readily canonized than works by female authors.

In order to appreciate the distinctive features of lesbian, gay, and queer criticism, we'll discuss them under separate headings. As you'll see, queer criticism – relatively speaking, a newer field of inquiry – is based on the insights of deconstruction and is relevant to issues of heterosexual identity as well as to issues of LGBTQ sexual identity.

Lesbian criticism

Perhaps because lesbian criticism and feminist criticism grew from the same soil – as responses to patriarchal oppression – and because lesbian critics are generally feminists, lesbian criticism is concerned with issues of personal identity and politics analogous to those analyzed by feminists (see Chapter 4). However, while feminism addresses issues related to sexism and the difficulties involved in carving out a space for personal identity and political action beyond the influence of sexist ideologies, lesbian critics address issues related to both sexism and heterosexism. In other words, lesbian critics must deal with the psychological, social, economic, and political oppression fostered not only by patriarchal male privilege, but by heterosexual privilege as well. And this second form of privilege has often put heterosexual and lesbian feminists at odds with each other.

Indeed, feminism has been, at various times, vulnerable to charges of heterocentrism in its tendency to focus on the oppression of heterosexual women rather than on the oppression of all women, including lesbians, and of heterosexism in the heterosexual orientation of its most visible leadership and in its legitimate fear of being "branded" a lesbian movement by the homophobic patriarchal power structure in America (legitimate because homophobia is such a pervasive and disarming force). Analogously, lesbians of color and working-class lesbians have suffered a history of marginalization, if not exclusion, within the lesbian-feminist movement, which, like the feminist movement, emerged largely from the white middle class and, therefore, has been limited – until relatively recently – by white middle-class perspectives and goals.

I mention these problems up front because, especially since the mid 1980s, lesbians have refused to be marginalized by heterosexual feminists; and lesbians of color and working-class lesbians have refused to be marginalized by white middle-class lesbians. As a result, lesbian criticism has become one of the richest and most exciting domains of theoretical inquiry and political activity. Questions that have long been central to lesbian critical inquiry – such as "What is a lesbian?" and "What constitutes a lesbian literary text?" – are problematized in very productive ways when lesbian critics take into account both the limitations imposed on their viewpoints by their class origins and race, and the beauty and importance of the complex heritage bestowed on all of us by the ultimate inseparability of race, class, gender, and sexual orientation in our daily lives.

In addition to generating fundamental issues of lesbian inquiry, the questions "What is a lesbian?" and "What constitutes a lesbian literary text?" belong to a self-questioning form of theoretical activity not generally performed by gay criticism. So let's take a closer look at these two questions.

Can a lesbian be defined as a woman who has sex with another woman? What activity constitutes sex? (Must there be genital contact?) How would such a definition work if we applied it to heterosexuality? Presumably, it would mean that virgins who thought of themselves as heterosexuals would have no right to call themselves heterosexuals unless and until they had genital sex with men. So one's sexuality must be defined, it seems, in terms of one's sexual desire.

Perhaps a better way to define a lesbian, then, is to say that she is a woman whose sexual desire is directed toward women. The advantage of a definition of this sort is that it allows us to recognize lesbian existence even within the confines of heterosexual marriage. For throughout history, women often have had to marry, whether they wanted to or not, in order to survive economically or because the rigid social system in which they lived offered them no other social or psychological option. And some of these women, though they may have loved and respected their husbands, were passionately attracted to women rather than to men. Virginia Woolf, who was married but who had a passionate, long-standing affair with Vita Sackville-West, is a case in point.

What if, however, there is evidence of a passionate attachment between two women – such as a long exchange of letters in which passionate love is expressed – but because the relationship occurred in a different historical period from our own, we can't be certain exactly what it was that was being expressed? For example, how do we interpret the "romantic friendships," as they are called, between women in nineteenth-century Britain and America – one embodiment of which was the "Boston marriage" discussed earlier – in which the most tender love or passionate attachment may have been expressed, but for which there is no concrete evidence of sexual activity or sexual desire?

The period is known for its overblown sentimentality and excesses of verbal expression, and effusions of physical affection between women were accepted, even encouraged, by patriarchy as charming displays of women's "overemotional nature."

So we can't assume with any certainty that women's exchanges of letters filled with exuberant expressions of passion – such as "I love you my darling, more than I can express, more than I am conscious of myself"[5] – are indicative of sexual desire, let alone sexual activity. On the other hand, many such relationships might have involved a sexual dimension to which nineteenth-century patriarchy would have been utterly blind. Indeed, given the nineteenth century's restriction of women's sexuality and sexual awareness, many women might have had enormous sexual desire for other women without ever recognizing it as such.

Thus, a strict focus on what we would define today as sexual activity or sexual desire runs the risk of erasing an important dimension of women's lives that very well might be understood fully only through a lesbian lens. In order to avoid this kind of erasure, and to promote solidarity among all women, some lesbian theorists have suggested that a lesbian is a *woman-identified woman*. Being a woman-identified woman is not restricted to the sexual domain but consists of directing the bulk of one's attention and emotional energy to other women and having other women as one's primary source of emotional sustenance and psychological support.[6]

Adrienne Rich makes use of this idea when she argues for the existence of what she calls a *lesbian continuum*. A lesbian continuum, Rich explains, "include[s] a range – through each woman's life and throughout history – of woman-identified experience, not simply the fact that a woman has had or consciously desired genital sexual experience with another woman" (239). Woman-identified experience includes, for example, emotional bonding through shared work or play, the giving or receiving of psychological support, and the shared experience of joy in any form. Woman-identification does not preclude sexual desire for or sexual activity with another woman, but neither does it require them. A woman can thus move in and out of the lesbian continuum throughout her life or remain within it entirely. From this perspective, women's romantic friendships during the nineteenth century, whether or not they involved sexual activity or desire, are indeed an appropriate subject for lesbian analysis.

Of course, to underplay the sexual dimension of lesbian experience is to underplay, some theorists argue, that which is most unique and liberating in lesbian life. In bonding with one another sexually and denying men access to their bodies, lesbians deny patriarchy one of its most powerful tools: heterosexuality. For heterosexuality is not a "natural" sexual orientation for "normal" women but a political institution that subordinates women to patriarchy in that women's subservience to men is built into heterosexual definitions of feminine sexuality. In other words, from this point of view, patriarchy and heterosexuality are inseparable. To resist the former, one must resist the latter.

For this reason, some lesbians are *separatists*. They disassociate themselves as much as possible from all men, including gay men, and from heterosexual women as well. They may also disassociate themselves from lesbians who don't share their views. Recalling the sexism of the male-dominated Gay Liberation Movement of the 1970s and, as we noted above, the heterosexist tendencies of feminism, lesbian separatists believe that only lesbian organizations will give priority to lesbian issues. For separatists, just as for the majority of lesbian feminists who are not separatists, lesbianism is a political stance, not merely an issue of personal sexuality.

Nevertheless, as Marilyn Frye argues, while separatism is a deliberate, systematic political policy, it is not the only form in which women's separation from patriarchal domination occurs. In fact, separation is enacted to varying degrees across a range of institutional practices that increase women's power, including, for example, the provision of shelters for battered women, divorce, the increased availability of day care, women's studies programs, women's bars, and the legalization of abortion. Even such apparently personal behaviors as breaking up a close relationship, excluding someone from one's house or one's company, withholding one's support, withdrawing one's loyalty, refusing to watch sexist television programs or listen to sexist music, and rejecting obnoxious individuals are all forms of separation from males or from male-dominated institutions that can increase women's power. As Frye puts it, "Access is one of the faces of Power. ... It is always the privilege of the master to enter the slave's hut. The slave who decides to exclude the master from her hut is declaring herself not a slave" (95–96). Thus, although most women do not choose separatist politics, neither should they find them completely alien to their own experience nor be unsympathetic to women who do choose them.

Clearly, attempts to define the word *lesbian*, or even to articulate the full political implications of various forms of women's separation, are as problematic as they are exciting. Equally difficult and equally rewarding are efforts to answer the question "What constitutes a lesbian literary text?" As we can't always be sure whether or not a particular writer was a lesbian, especially given the difficulties we've just discussed concerning the definition of that term, we can't depend on an author's sexual orientation, even if we know it, to tell us whether or not we are reading a lesbian text. Of course, how the critic defines *lesbian* will determine her or his definition of both lesbian writers and lesbian texts.

For example, a lesbian critic might argue that a writer known to have been a sexually active lesbian, such as Willa Cather, *coded* lesbian meaning in an apparently heterosexual narrative because she knew that she couldn't write about lesbian desire openly, at least not if she hoped to have her work published and to avoid public censure if not criminal prosecution. Judith Fetterly makes this argument in her interpretation of Cather's *My Ántonia* (1918). Among other codings, Fetterly argues that narrator Jim Burden, whose characterization is frequently contradictory and whom many critics have difficulty interpreting, can be understood if we see him as the embodiment of Cather's own lesbian desire. Fetterly notes, among other evidence, that despite Jim's frequent admissions of love for Ántonia and of his desire to have her as his sweetheart or his wife, for some unexplained reason he can't have her. Furthermore, he behaves in ways that are traditionally female. He spends most of his time in the kitchen, in women's space. We never see him participating in the male world of hunting and fishing. He doesn't identify with the men of his town and is hostile to the patriarchal privilege they abuse. And when Jim takes Ántonia's place in the home of Wick Cutter, her sexually predatory employer whose strange behavior is frightening her, Jim doesn't defend the woman he loves by beating up Wick. Instead, he is apparently raped in her place, for he runs home to his grandmother, repulsed and shamed by what he calls Cutter's disgusting behavior, and he begs his grandmother to tell no one, not even the doctor. Finally, Jim reveals a loathing of male sexuality, for example in his revulsion toward phallic masculinity evident in his description of "the extraordinarily phallic snake of Book I" (Fetterly 152):

> His abominable masculinity, his loathsome, fluid motion, somehow made me sick. He was as thick as my leg, and looked as if millstones couldn't crush the disgusting vitality out of him. ... He seemed like the ancient, eldest Evil.
>
> (Cather 45–47; quoted in Fetterly 152)

These narrative problems are resolved, Fetterly argues, when we realize that Jim is a stand-in for Cather, which makes even more sense when we learn that the tale is autobiographical.

Another task a lesbian critic might perform is to argue that a writer's literary output establishes her lesbian status even when available biographical material posits only a passionate emotional bond, a "romantic friendship," with another woman. For example, Paula Bennett argues persuasively that Emily Dickinson's poetic strategies reveal a homoerotic dimension of the author's poetry that is related, Bennett points out, to the "enormous amount of comfort, both emotional and sexual," she drew from her "relationships with women throughout her life" (109). For example, among other poetic strategies, Dickinson associates phallic imagery with fear and revulsion. As we see in "I started Early – Took my Dog" (poem #520), the speaker, pursued by the sea (whose "overflow" of "Pearl" is obviously male and obviously sexual), flees in terror because she fears it will consume her. Similarly, in "In Winter in My Room" (poem #1670), the speaker is disturbed by the presence of a "Worm—/ Pink, lank and warm" that terrifies and repels her when it transforms itself into "A snake ... ringed with power."

Conversely, Bennett observes, Dickinson links female sexual imagery – specifically, images associated with the clitoris and vaginal lips – with "Edenic pleasures" (111) that are "typically oral" and described in a manner that is "open, eager, and lush" (110). For example, "All the letters I can write" (poem #334) calls upon a lover (who is represented by the diminutive form of a hummingbird and whose gender is referred to, ambiguously, as "it") to "Play it ... / ... just sipped" her

"Depths of Ruby, undrained, I Hid, Lip, for Thee." Similarly, "I tend my flowers for thee" (poem #339) includes such female sexual images as "My Fuchsia's Coral Seams / Rip – while the Sower – dreams" and "My Cactus – splits her Beard / To show her throat." Whether or not the speaker in such poems adopts a male point of view, Dickinson's "focus is obviously on female sexuality itself" (111) and "bespeaks the poet's overwhelming physical attraction to her own sex" (110). Significantly, after Dickinson's death, family members requested that publication of the poet's letters be edited to suppress evidence of Dickinson's passionate love for Susan Gilbert, her lifelong friend.

Another task a lesbian critic might perform is to show the ways in which a text that is clearly heterosexual in its intention nevertheless has an important lesbian dimension. Using a definition of *lesbian* that does not require same-sex desire – for example, the woman-identified woman – Barbara Smith make this case for Toni Morrison's *Sula* (1973), in which two young black girls bond together to survive the racism and sexism that constrict their lives. In addition to what Smith notes as Morrison's "consistently critical stance toward the heterosexual institutions of male/female relationships, marriage, and the family" (165), this critic argues forcefully that the only deep and sustained love experienced in the novel is between two women: the main characters Nel and Sula. Their primary identification is with each other, their primary emotional sustenance comes from each other, and no man, including Nel's husband, is more influential or important in their lives than each other. In fact, both women's relationships with men are unsatisfactory. Finally, Sula's unconventional behavior – her refusal to marry and have children, her dismissive attitude toward the married men with whom she has one-night stands, and the like – represents a transgressive sexuality, a violation of patriarchal norms, that resonates strongly with lesbian violations of patriarchy. Indeed, Sula goes to bed with men, not in order to experience communion with them, which doesn't occur, but in order to learn about her own internal power and experience her own inner harmony.

Of course, lesbian literary critics perform a number of other tasks. Among other things, they try to decide what constitutes a lesbian literary tradition and what writers and works belong to it. They attempt to determine what might constitute a lesbian poetics, that is, a uniquely lesbian way of writing. They analyze how the sexual/emotional orientation of lesbian writers has affected their literary expression; how the intersection of race and sexual/emotional orientation has affected the literary expression of lesbians of color; and how the intersection of class, race, and sexual/emotional orientation has affected the literary expression of lesbians of working-class origins. Lesbian critics also analyze the sexual politics of specific texts by examining, for example, how lesbian characters or "masculine" women are portrayed in literature by and about lesbians. They study canonized heterosexual texts, too, in order to learn what attitudes toward lesbians they embody explicitly

or implicitly. And they identify and correct heterosexist interpretations of literature that fail to recognize or appreciate the lesbian dimensions of specific literary
works.

Clearly, these tasks do not exhaust the field. They are intended merely as a
representative sample. Only your own reading of the work done by lesbian critics
will acquaint you with the breadth and depth of their enterprise, which continues
to expand and evolve with each passing year.

In addition, you might want to acquaint yourself, if you haven't already done so,
with literary works by contemporary lesbian writers, who are receiving much cri-
tical acclaim. These writers include, among others, Jeanette Winterson, Gloria
Anzaldúa, Leslie Feinberg, Minnie Bruce Pratt, Rita Mae Brown, Paula Gunn Allen,
Dorothy Allison, Ann Allen Shockley, Monique Wittig, Jewelle Gomez, June Arnold,
Valerie Miner, Becky Birtha, Jane Rule, Bertha Harris, Sarah Shulman, Nicole
Brossard, Kitty Tsui, and, of course, Audre Lorde and Adrienne Rich.

Gay criticism

As we noted above, unlike lesbian criticism, gay criticism doesn't tend to focus on
efforts to define homosexuality. Sexual relations between men, or even just the
sexual desire of one man for another, is the generally accepted criterion of gayness
in white middle-class America today. Nevertheless, not all cultures share this definition. For example, in some Latin American cultures, the mere fact of sexual
activity with or desire for another male does not indicate that a man is homosexual. As long as he behaves in a traditionally masculine manner – strong, dominant, decisive – and consistently assumes the male sexual role as penetrator (never
allowing himself to be penetrated, orally or anally), a man remains a *macho*, a "real"
man. As a *macho*, a man can have sex with both men and women and not be considered
what North Americans call homosexual. The same definition of homosexuality was
used in white American working-class culture around the turn of the twentieth
century: only men who allowed themselves to be penetrated by a man during sex
and behaved in a traditionally feminine manner – submissive, coy, flirtatious,
"soft" – were considered homosexual.

A similar problem for contemporary white middle-class assumptions about
homosexuality is offered by ancient Athens, where there was no polar opposition
between homosexual and heterosexual behavior. Sexual partners were chosen along
caste lines, not according to their biological sex. In Athens, a member of the elite
male ruling class could have legitimate sexual relations only with his social inferiors:
women of any age and from any class, free-born boys past the age of puberty but
not old enough for citizenship, slaves, and foreigners.

In fact, it wasn't until the nineteenth century that the notion of homosexual
identity and even the word *homosexual* were adopted in Anglo-European and

American culture. Before that time, certain sexual acts – generally speaking, all forms of nonprocreative sex – were forbidden by church or state, but they weren't viewed as evidence of a specific sexual identity. The idea that one could be a homosexual came along with the idea, promoted by the medical professions, that such an identity was a form of pathology. This is why many gay men today prefer to refer to themselves as gay: the word *homosexual* is associated, for many, with the belief that homosexuality is a medical or psychological disorder.

Similarly, "the masturbator" also became a pathological sexual identity in the nineteenth century. An act that the medical professions today consider a normal, healthy outlet was considered so dangerous in the nineteenth century that children "suffering" from the "affliction" were tied to their beds at night to prevent their touching themselves, and there are several case histories of doctors' burning the genitals of little girls in order to "cure" them.

The point here is that attitudes toward homosexuality, like attitudes toward sexuality in general, differ widely from one place to another and from one historical period to another. The intense antigay sentiment that emerged in an especially concentrated and virulent form in America during the early 1950s and that lingers today does not represent some kind of universally held attitude toward, or even definition of, homosexuality.

The kinds of analyses that tend to engage the attention of gay critics often fall under the heading of *gay sensibility*. How does being gay influence the way one sees the world, sees oneself and others, creates and responds to art and music, creates and interprets literature, or experiences and expresses emotion? In a heterosexist culture such as the one we inhabit in the early decades of the twenty-first century in America, gay sensibility includes an awareness of being different, at least in certain ways, from the members of the mainstream, dominant culture, and the complex feelings that result from an implicit, ongoing social oppression. In other words, part of seeing the world as a gay man includes the ways in which one deals with being oppressed as a gay man. Among others, three important domains of gay sensibility, all of which involve responses to heterosexist oppression, are drag, camp, and dealing with the issue of AIDS.

Drag is the practice of dressing in women's clothing. *Drag queens* are gay men who dress in drag on a regular basis or who do it professionally. However, not all gay people cross-dress, not all cross-dressers are gay, and not all gay people approve of drag. But for some, it's a source of self-expression and entertainment that can also be a political statement against traditional gender roles. Drag doesn't necessarily involve (and perhaps never involves) the fantasy that one is a woman. Rather it is a way for a man to express his feminine side or his sense of the outrageous or his nonconformity. For other gay men, drag is a form of political activism used to draw attention to gay issues, criticize homophobic government and religious policies, and raise funds to fight AIDS. Whatever the purpose, drag is a way of refusing to be intimidated by heterosexist gender boundaries and a way of getting all of us to think about our own sexuality by challenging gender roles.

Lesbians sometimes cross-dress, too. In fact, there are some *drag kings*, such as Elvis Herselvis, who satirizes Elvis impersonators and includes in her act a discussion of Elvis' drug problem and sexual proclivities. However, drag doesn't seem to be for lesbians the major issue it is for gay men. One reason may be that, at least since the late 1960s, women's adoption of masculine attire and grooming is not considered outrageous or even unfashionable. Also, in general, the lesbian community's adoption of male clothing and grooming (for example, butch attire) or of androgenous clothing and grooming (for example, lesbian-feminist attire of the 1970s) has tended to be a matter of personal self-expression and/or quiet political statement that hasn't had the theatrical quality of gay drag. Therefore, although butch lesbians frequently have been beaten and raped, especially during such repressive periods as the 1950s, their cross-dressing never drew the national attention focused on gay drag.

The word *camp* refers to a kind of exuberant self-expression characterized by irreverence, artifice, exaggeration, and theatricality. Camp is ironic, witty, and humorous and often involves a blurring or crossing of gender lines. Indeed, when drag is practiced in a flamboyant, theatrical manner, it is generally considered camp. Think, for instance, of the role of Edna Turnblad, played by gifted actor and drag queen Divine, in John Waters' 1988 film classic *Hairspray*. In fact, the entire film – as well as the hit Broadway musical and 2007 remake it inspired – are generally appreciated for their camp qualities. Moreover, camp is subversive in that it mocks authority and traditional standards of behavior by imitating them in outrageous ways, often through the use of exaggerated gestures, postures, and voice. In addition to *Hairspray*, time-honored examples of camp include the well-known Monty Python skit entitled "Reenactment of the Battle of Pearl Harbor by the Townswomen's Guild of Sheffield in Yorkshire," in which six men, attired in the dresses and hats of middle-aged women from the 1950s, run into the middle of a field and beat one another with their handbags. (You can find the video on YouTube. I think you'll enjoy it.) Another example is "Three Gays of the Condo" – season 14, episode 17 of the long-lived animated television series *The Simpsons* – in which Homer Simpson has a fight with his wife and moves in with two gay men. Sir Elton John and Lady Gaga are camp icons. So is Dusty Springfield, pop/rock star of the 1960s, because, among other reasons, her signature bouffant hairstyles and extremely heavy makeup often gave her the onstage appearance of a beautiful drag queen. One doesn't have to be LGBTQ to behave in a manner that might be considered camp. Camp is as much, or more, in the eye of the beholder as in the intention of the beheld. Thus, the flamboyant theatricality of Judy Garland and Cher – and the flamboyant irreverence of Bette Midler and Madonna – are appreciated for their camp qualities by many gay fans. As in the case of drag, camp is a way of affirming one's difference from heterosexual culture. It's a way of disarming heterosexism and healing oneself through laughter. And thus it's a way of transforming victimhood into power.

Of course, living with the reality of AIDS, which includes AIDS-related discrimination, became part of gay sensibility during the 1980s. It can't help but affect the way gay men see the world to know that the federal government was reticent to fund AIDS research until the disease became a threat for heterosexual citizens as well, to be aware of the lingering reluctance of some medical professionals to treat AIDS patients or to treat them with respect, to encounter discrimination in the workplace against people who have AIDS or who are HIV positive (who do not have AIDS but who will presumably develop the disease at some future point), and to put forth the daily physical and emotional labor of caring for friends and loved ones dying of AIDS.

AIDS was first identified in 1981, and by the end of the decade a generation of men had died from it. The gay community's response to this national health emergency has been extremely active and positive. They have formed political organizations, such as the AIDS Coalition to Unleash Power (ACT UP), to publicize and gain support for their cause through public demonstrations and protests in an effort to get drug companies, insurance companies, government agencies, and the medical bureaucracy to respond appropriately to this epidemic. And as lesbians rallied to the support of gay men, joining their protests and playing a significant role in caring for the sick and dying, a new spirit of solidarity emerged between these two communities. As Margaret Cruikshank puts it, "those who had been labeled misfits and un-American perverts launched a typically American self-help movement which was probably one of the largest volunteer efforts in the nation's history" (182–83).

Despite their focus on different theoretical issues, there is a good deal of similarity in the way gay and lesbian critics approach literary texts. For example, like lesbian critics, gay critics attempt to determine what might constitute a gay poetics, or a way of writing that is uniquely gay; to establish a gay literary tradition; and to decide what writers and works belong to that tradition. Gay critics also examine how gay sensibility affects literary expression and study the ways in which heterosexual texts can have a homoerotic dimension. They try to rediscover gay writers from the past whose work was underappreciated, distorted, or suppressed, including gay writers who have been presumed heterosexual. They try to determine the sexual politics of specific texts, analyzing, for example, how gay characters or "feminine" men are portrayed in both gay and heterosexual texts. Finally, gay critics identify and correct heterosexist interpretations of literature that fail to recognize or appreciate the gay sensibility informing specific literary works. To get an idea of the kinds of insights into literature these approaches can produce, let's take a brief look at three specific examples: an analysis of Walt Whitman's poetic voice, a study of the representation of gay identity in the work of contemporary novelist Edmund White, and a defense of the gay sensibility in Tennessee Williams' plays.

In "Walt Whitman Camping," Karl Keller extends our understanding of Whitman's poetic project through his interesting analysis of the ways in which Whitman's poetic self-presentation is a form of camp. "We see this," Keller argues, "in the flamboyant gestures, the exaggerated tone, the operatic voice, the inflated role-playing, the dilation of language" (115) that frequently characterize Whitman's speaker, for example, the speaker in "Song of Myself" (1855). Keller says, "Those who have bemoaned the contradiction between Whitman's claim that his poetry … revealed his personality well and the paucity of autobiographical detail in the poems have only failed to look … at the workings of Whitman's voice" (115). "The poet is *performing*" (115), Keller asserts, and the camp quality of his performance reveals the seductive "come-on" (116) in his voice and in his pose that humorously sexualizes his transcendentalist ideals of bonding with nature and with other human beings. Whitman "is not making fun of the things he talks about but making fun out of them," Keller observes, in order to "intensif[y] his enjoyment of the world around him" (118). Referring to the poet as "the Mae West of American literature," Keller argues that Whitman reveals himself to the reader, not by "flashing his entire person at us," but by "showing the range of possibilities of his personality" (115).

Another representative example of gay literary criticism is Nicholas F. Radel's thoughtful essay "Self as Other: The Politics of Identity in the Works of Edmund White." "Gay identity," Radel observes, "is the explicit subject of many of White's works," and many of his gay characters "fail to achieve a coherent sense of self," a failure that "can be attributed to the politics of sexual and gender difference" (175). In other words, White examines the damaging effects of homophobic American culture on the gay men and boys who grow up within it, and its most damaging effect is the internalized homophobia, the learned self-hatred, of his gay characters. Indeed, Radel points out that White's gay characters experience a distinct split within themselves between what they consider their "essential selves" and "a homosexual self as Other that they themselves conceive as being separate" from them (176). This experience of being alienated from oneself undermines both gay identity and gay community. How can a man feel he belongs to a gay community if he is alienated from his own gayness? Furthermore, Radel argues, self-alienation in White's work is not due to individual psychological problems but is the direct result of the politics of heterosexist oppression. Therefore, "we might view White's novels as part of the historical apparatus for revealing a gay subject [selfhood] as it responds to political pressure from the culture at large" (176).

Finally, in "Camp and the Gay Sensibility," Jack Babuscio argues that gay sensibility has something to offer everyone: the relevance of its insights is not limited, as some critics believe, to the gay community. As a case in point, Babuscio observes that critics have failed to fully appreciate the insights into human life offered by

Tennessee Williams' heroines — the most famous of whom is probably Blanche Dubois in *A Streetcar Named Desire* (1947) — because these characters represent Williams' own emotions as a gay man. In other words, Williams' heroines are Williams himself in drag, so to speak, expressing his own anxieties about being gay: for example, his battle between the demands of the flesh and those of the spirit, his desire to be promiscuous and yet still keep his pride, and his fear of aging in a youth-oriented homosexual subculture. Critics have concluded therefore, Babuscio notes, that Williams' work is not relevant to mainstream heterosexual culture. In short, they believe that gay sensibility speaks only to gay men.

In contrast, Babuscio asserts that Williams' experience on the margins of mainstream America, as an object of "fear, suspicion, and, even, hatred" (34), gave him a privileged position from which to understand the conflicts of human life — the same privileged position occupied, for example, by members of racial minorities — because he had to deal with those conflicts in a particularly intense form. Furthermore, Babuscio notes, the act of literary creation involves, for all good writers, the transformation of their own experience into literary form. So when Maxine Faulk, in *The Night of the Iguana* (1962), says that we all reach a point in our lives, sooner or later, where we must settle for something that works for us, she is speaking not just to the gay community but to the entire human community.

Of course, just as in the case of our discussion of lesbian literary criticism, the examples of gay criticism provided here do not exhaust the field but are intended only as a representative sample of the kind of work done by gay critics. Your own reading of gay criticism will expand your understanding of this growing body of work.

In addition, you might want to acquaint yourself, if you haven't already done so, with literary works by contemporary gay writers, who are receiving much critical acclaim. These writers include, among others, David Feinberg, Tony Kushner, David Leavitt, Edmund White, Armistead Maupin, Paul Monette, Mark Doty, Randy Shilts, Dennis Cooper, Neil Bartlett, Allan Gurganus, David Sedaris, Andrew Holleran, Samuel R. Delany, Dale Peck, John Rechy, Paul Russell, Matthew Stadler, and Peter Weltner.

Queer criticism ③

One of the first questions asked by students new to the study of gay and lesbian criticism is why gay men and women have chosen the homophobic word *queer* to designate an approach within their own discipline. I think there are several answers to that question, and they will serve as an introduction to some of the basic premises of queer theory.

First, the use of the term *queer* can be seen as an attempt to reappropriate the word from what has been its homophobic usage in order to demonstrate that heterosexists shouldn't be allowed to define LGBTQ experience. The act of defining the terms of one's own self-reference is a powerful move that says, among other things, "We're not afraid to be seen!"; "You don't tell us who we are – we tell us who we are!"; and "We're proud to be different!" Or, as the popular queer slogan sums it up, "We're here, we're queer – get used to it!" As many members of the LGBTQ community have learned, the word *queer* is a tool of oppression, but it's also a tool of change.

Furthermore, some LGBTQ people have adopted the word *queer* as an inclusive category for referring to a common political or cultural ground shared by lesbian, gay, bisexual, transgender, and all people who, for whatever reasons, do not consider themselves heterosexual. Used in this way, the term *queer* tries to reunite the heretofore divided camps that resulted, in part, from the white middle-class roots of the gay liberation and lesbian feminist movements of the early 1970s. As products of the white middle class, these movements were unable to perceive their own white middle-class privilege. As a result, through the 1970s and into the 1980s, the experiences of gay people of color and of working-class gay men and lesbians were generally ignored, for these groups had little or no opportunity to assume visible leadership positions within the gay power structure. In addition, certain forms of gay sexual expression were excluded or marginalized, such as the butch–femme lesbian couples who played such an important role in lesbian culture during the 1950s and 1960s. Butch–femme couples resemble heterosexual couples in terms of clothing, grooming, and personal style. Although they did not necessarily resemble heterosexual couples in terms of emotional or sexual relatedness, it was usually assumed that they did, and they were therefore criticized for reproducing the same power imbalance generally found in heterosexual relationships. The word *queer*, then, as an inclusive term, seeks to heal these divisions by offering a collective identity to which all LGBTQ people can belong.

For the most part, however, the word *queer* is used to indicate a specific theoretical perspective. From a theoretical point of view, the words *gay* and *lesbian* imply a definable category – homosexuality – that is clearly opposite to another definable category: heterosexuality. However, for queer theory, categories of sexuality cannot be defined by such simple oppositions as homosexual/heterosexual. Building on deconstruction's insights into human subjectivity (selfhood) as a fluid, fragmented, dynamic collectivity of possible "selves," queer theory defines individual sexuality as a fluid, fragmented, dynamic collectivity of possible sexualities. Our sexuality may be different at different times over the course of our lives or even at different times over the course of a week because sexuality is a dynamic range of desire. Gay sexuality, lesbian sexuality, bisexuality, and heterosexuality are, for all of us, possibilities along a continuum of sexual possibilities. And what these categories mean to different individuals will be influenced by how they conceive their own racial and class identities as well. Thus, sexuality is completely controlled neither by our biological sex (male or female) nor by the way our culture translates biological sex into gender roles (masculine or feminine). Sexuality exceeds these definitions and has a will, a creativity, an expressive need of its own.

Moreover, heterosexuality is not a norm against which homosexuality can be defined because the range of human sexuality cannot be completely understood in terms of such limited concepts as homosexual and heterosexual. For one thing, these concepts reduce sexuality to the biological sex of one's partner, or, in psychological terms, one's *object choice*. There are a host of other factors that make up human sexual desire. As Eve Kosofsky Sedgwick argues, the intricacies of human sexuality could be understood just as well, or better, in terms of any number of paired opposites other than same-sex or different-sex object choice. For example, the definition of one's sexuality might be based on one's preference for someone older or younger, for a human or an animal, for a single partner or a group activity, for oneself alone (as in masturbation) or for a variety of different partners. Other dimensions of sexuality don't even involve object choice. For example, Sedgwick notes, the definition of one's sexuality might be based on such oppositions as "orgasmic/nonorgasmic, noncommercial/commercial, using bodies only/using manufactured objects, in private/in public, spontaneous/scripted" (57). Or the definition of one's sexuality might be based on one's preference for particular acts, sensations, or physical types.

For queer theory, then, our sexuality is socially constructed to the extent that it is based on the ways in which sexuality is defined by the culture in which we live. We saw examples of the social construction of sexuality earlier, when we discussed ancient Athens, where sexual categories were based on a caste system that didn't differentiate between male and female, and the very different definitions of homosexuality operating in some Latin American cultures, in early-twentieth-century working-class America, and in white middle-class America today. In short, our sexual orientation may indeed be inborn, but definitions of appropriate gender behavior are socially constructed. The belief that sexuality is, in this way, socially constructed is behind efforts to read literature from the past not just in terms of our own definitions of sexuality, but in terms of those definitions operating in the culture from which that literature emerged.

Clearly, the word *queer* has a range of meanings in literary studies today. As an inclusive term, it can refer to any piece of literary criticism that interprets a text from an LGBTQ perspective. Therefore, any of the examples of gay and lesbian criticism discussed earlier could be included in a collection of queer essays. However, if we restrict ourselves to its narrower theoretical meaning – its deconstructive dimension – queer criticism reads texts to reveal the problematic quality of their representations of sexual categories, in other words, to show the various ways in which the categories homosexual and heterosexual break down, overlap, or do not adequately represent the dynamic range of human sexuality. These kinds of readings can be rather complex. Here are a few simplified examples.

A queer reading of William Faulkner's "A Rose for Emily" (1931) might examine how traditional definitions of gender identity (masculine versus feminine) and sexuality (homosexual versus heterosexual) fail to explain or contain the character of Emily Greirson. Her gender categorization is not fixed but crosses back and forth between the masculine and the feminine. She's both the slender virgin in white dominated by her father and the defiant individualist who violates class norms and moral law to take what she wants from Homer Barron, including his life. She's both the childlike recluse who teaches the feminine art of china painting and the dominant presence with iron-gray hair, like that of a vigorous man, who imposes her will on the male power structure, including the post office, the tax collectors, the church, and, in the person of the pharmacist, the medical profession.

More tellingly, the characterization of Emily exceeds the opposition between homosexual and heterosexual. In terms of their biological sex, Homer and Emily are a heterosexual couple: he's a man; she's a woman. However, as we've just seen, the text constructs Emily's gender as a vacillation between the feminine and the masculine. Indeed, much of the powerfully defiant behavior traditionally associated with men is ascribed to Emily during her relationship with Homer. In terms of gender behavior, then, one might argue that Homer and Emily, symbolically at least, are a queer couple: they are both gendered as men. Thus, "A Rose for Emily," ostensibly a text about heterosexual passion and transgression, is also (or more so) a queer text that reveals the limits of traditional definitions of gender and sexuality.

Similarly, a queer reading of Walt Whitman's "Song of Myself" might examine how the poem's erotic dimension requires us to expand our understanding of the sexual. One of the hallmarks of Whitman's remarkable poem is its exuberant response to life: the speaker, who identifies himself as Whitman, revels in the beauty of nature, experiences spiritual union with fellow Americans from all walks of life, and celebrates the pure joy of just being alive. As we saw earlier, critic Karl Keller examines how Whitman's camp style reveals, among other things, a seductive tone of voice and pose that humorously sexualizes the poet's transcendentalist ideals of bonding with nature and with other human beings. Reading the poem through a queer lens, however, we might focus, in ways that Keller does not, on Whitman's eroticization of experience as it exceeds the contemporary white middle-class definition of homosexuality. For one might argue that the sexuality represented in "Song of Myself" is too fluid to be contained within the boundaries of male same-sex desire.

Indeed, the poem's implicit definition of sexuality includes many of those dimensions of erotic experience that, as we saw earlier, Eve Kosofsky Sedgwick argues have been neglected in sexual definitions structured by the homosexual/ heterosexual opposition. Under Whitman's gaze, almost all experience has an intensely erotic quality: he offers erotic descriptions not just of young men bathing in a river (a traditional homoerotic image), but of the young woman watching them from a distance, and of the natural setting itself, which is simultaneously private (isolated) and public (out in the open). Similarly, Whitman's gaze eroticizes not only the healthy bodies of men and women at their various modes of employment, but the modes of employment as well, and the places in which they perform them: the magnificent mountains, the fertile plains, the busy harbors, and the thriving cities. In addition, the poet eroticizes – among other persons, places, things, and activities – venerable old men and women, the strength and serenity of animals, the sea, and every conceivable zone of his own body. A queer reading of "Song of Myself" might argue, therefore, that Whitman's poem is not homoerotic but cosmically erotic or, perhaps more accurately, that Whitman's homoeroticism can be fully comprehended only by transcending definitions of human sexuality that rest on the biological sex of one's object choice or on object choice at all.

Finally, a queer reading of Toni Morrison's *Beloved* (1987) might explore the ways in which the novel's evocative richness and multilayered meanings depend in part on its crossing or transforming or abandoning traditional demarcations between same-sex and opposite-sex love and between the "natural" and the "unnatural." For example, imitating the mating turtles she sees in the woods (that is, imitating the natural), Beloved has sex with Paul D and presumably becomes pregnant as a result (witness her swollen belly near the novel's close and the reference to her pregnancy by the women who come to rescue Sethe). In a more meaningful sense, however, Beloved is "pregnant" with herself: she's trying to give birth to herself, to a new self able to take its place in the natural world inhabited by Sethe and Denver, and thereby emerge permanently from the ghostly, supernatural darkness that continually threatens to swallow her up. And this "pregnancy" has no father. Rather, it has two mothers: Beloved and Sethe. For Beloved, like a predatory lover, consumes Sethe's life in order to give birth to her own, which we see quite literally as Sethe grows thinner while Beloved grows larger. And this strand of the narrative occurs against a backdrop of same-sex love – a blend of familial and romantic devotion among Denver, Beloved, and Sethe – that is much more powerful than Beloved's zombielike sex with Paul D and that triumphs, at least temporarily, over the heterosexual coupling of Paul D and Sethe. Indeed, Beloved's passionate attachment to Sethe, like Denver's to Beloved, is described in romantic, even sexual, language that carries some of the most intense emotional charge of the novel. *Beloved* is thus infused with a queerness – with a refusal to limit itself to traditional notions of sexuality and of the natural – that is responsible for a good deal of the novel's narrative progression, thematic content, and emotional force.

If these examples of queer criticism seem more slippery, more indefinite, and more complicated than the examples of lesbian and gay criticism cited earlier, keep in mind that it is the slippery, indefinite, and complicated quality of human sexuality that queer criticism's deconstructive project tries to underscore. As the most recent and most philosophical trend in lesbian and gay literary studies, queer criticism promises us an exciting future of theoretical exploration and experimentation.[7]

(4)

Some shared features of lesbian, gay, and queer criticism

Regardless of the differences we've just seen among lesbian, gay, and queer criticism, there is a good deal of overlap in the ways all three domains approach literary interpretation. Note, for example, the similarities in the tasks performed by lesbian and gay critics discussed earlier. In addition, many gay and lesbian critics combine some of the deconstructive insights offered by queer theory with the social and political concerns associated with more traditional forms of lesbian and gay criticism. Indeed, many devotees of queer theory still refer to themselves as gay or lesbian critics.

Furthermore, critics from all three domains have taken an interest in recurring themes that appear throughout LGBTQ literature and that constitute part of an evolving literary tradition. These themes include the following: initiation, including discovering one's LGBTQ sexual orientation, experiencing one's first sexual encounters as an LGBTQ person, and "learning the ropes" in the LGBTQ subculture; coming out to family and friends; coming out at the workplace; dealing with homophobia and with heterosexist discrimination; the psychology of gay self-hatred; overcoming gay self-hatred; the role of camp and drag in gay life; dealing with loneliness and alienation; finding love; building a life with an LGBTQ partner; the quest to build a lesbian utopia; life before and after Stonewall; life before and after AIDS (in terms of both one's personal life and the collective life of the LGBTQ community); caring for loved ones with AIDS; mourning the death of AIDS victims; and the importance of LGBTQ solidarity. Of course, the themes in LGBTQ writing change over time as the social and political situation of LGBTQ writers changes. And themes that occur openly in contemporary works may appear, in literature from earlier periods, only in disguised forms (as we saw in our discussion of the work of Willa Cather) or in playful forms (consider, for example, the double meanings of the wordplay in Oscar Wilde's *The Importance of Being Earnest*, 1894).

Finally, lesbian, gay, and queer criticism often rely on similar kinds of textual evidence. For example, in addition to the more obvious forms of textual cues – such as homoerotic imagery and erotic encounters between same-sex characters – there are rather subtle textual cues that can create a homoerotic atmosphere even in an otherwise heterosexual text, as we saw in the examples of lesbian, gay, and queer criticism provided earlier. No single textual cue can stand on its own as evidence of a homoerotic atmosphere in a text. Nor can a small number of such cues support a lesbian, gay, or queer reading. But a preponderance of these cues, especially if coupled with other kinds of textual or biographical evidence, can strengthen a lesbian, gay, or queer interpretation even of an apparently heterosexual text. Let's take a closer look at a few of the most common examples of these subtle cues.

Homosocial bonding – The depiction of strong emotional ties between same-sex characters can create a homosocial atmosphere that may be subtly or overtly homoerotic. Whether homoerotic or not, however, the depiction of homosocial bonding foregrounds the profound importance of same-sex emotional ties in the development of human identity and community, which is a human potential often devalued, marginalized, or trivialized by the homophobic anxiety of heterosexist culture. Edna Pontellier and Adèle Ratignolle, in Kate Chopin's *The Awakening* (1899), share a homosocial bond, as do, in the same novella, Edna and Mademoiselle Reisz. Other examples of homosocial bonds among literary characters include those between Ishmael and Queequeg in Herman Melville's *Moby Dick* (1851), between Huck Finn and Jim in Mark Twain's *The Adventures of Huckleberry Finn* (1885), and between Nel and Sula in Toni Morrison's *Sula* (1973).

Gay or lesbian "signs" – Gay or lesbian signs are of two types. The first type consists of characteristics that heterosexist culture stereotypically associates with LGBTQ people, such as might be evident, for example, in the appearance and behavior of "feminine" male character or "masculine" female characters. The second type are coded signs created by the gay or lesbian subculture itself. For example, the word *gay*, as used in the writing of Gertrude Stein in the early decades of the twentieth century, may well have been an "in-group" coded sign that heterosexual culture of the period would not have recognized. And certainly the lesbian images in Emily Dickinson's poetry, discussed earlier, operate as coded signs generally not recognized by heterosexual readers. Interpreting both kinds of signs can be tricky because both the signs created by LGBTQ subcultures and the stereotypes created by heterosexist culture change over time. So we must use this kind of evidence cautiously and in conjunction with other forms of evidence. Some authors may have deliberately included gay or lesbian signs in their literary works because they felt it was the only safe way, in heterosexist culture, to express their own LGBTQ experience or to speak to an LGBTQ readership. Other authors may have included these signs for any number of conscious or unconscious reasons and may not have intended them as gay or lesbian signs. Whether or not we take into account an author's intention, our goal is to analyze how these signs function in the text to create the potential for a queer interpretation.

Same-sex "doubles" – A more subtle, somewhat abstract, form of gay and lesbian signs consists of same-sex characters who look alike, act alike, or have parallel experiences. Because gay and lesbian sexuality foregrounds sexual similarity, same-sex characters who function as some sort of "mirror image" of each other can also function as gay or lesbian signs. Same-sex doubles may share a homoerotic bond, a homosocial bond, or they may not know each other at all. Examples of same-sex doubles might include Edna Pontellier and Adèle Ratignolle in Kate Chopin's *The Awakening* (1899), as well as Robert Lebrun and Alcée Arobin in the same novella; Daisy Buchanan and Jordan Baker in F. Scott Fitzgerald's *The Great Gatsby* (1925); Quentin Compson and Dalton Ames in William Faulkner's

The Sound and the Fury (1929); and Miss China and Miss Poland in Toni Morrison's *The Bluest Eye* (1970).

Transgressive sexuality – A text's focus on transgressive sexuality, including transgressive heterosexuality (such as extramarital romance), throws into question the rules of traditional heterosexuality and thus opens the door of imagination to transgressive sexualities of all kinds. Of course, a great deal of literature deals with heterosexual transgression without necessarily having a queer subtext. But some representations of heterosexual transgression – for example, those that involve several characters, the leading of double lives, the relaxing of inhibitions associated with alcohol and riotous parties – create an atmosphere of sexual experimentation that sets the stage, so to speak, for a queer interpretation. While a set stage is not sufficient by itself for a queer reading, it can provide an evocative backdrop to complement more concrete textual evidence.

Clearly, the boundaries among lesbian, gay, and queer criticism remain somewhat fluid. Your purpose in using the kinds of textual evidence just described, as well as your own self-identified critical orientation, will determine whether your interpretation of a literary work is a lesbian, gay, or queer reading.

Some questions lesbian, gay, and queer critics ask about literary texts

The following questions are offered to summarize lesbian, gay, or queer approaches to literature. Question 7 – because it rests on a deconstructive view of sexuality – is the only question that falls within the narrower theoretical definition of queer criticism. The remaining questions can be answered from any one of the three perspectives.

1   What are the politics (ideological agendas) of specific gay, lesbian, or queer works, and how are those politics revealed in, for example, the work's thematic content or portrayals of its characters?
2   What are the poetics (literary devices and strategies) of a specific lesbian, gay, or queer work? What does the work contribute to the ongoing attempt to define a uniquely lesbian, gay, or queer poetics, literary tradition, or canon?
3   What does the work contribute to our knowledge of queer, gay, or lesbian experience and history, including literary history?
4   How is queer, gay, or lesbian experience coded in texts that are apparently heterosexual? (This analysis is usually done for works by writers who lived at a time when openly queer, gay, or lesbian texts would have been considered unacceptable, or it is done in order to help reformulate the sexual orientation of a writer formerly presumed heterosexual.)

5 How might the works of heterosexual writers be reread to reveal an unspoken or unconscious lesbian, gay, or queer presence? That is, does the work have an unconscious lesbian, gay, or queer desire or conflict that it submerges (or that heterosexual readers have submerged)?

6 What does the work reveal about the operations (socially, politically, psychologically) of heterosexism? Is the work (consciously or unconsciously) homophobic? Does the work critique, celebrate, or blindly accept heterosexist values?

7 How does the literary text illustrate the problematics of sexuality and sexual "identity," that is, the ways in which human sexuality does not fall neatly into the separate categories defined by the words *homosexual* and *heterosexual*?

Depending on the literary text in question, we might ask one or any combination of these questions. Or we might come up with a useful question not listed here. These are just some starting points to get us to look at literature through a lesbian, gay, or queer lens. Remember, not all these critics will interpret the same work in the same way, even if they use the same theoretical concepts. As in every field, even expert practitioners disagree. Our goal is to use lesbian, gay, and queer criticism to help enrich our reading of literary works, to help us see some important ideas they illustrate that we might not have seen so clearly or so deeply without these forms of criticism, and to help us appreciate the history and literary production of LGBTQ people.

The following reading of *The Great Gatsby* is offered as an example of what a queer interpretation of Fitzgerald's novel might yield. I call my reading queer in both the inclusive sense of the term – my discussion will not be limited to characters of a single sex or a single sexuality – and in its deconstructive sense: my reading explores the vagaries and instabilities of the novel's representation of sexuality. Specifically, I will argue that *The Great Gatsby* is a sexually ambiguous novel: it raises a number of questions about the sexuality of its characters, but it does not answer them. And I will argue that this ambiguity results from the delivery of a heterosexual plot through the medium of a closeted gay sensibility, that of narrator Nick Carraway. Finally, I will suggest that the novel's sexual ambiguity is a reflection of Fitzgerald's apparent conflicts concerning his own sexuality.

Will the real Nick Carraway please come out? A queer reading of *The Great Gatsby*

Certainly, we couldn't ask for a more overtly heterosexual plot than that of F. Scott Fitzgerald's *The Great Gatsby* (1925). The novel's narrative progression is driven by Jay Gatsby's tragic love for Daisy Fay Buchanan and by three overlapping heterosexual romantic triangles: Gatsby-Daisy-Tom, Tom-Myrtle-George, and Myrtle-Tom-Daisy. This heterosexual narrative is shadowed, however, by a homoerotic subtext, which, though it remains closeted, so to speak, by the spectacular twists and turns of the heterosexual plot, is a pervasive presence in the novel.

Specifically, I will argue that the novel's treatment of sexual transgression and its proliferation of gay and lesbian signs work together to create a homoerotic subtext that disrupts and destabilizes the heterosexual narrative, creating, in the process, a sexually ambiguous novel. And as we shall see, this homoerotic subtext finds its most complete embodiment in the characterization of narrator Nick Carraway, who is, I believe, unaware of his gay orientation. Put another way, *The Great Gatsby's* sexual ambiguity results from the delivery of a heterosexual plot through the medium of a closeted gay sensibility. In addition, I will suggest that the novel's sexual ambiguity mirrors the conflicts Fitzgerald apparently experienced concerning his own sexuality.

Although the depiction of transgressive heterosexuality cannot by itself create a queer subtext in a heterosexual novel, *The Great Gatsby's* apparent obsession with sexual transgression, which as we shall see includes intimations of gay and lesbian sexuality, sets the stage for a queer interpretation. For one thing, the three romantic triangles that generate most of the novel's action are all adulterous: Daisy, Tom, and Myrtle are all breaking their marital vows. And Daisy's illicit reunion with Gatsby is arranged by Nick, a male relative who, traditionally, should protect her virtue but, instead, facilitates her losing it. Furthermore, Gatsby had premarital sex with Daisy during their initial courtship, when "he took [her] one still October night, took her ... ravenously and unscrupulously ... because he had no real right to touch her hand" (156; ch. 8). And Nick and Jordan, too, are apparently engaged in a premarital affair, neither of them for the first time. Indeed, Nick believes that Jordan is sexually promiscuous: he speculates that she is "incurably dishonest" because she wants to "keep that cool, insolent smile turned to the world and yet satisfy the demands of her hard, jaunty body" (63; ch. 3).

Of course, the riotous parties depicted, both in Tom and Myrtle's apartment and on Gatsby's lawn, also contribute an ambience of sexual transgression. For example, Tom and Myrtle's party is an outgrowth of their illicit affair, about which they and their guests talk openly. And the descriptions of Gatsby's parties are peppered with sexually transgressive images, such as Tom's attempting to pick up a "common but pretty" young woman (112; ch. 6); Gatsby and Daisy's sneaking away from the party to be alone at Nick's cottage while Nick stands guard lest they be intruded upon; the unidentified man "talking with curious intensity to a young actress" while his wife "hisse[s] 'You promised!' into his ear" (56; ch. 3); "Beluga's girls" (66; ch. 4), with the implication that phrase carries of their being his sexual objects; and such implicitly transgressive couples as "Hubert Auerbach and Mr. Chrystie's wife" (66; ch. 4) and "Miss Claudia Hip with a man reputed to be her chauffeur" (67; ch. 4). What Nick says of New York City is thus true of the sexual atmosphere that pervades the novel: this is a place where "[a]nything can happen ... anything at all" (73; ch. 4).

Indeed, it is at these parties where we see the striking examples of gay and lesbian "signs" that initiate the development of the novel's homoerotic subtext. For example, at the party where Nick first meets Gatsby, he sees "two girls in twin yellow dresses who stopped at the foot of the steps. 'Hello!' they cried together" (47; ch. 3). These two young women are a striking example of same-sex "doubles" that function as lesbian signs: they look alike, talk alike, are dressed alike, are apparently inseparable, and turn out to be a "pair of stage 'twins'" who do "a baby act in costume" (51; ch. 3) at the party. In fact, the depiction of these two characters in the 1974 film version of the novel is that film's only concession to the possibility of a queer dimension in the story: in the film, the women are portrayed dancing together in a manner the sexual meaning of which cannot be missed.

At the party in Tom and Myrtle's apartment, we see a series of gay signs during the encounter between Nick and Mr. McKee, "a pale, feminine man" (34; ch. 2), who lives with his wife in a neighboring apartment. The encounter begins when McKee falls asleep in his chair. Nick tells us, "Taking out my handkerchief I wiped from his cheek the remains of the spot of dried lather that had worried me all the afternoon" (41; ch. 2). When McKee wakes up and leaves the party, he leaves his wife – whom Nick describes as "shrill, languid, handsome and horrible" (34; ch. 2) – behind. Nick "follow[s]" (42; ch. 2) McKee out, and the latter invites him to lunch one day. Nick agrees.

> "All right," I agreed, "I'll be glad to."
> ... I was standing beside his bed and he was sitting up between the sheets, clad in his underwear, with a great portfolio in his hands.
> "Beauty and the Beast ... Loneliness ... Old Grocery Horse ... Brook'n Bridge. ... "
> Then I was lying half asleep in the cold lower level of the Pennsylvania Station, staring at the morning *Tribune* and waiting for the four o'clock train.
> (Fitzgerald's ellipses, 42; ch. 2)

Obviously, both men are very drunk, and the scene easily can be interpreted as nothing more than a representation of their drunkenness. From this perspective, the ellipses refer to the memory lapses that commonly occur in such a state of inebriation. Nick is saying, in effect, "That's how drunk I was," and that's all he's saying.

Through a queer lens, however, the scene suggests another reading. The gay signs here are numerous, and the order in which they appear implies the progression of a homoerotic attraction between the two men, if not the equally likely possibility of a sexual encounter in McKee's bedroom. These signs include McKee's feminine appearance, the masculine (aggressive, overbearing, "handsome") quality of his wife, Nick's attention to the spot of lather on McKee's face (in other words, Nick's fastidious attention to McKee's grooming), Nick's "following" him out of the room, the lunch invitation, Nick's following McKee into his bedroom, McKee's sitting in bed attired only in his underwear, and Nick's remembering nothing else until he wakes up at four o'clock in the morning on the floor of the train station (so whatever occurred in the interim has the status of a repressed memory). None of these signs would carry much weight by itself. But when clustered in this fashion they suggest a homoerotic subtext that no queer critic would miss.

Perhaps the most numerous gay and lesbian signs are associated, however, with Jay Gatsby and Jordan Baker. Gatsby's fastidious grooming and flamboyant clothing and other possessions function effectively as gay signs. "[H]is short hair looked as though it were trimmed every day" (54; ch. 3), and his impeccable wardrobe features various shades of lavender and pink, two colors that have been long associated with gayness. We are told that Gatsby owns dozens of "shirts with stripes and scrolls and plaids in coral and apple green and lavender and faint orange with monograms of Indian blue" (97–98; ch. 5), and his pink suit is mentioned at least three times.

In fact, the manner in which Gatsby's pink suit is mentioned underscores its function as a gay sign. Nick's two references to the pink suit are phrased quite romantically, as if the clothing of a desirable woman were being described: "I could think of nothing but the luminosity of his pink suit under the moon" (150; ch. 7) and "[H]is gorgeous pink rag of a suit made a bright spot of color against the white steps" (162; ch. 8). And Tom's reference to the suit foregrounds its function as a gay sign because that seems to be precisely how Tom, who is clearly homophobic, sees it. Let's consider this last point a bit further.

Tom's numerous extramarital affairs with working-class women, whom he parades in public (28; ch. 2) and whose socioeconomic vulnerability gives him a great deal of power over them, suggests a need to reassure himself of his heterosexuality, as does his constant, aggressive assertion of his manhood, which we see throughout the novel. As Nick puts it,

> There was a touch of paternal contempt in [his voice], even toward people he liked ...
>
> "Now, don't think my opinion on these matters is final," he seemed to say, "just because I'm stronger and more of a man than you are."
>
> (11; ch. 1)

This kind of macho overcompensation is directly related to homophobia: Tom's need to prove his own manhood leads him to attack anything he perceives as an indication of homosexuality in others. So when Tom's contempt for Gatsby expresses itself in a derogatory reference to the latter's pink suit, it underscores the suit's function as a gay sign: "An Oxford man! ... Like hell he is! He wears a pink suit" (129; ch. 7).

Gatsby's other possessions also function as gay signs. Much of the decor of his house is extravagantly feminine: "Marie Antoinette music rooms and Restoration salons ... [and] period bedrooms swathed in rose and lavender silk and vivid with new flowers" (96; ch. 5). And Gatsby's car has the flamboyance, as Tom puts it, of a "circus wagon" (128; ch. 7): "It was a rich cream color," Nick says, "bright with nickel, swollen here and there in its monstrous length with triumphant hatboxes and supper-boxes and tool-boxes, and terraced with a labyrinth of windshields that mirrored a dozen suns" (68; ch. 4). In fact, the artifice and theatricality of the life Gatsby has created for himself has a camp quality about it, a quality evident even in the fictional "autobiography" in which Gatsby describes himself as a "young rajah ... collecting jewels, chiefly rubies, hunting big game, [and] painting" (70; ch. 4).

Analogously, Jordan Baker, whose name could belong to a man or a woman, is associated with numerous lesbian signs. She makes her living in the, then, male domain of professional golf. And just as Gatsby is frequently described in feminine terms, Jordan is frequently described in masculine terms. Upon first meeting her, Nick says, "I enjoyed looking at her. She was a slender, small-breasted girl with an erect carriage which she accentuated by throwing her body backward at the shoulders like a young cadet" (15; ch. 1), that is, like a young boy at military school. Even when dressed in her most feminine attire, she is described in rather masculine terms: "she wore her evening dress, all her dresses, like sports clothes — there was a jauntiness about her movements as if she had first learned to walk upon golf courses on clean, crisp mornings" (55; ch 3). Indeed, Nick's frequent descriptions of Jordan's appearance and behavior almost always evoke rather masculine images: she has a "hard, jaunty body" (63; ch. 3); "[h]er body asserted itself with a restless movement" (22; ch. 1); "her brown hand waved a jaunty salute" (57; ch. 3); she has a "wan, scornful mouth" (85; ch. 4); "her face [had] the same brown tint as the fingerless glove on her knee" (185; ch. 9); she "seemed to have mastered a certain hardy skepticism" (20; ch. 1); she's a "clean, hard, limited person" (84; ch. 4); and the like.

The possibility of a lesbian subtext in Jordan's characterization is reinforced by her relationships with men. As Nick observes, Jordan "instinctively avoided clever shrewd men ... because she felt safer on a plane where any divergence from a code would be thought impossible" (63; ch. 3). In other words, Jordan doesn't want to be seen through. She doesn't want to be thought to have a private life that "diverges" from the code, so she dates men she can manipulate, like the obviously immature escort who accompanies her to one of Gatsby's parties, "a persistent undergraduate given to violent innuendo" (49; ch. 3), or like Nick, who is "flattered" to be seen with "a golf champion" (62; ch. 3) and whom she can wrap around her little finger simply by saying "I like you" (63; ch. 3). In this context, and despite her sexual relationship with Nick, the "demands of her hard, jaunty body" that Jordan "satisf[ies]" by "dealing in subterfuges" (63; ch. 3) imply lesbian desire.

Given their function as repositories of gay signs, it is meaningful, from a queer perspective, that Gatsby and Jordan are the two characters in whom Nick takes the most personal interest. That Nick's attraction to Gatsby is homoerotic is suggested by his focus on Gatsby's feminine qualities, which mirrors his focus on McKee; his intense appreciation of Gatsby's "gorgeous" appearance and "romantic readiness" (6; ch. 1); his frequent, passionate, and often blind defense of Gatsby as the victim of others' selfishness and corruption; and the deep bond he feels with Gatsby after the latter's death, when it is "safe" to feel love for him. Similarly, Nick's attachment to Jordan seems as much the product of homoerotic as heterosexual attraction because he sees her primarily as a young boy.

In this context, Nick's successful effort to help Gatsby rekindle his affair with the unsuspecting Daisy also has a homoerotic subtext. Because of Nick's homoerotic attraction to Gatsby, he is likely to be curious about Gatsby's sexuality and to want to be involved in his personal life in any way he can. "Pimping" for Gatsby (which is what Nick's "procurement" of Daisy amounts to, as Gatsby's offer to pay him for the service suggests) may let Nick feel sexually close to him. (An analogous argument can be made, of course, that Jordan's interest in promoting Daisy's affair with Gatsby springs from Jordan's sexual attraction to and curiosity about Daisy.) In addition, by helping Daisy and Gatsby reunite in his own home, Nick may also experience a vicarious sexual thrill by identifying with Daisy during this episode. This is just what he seems to do as he chastises Gatsby for being insensitive to Daisy's feelings: "'Daisy's embarrassed too. ... You're acting like a little boy,' I broke out impatiently. 'Not only that, but you're rude. Daisy's sitting in there all alone'" (93; ch. 5). And during the subsequent tour of Gatsby's mansion, Nick's position is parallel to that of Daisy, as he, too, is getting a glimpse of Gatsby's private domain for the first time.

Indeed, Nick is a repository of gay signs, a fact that underscores the homoerotic dimension of his characterization. He is just turning 30, has never married or been engaged, and, his heterosexual affairs notwithstanding, he doesn't let his romantic relationships with women get serious. In fact, Nick fits the profile of thousands of young men who discovered their gay orientation during World War I. As George Chauncey observes in his gay history of New York City,

> [M]ilitary mobilization [during World War I], by removing men from the supervision of their families and small-town neighborhoods and placing them in a single-sex environment, increased the chances that they would encounter self-identified gay men and explore their homosexual interests. An extensive investigation of homosexuality among the men stationed at the Naval Training Station in Newport, Rhode Island, conducted by naval officials immediately following the war revealed that numerous sailors there had begun to forge [gay] identities ... after meeting other gay-identified sailors during the war, and

that a much larger number of men who did not consider themselves homo-sexual had nonetheless become familiar with the gay world and had homo-sexual experiences. Many of these men believed they could continue their homosexual lives only with great difficulty and circumspection if they returned to their home-towns, both because of the need to hide their homosexuality from their parents and because of the limited gay life available in most small towns.

Military mobilization also gave many recruits the chance to see the sort of gay life that large cities, especially New York [the major port from which American troops embarked for Europe], had to offer ... It is impossible to determine how many gay soldiers stayed in New York after the war, but the growing visibility of gay institutions in the city in the 1920s ... suggests that many of them did so – that it was, indeed, hard to keep them down on the farm after they'd seen gay New York.

(145)

Nick is a Midwesterner, and like the soldiers described above, he returned from the war unable to readjust to life in his hometown. Nick says,

I participated in that delayed Teutonic migration known as the Great War. I enjoyed the counter-raid so thoroughly that I came back restless. Instead of being the warm center of the world, the middle-west now seemed like the ragged edge of the universe – so I decided to go east. ...

(7; ch. 1)

And where in the East does he go? He goes to New York City, which both he and Jordan associate with transgressive sexuality. Nick says of New York, "I began to like ... the racy, adventurous feel of it at night" (61; ch. 3), and Jordan observes, "There's something very sensuous about it – overripe, as if all sorts of funny fruits were going to fall into your hands" (132; ch. 7).

More precisely, Nick works in New York City, where he also spends most of his evenings, and lives at West Egg, "this unprecedented 'place,'" as he puts it, "that Broadway had begotten upon a Long Island fishing village" (113–14; ch. 6), "a world complete in itself, with its own standards and its own great figures" (110; ch. 6), a world with a "raw vigor that chafed under the old euphemisms" (114; ch. 6). In other words, Nick is implying that he inhabits a transgressive subculture. And Nick's observation that Broadway is responsible for this subculture is noteworthy both because Broadway was a gay cruising area in New York City at this time (Chauncey 146) and because the theatrical profession has always been associated, whether accurately so or not, with sexual tolerance and experimentation.

Of course, when we analyze Nick, we're analyzing the novel's narrator. So it is Nick's point of view that produces the novel's sexual ambiguities. Let's take a moment to sum up those ambiguities. As we have seen, *The Great Gatsby* is a novel that seems obsessed with sexual transgression, but the nature of that transgression is not always clear. Nick sleeps with women but seems to be sexually attracted to McKee and, more profoundly, to Gatsby. Nick's attraction to Jordan seems to have a homoerotic dimension because of his fixation on her boyish appearance. Jordan, who is having an affair with Nick and could have married "several" men "at a nod of her head" (186; ch. 9), is a repository of lesbian signs. Gatsby, the novel's most important heterosexual romantic figure, is a repository of gay signs. Finally, Gatsby and Daisy, the heterosexual icon of the romantic couple, are brought together by Nick and Jordan, the novel's embodiment of closeted gay and lesbian desire.

The novel thus raises a number of questions about the sexuality of its characters, but it does not answer them. Is Nick heterosexual, gay, or bisexual? If there is a gay dimension to his sexuality, does he know it, and has he acted on it? What is Jordan's sexual orientation? Is she aware of it? What should we make of Gatsby's feminine, even camp, characteristics, given his romantic devotion to Daisy? Is the atmosphere of sexual freedom, even sexual license, that pervades the novel limited to the heterosexual domain, or does it include the gay world, and if so, in what ways?

The explanation that, I think, best accounts for most of the novel's sexual ambiguity is that Nick's sexual orientation is gay, and his gay sensibility influences his perception of the events he narrates. Thus, Gatsby and Jordan are repositories of gay and lesbian signs because we see them through Nick's eyes, and this is how he sees them. His perceptions may result from his own projection (he has gay desire, so he sees signs of it in others), or he may be sensitive to the queer aspects of Gatsby's and Jordan's sexuality because he shares them, or both. But Nick has closeted the queer dimension of his narrative and made it a subtext of the heterosexual love story because, I would argue, he has closeted his own gay desire. In other words, the novel's sexual ambiguity is the result of a heterosexual plot delivered by means of a gay sensibility that is hidden not only from others but from itself as well.

That Nick is denying his gay orientation is suggested not merely by his sexual affairs with women, which gay men in denial often have, but by his self-presentation, which seems to try too hard to convince us, and himself, of his conventionality. For example, concerning romantic matters, Nick represents himself as the conservative, almost puritanical, consciousness of the novel. When he learns that Tom is having an affair with "some woman in New York" (19; ch. 1), he says, "[M]y own instinct was to telephone immediately for the police" (20; ch. 1) and "It seemed to me that the thing for Daisy to do was to rush out of the house, child in arms – but apparently there were no such intentions in her head" (25; ch. 1). Similarly, before he allows himself to become romantically involved with Jordan, Nick feels that he must officially end his relationship with a young woman he'd been seeing back home because, as he puts it, "I am ... full of interior rules that act as brakes on my desires" (63–64; ch. 3). In fact, so repelled is Nick by the moral laxity of New York that when he returns to the Midwest after Gatsby's death, he tells us, "I wanted the world to be in uniform and at a sort of moral attention forever" (6; ch. 1).

At the same time, however, Nick seems to go out of his way to be sure we see him as an active heterosexual. For example, he tells us he "had a short affair with a girl who … worked in the accounting department" (61; ch. 3) at his place of employment. Why does he give us this apparently irrelevant bit of information except to make sure we know he's heterosexual? Having told us that the young woman he'd been seeing back home, whom everyone expected him to marry, was just "an old friend" (24; ch. 1), he wants to reassure us that he's capable of being more than just friends with a woman. Similarly, when he describes his evenings in New York City, "loiter[ing] in front of windows" (62; ch. 3) with other young men like himself, Nick deflates the homoerotic potential of the scene by relating in detail his fantasies about following "romantic women … to their apartments on the corners of hidden streets" (61; ch. 3).

Finally, when Nick talks about dating Jordan Baker he implies, as we saw earlier, that she is sexually promiscuous. And to make sure we know that Nick is a recipient of her sexual favors, chapter 4 ends with a description of his kissing Jordan during a romantic carriage ride through Central Park – "I drew up [Jordan] beside me, tightening my arms. … [She] smiled and so I drew her up again, closer, this time to my face" (85; ch. 4) – and chapter 5 opens by telling us how late Nick got home: "When I came home to West Egg that night. … [it was] [t]wo o'clock" (86; ch. 5) in the morning. In other words, Nick wants us to know that the kiss was just the beginning of his romantic encounter with Jordan.

Indeed, it seems that Nick insists on his "normality" and honesty rather too much. On the very first page of the novel Nick contrasts himself to the "wild, unknown men" at his college who wanted to reveal their "secret griefs" to him because they knew he was "inclined to reserve all judgments" (5; ch. 1). He says, "The abnormal mind is quick to detect and attach itself to this quality when it appears in a normal person" (5; ch. 1). That is, Nick may be surrounded by "abnormal" men who press themselves upon him, but he himself is "normal." Later, he tells us, "I am one of the few honest people that I have ever known" (64; ch. 3). And lest we forget, he reminds us in the very last chapter, "I'm thirty. … I'm five years too old to lie to myself and call it honor" (186; ch. 9). Jordan, however, finally sees through Nick's self-deception. She tells him,

> You said a bad driver was only safe until she met another bad driver? Well I met another bad driver, didn't I? I mean it was careless of me to make such a wrong guess. I thought you were rather an honest, straightforward person. I thought it was your secret pride.
>
> (186; ch. 9)

In other words, Jordan has come to believe that Nick is (as is she) transgressive and dishonest about his transgression. Through a queer lens, by this point in the narrative Jordan's observation carries some weight: Nick's insistence on his "normality" and honesty has worn rather thin.

It's interesting to note that Nick, apparently without intending it, is somewhat ambiguous about his sexuality in the passage in which he first realizes he wants to become involved with Jordan. He says,

> I knew that first I had to get myself definitely out of that tangle back home. I'd been writing letters once a week and signing them "Love, Nick," and all I could think of was how, when that certain girl played tennis, a faint mustache of perspiration appeared on her upper lip. Nevertheless there was a vague understanding that had to be tactfully broken off before I was free.
>
> (64; ch. 3)

In this passage Nick is, characteristically, emphasizing both his honesty and his heterosexuality. But his description of his response to that "faint mustache of perspiration" – an emblem of masculinity – is not particularly clear. If we look closely at the wording of the passage, we can see that Nick feels guilty writing weekly letters signed "Love, Nick" to a young woman back home when, in fact, he wants to date someone new. Nick's reference to the "tangle back home" is thus contrasted with his reference to "that certain girl," a phrase used, at least in the past, to describe a young man's attraction to a special young woman, in this case to Jordan. Yet the facts that the single sign of attraction he mentions is a "faint mustache of perspiration" and that he doesn't name "that certain girl" create a degree of ambiguity concerning which young woman develops a mustache of perspiration and how Nick feels about it. Certainly, a mustache of perspiration on a woman is not a classical male heterosexual turn-on. Indeed, in context of the interpretation of Nick being developed here it's a queer sign, which is why I would argue that he couches it in a passage that is not as clearly written as most of the rest of his narrative. I'm not surprised, then, when I hear some readers say that, on their first reading of the novel, they thought Nick was saying that the girl back home was the one who tended to develop a mustache of perspiration during tennis and that Nick didn't like it.

Of course, we can't be sure whether or not Nick is aware of the gay dimension of his sexuality. But I think if he were aware of it, he wouldn't insist so repeatedly on his heterosexuality, on his "normality," on his honesty. That is, his denial seems to go beyond the strategic need to hide his gay orientation from other characters or from heterosexist readers. His protestations of his own conventionality constitute a rhetoric of psychological denial that suggests he is hiding his gay orientation from himself as well. In keeping with the psychology of denial, I think Nick's blindness to his sexual orientation is precisely what gives his gay sensibility the power it has to project itself into his narrative so thoroughly, layering the novel with multiple meanings and infusing it with interpretive possibilities that, from a queer perspective, greatly enrich the reading experience it offers.

Interestingly, the sexual ambiguity Nick's gay sensibility creates in the novel as well as his apparent denial of his gay orientation mirror the conflicts Fitzgerald seemed to have experienced concerning his own sexuality. While we are not required to explain authors' representations of sexuality in terms of their own sexual orientations, in Fitzgerald's case, the correlations between his life and his work are too striking to be overlooked.

Much like *The Great Gatsby*, Fitzgerald himself seemed obsessed with transgressive sexuality. "For years Fitzgerald would annoy friends and new acquaintances by asking whether they had slept with their wives before they were married" (Bruccoli 114). And he sometimes seemed drawn to people who liked to talk of little else. According to his wife, Zelda, "all [Fitzgerald and his friends] talk[ed] about [wa]s sex – sex plain, striped, mixed, and fancy" (Mayfield 138). Fitzgerald seemed especially fascinated, however, by gay sexuality, toward which his attitude ranged, at different times during his life, from playful to homophobic.

As a Princeton undergraduate, Fitzgerald posed for a publicity photo, dressed as a showgirl, to advertise one of the university's all-male theatrical productions. The photo

> appeared in several newspapers, including *The New York Times,* and brought him
> fan letters from men who wanted to meet him and from an agent who offered
> to book him for a vaudeville tour as a female impersonator.
>
> (Bruccoli 62)

Although all the female roles at Princeton were played by male college students, Fitzgerald's experimentation with drag didn't stop there. He dressed as a woman and attended a fraternity dance at the University of Minnesota, where he "shocked his [male] dancing partners [who thought he was a young woman] with a racy line" (Bruccoli 65). And he kept the photos of himself dressed as a showgirl and liked to show them to friends (Mayfield 134).

Fitzgerald also liked to banter about himself as if he were gay. "While he was in the army, he sent Edmund Wilson [his friend and literary critic] two photographs of himself in a letter, saying that he enclosed the two pictures for Wilson to give to some poor, motherless ... fairy who had no dream" (Mayfield 134). Later, he told Wilson that one of his longings was "to go with a young man *affectueux* [affectionate] for a paid amorous weekend on the coast. It was, he added, deep calling to deep" (Mayfield 134). Certainly, Fitzgerald intended these remarks as "off-color jokes about himself" (Mayfield 134), but they reveal his curiosity about gay life as well as the gay dimension of his sexual imagination.

At other times, Fitzgerald's interest in homosexuality was clearly homophobic: "He had always been outspokenly contemptuous of 'fairies'" (Bruccoli 278), and he and Ernest Hemingway liked to joke "about pederasty, anal eroticism, and other forms of perversion" (Mayfield 133). Indeed, it was "the fairies" whom Fitzgerald blamed for "spoil[ing]" his close friendship with Hemingway (Mayfield 142). Presumably, Fitzgerald was referring to the rumors that he and Hemingway were gay, which upset Fitzgerald greatly (Bruccoli 278). Yet Fitzgerald was "not averse" to implying, himself, that Hemingway was gay, "referring to him as 'Hemophile, the Bleeding Boy'" (Mayfield 136).

Gay sexuality was also an issue of concern in Fitzgerald's marriage. Zelda believed that her husband "was involved in a homosexual liaison with Hemingway" (Bruccoli 278), and "to verify his masculinity, Fitzgerald decided to try sleeping with a whore and purchased condoms; Zelda found them, and a bitter argument ensued" (Bruccoli 279). Zelda also believed that she, herself, "was a latent lesbian," and "Fitzgerald was furious when Dolly Wilde, a notorious Paris 'amazon,' made a pass at Zelda" (Bruccoli 279).

Although it's impossible to draw any reliable conclusions about Fitzgerald's sexual orientation – there is no concrete data about his sexual activity, and evidence of his sexual desire is often marred by contradictory hearsay – we can very safely say that sexuality, especially gay sexuality, was an important issue for him. It is clear that he was intensely curious about gay life and intensely conflicted about it as well, for he was both drawn to and repulsed by the sexual possibilities it offered. And his homophobic response to the gay world reveals, if it reveals nothing else, that Fitzgerald did not want to admit the conflicts he experienced concerning his sexuality.

Given Fitzgerald's consistent reliance on his own personal experience for the material he used in his novels, it should not be surprising that *The Great Gatsby*'s focus on transgressive sexuality should include a queer dimension, whether the author intended it so or not. For as we have seen, Fitzgerald's fascination with transgressive sexuality was in no way limited to the heterosexual domain. And if, as the author's own life suggests, Jay Gatsby embodies Fitzgerald's capacity to devote himself to the pursuit of a heterosexual ideal, then surely Nick Carraway embodies his capacity to deny the gay dimension of his conflicted sexuality. Through a queer lens, then, the real Nick Carraway does come out – or at least comes into focus – as we see the ways in which his closeted gay sensibility opens one of America's best-known heterosexual love stories to queer interpretations.

Questions for further practice: lesbian, gay, and queer approaches to other literary works

The following questions are intended as models. They can help you use lesbian, gay, and queer criticism to interpret the literary works to which they refer or other texts of your choice. Your purpose in addressing these questions, the way in which you focus your essay, and your own self-identified critical orientation will determine whether your essay is considered an example of lesbian, gay, or queer criticism. Note, however, that the rejection of traditional definitions of homosexuality and heterosexuality referred to in question 2 is the primary tenet of queer theory.

1 How does Willa Cather's "Paul's Case" (1905) represent, among other things, the social and psychological conflicts of gay identity coming of age in a hetero-sexist world? In what ways might the story be said to illustrate the operations of compulsory heterosexuality?

2 How do representations of sexuality in Toni Morrison's *The Bluest Eye* (1970) exceed traditional definitions of homosexuality and heterosexuality? Consider, for example, the prostitutes' relationship to men, to sex, and to one another; Geraldine's relationship to her husband and to the cat; Cholly's relationship to the hunters, Darlene, Pauline, and Pecola; Pecola's relationship to the Mary Jane candies; Soaphead Church's relationship to Velma and to little girls; Mr. Henry's relationship to the prostitutes and to the MacTeer girls; and so forth. In other words, how does the novel reveal the inadequacy of the categories "heterosexual" and "homosexual" for our understanding of human sexuality?

3 Although Henry James apparently led a celibate life, many scholars claim his work for the gay canon because of its gay sensibility and because of the author's long-term relationships with the younger men whom he mentored and to whom he wrote letters expressing his love and devotion. The master–pupil relationship is also a recurring theme in James' fiction. Explore the author's representation of the master–pupil relationship in *The Turn of the Screw* (1898). Might Quint's relationship to Miles represent the dark potential of the master–pupil bond, while the governess (a stand-in for James?) illustrates its self-sacrificing devo-tion? From this perspective, what do we make of Miles' death? (It is interesting to note that the sudden, mysterious death of an exceptional male pupil is a recurring theme in James' fiction.)

4 Analyze the sexual politics of Jeanette Winterson's *Oranges Are Not the Only Fruit* (1985). What does the text want its readers to understand about the relation-ships among lesbian sexuality and such social/psychological/political forces as the heterosexual family and the church? How might the attitude of the repres-sive religious sect represented in the novel illustrate the oppression of lesbianism by society in general?

5 Examine the (apparently unconscious) homoerotic subtext of Mary Shelley's *Frankenstein* (1818). How might we argue that Victor's true love is Clerval (whose self-sacrificing care nurses the protagonist through a long illness) rather than Elizabeth? How is this same-sex bond paralleled in Walton's romantic admiration of Victor? What similarities might we find between Elizabeth's

relationship to Victor and Clerval, and Mary Shelley's relationship to her husband, Percy, and to their mutual friend and companion Lord Byron?

For further reading

Abelove, Henry, Michèle Aina Barale, and David M. Halperin, eds. *The Lesbian and Gay Studies Reader.* New York: Routledge, 1993.

Bristow, Joseph. *Sexuality.* 2nd ed. London and New York: Routledge, 2011. (See "Foucault's Exclusions [Gender Issues]," 169–96, and "Queer (Non)Identities," 197–215.)

Cruikshank, Margaret. *The Gay and Lesbian Liberation Movement.* New York: Routledge, 1992.

Faderman, Lillian. *Surpassing the Love of Men: Romantic Friendship and Love between Women from the Renaissance to the Present.* New York: William Morrow, 1981.

Frye, Marilyn. *Willful Virgin: Essays in Feminism.* Freedom, CA: Crossing, 1992.

Glover, David, and Cora Kaplan. *Genders.* 2nd ed. London and New York: Routledge, 2009.

Jay, Karla, and Joanne Glasgow. *Lesbian Texts and Contexts: Radical Revisions.* New York: New York University Press, 1990.

Lorde, Audre. *Sister Outsider: Essays and Speeches.* Trumansburg, NY: Crossing, 1984.

Meem, Deborah T., Michelle A. Gibson, and Jonathan F. Alexander. *Finding Out: An Introduction to LGBT Studies.* Thousand Oaks, CA: SAGE Publications, 2009.

Rich, Adrienne. *On Lies, Secrets, and Silence: Selected Prose.* New York: W. W. Norton, 1979.

Seidman, Steven. *The Social Construction of Sexuality.* 2nd ed. New York: Norton, 2010.

Zimmerman, Bonnie. *The Safe Sea of Women: Lesbian Fiction, 1969–1989.* Boston, MA: Beacon, 1990.

For advanced readers

Anzaldúa, Gloria. *Borderlands/La Frontera: The New Mestiza.* 4th ed. San Francisco: Aunt Lute Books, 2012.

Butler, Judith. *Gender Trouble: Feminism and the Subversion of Identity.* New York: Routledge, 1990.

Butters, Ronald R., John M. Clum, and Michael Moon, eds. *Displacing Homophobia: Gay Male Perspectives in Literature and Culture.* Durham, NC: Duke University Press, 1989.

Haggerty, George E., and Bonnie Zimmerman, eds. *Professions of Desire: Lesbian and Gay Studies in Literature.* New York: Modern Language Association, 1995.

Hall, Donald E. *Reading Sexualities: Hermeneutic Theory and the Future of Queer Studies.* London and New York: Routledge, 2009.

Hall, Donald E., and Annamarie Jagose, eds. *The Routledge Queer Studies Reader.* London and New York: Routledge, 2013. (See especially Johnson's "'Quare' Studies, or '(Almost) Everything I know about Queer Studies I Learned from my Grandmother,'" 96–118; Rodriguez's "Making Queer *Familia*," 324–32; and Halberstam's "Transgender Butch: Butch/FTM Border Wars and the Masculine Continuum," 464–87.)

Jagose, Annamarie. *Queer Theory: An Introduction.* New York: New York University Press, 1996.

Johnson, E. Patrick, and Mae G. Henderson, eds. *Black Queer Studies: A Critical Anthology.* Durham, NC and London: Duke University Press, 2005.

Menon, Madhavi, ed. *Shakesqueer: A Queer Companion to the Complete Works of Shakespeare.* Durham, NC and London: Duke University Press, 2011.

Nelson, Emmanuel S., ed. *Critical Essays: Gay and Lesbian Writers of Color.* New York: Haworth, 1993.

Sedgwick, Eve Kosofsky. *Epistemology of the Closet.* Berkeley: University of California Press, 1990.

Sullivan, Nikki. *A Critical Introduction to Queer Theory.* New York: New York University Press, 2003.

Notes

1 A transgender person's gender (masculine or feminine) doesn't match his or her biological sex (male or female). For example, a transgender man has the anatomy of a male but knows that, inside, he is a woman: his biological sex is male, but his gender is feminine. Furthermore, his transgender status doesn't indicate his sexual orientation. Finally, a transgender individual who has undergone the process of sex change is no longer transgender (for sex and gender now match) but transsexual.

The word *queer*, as you'll see in the "Queer criticism" section of this chapter, can have several different meanings. For example, *queer theory* refers to a perspective for understanding human sexuality that is not based on the biological sex of the people to whom one is sexually attracted. The word *queer* is also frequently used as a positive, inclusive term referring to LGBT (or GLBT) individuals *and* to anyone who is, in whatever way, not strictly heterosexual. The inclusive acronym, therefore, is LGBTQ (or GLBTQ). Although you may hear the term LGBT (or GLBT) used more frequently, for our purposes in this chapter we'll use the inclusive acronym LGBTQ. (The Q in LGBTQ can also refer to the word *questioning* – that is, to refer to people who are uncertain about their gender or their sexual orientation – or to refer to both *queer* and *questioning*.)

2 For a complete discussion of discrimination against lesbians and gay men, see Cruikshank.

3 Statistics concerning school dropout and suicide rates among LGBTQ adolescents and young adults can be found online at, for example, www.medicalxpress.com/news/2011–04-links-social-environment-high-suicide_1.html; www.pflagphoenix.org/education/youth_stats.html; and http://data/lambdalegal.org (under "LGBT Youth Fact Sheet.qxd").

4 The functions of "minoritizing" and "universalizing" views of homosexuality were developed by Eve Kosofsky Sedgwick in *Epistemology of the Closet*.

5 See *Selections from the Letters of Geraldine Endsor Jewsbury to Jane Welsh Carlyle*, edited by Mrs. Alexander Ireland (London: Longmans, Green and Co., 1892), p. 38. This quotation is taken from a letter dated October 29, 1841 (cited in Faderman 164).

6 For a complete discussion of the concept, see Radicalesbians' "The Woman Identified Woman." Full text available online at http://scriptorium.lib.duke.edu/wld/womid.

7 For a discussion of intersexuality, multiple genders, and similar issues, see "Gender studies and feminism" in Chapter 4.

Works cited

Babuscio, Jack. "Camp and the Gay Sensibility." *Gays and Films*. London: British Film Institute, 1977. Rpt. in *Camp Grounds: Style and Homosexuality*. Ed. David Bergman. Amherst: University of Massachusetts Press, 1993. 19–38.

Bennett, Paula. "The Pea That Duty Locks: Lesbian and Feminist-Heterosexual Readings of Emily Dickinson's Poetry." *Lesbian Texts and Contexts: Radical Revisions*. Eds. Karla Jay and Joanne Glasgow. New York: New York University Press, 1990. 104–25.

Bruccoli, Matthew J. *Some Sort of Epic Grandeur: The Life of F. Scott Fitzgerald*. New York: Harcourt Brace Jovanovich, 1981.

Cather, Willa. *My Ántonia*. 1918. Rev. 1926. Rpt. Boston: Houghton, 1980.

Chauncey, George. *Gay New York: Gender, Urban Culture, and the Making of the Gay Male World, 1890–1940*. New York: Basic Books, 1994.

Cruikshank, Margaret. "Gay and Lesbian Liberation as a Political Movement." *The Gay and Lesbian Liberation Movement*. New York: Routledge, 1992. 57–89.

Dickinson, Emily. *The Poems of Emily Dickinson*. Ed. Thomas H. Johnson. 3 vols. Cambridge, MA: Belknap Press of Harvard University Press, 1958.

Faderman, Lillian. "Boston Marriage." *Surpassing the Love of Men: Romantic Friendship and Love between Women from the Renaissance to the Present*. New York: William Morrow, 1981. 190–203.

Faulkner, William. "A Rose for Emily." 1931. *Selected Stories of William Faulkner.* New York: Random House, 1960. 49–61.

Fetterly, Judith. "*My Ántonia,* Jim Burden, and the Dilemma of the Lesbian Writer." *Lesbian Texts and Contexts: Radical Revisions.* Eds. Karla Jay and Joanne Glasgow. New York: New York University Press, 1990. 145–63.

Fitzgerald, F. Scott. *The Great Gatsby.* 1925. New York: Macmillan, 1992.

Frye, Marilyn. "Some Reflections on Separatism and Power?" *Sinister Wisdom* 6 (1978). Rpt. in *The Lesbian and Gay Studies Reader.* Eds. Henry Abelove, Michèle Aina Barale, and David M. Halperin. New York: Routledge, 1993. 91–98.

James, Henry. *The Bostonians.* New York: Macmillan, 1885.

Keller, Karl. "Walt Whitman Camping." *Walt Whitman Review* 26 (1981). Rpt. in *Camp Grounds: Style and Homosexuality.* Ed. David Bergman. Amherst: University of Massachusetts Press, 1993. 113–20.

Mayfield, Sara. *Exiles from Paradise: Zelda and Scott Fitzgerald.* New York: Delacorte, 1971.

Morrison, Toni. *Beloved.* New York: Alfred A. Knopf, 1987.

——. *Sula.* New York: Alfred A. Knopf, 1973.

Radel, Nicholas F. "Self as Other: The Politics of Identity in the Works of Edmund White." *Queer Words, Queer Images: Communication and the Construction of Homosexuality.* Ed. R. Jeffrey Ringer. New York: New York University Press, 1994. 175–92.

Radicalesbians. "The Woman Identified Woman." Pittsburgh: Know, Inc., 1970.

Rich, Adrienne. "Compulsory Heterosexuality and Lesbian Existence." *Signs* 5.4 (1980): 631–60. Rpt. in *The Lesbian and Gay Studies Reader.* Eds. Henry Abelove, Michèle Aina Barale, and David M. Halperin. New York: Routledge, 1993. 227–54.

Sedgwick, Eve Kosofsky. "Across Gender, Across Sexuality: Willa Cather and Others?" *Displacing Homophobia: Gay Male Perspectives in Literature and Culture.* Eds. Ronald R. Butters, John M. Glum, and Michael Moon. Durham, NC: Duke University Press, 1989. 53–72.

——. *Epistemology of the Closet.* Berkeley: University of California Press, 1990.

Smith, Barbara. "Toward a Black Feminist Criticism." 1977. *All the Women Are White, All the Blacks Are Men, But Some of Us Are Brave.* Eds. Gloria T. Hull, Patricia Bell Scott, and Barbara Smith. Old Westbury, NY: Feminist Press, 1982. 157–75.

Williams, Tennessee. *The Night of the Iguana.* New York: New Directions, 1962.

Whitman, Walt. "Song of Myself." *Leaves of Grass.* Brooklyn, NY: Rome Brothers, 1855.

11 African American criticism

Each semester I'm always alarmed to learn how many students in my critical theory course – including senior English majors of all races – are unacquainted or minimally acquainted with such milestones of African American history as the Middle Passage, the Underground Railroad, the Great Migration, the Harlem Renaissance, the Civil Rights Movement, the Black Power Movement, and the Black Arts Movement. Despite the increased focus on multicultural education in America's high schools and the increased provision of college courses in African American experience, history, and literature, educational efforts in these areas remain inadequate to the needs of students in a multicultural society such as ours, especially in light of their future role as world citizens of a rapidly shrinking globe.

Because African Americans constitute such a large part of the US population, and because they have contributed so much to the arts – including an enormous, internationally acclaimed literary output – I should be able to assume that my senior English majors have a certain amount of knowledge about African American history and literature on which I can build. But much of my job consists of providing background knowledge, for lack of a better term. And given the constraints of time, I often find myself outlining what I think students should know and, hopefully, promoting their desire to know it, so that they'll become interested enough in the field to pursue more knowledge on their own. In a sense, that's what I'll be trying to do here: acquaint you with the racial issues that have informed African American literary history, introduce you to the fundamental concerns of African American race theorists today, describe the range of interests of contemporary African American literary critics, and hope that you'll become interested enough to pursue this exciting field of literary study on your own.

Racial issues and African American literary history

The virtual exclusion of African American history and culture from American education, which began to be addressed only in the late 1960s, reflects the virtual exclusion of African American history and culture from official versions of American history before that time. Only over the past few decades have American history books begun to include information about black Americans that had been repressed in order to maintain the cultural hegemony, or dominance, of white America. For example, textbooks that were used to teach American history (which, more accurately, should have been called white American history) said little or nothing about the slave uprisings during the horrific Middle Passage (the transportation of African captives across the Atlantic Ocean), the numerous slave rebellions on the plantations, and the network of communication and resistance developed by slaves right under the noses of the slavemasters. And such accomplishments as the tremendous outpouring of creative enterprises – including, for example, black literature, music, painting, sculpture, philosophy, and political debate – associated with Harlem during the 1920s and known as the Harlem Renaissance were not given the attention they deserved.

I choose these two examples – slave resistance and the Harlem Renaissance – because I think they illustrate most clearly the political motives that lay behind the exclusion of African Americans from American history. A conscientious history of slave resistance would have blasted the racist stereotype of the contented, dim-witted slave who was grateful for the paternal guidance of the white master, without whom the slave would have been either a lost child or a dangerous savage. And a conscientious history of African American literary genius would have blasted the myth of African American inferiority on which so many racist policies and practices rested.

Given that so much African American literature deals with racism – as a literary record of African American experience, how could it not? – let's take a moment to define some key concepts concerning that issue about which many people still have misconceptions. *Racialism*, a word we don't often hear in everyday speech, refers to the belief in racial superiority, inferiority, and purity based on the conviction that moral and intellectual characteristics, just like physical characteristics, are biological properties that differentiate the races. *Racism* refers to the unequal power relations that grow from the sociopolitical domination of one race by another and that result in systematic discriminatory practices (for example, segregation, domination, and persecution). Therefore, although anyone can be a racialist, in order to be a racist – in order to be in a position to systematically segregate, dominate, or per-secute – one has to be in a position of power as a member of the politically dominant group, which in America usually means that one has to be white. In other words, the systematic practice of racism (for example, denying qualified persons of color employment, housing, education, or anything else to which they're entitled) can occur on a regular basis only when those who do it can expect, by and large, to get away with it. And those who do it can expect to get away with it when the group to which they belong controls most of the positions of power in the political, judicial, and law-enforcement systems.[1]

To put the matter another way, the systematic practice of racial discrimination can occur only when racism has become institutionalized. *Institutionalized racism* refers to the incorporation of racist policies and practices in the institutions by which a society operates: for example, education; federal, state, and local governments; the law, both in terms of what is written on the books and how it is implemented by the courts and by police officials; health care, which can be racially biased in everything from the allocation of research dollars to the location of hospitals to the treatment of individual patients; and the corporate world, which often practices racial discrimination in its hiring and promotion despite whatever equal-opportunity policies it officially claims to have.

One area in which institutionalized racism has been very effective in discriminating against African Americans is the American literary canon. As many of you probably know, the Western (British, European, and American) literary canon has been dominated by a *Eurocentric* definition of *universalism*: literary works have been defined as great art, as "universal" – relevant to the experience of all people – and included in the canon only when they reflect European experience and conform to the style and subject matter of the European literary tradition, that is, only when they resemble those European works already deemed "great." For *Eurocentrism* is the belief that European culture is vastly superior to all others. Although African Americans can boast a long and impressive literary history dating back to the eighteenth century, white American literary historians considered black writers, when they considered them at all, as a tributary or an offshoot rather than part and parcel of American literary history. Therefore, until recently, anthologies of American literature, including those used to teach high school and college courses, were confined largely to the work of white male writers. The literary canon has thus been used to maintain white cultural hegemony.

This situation has begun to change, of course, but that change is coming rather slowly. Although contemporary black American authors certainly hold top honors today – with, for example, Toni Morrison (who won the Nobel Prize for Literature in 1993), Alice Walker, John Edgar Wideman, Maya Angelou, Gloria Naylor, Ishmael Reed, Nikki Giovanni, Charles Johnson, Rita Dove, Sherley Anne Williams, August Wilson, June Jordan, Toni Cade Bambara, and Ernest J. Gaines among the most widely acclaimed American authors – works by black writers, past and present, are still too often underrepresented on course syllabi in American literature courses.

The promotion of racial discrimination by institutionalized racism is often mirrored in a society's racist stereotypes and in its adherence to a narrow standard of Anglo-Saxon beauty. Before "Black is beautiful!" and "Say it loud: I'm black and I'm proud!" sounded the call for a radical change in African American self-definition and self-perception in the late 1960s, many African Americans suffered from internalized racism. And despite the success of black-pride advocates, many people of color continue to suffer from it today. *Internalized racism* results from the psychological programming by which a racist society indoctrinates people of color to believe in white superiority. Victims of internalized racism generally feel inferior to whites, less attractive, less worthwhile, less capable, and often wish they looked more white, for example had lighter skin or straighter hair. Toni Morrison provides us with one of the most chilling portraits of internalized racism in *The Bluest Eye* (1970), in which Pecola Breedlove, a young black girl who can't see her own beauty, believes she would be pretty, happy, and loved if only she had blue eyes.

Internalized racism often results in *intra-racial racism*, which refers to discrimination within the black community against those with darker skin and more African features. We see this phenomenon illustrated in *The Bluest Eye* when Pecola is picked on by other black children for having dark skin, while another black child, the light-skinned Maureen Peal, is treated by the same black youngsters as if she were superior to them. Filmmaker Spike Lee also portrays intra-racial racism in *School Daze* (1988), in which students at a historically black college form two rival groups based on the relative "whiteness" or "blackness" of their physical appearance.[2] While the economic hardship and social marginalization caused by institutionalized racism are common knowledge, internalized racism and intra-racial racism illustrate the devastating psychological experiences that also result.

Given the multiple forms of racism with which African Americans have had to contend, it should come as no surprise that many African Americans experience what W. E. B. DuBois first described in *The Souls of Black Folk* (1903) as *double consciousness* or *double vision*, the awareness of belonging to two conflicting cultures: the African culture, which grew from African roots and was transformed by its own unique history on American soil, and the European culture imposed by white America. For many black Americans this means having one cultural self at home and another cultural self in white-dominated public space, such as the workplace and the school. And double consciousness sometimes involves speaking two languages. Black culture lived at home sometimes includes the use of *African American Vernacular English* (*AAVE*, also called *Ebonics* or *Black Vernacular English*), which fulfills all the grammatical criteria of a genuine language but is still dismissed by many white and some black Americans as substandard or incorrect English rather than recognized as a language in its own right.

For black writers, double consciousness has meant having to decide whether to write primarily for a black audience, a white audience, or both. This decision involves, in turn, the kind of language the writer uses. For example, Harlem Renaissance poet Countee Cullen chose to use highly polished, standard white English and a classically allusive style that conforms to the best of the European literary tradition. This style is evident, for example, in the Greek mythological allusions in the following lines from his sonnet "Yet Do I Marvel" (1925). The speaker, questioning why God would "make a poet black, and bid him sing," says that, if "He stoop[ed] to quibble," God could

> Make plain the reason tortured Tantalus
> Is baited by the fickle fruit, declare
> If merely brute caprice dooms Sisyphus
> To struggle up a never-ending stair.

Although most of Cullen's poetry contains political themes relating to race, he believed black authors should be as free as white authors to create according to the dictates of their own artistic inspiration without being obliged to consider the political needs of their people. Of course, this poet's use of formal English and Greek mythology raised questions about the validity of his artistic inspiration because it derived from the racist culture that had oppressed African peoples for centuries. But Cullen's classically crafted verse nevertheless demonstrated that African American writers were more than capable of writing in whatever style they preferred and thus provided a powerful argument against the racist assumption of African inferiority.

In contrast, much of the work of Langston Hughes, another writer who emerged during the Harlem Renaissance, uses vernacular English resonant with the rhythms of black speech patterns and blues music. His powerfully moving writing – which white readers, too, can appreciate and from which they can learn about the creativity of black culture – speaks of and for African Americans, celebrating their rich cultural heritage and calling for equal opportunity for black citizens. We see this style, for example, in the concrete imagery and the streetwise, vernacular quality of the voice in the following lines from "Good Morning" (1951). The speaker laments the dashed hopes of people of color, in search of a better life, who've "come dark / wondering / wide-eyed / dreaming / out of Penn Station" in New York:

> The gates open –
> but there're bars
> at each gate.
> What happens
> to a dream deferred?
> Daddy, ain't you heard?

Although our discussion of literary language and style is a discussion of poetics – that is, of literary devices and strategies – it is clearly also a discussion of politics, that is, of the realities of political, social, and economic power. For as the Cullen and Hughes examples demonstrate, the literary style black writers choose cannot be separated from their political views on the writer's role as a member of an oppressed group. Indeed, one of the oldest issues in the black literary community concerns the social role of the black writer in a racist society.

After all, African American writing began during the eighteenth century largely as the effort of African slaves to prove their humanity to whites. For slaveholders, as one of their many attempts to justify slavery, claimed that Africans weren't fully human because they couldn't write poetry! (Of course, slaveholders conveniently neglected to consider that they had made it illegal for slaves to learn even to read.) In fact, Phillis Wheatley's owners encouraged her to write poetry to prove this racist argument wrong. Slaves also wrote autobiographical narratives to alert white Northerners to their plight. Harriet Jacobs' *Incidents in the Life of a Slave Girl* (1861) is one such text. Yet so widespread was the belief, even in the North, that African slaves were incapable of writing, let alone of literary production, that many narratives were prefaced by the statements of white patrons, testifying to the identity of the writer and the authenticity of the narrative. Indeed, finding ways to pull white readers into texts they otherwise might have resisted has remained a task that many black writers still face.

The antiracist politics of early African American writers have remained relevant to the needs of black Americans over the long history of their struggle for justice. It is not surprising, therefore, that writing as a form of purely individual expression has been viewed by many African Americans as a luxury the race could not afford while so many of its members were oppressed.

The social role of the black writer remained an important issue during the *Black Arts Movement* of the 1960s, the literary and artistic offshoot of the Black Power Movement. Some of the most vocal spokespersons for the movement, such as the poet Amiri Baraka, believed that black writers have an obligation to help the race through such literary means as depicting the evils of racism, providing positive images of African Americans, and offering possible solutions to social problems confronting the black community. Similarly, the Black Arts Movement affected the role of African American literary critics by emphasizing their job as cultural critics. That is, black critics were called on to interpret literature in terms of its representation of and relationship to the political and economic situation of African Americans, a task analogous to that performed by Marxist critics but with the focus, of course, on race. For example, Afro-American critics analyzed the ways in which literary texts undermine or reinforce the racist ideologies that have kept black Americans politically oppressed and economically disadvantaged. This approach remains an important part of African American criticism today.

The Black Arts Movement also called into question the appropriateness of white critical theories for the interpretation of black literature. After all, it was a Eurocentric definition of "great" literature that marginalized black authors in American literary history and virtually excluded them from the American canon. And most contemporary mainstream critical theories, including all the theories discussed in the other chapters of this textbook, have European roots. The question of the appropriateness of white theories for the interpretation of black texts remains pertinent today in light of the reservations some critics have about the widespread influence of deconstructive theory on all forms of literary criticism. As Barbara Christian observes, the abstract discourse of deconstruction, which argues that such concepts as "center" and "periphery" are illusory and which allows those few who are especially fluent in deconstruction "to control the critical scene," emerged "just when the literature of peoples of color ... began to move to 'the centre'" (459). In addition, deconstruction critiques the concept of a stable, inherently meaningful cultural identity. Rather, as you may recall from Chapter 8, deconstruction defines the "self" as a fragmented collection of numerous "selves" that has no stable meaning or value except those we assign to it. And as Henry Louis Gates Jr. points out, it isn't fair "to deny [African Americans] the process of exploring and reclaiming our [cultural identity] before we critique it" ("The Master's Pieces" 32).

On the other hand, many African American critics believe that elements from any number of contemporary critical theories, including deconstruction, can be adapted for use by African American criticism. For despite the dangers involved in the uncritical application of European American theories to African American literature, many critics feel that the wholesale exclusion of white critical theory from the black critical repertoire would deny black critics some potentially useful critical tools and, in addition, would close off avenues of communication between African American critics and their colleagues. As Henry Louis Gates Jr. argues, "any tool that enables the critic to explain the complex workings of the language of a text is an appropriate tool. For it is language, the black language of black texts, that expresses the distinctive quality of our literary tradition" (*Figures in Black* xxi). And as we have seen in other chapters, most critical theories can be used to explain the operations of language, for example by calling our attention to the various ways in which language carries ideological content that can affect us without our even being aware of it.

The idea of the distinctiveness of black literature to which Gates refers was another important issue explored during the Black Arts Movement that remains with us today. In opposition to the notion of the "universality" of all "great" literature, many writers in the Black Arts Movement argued that African American literature has its own unique qualities, its own politics and poetics, that cannot be fully explained by or contained within the larger framework of European American literature. Some theorists believe that this uniqueness derives from the African American oral tradition of storytelling, folklore, and oral history, which has its roots in African culture and, according to some critics, relates to an essential, or inborn, "blackness," a way of thinking, feeling, and creating shared by all peoples of African descent. Others argue that there is no such thing as an essential blackness, that the qualities African American texts have in common result from the shared history and culture of their authors. For some of these critics, the distinctive quality of African American literature follows from its unique blending of both African and European American cultural traditions.

In either case, the *Afrocentricity* of African American texts – that is, the primacy of their relationship to African history and culture – must not be overlooked when we interpret them or we risk deforming African American literature in very important ways. For example, as John W. Roberts observes, the African American trickster tales that emerged during slavery, such as those about Br'er Rabbit, "exhibi[t] a close kinship to trickster tales in African oral tradition" (97). However, Eurocentric American folklorists, assuming that enslavement had abolished African Americans' cultural ties to Africa, argued that these tales derived from the European American tradition. Or they asserted that it didn't matter where the tales originated because slaves transformed them to fit a very specific psychological need: the need to compensate for their powerlessness under slavery by identifying with a small, disadvantaged animal who rebels against the moral order and, through cunning and deceit, fools the larger, more powerful animals, punishes them, takes their food, and so forth.

Afrocentric folklorists have corrected this misinterpretation, Roberts observes, by showing, among other things, that both African and African American trickster tales "revolv[e] around behaviors designed to compensate for chronic shortages of material necessities and existence in a rigid social hierarchy" (107). In short, the similarities between African and African American trickster tales derived from the fact that both populations, though for very different reasons, had to learn how to survive with an uncertain and often inadequate food supply. And the differences between the two groups of tales resulted from the differences between the strict social order of African culture, in which the welfare of the community always took precedence over individual gain, and the strict social order of American plantation culture, in which the individual gain of the slaveholder always took precedence over the welfare of the community of slaves that worked for him. An Afrocentric reading of the trickster tales thus accounts for both the continuity and the transformation of the tales without severing African American culture from its African roots.

Recent developments: critical race theory

Of course, times have changed in many ways over the past few decades. Extreme forms of overt violence against African Americans – such as lynching, the assassination of black leaders, the bombing of black churches, mob attacks on black homes "too near" white neighborhoods, and the brutal treatment of civil rights protestors – seem to be a thing of the past in the United States. In addition, racial discrimination against African Americans is now illegal: according to the law, people of color may live, work, shop, dine out, and so forth where they please. Therefore, many Americans – at least many white Americans – believe that racism, with the exception of white supremacist groups like the Ku Klux Klan, is a thing of the past. Certainly, we don't see reports of racial protests, sit-ins, or riots on the nightly news or read about them in the daily newspaper as we did during the 1950s and 1960s when the Civil Rights Movement was in its heyday. In fact, the Civil Rights Movement of the 1950s and 1960s is over, so isn't it logical to believe that it's no longer needed? Indeed, black American writers, jurists, scientists, philosophers, politicians, musicians, painters, dancers, actors, directors, athletes, and others who embody contemporary African American thought and the African American cultural tradition are famous both nationally and internationally. And the United States now has a large African American middle class. So why do we still need to concern ourselves with race at all, let alone study something called critical race theory?

As many Americans of all colors know, however, racism has not disappeared: it's just gone "underground." That is, racial injustice in the United States is still a major and pressing problem; it's simply become less visible than it used to be. Racial injustice is practiced on the sly, so to speak, to avoid legal prosecution, and it has flourished in ways that, in many cases, only its victims really know well. For example, as Richard Delgado and Jean Stefancic point out, African Americans and Latinos/as still have fewer chances of acquiring jobs, housing, and loans than whites with similar qualifications (10). In addition,

> The prison population is largely black and brown; chief executive officers [of corporations], surgeons, and university presidents are almost all white. ... [B]lack families have, on the average, about one-tenth of the assets of their white counterparts. They pay more for many products and services, including cars. People of color lead shorter lives, receive worse medical care, complete fewer years of school, and occupy more menial jobs than do whites. A recent United Nations report showed that African Americans in the United States [if thought of as comprising a nation of their own] would make up the twenty-seventh ranked nation in the world ... [in terms of] social well-being. Latinos would rank thirty-third.
>
> (Delgado and Stefancic 10–11)

I think the first fact listed in the passage just cited deserves further comment because the disproportionate number of prisoners of color in this country has encouraged, if not created, the misconception held by many white Americans that a disproportionate number of African Americans are criminals, in other words, that criminality is an African American trait. In order to show the flaws in this kind of thinking, let me offer just one striking example of why there is a larger proportion of African Americans than whites incarcerated in our country. The possession of 28 grams of crack cocaine (used predominantly by black Americans) automatically triggers a five-year mandatory prison sentence. However, it takes 500 grams of powder cocaine (used predominantly by white Americans) to trigger that same five-year mandatory prison sentence.[3] Discriminatory laws like these draw attention to the use of drugs in poor black neighborhoods, a situation that has resulted in increased police surveillance in these areas, while drug use in white neighborhoods is largely ignored. In fact, in the United States the majority of drug users (of all kinds) are white. Yet the majority of prisoners incarcerated for drug-related offenses are black. As this representative example illustrates, the racial bias of our legal system, not the "natural" criminality of African Americans, has put many black Americans behind bars who wouldn't be there if they were white.

Clearly, many African Americans are still routinely deprived of their civil rights despite the civil rights laws intended to guarantee these rights. Perhaps, then, one useful way to think of critical race theory is as a new approach to civil rights. Initiated by the work of Derrick A. Bell Jr. and others in the 1970s, critical race theory began at a time when the Civil Rights Movement of the 1950s and 1960s ceased to be a political or social force. And though critical race theory started out as a critique of constitutional law – that is, federal law, which is based on the Constitution and which the laws of individual states are not supposed to violate – it has spread to other disciplines, including those in the humanities. As we'll see, critical race theory concerns itself with every topic that is relevant to race. In addition to investigating such obvious issues as the kind of oppression described in the passage quoted above, critical race theory examines the ways in which details of our everyday lives are related to race, though we may not realize it, and studies the complex beliefs that underlie what seem to be simple, commonplace assumptions about race in order to show where and how racism still thrives in its "undercover" existence.

Let's start by examining what Delgado and Stefancic identify as the basic tenets of critical race theory. I'll list them for you here – don't expect to understand all of the vocabulary yet – and then we'll take a closer look at each one.

Basic tenets

1 *Everyday racism* is a common, ordinary experience for people of color in the United States.
2 Racism is largely the result of *interest convergence*, sometimes referred to as *material determinism*.
3 Race is *socially constructed*.
4 Racism often takes the form of *differential racialization*.
5 Everyone's identity is a product of *intersectionality*.

6 The experiences of racial minorities have given them what might be called a unique *voice of color*.

(6–9)

Critical race theorists don't all hold the same opinion regarding these tenets, but an understanding of these six points will be a very helpful means of introducing you to this growing discipline. We'll also take a look at a few additional topics as representative examples of the different kinds of issues that are of interest to critical race theorists.

1 *Everyday racism* – Many white Americans still think that the word racism applies only to very visible forms of racism, for example, physical or verbal attacks against people of color; the activities of white supremacist groups; the deliberate and overt exclusion of racial minorities from particular housing, restaurants, and social organizations open to the public; and the like. However, in many ways the most emotionally draining, stress-provoking forms of racism are the kinds that happen to people of color every day, and these forms of racism are the rule, not the exception. For instance, white store clerks or security personnel often watch, or even follow, African Americans who come into their stores. And members of minority groups frequently encounter a lack of common civility from their white fellow Americans – they're ignored, they see white people grimace or roll their eyes, they overhear sarcastic comments made at their expense – in the most mundane situations: while waiting in line at the supermarket or pharmacy, while paying for gas at the gas station, while asking for information at the bank, and so forth. Other common examples of everyday racist behavior exhibited by white people include "being patronizing, talking down, assuming lack of confidence, hiring token blacks ... or favoring whites. ... [and] contact avoidance [keeping a physical distance from a person of color or avoiding touch]" (Essed 205). A particularly damaging form of everyday racism consists of constantly underestimating the ability of minority persons, for example, immediately assuming that "typos in their writing are ... [due to] language deficiency" (Essed 206). This kind of behavior is especially destructive when it occurs in the classroom, when schoolteachers and college professors assume, often unconsciously, that students of color are in some way inferior: "less intelligent ... lack[ing] ... cultural sophistication ... work ethic, or social skills" (Essed 207). These kinds of unfounded assumptions can result in the teacher's grading unfairly, withholding information about scholarships, ignoring or lacking enthusiasm for the achievements of black students, and neglecting to include black students adequately in class discussions (Essed 207). Of course, most of us are also familiar with the continuing problem of exposing children and young people to racially unbalanced curriculum materials based too much

(and sometimes exclusively) on white experience as well as the continuing problem of white teachers who respond to black students as if those students "spoke for," or represented, their entire race.

One particularly revealing example of everyday racism is offered by Taunya Lovell Banks, a black woman law professor. One Saturday afternoon, Professor Banks and four of her fellow law professors, all African American women in their thirties and forties and all well dressed, had been visiting a colleague living in a luxury condominium in downtown Philadelphia. They got on a spacious elevator to leave. "A few floors later, the door opened and a white woman in her late fifties peered in, let out a muffled cry of surprise, stepped back and let the door close without getting on. Several floors later ... another white middle-aged woman ... also decided not to get on" (331). It couldn't have been the black women's clothing, age, sex, or locale that frightened the two white women. It had to have been nothing but their skin color alone. Yet their skin color alone was enough to overcome every other physical indication that the women on the elevator were not a threat to anyone. In fact, it's not unreasonable to assume that the two white women didn't even see the clothing, age, or sex of the elevator passengers or think about the well-protected nature of the luxury condominium in which they were all gathered: programmed by white society to react strongly to skin color, skin color was probably all they saw. It was certainly the only factor to which they reacted.

Perhaps one of the most distressing forms of everyday racism is white people's denial that racism exists or has occurred in a particular instance. Persons of color are accused of being oversensitive "about discrimination, ... ethnic jokes, ridicule in front of others, patronizing, [and] rudeness" (Essed 207). In other words, they're accused of seeing racism where it doesn't exist when, in fact, it does exist, but the white people exhibiting or witnessing it aren't able or don't choose to see it as racism. As Banks observes, when you are told by your co-worker that he doesn't think of you as black, you know that he is trying to say something positive, that he intends to tell you that your humanity matters to him, not your race. The underlying premise of such a statement, however, is that to be black is to be less than human (236). Then, of course, there's the difficulty of always wondering if the white person who gave you a mean look or said something rude to you was being racist or was just having a bad day. The emotional stress of trying to cope with being the target of everyday racism can damage the psychological and physical health of people of color because the effects of everyday racism are cumulative: "[o]ne event triggers memories of other, similar incidents" (Essed 207). Meanwhile, white perpetrators and witnesses of everyday racism might not even know that it's occurring. As Philomena Essed points out, though most people believe that racism should not exist, "there is insufficient inter/national commitment to educate children, inform adults, and provide citizens with relevant information about how to identify racism, how it is communicated, how it is experienced, and how it can be countered" (204).

2   *Interest convergence* – Derrick Bell uses this term to explain that racism is common in our country because it often converges, or overlaps, with the interest – with something needed or desired – of a white individual or group (*Brown v. Board of Education* 20–29). For example, racism is in the financial interest of upper-class whites who exploit black laborers by paying them less than their white counterparts, and it's in the psychological interest of working-class whites whose own experience of being underpaid and exploited by wealthy whites makes them need to feel superior to someone else. In other words, racism has many pay-offs for whites. This is why interest convergence is sometimes referred to as *material determinism* (Delgado and Stefancic 7). The desire to advance oneself in the *material* world – as we just saw, for example, the desire to advance oneself financially or to feel better about oneself psychologically – *determines* the ways in which the dominant society practices racism.

Even successes in the area of civil rights "coincide with ... white self-interest" (Delgado and Stefancic 18). For example, as Mary L. Dudziak's 1988 investigation of the US government's Cold War archives reveals, the Supreme Court's 1954 decision, *Brown v. Board of Education*, to legally desegregate our public school system was, as Derrick Bell had argued amid much controversy several years earlier (*Brown v. Board of Education* 20–29), not an issue of ethics but of politics. It wasn't altruism that led the Supreme Court finally to side with the National Association for the Advancement of Colored People (NAACP) in a school desegregation case for the first time in history. Rather, "a flood of secret cables" and "letters from US ambassadors abroad" as well as "foreign press reports" (Delgado and Stefancic 19) all indicated that the United States desperately needed to change its racist world image if it wanted to compete successfully with communist countries for the allegiance of uncommitted Third World nations, many of which were peopled by nonwhite inhabitants (Delgado and Stefancic 18–20). It should not be surprising that many critical race theorists consider interest convergence one of the primary causes, if not the primary cause, of racism.

3   *The social construction of race* – How can we define race as a matter of physical features when the physical differences between light-skinned blacks and dark-skinned whites, to cite just one example, are much fewer than the physical differences we often see among members of each group? (Delgado and Stefancic 75). Yet in 1790, the US Congress restricted naturalization (the acquisition of US citizenship) to white men, and this racial criterion, with only slight modifications, remained in effect until 1952. So over the course of those 162 years of racial restrictions the US judicial system frequently had to decide, among its

many applicants for citizenship, which men were white and which weren't. Are Arabs white? What about people from India? What if a given country contains both light- and dark-skinned people? To complicate matters, over the course of our history some groups have "become" white, so to speak. For instance, during our nation's early years, Italian, Jewish, and Irish people were considered nonwhite, that is, of the same status as African Americans (Delgado and Stefancic 76–77).

A look at the racial categories used by the US Census Bureau between 1790 and 1920 (the census is taken every ten years) should show us rather clearly that racial categorization doesn't reflect biological reality but rather the official beliefs about race at different times. For example, from 1790 to 1810, the Census Bureau designated the following populations as different races: (1) free whites, (2) all other free persons except Indians not taxed, and (3) slaves. From 1820 to 1840 racial categories were as follows: (1) free whites, (2) unnaturalized foreigners (foreigners who were not US citizens), (3) free colored, and (4) slaves. In 1850 and 1860 we had (1) whites, (2) blacks, (3) mulattos (half-white, half-black), (4) mulatto slaves, and (5) black slaves. From 1870 to 1920 we had (1) whites, (2) blacks, (3) mulattos, (4) quadroons (one-quarter black), (5) octoroons (one-eighth black), (6) Chinese, (7) Japanese, and (8) Indians. In short, our definitions of race change as economic and social pressures change (Ferrante and Brown, "Introduction to Part 2" 115–16). The dominant culture claims that "races" are fixed categories, but our history shows us that race in this country has always been a matter of definition. And if you find these facts rather intriguing, consider that "[i]n parts of the Caribbean class has shaped racial classification so that the richer one is, the whiter one is perceived to be" (Harding 219).

Throughout our history, moreover, many Americans have belonged to more than one race. However, until the 2000 census the Census Bureau did not allow Americans to check more than one box designating race, which since the nineteenth century has consisted of various forms of four racial categories – Caucasians, Africans, Asians, and Native Americans – to which it added, some decades back, "a fifth, Hispanics, who can be of any race" (Sollors 102). In fact, *Hispanic* is not a racial designation at all, though some people think it is. It's an ethnic designation for Spanish-speaking immigrants from a number of different countries, and though the designation includes all races, most Hispanics identify themselves as white (Muir 95).

Given that so many Americans belong to more than one racial category, the government's insistence, for more than two hundred years, on a single racial category for each person provides another illustration of how race is socially rather than biologically produced. That is, "the fact that everyone seemed (and still seems) to fit into a single racial category is really the result of the system of racial classification used in the United States" (Ferrante and Brown, "Introduction" 2). As a case in point, Naomi Zack observes that the way the black and white races are defined in America "precludes the possibility of mixed [black and white] race because cases of mixed race, in which individuals have both black and white forebears, are automatically designated as cases of black race," and it takes only "one black forebear, any number of generations back" to define an individual as black (cited in Sollors 101–2). Moreover, in the case of mixed race nonwhite children (for example, the offspring of an Asian and a black parent or the offspring of a black and a Native American parent), during some years the census classified the children according to the race of the mother, other years according to the race of the father (Ferrante and Brown, "Introduction to Part 2" 114–15).

Ironically, given the centuries of statistical contortions performed by the Census Bureau to classify Americans according to race, there is no biological or scientific evidence to support the idea that human beings belong to different races or that there is any such thing as "race." As Prince Brown Jr. explains,

[A]ll of the people in the world today ... regardless of their physical features readily exchange genes when they produce offspring. The variations in human traits ... evident when we look at each other are anatomical and physiological adaptations ... [to a] particular environment. ... No particular set of traits is limited to any one group or "race." ... For example, while grey eyes are associated with a light complexion, they do occur among dark complexioned people – as do brown eyes and black eyes. In the same vein, curly hair is associated with dark skin but we all know light complexioned people who also have curly hair. ... [N]o particular set of traits cluster together to form one group or "race." ... [Rather] [s]ome people share similar traits ... because they live in social isolation, which limits the availability of potential mates. ... [That is,] [t]he social rules (customs, laws) of their society ... prohibit them from mating with people whose features are different.

(144–45)

In other words, if a society's laws or customs forced all people with fair white skin, curly red hair, and blue eyes to live in separate communities and prohibited their marrying anyone other than people with fair white skin, curly red hair, and blue eyes, we would have, probably within a few generations and certainly within a few hundred years, a rather large population of people with fair white skin, curly red hair, and blue eyes. Would we say that these people belonged to a separate race? I don't think so.

From a strictly genetic perspective,

[I]f humans could be grouped into absolute "racial" categories ... [w]e would have groups of people unable to have children with any other groups ... [and]

[t]here would not be any differences between people in the same group. Instead what we find is that 75 percent of genes are identical … in all individuals regardless of the population to which they are socially assigned. The remaining 25 percent are genes which appear in more than one form. … for example … in the four (A, B, O, AB) different types of blood. That is, there is no gene for "race."

(Brown 145–46)

Indeed, the concept of race was originally introduced in the field of natural history merely as a convenient way to refer to groups of human beings in different geographic locations, not with the intention of separating human beings into physiologically distinct groups. However, by the nineteenth century, scientists were fixing these groups in permanent categories and claiming that physical differences corresponded to a cultural hierarchy based on biology: human beings, they asserted, belong to different races, and some races – in particular, the white race – are superior to others. It hardly seems a mere coincidence that members of the scientific community adopted this viewpoint at a time when US citizens were struggling with issues of race and racial superiority, at a time when most white Americans believed in a degree of black racial inferiority that justified, in their minds, racial segregation if not slavery (Muir 98).[4] Professionals in the natural sciences have eliminated from their discipline the concept of race as a biological category precisely because it is not a scientifically supportable concept. However, neither natural scientists nor anyone else has made any "organized effor[t] to bring this rejection to the attention of schools, government, general public, or even related disciplines" (Muir 102).

4   *Differential racialization* – Differential racialization refers to the fact that "the dominant society racializes [defines the racial characteristics of] different minority groups [in different ways] at different times, in response to [its] shifting needs" (Delgado and Stefancic 8). For example, it suited the needs of white plantation owners before the Civil War to depict Africans as simple-minded, in need of white supervision lest they revert to their "heathen" ways, and as happy to serve white people. This mythical stereotype helped justify, the plantation owners believed, their enslavement of Africans. Later, especially whenever they were thought to be in competition with whites for jobs, African Americans were stereotyped as threatening, prone to violence, and, often at the same time, lazy. The logic of this one seems rather skewed, to say the least (how can one be threatening and violent if one is lazy?), but stereotypes are often illogical because they grow from prejudice rather than from reality.

We see the same kind of differential racialization of other minority groups for analogous reasons. Depending on the historical moment and the needs of white society, Native Americans have been considered friendly and noble, lazy drunkards, thieving heathens, or bloodthirsty savages. Similarly, Chicanos/as have been stereotyped as devoutly religious and extremely family oriented, superstitious and gullible, or lazy, good-for-nothing freeloaders, depending on white society's need to see them one way or the other. Chinese American men have been stereotyped as wise, fatherly guides for youngsters of all races; Chinese American women have been stereotyped as submissive to men; and Chinese American men and women have both been stereotyped as sneaky and treacherous. And although Japanese Americans are generally considered hardworking and trustworthy, during World War II they were seen as dangerous potential traitors and put in internment camps for the duration of the war. German and Italian Americans were not racialized in this manner, though the United States was also at war with Germany and Italy. Could it be that Japanese Americans were more vulnerable because they were defined as nonwhite? Could it be that Japanese Americans were more vulnerable because they had been financially successful on the West Coast and owned considerable property and other financial assets, all of which – including their bank accounts and the furniture in their homes – were seized by the government never to be returned, not even after the war was over and Japanese Americans were released from the camps? Whatever the real motivation for Japanese American internment, the point is that, like all minority groups, they were racialized in a manner that served the perceived needs of mainstream white America.

5   *Intersectionality* – No one has a simple, uncomplicated identity based on race alone. Race *intersects* with class, sex, sexual orientation, political orientation, and personal history in forming each person's complex identity. "Everyone has potentially conflicting, overlapping identities, loyalties, and allegiances" (Delgado and Stefancic 9). For example, an individual may be a black, underemployed, working-class male or a Mexican American lesbian. Such persons will suffer oppression from more than one source and often have difficulty knowing the reason they are encountering discrimination in any given instance (Delgado and Stefancic 51–52). Am I being treated unfairly at work because of my race, class, or past employment? Have I been fired because of my sex, ethnicity, or sexual orientation? If I want to sue, on which basis do I do so if I can't be sure on which basis I encountered discrimination?

Kimberlé Williams Crenshaw offers an example that illustrates how easily one's intersectionality can result in one's falling through the cracks of government bureaucracy and how dangerous it can be to life and limb when this situation occurs. Specifically, she examined what can happen when immigrant working-class women of color are victims of domestic violence. In 1990 "Congress amended the marriage fraud provisions of the Immigration and Nationality Act to protect immigrant women who were battered or exposed to extreme cruelty by the US citizens or permanent residents" (358–59) they had come to the United States to marry. Formerly, "a person who immigrated to the United States to marry a US citizen or permanent resident had to remain 'properly' married for two years before even applying for permanent resident status" (359) at which time both husband and wife had to apply for the wife's permanent status. To put a stop to the exploitation of these women, who accepted spousal abuse rather than lose their chance at permanent US residency, Congress voted to allow for a waiver of the two-year requirement in cases of domestic violence. However, Crenshaw found that "[i]mmigrant women who are socially, culturally, or economically privileged are more likely to be able to ... satisfy the waiver requirements" (360), which consist, for example, of reports from social service agencies, police, healthcare providers, psychologists, or school officials (359). "Those women who are least able to take advantage of this waiver – women who are socially or economically the most marginal – are the ones most likely to be women of color" (360). These are women who don't have connections in the United States besides their husbands, so their husbands are their only link to the outside world. They're women who don't know where to go for help and who might not even know that help is available. Because the 1990 waiver to protect immigrant women from domestic violence neglects to consider the inter-sectionality of sex with race and class, it renders this legal safety net the least accessible to those who need it the most.

6 *Voice of color* – Many critical race theorists believe that minority writers and thinkers are generally in a better position than white writers and thinkers to write and speak about race and racism because they experience racism directly. This positionality is called the *voice of color*. Indeed, "black, Indian, Asian, and Latino/a writers and thinkers may be able to communicate to their white counterparts matters that the whites are unlikely to know" (Delgado and Stefancic 9). One might argue that the logic of this idea seems so strong that the phrase *matters that the whites are unlikely to know* could be accurately replaced with *matters that most whites almost certainly don't know.* White people can and do know about many kinds of oppression – for instance, oppression due to class, sex, sexual orientation, ethnicity, religion, and so forth – and all forms of oppression are horrific. But to think that racial oppression isn't unique in myriad important ways is to ignore over three hundred years of American history regarding race.

It is interesting to note that Delgado and Stefancic believe the voice-of-color thesis "[c]oexist[s] in somewhat uneasy tension with anti-essentialism" (9). That is, because antiessentialism, which critical race theory embraces, holds that there are no essential, or inborn, genetic character traits associated with what we define as race, it may seem self-contradictory to assert that there is such a thing as a voice of color. For the term *voice of color*, taken out of context, implies that because some people are born with black or brown skin, they are born with some kind of natural racial insight into the operations of oppression. One might argue, however, that there is no self-contradiction here because Delgado and Stefancic are not positing that the voice of color is an essential – that is, an inborn, or genetic – quality. Rather, it is learned through the experience of racial oppression. In other words, the voice of color – the enhanced ability to speak and write about race and racism due to the experience of racial oppression – is socially, not biologically, acquired. So it is reasonable to argue that the voice-of-color thesis is not an example of essentialism and thus does not contradict critical race theory's antiessentialist philosophy.

Of course, we must remember that even members of the same minority group will not necessarily experience the same kind or amount of oppression and that individuals will handle their experiences differently. For this reason, members of a minority group who deny the racial oppression they've encoun-tered, or who deny that racial oppression is still a problem today, obviously would not be useful examples of the voice-of-color thesis. But those who seek to use the voice of color to inform others of the racial injustice they've experi-enced are being encouraged to tell their stories. "The 'legal storytelling' move-ment urges black and brown writers to recount their experiences with racism and the legal system and to apply their own unique perspectives to assess law's master narratives" (Delgado and Stefancic 9), that is, to assess the ways in which the law is not the colorblind, neutral instrument of justice it claims to be. In the frontline of this movement are, among others, Derrick Bell, Patricia Williams, and Richard Delgado. Delgado, for example, wrote an article "pointing out that white-collar and corporate/industrial crime – perpetrated mostly by whites – causes more personal injury, death, and property loss than all street crime combined" (cited in Delgado and Stefancic 43). Yet it's the black, relatively small-time lawbreakers that are filling our prisons today, while white big-time corporate criminals are rarely pursued by our legal system.

I hope these six tenets have given you a fairly clear idea of the general perspec-tive and goals of critical race theory. To expand on that understanding, let's take a brief look at a few representative examples of the kinds of issues that continue to engage many critical race theorists. Specifically, we'll examine the issues of white privilege, the problem with liberalism, and racial realism.

White privilege can be defined as "the myriad of social advantages, benefits, and courtesies that come with being a member of the dominant race" (Delgado and Stefancic 78). Peggy McIntosh, whose famous list is frequently mentioned by cri-tical race theorists, "identified forty-six advantages available to her as a white person that her African American coworkers, friends, and acquaintances could not count on" (Wildman 18). They include, for example, being told that people of her race were responsible for America's heritage (just think back to the history books we've all read that purported to give a balanced picture of America's past but in reality focused on white American accomplishment); not having to explain to her children, for their own protection, the many modes of white racism; never being asked to speak for her race (cited in Wildman 18); knowing that her achievements will not be considered exceptions to the rule for people of her color; assuming that her occasional errors will not be viewed as signs of her racial inferiority; and expecting that she will be treated with common courtesy – rather than with fear, suspicion, or discomfort – by the individuals she encounters in public places over the course of her day (cited in Delgado and Stefancic 78). White privilege, McIntosh observes, also allows whites to expect that their children will be able to find summer employment of some sort from their unofficial network of white neighbors or from the friends and acquaintances of those neighbors; to feel reasonably confident that their children will get help from a white teacher, if only in the form of an extra-credit assignment to raise a borderline grade; and to rely on a quiet network of favoritism – a kind of "club" – that would help a borderline white candidate receive an important promotion (cited in Delgado and Stefancic 78–79). "This [last] example becomes especially telling when one considers that most corporate positions of power, despite token inroads, are still held by whites" (Delgado and Stefancic 78).

White privilege is a form of everyday racism because the whole notion of privilege rests on the concept of disadvantage. That is, one can be privileged only in contrast with someone else who is not privileged. So if whites enjoy a system of everyday privileges because they are white, this means that blacks are deprived of these privileges because they are black. And this is, of course, a form of racism. More often than not, white privilege is unconscious because it is taken for granted, seen as a natural part of daily life, by those who have it (Essed 205). The unconscious nature of white privilege is often what makes it so difficult for whites to spot, let alone to address.

During group discussions of race and racism in my own classroom, for example, it is not uncommon for a good-hearted, well-intentioned white student to tell the class, "I don't really notice people's race; I don't even think about race most of the time." I have no doubt that such students are sincere in their feelings and are most certainly telling the truth. But they're missing the point. So I always reply to them by asking, "Do you think you would notice people's race and think about race a good deal of the time if you were black?" So far, this question has never failed to achieve its goal. Students invariably answer, "Yes." Yes, if they were black they would notice people's race, and race would often be on their mind. And I see a light bulb go on over their heads as they realize what a luxury it is for them to not *have* to notice or think about race. Not having to notice others' race or think about race is a white privilege. Black people, unless they're in an all-black environment, have to notice the race of others and think about the racial implications of their daily experiences because they're always, "no matter [their] prestige or position ... no more than a few steps away from a racially motivated exclusion, restriction, or affront" (Bell, "Racial Realism" 306).

We might add that black Americans are, at any given moment, little more than one step away from a racially motivated insult that the white perpetrator may not even be conscious of communicating. The black youngster selling candy for his school for whom too many doors remain closed in the white neighborhood; the black teenager in her high school composition class whose white female discussion-group members suddenly become uncomfortably quiet because they realize that their animated talk about hairstyles does not apply to her "different" hair, which is assumed to be somehow less attractive; the black college student in his literature class whose white classmate is in the process of explaining how the story they've just read makes sense if you realize that black symbolizes evil and white symbolizes good; and the parents of these young people of color, who must try to help their children deal with hurtful racial experiences just as they must deal with their own hurtful racial experiences – these are just a few examples of the incidents that many black people must anticipate on a daily basis. White people, in contrast, have the privilege of not having to think about it. In other words, white people have the privilege of not having to think about – or even know about – everyday racism.

Ironically, as Stephanie M. Wildman points out, often "those of us with privilege so earnestly want not to discriminate that we privilege our conduct by failing to examine it critically. Without this examination, the systems of privilege are repli-cated and the cycle of exclusion continues" (179). So what can those who have white privilege do about it? "'Just give up the privilege' seems both obvious and impossible" (Wildman 180) because white privilege is built into every aspect of American culture, and as long as most white people remain by and large unaware of white privilege, all white people will benefit from it whether they want to or not.

> But one small way to give up white privilege is to stop pretending that race does not matter, even though our aspiration continues to be that it should not matter. If we stop pretending that race does not permeate our daily lives, our classrooms, and the affairs of government, perhaps we will start to see the operation of white privilege ... more clearly. ... We need ... the discussion to take place everywhere: in classrooms, workplaces, and meetings ... [so that we can] take our first steps toward dismantling this world of invisible ... privilege.
> (Wildman 180)

Taking steps toward racial justice, but taking too few and taking them too slowly, is seen by many critical race theorists as part of the *problem with liberalism*. Although conservative politics is by no means preferable, given that the conservative viewpoint generally opposes change that would benefit only oppressed people, liberalism has tended to be too moderate, too conciliatory, too cautious when it comes to racial issues. Attempting to accomplish change in small increments doesn't work because the kinds of changes needed for racial justice in this country cannot be contained in small increments: "the system merely swallows up the small improvement ... and everything remains the same" (Delgado and Stefancic 57).

Brown v. Board of Education (1954), for example, seemed like a big improvement because, as we saw earlier, the Supreme Court declared the racial segregation of public schools illegal. That decision hit the nation with enormous impact: many Americans celebrated the decision; others mourned it. However, this Supreme Court decision did nothing to remedy the fact that public schools are still largely segregated, not by law but by poverty. Most children living in poor urban locations are African American and Latino/a. Most children living in wealthy suburban neighborhoods are white. Because children go to school in the school district in which they live, we still have public schools that are largely all white or all non-white. Of course, given that school funding derives from local taxes, the nonwhite schools in the poor districts are woefully underfunded.

From this perspective, *Brown v. Board of Education* was not only a small step, but it was also a misleading step. Many liberals thought it solved the problem, and they went about addressing other national concerns (Delgado and Stefancic 24). In this way, such "solutions" can be compared to quackery in the medical profession. The "quack" doctor not only prescribes medicine that doesn't work but, by convincing the patient that the problem has been addressed, prevents the sufferer from receiving medical aid that might really help.

Critical race theory also opposes the kind of liberalism that believes constitutional law is "color-blind," or neutral in terms of race. For although we do have laws now that guarantee equal opportunities for all, these laws do nothing to support programs to ensure that such opportunities actually are available to all. As most of us know, although racial discrimination in housing and employment is illegal, it still occurs regularly (Delgado and Stefancic 21–23). The white landlord need only tell the applicant of color, politely of course, that there are no vacancies or that the dwelling has just been rented or sold. The white employer need only tell the applicant of color that the job has just been taken but the applicant can leave his or her phone number in case something else comes up. Sometimes these ploys are convincing. Most often they're not. But for the applicant of color to get justice, he or she would need the time and money it takes to hire a lawyer and go to court, where the case may be lost if the lawyer can't prove that there was an intention to discriminate racially on the part of the landlord or employer. How many individuals seeking a job or in need of housing are in a position, financially or psychologically, to take this step? As Delgado and Stefancic argue, "[o]nly aggressive, color-conscious efforts to change the way things are will do much to ameliorate misery" (22). They point to a strategy suggested by one of their colleagues "that society 'look to the bottom' in judging new laws. If [new laws] would not relieve the distress of the poorest group – or, worse, if they compound it – we should reject them" (22).

Although classic, cautious liberalism remains a problem for the kind of meaningful racial progress many critical race theorists want to see, the larger obstacle to racial justice today is the

> rampant, in-your-face conservatism that co-opts Martin Luther King, Jr.'s language, has little use for welfare, affirmative action, or other programs vital to the poor and minorities, and wants to militarize the border and make everyone speak English when businesses are crying for workers with foreign-language proficiency. Some critical race theorists, accordingly, have stopped focusing on liberalism and its ills and begun to address the conservative tide.
>
> (Delgado and Stefancic 24–25)

Many of the problems, issues, and concepts we've encountered so far in our discussion of critical race theory have implied a belief in *racial idealism*: the conviction that racial equality can be achieved by changing people's (often unconscious) racist attitudes through such means as education, campus codes against racist speech, positive media representations of minority groups (Delgado and Stefancic 20), and the use of the law (Bell, "Racial Realism" 308). In short, if our attitudes toward race are constructed by society, then society can reconstruct them. This perspective on racial issues is embraced by the majority of Americans, black and white alike, who want to see racial equality become a reality. *Racial realism*, in sharp contrast, is the conviction that racial equality will never be achieved in the United States and that African Americans should, therefore, stop believing that it will. I'm sure that, for many readers, this position initially might seem shocking, overly pessimistic, even illogical and self-defeating. But I hope you'll wait until you hear more of the argument before you make up your mind.

Racial realism, a philosophy described in an essay aptly entitled "Racial Realism," grew out of the long experience and committed work of New York University law professor Derrick A. Bell Jr., formerly a distinguished civil rights attorney and, as we noted earlier, one of the founders of the critical race theory movement. As Bell points out, "There is little reason to be shocked at my prediction that blacks will not be accepted as equals, a status that has eluded us as a group for more than three hundred years. The current condition of most blacks provides support for this position" (306). The appallingly higher rate of mortality, unemployment, poverty, job discrimination, and the like for African Americans than for white Americans has been documented by reputable sources many times over. Yet these "shocking disparities ... have little effect on policymakers or the society in general" (306) now or in the past. Indeed, Bell notes, history itself should "trigger civil rights advocates to question the efficacy of equality theory. After all, it is an undeniable fact that the Constitution's Framers initially opted to protect property, including enslaved Africans in that category, through the Fifth Amendment" (307). And "[t]hose committed to racial equality also had to overlook the political motivations for the Civil War amend-ments – self-interested motivations almost guaranteeing that when political needs changed, the protection provided the former slaves would not be enforced" (307).

Here Bell is referring to the various amendments to the Constitution passed during and after the Civil War largely for the purpose of punishing the South and ensuring black support for Northern political candidates. For example, the slaves were declared free in 1863, two years before the war ended, only in those states that did not secede from the Union; black men were given the vote in the belief that they would vote for Northern candidates; and so forth. The presence of Northern political administrators and troops stationed in the South during the decade-long Reconstruction period that followed the Civil War was the means by which, among other things, freed slaves were protected from Southern whites. However, as soon as the political support of Southern whites in Congress was needed by a white Northern presidential candidate, things changed.

> With an eye toward ensuring the victory of the Republican Rutherford B. Hayes in a disputed presidential election, the North was more than ready to agree to a compromise that ill served blacks. Among other things, [the Hayes-Tilden Compromise of 1877] promised ... both removal of remaining federal troops from the southern states and freedom from intervention in "political affairs" in those states.
>
> (Bell, "Racial Realism" 312, n. 28)

This change in federal policy meant that freed Southern blacks were left at the mercy of a white population who hated and feared them. Many of us are aware of the holocaust of lynching, black disenfranchisement (being deprived of the vote), humiliating racial segregation laws, and impoverishing racial discrimination that followed.

Of course, the problem of laws officially intended to aid black Americans giving way to the needs of the white power structure is not confined to the past. Bell sees the problem as systemic and due to the formalistic nature of the law, that is, due to the use of abstract language by which the law assumes it provides neutral (unbiased) protection to all citizens. The problem is that the law's abstract language leaves it particularly open to the interpretation of the judges who administer it, and judges have tended to use the law's abstract language to hide the personal value judgments behind their "neutral" decisions, decisions that almost always favor the white power structure.

As a representative example, Bell cites the case of *Regents of the University of California v. Bakke* (1978). Bakke, a white applicant to the University of California's School of Medicine, sued the university on the grounds that its affirmative action policy, intended to help ensure that qualified minority candidates were accepted to the university, discriminated against him because he was white. Hiding behind an abstract application of the notion of equality and "ignoring social questions about which race in fact has power and advantages and which race has been denied entry for centuries into academia, the court held that an affirmative action policy may not unseat white candidates on the basis of their race" (304). The court thus made a landmark decision that relied on an abstract notion of equality in order to side-step the real issues of equality that affirmative-action policies were designed to defend. In fact, Bell observes, "[t]he protection of whites' race-based privilege, so evident in the *Bakke* decision, has become a common theme in civil-rights decisions, particularly in many of those decided by an increasingly conservative Supreme Court" (304). Indeed, Bell notes, the appointment of Judge Clarence Thomas to the Supreme Court "is particularly unkind because the choice of a black like Clarence Thomas replicates the slave-masters' practice of elevating those slaves willing to mimic the masters' views, carry out orders, and by their presence provide a perverse legitimacy to the oppression they aided and approved" (304).

For all of these reasons, Bell urges black Americans to "vie[w] the law – and, by extension, the courts – as instruments for preserving the status quo and only periodically and unpredictably serving as a refuge of oppressed people" so that blacks can "challenge ... the principle of racial equality ... and have their voice and outrage heard" (302). Bell writes,

> I am convinced that there is something real out there in America for black people. It is not, however, the romantic love of integration; it is surely not the long-sought goal of equality under law, though we must maintain the struggle against racism, else the erosion of black rights will become even worse than it is now. The Racial Realism that we must seek is simply a hard-eyed view of racism as it is and our subordinate role in it. We must realize, as our slave forebears did, that the struggle for freedom is, at bottom, a manifestation of our humanity which survives and grows stronger through resistance to oppression, even if that oppression is never overcome.
>
> (308)

For Bell, then, keeping one's "eyes on the prize" does not refer to the prize of racial equality. For the continued expectation of a prize that one has earned but will never receive leads only to "discouragement and defeat" (308). Ironically, then, the belief in racial equality – because it is not now, never has been, and never will be forthcoming – actually can tend to create a kind of apathy or moral paralysis in people who need to keep fighting. The prize Bell has in mind consists of the strengthened humanity and moral "triumph" (309) of facing the realities of and continuing to struggle against racism in all its forms without the illusion that the white power structure will ever be dismantled.

Although I think we've covered a good deal of important ground in our attempt to become acquainted with critical race theory, in many ways we've only scratched the surface. There is so much more to read about each of the issues we've discussed, and there are so many more issues about which we can still learn, issues such as black nationalism versus assimilation, America's black-and-white binary vision regarding race, the role of revisionist history in critical race theory, unconscious racism, and many more. While critical race theory doesn't address itself directly to literary studies, it has significant implications for our interpretation of literature because, as we have seen, it offers us a number of new perspectives from which to understand race and, therefore, from which to understand human relations. And the quest to understand human relations, one might argue, is the reason why most authors write as well as the reason why most readers read.

African American criticism and literature

Whether African American literary critics have sought to explain the unique quality of African American literature by citing its African sources or its African and European American sources, much effort has been expended in delineating the distinguishing features of what has been identified as the African American literary tradition. Generally speaking, critics agree that African American literature has focused on a number of recurring historical and sociological themes, all of which reflect the politics – the realities of political, social, and economic power – of black American experience. Among these themes are the following: reclaiming the African past; surviving the horrors of the Middle Passage; surviving the ordeal of slavery; the quest for freedom from slavery and from other forms of oppression; the quest for literacy; the experience of African Americans during the Civil War and Reconstruction; surviving life in the South under segregation; the problems and conflicts of mulattoes in a racist society; the difficulties of economic survival; the migration North and the related themes of urbanization, alienation, and the quest to reconcile double consciousness; the role of religion in personal and collective survival; the importance of cultural heritage; the importance of family and community; and surviving the combined oppression of racism, classism, and sexism. Until the mid twentieth century, however, black writers often treated the subject of racism carefully or encoded it in their writing in order to be published by white editors and read by white audiences. That is, black writers often represented the evils of racism indirectly through subtle references that black readers and sympathetic white readers would catch but that unsympathetic white readers wouldn't readily notice. We see this strategy quite clearly in, for example, Charles Waddell Chesnutt's story "Po Sandy" (1899), in which the "tall tale" genre is used to convey a rather guarded portrait of the horrors of slavery. Indeed, when Chesnutt became overt in his portrayals of racism, he was unable to find a press to publish his work.

As these themes suggest, the political content of African American literature includes correcting stereotypes of African Americans; correcting the misrepresentation of African Americans in American history and the omission of African Americans from American history; celebrating African American culture, experience, and achievement; and uncovering the social and psychological operations of racism. You'll notice, too, that many of these themes involve surviving life's negative experiences and questing for the positive. For spiritual survival and the realization of African Americans' full human potential are values frequently celebrated in African American writing.

In terms of its poetics, or stylistic elements, the African American literary tradition is distinguished by, among other characteristics, two prominent features: orality and folk motifs. *Orality*, or the spoken quality of its language, gives a literary work a sense of immediacy, of human presence, by giving readers the feeling they are hearing a human voice. In African American literature, orality is usually achieved by using Black Vernacular English and by copying the rhythms of black speech, including, for example, the repetition of important phrases and alternating voices, devices associated with church sermons and with blues, jazz, and rap music. As we saw earlier, the work of Langston Hughes is noted for its orality, and so is the poetry of Sonia Sanchez and Nikki Giovanni. Toni Morrison's *The Bluest Eye* (1970), too, offers us a striking example of orality in the range of black voices it represents, the most "audible" of which include those of Mrs. MacTeer, Pauline Breedlove, and Miss Marie.

The use of folk motifs includes a wide range of character types and folk practices and creates a sense of continuity with the African and African American past. These character types include, for example, the local healer, the conjurer, the matriarch, the local storyteller, the trickster, the religious leader, and the folk hero. Folk practices include, for example, singing worksongs, hymns, and the blues; engaging in folk and religious rituals as a way of maintaining community and continuity with the past; storytelling as a way of relating personal and group history and passing down traditional wisdom; passing down folk crafts and skills, such as quilting, furniture making, and the preparation of traditional foods; and emphasizing the importance of naming, including pet names, nicknames, and being called out of one's name (being called a derogatory name).

Among the best-known attempts to analyze the African American literary tradition are *The Signifying Monkey*, by Henry Louis Gates Jr., and Houston A. Baker Jr.'s *Blues, Ideology, and Afro-American Literature*. Gates attempts to chart African American literary history as a history of relationships among literary texts. He argues that black texts "talk" about one another – for example, by copying, altering, or parodying one another's literary devices – the same way that black people talk about one another when they engage in the African American folk practice called *signifying*.

Signifyin(g), which Gates spells in this manner to emphasize the folk pronunciation of the word and to distinguish it from other definitions of the term, refers to various indirect, clever, ironic, and playful ways of giving your opinion about another person – for example, insulting someone, deflating someone's pretentiousness, or paying someone a compliment – without saying explicitly what you mean. To cite the simplest example, if you want to tell your roommate to quit hogging all the ice cream, you can say to a third party, in your roommate's presence, "Something must be wrong with this freezer because every time I put a half-gallon of chocolate-chip-mint in here it turns into a pint overnight." When your roommate responds with "I don't eat all the ice cream," you can then say, "Did I mention your name? I wasn't even talking to you! You must have a guilty conscience!" This would be called signifying on your roommate. The figure Gates chooses to embody this process of indirect communication is the Signifying Monkey, the master trickster of African American folk tales. Let's look briefly at a literary application of Gates' theory.

Richard Wright and Ralph Ellison, two great African American writers who emerged during the 1940s and 1950s, disagreed about how black experience should be rendered in literature. Wright was a naturalist: he believed that the harsh, inescapable realities of racist oppression should be represented in straightforward, stark language in order to convey as powerfully as possible the evils of racism and the depth of black suffering. This is exactly what Wright did in works like *Native Son* (1940) and *Black Boy* (1945). Ralph Ellison, in contrast, was a modernist: he believed that the complexities, ambiguities, and uncertainties of human experience could best be represented by ambiguous, metaphorical language and a complex narrative with multiple layers of meaning. In *Invisible Man* (1952), Ellison "signifies upon Wright by parodying Wright's literary structures through repetition and difference" (Gates, *Signifying Monkey* 106). That is, *Invisible Man* indirectly and cleverly reveals Ellison's disagreement with Wright's literary vision by echoing certain key elements in Wright's texts in a manner that reverses them.

For example, Gates explains, Wright's titles, *Native Son* and *Black Boy,* suggest a concrete, visible, racial presence. Ellison signifies on these titles by calling his novel *Invisible Man*. While *man* "suggests a more mature and stronger status than either *son* or *boy*" (*Signifying Monkey* 106), Ellison's *man* is "invisible," an absence rather than a presence, which is how black people historically have been treated by white America: as if they were invisible. Ellison also signifies on Wright's protagonist, Bigger Thomas. Bigger is "voiceless": he never speaks up for himself and, indeed, rarely speaks at all. He doesn't act so much as react to the circumstances around him. Ellison responds with a protagonist who "is nothing but voice": we are never told his name, but "it is he who shapes, edits, and narrates his own tale" (*Signifying Monkey* 106). In short,

> Bigger's voicelessness and powerlessness to act (as opposed to react) signify an absence, despite the metaphor of presence found in the novel's title; the reverse obtains in *Invisible Man*, where the absence implied by invisibility is undermined by the presence of the narrator as the author of his own text.
>
> (*Signifying Monkey* 106)

Gates points out numerous other ways in which the works of Ellison signify upon those of Wright in Ellison's attempt to show that naturalism's unrelenting gloom does not adequately represent black experience. In fact, disagreements over the best way to represent black experience form the contested ground on which Gates maps all the acts of literary signifyin(g) he analyzes, including, in addition to Ralph Ellison's, those of Richard Wright, Zora Neale Hurston, Jean Toomer, Paul Laurence Dunbar, Ishmael Reed, Alice Walker, and others.

Houston Baker also attempts to relate the African American literary tradition to an African American folk art: the blues. Baker argues that the blues are a form of African American cultural self-expression that both influences and is influenced by, that both affects and reflects, all other forms of African American expressive culture. The blues are a "matrix" — "a womb, a network ... a point of ceaseless input and output" (3) — and as such, they are also a metaphor for African American culture as a whole. In short, the blues are a language, a cultural code that gets "spoken" in many different ways by many different African American art forms, including literature. Thus, the blues offer a specifically African American approach to African American literary history. Let's take a brief look at one of Baker's many different examples of the complex relationship between the blues and African American literature.

Throughout African American literary history, Baker observes, we find texts with a thematic structure akin to that of the blues. Blues songs, he notes, generally have a double theme: a spiritual theme, usually about loss and desire, and a material theme, usually about the exigencies of economic necessity. Baker sees this same doubleness in African American literary texts, in which the material theme is the subtext that drives the work's overt spiritual theme. For example, *The Life of Olaudah Equiano, or Gustavus Vassa, the African. Written by Himself* (1789), Frederick Douglass' *Narrative of the Life of Frederick Douglass, An American Slave* (1845), and Harriet Jacobs' *Incidents in the Life of a Slave Girl* (1861) share a common spiritual theme: the journey to spiritual awakening, to finding oneself, which is an important dimension of their journey to freedom. Their common subtext, which lies below the spiritual theme and quietly competes with it, is the economic reality on which the protagonists' spiritual quests depend. Equiano, Douglass, and Jacobs' Linda Brent must all find ways to get the money they need in order to achieve their freedom, which is the soil in which their spiritual goals are planted.

Of course, the economic subtext of all African American texts does not lie in the financial requirements of escaping from or buying oneself out of slavery. But Baker nevertheless refers to the "economic grounding" (39) of African American literature as the "economics of slavery" (13) because the economic oppression of black Americans is slavery's legacy, and economic oppression is itself a form of bondage. Baker's project, then, is to chart those moments in African American literary history when the blues, in one form or another, are being played: "when personae, protagonists, autobiographical narrators, or literary critics successfully negotiate an obdurate 'economics of slavery' and achieve a resonant, improvisational expressive dignity" (13). In contemporary literature, we might say that such a moment occurs, for example, when *Beloved*'s Baby Suggs, who administers to the emotional deprivations of the former slaves, urges them, in improvisational blues fashion, to laugh and cry at the same time.

There has also been a good deal of work done to define the contours of a literary tradition specific to the writing of African American women, who were excluded from or marginalized by the African American literary canon as defined both by black male writers and by the white literary establishment. Furthermore, in literary works by white authors and black male authors alike, the representations of African American women generally were restricted to minor or stereotyped characters. As a result, black women writers have been concerned, throughout their literary history, to portray black women as real people with all the complexity and depth that black women have. As Mary Helen Washington puts it, "[O]ne of the main preoccupations of the Black woman writer has been the Black woman herself – her aspirations, her conflicts, her relationship to her men and her children, her creativity" (*Black-Eyed Susans* x).

Relationship is a key word in Washington's statement. For as we saw in Chapter 4, "Feminist criticism," black women must negotiate the conflicting requirements of their relationship to the black community as a whole – their solidarity with black men against racist oppression – and their relationship to women of all races in an effort to resist sexist oppression. In particular, the dilemma created by the conflicting requirements of black men's demands for racial solidarity and white feminists' demands for gender solidarity has forced many African American women engaged in literary criticism to address gender issues in black women's writing without mentioning feminism. (See Chapter 4 for further discussion of this issue.)

The focus on black women's identity in writing by African American women is embodied in a number of recurring themes. Among them are the following: the victimization of black women as underpaid workers forced into the lowliest jobs and as victims of violence and sexual exploitation; the black woman as suppressed artist; the importance of black women's community for psychological (and sometimes physical and economic) survival, which includes relationships among grandmothers, mothers, and daughters; the initiation of young black girls into the harsh realities of racism and sexism; the role of skin color, hair texture, and white standards of beauty in the black woman's self-perception and status within the community; the importance of the relationships between black women and men; and a more sustained focus on the combined oppression of racism, sexism, and classism than we find in the work of black male writers or white writers. In earlier literary works by black women we also see the theme of passing for white. And in literature written over the past two decades the theme of lesbian relationships has emerged. In addition, "[l]argely because degraded images of black women have persisted throughout history, both in and out of literature," Deborah E. McDowell observes, "Black women novelists [and, we might add, poets and playwrights as well] have assumed throughout their tradition a revisionist mission aimed at substituting reality for stereotype" (94–95).

This revisionist mission has included the provision of realistic female character types. In "Teaching Black-Eyed Susans," Mary Helen Washington draws on the insights of Alice Walker to describe three salient types, which frequently have been used by black women writers to represent black women from different historical periods. The first is the "suspended woman," the victim of men and of society as a whole, with few or no options, "suspended" because she can't do anything about her situation. This type is often found in works set in the nineteenth and early twentieth centuries. Examples include Nannie in Zora Neale Hurston's *Their Eyes Were Watching God* (1937) and Pauline Breedlove in Toni Morrison's *The Bluest Eye* (1970). The second type is the "assimilated woman," who is not victimized by physical violence and has much more control of her life, but who is victimized by psychological violence in that she is cut off from her African American roots by her desire to be accepted by white society. This type is often found in works set in the 1940s and 1950s. Examples include Mrs. Turner in *Their Eyes Were Watching God* and Geraldine in *The Bluest Eye*. Finally, the third character type is the "emergent woman," who is coming to an awareness of her own psychological and political oppression and becoming capable of creating a new life and new choices for herself, usually through a harsh experience of initiation that makes her ready for the change. This type is often found in works set in the 1960s. Examples include Meridian in Alice Walker's *Meridian* (1976) and Janie in *Their Eyes Were Watching God*. As the example of Janie illustrates, these character types are not confined to the historical settings with which they are generally associated.

Some critics might argue, I think, that we should add a fourth character type to this useful list: that of the "liberated woman," who has discovered her abilities, knows what she needs, and goes about getting it. We might say, in short, that the "liberated woman" has already found herself and likes what she has found. Although we might expect that this character type would appear most often, or most visibly, in black women's writing set in the 1970s and later, I think she can be found in works set in earlier periods as well. Examples of the "liberated woman" include Shug Avery in Alice Walker's *The Color Purple* (1982) and Pilate in Toni Morrison's *Song of Solomon* (1977), both of which are set in the decades of the first half of the twentieth century.

Finally, African American women's poetics traditionally include a number of recurring literary strategies. For example, black women writers frequently use a black female character as the narrator in a novel or work of short fiction or as the speaker in a poem or dramatic monologue in order to give black women authority as the tellers of their own stories. When third-person narration is used, the point-of-view character (the character through whose eyes we see the story) is usually a black woman or girl. To emphasize the importance of relationships between black women, sometimes the narrative is framed as a conversation (a real conversation, one imagined by the protagonist, or one that takes place through letters) between two black women or girls.

In order to evoke a world that resonates with black women's experience, the use of imagery associated with black women's domestic space and activity is also a frequently employed literary strategy: for example, imagery associated with the kitchen and other locations within the home where such traditional skills as quilting, canning, the performance of garden and farm chores, and the passing down of family and cultural heritage to children occur. Or the world of black women may be evoked by imagery associated with black women's physical appearance, such as clothing, hairstyles, skin color, cosmetics, and the like.

Generally speaking, all the literary devices we've discussed emphasize the struggle of black women to assert their own identity. That identity may take the form of sacrificing oneself for the good of the family, the community, or the race, as it does in many earlier works. Or it may take the form of exploring one's own abilities, needs, and desires, as it does in many contemporary literary texts. But whatever form it takes, the complex psychological, social, and economic dynamics of black women's self-definition occupy an important place in their writing.

Of course, the unique perspectives of African American criticism can also offer us insights into literary works by white American writers. In *Playing in the Dark: Whiteness and the Literary Imagination*, Toni Morrison offers us a very productive approach to reading white mainstream literature from an African American perspective that reveals the ways in which white texts construct, for their own purposes, what she calls the *Africanist* presence in American history. Morrison uses the word Africanist as "a term for the denotative and connotative blackness that African peoples have come to signify as well as the entire range of views, assumptions, readings, and misreadings that accompany Eurocentric learning about these people"

(6–7). In short, *Africanism*, in Morrison's sense of the word, is a white conception (or, more accurately, misconception) of African and African American people on which white authors have projected their own fears, needs, desires, and conflicts.

In white mainstream literature, an Africanist presence can take the form of black characters, stories about black people, representations of black speech, and images associated with Africa or with blackness. In calling for investigations of how these devices function in the work of white writers, Morrison is not suggesting that we analyze racism in literature – such analyses have been and are being conducted – nor that we judge the quality of a work based on its representation of nonwhite characters. Rather, she encourages us to examine the ways in which

> the major and championed characteristics of our national [white] literature – individualism, masculinity, social engagement versus historical isolation; acute and ambiguous moral problematics; the thematics of innocence coupled with an obsession with figurations of death and hell – are ... responses to a dark, abiding ... Africanist presence.
>
> (5)

That is, Morrison wants to analyze the ways in which canonized white American literature has defined a positive "quintessential American identity" (44) by contrast with an invented Africanist identity, "raw and savage ... bound and unfree, rebellious but serviceable" (45), against which whites have been able to define their own civilized virtues. "These topics," Morrison observes, "seem to me to render the nation's literature a much more complex and rewarding body of knowledge" (53).

Among the many ways in which white writers have employed the Africanist presence, Morrison notes, is the use of black characters as a sign of and "vehicle for," among other things, "illegal sexuality, fear of madness, expulsion, [and] self-loathing" (52) as well as "to define the goals and enhance the qualities of white characters" (52–53). For example, Morrison argues that Ernest Hemingway's *To Have and Have Not* (1937), among other strategic uses of Africanist characters, employs a black crewman on a fishing boat to "solicit our admiration" (80) for the boat's white captain, protagonist Harry Morgan, a deep-sea fisherman. "Harry Morgan," Morrison notes,

> seems to represent the classic American hero: a solitary man battling a government that would limit his freedom and his individuality. He is romantically ... respectful of the nature he destroys for a living ... competent ... virile, free, brave, and moral.
>
> (70)

How does Hemingway show the reader that Harry has these qualities? He does so largely by contrasting the protagonist with a "'nigger' in his crew, a man who, throughout all of part one, has no name" (70). In part two, when Hemingway switches from Harry's first-person narration to a third-person narrator, the black character is "named" in two different ways: "Harry says 'Wesley' when speaking to the black man in direct dialogue; Hemingway *writes* 'nigger' when as narrator he refers to him" (71). The word *man*, however, is reserved for Harry.

Furthermore, "[t]his black character either does not speak (as a 'nigger' he is silent) or speaks in very legislated and manipulated ways (as a 'Wesley' his speech serves Harry's needs)" (71). Even when the black man is the first to spot the flying fish for which everyone on board has been waiting, Hemingway does not let him "cry out at the sighting" (73), which would be the natural thing for him to do. Instead, the author gives Harry the awkwardly constructed phrase, "I looked and saw he had seen a patch of flying fish" (Hemingway 13) because "the logic of the narrative's [racial] discrimination" dictates that it must be Harry, "the powerful one, the authoritative one, who sees," even if it requires a less "graceful" syntax to achieve this goal (73).

Finally, when the black crewman finally does begin to speak a good deal, after their boat has been fired upon, it serves the clear purpose of foregrounding Harry's bravery. Morrison points out that

> [w]e hear the grumbles, the groans, the weakness as Wesley's responses to his gunshot wounds for three pages before we learn that Harry is also shot, and much worse than Wesley is. By contrast, Harry has not only not mentioned his own pain, he has taken Wesley's whining with compassion and done the difficult work of steering and tossing the contraband [the illegal goods the boat is transporting] overboard in swift, stoic gestures of manliness.
>
> (74–75)

Thus, we admire Harry the more because we don't admire Wesley, who is depicted as his opposite. Harry's narrative power, so to speak – his authority, strength, and bravery – are enhanced by the black character's silence, weakness, and cowardice. This is just one of the many ways in which an Africanist presence performs a major function in white mainstream literature, a function that merits further study. As Morrison puts it, "All of us, readers and writers, are bereft when criticism remains too polite or too fearful to notice a disrupting darkness before its eyes" (90–91).

Before we draw this section to a close, let me pause here to answer a question frequently asked by students: why are we studying African American criticism and not the criticism of other ethnic literatures as well? Certainly, African Americans aren't the only American ethnic minority to produce a body of exquisite literature. Among others, Native Americans, Asian Americans, Chicanos/as, and Latinos/as have contributed a great deal to the literary output of the United States. African American literature, however, has played a significant role in American history since the eighteenth century, and Black Studies has been an important field in American academia since the 1960s. In contrast, theoretically oriented bodies of criticism of these other wonderful literatures are just beginning to emerge. So it seems logical at this point in time to focus our attention on African American criticism, both to acquaint you with the work being done in this exciting field and to encourage you to investigate the literature and criticism of other American ethnic minorities, an endeavor for which a thorough grounding in African American criticism can serve as both a useful model and as a point of departure for comparison and contrast with other American literatures.

Some questions African American critics ask about literary texts

The following questions are offered to summarize African American approaches to literature. Keep in mind that, like feminist, lesbian/gay/queer, postcolonial, or any criticism that analyzes the writing of a specific group of historically oppressed people, African American criticism is both a subject matter – the study of a body of literature written by a specific group of marginalized people – and a theoretical framework. As a subject matter, any analysis of a literary work written by an African American, regardless of the theoretical framework used, might be called African American criticism, even if no attention is paid to elements in the text that are specifically African American. However, as a theoretical framework – and this is our primary concern here – African American criticism foregrounds race (racial identity, African American cultural traditions, psychology, politics, and so forth) as the object of analysis because race, in America, informs our individual and cultural psychology, and therefore our literature, in profound ways. As a theoretical framework, then, African American criticism can be used to analyze any literary text that speaks to African American issues, regardless of the race of its author, although the work of African American writers is the primary focus.

1 What can the work teach us about the specifics of African heritage, African American culture and experience, and/or African American history (including but not limited to the history of marginalization)?

2 What are the racial politics (ideological agendas related to racial oppression or liberation) of specific African American works? For example, does the work correct stereotypes of African Americans; correct historical misrepresentations of African Americans; celebrate African American culture, experience, and achievement; or explore racial issues, including, among others, the economic, social, or psychological effects of racism? Or as can be seen in the literary production of many white authors, does the work reinforce racist ideologies?

3 What are the poetics (literary devices and strategies) of specific African American works? For example, does the work use Black Vernacular or standard white English? Does the work draw on African myths or African American folk tales or folk motifs? Does the work provide imagery that resonates with African American women's domestic space, African American cultural practices, history, or heritage? What are the effects of these literary devices and how do they relate to the theme, or meaning, of the work?

4 How does the work participate in the African American literary tradition? To what group of African American texts might we say it belongs in terms of its politics and poetics? How does it conform to those texts? How does it break with them, perhaps seeking to redefine literary aesthetics by experimenting with new forms? In short, what place does it occupy in African American literary history or in African American women's literary history?

5 How does the work illustrate interest convergence, the social construction of race, white privilege, or any other concept from critical race theory? How can an understanding of these concepts deepen our interpretation of the work?

6 How is an Africanist presence – black characters, stories about black people, representations of black speech, images associated with Africa or with blackness – used in works by white writers to construct positive portrayals of white characters?

Depending on the literary work in question, we might ask one or any combination of these questions. Or we might come up with a useful question not listed here. These are just some starting points to get us thinking productively about literary texts from an African American perspective. Remember, not all African American critics will interpret the same work in the same way, even if they employ the same theoretical concepts. As always, even expert practitioners disagree. Our goal in using African American criticism is to learn to see some important aspects of literature that we might not have seen so clearly or so deeply without this theoretical perspective and to understand the challenges, responsibilities, and opportunities of living in an ethnically diverse society.

The following reading of F. Scott Fitzgerald's *The Great Gatsby* is offered as an example of what an African American interpretation of that work might yield. It focuses on what I will argue is the novel's racist response to its own setting. By omitting the place – Harlem – and the people – African Americans – responsible for the Jazz Age the novel purports to represent, *The Great Gatsby* gives us a historically inadequate, even inaccurate, portrait of New York City in the early 1920s. Because Fitzgerald is known for his scrupulous attention to the cultural details of setting, this "oversight" raises questions about the author's own racial politics.

While I believe that one of the most important products of African American criticism is its potential to bring the works of marginalized American writers of

color to the fore, I hope that my interpretation of Fitzgerald
antiracist purpose by illustrating some of the ways in which ra
literary work, not just in its use of racist stereotypes or theme
ulation of setting as well. For this latter technique is often mor
more difficult to articulate, and therefore usually more of a cl
efforts in the academic community.

But where's Harlem? An African American reading of *The Great Gatsby*

One of the hallmarks of the writing of F. Scott Fitzgerald is its strong evocation of sense of place. Through the author's scrupulous representation of cultural details very specific to the time and locale in which he places his characters, his novels and stories offer readers the opportunity to feel that they are experiencing a particular moment in history. "Great fiction," says Matthew J. Bruccoli, "is great social history; Fitzgerald's work has become automatically identified with an American decade: ... The Roaring Twenties" ("Preface" ix). Or as Malcolm Bradbury puts it, "The writer of the nineteen twenties who most obviously feels the intensity of modern American experience in all its specified and evolving detail is Scott Fitzgerald" (141). Indeed, Bradbury notes,

> The great fact of his work is that he was able, as a young man in his twenties, to humanize and internalize his times, to follow out their running sequences, catching the right tunes for the year and the right fashions and tones of voice. ... [W]ith a tigh[t] [attention to] social detail, he follows out the psychic history of the times, the history of the great gaudy spree.
>
> (144)

Because of this signature aspect of his writing, Fitzgerald has been dubbed by many the "chronicler ... of his times" (Bradbury 141).

This claim seems especially descriptive of his best-known novel, *The Great Gatsby* (1925), which long has been considered the representative American novel of the Jazz Age, a term Fitzgerald coined to describe the 1920s. For as we shall see, *The Great Gatsby*, which is set in the borough of Manhattan in New York City and on nearby Long Island during the summer of 1922, paints a portrait of that time and place so rich in detail that, arguably, it renders this novel his most memorable work. Yet *The Great Gatsby* omits all reference to, let alone description of, Harlem, which is located in Manhattan and is one of the primary places responsible for the Jazz Age. It's the place where, at that very time, the Harlem Renaissance – that great outpouring of African American literature, music, painting, sculpture, philosophy, and political debate, among other creative enterprises – was in progress.

.d it's the place that was famous for attracting white folks to its nightclubs in droves – especially white folks with money like *The Great Gatsby*'s Tom and Daisy Buchanan, Jay Gatsby, Jordan Baker, and narrator Nick Carraway – where they would hear the latest jazz tunes, see and be seen by the in-crowd, and drink the bootlegged liquor that flowed as freely in Harlem as it flowed in every sophisticated metropolis of Prohibition America. So if it's reasonable to consider Fitzgerald the chronicler of his times, the writer who evoked an unusually strong sense of place through his meticulous attention to social detail, then it's also reasonable to ask, "But where is Harlem?" As this essay will argue, in its total omission of the Harlem of the 1920s – indeed, in its virtual erasure of the African American population of Manhattan at that time – *The Great Gatsby* falls short of the requirements of its setting, especially as Fitzgerald conceived of setting, in a way that raises questions about the author's attitude toward African Americans.

That the novel is bursting with the kind of contemporary cultural detail for which Fitzgerald is known is obvious to anyone who reads it with an eye to cultural history. Among other things, *The Great Gatsby* shows us the early 1920s through its references to the significant events and people of the period as well as through the glimpses it provides of the everyday world at that time: the fashions of the early twenties, references to the period's popular songs, dances, consumer crazes, and reading materials; and descriptions of specific places in 1920s New York. Although we'll devote several paragraphs to establishing the novel's strong sense of place – and I hope you'll bear with me in this effort – do keep in mind that we'll be only scratching the surface of the innumerable ways in which Fitzgerald evokes this specific place and time.

Perhaps the most obvious and pervasive sign of the times in the early 1920s was Prohibition, the passing of the 1919 federal law that made the production and consumption of alcohol illegal but that was treated by the fashionable set as a scoff law. Indeed, breaking this law became the fashionable thing to do. And Prohibition makes its presence known throughout the novel. We see it, for example, in the heavy drinking that occurs at every party depicted in the novel and in the availability of alcohol almost everywhere else; in the bottle of whiskey "wrapp[ed] ... in a towel" (127; ch. 7) that Tom brings along when the main characters drive into New York on the fateful day that will end with Myrtle Wilson's death; in Tom's revelation that Gatsby and Meyer Wolfsheim "bought up a lot of side-street drug stores here and in Chicago and sold grain alcohol over the counter" (141; ch. 7), a common practice during Prohibition; and even in Nick's mention of "the 'underground pipe-line to Canada,'" the "[c]ontemporary legend" (103; ch. 6) that liquor was somehow being "piped in" to the United States from Canada.

The expansion of organized crime that accompanied Prohibition in the 1920s is present in *The Great Gatsby* most obviously in the character of Meyer Wolfsheim, a stand-in for Arnold Rothstein, the notorious gambler and racketeer credited by many people at that time, as well as by Gatsby (78; ch. 4), with bribing the Chicago White Sox to throw the 1919 World Series (Bruccoli, "Explanatory Notes" 211–12). The rise of organized crime is also present in the character of Gatsby himself, through his bootlegging activities, as we saw above; in his longtime criminal connection with a gangster like Wolfsheim (179; ch. 9); and in his own operation involving the sale of fake bonds (174; ch. 9), a popular illegal money-maker at that time and one that resonates strongly with the get-rich-quick aspirations of the 1920s, aspirations that are also recalled by the novel's mentions of oil magnate John D. Rockefeller (31; ch. 2) and railroad tycoon James J. Hill (176; ch. 9). Organized crime, of course, is associated with violence as well as with police corruption, and we get a hint of this world in Wolfsheim's reminiscence about the unexpected street shooting of gambler Rosy Rosenthal, for which four gangsters were executed or, as Wolfsheim points out, "Five, with Becker" (75; ch. 4), a corrupt New York police lieutenant who allegedly ordered the murder presumably because Rosenthal had complained to the newspapers about police corruption ("Charles Becker").

Similarly, the effects on 1920s America of World War I, which ended less than four short years before *The Great Gatsby*'s summer of 1922, are effectively evoked in the novel by means of both Gatsby's war record – the honors he accrued and the famous battles in which he fought – and his war-related experiences, including his brief attendance at England's Oxford University after the war (136; ch. 7). The effects of the Great War, as it was then called, are also seen in the "number of young Englishmen" Nick sees at Gatsby's parties, "all looking a little hungry and all talking in low earnest voices to solid and prosperous Americans. ... They were all selling something ... agonizingly aware of the easy money in the vicinity and convinced that it was theirs for a few words in the right key" (46; ch. 3). This reference reminds us of the economic devastation suffered by Great Britain and Europe during the war, as does Gatsby's purchase of "a high Gothic library, panelled with carved English oak, and probably transported complete from some ruin overseas" (49; ch. 3). It was not an uncommon practice for wealthy Americans in the 1920s to take advantage of postwar economic conditions abroad in order to purchase heirlooms that would otherwise not have been for sale. Finally, that people are still thinking a good deal about the Great War in the summer of 1922 is also evident in the speculations of Gatsby's acquaintances concerning the origin of his wealth: for instance, one acquaintance believes that "he's a nephew or cousin of Kaiser Wilhelm's" (37; ch. 2), Germany's monarch during the Great War; another suggests that he's "nephew to von Hindenburg" (65; ch. 4), the highest-ranking German officer during the war; and yet another thinks "he was a German spy during the war" (48; ch. 3).

Current fashions, though in some ways less important than famous historical events and the people who made them happen, nevertheless render an important aspect of cultural history by giving us a sense of the era's collective self-perception and attitude toward life. For example, after World War I and especially with the advent of the 1920s, fashionable women cut their long hair into chin-length, loosely hanging "bobs," which Daisy and Jordan surely wear and which we see specifically in the description of Myrtle Wilson's sister Catherine with her "sticky bob of red hair" (34; ch. 2). At Gatsby's parties, too, the women have "hair shorn in strange new ways" (44; ch. 3). Similarly, makeup became popular during the 1920s, and we see it, for example, in Catherine's use of eyebrow pencil and face powder (34; ch. 2) as well as in the mascara on the "heavily beaded eyelashes" (56; ch. 3) of one of Gatsby's inebriated party guests. Women's clothing, unlike that of yesteryear, is "gaudy with primary colors" and modern designs, such as the "gas blue" dress "with lavender beads" and the "shawls beyond the dreams of Castile" we see at Gatsby's parties (44; ch. 3). And certainly, before World War I women didn't wear the "small tight hats of metallic cloth" sported by Daisy and Jordan nor the "light capes [draped] over their arms" (127; ch. 7), which they might need even on this hot summer night because their modern attire is so thin and spare.

Analogously, the fashionable summer attire for young men on occasions requiring "casual elegance" in the early 1920s was a lightweight white suit referred to as "white flannels," which we see on both Nick (46; ch. 3) and Gatsby (89; ch. 5), who also sport the straw hats popular during this period (121; ch. 7). In addition, Gatsby's short hair (54; ch. 3) is in keeping with the new fashion for men in post-World War I America, and there is an accurate absence, throughout the novel, of the kinds of facial hair – for example, full beards and "mutton chops" – that were no longer worn by fashionable men after the war.

The popular songs, dances, and consumer crazes referred to in the novel also help create the work's strong sense of place because they give us a sense of the sounds and sights of the leisure world of the early 1920s. In addition to the novel's several references to jazz, which was the music of the decade, we find mention of specific popular songs of the period, all written in the years from 1920 to 1922: "The Sheik of Araby" (83; ch. 4), "The Love Nest" (100; ch. 5), "Ain't We Got Fun?" (101–2; ch. 5), and "It's Three o'clock in the Morning" (115: ch. 6). There are also various improvisational dances that occur at Gatsby's parties (45, 51; ch. 3) – again, typical of the period – and we see Gatsby and Daisy dancing the fox-trot (112; ch. 6), a popular ballroom dance of the time. Moreover, there are references to the period's popular New York entertainments: for example, Gilda Gray (45; ch. 3), the lead dancer at Broadway's "Ziegfeld Follies"; Joe Frisco (45; ch. 3), a well-known comedian and dancer; and David Belasco (50; ch. 3), a Broadway producer known for his realistic sets (Bruccoli, "Explanatory Notes" 209).

We see the period's fascination with all things mechanized, electrified, or "new and improved" in the novel's references to trendy consumer items, for those who could afford them: for instance, Gatsby's motor boats (43; ch. 3), his hydroplane (52; ch. 3), his aquaplane (43; ch. 3), and his electric juicer (43–44; ch. 3), the latter of which is certainly not as glamorous as his other possessions but nevertheless indicative of the modern gadgetry of the 1920s. Perhaps the most significant consumer craze of the early 1920s, however, was the automobile.

By the early 1920s, the automobile had become the new machine that everyone wanted. Unlike the American landscape of just 15 years earlier, in which cars were an oddity, in 1920 cars could be seen everywhere, and traffic jams were not uncommon in American cities (O'Meara 53). In *The Great Gatsby*, in addition to the autos owned by the main characters, cars on the road are routinely mentioned whenever the characters drive into Manhattan. Moreover, Nick mentions traffic jams at least twice: he reports that the cars "parked five deep" (44: ch. 3) in Gatsby's driveway one Saturday evening become tied up in a traffic jam when the party is over (58; ch. 3), and Nick tells us that he likes to walk up 5th Avenue at eight o'clock in the evening when "the dark lanes of the Forties [are] five deep with throbbing taxi cabs, bound for the theatre district" (62; ch. 3). Indeed, on their way to Manhattan, the two cars carrying Gatsby, Daisy, Tom, Nick, and Jordan can't even pull up side by side for a brief exchange of words without "a cursing whistle [from a truck] behind [them]" (132; ch. 7). No doubt, modern times have arrived.

Although the reading materials mentioned in *The Great Gatsby* are not numerous, they are significant in terms of their contribution to the novel's sense of place, for they offer us a glimpse of the beliefs that were prevalent among many Americans at that time. For example, Tom's reference to *The Rise of the Coloured Empires* by Goddard, which echoes the sentiments of *The Rising Tide of Color* (1920) by Theodore Lothrop Stoddard, bespeaks an opinion widely held in the 1920s that "the dominant 'Nordic' race was being threatened by the intermarriage … with persons of 'inferior' races" (Gidley 173). Indeed, *The Saturday Evening Post*, which is also mentioned in the novel (22; ch. 1) and which was the most popular magazine in the United States at that time, began in 1920 to recommend the ideas of a similarly racist book Madison Grant published in 1916 entitled *The Passing of the Great Race* (Gidley 173). In fact, the popularity of Nordicism – the belief that the United States was founded and developed by the "Nordic race" and that the "cross-breeding" of this "superior" race with other races would result in the disappearance of the "Nordic race" (Decker 122) – was so widespread in the early 1920s that a restrictive Immigration Bill was passed in 1924 and supported by President Coolidge, who said that "America must be kept American" (cited in Decker 123).

Mention of the popular New York newspapers of the day, the *Tribune* (42; ch. 2) – presumably the *New York Tribune* or the *New York Herald Tribune*, which absorbed the former in 1922 (see "New York Herald Tribune") – and the *Journal* (89; ch. 5), presumably the *New York Journal American*, as well as *Town Tattle* and similar "scandal magazines of Broadway" (31; ch. 2), also contribute to the novel's evocation of place: these are newspapers and magazines published in New York with an eye to news likely to be of interest to New Yorkers. An analogous claim can be made for the novel's reference to Robert Keable's *Simon Called Peter* (1921), a popular novel of the day. Its plot concerns "an army chaplain who becomes involved in passionate episodes" (Bruccoli, "Explanatory Notes" 209), a subject that clearly resonates with the 1920s reputation for living life in the fast lane and breaking all the old rules.

Finally, places mentioned in the novel are often so specifically located that we could probably find our way to them, in 1922 at least, with just a copy of *The Great Gatsby* as our guide. To cite just a few of the novel's many examples, we learn that the Plaza Hotel fronts "the south side of Central Park" (132; ch. 7), that movie stars – many movies were made in New York in those days – lived in "tall apartments ... in the West Fifties" (83; ch. 4), that we can go to a movie in one of the "big" movie theaters "around Fiftieth Street" (132; ch. 7), that the old Murray Hill Hotel is located on Madison Avenue within walking distance from the financial district in lower Manhattan, and that Pennsylvania Station is on West Thirty-third Street (61; ch. 3). And if we can get a member to sponsor us, we can visit the Yale Club, where Nick usually eats dinner, and see its library, which is still located on the second floor, where Nick "studied investments and securities" after his evening meal (61; ch. 3). We also learn that we can get from Great Neck (West Egg) or Manhasset Neck (East Egg), Long Island, to Manhattan by crossing the Queensboro Bridge (73; ch. 4). And we'd recognize the view of the city, as Nick describes it from that bridge – buildings "rising up ... in white heaps and sugar lumps" (73; ch. 4) – because the buildings actually had "[w]hite and light ... finishes" (O'Meara 58). Indeed, on our way from Long Island to the Queensboro Bridge, we're even prepared to pass by the unpleasant sights and smells of the Corona dump, known in the novel as the "valley of ashes" (27; ch. 2), which was "a swamp ... being filled with ashes, garbage, and manure" (Bruccoli, "Explanatory Notes" 208). As I mentioned earlier, the cultural details noted here are but a small sampling of *The Great Gatsby*'s evocation of 1920s Manhattan, a city with which the novel's main characters are well acquainted.

Although in point of fact, Manhattan is just one of five boroughs of New York City (the others are Queens, the Bronx, Brooklyn, and Staten Island), *The Great Gatsby*'s characters refer to Manhattan, just as we do today, as *New York City, New York, the city,* or even just *town.* And they know that it's the place to go for fun as well as to conduct business. As early as page 15 (ch. 1), Daisy responds to Jordan's complaint about lying on the sofa all afternoon by saying, "Don't look at me. ... I've been trying to get you to New York all afternoon." Nick works in New York, of course, but he also spends much of his leisure time there, dining at the Yale Club after work, walking around lower Manhattan after dinner (61; ch. 3), and "trotting around with Jordan" (107; ch. 6). We even see the couple driving through Manhattan's Central Park in a horse-drawn Victoria (83; ch. 4), a vehicle similar to the horse-drawn hansom cabs in which twosomes tour the park today. Myrtle, who lives in the borough of Queens, often visits her sister in New York, and it was on the train to New York that she first met Tom (40; ch. 2). West 158th Street in Manhattan is the location of the apartment Tom keeps for his trysts with Myrtle (32; ch. 2), which means that their taxi has to pass right by Harlem, if not pass through it, to get to their destination. Moreover, we're told that he frequently takes his mistress to "popular restaurants" in the city, to the chagrin of his "acquaintances" who see them there (28; ch. 2). Clearly, Tom spends a good deal of time in Manhattan. Nick and Gatsby even run into him in the Forty-second Street restaurant where they meet for lunch and where Nick is introduced to Meyer Wolfsheim (73; ch. 4). And certainly Gatsby visits New York City to meet with Wolfsheim. In addition, the confrontation scene between Tom and Gatsby, one of the novel's pivotal events, occurs in the Plaza Hotel in Manhattan (132; ch. 7). Even most of Gatsby's party guests (44; ch. 3), as well as the "crates of oranges and lemons" (43; ch. 3) that garnish their hors d'oeuvres and drinks, come from New York.

How, then, can narrator Nick Carraway and his friends have missed Harlem? Harlem's nightclubs, which offered such jazz greats as Eubie Blake, Fats Waller, Louis Armstrong, Bessie Smith, Duke Ellington, and Cab Calloway (Lewis 91, 120, 183, 210), attracted white people from all over the city and beyond. Nightspots like Barron's Little Savoy, the Douglass Club (Lewis 28), Connie's Inn (Stovall 29), and the Exclusive Club (Stovall 44), among others, could boast among their clientele "white debutantes, socialites, politicians, [and] performers" (Stovall 29). And Harlem's theaters offered the talents of such time-honored actors as Paul Robeson, Ethel Waters, and Bill "Bojangles" Robinson (Lewis 120). As Jervis Anderson puts it, "Harlem was Manhattan's capital of gaiety and amusement. ... [T]here was no livelier place in all of New York City, especially after dark. Nightly, thousands of white visitors – most from downtown, some from other parts of the country, a few from cities abroad – made their way to Harlem" (139). Among the throngs of ordinary folk and wealthy whites who visited Harlem's nightspots, David Levering Lewis reports, were the very famous, including such notables of the period as John and Ethel Barrymore, Charlie Chaplin (105–6), the famous composer Maurice Ravel (173), George Gershwin (183), Jimmy Durante, Joan Crawford, Benny Goodman, bandleaders Tommy and Jimmy Dorsey, future mayor of New York Fiorello LaGuardia, Mae West, Tallulah Bankhead, and Emily Vanderbilt (209).

In fact, when the African American musical comedy *Shuffle Along* opened, it took all of New York City by storm. Written, produced, and performed exclusively by black people, the show appeared in the long unused Sixty-third Street Theatre, which was considered rather far uptown for Broadway audiences to attend. Nevertheless, "[w]ithin a few weeks *Shuffle Along* made the Sixty-third Street

Theatre one of the best-known houses in town and made it necessary for the Traffic Department to declare Sixty-third Street a one-way thoroughfare" to handle the traffic (Johnson 188). The musical comedy opened in the summer of 1921 and ran for two years before going on the road. This means that it was running in the summer of 1922, when Nick Carraway was living on Long Island and spending most of his time in New York. Although it was a "record-breaking, epoch-making" show that eclipsed all other New York theatricals at that time – in fact, "some of its tunes ... went round the world" (Johnson 186) – there is no mention of it in *The Great Gatsby*.

The white population of New York didn't have to depend on word of mouth to know what was transpiring in Harlem, though word of mouth was certainly active. They could read about it in such mainstream newspapers as the *Daily News*, *The New York World*, *The New York Times*, and *Variety* (Lewis 22, 61, 73). And the white literary world, including white publishers, took great interest in the literary creations of Harlem. Among the noteworthy white writers who encouraged the black literati of Harlem were Pearl Buck, Dorothy Parker, Sinclair Lewis, Sherwood Anderson, Hart Crane, and Eugene O'Neill (Lewis 98–99). Among the great writers of the Harlem Renaissance – referred to at the time as the New Negro Movement – who attracted white attention were Claude McKay, Jean Toomer, Langston Hughes, Countee Cullen, Jesse Fauset, James Weldon Johnson, Arna Bontemps, and Zora Neale Hurston. In fact, while Fitzgerald was in the initial stages of planning and writing *The Great Gatsby* in 1923, Jean Toomer's novel *Cane* was released to "outstanding" critical response, including high praise by renowned white critic Allen Tate and playwright Eugene O'Neill (Lewis 70), and Countee Cullen was interviewed in New York's premier mainstream newspaper *The New York Times* (Lewis 77).

Although Harlem was a relatively small section of Manhattan, it was really a city within a city, and like any other city it had its underemployed poor, especially as its population increased (Anderson 139). "[L]ess than two square miles" in size during the early 1920s, it was home to a black population that numbered "more than two hundred thousand" (Johnson 147). However, situated at the north end of Central Park, "in the heart of Manhattan," 1920s Harlem was "not a fringe, ... not a slum, nor [was] it a 'quarter' consisting of dilapidated tenements. It [was] a section of ... apartment houses and handsome dwellings, with streets as well paved, as well lighted, and as well kept as in any other part of the city" (Johnson 146). Celebrated people, black and white, from the world of literature, theater, and academia could be seen at any time of the day or night strolling the streets of Harlem or giving public lectures, such as that given by John Dewey at the Harlem YMCA (Lewis 104).

Harlem even had its own newspapers and magazines, including *Crisis, Fire!, Messenger* (Douglas 312–13), and *Opportunity* (Lewis 120). And Harlem boasted famous black artists as well as writers, musicians, and actors, including painters Romare

Bearden, Aaron Douglas, and Laura Wheeler Waring and sculptors Sargent Johnson, Elizabeth Prophet, and Augusta Savage. Just to give you an idea of how productive the Harlem Renaissance was, even in terms of its painters and sculptors (a category that has tended to receive less attention than that of writers and performing artists), by the end of the decade over one hundred Harlem painters and sculptors were entering their works in annual contests and exhibitions (Lewis 261–62).

The creative output of the Harlem Renaissance was, as we have seen, well known to white New Yorkers and to the Western world at large. So how can a Yale graduate like Nick Carraway – well-educated, sensitive, curious, and, as he tells us, "rather literary" (8; ch. 1) – be completely oblivious to the existence of Harlem? Even if Nick somehow overlooks the celebrated outpouring of Harlem's "high" culture – its literature, philosophical and political writing, painting, sculpture, and the like – he certainly can't work and play in New York City without knowing about Harlem's nightlife. From a historical perspective, such an oversight is virtually impossible. Had Fitzgerald remained true to form in his description of cultural reality, Nick and his friends would have visited, or at least mentioned having visited, a Harlem nightclub. Surely, he would have taken Jordan there on one of their numerous New York dates. And there's no way that Tom and Daisy, who consider themselves so fashionably modern, would have missed Harlem. Indeed, Nick tells us that the Buchanans "drifted here and there unrestfully wherever people played polo and were rich together" (10; ch. 1). If Tom and Daisy go where other wealthy whites of the period go to be "rich together," they would have visited Harlem nightspots on a fairly regular basis. They at least would have gone to the most expensive and exclusive nightspots, like Barron's Little Savoy and Connie's Inn, which catered to a segregated white clientele (Lewis 106). As Tyler Stovall puts it, "During [the 1920s] it became the custom for wealthy and prominent white New Yorkers to finish up an evening on the town listening to jazz in one of Harlem's many speakeasies" (29).[5]

The enormous population of African Americans inhabiting Harlem in the 1920s, moreover, was not confined to that neighborhood. In fact, African Americans from Harlem and from elsewhere in New York worked, played, and shopped all over Manhattan. Yet the only vivid representation of African Americans in the novel occurs when Gatsby and Nick are driving into New York City to have lunch. Nick sees "three modish [fashionable] Negroes" in "a limousine ... driven by a white chauffeur" (73; ch. 4). He describes them as "two bucks and a girl" and says, "I laughed aloud as the yolks of their eyeballs rolled toward us in haughty rivalry" (73; ch. 4).[6] Of course, Nick's unselfconscious racism is obvious in his reaction to these characters: the black men are "bucks" – animals rather than men – and the description of their wide-stretched, rolling eyes resonates strongly with racist stereotypes that portrayed African Americans as foolish, childish, overly dramatic, comic characters.

In addition, Nick's description of these characters fulfills the kind of narrative function Toni Morrison describes in her analysis of the Africanist presence in white American literature. These black characters – fashionably dressed, riding in a chauffeured limousine, very conscious of their social status in the eyes of others – are the mirror and shadow of Gatsby. The only obvious difference between them is that Gatsby can hide his origins, which he does, whereas they can't because they can't hide their color. From Nick's point of view, despite Gatsby's "elaborate formality of speech [that] just missed being absurd" (53; ch. 3), his ridiculous fabrication of wealthy "ancestors" (69; ch. 4), his "circus wagon" (128; ch. 7) of a car, as Tom calls it, and all his other ludicrous affectations, he is the romantic embodiment of success. The black characters, however, are its parody. In barely more than one sentence, in the single image with which Nick describes the black characters, he projects onto them everything about Gatsby that he, and perhaps the reader, hold in contempt. *They* are preposterous, not Gatsby. Thus, Nick's racist attitude toward these characters facilitates their function as scapegoats sacrificed to Nick's, and the text's, recuperation of Gatsby. To put the matter another way, the novel erases real African Americans, who were a very visible and important presence in New York City during the 1920s where, as we have seen, much of the novel is set, and substitutes in their place a comic stereotype that reinforces white superiority. This is no small move, given the historical reality of New York City during the 1920s.

Apparently, Fitzgerald decided not only to remove African Americans from his representation of the Jazz Age, but he also decided to remove jazz from the hands of the African Americans who invented it. For the novel gives the credit for jazz symbolically to whites. The only musicians we see playing jazz are the white musicians at Gatsby's party. And they are "no thin five-piece affair," Nick tells us, "but a whole pit full of oboes and trombones and saxophones and viols and cornets and piccolos and low and high drums" (44; ch. 3). In other words, jazz has been "elevated" to the status of high culture in the form of an orchestra, and high culture belongs to white, not black, Americans. Significantly, the orchestra spotlights its performance of a piece that, the conductor informs us, was played at Carnegie Hall: "Vladimir Tostoff's Jazz History of the World" (54; ch. 3). Could Fitzgerald have found a more conspicuously European – that is, white – name than Vladimir Tostoff? There's no way a reader could mistake him for an African American. In the world of this novel, jazz is, symbolically at least, a European invention. Thus, Tom's warning that "[i]t's up to us who are the dominant race to watch out or these other races will have control of things" (17; ch. 1), though mocked by Nick and by the novel's unflattering characterization of Tom, is an attitude the novel unconsciously shares.

What could be responsible for such a glaring omission on the part of an author known for his accurate renditions of setting? Certainly, as Lauraleigh O'Meara notes, Fitzgerald was personally familiar with Manhattan in all its "remarkabl[e] divers[ity]" (34). Scott and Zelda Fitzgerald were married in New York City in April 1920 and spent the first month of their married life at the Biltmore and Commodore hotels in New York City. Although they spent the next several months in Westport, Connecticut, Manhattan was a mere 50 miles away, and they frequently went to the city for fun. Moving back to New York City in October 1920, they remained there, in an apartment on West Fifty-ninth Street, until they left for Europe for the summer of 1921, but by 1922 they had returned to Manhattan. Although the couple lived in Great Neck, Long Island, from October 1922 to April 1924, they often partied in New York City (O'Meara 33–34). Indeed, from their home on Long Island, New York was too nearby and too inviting, which is why they again left for France in April 1924 (O'Meara 50).

Fitzgerald's personal acquaintance with New York City included a personal acquaintance with Harlem as well through his friendship with white writer, critic, and photographer Carl Van Vechten. Van Vechten was fascinated by Harlem and was very well known there. By the mid 1920s, Van Vechten had become "Harlem's most enthusiastic and ubiquitous Nordic" (Lewis 182). Fitzgerald attended Van Vechten's parties, which were given in his own home on New York's west side for both white and black guests, including, of course, Van Vechten's friends and acquaintances from Harlem (Lewis 182–84). In fact, Fitzgerald refers specifically to the diversity of New York City, including Harlem, in his 1922 novel *The Beautiful and Damned*, and Fitzgerald is known to have based that novel, like so much of his other work, on his personal experience (O'Meara 34).

Even the time Fitzgerald spent in Paris contributed to his awareness of Harlem because, as Tyler Stovall points out, African Americans, many of whom were from Harlem, established an expatriate artists' colony in Paris – consisting of African American jazz musicians, writers, painters, sculptors, and athletes – just as Fitzgerald, Hemingway, Stein, and other members of the "Lost Generation" established a writers' colony there (26). Stovall claims, in fact, that "few of the tens of thousands of illustrious exiles in Paris during the 1920s had a greater impact on the city than the hundreds of African Americans who chose to call it home in those years" (25–26). "[B]lackness became the rage in Paris during the 1920s," for "Parisian intellectuals took black culture seriously, considering it to represent the spirit of the age" (Stovall 32). Fitzgerald, who himself wanted to represent the spirit of the age in his novels, could not have failed to notice that the 1921 Prix Goncourt for literature, "the most prestigious literary award in France" went "to the novel *Batouala* by René Maran ... a black Frenchman ... [b]orn in Martinique" (Stovall 32).

Fitzgerald's personal acquaintance with Harlemites in Paris resulted from his frequent visits to jazz clubs in Montmartre, a section in the northern part of the city where most African Americans in Paris lived during the 1920s (Stovall 39). In a very real sense, Montmartre reproduced the nightlife available in Harlem by reproducing the same kind of jazz clubs and by employing many of the same jazz musicians available in Harlem. "White American expatriates frequently visited Mon-tmartre's nightclubs" (Stovall 78), and Fitzgerald was particularly fond of a famous African American jazz singer there called Bricktop, so named for her red hair, who also sang in Harlem clubs when she was in the United States (Stovall 78–79).

A rather obvious question, then, seems to present itself: Why does *The Great Gatsby*, Fitzgerald's great novel of the Jazz Age, omit entirely any reference to Harlem, imply that jazz was a product of white culture, and limit its only vivid representation of African Americans in 1920s New York City to a negative "comic" stereotype? In other words, what was Fitzgerald's attitude toward African Amer-icans while he was writing his most famous novel? Although Robert Forrey and Alan Margolies, for example, agree that Fitzgerald "show[ed] signs," toward the end of his life, of "outgrowing" his racist attitude (Forrey 296), it seems evident that *The Great Gatsby*, written when the author was in his twenties, arrived too early in Fitzgerald's career to benefit from his later change in perspective. There is, indeed, a good deal of evidence to suggest that *The Great Gatsby* suffers from the omissions and misrepresentations noted above because its author, consciously or uncon-sciously, wanted to erase from his novelistic field of vision the African Americans who so visibly populated the real New York, the New York that plays such an important role in his novel's sense of place. As we shall see, Fitzgerald believed that African Americans were woefully inferior to whites. And although the psychological motives for the author's racism are not the issue here, it is possible that beneath his belief in the superiority of his race lay a deep-seated insecurity about his own lit-erary value in face of the outstanding achievements of African Americans in arts and letters, which he was witnessing in Paris as well as in New York. Whatever the reason, it is evident that Fitzgerald's attitude toward African Americans, for the greater part of his life, was decidedly racist.

As Robert Forrey observes, the black characters in Fitzgerald's numerous short stories "are almost always menial characters who are referred to disparagingly – sometimes by the author himself in the third person – as 'coons,' 'niggers,' 'pick-aninnies,' or 'Samboes.' Their function is usually to create a comic effect" (293). Tyler Stovall concurs, observing that Fitzgerald's *Tender Is the Night*, "one of the great novels of American expatriate life," contains "notoriously racist passages about blacks" (80). And "[i]n real life, as in fiction," Forrey adds, "the appearance of a Negro was usually the signal for Fitzgerald to promote a prank" (294). Citing Andrew Turnbull's 1962 biography *Scott Fitzgerald*, Forrey notes that, on one occa-sion, Fitzgerald "introduced an unsuspecting Negro clergyman, soliciting funds for a local orphanage, as a distinguished visitor from Africa. Polite but panic-stricken, the clergyman fled the premises" (294). Another time, Fitzgerald made his African American chauffeur, who had a speech impediment, repeat over and over again a sentence filled with words he was unable to pronounce correctly (Turnbull, cited in Forrey 294). And certainly Fitzgerald's attitude toward Bricktop, the African American singer whom, as we noted earlier, he greatly admired, is revealing: although he was a great fan of her work and frequented the club where she sang, "she came to [his] hom[e] as a hired musician, not as a friend and equal" (Stovall 80).

Drawing on Andrew Turnbull's 1963 *The Letters of F. Scott Fitzgerald*, M. Gidley underscores a telltale passage in a letter from Fitzgerald to his friend Edmund Wilson concerning the author's racial philosophy:

> God damn the continent of Europe. ... The Negroid streak creeps northward to defile the Nordic race. Already the Italians have souls of blackamoors [black or dark-skinned people]. Raise the bars of immigration [in the United States] and permit only Scandinavians, Teutons [people of Germanic or Celtic origin], Anglo-Saxons and Celts [British, Scottish, or Irish people] to enter.
>
> (178)

In another letter to Edmund Wilson, Fitzgerald wrote, "We [Anglo-Saxons, Celts, and the like] are as far above the modern French man as he is above the Negro. Even in art!" (Turnbull, *Letters*, cited in Gidley 178).

Equally revealing of Fitzgerald's attitude toward African Americans, I think, is his response to a book written by his friend Carl Van Vechten. As we saw earlier, Van Vechten spent a good deal of time in and had a great deal of enthusiasm for Harlem. In 1926 Van Vechten came out with a novel about Harlem entitled *Nigger Heaven*. The title alone is revealing, and W. E. B. DuBois wrote that the book "is a blow in the face ... an affront to the hospitality of black folk [who had welcomed Van Vechten into their community] and to the intelligence of white[s]. ... I find the novel neither truthful nor artistic. ... It is a caricature" (cited in Anderson 219). According to David Levering Lewis, "[t]he plot is sheer melodrama," and "90 percent of the [black] race ... saw the book as DuBois did" (181).

Many white readers and literary critics disagreed, however, and Fitzgerald was among them. He called *Nigger Heaven* "a work of art" (Anderson 217) and praised it for its representation of "the northern nigger or, rather the nigger in New York" (Turnbull, *Letters*, cited in Gidley 181). According to Lewis, Fitzgerald "adored the novel because, for [him] it confirmed the Afro-American grotesqueries produced by civilization and the durability of ... the 'unspoiled Negro'" (188). In other words, Fitzgerald believed that African Americans were unable to truly internalize white culture – they remained primitive, or "unspoiled" – and therefore Harlem was merely their attempt to copy white culture. For Fitzgerald, "Harlem [was] aping ... white ways, as if white culture had been dug out of its context and set down against an accidental and unrelated background" (Carl Van Vechten Collection, N.Y. Public Library, cited in Lewis 188).

This last statement is as revealing, it seems to me, as it is startling. African Americans invented jazz, which can hardly be said to be a copy of white music. The

Harlem Renaissance produced writers like Langston Hughes, Zora Neale Hurston, and Claude McKay, who expanded on an African American literary tradition that was by no means a copy of white literary culture. On the contrary, white societies outside the United States often recognized the originality of African American culture. As we saw earlier, for example, Jazz Age Paris greatly admired the unique quality of African American culture. Yet Fitzgerald was unable or unwilling to see Harlem in its own right. Clearly, he wanted to continue believing the white stereotype of African Americans as uncivilized and uncultured. If he saw anything in Harlem other than this stereotype, he chalked it up, as we noted above, to African Americans' "aping" whites, a word choice that, in this context, also reveals Fitzgerald's racist perspective.

It is ironic, then, to say the least, that "*The Great Gatsby* has become an international source for American social history and is read as a record of American life at an actual time and place" (Bruccoli, "The Text of *The Great Gatsby*" 193). For if this is the case, then the world has a record of American life during the Jazz Age that omits the place and the people largely responsible for creating the era that the novel examines. M. Gidley says, "Fitzgerald, who was known ... as the 'laureate of The Jazz Age,' so much of the quality of which era emanated originally from the night life of Harlem, strikes us now, I would suggest, as a prisoner of prejudice who yet sees beyond his own chains" (181). Fitzgerald may indeed have been a prisoner of prejudice, but at least in terms of the textual evidence offered in *The Great Gatsby*, it is evident that he was unwilling or unable to see beyond the narrow boundaries set by his racial biases.

Questions for further practice: African American approaches to other literary works

The following questions are intended as models. They can help you use African American criticism to interpret the literary works to which they refer or other texts of your choice.

1 In what ways does Toni Morrison's *The Bluest Eye* (1970) participate in the African American literary tradition? For example, you might analyze the novel's antiracist politics. (Morrison is known for her insights into the psychology of internalized racism.) Or you might analyze its poetics, for example, its orality, its folk motifs, and the ways in which the novel's use of these devices relates to the meaning of the work. Or you might want to argue that Morrison's novel participates more specifically in the tradition of African American women's writing.

2 In his play *The Piano Lesson* (1990), August Wilson sets up a conflict between two recurring African American themes: the importance of cultural heritage and

the difficulties of economic survival. Analyze how the play represents and sustains this conflict without letting us resolve it in favor of one side or the other. (Or if you think the play does resolve the conflict, argue for that interpretation instead.) How might you relate Wilson's use of these themes to Houston Baker's observations about the relationship between the spiritual quest and its economic subtext in African American literature? If you don't think the play quite fits this particular schema of text and subtext, improvise, as Baker would say, a schema of your own, explaining how yours differs from Baker's.

3   Use Mary Helen Washington's description of recurring character types in African American women's writing – the "suspended woman," the "assimilated woman," and the "emergent woman" – to analyze the female characters in Alice Walker's *The Color Purple* (1982), Zora Neale Hurston's *Their Eyes Were Watching God* (1937), or any other African American work that will lend itself to such a study. Which of these types appear in the text, and how do they relate to the meaning of the work as a whole? That is, how do these types function in the text to convey some sort of moral or lesson or theme?

4   Use such concepts from critical race theory as intersectionality, white privilege, the social construction of race, or any others you find helpful, to analyze the experience of black and/or white characters in Charles Johnson's *Middle Passage* (1990), Kate Chopin's *The Awakening* (1899), or Flannery O'Connor's "Judgment Day" (1965). How do these concepts help clarify certain aspects of characterization?

5   Using Toni Morrison's theory of the Africanist presence in white mainstream American literature (the function of black characters, of stories about black people, of representations of black speech, or of images associated with Africa or with blackness), analyze the Africanist presence in a literary text by a white American author. F. Scott Fitzgerald's "The Off-shore Pirate" (1920), "Family in the Wind" (1932), or *Tender Is the Night* (1934) might work well for this purpose.

For further reading

Awkward, Michael. *Inspiriting Influences: Tradition, Revision, and Afro-American Literature*. New York: Columbia University Press, 1989.

Bell, Bernard W. *The Folk Roots of Contemporary Afro-American Poetry*. Detroit, MI: Broadside, 1974.

———. *The Afro-American Novel and Its Tradition*. Amherst: University of Massachusetts Press, 1987.

Delgado, Richard, and Jean Stefancic. *Critical Race Theory: An Introduction*. New York: New York University Press, 2001.

Ferrante, Joan, and Prince Brown Jr., eds. *The Social Construction of Race and Ethnicity in the United States*. 2nd ed. Upper Saddle River, NJ: Prentice Hall, 2001.

Gates Jr., Henry Louis. "African American Criticism." *Redrawing the Boundaries: The Transformation of English and American Literary Studies*. Eds. Stephen Greenblatt and Giles Gunn. New York: Modern Language Association, 1992. 303–19.

hooks, bell. *Ain't I a Woman: Black Women and Feminism*. 1981. Boston: South End Press, 1999.

Hull, Gloria T., Patricia Bell Scott, and Barbara Smith, eds. *All the Women Are White, All the Blacks Are Men, But Some of Us Are Brave: Black Women's Studies.* Old Westbury, NY: Feminist Press, 1982.

Ikard, David. *Breaking the Silence: Toward a Black Male Feminist Criticism.* Baton Rouge: Louisiana State University Press, 2007.

McNeil, Elizabeth, Neal A. Lester, DoVeanna S. Fulton, and Lynette D. Myles. *Sapphire's Literary Breakthrough: Erotic Literacies, Feminist Pedagogies, Environmental Justice Perspectives.* Basingstoke and New York: Palgrave Macmillan, 2012.

Mitchell, Angelyn, ed. *Within the Circle: An Anthology of African American Literary Criticism from the Harlem Renaissance to the Present.* Durham, NC: Duke University Press, 1994.

Morrison, Toni. *Playing in the Dark: Whiteness and the Literary Imagination.* New York: Vintage, 1993.

Tate, Claudia. *Psychoanalysis and Black Novels: Desire and the Protocols of Race.* New York and Oxford: Oxford University Press, 1998.

For advanced readers

Ahad, Badia Sahar. *Freud Upside Down: African American Literature and Psychoanalytic Culture.* Urbana: University of Illinois Press, 2010.

Baker Jr., Houston A. *Blues, Ideology, and Afro-American Literature: A Vernacular Theory.* Chicago: University of Chicago Press, 1984.

Camara, Babacar. *Marxist Theory, Black/African Specificities, and Racism.* Lanham, MD: Lexington Books, 2008.

Collins, Patricia Hill. *Black Feminist Thought: Knowledge, Consciousness, and the Politics of Empowerment.* 1990. London and New York: Routledge, 2008.

Crenshaw, Kimberlé Williams, Neil Gotanda, Gary Peller, and Kendall Thomas, eds. *Critical Race Theory: The Key Writings That Formed the Movement.* New York: New Press, 1995.

Gates Jr., Henry Louis. *The Signifying Monkey: A Theory of African-American Literary Criticism.* New York: Oxford University Press, 1988.

Goldberg, David Theo, and John Solomos, eds. *A Companion to Racial and Ethnic Studies.* Malden, MA: Blackwell, 2002.

James, Joy, and T. Denean Sharply-Whiting, eds. *The Black Feminist Reader.* Malden, MA: Blackwell, 2000.

Johnson, Patrick E., and Mae G. Henderson, eds. *Black Queer Studies: A Critical Anthology.* Durham, NC and London: Duke University Press, 2005.

Nelson, Emmanuel S., ed. *Critical Essays: Gay and Lesbian Writers of Color.* New York: Haworth, 1993.

Spillers, Hortense. *Black, White, and in Color: Essays on American Literature and Culture.* Chicago: University of Chicago Press, 2003.

Notes

1 In our everyday speech, of course, most people use the word *racist* to refer both to the belief in racial superiority and to the unfair race-based attitudes and practices of any race against any other. In differentiating between racism and racialism, my effort is to foreground the enormous difference between, for example, white racist attitudes and behaviors, which are backed up by the institutionalized power structure, and African American "racist" attitudes and behaviors, which are not institutionally supported.

2 Students often have asked whether or not white people have some form of color prejudice within the white race comparable to the intra-racial racism of African Americans discussed here. Indeed, they have, and it's called *Nordicism*. Although we no longer frequently hear the word today,

Nordicism still plays a powerful role in most if not all white cultures. From a Nordicist perspective, not only is the Caucasian race genetically superior to all other races, but Nordics – Germanic peoples of Northern Europe – are the most genetically superior Caucasians: they are born with superior intelligence, physical strength, and beauty. In terms of physical appearance, the word *Nordic* is associated with persons of tall stature, long rather than round facial structure, fair skin, blond or brown hair, and light-colored eyes. For a more thorough discussion of Nordicism, see "Colonialist ideology and postcolonial identity" in Chapter 12 of this book.

3 A full discussion of mandatory sentencing for the possession of cocaine is available online at *The Sentencing Project*, http://sentencingproject/CRACKREFORM/.

4 It is interesting to observe that Muir here refers specifically to the official racial tenets of the American *scientific* community in the nineteenth century. Many readers will recall, I'm sure, that the racist ideology he describes had been present in various forms among the white American public since the days of the American colonies.

5 During the 1920s, some Harlem nightclubs had black owners, some had white, but almost all were segregated in terms of their clientele. Typically, the musicians and others who worked in the clubs were African American; the customers were white. Therefore, wealthy people like the Buchanans would have gone to Harlem nightclubs, not to mix with an interracial crowd and broaden their social experience, but to see and be seen by other wealthy or important whites.

6 As my students have reminded me, the scene of Myrtle Wilson's hit-and-run death includes "[a] pale, well dressed Negro [who] step[s] near" a police officer in order to tell what he witnessed. And the officer is eager to take this character's information (147; ch. 7). While this brief passage confers some authority on the black character, the racial atmosphere pervading the novel suggests that he wouldn't have been taken seriously had he not had light skin and worn good clothing. Indeed, one could argue that Fitzgerald portrayed him in this manner so that the officer, and the (white) reader, would have reason to believe his testimony.

Works cited

Anderson, Jervis. *This Was Harlem: A Cultural Portrait, 1900–1950*. New York: Farrar Strauss Giroux, 1982.

Baker Jr., Houston A. *Blues, Ideology, and Afro-American Literature: A Vernacular Theory*. Chicago: University of Chicago Press, 1984.

Banks, Taunya Lovell. "Two Life Stories: Reflections of One Black Woman Law Professor." *Critical Race Theory: The Key Writings That Formed the Movement*. Eds. Kimberlé Williams Crenshaw, Neil Gotanda, Gary Peller, and Kendall Thomas. New York: New Press, 1995. 329–36.

Bell Jr., Derrick A. "Brown v. Board of Education and the Interest-Convergence Dilemma." 93 *Harvard Law Review* 518 (1980). Rpt. in *Critical Race Theory: The Key Writings That Formed the Movement*. Eds. Kimberlé Williams Crenshaw, Neil Gotanda, Gary Peller, and Kendall Thomas. New York: New Press, 1995. 20–29.

——. "Racial Realism." From *Critical Race Theory: The Key Writings That Formed the Movement*. Eds. Kimberlé Williams Crenshaw, Neil Gotanda, Gary Peller, and Kendall Thomas. New York: New Press, 1995. 302–12.

Bradbury, Malcolm. "The High Cost of Immersion." *Readings on* The Great Gatsby. Ed. Katie de Koster. San Diego: Greenhaven Press, 1998. 141–46. Excerpted from Malcolm Bradbury, "Style of Life, Style of Art, and the American Novelist of the Nineteen Twenties." *The American Novel and the Nineteen Twenties*. Eds. Malcolm Bradbury and David Palmer. London: Edward Arnold, 1971.

Brown Jr., Prince. "Biology and the Social Construction of the 'Race' Concept." *The Social Construction of Race and Ethnicity in the United States*. 2nd ed. Eds. Joan Ferrante and Prince Brown Jr. Upper Saddle River, NJ: Prentice Hall, 2001. 144–50.

Bruccoli, Matthew J. "Explanatory Notes." *The Great Gatsby*. 1925. New York: Macmillan, 1992. 207–14.

——. "Preface." *The Great Gatsby*. 1925. New York: Macmillan, 1992. vii–xvi.

——. "The Text of *The Great Gatsby*." *The Great Gatsby*. 1925. New York: Macmillan, 1992. 191–94.

Christian, Barbara. "The Race for Theory." *Cultural Critique* 6 (1987): 51–63. Excerpted in *The Post-Colonial Studies Reader*. Eds. Bill Ashcroft, Gareth Griffiths, and Helen Tiffin. New York: Routledge, 1995. 457–60.

Crenshaw, Kimberlé Williams. "Mapping the Margins: Intersectionality, Identity Politics, and Violence against Women of Color." *Critical Race Theory: The Key Writings That Formed the Movement*. Eds. Kimberlé Williams Crenshaw, Neil Gotanda, Gary Peller, and Kendall Thomas. New York: New Press, 1995. 357–83.

Cullen, Countee. "Yet Do I Marvel." *Color*. New York: Harper & Row, 1925.

Decker, Jeffrey Louis. "Corruption and Anti-Immigrant Sentiments Skew a Traditional American Tale." *Readings on* The Great Gatsby. Ed. Katie de Koster. San Diego: Greenhaven Press, 1998. 121–32. Excerpted from Jeffrey Louis Decker. "Gatsby's Pristine Dream: The Diminishment of the Self-Made Man in the Tribal Twenties." *Novel: A Forum on Fiction* 28.1 (Fall 1994).

Delgado, Richard, and Jean Stefancic. *Critical Race Theory: An Introduction*. New York: New York University Press, 2001.

Douglas, Ann. *Terrible Honesty: Mongrel Manhattan in the 1920s*. New York: Farrar, Straus and Giroux, 1995.

DuBois, W. E. B. *The Souls of Black Folk: Essays and Sketches*. 1903. New York: Kraus, 1973.

Essed, Philomena. "Everyday Racism." *A Companion to Racial and Ethnic Studies*. Eds. David Theo Goldberg and John Solomon. Malden, MA: Blackwell, 2002. 202–16.

Ferrante, Joan, and Prince Brown Jr. "Introduction." *The Social Construction of Race and Ethnicity in the United States*. 2nd ed. Eds. Joan Ferrante and Prince Brown Jr. Upper Saddle River, NJ: Prentice Hall, 2001. 1–12.

——. "Introduction to Part 2." *The Social Construction of Race and Ethnicity in the United States*. 2nd ed. Eds. Joan Ferrante and Prince Brown Jr. Upper Saddle River, NJ: Prentice Hall, 2001. 113–28.

Fitzgerald, F. Scott. *The Great Gatsby*. 1925. New York: Macmillan, 1992.

Forrey, Robert. "Negroes in the Fiction of F. Scott Fitzgerald." *Phylon* 28.3 (1967): 293–98.

Gates Jr., Henry Louis. *Figures in Black: Words, Signs, and the "Racial" Self*. New York: Oxford University Press, 1987.

——. *The Signifying Monkey: A Theory of African-American Literary Criticism*. New York: Oxford University Press, 1988.

——. "The Master's Pieces: On Canon Formation and the Afro-American Tradition." *The Bounds of Race: Perspectives on Hegemony and Resistance*. Ed. Dominick LaCapra. Ithaca, NY: Cornell University Press, 1991. 17–38.

Gidley, M. "Notes on F. Scott Fitzgerald and the Passing of the Great Race." *Journal of American Studies* 7.2 (1973): 171–81.

Harding, Sandra. "Science, Race, Culture, Empire." *A Companion to Racial and Ethnic Studies*. Eds. David Theo Goldberg and John Solomon. Malden, MA: Blackwell, 2002. 217–28.

Hemingway, Ernest. *To Have and Have Not*. New York: Grosset and Dunlap, 1937.

Hughes, Langston. "Good Morning." *Montage of a Dream Deferred*. New York: Henry Holt, 1951.

Johnson, James Weldon. *Black Manhattan*. 1930. Rpt. New York: Arno Press and *The New York Times*, 1968.

Lewis, David Levering. *When Harlem Was in Vogue*. New York: Knopf, 1981.

Margolies, Alan. "The Maturing of F. Scott Fitzgerald." *Twentieth Century Literature* (Spring 1997). Available online at www.findarticles.com/p/articles/mi_m0403/is_1_43/ai_5675 (accessed July 31, 2005).

McDowell, Deborah E. "The Changing Same: Generational Connections and Black Women Novelists." *New Literary History* 18 (1987): 281–302. Rpt. in *Reading Black, Reading Feminist: A Critical Anthology*. Ed. Henry Louis Gates Jr. New York: Meridian, 1990. 91–115.

Morrison, Toni. *The Bluest Eye*. New York: Holt, Rinehart, and Winston, 1970.

——. *Playing in the Dark: Whiteness and the Literary Imagination*. New York: Vintage, 1993.

Muir, Donal E. "Race: The Mythic Root of Racism." *Sociological Inquiry* 63.3 (August 1993). Rpt. in *Critical Race Theory: The Concept of "Race" in Natural and Social Science*. Ed. E. Nathaniel Gates. New York: Garland, 1997. 93–104.

O'Meara, Lauraleigh. *Lost City: Fitzgerald's New York*. New York: Routledge, 2002.

Roberts, John W. "The African American Animal Trickster as Hero." *Redefining American Literary History*. Eds. A. LaVonne Brown Ruoff and Jerry W. Ward Jr. New York: Modern Language Association, 1990. 97–114.

Sollors, Werner. "Ethnicity and Race." Drawn from his introduction to *Theories of Ethnicity: A Critical Reader*. 1997. Rpt. in *A Companion to Racial and Ethnic Studies*. Eds. David Theo Goldberg and John Solomon. Malden, MA: Blackwell, 2002. 97–104.

Stovall, Tyler. *Paris Noir: African Americans in the City of Light*. Boston, MA: Houghton Mifflin, 1996.

Washington, Mary Helen, ed. *Black-Eyed Susans: Classic Stories by and about Black Women*. Garden City, NY: Doubleday, 1977.

——. "Teaching Black-Eyed Susans: An Approach to the Study of Black Women Writers." *All the Women Are White, All the Blacks Are Men, but Some of Us Are Brave: Black Women's Studies*. Eds. Gloria T. Hull, Patricia Bell Scott, and Barbara Smith. Old Westbury, NY: Feminist Press, 1982.

Wikipedia. "Charles Becker." http://en.wikipedia.org/wiki/Charles_Becker. n.d.

——. "New York Herald Tribune." http://enwikipedia.org/wiki/New_York_Herald_ Tribune. n.d.

Wildman, Stephanie M. *Privilege Revealed: How Invisible Preference Undermines America*. New York: New York University Press, 1996.

12 Postcolonial criticism

Perhaps one of the most important abilities critical theory develops in us is the ability to see connections where we didn't know they existed: for example, connections between our personal psychological conflicts and the way we interpret a poem, between the ideologies we've internalized and the literary works we find aesthetically pleasing, between a nation's political climate and what its intellectuals consider "great" literature, and so forth. Most of the critical theories we've studied so far have encouraged us to make connections along one or more of these lines. Postcolonial criticism is particularly effective at helping us see connections among all the domains of our experience – the psychological, ideological, social, political, intellectual, and aesthetic – in ways that show us just how inseparable these categories are in our lived experience of ourselves and our world. Indeed, that's why postcolonial criticism asks us to think of ourselves and others in terms of what it calls cultural difference: the ways in which race, class, sex, gender, sexual orientation, religion, cultural beliefs, and customs combine to form individual identity. In addition, postcolonial theory offers us a framework for examining the similarities among all critical theories that deal with human oppression, such as Marxism; feminism; gay, lesbian, and queer theories; and African American theory.

In fact, because postcolonial criticism defines formerly colonized peoples as any population that has been subjected to the political and economic domination of another population, you may see postcolonial critics draw examples from the literary works of African Americans as well as from, for example, the literature of Aboriginal Australians or the formerly colonized population of India. However, the tendency of postcolonial criticism to focus on global issues, on comparisons and contrasts among various peoples, means that it is up to the individual members of specific populations to develop their own body of criticism on the history, traditions, and interpretation of their own literature. Of course, this is precisely what African American critics have been doing for some time, long before postcolonial criticism emerged as a powerful force in literary studies in the early 1990s.

To place postcolonial criticism in a historical context of its own, however, let's take a minute and think back to our high school history classes. As most of us can recall from our high school education, European domination of the New World began in the late fifteenth century. Spain, France, England, Portugal, and the Netherlands were the main contenders for the plunder of natural and human resources, and over the next few centuries European empires extended themselves around the globe. During the nineteenth century Britain emerged as the largest imperial[1] power, and by the turn of the twentieth century the British Empire ruled one quarter of the earth's surface, including India, Australia, New Zealand, Canada, Ireland, and significant holdings in Africa, the West Indies, South America, the Middle East, and Southeast Asia. British colonial domination continued until the end of World War II, when India gained independence in 1947, and other colonies gradually followed suit. By 1980 Britain had lost all but a few of its colonial holdings.

Although postcolonial criticism didn't become a major force in literary studies until the early 1990s, the cultural analysis of colonialism on which it draws has played an important role in anticolonial political movements everywhere and took its place as a field of intellectual inquiry when colonial regimes began to topple after World War II. As a domain within literary studies, postcolonial criticism is both a subject matter and a theoretical framework. As a subject matter, postcolonial criticism analyzes literature produced by cultures that developed in response to colonial domination, from the first point of colonial contact to the present.[2] (You may recall reading postcolonial literature under the heading of "Commonwealth literature," which it was called until the 1980s.) Some of this literature was written by the colonizers. Much more of it was written, and is being written, by colonized and formerly colonized peoples. As a subject matter, any analysis of a postcolonial literary work, regardless of the theoretical framework used, might be called postcolonial criticism. For English majors, of course, postcolonial criticism focuses on the literature of cultures that developed in response to British colonial domination because English departments study, for the most part, literatures written in English.

However, as a theoretical framework, and this is our primary concern here, postcolonial criticism seeks to understand the operations – politically, socially, culturally, and psychologically – of colonialist and anticolonialist ideologies. For example, a good deal of postcolonial criticism analyzes the ideological forces that, on the one hand, pressed the colonized to internalize the colonizers' values and, on the other hand, promoted the resistance of colonized peoples against their oppressors, a resistance that is as old as colonialism itself. And as we'll see, because colonialist and anticolonialist ideologies can be present in any literary text, a work doesn't have to be categorized as postcolonial for us to be able to use postcolonial criticism to analyze it.

Colonialist ideology and postcolonial identity

That so many peoples formerly colonized by Britain speak English, write in English, use English in their schools and universities, and conduct government business in

English, in addition to the local languages they may use at home, is an indication of the residual effect of colonial domination on their cultures. In fact, the dynamic psychological and social interplay between what ex-colonial populations consider their native, indigenous, precolonial cultures and the British culture that was imposed on them constitutes a large portion of the field of study for postcolonial critics. For postcolonial cultures include both a merger of and antagonism between the culture of the colonized and that of the colonizer, which, at this point in time, are difficult to identify and separate into discrete entities, so complete was the British intrusion into the government, education, cultural values, and daily lives of its colonial subjects.

In short, although the colonizers retreated and left the lands they had invaded in the hands of those they had colonized, decolonization often has been confined largely to the removal of British military forces and government officials. What has been left behind is a deeply embedded *cultural colonization*: the inculcation of a British system of government and education, British culture, and British values that denigrate the culture, morals, and even physical appearance of formerly subjugated peoples. Thus, ex-colonials often were left with a psychological "inheritance" of a negative self-image and alienation from their own indigenous cultures, which had been forbidden or devalued for so long that much precolonial culture has been lost.

Given that a good deal of postcolonial criticism addresses the problem of cultural identity as it is represented in postcolonial literature, let's take a closer look at the issue of postcolonial identity. In order to do so, however, we must first understand colonialist ideology, the various reactions to which, in large part, constitute the origins of postcolonial identity for individual human beings as well as for communities. As we begin to use the following concepts, however, we must remember that we are applying generalizations to groups of people that differ greatly in terms of their history and experience before, during, and after colonial rule. Thus, such postcolonial terms as *unhomeliness* and *mimicry*, which we'll discuss shortly, are only "a helpful shorthand, because they do not allow for the differences between distinct kinds of colonial situations, or the workings of class, gender, [geographical] location, race, caste or ideology among people whose lives have been restructured by colonial rule" (Loomba 19).

Colonialist ideology, often referred to as *colonialist discourse* to mark its relationship to the language in which colonialist thinking was expressed, was based on the colonizers' assumption of their own superiority, which they contrasted with the alleged inferiority of native (indigenous) peoples, the original inhabitants of the lands they invaded. The colonizers believed that only their own Anglo-European culture was civilized, sophisticated, or, as postcolonial critics put it, *metropolitan*. Therefore, native peoples were defined as savage, backward, and undeveloped. Because their technology was more highly advanced, the colonizers believed that their whole culture was more highly advanced, and they ignored or swept aside the religions, customs, and codes of behavior of the peoples they subjugated. So the colonizers saw themselves at the center of the world; the colonized were at the margins. The colonizers saw themselves as the embodiment of what a human being should be, the proper "self"; native peoples were considered "other," different, and therefore inferior to the point of being less than fully human.

This practice of judging all who are different as less than fully human is called *othering*, and it divides the world between "us" (the "civilized") and "them" (the "others," the "savages"). When Europeans first arrived in the "New World," for example, land that wasn't occupied by Christians was considered "empty land" and, therefore, theirs for the taking. In other words, native inhabitants of these lands were so othered by the colonizers that they didn't officially exist. Native inhabitants were certainly physically present – indeed, European conquerors often used them as slaves, and European missionaries arrived to Christianize them – but as non-Christian "savages," they didn't count. The "savage" was usually considered evil (the demonic other) as well as inferior. But sometimes the "savage" was perceived as possessing a "primitive" beauty or nobility born of a closeness to nature (the *exotic other*). In either case, however, the "savage" remained other and, therefore, not fully human.

Today, this attitude – the use of European culture as the standard to which all other cultures are negatively contrasted – is called *Eurocentrism*. A common example of Eurocentrism in literary studies is the longstanding philosophy of so-called *universalism*. British, European, and, later, American cultural standard-bearers judged all literature in terms of its "universality": to be considered a great work, a literary text had to have "universal" characters and themes. However, whether or not a text's characters and themes were considered "universal" depended on whether or not they resembled those from European literature. Thus, the assumption was that European ideas, ideals, and experience were universal, that is, the standard for all humankind.

An example of Eurocentric language can be seen in the term I used earlier – *New World* – to denote the very old worlds of the Americas, a land which was "new" only to the Europeans. Similar examples of Eurocentric language can be seen in the terms *First World*, *Second World*, *Third World*, and *Fourth World* to refer to, respectively, (1) Britain, Europe, and the United States; (2) the white populations of Canada, Australia, New Zealand, and southern Africa (and, for some theorists, the former Soviet bloc); (3) the technologically developing nations, such as India and those of Africa, Central and South America, and Southeast Asia; and (4) the indigenous populations on every continent who were subjugated by white settlers and are marginalized today by the majority culture that surrounds them, such as Native Americans and Aboriginal Australians (and, for some theorists, nonindigenous populations who have the status of racial minorities in First World countries, such as African Americans). Although these four "worlds" are commonly referred to today, and we'll use these terms in this chapter, we should remain aware of their

Eurocentric implications. Such language makes sense only if history begins with Europe and is organized in terms of European colonial conquest. It ignores the existence of earlier worlds – such as those of Greece, Egypt, Africa, the Middle East, China, and the Americas – and it privileges European military conquest as the primary means of organizing world history.

Orientalism is an example of Eurocentric othering, analyzed by Edward Said (pronounced sah-eed), which has been practiced in Europe, Britain, and America. Its purpose is to produce a positive national self-definition for Western nations by contrast with Eastern nations on which the West projects all the negative characteristics it doesn't want to believe exist among its own people. Thus the Chinese or the Arabs, or whatever Asian or Middle Eastern population is politically convenient, are defined as cruel, sneaky, evil, cunning, dishonest, given to sexual promiscuity and perversion, and the like. (Think of the cruel, deceitful Arab merchant in Mary Shelley's *Frankenstein*, published in 1818, who is saved from prison by the young DeLacey, a European, whom the Arab subsequently betrays.) Citizens of the West then define themselves, in contrast to the imaginary "oriental" they've created, as kind, straightforward, good, upright, honest, and moral. In short, the "oriental" is an invention of the West, by contrast to whom it has been able to define itself positively and justify any acts of military or economic aggression it has found advantageous.

Finally, *Nordicism* is an ideology that might be seen as an example of Eurocentric othering taken to its logical extreme. While many students have never heard the term *Nordicism*, it plays a powerful role in most if not all white cultures. From a Nordicist perspective, not only is the Caucasian race genetically superior to all other races, but Nordics – Germanic peoples of Northern Europe – are the most genetically superior Caucasians: they are born with superior intelligence, physical strength, and beauty. Although Nordicists sometimes disagree on which countries should be considered Nordic, most agree that Norway, Sweden, Denmark, and Iceland belong to this group. Our nationality, however, is not important in determining our membership in this "superior race." Human beings have been migrating around the globe so much for so long that our place of birth, or even our great-great-great grandparents' place of birth, is not a reliable indicator of our racial heritage. The only factor that can be counted on to reveal our racial makeup is our physical appearance. Specifically, the word *Nordic* is associated with persons of tall stature, long rather than round facial structure, fair skin, blond or brown hair, and light-colored eyes. If we have this combination of physical features, it is assumed that we are of Nordic ancestry and, therefore, genetically superior to all others. The US Immigration Act of 1924, which gave immigrants from Northern Europe favored status while restricting the immigration of peoples from Southern and Eastern Europe, is a well-known example of the Nordicism that pervaded the United States during the 1920s. Another example of Nordicism is Hitler's Aryanism, or master-race theory, which fueled the Holocaust during the late 1930s and early 1940s. Nordicism is still alive and well throughout the world today in many neo-Nazi, white nationalist, and white supremacist groups. And I think it's reasonable to argue that it still plays a role, even if it's an unconscious role, in our everyday lives, for instance in the idealization of "fair-haired boys" and "golden girls" and in the staying power of blond, blue-eyed Barbie dolls.

Colonialist ideology, which is inherently Eurocentric, was a pervasive force in the British schools established in the colonies to inculcate British culture and values in the indigenous peoples and thereby forestall rebellion. It's difficult to rebel against a system or a people one has been programmed, over several generations, to consider superior. The plan was extremely successful and resulted in the creation of *colonial subjects*, colonized persons who did not resist colonial subjugation because they were taught to believe in British superiority and, therefore, in their own inferiority. Many of these individuals tried to imitate their colonizers, as much as possible, in dress, speech, behavior, and lifestyle. Postcolonial critics refer to this phenomenon as *mimicry*, and it reflects both the desire of colonized individuals to be accepted by the colonizing culture and the shame experienced by colonized individuals concerning their own culture, which they were programmed to see as inferior. Postcolonial theorists often describe the colonial subject as having a *double consciousness* or *double vision*, in other words, a consciousness or a way of perceiving the world that is divided between two antagonistic cultures: that of the colonizer and that of the indigenous community.[3]

Double consciousness often produced an unstable sense of self, which was heightened by the forced migration colonialism frequently caused, for example, from the rural farm or village to the city in search of employment. (Forced migration, either as a quest for employment, including indentured servitude, or as the result of enslavement, scattered large numbers of peoples around the globe, and large populations of their descendants have remained in the *diaspora*, or separated from their original homeland.) This feeling of being caught between cultures, of belonging to neither rather than to both, of finding oneself arrested in a psychological limbo that results not merely from some individual psychological disorder but from the trauma of the cultural displacement within which one lives, is referred to by Homi Bhabha and others as *unhomeliness*. Being "unhomed" is not the same as being homeless. To be unhomed is to feel not at home even in your own home because you are not at home in yourself: your cultural identity crisis has made you a psychological refugee, so to speak.

Double consciousness and unhomeliness persist in decolonized nations today. Among the tasks formerly colonized peoples face is the rejection of colonialist ideology, which defined them as inferior, and the reclamation of their precolonial past. Both tasks involve many complex problems of interest to postcolonial critics. For example, in order to reject colonialist ideology and embrace their precolonial cultures, some native authors, such as Kenyan writer Ngugi wa Thiong'o, write in their own local languages. When they do so, however, they face the difficulty of surviving in a publishing industry, both in their own countries and internationally, that requires the use of English. The use of native languages often requires native writers to put forth the double effort of writing in their indigenous languages and then translating their work into English or having it translated.

On the other hand, many indigenous writers from former British colonies prefer to write in English because that is the language in which they first learned to write. As Nigerian writer Chinua Achebe observes, "[F]or me there is no other choice. I have been given the language and I intend to use it" (*Morning Yet on Creation Day* 62). Some also argue that English provides a common language for the various indigenous peoples within Third and Fourth World nations, who speak a number of different local languages, to communicate with one another. And they point out that English, as a world language, facilitates the emergence of those nations into global politics and economics.

Another problem that complicates the desire to reclaim a precolonial past is that it is not always easy to discover that past. As we noted earlier, much precolonial culture has been lost over many generations of colonial domination. In addition, many postcolonial theorists argue that, even had there been no colonization, the ancient culture would have changed by now: no culture stands still, frozen in time. Furthermore, most cultures are changed by cross-cultural contact, often through military invasion. For example, ancient Celtic culture was changed by the Roman legions who occupied the British Isles. And Anglo-Saxon culture was changed by the many generations of French rule that followed the Norman conquest of that same territory in the eleventh century. By the same token, the precolonial cultures of colonized peoples influenced European culture. For example, Picasso's art was greatly influenced by his study of African masks. Therefore, many postcolonial theorists argue that postcolonial identity is necessarily a dynamic, constantly evolving *hybrid* of native and colonial cultures. Moreover, they assert that this *hybridity*, or *syncretism* as it's sometimes called, does not consist of a stalemate between two warring cultures but is rather a productive, exciting, positive force in a shrinking world that is itself becoming more and more culturally hybrid. This view encourages ex-colonials to embrace the multiple and often conflicting aspects of the blended culture that is theirs and that is an indelible fact of history.

It is important to note, however, that these arguments don't take into account the need of formerly colonized peoples to rediscover and affirm their precolonial civilizations for the very good reason that the colonizers told them they didn't have any precolonial civilizations. Before colonization, the colonizers claimed, native peoples lived barbarically, without any systems of government, religion, or rational customs. Or if colonizers acknowledged that a native culture existed, they claimed that such cultures were not worth sustaining in the face of the "superior" civilization offered by the Europeans. Many ex-colonials therefore feel they must assert a native culture both to avoid being swamped by the Western culture so firmly planted on their soil and to recuperate their national image in their own eyes and in the eyes of others. This emphasis on indigenous culture, especially when accompanied by the attempt to eliminate Western influences, is called *nativism* or *nationalism*. From a nativist perspective, there is a big difference between a culture changing over time and a people being cut off from their culture.

If you've read Chapter 4, "Feminist criticism," you've probably noticed by now, as many postcolonial critics have, a number of similarities in the theoretical issues that concern feminist and postcolonial critics. For example, patriarchal subjugation of women is analogous to colonial subjugation of indigenous populations. And the resultant devaluation of women and colonized peoples poses very similar problems for both groups in terms of achieving an independent personal and group identity; gaining access to political power and economic opportunities; and finding ways to think, speak, and create that are not dominated by the ideology of the oppressor.

These parallels between feminist and postcolonial concerns underscore the double oppression suffered by postcolonial women, often referred to as *double colonization*. For they are the victims of both colonialist ideology, which devalues them because of their race and cultural ancestry, and patriarchal ideology, which devalues them because of their sex. Sadly, postcolonial women have suffered patriarchal oppression not only at the hands of colonialists, but within their own patriarchal cultures as well. Gender inequities are often particularly visible in rural communities where women are expected to do most or all of the agricultural work, in addition to the considerable work associated with taking care of homes and families, without compensation comparable to the familial authority, community leadership roles, or economic opportunities afforded their male counterparts.

It is clear, nevertheless, that postcolonial women are very capable of effective leadership when circumstances offer the opportunity. For example, much of the grassroots resistance to the destruction of local environments in the Third World was started by village women and consists today mostly of village women. The Chipko Movement in India, for instance – which grew from a spontaneous protest by local women in 1973 against the continued and excessive felling of local trees for commercial purposes – employs the strategies of nonviolent resistance to prevent the deforestation of large wooded regions critical to the survival of the rural environment and of the Indian people who inhabit it. And the Green Belt Movement – begun in Kenya in 1977 by Wangari Maathai to restore, seedling by seedling, those areas already suffering the dreadful effects of deforestation – has spread throughout her country and gained international influence.[4] When it comes, however, to the distribution of financial opportunities, international aid to technologically developing countries has tended to reinforce the patriarchal belief that women are naturally less capable than men by giving the money, the machinery, and the training to men alone, even in Africa, where "women farmers produce 65–80 percent of all agricultural produce, yet do not own the land they work, and are consistently by-passed by aid programs and 'development' projects" (McClintock 298). So the double colonization of women continues. As Anne McClintock observes, "In a world where women do two-thirds of the world's work, earn 10 percent of the world's income, and own less than 1 percent of the world's property, the promise of 'post-colonialism'" – that is, the promise of a better life for all once the colonizers were gone – "has been a history of hopes postponed" (298).

Foundational postcolonial debates

Perhaps you have noticed that a good deal of the material we've discussed so far involves issues that seem to be under debate. For example, how important is it that postcolonial peoples seek lost evidence of their precolonial past? How much of their precolonial past is really available to them? Should postcolonial authors write in English, in their native languages, or in both? What should a postcolonial writer do who was raised with English as his or her first language? Is hybridity, as postcolonial theorists define the term, a realistic alternative for postcolonial individuals who feel unhomed? And so forth.

Many postcolonial issues, like many of the theoretical issues we've discussed in other chapters, are matters of some disagreement among those who study the field. But before we move on to issues that are of somewhat more recent origin in postcolonial studies, let's take a brief look at three of the important debates that have helped form the field of postcolonial theory from the beginning: Which peoples – and, therefore, which literary works – should be considered postcolonial? Is postcolonial theory in danger of marginalizing the real concerns of postcolonial peoples? Finally, is postcolonial criticism in danger of marginalizing the work of postcolonial writers?

As you may have noticed, our focus in this chapter, so far, on the political, social, cultural, and psychological colonization of indigenous peoples has limited our discussion to *invader colonies* – colonies established among nonwhite peoples through the force of British arms, such as those established in India, Africa, the West Indies, South America, the Middle East, and Southeast Asia – for no one debates the inclusion of literature from these cultures in postcolonial literary studies. There is also a general consensus that the United States and Ireland are not postcolonial nations, the first because it has been independent for so long and has itself colonized others, the second because it has long been an integral part of British culture (though some Irish people, especially in Northern Ireland, would surely disagree with this assessment, and many postcolonial critics cite the work of Irish poet W. B. Yeats as emblematic of anticolonialist nationalism). However, there has been much debate among postcolonial critics concerning whether or not the literature of *white settler colonies* – specifically, those established in Canada, Australia, New Zealand, and southern Africa – should be included in the study of postcolonial literature.

Those who argue that the term *postcolonial* should be reserved for Third and Fourth World writers observe that white settler cultures share a tremendous common ground with Britain, including race, language, and culture. These colonies viewed Britain as the "mother country," not as an imperial invader, and they were treated very differently from the nonwhite colonies Britain controlled. For example, white settler colonies were permitted a good deal of self-government and were granted Dominion status (political autonomy within the British Commonwealth) without having to take up arms to achieve it. Indeed, it was white settlers who, as Britain did elsewhere, subjugated nonwhite indigenous peoples and took their land and natural resources. In other words, these theorists argue, the inclusion of white settler cultures under the postcolonial rubric ignores the enormous difference race has played in the history of colonization and continues to play today in the racist attitudes that keep Third and Fourth World peoples economically oppressed.

On the other hand, theorists who believe white settler cultures should be included under the rubric *postcolonial* argue that the foundational concept of post-colonial criticism is anticolonial resistance, and the literatures of white settler cul-tures have a good deal to teach us about the complexities of anticolonial resistance because their own resistance to cultural obliteration by an overwhelming British cultural presence has occurred without the help of a clear distinction between colonized and colonizer, a distinction that nonwhite invader colonies have been able to count on. In other words, white colonial subjects experience – in a subtler, less clearly demarcated form – the same double consciousness experienced by nonwhite colonial subjects. From this perspective, we can't simply ignore the anticolonialist literature produced by the Second World while we uncritically assume that all the literature produced by nonwhite postcolonial peoples is necessarily a literature of resistance.

Another debate that has engaged the attention of postcolonial theorists involves the concern that postcolonial theory is itself in danger of marginalizing the voices of those it wishes to bring into the spotlight. For one thing, most postcolonial theorists – including those born in formerly colonized nations, many of whom were educated at European universities and live abroad – belong to an intellectual elite, an academic ruling class that has, it would seem, little in common with *subalterns*, or people of inferior status, that is, with the majority of poor, exploited ex-colonial peoples who are the object of their concern.

Furthermore, postcolonial criticism's analysis of the problem of cultural iden-tity – specifically, its focus on the fluid, dynamic, hybrid forms of cultural identity – is largely a product of the poststructuralist, deconstructive theory of the First World. As you may recall from Chapter 8, deconstruction defines the self as a fragmented pastiche of numerous "selves" within a world that has no stable meaning and no value beyond that which we assign it. Such a theory is extremely helpful in allowing us to understand how we construct the illusion of our own identity out of the ideological materials provided by our culture. And deconstruction has been used effectively to reveal the Eurocentrism of the Western philosophy and literature that have been imposed on the rest of the world. However, it is understandable that nations struggling to define their cultural identity might not find this destabilizing theory very attractive and might mistrust Western theories in general, having suffered Western domination for so long.

Finally, because postcolonial criticism can be used to interpret literature in the Western literary canon, some theorists have been long concerned that it will become just one more way to read the same First World authors we've been reading for years, rather than a method that brings to the fore the works of post-colonial writers. Happily, it seems unlikely that this fear will be realized, given the international success of such postcolonial authors as, to name but a few, Chinua Achebe (Nigeria), Salman Rushdie (India), Jamaica Kincaid (Antigua, West Indies), Bessie Head (South Africa), Bharati Mukherjee (India), Tsitsi Dangarembga (Zimbabwe), Leslie Marmon Silko (Laguna Pueblo tribe, United States), Flora Nwapa (Nigeria), Zakes Mda (South Africa), Edward Kamau Brathwaite (Barbados), Arundhati Roy (India), Linda Hogan (Chickasaw Nation, United States), and Ngugi wa Thiong'o (Kenya).

Indeed, the Nobel Prize for literature was won by Wole Soyinka (Nigeria) in 1986, by Nadine Gordimer (South Africa) in 1991, by Derek Walcott (St. Lucia, West Indies) in 1992, by Toni Morrison (United States) in 1993,[5] by V. S. Naipaul (Trinidad) in 2001, and by J. M. Coetzee (South Africa) in 2003. And there has been such a great increase in the number of colleges offering courses in postcolonial literature that the field has become an international staple.

Nevertheless, it's not unreasonable to be apprehensive that postcolonial literature will be "colonized," that is, interpreted according to European norms and standards. For cultural Eurocentrism still dominates literary education and literary criticism the world over.

As you think about all of these issues, keep in mind that the phrase *foundational debates* does not have the same meaning as the phrase *former debates*. Many of the arguments that helped form the foundation of postcolonial thinking are still vital issues today. C. Michael Hall and Hazel Tucker's observation that "the central question – what constitutes a postcolonial text – remains a contentious issue" (1) can be said of much of postcolonial theory's foundational philosophy. This willingness to see the core elements of one's field as questions rather than as premises, or "givens," is surely one of the reasons why so many postcolonial theorists and literary critics continue to respond to our rapidly changing world with such insight and personal engagement.

Globalization and the "end" of postcolonial theory

Perhaps one of the most interesting developments engaging the attention of post-colonial critics today is what some economists, among others, consider the out-dated quality of the field of postcolonial theory as a whole. Colonialism, the argument goes, ended, by and large, shortly after World War II. And the efforts of formerly colonized peoples to create their own governments, establish their own cultural heritage, and the like, have been overshadowed by – or perhaps more accurately, absorbed within – the worldwide spread of international culture and global economics that have affected *all* peoples, whether postcolonial or not. As you've probably noticed, cultural production – for example, music, movies, literary works, fashion, and a variety of consumer products – has gone global due largely to the continually increasing global access to the Internet and other forms of electronic information and communication. Indeed, the geographic borders that separate the nations of the world today are becoming, in many ways, less important than the Internet capabilities that connect the peoples of the world.

Furthermore, this kind of cultural *globalization* – or worldwide spread of technolo-gies, products, and ideas – is due largely to the globalization of economics, which can be defined as the worldwide spread of capitalism with minimal interference from national governments. And how did the globalization of economics come about? It was created by the success of multinational corporations such as General Electric, ExxonMobil, British Petroleum, and Toyota.[6] For multinational corpora-tions, with those based in the United States leading the way, develop technology and manufacture products in countries that never before housed these industries and, in turn, sell products in countries that never before had markets for them. As their spokespersons point out, multinational corporations contribute to the econo-mies of developing nations by building local factories and other kinds of work-places, by creating local jobs, and by training local workers. So, they conclude, if we want to talk about the transformation of culture and the development of individual identity in the world today – whether we believe these changes are for good or ill – we need to realize that the postcolonial world is long gone, and with it has gone the usefulness of postcolonial theory. In short, the argument goes, in an age of globalization we need a theory of globalization, perhaps along the lines of international relations theory, but we don't need postcolonial theory.

The question must be raised, however: Why does globalization mean that post-colonial theory is no longer relevant? Is this conclusion an accurate one? It's true that colonialism is no longer practiced as it was between the late fifteenth and mid-twentieth centuries, through the direct, overt administration of governors and educators from the colonizing country. Today, nevertheless, the same kind of poli-tical, economic, and cultural subjugation of vulnerable regions occurs, through different means, at the hands of the very multinational corporations whose success has called into question the relevance of postcolonial criticism. These means include what postcolonial critics call *cultural imperialism* and *neocolonialism*.

You're probably already aware of some examples of *cultural imperialism*, sometimes called *cultural colonization,* although you might not have heard these two terms before. Cultural imperialism is often a result of the kind of economic domination frequently imposed by multinational corporations. It consists of the "takeover" of one culture by another: the food, clothing, customs, recreation, and values of the economically dominant culture increasingly replace those of the economically vulnerable culture until the latter appears to be a kind of imitation of the former. American cultural imperialism has been one of the most pervasive forms of this phenomenon, as we see American fashions, movies, music, sports, fast food, consumer products, and definitions of personal beauty and success squeeze out regional and national cultural traditions all over the world. Recently, I heard some of my students joking that no one need worry about a single country "taking over the world" because Coca Cola and Nike have already done it. I don't think they realized it, but they were talking about signs of cultural imperialism.

Perhaps less obvious to many of us, but certainly more wide-ranging in its worldwide effects, is the fact that corporate globalization frequently operates as a form of *neocolonialism*. *Neo* – that is, *new* – colonialism consists of the exploitation of the cheap labor available in developing countries, often at the expense of those countries' own struggling businesses, cultural traditions, and ecological well-being. Multinational corporations may form partnerships with the governments of the nations into which they want to expand, or they may gain the support of the relatively wealthy, and relatively few, individuals who will benefit financially from their corporate presence. But the subaltern majority of the country's inhabitants do not necessarily derive any benefit. Indeed, even when a multinational corporation partners with a national government, it doesn't mean that the nation's subaltern inhabitants or natural resources are protected. For example, an entire community, or several communities, may be driven from their homes, farms, and fisheries – driven away only to add to the population of slum dwellers in the big cities – by a corporation's need for land or for new mega-dams to create waterpower. And while jobs are frequently created, child labor is often used, and whether the workers are children or adults, they usually receive low pay, work long hours, and endure unsafe working conditions. Sometimes natural resources – in the form of timber, oil, minerals, and precious metals – are themselves the desired commodities to be "harvested" and taken away. Sometimes natural resources – in the form of soil, water, air, animals, and vegetation – are imperiled or destroyed by the pollution, soil erosion, and reduction of animal habitat that result from industrial operations. To give you an idea of the scope of this problem, let's take a brief look at three representative examples – there are hundreds more – of the damage often done by unregulated or under-regulated multinational corporate activity in Third World nations. Our first example comes from the global oil industry, our second from the global garment industry, and our third from global agribusiness, which consists of the wide-scale, high-tech, commercial production and distribution of agricultural crops and machinery.

In the Niger Delta region of Nigeria, Royal Dutch Shell, an Anglo-Dutch oil company, has destroyed farmers' lands, forestland, and fish populations through the unchecked dumping of petroleum waste, frequent oil spills due to corroded pipelines, and natural gas emissions that result from oil extraction. Local residents receive no benefit whatsoever from the presence of the oil industry on their land, but they are the ones who suffer the consequences of that presence: their air is no longer fit to breathe, much of their land will no longer produce agricultural crops, the local fish population has all but disappeared, and their water is no longer drinkable. As Amnesty International points out, this kind of pollution and environmental damage, which has been ongoing since the 1950s, has resulted in human rights violations, including the violation even of the local residents' right to their own food and water.[7] A different kind of ongoing devastation has been occurring in Bangladesh, where garments are manufactured in unsafe buildings under dangerous working conditions by underpaid local workers, many in their teens and early twenties, for such American brands as Wal-Mart, Sears, and the Gap; such British brands as Bonmarché and Primark; and such European brands as Mango, C&A, and Benetton. At least 112 workers, unable to escape their burning factory, were killed in the infamous Tazreen factory fire on November 24, 2012, and on April 24, 2013, over 1,000 workers were killed when the poorly constructed, eight-story Rana Plaza, which housed five garment factories, collapsed. These are just two in a long series of disasters related to the garment industry in Bangladesh.[8] Finally, Nestlé, the multinational Swiss food and beverage company, has a decades-long history of destroying indigenous dairy industries in such countries as Colombia, Sri Lanka, and the Philippines by replacing locally made dairy products with the mass distribution of Nestlé's processed, often imported, milk and milk substitutes. When local fresh-milk dairy farms are thereby eliminated, the prices of Nestlé's milk products go up. In tandem with the squeezing out of local dairy farmers is the company's fraudulent marketing campaign to convince Third World mothers to feed their babies Nestlé's infant formula instead of breast milk. The success of this campaign has resulted in hundreds of thousands of infant deaths from infectious diseases caused by the necessity of mixing the formula with local water and by the absence of the immunities that would have been provided by breast milk. Nestlé's unethical practices have resulted in a longstanding global boycott of their products, but the company's response to this outcry remains grossly inadequate.[9]

As these examples illustrate, the well-being of corporate profits, not of the local peoples or the local environment, is the only real concern of neocolonialist multinational corporations. Indeed, when the need arises, neocolonialist corporate

enterprise is supported by bribery (officials at every level of government, if necessary, paid by a corporation to support its interests) and by overt or covert armed
intervention (sometimes in the form of financing local police and military troops to
protect corporate political interests, sometimes in the form of enlisting military aid
from the Western power most closely aligned with the corporation's concerns).
Although there is a decades-long history of organized grassroots local resistance to
the destruction wreaked by neocolonialist corporate enterprise,[10] there is big money
to be made in this game, and the major players are too powerful to be bound by any
rules of fair play.

In short, what many multinational corporations, and the governments with
which they partner, refer to as their "development" projects – they are "developing" poor regions by modernizing them – are anything but for the poor people
who inhabit those regions. Clearly, the political, economic, and cultural realities of
colonialist exploitation and postcolonial resistance have taken new forms, but they
are still with us. The danger in abandoning the insights offered by postcolonial
theory is that it will become increasingly difficult to recognize, and therefore to
respond to, these realities.

Postcolonial theory and global tourism

As you were reading the previous section and thinking about multinational corporations,
did names like *Disney* or *Club Med* or *Viking River Cruises* occur to you? Probably
not. We don't tend to associate the rather intimidating, stern-sounding phrase
multinational corporation with images of clear blue skies, sparkling white beaches,
spotless putting greens, or smiling people in sports clothes enjoying themselves at a
beautiful vacation spot. Nevertheless tourism has become an industry, that industry
has gone global, and it isn't always just "fun in the sun" – at least not for everyone
involved. Think about it. In any given instance, who benefits from and who is hurt
by the development of a tourist resort?

Well, surely there are many times when few or none are hurt while many people
benefit from tourism, for example in the case of locally controlled tourist attractions – such as lovely lakefronts, forested parks, interesting historical sites, camp-
grounds, and the like – all open to and affordable by the general public. In such
cases, local businesses receive a boost, local economies are supported or improved,
and local inhabitants are benefitted. For example, local residents can themselves
spend leisure time locally, can take jobs created by local tourism, or can start their
own small tourist-related businesses.

In contrast, many global tourist attractions – geared to an international tourist
market and often supported by foreign investors in conjunction with local bankers,
local real-estate companies, or other elite local financiers – are beyond both the
influence and the pocketbooks of the general local population. "[E]lites in

developing countries consistently gain disproportionately more [than the general population] from tourism development, as for example through soaring land values and from favouritism in the participation in investments from abroad" (M. Smith, cited in Jaakson, 170). Thus, while "[i]ncome may increase overall in a country ... the wealth gap may remain the same or may even widen" (Jaakson, 170). Many kinds of global tourism fit this model, from those that market the grandeur of natural wonders or the beauty of scenic locales, to those that market the range of large wildlife available for shooting with camera or gun, to those that market the perceived "exotic" quality of the local inhabitants and their cultures. Of course, there are many varieties of global tourism,[11] and each has its history of conflicts, compromises, and partnerships with national governments and with the local peoples whose homelands – for good or ill – have become either mass-market tourist destinations or upscale vacation locations for the wealthy elite.

Unfortunately, it is often the case that local peoples are denied access to their ancestral forests, jungles, and pasturelands to make way for paying tourists, and many rural peoples have been simply evicted from their homes and their traditional livelihoods to make way for tourist accommodations, which often include luxury hotels and condominiums built near, if not within, tourist attractions. Of course, a struggling economy makes a developing nation vulnerable to such exploitation, and its technologically undeveloped, biologically diverse lands make it attractive to those who would profit by that vulnerability. So the nations that incur the most negative effects of global tourism are those of the Third World whose history of colonial exploitation has left them so economically disadvantaged that their governments embrace, even seek, investors to "develop" and market their potential global tourist attractions. For global tourism is seen as perhaps the only means by which such countries can improve their economic standing in the global marketplace, albeit too often at the expense of their own rural inhabitants. In this context, the global tourism industry is of great interest to postcolonial theory: too often, the industry's presence in vulnerable postcolonial nations today has much the same negative impact as the presence of Anglo-European colonial forces had in centuries past.

As a case in point, consider the situation of the people of Hacienda Looc (pronounced *low-ahk*) in the Philippines.[12] This rural community, located on the South China Sea about 60 miles southwest of Manila, consists of four villages inhabited by roughly 10,000 people and occupying 8,650 hectares (1 hectare = 2.47 acres) of ancestral coastal farmland, which the inhabitants have successfully and sustainably farmed and fished for many generations. Between 1991 and 1993, the Philippine Department of Agrarian Reform issued the villagers Certificates of Land Ownership Awards for 5,000 hectares of Hacienda Looc. The government also sold what is called an Indefinite Quantity Contract for all 8,650 hectares of Hacienda Looc to two real-estate developers, Fil-Estate and Manila Southcoast Development Corporation. Now, stay with me here. This contract, which might be thought of as a purchase made on speculation, gave developers the right to proceed with the building of tourist attractions and accommodations on the 3,650 hectares of Hacienda Looc not protected by the farmers' certificates of land ownership, which is what developers proceeded to do. The contract also gave them the right to develop whatever portions of the farmers' *protected* land that they could show were not suitable for farming, and in 1996 Fil-Estate and Manila Southcoast Development Corporation won their joint suit to develop 1,219 hectares of Hacienda Looc that had been thus far protected by farmers' certificates of ownership. The certificates for these parcels were cancelled because, it was argued, the land therein had an average slope of 18 percent or more and had not been used for agricultural crops. Wooded land containing a variety of fruit trees, managed by the inhabitants and providing important staples in their diet, was among the land that could be converted into tourism sites. In short, developers took well-maintained, productive coastal lands away from the people who have inhabited them, gained their livelihoods from them, and preserved them for generations. Indeed, it was the excellent condition of the land and the coastal waters that made the area attractive to developers in the first place.

When inhabitants of Hacienda Looc refused to leave, kept working their farms and fisheries, and began to file appeals to regain their land, they could not know what trouble awaited them. National police officers, members of the Philippine military, and security guards hired by the developers were sent in to "keep the peace." Subsequently, farmers and fisherfolk have been harassed by these heavily armed deputies: they've been verbally threatened by armed guards; their homes have been subject to illegal searches; many of their dwellings have been destroyed; many of the fisherfolk have been prevented from fishing; and at least seven inhabitants, all of whom spoke out against the seizure of their land, have been killed in incidents that were not investigated. Some inhabitants have moved away as a result of this intimidation. Some have moved away because a residential beach resort has been built on their homeland, a resort which includes nine six- and seven-story buildings housing luxury residential condominiums, a luxury hotel with country club and spa, and two golf courses, designed by champion golfers Hale Irwin and Fred Couples, that occupy large tracts of former farmland and forest. With their farming and fishing skills no longer of any use to them, some inhabitants have taken what low-paying jobs they could find in Manila and now live in the city's impoverished areas. Those who remain in Hacienda Looc are subject to soil erosion, floods, and landslides, caused by the bulldozing of forests, and to the water and air pollution caused by the two tons of weed-killers and insecticides sprayed on the golf courses annually. Peasants' rights organizations – at the local, national, and international level – continue to seek justice for the people of Hacienda Looc. The state of conflict in which the locals live, however, remains unsettled.

Sadly, the land-grabbing from which the people of Hacienda Looc are suffering is occurring throughout the rural Philippines and throughout the world. India, Tibet, and the nations of Southeast Asia, Africa, Central and South America, the Caribbean, and more, have had and still have regions undergoing these kinds of changes. Even ecotourism – although intended as a sustainable, eco-friendly form of tourism respectful of the natural beauty opened to global visitors – is too often neither sustainable nor eco-friendly. For example, in a letter to the United Nations, Third World Network (TWN) reported that in Thailand an "upsurge of ecotourism demand had resulted in a construction frenzy in rural and natural areas to provide accommodation and infrastructure [such as roads, electricity, and sewers] for visitors" (cited in Higham 11).[13] And the international market for unspoiled rural land in Third World countries is growing. For instance, the appeal of luxury "vacation ownership" is on the rise: a relatively small but very wealthy population of clients is increasing the marketability of, among other things, rural lands in economically underdeveloped, warm-climate countries for the creation of such luxury developments as "golf leisure communities," "residential beach resorts," and "hobby" or "leisure farms." As we see in the online ad for Pico de Loro's luxury beach resort at Hamilo Coast in the Philippines, clients can have the "complete modern comforts and luxuries of a vacation destination in a breathtaking natural setting."[14] Hamilo Coast used to be called Papaya, one of the four villages of Hacienda Looc.[15]

As we have seen, the incentive for a good deal of global tourism development in economically vulnerable postcolonial nations is, at least, threefold: postcolonial governments want to improve poor national economies; elite individual investors want to make large amounts of money; and a very wealthy though relatively small international clientele want to buy their own private, unspoiled tropical paradises. In addition, the impetus for such development comes from political forces beyond national borders. To cite just one example, consider the position on Hacienda Looc taken by the United States Agency for International Development (USAID). USAID was formed in 1961 to provide technical assistance and training, resource-management advice, and financial aid to struggling nations. As the narrator of the 1999 documentary film *The Golf War* tells us, in 1991 USAID released a report concluding that "the Hacienda Looc area is right for tourism and land conversion," that is, the conversion of farmland and woodland into tourist attractions and accommodations.

From the perspective of postcolonial theory, however, rural areas throughout the Third World – areas threatened by or already undergoing fates similar to that of Hacienda Looc – are "right for tourism and land conversion" only if we see the world through the lens of colonialist ideology, a lens through which the worldwide rural poor are considered better off as a result of global tourism development, or collateral damage from the forward march of progress, or not important enough to be considered at all. Sound familiar? It should. If we substitute the word *civilization* for *global tourism development* and *progress*, we will see that this perspective on the Third World rural poor today is much like that of the first Anglo-European colonizers who viewed the "New World" as "empty land" – that is, uninhabited land available to them for any purposes they desired – because, in effect, the native inhabitants were not Anglo-European and, therefore, not fully human. As Hall and Tucker aptly put the matter, "the practice of contemporary international tourism indicates that the economic structures, cultural representations and exploitative relationships that were previously based in colonialism are far from over" (185).[16]

Postcolonial theory and global conservation

Certainly, the continued relevance of postcolonial theory can be seen today as we attempt to address the global catastrophe of environmental destruction. For as many postcolonial critics point out, the losses endured by colonized peoples included the depletion or destruction of the natural environments they inhabited and the consequent loss of their homelands and often their lives. And as we saw earlier in this chapter, the problem persists today: the growth of multinational corporations and the expansion of the global tourism industry continue to deplete or destroy "undeveloped" regions of the Third World, thereby jeopardizing the human life those regions had sustained for countless generations. Indeed, conservationism[17] and postcolonialism might be seen as areas of ethical concern that never should have been separated in thought because they never have been separated in reality: the conservation of nature and the preservation of human life.

Why have conservationism and postcolonial criticism been considered, and continue to be considered by many people, separate and even adversarial areas of enquiry? A number of reasons for the divide grew from the European and Anglo-American belief that the words *nature* and *human* represent diametrically opposed concepts. In terms of the environment, for example, postcolonial criticism tends to emphasize the human element: for instance, the struggle of native communities to survive in natural environments invaded by the global spread of industrialization and commercialization. In contrast, conservationism, which grew from the philosophies of such American writers as Ralph Waldo Emerson and Henry David Thoreau, tends to focus on the natural environment itself: the desire for "virgin wilderness and the preservation of 'uncorrupted' last great places" where one can pursue "timeless, solitary moments of communion with nature" (Nixon 236).[18] Global conservation organizations share this desire for the protection of pristine nature. Modeled upon the American national park system, they focus their efforts almost exclusively on the preservation of wilderness areas. And when, as almost always happens, indigenous[19] inhabitants have stewarded and preserved, since precolonial times, the very lands that conservationists believe are endangered by human presence, the result usually has been a turf war that indigenous inhabitants generally have lost.

Indeed, many postcolonial thinkers see the word *wilderness*, as it is defined by most conservationists, as a major cause of the antagonism between the goals of global conservation organizations and postcolonialist concerns about human rights. According to Part C of The Wilderness Act of 1964 (US Public Law 88–577), which is the source of the definition used today by most American and global conservation organizations,

> wilderness, in contrast with those areas where man and his works dominate the landscape, is hereby recognized as an area where the earth and its community of life are untrammeled by man, where man himself is a visitor who does not remain. An area of wilderness is further defined to mean in this Act an area of undeveloped Federal land retaining its primeval character and influence, without permanent improvements or human habitation, which is protected and managed so as to preserve its natural conditions and which (1) generally appears to have been affected primarily by the forces of nature, with the imprint of man's work substantially unnoticeable; (2) has outstanding opportunities for solitude or a primitive and unconfined type of recreation; (3) has at least five thousand acres of land or is of sufficient size as to make practicable its preservation and use in an unimpaired condition; and (4) may also contain ecological, geological, or other features of scientific, educational, scenic, or historical value.

In short, a wilderness is a large, beautiful tract of unspoiled land that the colonizing forces of homesteading or business development have not yet acquired. The traditional dwellings of native peoples are not "permanent" structures and, therefore, are not taken into consideration.

Conservationists who insist on preserving a wilderness free of human habitation either don't know or don't care about the native dwellers evicted in the process. For example, the myth that the region now covered by Yosemite National Park was originally uninhabited by humans was successfully fostered by the breathtaking images of the region created by celebrated photographer Ansel Adams, among others, who

> assiduously avoided photographing any of the local Miwok who were rarely out of his sight as he worked Yosemite Valley. He filled thousands of human-free negatives with land he knew the Miwok had tended for at least four thousand years. And he knew that the Miwok had been forcibly evicted from Yosemite Valley, as other natives would later be from national parks yet to be created, all in the ... [supposed] ... interest of protecting nature from human disturbance.
> (Dowey 16)

Despite the fact that native peoples had lived sustainably on this land and had stewarded its wildlife, its forests, and its waters from time out of mind, park preservationists believed that the indigenous inhabitants' continued presence would harm the natural setting. Certainly, their continued presence would have meant that Yosemite could not have been described as a true wilderness – a wilderness without human inhabitants – and a true wilderness is what was wanted. Having seen so much of the nation's natural resources destroyed by urbanization, industrialization, and commercialization, American naturalists wanted to preserve, as a national heritage, as much as possible of the remaining natural environment so that Americans (or, more precisely, white Americans) could forever visit, learn from, and be morally refreshed by the wonders of nature.[20] Thus, tourists could visit the new park, even for extended stays, but the people for whom it was homeland had to leave.

The colonialist attitude toward the original inhabitants of Yosemite National Park has remained the dominant attitude toward native inhabitants of lands set aside for wilderness preservation by conservation organizations throughout the world. To obtain the land it wants, a conservation organization might, for example, pay off a portion of a poor country's foreign debt, or provide some other economic incentive, in exchange for the desired acreage.[21] Sometimes land is obtained by sanitizing the process with "terms such as *voluntary relocation*, or [by] veil[ing] it behind a so-called *co-management* project where a government imposes strict livelihood restrictions (e.g., no hunting, fishing, gathering of certain plants, agricultural practices)" (Dowie, xxii–xxiii) until native inhabitants are driven away by starvation. The result has been the continuing worldwide eviction of millions of native peoples from their ancestral lands to live in poverty just outside the confines of what is now the park; to take low-paying jobs as waiters, porters, or day laborers within the park; or to drift into poverty in the cities.

Without the presence of indigenous peoples to safeguard areas designated as wilderness, however, many tracts of preserved land too big to patrol effectively have fallen victim to invasion by the very evictees who used to steward them. For instance, some desperate evictees reenter, as commercial poachers, areas that used to be their own hunting grounds. Others

> sneak back into the forest to harvest medicinal plants and firewood at the risk of being legally killed by eco-guards hired and paid by conservation agencies. And much less desirable groups – colonists, renegade loggers, exotic animal hunters, cash-crop farmers, and cattle ranchers – are moving into unpatrolled protected areas the world over. As they often share ethnicity with the ruling class of the nation involved, the new settlers are generally favored in territorial conflicts with … aboriginals who are arrested or expelled for doing the same things.
>
> (Dowie xxvii)

The tragic result for these areas is rapid ecological decline where there could be, instead, a cooperative relationship between native inhabitants and conservationists that would allow the ecological preservation of indigenous lands, in indigenous hands, to continue. Indeed, indigenous leaders have been traveling the globe for "a quarter of a century," Mark Dowie observes, to bring the message to conservation organizations everywhere: "We have proven ourselves good stewards, otherwise you wouldn't have selected our land for conservation. Let us stay where our ancestors are buried and we will help you preserve the biological diversity we all treasure" (xvi–xvii). As Australian Aboriginal philosopher Bill Neidjie explains, his people care for the land because "Earth [is] like your father or brother or mother ... your bone, your blood" (cited in Plumwood 226).

Many international agencies – including the world's five biggest conservation organizations: Conservation International (CI), The Nature Conservancy (TNC), the Worldwide Fund for Nature (WWF), the African Wildlife Foundation (AWF), and the Wildlife Conservation Society (WCS) – have made formal announcements supporting the territorial rights of indigenous peoples. In addition, the United Nations Declaration of the Rights of Indigenous Peoples, an issue under debate since the early 1980s, was finally approved by the UN General Assembly in 2007. None of these documents, however, is legally binding. Therefore,

> [t]ribal people, who tend to think and plan in generations rather than weeks, months, and years, patiently await the consideration promised in these thoughtful declarations and pronouncements. Meanwhile, the human rights and global conservation communities remain at serious odds over the question of displacement [the removal of indigenous people from their homeland], each side blaming the other for the particular crisis they perceive.
>
> (Dowie xxv)

Ironically, wilderness preservation is not the same thing as environmental protection, though the two are often confused. Wilderness preservation alone can neither protect the global environment nor remedy the damage it has already suffered. In fact, as Ramachandra Guha observes, the single-minded focus on wilderness preservation has deflected attention from two much more dangerous and "fundamental ecological problems facing the globe": increasing "overconsumption by the industrialized world and by urban elites in the Third World" and "growing militarization, both in a short-term sense (i.e., ongoing regional wars) and in a long-term sense (i.e., the arms race and the prospect of nuclear annihilation)" ("Radical American Environmentalism" 95). Let's think about these two points for a minute. First, the global spread of industrialization is fueled by, and in turn fuels, the global spread of rampant consumerism, or what might be called purchase for the sake of purchase. In short, those who can afford it are rapidly using up the planet to get for themselves ever more extravagant versions of "the good life." Such runaway global wastefulness – in addition to decreasing the availability of food, water, and shelter for the world's poor – increases the pollution of soil, water, and air as well as the destruction of other natural resources. Second, the continued creation and dissemination of nuclear weapons is putting the planet in catastrophic ecological jeopardy. And even the weapons used in non-nuclear, relatively small-scale wars – in addition to destroying human life and property – fill the global atmosphere with large quantities of pollutants. Neither of these pressing environmental issues is addressed by, or even related to, the preservation of wilderness areas.

It hasn't helped matters that mainstream news media have done little to increase public awareness of the plight of native peoples unjustly and unwisely evicted from their homelands in the name of conservation. "In an age when media venerate the spectacular" event, Rob Nixon argues, "[f]alling bodies, burning towers, exploding heads, avalanches, volcanoes and tsunamis have a[n] … eye-catching and page-turning power" that cannot be matched by what he calls "slow violence" (3). Slow violence, Nixon explains, is "a violence that occurs gradually and out of sight, a violence of delayed destruction that is dispersed across time and space," a violence that kills, but "that is typically not viewed as violence at all" (2). He's talking here about the ecological devastation of the Third World – caused by, for example, under-regulated foreign industrialism – and the environmental consequences suffered by the poor who live there. But his analysis of the "invisibility" of long-term ecological destruction also applies to the "invisibility" of the millions of aboriginal peoples who have been and are being evicted from their lands all over the world. Conservation organizations have not used military weapons of mass destruction to rid lands earmarked for wilderness preservation of their native human inhabitants. If they had, we surely would have heard about it on the nightly news. As we have seen, however, conservation organizations have succeeded, slowly and methodically, in getting those inhabitants evicted, despite the human or even – in cases where preserves are too big to be adequately patrolled – the environmental consequences. Thus, while many of us are gratefully aware of the millions of square miles of "wilderness" worldwide that have been set aside for preservation, very few of us know how that "wilderness" was created or what has become of it without its native stewards.

Indigenous activists have been making a concerted effort to get justice for their peoples since the 1960s. Their efforts have grown into an international indigenous movement: a steadily growing, worldwide web of communication among indigenous peoples in an attempt to unify indigenous interests within and across national borders. One of the movement's major goals is to replace the colonial model of wilderness conservation, dominant since the creation of Yosemite National Park, with a cooperative model that would both keep indigenous people in control of their lands and satisfy the concerns of international conservation organizations. The Indigenous Protected Area (IPA) concept, invented by Australian Aboriginals, is one example of the cooperative model. According to IPA values, conservation reserves are not thought of as "wilderness" areas but as *country* – a term including both land and the sea it borders – that is cared for by the native peoples who already inhabit it or by indigenous evictees who have been resettled in their ancestral homelands. IPAs in Australia are created voluntarily by Aboriginal communities who designate an area they want to protect within or bordering their ancestral lands. They map the proposed area; draw up rules of operation, which they will be responsible for enforcing; and submit a management plan to the Australian government for the conservation of biodiversity.[22] Although land titles have not been granted to these original owners, the Australian Homelands Movement, which has been resettling indigenous peoples on their ancestral lands for over 30 years, continues working toward the restoration of all Aboriginal custodial rights. Various versions of Australia's IPAs have been created and are being created around the world (Dowie 237–39).

Such gains as these, while relatively small, are encouraging. Yet when we consider that the powerful groups vying for control of the natural environment include government agencies, narrowly focused conservation organizations, and the multi-national corporations and global tourism companies discussed earlier in this chapter, the chances that a globally significant number of native communities will be allowed to continue, or return to, stewarding their own lands seem slim indeed. Still, Mark Dowie hasn't lost hope: "[i]ndigenous peoples' presence ... may offer the best protection that protected areas can ever receive. That's a possibility that international conservationists have begun to consider" (xxvii). From a postcolonial perspective, that possibility can't be considered soon enough.[23]

Postcolonial criticism and literature

Wherever postcolonial critics place themselves in terms of the postcolonial issues we've been discussing, most interpret postcolonial literature in terms of a number of overlapping topics. These include, among others, the following common topics, which illustrate postcolonial criticism's recognition of the close relationship between psychology and ideology or, more specifically, between individual identity and cultural beliefs:

1 the native people's initial encounter with the colonizers and the disruption of indigenous culture;
2 the journey of the European outsider through an unfamiliar wilderness with a native guide;
3 othering (the colonizers' treatment of members of the indigenous culture as less than fully human) and colonial oppression in all its forms;
4 mimicry (the attempt of the colonized to feel that they belong – to feel that they are not inferior – by imitating the dress, behavior, speech, and lifestyle of the colonizers);

5   exile (the experience of being an "outsider" in one's own land or a foreign
    wanderer in Europe);
6   post-independence exuberance followed by disillusionment;
7   cultural difference (the ways in which race, class, sex, gender, sexual orientation,
    religion, cultural beliefs, and customs combine to form individual identity);
8   the struggle for individual and collective cultural identity and the related
    themes of alienation, unhomeliness (feeling that one has no cultural "home," or
    sense of cultural belonging), double consciousness (feeling torn between the
    social and psychological demands of two antagonistic cultures), and hybridity
    (experiencing one's cultural identity as a hybrid of two or more cultures, which
    feeling is generally considered a positive alternative to unhomeliness);
9   double colonization, or the experience of postcolonial women under the dual
    subjugation of colonialist and patriarchal ideologies;
10 the role of the natural environment, and the loss thereof, in the culture and
    experience of postcolonial peoples;
11 the need for continuity with a precolonial past and self-definition of the political
    future;
12 the ways in which a literary text is itself colonialist or anticolonialist.

This last item on our list requires discussion. For most postcolonial critics, whatever the topic or topics on which they focus, also analyze the ways in which a literary
text is colonialist or anticolonialist, that is, the ways in which the text reinforces or
resists colonialism's oppressive ideology. For example, in the simplest terms, a text
can reinforce colonialist ideology through positive portrayals of the colonizers,
negative portrayals of the colonized, or the uncritical representation of the benefits
of colonialism for the colonized. Analogously, texts can resist colonialist ideology by
depicting the misdeeds of the colonizers, the suffering of the colonized, or the
detrimental effects of colonialism on the colonized.

Such analysis is not always as straightforward as this simple outline might lead
you to expect, however. For the ideological content of literary texts is rarely able
to confine itself to such tidy categories. Joseph Conrad's *Heart of Darkness* (1902),
for example, is extremely anticolonialist in its negative representation of the colonial
enterprise: the Europeans conducting the ivory trade in the Congo are portrayed as
heartless, greedy thieves who virtually enslave the indigenous population to help
collect and transport the Europeans' "loot," and the negative effects of the European presence on the native peoples are graphically depicted. However, as Chinua
Achebe observes, the novel's condemnation of Europeans is based on a definition of
Africans as savages: beneath their veneer of civilization, the Europeans are, the novel
tells us, as barbaric as the Africans. And indeed, Achebe notes, the novel portrays
Africans as a prehistoric mass of frenzied, howling, incomprehensible barbarians:
"Africa [is a] setting and backdrop which eliminates the African as human factor.

Africa [is] a [symbolic] battlefield devoid of all recognizable humanity, into which the wandering European enters at his peril" ("An Image of Africa" 12). In other words, despite *Heart of Darkness*'s obvious anticolonialist agenda, the novel points to the colonized population as the standard of savagery to which Europeans are compared. Thus, Achebe uncovers the novel's colonialist subtext, of which the text does not seem to be aware.

Let's look at a few more brief examples of postcolonial interpretations of literary texts. Homi Bhabha gives us a wonderful example of the global orientation of much postcolonial criticism when he offers a new way to analyze world literature, not in terms of national traditions, which is how it generally has been studied, but in terms of postcolonial topics that cut across national boundaries. For example, Bhabha suggests that world literature might be studied in terms of the different ways cultures have experienced historical trauma, perhaps such traumas as slavery, revolution, civil war, political mass murder, oppressive military regimes, the loss of cultural identity, and the like. Or world literature might be seen as the study of the ways in which cultures define themselves positively by "othering" groups whom they demonize or otherwise devalue for that purpose. Or we might analyze world literature by examining the representations of people and events that occur across cultural boundaries, rather than within them, such as representations of migrants, political refugees, and colonized peoples. "The center of such a study," Bhabha says, "would neither be the 'sovereignty' of national cultures, nor the universalism of human culture, but a focus on … the unspoken, unrepresented pasts that haunt the historical present" (12). That is, we might study what world literature tells us about the personal experience of people whom history has ignored – the disenfranchised, the marginalized, the unhomed – such as are found in the work of South African writer Nadine Gordimer and African American writer Toni Morrison.

For example, Bhabha argues that Gordimer's *My Son's Story* (1990) and Morrison's *Beloved* (1987) are unhomely novels in which the female protagonists – Aila and Sethe, respectively – live in the hinterland between cultures. Aila is unhomed because she is imprisoned for using her house as a cover for gun-running in an effort to resist South Africa's racist government; Sethe, because she has killed her baby daughter in order to save the child from the abuses of a cruel slavemaster. Thus, Bhabha observes, these two characters are doubly marginalized: first as women of color living in racist societies, second as women whose actions have placed them outside the circle of their own communities. In representing the psychological and historical complexities of these characters' ethical choices, both novels reveal the ways in which historical reality is not something that happens just on the battlefield or in the government office. Rather, historical reality comes into our homes and affects our personal lives in the deepest possible ways. Marginalized people may be more aware of this fact because it is pressed on them by violence and oppression, but it is true for everyone.

Another attempt to find a common denominator in postcolonial literature is made by Helen Tiffin, who claims that the "subversive [anticolonialist] manoeuvr[e] ... characteristic of post-colonial texts" does not lie in "the construction or reconstruction" of national cultural identity, but rather in "the rereading and rewriting of the European historical and fictional record" (95). Tiffin argues that, as it is impossible to retrieve a precolonial past or construct a new cultural identity completely free of the colonial past, most postcolonial literature has attempted, instead, "to investigate the means by which Europe imposed and maintained ... colonial domination of so much of the rest of the world" (95). One of the many ways postcolonial literature accomplishes this task, Tiffin maintains, is through the use of what she calls "canonical counter-discourse," a strategy whereby "a post-colonial writer takes up a character or characters, or the basic assumptions of a British canonical text, and unveils [its colonialist] assumptions, subverting the text for post-colonial purposes" (97).

Tiffin sees this kind of "literary revolution" (97) in, for example, *Wide Sargasso Sea* (1966) by Jamaican-born writer Jean Rhys. Rhys' novel, a postcolonial response to Charlotte Brontë's *Jane Eyre* (1847), "writes back" (98) to Brontë's novel by, among other things, reinterpreting Bertha Mason, Rochester's West Indian wife. Brontë's novel portrays Bertha, the descendent of white colonial settlers, as an insane, drunken, violent, and lascivious woman who tricked Rochester into marriage and whom her husband must keep locked in the attic for her own and everyone else's protection. In contrast, Rhys' novel depicts Bertha, in Gayatri Spivak's words, as a "critic of imperialism" (Spivak 271), a sane woman driven to violent behavior by Rochester's imperialist oppression. Rhys' narrative thereby unmasks the colonialist ideology informing Brontë's narrative. And part of *Jane Eyre*'s colonialist ideology, we might add, is revealed when the novel associates Bertha with the nonwhite native population as seen through the eyes of colonialist Europe: Bertha's face is a "black and scarlet visage" (Brontë 93; ch. 27, vol. II), and the room she inhabits is "a wild beast's den" (Brontë 92; ch. 27, vol. II). In other words, according to the colonialist discourse in which *Jane Eyre* participates, to be insane, drunken, violent, and lascivious is the equivalent of being nonwhite.

Tiffin notes that similar canonical counter-discourse can be found, for example, in *Foe* (1988), by South African writer J. M. Coetzee, in the way the novel reveals the colonialist ideology of Daniel Defoe's *Robinson Crusoe* (1719), an ideology manifest in Crusoe's colonialist attitude toward the land on which he's shipwrecked and toward the black man he "colonizes" and names Friday. And of course, canonical counter-discourse occurs in the numerous modern Caribbean and South American performances of Shakespeare's *The Tempest* (1611), which reveal the political and psychological operations of Prospero's colonialist subjugation of Caliban in the original play. As Tiffin observes, canonical counter-discourse doesn't unmask merely the literary works to which it responds, but the whole fabric of colonialist discourse in which those works participate.

Finally, Edward Said demonstrates how postcolonial criticism of a canonized literary work often involves moving the "margins" of the work (for example, minor characters and peripheral geographical locations) to the center of our attention. This is what he does in his analysis of Jane Austen's *Mansfield Park* (1814). The entire novel is set in England around the turn of the nineteenth century, most of it on the sizable estate of the wealthy Sir Thomas Bertram, who epitomizes the positive image of the traditional English gentleman of property: he is well bred, rational, honorable, and highly moral, and is the proper patriarchal head of his home and of the overseas agricultural enterprise that financially sustains that home.

This enterprise is in Antigua, in the Caribbean British colonies, and it is maintained by slave labor. But things are not going well in Antigua, and Sir Thomas must travel there to take control personally. And take control he does, apparently with the same efficiency with which he rules his home. For having set his "colonial garden" (*Culture and Imperialism* 86) in order, as Said puts it, Sir Thomas returns home to quickly set to rights his household, which, without his paternal guidance, has gotten out of order: his grown children have fought among themselves, engaged in clandestine courtships, and generally created a domestic uproar. Thus, among other things, Said notes that the novel draws a strong parallel between "domestic [and] international authority" (*Culture and Imperialism* 97). For the financial well-being of the British estate depends on the success of the colonial enterprise, and the orderly operation of both depends on the guidance of the British patriarch.

Although Sir Thomas' trip to Antigua is peripheral to the narration – it is mentioned only in passing and we see nothing that goes on there – it is "absolutely crucial to the action" (*Culture and Imperialism* 89). In Said's words,

> *Mansfield Park* [is] part of the structure of [Britain's] expanding imperialist venture. ... [And] we can sense how ideas about dependent races and territories were held [not only] by foreign-office executives, colonial bureaucrats, and military strategists [but also] by intelligent novel-readers educating themselves in the fine points of moral evaluation, literary balance, and stylistic finish.
>
> (*Culture and Imperialism* 95)

In other words, the colonialist ideology contained in literature is deposited there by writers and absorbed by readers without their necessarily realizing it.

Some questions postcolonial critics ask about literary texts

The questions that follow are offered to summarize postcolonial approaches to literature. Keep in mind that most postcolonial analyses, regardless of the issues on which they focus, will include some attention to whether the text is colonialist, anticolonialist, or some combination of the two, that is, ideologically conflicted.

1 How does the literary text, explicitly or allegorically, represent various aspects of colonial oppression? Special attention is often given to those areas where political and cultural oppression overlap, as it does, for example, in the colonizers' control of language, communication, and knowledge in colonized countries.

2 What does the text reveal about the problematics of postcolonial identity, including the relationship between personal and cultural identity and such issues as double consciousness and hybridity?

3 What does the text reveal about the politics and/or psychology of anticolonialist resistance? For example, what does the text suggest about the ideological, political, social, economic, or psychological forces that promote or inhibit resistance? How does the text suggest that resistance can be achieved and sustained by an individual or a group?

4 What does the text reveal about the operations of cultural difference – the ways in which race, religion, class, gender, sexual orientation, cultural beliefs, and customs combine to form individual identity – in shaping our perceptions of ourselves, others, and the world in which we live? *Othering* might be one area of analysis here.

5 How does the text respond to or comment on the characters, topics, or assumptions of a canonized (colonialist) work? Following Helen Tiffin's lead, examine how the postcolonial text reshapes our previous interpretations of a canonical text.

6 Are there meaningful similarities among the literatures of different postcolonial populations? One might compare, for example, the literatures of native peoples from different countries whose land was invaded by colonizers, the literatures of white settler colonies in different countries, or the literatures of different populations in the African diaspora. Or one might compare literary works from all three of these categories in order to investigate, for example, if the experience of colonization creates some common elements of cultural identity that outweigh differences in race and nationality.

7 How does the text represent relationships between the characters it portrays – for example, culturally dominant characters, subalterns, and cultural outsiders – and the land these characters inhabit? Does the natural setting change over time and, if so, what is the cause? Does the narrator's attitude toward the natural setting, or the attitude of any character toward the natural setting, change over time? What kinds of relationships between human beings and nature does the text seem to promote? Questions like these can help you think about a text in terms of postcolonial criticism's environmental concerns.[24]

8 How does a literary text in the Western canon reinforce or undermine colonialist ideology through its representation of colonization and/or its inappropriate

silence about colonized peoples? Does the text teach us anything about colonialist or anticolonialist ideology through its illustration of any of the postcolonial concepts we've discussed? (A text does not have to treat the subject of colonization in order to do this.)

Depending on the literary work in question, we might ask one or any combination of these questions. Or we might come up with a useful question not listed here. These are just some starting points to get us thinking productively about literature from a postcolonial perspective. Keep in mind that not all postcolonial critics will interpret the same text in the same way, even if they focus on the same postcolonial concepts. As in every field, even expert practitioners disagree.

Whatever ways we may choose to apply postcolonial criticism, our goal in using this approach is to learn to see some important aspects of literature that we might not have seen so clearly or so deeply without this theoretical perspective; to appreciate the opportunities and the responsibilities of living in a culturally diverse world; and to understand that culture is not just a fixed collection of artifacts and customs frozen in time but a way of relating to oneself and to the world, a psychological and social frame of reference that necessarily alters in response to cross-cultural encounters, whether those encounters occur in our community or on the pages of a literary text.

The following reading of F. Scott Fitzgerald's *The Great Gatsby* is offered as an example of what a postcolonial interpretation of that novel might yield. You'll notice that my postcolonial reading relies a good deal on psychological analysis and is similar, in some ways, to my discussion of the novel in Chapter 3, "Marxist criticism." In addition, my postcolonial interpretation includes both an analysis of the novel's three minor black characters and its erasure of the African American presence in Jazz Age New York City, an analysis you will also find as part of my African American reading of the novel in Chapter 11. This kind of theoretical "overlap" is quite common for a postcolonial interpretation because postcolonial criticism draws on these three theories, among others, in its attempt to analyze all aspects of colonialist and anticolonialist ideologies. In short, my postcolonial interpretation of Fitzgerald's novel focuses on what I will argue is the work's colonialist ideology, an ideology that can subjugate minority populations within a nation's borders as well as colonized populations elsewhere on the globe. Indeed, as I will argue, the novel illustrates some of the ways in which colonialist ideology is also a psychological state – not just a way of thinking but a way of being – that is detrimental to those who oppress others as well as to those who are oppressed.

Although I believe that one of the greatest products of postcolonial criticism is its potential to bring the work of writers from formerly colonized societies, especially the work of marginalized postcolonial writers, to the fore, I hope that my reading of *The Great Gatsby* serves anticolonialist intellectual efforts by illustrating the ways in which colonialist ideology is inherently racist, classist, and sexist and is a fundamental element lurking at the core of American cultural identity. As many postcolonial critics attest, the key concern of postcolonial criticism is resistance to colonialist ideology in all its forms, and we can't resist an ideology until we know where it's hiding.

The colony within: a postcolonial reading of *The Great Gatsby*

As such critical frameworks as Marxism, feminism, lesbian/gay/queer theory, and African American criticism have taught us, no ideology is really separate from the psychology it produces. Ideology cannot exist without the psychology appropriate to it, without the psychology that sustains it. Thus, such ideologies as classism, sexism, heterosexism, and racism are not merely belief systems. They are also ways of relating to oneself and others and, as such, involve complex psychological modes of being.

Perhaps nowhere is the intimate connection between ideology and psychology demonstrated more clearly than in postcolonial criticism. For one of postcolonial theory's most definitive goals is to combat colonialist ideology by understanding the ways in which it operates to form the identity – the psychology – of both the colonizer and the colonized. And as a pervasive force in Western civilization, colonialist ideology can be found operating, sometimes invisibly but almost always effectively, even in those cultural practices and productions in which we would not expect to find it, for example in an American novel that doesn't seem concerned with colonialism at all: F. Scott Fitzgerald's *The Great Gatsby* (1925). When looked at through a postcolonial lens, Fitzgerald's famous novel about the American Jazz Age is the quintessential text about othering, a psychological operation on which colonialist ideology depends and that is its unmistakable hallmark.

As the history of Western civilization has shown repeatedly, in order to subjugate an "alien" people, a nation must convince itself that those people are "different," and "different" must mean inferior to the point of being less than fully human. In postcolonial terminology, the subjugated people must be *othered*. In our own country, for example, the justification for exterminating some Native American nations and assimilating others through compulsory colonialist education was that Native Americans were "savages," literally inhuman. Similarly, the enslavement of Africans and their indoctrination in the colonialist ideology of white superiority was justified by officially defining Africans as only three-fifths human. As our own national history reveals, then, colonialism doesn't require a colonized population beyond a nation's geographical borders. Colonized populations can exist within the geographical borders of the colonizing nation.

As *The Great Gatsby* illustrates, colonialism exists "within" in another sense of the term as well: it exists within the individual psyche, where it influences our personal identity and our perceptions of others. Specifically, I will argue that Fitzgerald's novel reveals the colonialist ideology hiding at the heart of American culture by revealing the colonialist psychology that lurks at the core of American cultural identity.

As might be expected, colonialist psychology consists of, among other things, those (often unconscious) attitudes and behaviors by which a culturally privileged group others a culturally subordinate group, that is, by which the culturally privileged distance themselves emotionally from populations over whom they want to gain or maintain control. There are many political and economic motives for othering, but the primary psychological motive seems to be the need to feel powerful, in control, and superior. Thus, colonialist psychology finds in the insecure individual fertile ground on which to establish itself. And as we shall see, colonialist psychology is self-perpetuating: it encourages the personal insecurity that facilitates its operations. Because othering is the activity that both fuels and expresses it, colonialist psychology depends heavily on racism and classism, two very successful forms of othering. Of course, sexism often overlaps with racism and, as we shall see below, with classism, thus subjecting women from culturally subordinate groups to complex forms of multiple othering. Indeed, it is the practice of multiple forms of othering that distinguishes colonialist psychology.

In *The Great Gatsby*, colonialist psychology is not confined to the depiction of characters the novel itself discredits, such as Tom Buchanan. Rather, colonialist psychology is a pervasive presence in the narrative as a whole because that psychology is central to the characterization of the narrator, Nick Carraway. In addition, the novel helps us understand colonialist psychology from the viewpoint of the colonial subject, who, remaining a cultural outsider whether or not he achieves financial success, wants only to be accepted by the cultural elite, a position epitomized by the character of Jay Gatsby. Finally, in the character of Tom Buchanan, *The Great Gatsby* reveals the detrimental effects of colonialist psychology even on the culturally privileged who seem to be its beneficiaries.

Nick Carraway strikes many readers, as indeed he wants to strike them, as a very tolerant person. Because, as he says, he is "inclined to reserve all judgments," he "was privy to the secret griefs" (5; ch. 1) of his acquaintances when he was a Yale undergraduate. And so is he still when we meet him in the novel as a man just turning 30. Almost all the main characters confide in Nick. Daisy tells him about her marital troubles; Tom talks to him about Myrtle; Gatsby tells him the truth about his past life and his initial relationship with Daisy; and even Myrtle describes to him her excitement at meeting Tom and having an extra-marital affair for the first time. And though Nick functions as the novel's moral center – he's the only character who cares about others, who takes a genuine personal interest in their happiness and their sorrows, and who expresses strong ethical reservations about their obvious selfishness – he is extremely tolerant of the personal choices they make in their private lives. While he feels he must break off his correspondence with a young woman he knew back home before he can date Jordan, he seems perfectly comfortable with the very different lifestyle of the group he has fallen in with on Long Island. Indeed, Nick agrees to arrange Gatsby's reunion with Daisy and to stand guard while the two meet at his cottage during one of Gatsby's parties.

So it seems especially significant that there is one area in which Nick continually makes judgments about others with no apparent consciousness of doing so: in his numerous references to the plethora of minor characters who are in some way foreign, in some way alien, to the privileged cultural group of his day, of which he is a member: white, upper-class, Anglo-Saxon Protestants, born of families who had prospered in America for several generations. Whenever Nick has cause to mention people from a different culture, he emphasizes their ethnicity as if that were their primary or only feature and thus foregrounds their "alien" quality. For example, the woman he has hired to keep his house and cook his breakfast, whom he sees every day, is referred to six different times and always by such appellations as "my Finn" (88; ch. 5) and "the Finn" (89; ch. 5). Her language consists of "mutter[ing] Finnish wisdom to herself over the electric stove" (8; ch. 1), and even her walk – "the Finnish tread" (89; ch. 5) – is described in a way that foregrounds her ethnic difference.

Similarly, Wolfsheim's secretary is "a lovely Jewess" (178; ch. 9); the witness talking to the police officer at the scene of Myrtle's death is "the Negro" (148; ch. 7); the youngster playing with fireworks in the "valley of ashes" (27; ch. 2) is "a gray, scrawny Italian child" (30; ch. 2); and the people in the funeral procession Nick sees one day on his way to New York City have "the tragic eyes and short upper lips of south-eastern Europe" (73; ch. 4). While Nick's choice of words is certainly effective as colorful description, its relentless focus on the ethnicity of characters outside the dominant culture of Jazz Age America hints at a disquieting dimension of his attitude toward "foreigners," a dimension that becomes clear when he speaks of Meyer Wolfsheim.

Nick introduces Wolfsheim to us as a "small flat-nosed Jew" (75; ch. 4), and we are told very little else about his appearance except for his nose. But his nose is mentioned so frequently and in such descriptive detail that Wolfsheim is reduced to the single physical feature that, as the statement just cited indicates, Nick finds the most unattractive and associates the most strongly with Wolfsheim's ethnicity. For example, Nick says, Wolfsheim raised his "head and regarded me with two fine growths of hair which luxuriated in either nostril" (73–74; ch. 4), and "dropp[ing] my hand [he] covered Gatsby with his expressive nose" (74; ch. 4). Apparently, all of Wolfsheim's expressiveness, in Nick's opinion, resides in his nose, for when Nick wants to tell us that Wolfsheim has become angry, he says, "Mr. Wolfsheim's nose flashed at me indignantly" (75; ch. 4). When Wolfsheim is interested in something Nick has said, Nick reports, "His nostrils turned to me in an interested way"

(75; ch. 4). When Wolfsheim is emotionally moved, Nick communicates this fact by saying, "[H]is tragic nose was trembling" (77; ch. 4) or "The hair in his nostrils quivered slightly" (180; ch. 9).

Nick is clearly othering Wolfsheim, as he others almost all the ethnic characters he sees. And in doing so he dehumanizes them. Othering dehumanizes because it permits one to identify oneself as "the human being" and people who are different as something "other" than human. Othering thus facilitates the demonization of people we define as different from us, as we see when Nick's description of Wolfsheim turns that character into a version of "the Jew as monster," a form of othering that served Hitler well in Nazi Germany. Nick achieves this effect, apparently with no consciousness of doing anything amiss, with the only descriptions we get of Wolfsheim that do not include his nose: in Nick's words, Wolfsheim has a "large head" (73; ch. 4), "tiny eyes" (74; ch. 4), "bulbous fingers" (179; ch. 9), and finally, "cuff buttons" made of "human molars" (77; ch. 4). Of course, Nick is demonizing Wolfsheim because this character is a criminal of rather vast proportions. But Nick foregrounds Wolfsheim's Jewishness to such a degree that even Wolfsheim's criminal status becomes associated with his ethnicity.

Another significant example of Nick's othering of ethnic characters occurs when Gatsby is driving him to New York City in his enormous luxury car. Nick sees "three modish [fashionable] Negroes" in "a limousine ... driven by a white chauffeur" (73; ch. 4). He describes them as "two bucks and a girl" and says, "I laughed aloud as the yolks of their eyeballs rolled toward us in haughty rivalry" (73; ch. 4). Of course, Nick's unselfconscious racism is obvious in his othering of these characters: the black men are "bucks" – animals rather than men – and the description of their wide-stretched, rolling eyes resonates strongly with racist stereotypes that portrayed African Americans as foolish, childish, overly dramatic, comic characters.[25]

In addition, Nick's description of these characters fulfills the kind of narrative function Toni Morrison describes in her analysis of the Africanist presence in white American literature. These black characters – fashionably dressed, riding in a chauffeured limousine, very conscious of their social status in the eyes of others – are the mirror and shadow of Gatsby. The only obvious difference between them is that Gatsby can hide his origins, which he does, whereas they can't because they can't hide their color. From Nick's point of view, despite Gatsby's "elaborate formality of speech [that] just missed being absurd" (53; ch. 3), his ridiculous fabrication of wealthy "ancestors" (69; ch. 4), his "circus wagon" (128; ch. 7) of a car, as Tom calls it, and all his other ludicrous affectations, he is the romantic embodiment of success. The black characters, however, are its parody. In barely more than one sentence, in the single image with which Nick describes the black characters, he projects onto them everything about Gatsby that he, and perhaps the reader, hold in contempt. *They* are preposterous, not Gatsby. Thus, Nick's othering of these characters facilitates their function as scapegoats sacrificed to Nick's, and the text's, recuperation of Gatsby.

To put the matter another way, the novel erases real African Americans, who were a very visible and important presence in New York City during the 1920s, where much of the novel is set, and substitutes in their place a comic stereotype – a colonialist other – that reinforces white superiority. This is no small move, given the historical reality of New York City during the 1920s, which was home to the Harlem Renaissance as well as to sites of black cultural production like The Cotton Club, where African American jazz greats attracted wealthy white patrons in droves. In fact, given Fitzgerald's penchant for creating a strong sense of place through the evocation of specific cultural details, it wouldn't be unreasonable to argue that the text falls short of the demands of its setting by not having one of the main characters visit a Harlem nightclub, or at least refer to a visit there, for that is surely what fashionable young white people such as the Buchanans, Nick, and Jordan would have done. The novel's erasure of African Americans becomes even more ironic when we consider that *The Great Gatsby* is credited with representing the Jazz Age, a term coined by Fitzgerald. Yet black Americans, who invented jazz and who were its most famous musicians, are conspicuously absent from the text.

Indeed, the novel's erasure of this local, "colonized" population is a feature of colonialist ideology that often accompanies othering. The colonized other doesn't count, becomes invisible to the eyes of the colonizer, who not only takes the fruits of colonized labor but also takes credit for those fruits. It should be no surprise, then, that the novel gives the credit for jazz symbolically to whites. The only musicians we see playing jazz are the white musicians at Gatsby's party. And they are "no thin five-piece affair," Nick tells us, "but a whole pit full of oboes and trombones and saxophones and viols and cornets and piccolos and low and high drums" (44; ch. 3). In other words, jazz has been "elevated" to the status of high culture in the form of an orchestra, and high culture belongs to white, not black, Americans.

Significantly, the orchestra spotlights its performance of a piece that, the conductor informs us, was played at Carnegie Hall: "Vladimir Tostoff's Jazz History of the World" (54; ch. 3). Could Fitzgerald have found a more conspicuously European – that is, white – name than Vladimir Tostoff? There's no way a reader could mistake him for an African American. In the world of this novel, jazz is, symbolically at least, a European invention. Thus, Tom's warning that "[i]t's up to us who are the dominant race to watch out or these other races will have control of things" (17; ch. 1), though mocked by Nick and by the novel's unflattering characterization of Tom, is an attitude the novel seems, unconsciously, to share.

Even the sympathetically portrayed "young Greek, Michaelis, who ran the coffee joint" (143; ch. 7) next to George Wilson's garage, is not entirely immune from

Nick's othering of ethnic characters. Michaelis spends the whole night sitting up with George Wilson, trying to help and comfort him, after Myrtle is killed. He cooks breakfast for himself, George, and "one of the watchers of the night before" (168; ch. 8) who returns the next morning to help out. And the text gives Michaelis some authority by making him "the principal witness at the inquest" (143; ch. 7) concerning Myrtle's death. Nevertheless, Michaelis retains the status of the immigrant other. First, he embodies the assumption that all Greek Americans run restaurants, which foregrounds his ethnicity. Moreover, while in point of fact the number of *successful* Greek American restaurants rose sharply during the 1920s (Moskos 123), the novel dooms Michaelis' small eatery to economic obscurity in the Valley of Ashes, which foregrounds his economic failure. Finally, given the time and place in which the novel is set, Michaelis' nurturing qualities can be seen as feminine qualities, which foregrounds his difference from "real" American men. Indeed, from the perspective of the novel's 1920s setting, Michaelis is accepted as the "principal witness at the inquest" (143; ch. 7) into Myrtle's death because Myrtle, as a female resident of the Valley of Ashes, doesn't deserve better.

Why does Nick engage in this kind of ethnic othering? Of course, one important reason is that, as a member of the dominant cultural group, he was programmed to do so. However, Nick also has some personal insecurity that makes him need to feel he is in control, that makes him need to feel superior to others in some way, and therefore that makes him especially vulnerable to colonialist psychology. At the age of 30, Nick is still being financed by his father while he tries to figure out what he should do with himself. His summer in New York is just the latest in a series of experiences failing to produce either a promising career or a lasting romance. Nick fears that all he has to look forward to is, as he puts it, "a thinning list of single men to know, a thinning briefcase of enthusiasm, thinning hair" (143; ch. 7). In addition, though Nick comes from the "right" family and the "right" background, apparently he doesn't expect a large inheritance. He needs to find a profession and, while he searches, his family funding goes only so far as to provide a modest cottage and pay his expenses. Certainly, this is no small feat, especially as Nick's expenses include courting Jordan. But given the cultural milieu in which he was raised, he doubtless has had many friends who come from families immensely more wealthy than his. As a member of the cultural elite, Nick knows the importance of gradations in social rank and must therefore be aware that his lack of fortune, relative to his peers, puts him at a social disadvantage. Thus, Nick has at least two important reasons to feel the need to assert his superiority and thereby assert his control. And the othering of ethnic subalterns offers him precisely this feeling.

The novel also helps us understand colonialist psychology from the viewpoint of the colonial subject, the cultural outsider who wants only to be accepted by the cultural elite. Although Gatsby has two important characteristics that place him, geographically, among the cultural elite in the text – he's white and wealthy enough to buy a mansion on Long Island Sound – he has far more in common with the colonial subject. For the culture to which Gatsby aspires, the culture to which Daisy Fay Buchanan belongs, is not his own. Its subtle social codes and gradations of social status are unfamiliar to him, and he can't quite get the hang of them. He is oblivious, for example, to the important social distinction between the upper-crust East Eggers and those who live at "the less fashionable" (9; ch. 1) West Egg, where he resides, just as he is oblivious to the gradations of class among the "menagerie" (114, ch. 6), as Tom calls them, who attend his parties. And it doesn't even seem to occur to Gatsby that a person of Nick's background – a Yale graduate from a socially established family, related to Daisy – might not be interested in selling fake bonds, a criminal enterprise in which Gatsby offers to include him in return for Nick's arranging Gatsby's reunion with Daisy.

In short, Gatsby lacks the proper bloodline, class origin, upbringing, and education for Daisy's set. He has lied and faked his way into her life, both during their initial courtship and again after their reunion. And as a result, Gatsby is unhomed: he feels he belongs nowhere because he is caught between two antagonist cultures, that into which he was born and that to which he aspires. Indeed, his personality is dominated by an endless struggle to rid himself of his own roots, his own identity as a poor boy from a family of "shiftless and unsuccessful farm people" (104; ch. 6) in North Dakota. When he tells Nick that his "family all died" (70; ch. 4), the lie carries with it the weight of unconscious psychological desire: Gatsby would like to eradicate all trace of his social origins.

We can see the force of this desire in the excessive quality of Gatsby's mimicry, his elaborate attempt to imitate the dress, speech, behavior, and lifestyle of the culturally privileged. For example, Gatsby fabricated an upper-class family and invented a past that includes an Oxford education; big-game hunting; living "like a young rajah in all the capitals of Europe"; jewel collecting, "chiefly rubies"; and "painting a little, things for myself only" (70; ch. 4). He created a new, more fashionable-sounding name for himself. He adopted numerous affectations of upper-class speech and "correct" manners, including calling everyone "old sport" and "excus[ing] himself" from his party guests "with a small bow that included each of us in turn" (53; ch. 3). And he purchased an enormous mansion and many very expensive possessions that he uses for display only. Even Gatsby's blind devotion to the selfish and shallow Daisy can best be explained by her symbolic quality, in Gatsby's eyes, as a princess "[h]igh in a white palace[,] the king's daughter, the golden girl" (127; ch. 7). If Gatsby can win Daisy, then he has proof that he belongs to the cultural elite she represents for him, that he is no longer a poor farm boy, a "Mr. Nobody from Nowhere" (137; ch. 7), as Tom calls him. Clearly, Gatsby is trying to stop being Jimmy Gatz as much as he is trying to become Jay Gatsby. For as his characterization illustrates, mimicry involves not only the laborious attempt to be accepted by a culture different from the one into which one was born but a simultaneous attempt to rid oneself of everything one has identified as other than that culture. Mimicry thus involves the othering of oneself.

Gatsby's characterization also suggests that mimicry is inseparable from unhomeliness, for one wouldn't engage in mimicry if one didn't feel unhomed. Mimicry is an attempt to find a home, psychologically, by finding a culture to which one can feel one belongs. But the conviction of one's own inferiority that produces mimicry also requires one to seek that home in a culture one deems superior to oneself. Therefore, as the portrayal of Gatsby illustrates, mimicry is an attempt to belong that is doomed to failure because, even if one succeeds in adopting the "superior" culture, one's feelings of inferiority will ensure that one is never at home in it. Indeed, Gatsby, who actually succeeds in acquiring the literal home he seeks, the mansion – the "colossal affair by any standard ... with a tower on one side ... and a marble swimming pool and more than forty acres of lawn and garden" (9; ch. l) – does not really occupy his home.

For example, among all the "Marie Antoinette music rooms and Restoration salons ... [and] period bedrooms swathed in rose and lavender silk ... [and] dressing rooms and poolrooms, and bathrooms with sunken baths" (96; ch. 5), the only area that shows any signs of Gatsby's occupancy is a small "apartment, a bedroom and a bath and an Adam study" (96; ch. 5). Furthermore, Gatsby doesn't seem to notice the difference between, on the one hand, the well-ordered cleanliness of his home under the care of the trained servants he fires and, on the other hand, the disarray into which it falls at the hands of the nonprofessional crew supplied him by Wolfsheim: "There was an inexplicable amount of dust everywhere," Nick observes, "and the rooms were musty as though they hadn't been aired for many days" (154–55; ch. 8). In fact, "[t]he grocery boy reported that the kitchen looked like a pigsty" (120; ch. 7). Neither does Gatsby seem at all perturbed by the prolonged presence of Mr. Klipspringer, evidently a party guest with no place else to go who took it upon himself to stay in one of his host's empty bedrooms. Gatsby doesn't respond to these rather radical alterations in his home because, emotionally, he's not really there. He can't be at home in his home because it's not his home: it's a form of mimicry. And mimicry is too outer-directed to provide any space for one's inner life.

Finally, *The Great Gatsby* reveals, in the character of Tom Buchanan, the detrimental effects of colonialist psychology even on the culturally privileged who are its apparent beneficiaries. Tom is clearly the most culturally privileged character in the novel. Despite his lack of personal refinement and his "ungentlemanly" behavior, he has all the cultural advantages afforded by race, ethnicity, socioeconomic class, gender, family, and education. In addition, his inherited wealth, which he need not lift a finger to maintain, is enormous. "[F]or instance," Nick reports, Tom "brought down a string of polo ponies from Lake Forest. It was hard to realize that a man in my own generation was wealthy enough to do that. ... [E]ven in college his freedom with money was a matter for reproach" (10; ch. 1).

Tom is also the character who most overtly exhibits the attitudes and behaviors associated with colonialist psychology. For one thing, as we saw earlier, he fervently believes in white supremacy, a colonialist ideology that others nonwhite people in order to justify subordinating them. Indeed, Tom has emotionally invested in a very specific form of white supremacist ideology called *Nordicism*, which refers to the belief not only that whites are genetically superior to all other races, but that Nordics – tall people with fair skin, light-colored hair and eyes, and long, rather than round, facial structure – are the most genetically superior Caucasians: they are born with superior intelligence, physical strength, and beauty. Paraphrasing the racist *The Rise of the Coloured Empires* by Goddard, a fictional stand-in for *The Rising Tide of Color* by Stoddard (Bruccoli 208), Tom tells Nick, "[W]e're Nordics ... and we've produced all the things that go to make civilization – oh, science and art and all that" (18; ch. 1), but "if we don't look out the white race will be ... utterly submerged" by "these other races" (17; ch. 1).

In addition, Tom is a classist, and the belief in the inherent superiority of the upper class is one way in which colonialism justifies the domination of colonized peoples. Indeed, Tom holds everyone in contempt who is beneath him in social class, including "these newly rich people," as he calls those who have acquired their own wealth. He says that "[a] lot of [them] are just big bootleggers" (114; ch. 6). While it is true that a number of people acquired a fortune through bootlegging in the 1920s, the implication here is that people who have not inherited their wealth as Tom has done are not to be trusted. In fact, Tom's mistrust of Gatsby, to whom Tom's comment about the newly rich specifically refers, is the product of his classism. And that mistrust occurs long before Tom learns, to his enormous surprise, that Gatsby is his rival for Daisy's affections.

Tom knows that Gatsby is a West Egger and not a member of his own set, a social distinction made painfully clear to the reader, though apparently not to Gatsby, when Tom and two friends, all on horseback, drop by Gatsby's house one afternoon for something to drink. All three treat Gatsby disdainfully. Tom's friend, Mr. Sloane, doesn't even speak to Gatsby but just "lounge[s] back haughtily in his chair" (108–9; ch. 6). When Sloane's ladyfriend becomes tipsy and invites Gatsby to join them for dinner, Mr. Sloane hurries her outside while Gatsby goes to get his coat, and the three riders depart before Gatsby is able to join them. Tom is outraged that Gatsby doesn't realize he's unwelcome: "'My God, I believe the man's coming,' said Tom. 'Doesn't he know she doesn't want him?'" (109; ch. 6). Tom can't imagine "where in the devil" (110; ch. 1) Daisy could have met Gatsby and writes it off to "women run[ning] around too much these days" and therefore meeting "all kinds of crazy fish" (110; ch. 6). Tom is standing in Gatsby's enormous, lavishly furnished mansion set on a 40-acre estate, and yet he knows, and quite correctly, that Gatsby is his social inferior. Indeed, Gatsby is unaware of the social distinctions so important to Tom, distinctions that are largely responsible for the mocking references Tom makes to Gatsby's parties, possessions, and probable social origins. For Tom needs everyone to know exactly in what manner he outranks them.

Classism, like racism, is an ideology that others people, a fact illustrated with particular clarity in the language Tom uses when referring to Gatsby. As we have seen, Tom calls Gatsby's parties "menagerie[s]" (114; ch. 6), that is, collections of animals. He refers to Gatsby's car as a "circus wagon" (128; ch. 7), in other words, something used to transport animals or human "freaks." And he refers to Gatsby as a "crazy fish" (110; ch. 6). Gatsby cannot have fully human status in Tom's eyes because he doesn't have the social rank such a status requires. Surely, Tom's classist othering of Gatsby is also one of the reasons Tom is able to dispose of him without a moment's hesitation when he sends Wilson, armed and crazed, to Gatsby's house, knowing that Wilson intends to murder Gatsby yet taking no action to prevent it.

The connection between classism and colonialist psychology is especially evident in the nature of Tom's womanizing. He doesn't pick on women from his own cultural milieu. He seduces only working-class women: for example, "one of the chambermaids in the Santa Barbara Hotel" (82; ch. 4), where Tom and Daisy stayed upon returning from their honeymoon; Myrtle Wilson; and the "common but pretty" (112; ch. 6) young woman Tom tries to pick up at Gatsby's party. What seems to attract Tom most to these women is their powerlessness, which augments his own power. He can do what he wants with them. He flagrantly lies to Myrtle. He keeps her at his beck and call. He can even break her nose and get away with it. And the reason he breaks Myrtle's nose – because she dares to say Daisy's name, that is, because she thinks she's as good as Daisy – suggests that Tom sees working-class women as "bad girls," as sexual objects and nothing more, who are in a separate category altogether from "good girls" like his wife and Jordan Baker. Because his mistresses are his social inferiors, he feels they don't deserve the respect reserved for upper-class women. In other words, Tom's classism and sexism are merged, and his womanizing is a form of classist othering. For in terms of Tom's privileged cultural milieu, working-class women are cultural outsiders. That is, Tom's classist victimization of working-class women resembles the white colonial official's racist victimization of women from the indigenous colonized population: both define their prey as "bad girls" and are thereby able to other them, thus allowing themselves to sexually exploit their victims while relieving themselves of all responsibility toward these women as human beings.

Certainly, Myrtle behaves like a colonial subject. She seems to have internalized the same colonialist psychology Tom has. But because she's on the bottom rung of the social hierarchy, that psychology disempowers her and makes her especially vulnerable to Tom: she considers his social superiority such a valuable asset that she will do anything to keep him. We see Myrtle as the colonial subject most clearly during the party at the small, three-room apartment Tom keeps for their trysts, where she engages in her own form of mimicry.

> Mrs. Wilson ... was now attired in an elaborate afternoon dress of cream-
> colored chiffon ... With the influence of the dress her personality had also
> undergone a change ... Her laughter, her gestures, her assertions became more
> violently affected moment by moment.
>
> (35; ch. 2)

Behaving as she imagines the very wealthy behave, Myrtle complains about the
elevator boy as if he were her servant, "rais[ing] her eyebrows in despair at the
shiftlessness of the lower orders. 'These people! You have to keep after them all the
time,'" she says (36; ch. 2). Then she "swept into the kitchen, implying that a dozen
chefs awaited her orders there" (36; ch. 2). Clearly, Myrtle behaves in such an
artificial manner because she believes that her "real self" isn't good enough, because
she feels inferior to Tom and his social set.

However much freedom and power colonialist psychology affords Tom, though,
it comes at a cost. Besides the obvious spiritual or moral damage colonialist psychology does to the culturally privileged by facilitating and providing a rationale for
unethical behavior, it also can produce a tormented inner life. This is precisely what
it does to Tom Buchanan.

There could be no cultural superiority if there were no cultural inferiority to
contrast with it. And no one internalizes this idea more thoroughly than Tom. He
behaves as if his social status depended on othering everyone "beneath" him and
then showing his "superiority" through some form of aggression. He doesn't merely
harbor racist, classist, and sexist attitudes; as we have seen, he continually and
aggressively displays them. And it's the recurrent and petty nature of these displays
that suggests the existence of a strong psychological motive.

For example, Tom takes cruel advantage of George Wilson's poverty, not only by
stealing his wife but also by tormenting George about the car George would like to
buy from Tom. George thinks he can resell the car at a profit, which he badly
needs, and Tom toys with him repeatedly concerning whether or not he will let
George have the vehicle, even offering to sell him Gatsby's enormous luxury car so
that George will have to admit he can't afford it. Indeed, Tom can't even buy a
puppy from a poor old man without insulting him to show that the man has not
fooled Tom about the value of the dog: "Here's your money," Tom snaps as he gives
the man ten dollars; "[g]o and buy ten more dogs with it" (32; ch. 2). There are
many more examples of Tom's unnecessary and open hostility toward his social
inferiors, but the point is that he wouldn't need to display his social superiority so
aggressively if he were secure in it.

One explanation for Tom's insecurity is that he is from the Midwest, and
therefore he can never have the cultural status that, in his day, belonged only to the
wealthy old blueblood families who had lived in the East since their forebears
arrived in America so long ago. He attended Yale and must know, as Fitzgerald

painfully knew as a Midwesterner at Princeton, that this is the one kind of cultural superiority he can never have, no matter how many millions he has or how lavishly he lives. In this one way, Tom himself is other, a fact that must be especially disconcerting since his recent move east. And I think it is this knowledge, whether it is conscious or unconscious, that makes him feel insecure enough to need to prove his social superiority at every conceivable opportunity.

Nick senses the problem when he says, referring to Tom's comments about *The Rise of the Coloured Empires*, "There was something pathetic in his concentration as if his complacency [self-satisfaction] … was not enough to him any more" (18; ch. 1). "Something," Nick adds, "was making him nibble at the edge of stale ideas as if his sturdy physical egotism no longer nourished his peremptory [dictatorial] heart" (25; ch. 1). Nick can't explain Tom's problem, but we can: the colonialist psychology that empowers Tom also undermines his confidence because it simultaneously tells him, "If you're not on top, you're nobody" and heightens his awareness of any way in which he might not be "on top."

As I hope this reading of *The Great Gatsby* makes clear, I'm not suggesting that Fitzgerald's novel can be read as a colonialist allegory, that its characters can be interpreted as symbolic stand-ins for colonialist types the way that characters in, for example, Hawthorne's "Young Goodman Brown" (1835) or "The Minister's Black Veil" (1836) are symbolic stand-ins for abstract moral concepts like good and evil. Rather, I'm suggesting that *The Great Gatsby* reveals the ways in which colonialist psychology, on which colonialist ideology depends, operates on the home front to sustain the imbalances of cultural power that have characterized America since its inception. For although the founders of this nation broke with Anglo-European political philosophy when they framed the American Constitution, they nevertheless inherited many aspects of Anglo-European cultural philosophy.

Most conspicuously, they inherited the belief that members of the white race are God's chosen people and the natural rulers of the world. That is, they inherited Anglo-European colonialist ideology, which permitted a small group of small nations – England, France, Spain, Portugal, and the Netherlands – to dominate most of the globe from the mid eighteenth to the mid twentieth century and which permitted white Americans, in turn, to dominate the Native American lands we now call the United States of America and to hold African captives as slaves. An ideology this successful dies hard. And as *The Great Gatsby* illustrates, one reason colonialist ideology is so successful is that it is supported by a complex psychology that strongly influences the way we perceive ourselves and others.

Is colonialist psychology as pervasive a presence in America today as *The Great Gatsby* suggests it was during the 1920s? Certainly, the othering of American citizens is no longer supported by law, as it was in the legal discrimination that subjugated all nonwhite Americans, and many white immigrants, before the Civil Rights Movement of the 1960s. And respect for cultural difference is promoted by our government, our media, and our educational system as it has never been before. Surely, these changes constitute a significant improvement.

Yet white supremacist backlash, for example as witnessed in the proliferation of racist hate groups; the persistence of covert racial discrimination, for example in housing, employment, and education; the othering of the homeless, indeed their virtual erasure from American consciousness and conscience; and all the forms of othering that still flourish in this country today make it clear that America's neo-colonialist enterprises around the globe will be accompanied by versions thereof at home for a long time to come. For colonialist psychology and the discriminatory ideologies it supports are part of our historical and cultural legacy, as *The Great Gatsby* illustrates. And this is a reality that will have to be confronted anew by each generation of Americans.

Questions for further practice: postcolonial approaches to other literary works

The following questions are intended as models. They can help you use postcolonial criticism to interpret the literary works to which they refer or other texts of your choice.

1   Analyze the anticolonialist agenda of Chinua Achebe's *Things Fall Apart* (1958). In order to accomplish this task, examine the novel's representation of pre-colonial tribal life in Africa. What is lost as a result of colonial contact? What are the colonizers' strategies in indoctrinating the native population to their way of thinking? Why are the colonizers so successful?

2   What does Jamaica Kincaid's *The Autobiography of My Mother* (1996) suggest about the social and psychological effects of colonialism on the colonizers (Philip and Moira) and, primarily, on the colonized? Analyze, for example, the problems of corruption, class division, and colonial education as they are revealed in the characterizations of Xuela, the narrator; her father and stepmother; her lover, Roland; and Monsieur and Madame LaBatte. How does Xuela manage to survive psychologically and achieve personal independence and self-confidence?

3   Analyze the themes of unhomeliness and mimicry as they apply to V. S. Naipaul's *The Mimic Men* (1967). How might we say that colonialism has robbed the narrator of a stable (or of any) sense of himself? How does he try to find an identity? Does he ever succeed? Why or why not? How does the narrator's language (word choice, tone, imagery) reveal his emotional distance from his own experience, and what does this add to our understanding of the novel?

4   What does Mary Shelley's *Frankenstein* (1818) reveal about the ideological and psychological operations of "othering"? For example, how does Shelley's por-trayal of the European landed gentry, embodied in Alphonse Frankenstein and

his family, represent the rightful "self" in contrast with an alien "other" embodied in, for example, the Arab merchant (among other things, note the contrast between the Arab and his Christian wife), the peasants who raised Elizabeth, the peasants among whom Victor lived while he worked on the female monster, and the peasants he met after the death of Clerval? In what ways might Safie be viewed as resisting a kind of colonial subjugation? In what ways might she be viewed as seeking it? How should we interpret the monster in this context? Might he be seen as the novel's postcolonial critic, the unhomely "other" who will not accept colonialist domination? In what ways does he not fit this role?

5   What does Zakes Mda's *The Heart of Redness* (2000) suggest about the relationship among cultural beliefs, economic loss and gain, and the ownership and use of land? For example, how might we account for, on the one hand, the conflict between the local people and the land-developers and, on the other hand, the conflict among the local people themselves? What kinds of relationships between human beings and nature does the novel seem to promote? What role do descriptions of setting, especially of the natural setting, play in our response to this aspect of the novel?

For further reading

Ashcroft, Bill, Gareth Griffiths, and Helen Tiffin. *The Empire Writes Back: Theory and Practice in Post-Colonial Literatures*. 2nd ed. London and New York: Routledge, 2002.

———, eds. *The Post-Colonial Studies Reader*. 2nd ed. London and New York: Routledge, 2006.

Cook-Lynn, Elizabeth. *A Separate Country: Postcoloniality and American Indian Nations*. Lubbock: Texas Tech University Press, 2012.

Dowie, Mark. *Conservation Refugees: The Hundred-Year Conflict between Global Conservation and Native Peoples*. Cambridge, MA: MIT Press, 2009.

Hall, C. Michael, and Hazel Tucker, eds. *Tourism and Postcolonialism: Contested Discourses, Identities and Representations*. London and New York: Routledge, 2004.

Irele, F. Abiola. *The African Imagination: Literature in Africa and the Black Diaspora*. New York: Oxford University Press, 2001.

Kincaid, Jamaica, *A Small Place*. 1988. New York: Farrar Straus Giroux, 2000.

LaCapra, Dominick, ed. *The Bounds of Race: Perspectives on Hegemony and Resistance*. Ithaca, NY: Cornell University Press, 1991. (See especially Appiah's "Out of Africa: Topologies of Nativism," 134–63; McClintock's "'The Very House of Difference': Race, Gender, and the Politics of South African Women's Narrative in *Poppie Nongena*," 196–230; Clingman's "Beyond the Limit: The Social Relations of Madness in Southern African Fiction," 231–54; Piedra's "Literary Whiteness and the Afro-Hispanic Difference," 278–310; and Mohanty's "Drawing the Color Line: Kipling and the Culture of Colonial Rule," 311–43.)

Loomba, Ania. *Shakespeare, Race, and Colonialism*. Oxford and New York: Oxford University Press, 2002.

———. *Colonialism/Postcolonialism*. 2nd ed. London and New York: Routledge, 2005.

Mohanty, Chandra Talpade, Ann Russo, and Lourdes Torres, eds. *Third World Women and the Politics of Feminism*. Bloomington: Indiana University Press, 1991.

Poddar, Prem, and David Johnson, eds. *A Historical Companion to Postcolonial Thought in English*. New York: Columbia University Press, 2005.

For advanced readers

Bhabha, Homi K. *Nation and Narration*. New York: Routledge, 1990.

——. *The Location of Culture*. New York: Routledge, 1994.

Braithwaite, Kamau. *The History of the Voice*. 1979. Rpt. *Roots*. Ann Arbor: University of Michigan Press, 1993.

DeLoughrey, Elizabeth, and George B. Handley, eds. *Postcolonial Ecologies: Literatures of the Environment*. New York: Oxford University Press, 2011.

Fanon, Frantz. *The Wretched of the Earth*. 1961. Trans. Constance Farrington. New York: Grove, 1963.

Huggan, Graham, and Helen Tiffin. *Postcolonial Ecocriticism: Literature, Animals, Environment*. London and New York: Routledge, 2010.

Mohanty, Chandra Talpade. *Feminism without Borders: Decolonizing Theory, Practicing Solidarity*. Durham, NC and London: Duke University Press, 2003.

Nixon, Rob. *Slow Violence and the Environmentalism of the Poor*. Cambridge, MA: Harvard University Press, 2011.

Said, Edward W. *Orientalism*. New York: Pantheon, 1978.

——. *Culture and Imperialism*. New York: Knopf, 1994.

Spivak, Gayatri Chakravorty. *In Other Worlds: Essays in Cultural Politics*. New York: Routledge, 1987.

Walcott, Derek. "The Muse of History." *Is Massa Day Dead?: Black Moods in the Caribbean*. Ed. Orde Coombs. New York: Anchor, 1974.

Notes

1 Today, the words *imperialism* and *colonialism* are often used interchangeably. Before World War II, however, when Britain still had extensive colonial holdings, the distinction between the two terms was fairly clear. Strictly speaking, imperialism is the system of forming and maintaining an empire (a collection of territories under the control of a single ruler) through such means as military conquest, the control of natural resources, the control of world markets, and colonization. Colonialism (the extension of territorial control through the establishment of colonies) is merely one form of imperialism. In the decades since World War II, however, such concepts as neocolonialism, cultural imperialism, and cultural colonization – all of which involve the economic and cultural domination of one society by another without the extension of territorial control – have blurred the distinction between the terms *imperialism* and *colonialism*.

2 As a historical term, the word post-colonial (hyphenated) generally refers to the cessation of colonialist domination of one country by another. For literary criticism and other forms of cultural studies, however, post-colonial is a problematic term. For as this chapter explains, the cessation of colonialist domination – the liberation of a colonized nation by the removal of the colonizers' military and governmental forces – does not automatically result in the cessation of the cultural, social, or economic exploitation of the liberated nation by more technologically developed countries. And it is difficult to say that a nation is truly post-colonial if it continues to be exploited by, for example, multinational corporations taking unfair advantage of its cheap labor and its lack of environmental protection laws. By employing the term postcolonial (without the hyphen), as we do here, to name a theoretical framework used to analyze literature and other cultural productions, we are not limiting ourselves to texts written after the removal of the colonizers' military and governmental forces. Rather, we're interested in analyzing writing produced as a result of colonization, which means we're interested in literature written at any time following a nation's initial contact with a colonialist oppressor.

3 It is interesting to note that the concept of double consciousness was first articulated in 1903 by African American writer W. E. B. DuBois in *The Souls of Black Folk*.

4 A brief history of the Chipko Movement is available online at www.iisd.org/50comm/commdb/desc/d07.htm. For a more comprehensive discussion of the movement see Guha's *The Unquiet*

Woods. You can read about the Green Belt Movement online at www.greenbeltmovement.org and in Maathai.

5 I include Morrison in this list of Fourth World Nobel laureates because many postcolonial thinkers find that her work, as the work of an African American author writing about African American experience, illuminates a number of Fourth World issues. From whatever perspective we consider her astounding corpus, her work offers a great deal of insight into the social and psychological manifestations of such postcolonial concepts as othering, unhomeliness, mimicry, cultural colonization, and the like.

6 Additional multinational corporations with which you might be familiar include Bank of America, Nestlé, JPMorgan Chase, Wells Fargo, Chevron, Apple, Wal-Mart Stores, AT&T, IBM, Microsoft, Ford Motor, Samsung Electronics, and Johnson & Johnson. As the term implies, *multinational corporations*, though they usually have a home base in a single country, have substantial operations in a number of nations. (You can get an online list of the top 2,000 multinational corporations for a given year at www.forbes.com/global2000/.) For an example of opposing viewpoints on the benefits of globalization, see Hobson and Bhagwati.

7 See, also, Vidal and BBC News: In pictures.

8 For more information about these two events, see Greenhouse, Hossain, and Manik and Yardley.

9 See, for example, Baby Milk Action, INFACT Canada, and Krasny.

10 Examples of local grassroots resistance, often called *peasant resistance*, include the Chipko Movement in India (see Guha's *The Unquiet Woods*, and go online to www.iisd.org/50comm/commdb/desc/d07.htm); the Narmada Bachao Andolan, or the Save the Narmada Movement, also in India (go online to www.narmada.org); the Green Belt Movement in Kenya (see Maathai, and go online to www.greenbeltmovement.org); the American Indian Movement in the United States (go online to www.aimovement.org); and the Movimento Sem Terra, or the Movement of Landless Rural Workers, in Brazil (see Carter, and go online to www.mstbrazil.org/about-mst/history).

11 For a discussion of these and other issues raised by the tourism industry's international marketing of indigenous lands and cultures, see Hall and Tucker. For example, as you'll see among the essays included in this anthology, some promoters of cultural tourism – which is intended to honor the peoples whose traditional arts, crafts, dress, dwellings and customs are on display for global visitors – are, in fact, exploiting these peoples in a variety of ways.

12 Information concerning the history of recent events at Hacenda Looc comes from the following overlapping sources: Marbella, Olea, Republic of the Philippines Department of Agrarian Reform, Schradie and DeVries, and Vohra, *et al.*

13 For a summary of divergent perspectives on ecotourism, see Higham.

14 The ad for Pico de Loro can be seen online at www.youtube.com/watch?v=t6Tf XV_QSk.

15 The following are just a small sampling of tourism companies with upscale, luxury offerings in heretofore unspoiled, rural, or developing regions of the world: Club Méditerranée (Club Med), Hayes & Jarvis, Wyndham Vacation Ownership, Landco Pacific Corporation, Kuoni Travel, Lonrho Corporation, Sterling Holidays, and SM Land Inc.

16 To learn more about human rights issues related to a variety of forms of global tourism in the Third World, you might begin with the following organizations: Third World Network (www.twnside.org.sg), People's Coalition on Food Sovereignty (www.foodsov.org), and Asian Peasants Coalition (www.asianpeasant.org).

17 Like all of the terminology discussed below, the word *conservationism* has had different meanings at different times and in different places. Today, especially in the United States, *conservationism* often refers to efforts to promote sustainability: the conscientious use and management of such natural resources as air, water, soil, timber, renewable and nonrenewable energy sources, and metal and other mineral ores so that they will continue to be available for use by future generations. However, from the perspective of conservation organizations in the US and around the world, *conservationism* means the setting aside of large tracts of unspoiled land as protected areas for the preservation of all the forms of plant and nonhuman animal life it supports – that is, for the preservation of its biodiversity – both for its own sake and for the environmental well-being of the planet. It is the second meaning of the word we are using here. Related, and often overlapping, terms include *ecology, environmentalism,* and *ecocriticism.*

Ecology is the scientific study of the complex web of relationships among living things (for example, among animals, human animals, insects, plants, and microorganisms) and the specific environments – living and non-living – they inhabit. The field of ecology includes the study of the harmful effects of human mismanagement on the natural environment and how the natural environment might be preserved or recuperated.

Environmentalism generally refers to organized advocacy for the protection of nature – the natural *environment*, which consists of all nonhuman forms of life – from the destructive forces of pollution and other human damage. Environmental activists lobby government officials, organize protests, and raise funds to support their work, which includes the preservation and restoration of native plant and nonhuman animal life.

Ecocriticism, which emerged in literary studies during the 1990s, focuses on literary representations of the environment and what those representations suggest about the literary work's attitude toward nature. Ecocritics believe strongly in the preservation of the natural world and in the proposition that human culture should respect and harmonize with nature. Ecocriticism is, as Cheryll Glotfelty puts it, "an earth-centered approach to literary studies" (xviii). Foundational texts include Lawrence Buell's *The Environmental Imagination: Thoreau, Nature Writing, and the Formation of American Culture* (1995) and Cheryll Glotfelty and Harold Fromm's *The Ecocriticism Reader: Landmarks in Literary Ecology* (1996).

18 For a thorough discussion of the divide between postcolonial and conservationist concerns about the environment, see Nixon (233–62).

19 According to the United Nations Permanent Forum on Indigenous Issues, "It is estimated that there are more than 370 million indigenous people spread across 70 countries worldwide. Practicing unique traditions, they retain social, cultural, economic and political characteristics that are distinct from those of the dominant societies in which they live. Spread across the world from the Arctic to the South Pacific, they are the descendants – according to common definition – of those who inhabited a country or a geographical region at the time when people of different cultures or ethnic origins arrived. The new arrivals later became dominant through conquest, occupation, settlement or other means" (Fifth Session, May 2006). Indigenous peoples – also referred to as native peoples, first peoples, first nations, and tribal peoples – include, for example, those of the Americas (for instance, the Lakota in the United States, the Maya in Guatemala, and the Aymara in Bolivia); the Inuit of the Arctic circle; the Saami of northern Europe; the Maasai of Kenya and Tanzania; the Katawhang Lumad of the southern Philippines; the Santal of India, Bangladesh, and Nepal; the Arrernte of central Australia; and the Maori of New Zealand.

20 White Americans became interested in the Yosemite region for tourist purposes during the 1850s. In 1864, a portion of the area was set aside as a park under the management of the state of California. In 1890 Yosemite National Park – today comprising 1,169 square miles – was created. In 1916, the National Park Service, which oversees the management of America's national parks, was established. Adams' famous photographs of the area were published in 1927.

21 The first "debt-for-nature swap" occurred in 1987 when Conservation International (CI) paid a portion of Bolivia's foreign debt in exchange for that country's agreement to invest in the protection of lands in northern Bolivia in and adjacent to what is now called the Beni Biosphere Reserve. Since then, over a billion dollars have been spent in debt-for-nature swaps worldwide. For CI's view of this practice, go online to www.conservation.org/global/gcf/ … /GCF_debtfor-nature_overview.pdf. For a critical view of this practice, including its negative effects on indigenous peoples, see Knicley.

22 For more details about Australia's Indigenous Protected Areas, go online to www.environment.gov.au/indigenous/ipa.

23 The following social justice organizations can help you begin to learn about indigenous peoples and their concerns: Cultural Survival (www.culturalsurvival.org); First Peoples Worldwide (www.firstpeoples.org); Forest Peoples Programme (www.forestpeoples.org); International Work Group for Indigenous Affairs (www.iwgia.org); Survival International (www.survival-international.org); and Tebtebba: Indigenous Peoples' International Centre for Policy Research and Education (www.tebtebba.org).

24 Among the numerous literary works that include representations of postcolonial concerns about the environment are Helon Habila's *Oil on Water: A Novel* (2010), Linda Hogan's *People of the Whale* (2008), Indra Sinha's *Animal's People* (2007), Kiran Desai's *The Inheritance of Loss* (2006), Amitav Ghosh's *The Hungry Tide* (2004), Zakes Mda's *The Heart of Redness* (2000), J. M. Coetzee's *The Lives of Animals* (1999), Arundhati Roy's *The God of Small Things* (1997), Derek Walcott's *Collected Poems 1948–1984* (1986), Ah Cheng's "The King of Trees" (1985), Ngugi wa Thiong'o's *Petals of Blood* (1977), Flora Nwapa's *Efuru* (1966), and Alejo Carpentier's *The Lost Steps* (1953).

25 As my students have reminded me, the scene of Myrtle Wilson's hit-and-run death includes "[a] pale, well dressed Negro" who is not othered. This character "step[s] near" a police officer in order to tell what he witnessed, and the officer is eager to take the man's information (147; ch. 7). This brief passage thus confers some authority on the black character. Nevertheless, the racial atmosphere pervading the novel suggests that he wouldn't have been taken seriously had he not had light skin and worn good clothing. Indeed, one could argue that Fitzgerald portrayed him in this manner so that the officer, and the (white) reader, would have reason to believe his testimony.

Works cited

Achebe, Chinua. *Morning Yet on Creation Day.* Garden City, NY: Doubleday, 1975.

———. "An Image of Africa: Racism in Conrad's *Heart of Darkness.*" *Massachusetts Review* 18 (1977): 782–94. Rpt. in *Hopes and Impediments, Selected Essays.* New York: Anchor, 1989. 1–20.

Amnesty International. "Oil industry has brought poverty and pollution to Niger Delta." June 30, 2009. (Available online at www.amnesty.org/en/news-and-updates/news/oil-industry-has-brought-poverty-and-pollution-to-niger-delta-20090630.)

Austen, Jane. *Mansfield Park.* London: T. Egerton, 1814.

Baby Milk Action. "The Nestlé Boycott." (Available online at www.babymilk.org/pages/boycott.html.) n.d.

BBC News: In pictures. "Living on oil." (Available online at http://news.bbc.co.uk/1/shared/spl/hi/picture_gallery/04/africa_polluting_nigeria/html/1.stm.) n.d.

Bhabha, Homi K. *The Location of Culture.* New York: Routledge, 1994.

Bhagwati, Jagdish. *In Defense of Globalization.* New York: Oxford University Press, 2007.

Brontë, Charlotte. *Jane Eyre.* 1847. New York: Alfred A. Knopf, 1991.

Bruccoli, Matthew J. "Explanatory Notes." *The Great Gatsby.* 1925. New York: Macmillan, 1992. 207–14.

Carter, Miguel, ed. *Challenging Social Inequality: The Landless Rural Workers Movement and Agrarian Reform in Brazil.* Durham, NC: Duke University Press Books, 2013.

Conrad, Joseph. *Heart of Darkness.* 1902. New York: Norton, 1988.

DeLoughrey, Elizabeth, and George B. Handley, eds. *Postcolonial Ecologies: Literatures of the Environment.* New York: Oxford University Press, 2011.

Dowie, Mark. *Conservation Refugees: The Hundred-Year Conflict between Global Conservation and Native Peoples.* Cambridge, MA: MIT Press, 2009.

DuBois, W. E. B. *The Souls of Black Folk: Essays and Sketches.* 1903. New York: Kraus, 1973.

Fitzgerald, F. Scott. *The Great Gatsby.* 1925. New York: Macmillan, 1992.

Glotfelty, Cheryll. "Introduction: Literary Studies in an Age of Environmental Crisis." *The Ecocriticism Reader: Landmarks in Literary Ecology.* Eds. Cheryll Glotfelty and Harold Fromm. Athens: University of Georgia Press, 1996.

Gordimer, Nadine. *My Son's Story.* New York: Farrar Straus Giroux, 1990.

Greenhouse, Steven. "2nd Supplier for Walmart at Factory That Burned." *The New York Times,* December 10, 2012. (Available online as "Documents Reveal New Details about Walmart's Connection to Tazreen Factory Fire" at www.nytimes.com.)

Guha, Ramachandra. *The Unquiet Woods: Ecological Change and Peasant Resistance in the Himalya.* Berkeley: University of California Press, 1989.

————. "Radical American Environmentalism and Wilderness Preservation: A Third World Critique." *Varieties of Environmentalism: Essays North and South*. Ramachandra Guha and Juan Martinez-Alier. London: Earthscan, 1997. 92–108. An earlier version of this essay appeared in *Environmental Ethics* 11.1 (1989): 71–83.

Hall, C. Michael, and Hazel Tucker, eds. *Tourism and Postcolonialism: Contested Discourses, Identities and Representations*. London and New York: Routledge, 2004.

Higham, James. "Ecotourism: Competing and Conflicting Schools of Thought." *Critical Issues in Ecotourism: Understanding a Complex Tourism Phenomenon*. Oxford: Elsevier, 2007. 1–19.

Hobson, Ira R. "The Unseen World of Transnational Corporations' Powers." *The Neumann Business Review: Journal of the Division of Business and Information Management* 1 (Spring 2006): 23–31. (Also available online at www.neumann.edu.)

Hossain, Emran. "Bangladesh Building Collapse Leaves Hundreds Missing as Search Ends." *The Huffington Post*, May 15, 2013. (Available at www.huffingtonpost.com.)

INFACT (Infant Feeding Action Coalition) Canada. "Nestlé Boycott Home." (Available online at www. infactcanada.ca/nestle_boycott.htm.) n.d.

Jaakson, Reiner. "Globalisation and Neocolonialist Tourism." *Tourism and Postcolonialism: Contested Discourses, Identities and Representations*. Eds. Michael C. Hall and Hazel Tucker. London and New York: Routledge, 2004.

Knicley, Jared E. "Debt, Nature, and Indigenous Rights: Twenty-five Years of Debt-for-Nature Evolution." *Harvard Environmental Law Review* 36.1 (2012): 79–122. (Available online at www3.law.harvard.edu/journals/eir/archive/volume-36-volume-1-2012.)

Krasny, Jill. "Every Parent Should Know the Scandalous History of Infant Formula." *Business Insider*, June 25, 2012. (Available online at www.businessinsider.com/nestles-infant-formula-scandal-2012-6?op-1.)

Loomba, Ania. *Colonialism/Postcolonialism*. 2nd ed. London and New York: Routledge, 2005.

Maathai, Wangari. *The Greenbelt Movement: Sharing the Approach and the Experience*. New York: Lantern Books, 2003.

Manik, Jufikar Ali, and Jim Yardley. "Building Collapse in Bangladesh Kills Scores of Garment Workers." *The New York Times*, April 24, 2013. (Available online as "Building Collapse in Bangladesh Leaves Scores Dead" at www.nytimes.com.)

Marbella, Wilfredo. *Petition to Stop Landgrabbing in Hacienda Looc*. August 8, 2012. (Available online at www.asianpeasant.org/petition/petition-stop-landgrabbing-hacienda-looc.)

McClintock, Anne. "The Angel of Progress: Pitfalls of the Term 'Post-colonialism.'" *Social Text* (Spring 1992): 1–15. Rpt. in *Colonial Discourse and Post-Colonial Theory*. Eds. Patrick Williams and Laura Chrisman. New York: Columbia University Press, 1994. 291–304.

Morrison, Toni. *Beloved*. New York: Alfred A. Knopf, 1987.

————. *Playing in the Dark: Whiteness and the Literary Imagination*. New York: Vintage, 1993.

Moskos, Charles C. *Greek Americans: Struggle and Success*. 2nd ed. Piscataway, NJ: Transaction Publishers, Rutgers – The State University, 2009.

Nixon, Rob. "Environmentalism, Postcolonialism, and American Studies." *Slow Violence and the Environmentalism of the Poor*. Cambridge, MA: Harvard University Press, 2011.

Olea, Ronalyn V. "Int'l Mission Urges Gov't to Stop Land-use Conversion in Hacienda Looc." *Bulatlat*. February 17, 2012. (Available online at www.bulatlat.com/news/4-43/4-43-looc.html.)

Plumwood, Val. *Environmental Culture: The Ecological Crisis of Reason*. London and New York: Routledge, 2002.

Republic of the Philippines Department of Agrarian Reform. *O.P. Case No. 99-E-8734*, July 5, 2000. (Available online at www.lis.dar.gov.ph/home/document_view/1559.)

Rhys, Jean. *Wide Sargasso Sea*. London: Deutsch, 1966.

Said, Edward W. *Orientalism*. New York: Pantheon, 1978.

———. *Culture and Imperialism*. New York: Knopf, 1994.

Schradie, Jen, and Matt DeVries, filmmakers. *The Golf War*. 1999. (Available online at www.golfwar. org and on YouTube: enter "link tv documentary the golf war.")

Shelley, Mary. *Frankenstein*. London: Lackington, Hughes, Harding, Mavor, & Jones, 1818.

Smith, M. E. "Hegemony and Elite Capital: The Tools of Tourism." *Tourism and Culture: An Applied Perspective*. Ed. E. Chambers. Albany: State University of New York Press, 1997. 199–214.

Tiffin, Helen. "Post-Colonial Literatures and Counter-Discourse." *Kunapipi* 9.3 (1987): 17–34. Excerpted in *The Post-Colonial Studies Reader*. Eds. Bill Ashcroft, Gareth Griffiths, and Helen Tiffin. New York: Routledge, 1995. 95–98.

United Nations Permanent Forum on Indigenous Issues. Factsheet: "Who Are Indigenous Peoples?" Fifth Session, May 2006. (Available online at www.un.org/esa/socdev/unpfii/documents/5session_factsheet1.pdf.)

Vidal, John, "Shell Settlement with Ogoni People Stops Short of Full Justice." *Guardian*, June 10, 2009. (Available online at www.guardian.co.uk.)

Vohra, Baljit, *et al*. *Evaluation of the USAID/Philippines Privatization Project, Project No. 492–0428*. Intrados/International Management Group. September 1992. Appendices VII and VIII. (Available online at http://pdf.usaid.gov/pdf_docs/XDABG759A.pdf).

13 Gaining an overview

If you've read several of the preceding chapters, you may be feeling a bit over-whelmed both by the amount of information you've consumed and by the various ways in which many critical theories overlap with one another. The following questions are offered, not as a summary of the schools of criticism we've discussed but as ways to organize your thoughts as you reflect on what you've learned and decide which theories you'd like to pursue further. Certainly, "Some Questions Critics Ask about Literary Texts" and "Questions for Further Practice" (which preceding chapters provide as specific guidelines for applying the critical theories they describe) are more thorough than the brief questions listed below. However, the questions that follow offer you a kind of bird's-eye overview of the theories we've studied and, therefore, an opportunity to see more generally the ways in which critical theories both resemble and differ from one another.

Psychoanalytic Criticism – How is the text shaped by its (intentional or uninten-tional) representation of the psychological desires, needs, and conflicts of its characters (or the psychological desires, needs, and conflicts of its author)?

Marxist Criticism – How is the text shaped by its (intentional or unintentional) representation of capitalism and/or classism? Does this representation support or undermine these oppressive socioeconomic ideologies?

Feminist Criticism – How is the text shaped by its (intentional or unintentional) representation of patriarchal norms and values? Does this representation support or undermine these oppressive norms and values?

New Criticism – Is the text a great work of literature? That is, does it have both organic unity and a theme of universal significance?

Reader-Response Criticism – How do readers make meaning as they read the text, and what is the relationship between the meaning they make and the text?

Structuralist Criticism – What is the underlying structural system (for example, archetypal, modal, or narratological) by which we make sense of the text? Structuralist critics often refer to a text's underlying structure as its grammar, which might be expressed as a kind of "mathematical formula" that represents the functions of characters and their actions.

Deconstructive Criticism — What do we learn about the ideology (or ideologies) operating in the text by analyzing the text's self-contradictions rather than by trying to resolve those contradictions into some overarching theme?

New Historicism — How does the text participate in the interpretation of history? Specifically, what role does the text play in the circulation of discourses (ways of using language that are associated with particular ideologies, such as the discourses of liberal humanism, Christian fundamentalism, or white supremacy) prevalent in the culture from which the work emerged and/or prevalent in the culture(s) in which the work is interpreted?

Cultural Criticism — Especially in regard to working-class cultural productions (such as popular fiction and movies) and to comparisons of working-class productions with the productions of "high" culture (such as canonized literature), what cultural work does the text perform? That is, how does the text transmit and transform the ideologies that support and/or undermine the sociopolitical power structure at the time the text was produced and/or over the course of its reception?

Lesbian, Gay, and Queer Criticism — How is the text shaped by its (intentional or unintentional) representation of LGBTQ sexuality? Does this representation support or undermine heterosexism? For queer theory, specifically, how does the text illustrate the inadequacy of our traditional way of thinking about sexuality and sexual orientation?

African American Criticism — How is the text shaped by its (intentional or unintentional) representation of race and racial difference? Does this representation support or undermine racist ideologies?

Postcolonial Criticism — How is the text shaped by its (intentional or unintentional) representation of cultural difference (the ways in which race, class, sex, gender, sexual orientation, religion, cultural beliefs, and customs combine to form individual identity)? Does this representation support or undermine colonialist ideologies?

Although these questions focus on the interpretation of literary texts, I trust that by this point you are fully aware that each theoretical lens alters the way we perceive ourselves and our world as well. To cite just one example, African American criticism, considered in its broadest context, asks us to see what we can learn by examining the ways in which race (for example, perceptions of racial difference, the history of race in America, and racism) informs our individual and collective identity; our interpersonal relationships; our history; and our cultural productions, including but not limited to literature. Thus, taken together, critical theories enlarge our understanding not only of literary works, though that is a worthwhile end in itself, but also of human experience in general.

I'm sure you've noticed that some of the schools of criticism listed above are overtly political: their goal is to change society for the better in some way. Other theories see themselves as "apolitical," as removed from the forces that shape history and politics. A striking example of this kind of theory is New Criticism, which was the dominant force in literary studies in the late 1940s and 1950s and which saw itself as occupying a purely aesthetic realm. However, most critical theorists today recognize that all critical theories are produced by historical realities and have political implications whether or not their advocates are aware of those realities and implications.

For example, many politically oriented theorists believe that the creation of a purely aesthetic realm of literary analysis is itself a political move that reflects a desire to escape history, a desire to carve out a "safe" space where one can feel protected from the unpredictable and often frightening realities of the world. However, a critical practice that ignores political reality does not thereby remove itself from politics. It merely protects, however inadvertently, whatever power structure is in place by drawing our attention away from that power structure. From this perspective, it is not surprising that New Criticism rose to prominence and that structuralism emerged in the years following World War II, when the fear of nuclear holocaust was at its height and, therefore, the belief in a permanent realm of ideas beyond the reach of human events was especially appealing. Indeed, "apolitical" theories always serve conservative power structures.

One could analyze, in a similar fashion, the historical roots and political implications of any critical theory. Of course, the historical roots and political implications of some critical theories are more obvious than those of others. For example, feminist criticism, African American criticism, and lesbian, gay, and queer criticism grew directly out of political movements: respectively, the women's liberation, Black Power, and gay and lesbian liberation movements of the late 1960s, although the intellectual roots of all three schools of criticism are as old as the struggle for equality regardless of sex, race, or sexual orientation. Similarly, Marxist criticism is a response to social injustice, as are, in large part, postcolonial, new historical, and cultural criticism.

On the other hand, the political or "apolitical" orientation of psychoanalytic, reader-response, and deconstructive criticism depends entirely on the individual critic and the purpose for which the theory is used. For example, the psycho-analytic reading of *The Great Gatsby* offered in Chapter 2 is "apolitical" (that is, it ignores politics and thus does nothing to alter the political status quo) because it focuses on dysfunctional love as an individual, or familial, disorder. Had I, instead, examined the novel's representation of dysfunctional love as a product of modern American culture – perhaps as a product of the intersection of capitalism, patriarchy, and other ideological forces – I would have produced an overtly political psychoanalytic reading (or, depending on how I focused the essay, a psychoanalytically oriented Marxist or feminist reading).

Similarly, reader-response criticism can function "apolitically" when, for example, it examines how texts elicit particular reading experiences, as we saw in the section on affective stylistics in Chapter 6. Or reader-response criticism can have a political function when, for example, it examines the ideological motives informing the way certain literary works have been read by whole generations of critics. Deconstruction, too, is "apolitical" when it is used to show that the meaning of a text is undecidable: the text's meaning can't be pinned down and, therefore, the text has no meaning in the traditional sense of the word. Certainly, if a text has no meaning, it has no politics. In the hands of other practitioners, however, deconstruction can be a powerful political tool when it is used to reveal the ideological contradictions – the hidden politics – operating in a text, as we saw in the deconstructive reading of *The Great Gatsby* offered in Chapter 8.

In short, the meaning and power of every critical theory depend largely on you. Critical theories are tools in your hands, no more, no less. You can choose one theory and interpret literature through that lens alone, or you can become adept at using two, three, or more theories, even combining the insights they offer as you interpret a single literary work. You might produce, for example, an African American reading that draws on Marxist, psychoanalytic, and feminist concepts in order to interpret the representation of racial difference in a literary work. Or you might produce a feminist reading that draws on postcolonial and reader-response concepts in order to analyze what you consider a recurrent misreading of a literary work written, for example, by a West Indian woman. In fact, it is not unreasonable to argue that, in order to be really proficient at applying some critical theories, it is necessary that you familiarize yourself with the theories on which they draw. For many Marxist, feminist, postcolonial, African American, and lesbian/gay/queer critics draw on one another's theoretical frameworks as well as on such theories as psychoanalysis, deconstruction, reader-response theory, and semiotics in order to analyze the myriad forms and processes of oppression and the resistance to oppression.

The theory or theories you choose to use for a particular reading, however, should depend mainly on two factors: (1) your own ability to use the theory, and (2) the literary text to which you plan to apply it. For in order to produce a useful reading you need a good fit, both between yourself and the theory you choose and between the theory you choose and the literary text. Not all literary texts lend themselves equally well to all theories. So part of your skill must involve recognizing when to apply which theory. Like any skill worth acquiring, it takes practice. Don't be discouraged by initial difficulties you may encounter. Your violin has to squeak quite a bit before you learn to play Mozart.

And if I may offer one more warning, don't dismiss a theory because you find it has some flaws. It's easy to find fault with critical theories. They all have flaws. That's part of what it means to be a theory rather than a fact. For example, how can a literary work be its own context, as New Criticism claims it is? Isn't that a logical absurdity, a violation of the definition of context? Or how can psychoanalysis omit or marginalize sociological factors in the creation of the psyche, when the family (which psychoanalysis holds responsible for the formation of the psyche) is itself a sociological entity?

Finding faults in a theory, however, does not necessarily render that theory less helpful for literary interpretation. And if we practice faultfinding too soon in our learning process, we can overlook the enormous usefulness of many theories as our tendency to dismiss them grows, a tendency that is fed, it seems to me, by our understandable desire to feel less intimidated by critical theory. The logic is inviting but very self-defeating: if a critical theory is flawed, then it's not so important that I become proficient at it, and I don't have to worry about my difficulties with it. So I urge you very strongly to postpone the "critique mode" for a while, at least until you have thoroughly familiarized yourself with a range of theories by using them to interpret literature.

Before I send you off on your own to do those readings, however, I'd like to share with you a recent experience that I think reflects both the personal and the political nature of critical theory and literary interpretation. I briefly described my feminist, postcolonial, and queer readings of *The Great Gatsby* to an interested friend who loves to read literature but who knows nothing about critical theory. He immediately asked, "Are any of the theories you use in your textbook in harmony with the novel?" "They all are," I hastened to assure him. "I wouldn't apply a theory to a literary work if it distorted the work," I explained. "No," he said, "I mean, do all the theories find something *wrong* with the novel?"

Then it hit me. He's right! Almost all the theories I used have led me to conclude, in effect, that the novel is ideologically flawed in some way. If I put all these flaws together, I come up with a statement something like this: "*The Great Gatsby* is a classist, sexist, homophobic, racist, colonialist novel that romanticizes the evils of capitalism, glorifies dysfunctional love, and, as if that weren't enough, creates an indeterminate reading experience that invites us to project our own beliefs and desires onto the text." Yet *The Great Gatsby* is also one of the most moving and exquisitely written literary works it's ever been my pleasure to read. How can that be?

Perhaps the better question is, How can that not be? Few critics would deny that Fitzgerald had one of the best ears for language ever bestowed on an American writer or that *The Great Gatsby* is one of the most lyrically beautiful, masterfully crafted works ever produced. At the same time, the novel was written in 1924 by a young white man struggling for acceptance by the upper class and for literary recognition that he did not achieve during his lifetime. And if his biographers are to be believed, including those biographers who admire his work and appreciate the difficulties he suffered in life, Fitzgerald was a man of his time who had all the ideological biases that a man of his time could possibly possess. How could these elements not appear in the work that he believed would be his greatest achievement and into which he poured himself so completely? In fact, even had Fitzgerald not shared all the ideological biases that inform his novel, those biases would have appeared in the work in some form because *The Great Gatsby* was intended as a chronicle of the 1920s, of the author's own generation – or at least of the elite white population with whom the author was acquainted – and Fitzgerald was an extremely accurate observer of human behavior. In short, the times were ideologically flawed even if the author hadn't been.

Yet I didn't really see these flaws as "something wrong with the novel," as my friend put it. I was so excited by my ability to see the appalling ideologies my theories were helping me uncover that I forgot to be appalled by them. Yes, the novel is ideologically appalling, a fact we mustn't forget. And the novel is intensely beautiful as well. This is the contradiction I try to sustain as I continue to appreciate both the incomparable artistry of *The Great Gatsby* and the theories that show me the multiple layers of its disquieting subtext. Sustaining that contradiction in Fitzgerald's novel and in all the literature I read is, I believe, one of the greatest pleasures that reading through a theoretical lens offers us. It may be an acquired taste. If so, I would be very happy if the book you hold in your hands helped you acquire it.

Index

Please note that page numbers relating to Notes will have the letter "n" following the page number.

abandonment, fear of: in psychoanalysis 16, 17, 22; in *Frankenstein* 35–6; parental role 13, 23

Aboriginal Australians 398, 401, 420; *see also* Australia

Absalom, Absalom! (Faulkner) 96

abstraction: in psychoanalysis 21–2; in French feminism 100

Achebe, Chinua 278, 404, 408, 422–3, 440

actants in structuralist narratology 212

activism 88, 108–9

Adams, Ansel 417

adultery, theme of 135

Adventures of Huckleberry Finn (Twain) 209–10, 307, 325

affectation 42

affective fallacy 131

affective stylistics, reader-response theory 166–9

African American criticism/African Americans 34, 141, 343–97, 449; African American feminists 101–3; basic tenets of critical race theory 352–68; black writers 345, 347–8, 372–3; critical race theory 350–68; folk motifs 369, 392; *Great Gatsby*, African American reading 280, 378, 379–92; literary texts, questions asked by African American critics 377–9; and literature 368–77; orality 369, 392; oral tradition 349; other literary works, African American approaches to 392–3; qualities of African American texts 349–50; racial issues and African American literary history 343–50; spiritual themes 371–2, 393; stereotypes 358, 369, 379; trickster tales 350; women (black), marginalization of 101–2, 372–3; *see also* racial issues; racism

African American history: exclusion from American history books 343–4; key milestones 343; and racial issues *see* racial issues; slavery 344, 348, 350; *see also* African American criticism/African Americans; racism

African American Vernacular English (AAVE) 346, 347, 378

Africanism 374, 375

African Wildlife Foundation (AWF) 419

Afrocentricity 350

Age of Innocence, The (Wharton) 209

AIDS *see* HIV/AIDS

AIDS Coalition to Unleash Power (ACT UP) 317

Albee, Edward 302

Alger, Horatio 287, 290, 291

Allen, Paula Gunn 314

Allison, Dorothy 314

ambiguity: in language 237–8; in literary texts 133–4, 135

American Civil War (1861–65), and African American history 358, 366, 368

American dream, ideology of 55–6, 58, 62

American Psychiatric Association, and homosexuality 304

American Revolution (1775–83), and new historicism 273

America's Castles (television series) 296

anal developmental stage 24

Anatomy of Criticism (Frye) 226, 233n

Anderson, Jervis 385

Anderson, R. C. 195n

Anderson, Sherwood 386

androgyny 110

Angelou, Maya 345

Animal Farm (Orwell) 209

anthropology, structural 203–4

anticolonialism 278, 399, 406, 424, 426, 427–8

anxiety, in psychoanalysis 16, 17

Anzaldúa, Gloria 314
Apocalypse Now (Coppola) 283
archetypes/archetypal criticism 211, 233n
Armour, Philip 287, 291
Armstrong, Louis 385
Arnold, June 314
Aryanism 402–3
Asian Americans 376
"assimilated woman," in African American
    literature 373, 393
attributes, in structuralist narratology 214–15
Auden, W. H. 302
Austen, Jane 133, 425
Australia: Aboriginal Australians 398, 401, 420;
    Australian Homelands Movement 421;
    Indigenous Protected Areas 421, 444n
authorial intention 130, 131
Autobiography of My Mother, The (Kincaid) 440
autumn, mythos of 210
avoidance, in psychoanalysis 15
Awakening, The (Chopin) 33, 298, 307, 325, 393

Babuscio, Jack 318–19
Baker, Houston A. 369, 371, 372, 393
Baldwin, James 302
Ballard-Reisch, Deborah 111
Bambara, Toni Cade 76, 158, 345
Bankhead, Tallulah 385
Banks, Taunya Lovell 354
Baraka, Amiri 348
Barnes, Djuna 80
Barrymore, John and Ethel 385
Barthelme, Donald 218
Barthes, Roland 205
Bartlett, Neil 319
Bearden, Romare 386–7
Beautiful and Damned, The (Fitzgerald) 389
Beauvoir, Simone de 89, 92, 93, 99
Before Reading (Rabinowitz) 196n
Bell, Derrick A. 352, 355, 361, 366, 367–8
Beloved (Morrison) 48, 96, 125, 179, 231, 283,
    323, 423; New Criticism 133–4; new
    historicism 277, 278, 279
Bennett, Paula 312
Bernanos, Georges 213, 214
Bethel, Lorraine 102
betrayal, fear of: in psychoanalysis 16
Bewley, Marcus 191, 294
Bhabha, Homi 403, 423
Bierbower, Austin 288
"Big, Two-Hearted River" (Hemingway) 136
binary oppositions 95–6, 202, 212; and
    deconstruction 240–1, 248, 249, 250; in
    Great Gatsby 256, 258–9, 260–1, 262, 264

biographical-historical criticism 129–30
biological essentialism 81, 306
Birtha, Becky 314
Bishop, Elizabeth 302
Black Arts Movement (1960s) 343, 348, 349
Black Boy (Wright) 370
Black Power Movement 343, 348
Black Vernacular English 346, 347, 378
black women, marginalization 101–2, 372–3
Blake, Eubie 385
Blake, William 265, 298
Bleich, David 169–73, 178
Blues, Ideology, and Afro-American Literature
    (Baker) 369
blues music, and African American literature
    371, 372
Bluest Eye, The (Morrison) 6, 35, 64, 113;
    African American criticism 346, 373, 392;
    lesbian, gay and queer criticism 307, 326,
    339; new historicism and cultural criticism
    297–8; reader-response criticism 174–5, 194
Boccaccio, Giovanni 214–15
Bonmarché 411
Bontemps, Arna 386
Booth, Wayne 196n
"Boston marriage" 303, 309
bourgeoisie, in Marxism 52, 53
Bradbury, Malcolm 379
Brannon, Linda 105
Brathwaite, Edward Kamau 408
bricolage 239
British colonies 399–400, 403, 404, 407, 425
British Commonwealth 407
British Petroleum 409
Brontë, Charlotte 424
Brossard, Nicole 314
Brown, Prince 357–8
Brown, Rita Mae 314
Brown v. Board of Education 355, **364**
Bruccoli, Matthew J. 80, 192, 379, 392
Buck, Pearl 386
buildings, dreams about 20
bullying, of LGBTQ adolescents and young
    adults 304–5
Bunyan, John 209
Burnam, Tom 294
Burroughs, William S. 302

Calloway, Cab 385
camp 316–17
"Camp and the Gay Sensibility" (Babuscio)
    318–19
Cane (Toomer) 386
canonical counter-discourse 424–5

capitalism/capitalist ideology: in *Great Gatsby* 66, 72, 75; and Marxism 58, 59, 60, 61, 64, 66, 72
Carnegie, Andrew 287, 289, 291, 293, 299n
Carpentier, Alejo 445n
Cartwright, Kent 191, 295
castration anxiety 14, 25, 97
Cather, Willa 80, 302, 311–12, 324, 339
Certificates of Land Ownership Awards, Philippines 413
Chaplin, Charlie 385
character functions, in structuralist narratology 212
Chase, Richard 192
"Chase, The" (Moravia) 135
Chauncey, George 332–3
Cheng, Ah 445n
Cher 316
Chesnutt, Charles Waddell 369
Chicanos/as 359, 376
Chipko Movement, India 405, 442n, 443n
Chopin, Kate 85–6, 264; *The Awakening* 33, 298, 307, 325, 393; "The Storm" 76, 125–6, 135, 158, 193
Christian, Barbara 349
"Cinderella," and feminism 84, 85
Civil Rights Movement (1950s and 1960s) 343, 351, 352, 439
Cixous, Hélène 95–6, 97
class consciousness, in Marxism 52
classism 56, 57, 428; in *Great Gatsby* 72–3, 437
Clifton, Lucille 137–41
close reading 129, 135
Coca Cola 410
Coetzee, J. M. 408, 424
Colette (Sidonie-Gabrielle Colette), female writer 96
colonialism: anticolonialism 278, 399, 406, 424, 426, 427–8; colonialist discourse 400; and globalization 409; in *Great Gatsby* 428–9; ideology 399–406, 424, 426, 427; neocolonialism 410–11, 442n; terminology 442n; *see also* postcolonial criticism
colonialist psychology 429, 435, 437, 439
colonial subjects 400, 403, 407, 429
colonies 60, 258, 442n; American 61, 268, 395n; British 399–400, 403, 404, 407, 425; invader 406; white settler 407, 426
colonization 404, 426; cultural 400, 410, 443n; double 405, 406
Color Purple, The (Walker) 374, 393
Comedy of Errors (Shakespeare) 210
Commager, Henry Steele 295

commodity/commodification 59, 60; in *Great Gatsby* 66–7, 68, 69, 70–1, 75; people, as commodities 68
condensation, in dreams 18, 29
conditions, in structuralist narratology 215
connotation vs. denotation 132
Conrad, Joseph 48, 125, 169, 193, 231, 277, 283, 421
conscience vs. superego 24
consciousness 61; double consciousness 346, 403, 407, 426; false 56; structures of 199, 200
conservation, global 416–21
Conservation International (CI) 419, 444n
conservationism 416, 418–19, 443n
conspicuous consumption 60
consumerism ("shop-'til-you-drop-ism") 58, 74, 419
contractual structures 213
Cooke, Jay 291
Coolidge, President Calvin 383
Cooper, Dennis 319
Coppola, Francis Ford 283
core issues, in psychoanalysis 16–18
Country Wife, The (Wycherley) 210
Couples, Fred 414
Crane, Hart 302, 386
Crawford, Joan 385
Crenshaw, Kimberlé Williams 359–60
critical race theory 350–2, 364–5; basic tenets 352–68
critical theory 1–10, 34, 67, 100, 143, 177, 281, 302, 414, 450, 451, 452; flawed 452; *see also* African American criticism/African Americans; critical race theory; cultural criticism; deconstruction/deconstructive criticism; feminist criticism/feminism; lesbian, gay and queer criticism; Marxist criticism/Marxism; New Criticism; new historicism; postcolonial theory/criticism; psychoanalytic criticism/psychoanalytic theory; reader-response criticism/theory; structuralism/structuralist criticism
Crockett, Davy 192
cross-dressing 111, 316
Cruikshank, Margaret 317
Crying of Lot 49, The (Pynchon) 226
Cullen, Countee 346–7, 386
Culler, Jonathan 195n, 217–20
cultural colonization 400, 410, 443n
cultural criticism 280–2, 449; examples 280–1; literary texts, questions asked 285–7; and literature 282–5; new historicism compared 281–2; other literary works, cultural critical

approaches to 297–8; *see also* new
historicism
cultural difference 426, 439–40
cultural displacement 403
cultural identity 407
cultural imperialism 410
cultural productions 58
Cultural Survival 444n
culture: cultural heritage, importance 392; and
gender 88; "high" and "low" forms 281, 283;
patriarchal 97; popular 287; as process 281;
see also cultural criticism
Culture and Imperialism (Said) 425

Dangarembga, Tsitsi 408
death: death drive 21; death work 21, 23;
meaning of 21–3
Death of a Salesman (Miller): feminist criticism
111, 112; Marxist criticism 62, 64; New
Criticism 134, 158; psychoanalytic criticism
15, 34–5; reader-response criticism 165, 166
"death of the author" 1–2
"debt-for-nature swaps" 444n
Decameron, The (Boccaccio) 214–15
deconstruction/deconstructive criticism 89–90,
100, 235–65, 449; and African American
criticism 349; binary oppositions 240–1;
concepts 242; and feminism 90, 235; *Great
Gatsby*, deconstructive reading 251, 252–64;
human identity, deconstructing 243–4;
ideology 239, 240–1, 245–6, 248; language,
deconstructing 235–41; literature,
deconstructing 244–6; meaning-making 236,
237, 238, 239, 242, 244–5; and New
Criticism 246, 248, 249, 250; origins of
deconstruction 235; other literary works,
deconstructive approaches to 264–5;
philosophy 242; poststructuralist theory,
deconstruction as 243; self, definition
407–8; text deconstructing itself 251; world,
deconstructing 241–3; *see also* language
defense mechanisms, in psychoanalysis 11,
15–16, 17, 18, 23
defense mode, in psychological reader-response
theory 175
Defoe, Daniel 424
Delany, Samuel R. 319
Delgado, Richard 351, 352, 355, 359–60, 361,
362, 364, 365
DeLillo, Don 226
Delphy, Christine 93–4
Denard, Carolyn 102
denial, in psychoanalysis 15, 46, 336
Denmark 402

denotation, vs. connotation 132
Derrida, Jacques 6, 9, 100, 235, 239, 240
Desai, Kiran 445n
Descartes, René 242
Desire of the Mother, Lacanian psychoanalysis
27, 30
determinate meaning 165, 166
developmental stages, in psychoanalysis 14
diaspora 403, 426
DiCaprio, Leonardo 296
Dickinson, Emily 48, 178, 312, 313
Didion, Joan 226
différance 239
differential racialization 352, 358–9
Dillon, Andrew 74, 191, 295
discourse 242, 270, 271, 400; canonical
counter-discourse 424–5
discrimination: AIDS-related 304; gender 111;
institutionalized 305; against LGBTQ people
304, 305; racial 345, 350–1; *see also* gender;
racial issues
disjunctive structures 213
displacement/dream displacement 15, 18,
29, 62
distance, in structuralist narratology 216, 218
Doctor Faustus (Mann) 179
domestic work 93–4
Doolittle, Hilda (H. D.) 80, 302
Dorsey, Tommy and Jimmy 385
Doty, Mark 319
double colonization 405, 406
double consciousness/double vision 346, 403,
407, 426
Douglas, Aaron 387
Douglass, Frederick 371
Dove, Rita 345
Dowie, Mark 417, 418, 419, 421
drag/drag queens and kings 315–16
dreams/dream symbols 18–21, 37, 48;
condensation 18, 29; displacement 18, 29
DuBois, W. E. B. 346, 442n
Dudziak, Mary L. 355
Dunbar, Paul Laurence 371
Durante, Jimmy 385
Duras, Marguerite 96
duration, in structuralist narratology 216
Dyson, A. E. 192

Ebonics 346
ecocriticism 443n, 444n
ecology 443n, 444n
economic power, in Marxism 51–2
écriture féminine 96, 99, 125
educated reader 178

ego 25, 56
"Elegiac Stanzas" (Wordsworth) 130
Eliot, T. S. 302
Elizabethan World Picture (Tillyard) 299n
Ellington, Duke 385
Ellison, Ralph 210, 370–1
"emergent woman," in African American
    literature 393
Emerson, Ralph Waldo 416
environmentalism 426, 443n, 444n
Epistemology of the Closet (Sedgwick) 341n
Equiano, Olaudah 371
Essed, Philomena 354–5
Eurocentrism 278, 345, 374–5, 401, 402
everyday racism 352, 353–5, 362
exchange value 59, 60
experience oriented response statements
    171–2
extrinsic criticism 142
ExxonMobil 409

Faderman, Lillian 303–4
Faerie Queen, The (Spenser) 209
fairy tales, feminist reading 84–5, 88
false consciousness 56
family, the 61; unresolved conflicts with parents
    13, 14, 18
"Family in the Wind" (Fitzgerald) 393
fantasy mode, in psychological reader-response
    theory 175
Faulkner, William 76, 96, 126, 142, 231,
    321–2, 325–6
Fauset, Jesse 386
Fausto-Sterling, Anne 108
fear: of abandonment 16, 17, 22; of betrayal
    16; of death 22; of intimacy 15–16, 22–3; of
    loss 23; of risk 23; unconscious 20
Federal Bureau of Investigation (FBI), definition
    of hate crime 124
Feinberg, David 319
Feinberg, Leslie 314
female imagery, in dreams 20
feminist criticism/feminism 34, 79–128, 448;
    African American feminists 82, 91, 101, 103;
    and deconstruction 90, 235; equality
    legislation 81; fairy tales 84–5, 88; feminisms
    79; French feminism 91–100; and gender
    studies 103–12; "good-girl/bad-girl" 14–15,
    85, 86; *Great Gatsby*, feminist reading
    115–25, 280; and heterocentrism 308;
    literary texts, questions asked by feminist
    critics 114–15; and literature 112–14;
    marginalization of female writers 80;
    marriage 92, 93, 95; and Marxism 89, 267;

masculine pronoun, use of to portray men
    and women 79–80; multicultural feminism
    100–3; oppression of women 87, 92–3, 100;
    patriarchy *see* patriarchy; and postcolonial
    criticism 405; premises of feminism 87–8;
    and reader-response criticism 161; sexuality
    85, 86, 87; strengths of feminism 90;
    subjugation of women, recognition 92–3;
    traditional gender roles 25, 81–7, 117;
    universality, standards of 80; white
    mainstream feminism 101; white male
    authors, as standard of universality
    (pre-1960s) 80; women's work 93–4;
    see also gender
Fetterly, Judith 311–12
Fielding, Henry 210
figurative language 135–6
Fil-Estate 414
Finnegan's Wake (Joyce) 96
First Peoples Worldwide 444n
First World 401, 407
First World War, in *Great Gatsby* 381, 382
Fish, Stanley 167, 176, 177
Fisk, Jim 287, 291
Fiske, John 284–5
Fitzgerald, F. Scott 75, 192, 389; *The Beautiful
    and Damned* 389; *The Great Gatsby see Great
    Gatsby, The* (F. Scott Fitzgerald); *Tender Is the
    Night* 117, 390, 393
Fitzgerald, Zelda 117, 337, 338, 389
Foe (Coetzee) 424
folk motifs, in African American literary
    tradition 369, 392
Forest Peoples Programme 444n
formal elements of a literary work 131, 135–7,
    138, 140
formalism 135
Forrey, Robert 390–1
Foucault, Michel 270, 280
Fourth World 401, 404, 407, 443n
Frankenstein (Shelley) 6, 64, 179, 210, 265, 402;
    feminist criticism 113–14; lesbian, gay and
    queer criticism 339–40; postcolonial
    criticism 440–1; psychoanalytic criticism
    35–6, 48
Franklin, Benjamin 255
French feminism 91–100; materialist 91, 92,
    93, 94, 95, 98; psychoanalytic 91, 95–6,
    99, 100
frequency, in structuralist narratology 216
Freud, Sigmund/Freudian theory 11–12, 14,
    24, 25, 36, 97
Frost, Robert 175–6, 264–5, 302; "Mending
    Wall," deconstructive reading 246–51

Frye, Marilyn 311
Frye, Northrop 209–12, 220, 226, 228, 231, 232
Fussell, Edwin 192

Gaines, Ernest J. 345
Gallo, Rose Adrienne 191, 294
Gap (clothing company) 411
Garland, Judy 316
Gates, Henry Louis 349, 369–70, 371
gay criticism 314–19
gay drag 316
Gay Liberation Movement 304, 311
gay sensibility 315
Geertz, Clifford 274
gender: American gender system 105–6, 107; as binary system 105, 110; concept 110; and culture 88; discrimination 111; gender equality legislation 81; gender studies, and feminism 103–12; and identity 103, 110; intersexuality 108, 109, 110; Native North American societies 107; non-binary systems 105–7; and sexuality 104; traditional gender roles 25, 81–7, 117, 321; *see also* feminist criticism/feminism
General Electric 409
Genet, Jean 96
Genette, Gérard 212, 215–17, 231
genital altering surgery 109
genital developmental stage 24
genres, theory of (Frye) 233n
Gerai people, Indonesia 106
Gershwin, George 385
Ghosh, Amitav 445n
Gidley, M. 391, 392
Gilbert, Susan 313
Ginsberg, Allen 302
Giovanni, Nikki 345
Glasgow, Ellen 80
Glaspell, Susan 80
global conservation, and postcolonial theory 416–21
globalization, and "end" of postcolonial theory 409–12
global tourism 412–16, 443n
Glotfelty, Cheryll 444n
Gomez, Jewelle 314
"good-girl/bad-girl" attitude 14–15, 85
Goodman, Benny 385
Gordimer, Nadine 408, 423
Gould, Jay 287, 291
grammar, narrative 221, 222
Grant, Madison 383
Grapes of Wrath, The (Steinbeck) 76, 232, 298

Great Chain of Being, Renaissance notion of 268
Great Gatsby, The (F. Scott Fitzgerald): African American reading 280, 378, 379–92; binary contrasts/oppositions in 256, 258–9, 260–1, 262, 264; class system portrayed in 44, 119, 253–4, 436; deconstructive reading 251, 252–64; female characters in 117–18, 119, 124–5; feminist reading 80, 91, 115–25, 280; imagery 145, 146, 147–8, 150–1, 152, 155–6; Marxist reading 6–7, 65, 66–75, 251–2, 280; modern world, depicting spiritual poverty of 145, 226–8, 252–6, 258, 261, 262; narration/narrator (Nick Carraway character) 183–6, 188, 191, 212, 215, 221–3, 224, 228, 229, 252–3, 254–5, 256, 257, 259, 293–4, 296, 297, 327–38, 385; New Critical reading 144–57; new historical reading 286, 287–97; postcolonial reading 427, 428–40; psychoanalytic reading 28, 38–48, 281, 450; queer reading 280, 325, 327–38; reader-response analysis 181–93; seek-find-lose grammars 223, 224, 225; self-made man discourse 287–97; setting 153–4, 155; sexual ambiguity 328, 333–4; structuralist reading 208, 212, 213, 215, 221–31; unfulfilled longing theme 146, 148, 149–50, 151–2, 153, 154–5, 157; "valley of ashes" 69, 70, 72, 119, 145, 148–9, 188, 227, 229, 254, 384, 430, 433
Green Belt Movement, Kenya 405, 443n
Greenblatt, Stephen 282
Greimas, A. J. 212, 213–14, 215, 217
Gross, Barry Edward 294
Guha, Ramchandra 419, 442–3n
Guillaumin, Colette 94–5
Gulliver's Travels (Swift) 209
Gurganus, Allan 319
gynocriticism 114
gynophobia (fear and loathing of women as sexual and reproductive beings) 113

Habila, Helon 445n
Hacienda Looc, Philippines 413–14, 415, 443n
Hairspray (film) 316
Hall, C. Michael 408
Hamilo Coast 415
Hamlet (Shakespeare) 130–1, 210
Hansen, Jennifer 92
Harlem/Harlem Renaissance 343, 344, 386, 386–7, 391–2; and *Great Gatsby* 379, 385, 390; nightclubs 385, 390, 395n
Harris, Bertha 314
Hart, Jeffrey 191
Hartman, Geoffrey 235

Hawthorne, Nathaniel 297
Hayden, Robert 131, 193
Head, Bessie 408
Heart of Darkness (Conrad) 48, 125, 169, 193, 231, 283; and new historicism 277–9; and postcolonial criticism 421, 422
Heart of Redness, The (Mda) 441
Heller, Joseph 226
Helliwell, Christine 106
Hemingway, Ernest 136, 375–6
heresy of paraphrase 131
Herselvis, Elvis 316
heterocentrism 305–6
heteronormativity 305, 306
heteropatriarchy 305
heterosexism 306, 308, 325, 428
heterosexuality: assumption of 110, 111, 302, 305, 306; compulsory 305
Hill, James J. 287, 291, 382
Hispanic Americans 356
historical situation, in Marxism 52
history: African American, and racial issues 343–50; complexity 269; history as narrative/text 272–3; limitations of traditional history 271–2, 275; marginalized peoples, narratives 273; primary and secondary sources of historical information 272–3; traditional view 268, 269, 271–2, 279; *see also* new historicism
HIV/AIDS 304, 317
Hogan, Linda 408, 445n
Holland, Norman 173–6, 178
Holleran, Andrew 319
homoerotica 306–7, 325; in *Great Gatsby* 327–8, 332
homophobia 304, 305, 306, 308, 318, 319, 325; in *Great Gatsby* 330, 338
homosexuality 83, 84, 271; gay criticism 314–15; minoritizing or universalizing views 306, 341n; removal from APA list of psychological disorders (1974) 304; *see also* lesbian, gay and queer criticism; LGBTQ (lesbian, gay, bisexual, transgender and queer) people
homosocial 307
homosocial bonding 324–5
homosocial views 306, 307
House of Mirth (Wharton) 133
How to Succeed (Bierbower) 288
Hughes, Langston 76, 158, 302, 347, 386, 392
Hurston, Zora Neale 371, 373, 386, 392, 393
hybridity/syncretism 404, 426
hysteria, feminist critique 81–2

id, the 25
ideal reader 178
identity: black women, literary representations 374; cultural 407; and gender 103, 110; human identity, deconstructing 243–4; individual, and cultural beliefs 421–2; personal 275–6; postcolonial 399–406; and sexuality 24, 327
identity themes, in psychological reader-response theory 175, 176
ideology: American dream as 55–6, 58, 62; capitalist 58; colonialist 399–406, 424, 426, 427; deconstruction 239, 240–1, 245–6, 248; defined 54; and language 235; in Marxism 54–9; and nature 54, 55; and new historicism 270; overt ideological project of text 248, 251; patriarchal 85, 87–8, 89, 112, 113, 124; patriotism 57; and the Real 31; and religion 57; repressive 54–5, 58; sexist 54, 85, 125, 308
imagery 135–6, 143, 312–13; in *Great Gatsby* 145, 146, 147–8, 150–1, 152, 155–6
Imaginary Order, Lacanian psychoanalysis 27, 31, 32, 33, 37, 48
Immigration Act (1924) 383, 402
Immigration and Nationality Act (1952 and 1965) 359–60
imperialism 60, 410, 442n
implied reader 179
Importance of Being Earnest, The (Wilde) 324
Incidents in the Life of a Slave Girl (Jacobs) 348, 371
Indefinite Quantity Contract, Philippines 413–14
indeterminacy/indeterminate meaning 165–6, 188, 189, 190, 191
index, in semiotics 206
India: Chipko Movement 405, 442n, 443n; Save the Narmada Movement 443n
indigenous activists 420, 443n
Indigenous Protected Area (IPA) concept 420–1, 421, 444n
individualism, rugged 55, 57, 192
industrialism 59, 419, 420
infants: Lacanian psychoanalysis 26, 27, 30, 31; language 99; pre-verbal feelings 27, 30, 31; as sexual beings 24
informed reader 178
institutionalized discrimination, against LGBTQ people 304–5
institutionalized racism 345
intentional fallacy 130
interest convergence 352, 355

internalized homophobia 305
internalized racism 346
international aid, postcolonial women 405–6
International World Group for Indigenous Affairs 444n
Interpretation of Cultures, The (Geertz) 274
interpretive community 176
intersectionality 352, 359–60
intersexuality 108, 109, 110
intimacy, fear of, in psychoanalysis 15–16, 22–3; in *Great Gatsby* 39–40, 42, 43, 44, 47
intra-racial racism 346, 394n
intrinsic criticism 142
invader colonies 406
Invisible Man (Ellison) 210, 370
Ireland, and postcolonial theory 406
Ireland, Alexander 341n
Irigaray, Luce 97–8, 235
irony, and the structure of literary genres 209, 210
Irwin, Hale 414
Iser, Wolfgang 165, 179, 195n
"I Stand Here Ironing" (Olsen) 231–2

Jacobs, Harriet 348, 371
James, Henry 303–4, 339
Jane Eyre (Brontë) 424
Japanese Americans, and World War Two 359
Jazz Age (1920s), and *Great Gatsby* 116, 144, 157, 192, 226, 256, 379, 380, 382–3, 388, 392, 428
jazz music, in *Great Gatsby* 388, 432
Jewett, Sarah Orne 302
"Jilting of Granny Weatherall, The" (Porter) 231–2
John, Sir Elton 316
Johnson, Charles 345, 393
Johnson, James Weldon 386
Johnson, Sargent 387
Jordan, June 345
Josephson, Matthew 291–2
Joyce, James 96
Jung, Carl G. 233n

Keable, Robert 384
Keller, Karl 318, 322
Kenya, Green Belt Movement 405
Kincaid, Jamaica 408, 440
Kristeva, Julia 98, 99
Kushner, Tony 319

Lacan, Jacques 100; *see also* Lacanian psychoanalysis
Lacanian psychoanalysis 25–33, 48; Desire of the Mother 27, 30; Imaginary Order 27, 31, 32, 33, 37, 48; literary interpretation 32–3; loss or lack in 28, 29–30; Mirror Stage 26, 27, 37; Name-of-the Father 30; *objet petit a* ("object small a") 27–8, 33, 38, 48; Real, notion of 31–2; Symbolic Order 27, 28, 30, 31, 32, 37, 48
Lady Gaga 316
LaGaurdia, Fiorello 385
language: ambiguity 237–8; Black Vernacular English 346, 347, 378; deconstructing 235–41; Eurocentric 401; everyday 131–2; figurative 135–6; in French feminism 95–9; and ideology 239, 240; in Lacanian psychoanalysis 27, 28; literary, and organic unity 131–7, 143; scientific 131, 132; stretching 239; and structuralism 201; structural linguistics 201–3; and unconscious 29; *see also* deconstruction/deconstructive criticism; semiotics; signified and signifiers
langue 201, 203, 204, 208, 220
Larsen, Nella 80
latent content, dreams 18
Latinos/as 376
Lawrence, D. H. 226
Leavitt, David 319
Lee, Spike 346
legal storytelling movement 361
Le Morte d'Arthur (Malory) 209
Lepowsky, Maria Alexandra 106
lesbian, gay and queer criticism 103, 302–42, 449; gay criticism 314–19; gay men, and lesbians 307–8; gay or lesbian "signs" 325, 329–30, 331, 332; *Great Gatsby*, queer reading 327–38; lesbian criticism 308–14; literary texts, questions asked by lesbian, gay and queer critics 326–7; marginalization of LGBTQ people 303–8; other literary works, lesbian, gay and queer approaches 338–40; portrayal of lesbian characters 313; queer criticism 319–23; sexual orientation of writers 302–3, 314, 319; shared features 324–6; *see also* LGBTQ (lesbian, gay, bisexual, transgender and queer) people
lesbian continuum 310
lesbian criticism 308–14
Lessing, Doris 218
"Lesson, The" (Toni Cade Bambara) 76, 158
Letters of F. Scott Fitzgerald, The (Turnbull) 391
Lévi-Strauss, Claude 203, 204
Le Vot, André 191, 294–5

Lewis, David Levering 385

Lewis, Sinclair 386

LGBTQ (lesbian, gay, bisexual, transgender and queer) people 57, 109, 303, 324; adolescents 304–5, 341n; "closeting" (posing as heterosexuals) 308; definitions 309, 313; friendship 307; hate crimes 304; heterocentrism 305–6; marginalization 303–8; as members of racial minorities 305, 308–9, 313; police harassment 304; same-sex desire 313; same-sex "doubles" 325–6; separatists, lesbians 310–11; subcultures 325; woman-identified women 310, 313; working-class 308, 309, 313; *see also* lesbian, gay and queer criticism

"liberated woman," in African American literature 373–4

Life of Olaudah Equino, or Gustavus Vassa, the African (Equino) 371

Lindberg, Stanley W. 295

linguistics, structural 201–3

Lispector, Clarice 96

literary competence 178, 218, 220

literary criticism 2, 5, 6, 12, 178, 212, 408; *see also* African American criticism/African Americans; cultural criticism; deconstruction/deconstructive criticism; feminist criticism/feminism; lesbian, gay and queer criticism; Marxist criticism/Marxism; New Criticism; new historicism; postcolonial theory/criticism; psychoanalytic criticism/ psychoanalytic theory; reader-response criticism/theory; structuralism/structural criticism

literary genres, structure 209–12

literary texts: ambiguity in 133–4; blueprint function 165; close reading 129, 135; complexity 132–3, 134; determinate meaning 165, 166; formal elements 131, 140; "gaps" in 165–6; ideological conflicts of culture, reflecting 117; indeterminate meaning 165–6, 188, 189, 190; irony in 133, 135; overt ideological project 248, 251; paradox in 132, 135, 138; questions asked about *see* literary texts, questions asked; as self-sufficient verbal objects 131; stimulus function 165; symbols in 206; tension in 134, 138, 145, 246, 248, 250; text as an event, not an object 164; themes 135, 140, 169, 248–9; undecidability 245, 251

literary texts, questions asked: by African American critics 377–9; by feminist critics 114–15; by lesbian, gay and queer critics 326–7; by Marxist critics 65–6; by New Critics 143–4; by new historical and cultural critics 285–7; by postcolonial critics 425–8; by psychoanalytic critics 36–8; by reader response critics 180–1; by structuralist critics 220–1; *see also* literary works, other; literature

literary theory *see* critical theory

literary works, other: African American approaches to 392–3; deconstructive approaches to 264–5; feminist approaches to 125–6; lesbian, gay and queer approaches to 338–40; Marxist approaches to 76; New Critical approaches to 157–8; new historical and cultural criticism, approaches of 297–8; postcolonial approaches to 440–1; psychoanalytic approaches to 48; reader-response approaches to 193–4; structuralist approaches to 231–2

literature: and African American criticism 368–77; and classical psychoanalysis 33–6; and cultural criticism 282–5; deconstructing 244–6; and feminism 112–14; and language 207–8; and Marxism 62–5; and new historicism 276–80; and postcolonial criticism 421–5; and structuralism 207–9; *see also Great Gatsby, The* (F. Scott Fitzgerald); literary texts, questions asked; literary works, other

"Little Black Boy, The" (Blake) 265, 298

logocentrism 242

Lorber, Judith 107

loss, fear of 23

loss or lack, in Lacanian psychoanalysis 28, 29–30

"Los Vendidos" (Valdez) 264

Lowe-Evans, Mary 179

Lowell, Amy 302

Maathai, Wangari 405

McClintock, Anne 406

McCullers, Carson 302

McDowell, Deborah E. 373

McGuffey Readers (elementary school books) 287, 291, 295, 296

McIntosh, Peggy 361–2

McKay, Claude 386, 392

Madonna (singer) 316

Maecenas (mythical figure) 148

male gaze 97

male imagery: in dreams 19; in *My Ántonia* (Cather) 312

Malkovich, John 283

Malory, Sir Thomas 209
manifest content, dreams 18, 19
Manila Southcoast Development Corporation 414
Mann, Thomas 179
Mansfield Park (Austen) 425
Marland, E. W. 296
marriage, and French materialist feminism 92–5
Marx, Karl 51, 57, 59, 89
Marxist criticism/Marxism 5, 34, 51–78, 448; base/superstructure model 51; *bourgeoisie* and *proletariat* 52, 53; commodity/ commodification 59, 60; consciousness 52, 56, 61; and deconstruction 235; family 61; and feminism 89, 267; fundamental premises of Marxism 51–2; *Great Gatsby*, Marxist reading 6–7, 65, 66–75, 251–2, 280; human behavior 59–60; ideology, role of 54–9; literary texts, questions asked by Marxist critics 65–6; literature and Marxism 62–5; other literary works, Marxist approaches to 76; and psychoanalytic theory 62–3, 267; United States, class system in 52–5, 57
masculine pronoun, use of to portray men and women 79–80
master narrative 273
master-race theory 402–3
masturbation, as sexual pathology 315
material circumstances, in Marxism 52
material determinism 352, 355
materialist feminism, French 91, 92, 93, 94, 98
Matlock (American television series) 296
Maugham, Somerset 302
Maupin, Armistead 319
Mda, Zakes 408, 441, 445n
meaning-making: death 21–3; deconstruction 236, 237, 238, 239, 242, 244–5; determinate meaning 165, 166; in *Great Gatsby* 182, 190, 191; indeterminate meaning 165–6, 188, 189, 190; "moments" of meaning 245, 251; in reader-response criticism 165–6, 167, 180, 182; sexuality 23–5
media, representation of death/death work 23
Melville, Herman 325
Memoirs of a Survivor (Lessing) 218
memory, selective 15
men: display of emotions by 83–4; male programming 84
"Mending Wall" (Robert Frost) 246–51; binary oppositions 248, 249, 250; nonconformity and conformity conflict within poem 249, 250, 265

Meridian (Walker) 373
Merrill, James 302
metaphorical coherence, rule of 219
metaphors 29, 30, 135, 136–7; in *Great Gatsby* 145; in "There Is a Girl Inside" 139
metonymy 29, 30
Midas (mythical figure) 148
middle classes, in United States 53, 54–5, 86–7
Middle Passage 343, 344, 368
"Middle Passage" (Hayden) 131
Midler, Bette 316
Midsummer Night's Dream (Shakespeare) 210
Miller, Arthur, *Death of a Salesman see Death of a Salesman* (Miller)
mimicry, in postcolonial theory 403, 421, 435, 437, 443n
Miner, Valerie 314
minoritizing views of homosexuality 306, 341n
Mirror Stage, Lacanian psychoanalysis 26, 27, 37
misogyny (hatred of women) 113
Mitchell, Joni 132
Moby Dick (Melville) 325
modernist worldview 226
modes, theory of 211, 232, 233n
Moi, Toril 96
Monette, Paul 319
Montrose, Louis 275
mood 216, 217
Moore, Marianne 80
Moravia, Alberto 135, 158
Morgan, J. P. 287
Morrison, Toni 102, 133, 345, 375, 376, 388, 408, 431, 443n; *Beloved* 48, 96, 125, 133–4, 179, 231, 277, 283, 423; *The Bluest Eye* 6, 35, 64, 113, 174–5, 194, 297–8, 307, 326, 339, 346, 373, 392; *Playing in the Dark: Whiteness and the Literary Imagination* 374–6; *Song of Solomon* 374; *Sula* 313, 325
Movement of Landless Rural Workers, Brazil 443n
Mrs Dalloway (Woolf) 96
Mukherjee, Bharati 408
multicultural feminism 100–3
multinational corporations 409–11, 412, 443n
My Ántonia (Cather) 311–12
My Son's Story (Gordimer) 423
mythemes 204
mythoi, theory of (Frye) 209, 210, 226, 231, 232, 233n
myths, theory of 209

Naipaul, V. S. 408, 440
Name-of-the-Father, Lacanian psychoanalysis 30

narrative: grammar 221, 222; master 273; structure of (structuralist narratology) 212–17

Narrative as Rhetoric (Phelan) 195–6n

Narrative of the life of Frederick Douglass, An American Slave (Douglass) 371

narratology, structuralist 212–17

Nash, Charles C. 191

National Association for the Advancement of Colored People (NAACP) 355

National Park Service 444n

Native Americans 107, 271, 356, 376, 401

Native Son (Wright) 209, 226, 370

naturalization 218–19

natural resources 410

nature, and ideology 54, 55

Naylor, Gloria 345

Nazis 271

"Negro Speaks of Rivers, The" (Langston Hughes) 158

neocolonialism 410–11, 442n

New Criticism 8–9, 10n, 129–60, 448; authorial intention 130, 131; contribution to literary studies 129; and deconstruction 246, 248, 249, 250; formal elements 131, 140; *Great Gatsby*, New Critical reading 144–57; as intrinsic, objective criticism 141–2; length of work 142–3; literary language and organic unity 131–7, 143; literary texts, questions asked by New Critics 143–4; and new historicism 276, 277; as no longer practiced by literary critics 129; and reader-response criticism 162; single best interpretation 142–3; tension, in literary texts 134, 138, 145, 246, 248, 250; text itself, focus on 129–31, 143; "There Is a Girl Inside," New Critical reading 137–41; universal significance concept 134, 141, 159n, 448; *see also* literary texts

new historicism 267–76, 449; cultural criticism compared 281–2; definitions 273–4; and feminism 90; *Great Gatsby*, new historical reading 286, 287–97; and interpretation of historical events 269, 273, 279–80; key concepts 275–6; literary texts, questions asked 285–7; and literature 276–80; and New Criticism 276, 277; non-linear view of history 268–9, 275; objective analysis, belief in impossibility of 269, 271; other literary works, new historical approaches to 297–8; and power 270, 271, 275; and subjectivity 269–70, 275, 276; thick description 274, 285;

versus traditional view of history 268, 269; *see also* cultural criticism; history

New Negro Movement 386

New Woman 116, 117, 119, 123

"New World" 401, 416

New York City 332–3, 378, 386, 431, 432; Bronx 384; Brooklyn 384; Central Park 384, 385; and Fitzgerald 389; Long Island 379, 384, 389; Madison Avenue 384; Manhattan 379, 383, 384, 385, 386, 387, 388–9; newspapers 383–4, 386; Queens 384; Staten Island 384; *see also Great Gatsby, The* (F. Scott Fitzgerald); Harlem/Harlem Renaissance; United States

Ngugi wa Thiong'o 404, 408, 445n

Nigger Heaven (Van Vechten) 391

Night of the Iguana, The (Williams) 319

Nike 410

1920s period *see* Jazz Age (1920s)

Nixon, Rob 420, 444n

Nordicism 383, 389, 394–5n, 402–3, 436

Northern Ireland, and postcolonial theory 406

Nwapa, Flora 408, 445n

objective criticism 142

"objective" knowledge 170–1

objects, real and symbolic 170

objet petit a ("object small a"), Lacanian psychoanalysis 27–8, 33, 38, 48

O'Connor, Flannery 393

oedipal conflict 13, 14, 16, 37; and Marxism 62

Oedipus myth 204

Oedipus the King (Sophocles) 210

"Off-shore Pirate, The" (Fitzgerald) 393

Of Mice and Men (Steinbeck) 209

Olsen, Tillie 231–2

O'Meara, Lauraleigh 388–9

O'Neill, Eugene 386

"On the Road" (Hughes) 76

optimal reader 178

oral developmental stage 24

orality, in African American literary tradition 369, 392

Oranges Are Note the Only Fruit (Winterson) 339

order, in structuralist narratology 216

organic unity 132, 143

organized crime, in *Great Gatsby* 380–1

orientalism 402

Orwell, George 209

Othello (Shakespeare) 210

othering 401, 402, 421, 426, 443n; in *Great Gatsby* 429, 431, 433

paradox, in literary texts 132, 135, 138
paraphrase, heresy of 131
parents/parental figures: abandonment 13, 23;
    unresolved conflicts with 13, 14, 18
Paris 389–90, 392
Parker, Dorothy 386
parole (speech) 201, 203
Passing of the Great Race, The (Grant) 383
patriarchy: binary oppositions, hierarchical
    95–6; culture 97; femininity, patriarchal
    concept 84; getting beyond 88–91;
    heteropatriarchy 305; ideology 85, 87–8, 89,
    112, 113, 124; male desire 85; norms and
    values 81; oppression, patriarchal 87, 92–3,
    100; patriarchal programming 82, 83, 88–9;
    patriarchal society 92; patriarchal woman 81,
    82; and postcolonial criticism 405; power
    structures 96; and reader-response criticism
    161; as sexist 81, 87; threats to 122; *see also*
    feminism
patriotism 57
"Paul's Case" (Cather) 339
peasants' rights organizations 414, 443n
Peck, Dale 319
penis envy/power envy 14, 25, 89
perception, selective 15
performative structures 213
Perkins Gilman, Charlotte 32, 125, 302
Perry, Linda A. M. 111
perspective, in structuralist narratology 216
phallic symbols; in *My Ántonia* (Cather) 19
phallogocentric thinking 87–8
Phelan, James 195–6n
phenomenology 195n
Philippines Department of Agrarian Reform
    413, 443n
phonemes 199
Piano Lesson, The (Wilson) 392–3
Pichert, J. A. 195n
Pilgrim's Progress, The (Bunyan) 209
Plato 242
*Playing in the Dark: Whiteness and the Literary
    Imagination* (Morrison) 374–6
Play It as It Lays (Didion) 226
Poe, Edgar Allan 142
political power, in Marxism 51
Porter, Katherine Anne 231–2
"Po Sandy" (Chesnutt) 369
postcolonial theory/criticism 141, 398–447,
    449; colonialist ideology and postcolonial
    identity 399–406; foundational postcolonial
    debates 406–8; globalization and "end" of
    postcolonial theory 409–12; *Great Gatsby*,
    postcolonial reading 427, 428–40; literary

texts, questions asked by postcolonial
    critics 425–8; and literature 421–5;
    othering 401, 402, 421, 426, 429, 431,
    433, 443n; other literary works, postcolonial
    approaches 440–1; postcolonial theory
    and global conservation 416–21;
    postcolonial theory and global tourism
    412–16; terminology 442n
poststructuralist theory, deconstruction
    as 243
poverty/the poor, in United States 53–5, 57
power: economic 51–2; new historicism 270,
    271, 275; patriarchy 96; political 51; and
    racial issues 344; social 51, 270–1; and
    transforming victimhood 316–17
Pratt, Minnie Bruce 314
praxis, Marxist 52
Preeves, Sharon 108, 110
pre-verbal feelings 27, 30, 31
Primark (clothing company) 411
primary revision, dreams 18
prisoners, disproportionate number of people
    of color 351–2
"Professing the Renaissance: The Poetics and
    Politics of Culture" (Montrose) 275
Prohibition, in *Great Gatsby* 380
projection, in psychoanalysis 15
proletariat, in Marxism 52, 53
propositions, in structuralist narratology 214
Proust, Marcel 28, 215, 217
psychoanalytic criticism/psychoanalytic
    theory 11–50, 448; anxiety 16; classical
    psychoanalysis 12, 25, 33–6; common
    terminology 11; core issues 16–18; death,
    meaning 21–3; defense mechanisms 11,
    15–16, 17, 18, 23; dreams/dream
    symbols 18–21; familiarity of psychoanalytic
    thinking 11; and feminism 89, 95–6, 99,
    100; goal of psychoanalysis 12; *Great Gatsby*,
    psychoanalytic reading 28, 38–48, 450;
    and human behavior 12, 36; Lacanian
    psychoanalysis 25–33; literary texts,
    questions asked by psychoanalytic
    critics 36–8; literature and classical
    psychoanalysis 33–6; and Marxism
    62–3, 267; other literary works,
    psychoanalytic approaches to 48;
    psychoanalytic feminism 91; psychoanalytic
    principles 11–12, 34; and reader-response
    criticism 161; sexuality, meaning 23–5;
    unconscious, origins 12–15
"psychobabble" 11
psychological reader-response theory 173–6
Pynchon, Thomas 226

qualities, in structuralist narratology 214–15
queer criticism 319–23; definitions/
    terminology 320, 321; *see also* lesbian, gay
    and queer criticism
queer theory 320, 321, 339
questioning, and LGBTQ terminology 110–11
quest-myth/formula 210, 225, 226
quest-romance 227, 228

Rabinowitz, Peter 196n
racial issues: ability of minority persons,
    underestimating 353; and African American
    literary history 343–50; assumption of
    African inferiority 347; classification of
    Americans according to race 356–7; concept
    of race 358; critical race theory 350–68;
    differential racialization 352, 358–9;
    education 353–4; injustice 351; interest
    convergence 352, 355; intersectionality 352,
    359–60; liberalism, problem with 361,
    363–5; prisoners, disproportionate number of
    people of color 351–2; racial discrimination
    345, 350–1; racial idealism 365; racialism
    344; racial realism 361, 365–8; social
    construction of race 352, 353–8; voice of
    people of color 353, 361; white privilege
    361–3, 367; *see also* racism
racial realism 361, 365–8
racism 35, 344, 345, 394n, 428; black writers,
    treatment by 368–9; and classism 437;
    denial of existence 354–5; everyday 352,
    353–5, 362; of Fitzgerald 390–1; as going
    underground 351, 352; institutionalized 345;
    internalized 346; intra-racial 346, 394n
Radel, Nicholas F. 318
Radical American Environmentalism 419
Ravel, Maurice 385
reader oriented response statements 171
reader-response criticism/theory 34, 161–97,
    448, 450–1; affective stylistics 166–9;
    classification 164; contribution to literary
    studies 161; defining readers 178–80;
    definition and function of text 162;
    experience of reading 168–9; goal 179–80;
    Great Gatsby, reader-response analysis 181–93;
    "house passage" (reader-response exercise)
    162–4, 195n; hypothetical ideal reader 178;
    interpretation 166, 173, 174, 175, 176, 177,
    178, 179; literary texts, questions asked by
    reader-response critics 180–1; meaning-
    making in 165–6, 167, 180, 182; other
    literary works, reader-response approaches
    to 193–4; psychological reader-response
    theory 164, 173–6; reading-as-projection

193; reading process 162, 179–80; rhetorical
    195–6n; social reader-response theory 164,
    176–8; and structuralism 208, 219–20;
    subjective reader-response theory 164,
    169–73; transactional reader-response
    theory 164, 165–6
Real, notion of in Lacanian psychoanalysis 31–2
Realism, in Marxist theory 63–4
reality oriented response statements 171
Rechy, John 319
Redford, Robert 296
Reed, Ishmael 345, 371
Regents of the University of California v. Bakke 367
regression, in psychoanalysis 15
Remembrance of Things Past (Proust) 28, 215, 217
repression: in psychoanalysis 12, 13, 15, 17, 25,
    48; in *Great Gatsby* 43, 47–8, 330; in
    Lacanian psychoanalysis 28–9, 31; repressive
    ideologies 54–5, 58, 72
response statements: experience oriented
    171–2; focus of 194; reader oriented 171;
    reality oriented 171; writing 173, 194
restaurant menus, semiotic analysis 207
resymbolization 170
rhetorical analysis 286
rhetorical reader-response criticism 195–6n
Rhetoric of Fiction, The (Booth) 196n
Rhys, Jean 424
Rich, Adrienne 302, 310, 314
Riggs, Rolla Lynn 80
Rising Tide of Color, The (Stoddard) 383, 436
"Road Not Taken, The" (Frost) 264–5
"Road to Business Success, The" (Carnegie) 289
Roaring Twenties *see* Jazz Age (1920s)
Roberts, Elizabeth Maddox 80
Roberts, John W. 350
Robeson, Paul 385
Robinson, Bill "Bojangles" 385
Robinson Crusoe (Defoe) 424
Rockefeller, John D. 287, 291, 382
Room of One's Own, A (Woolf) 89
"Rose for Emily, A" (Faulkner) 76, 126, 142,
    231, 321–2
Rosenblatt, Louise 6, 165, 166, 195n
Rothstein, Arnold 381–2
Roy, Arundhati 408
Royal Dutch Shell 411
rugged individualism 55, 57, 192
Rule, Jane 314
Rushdie, Salman 408
Russell, Paul 319

Said, Edward 402, 425
"Sandman, The" (Barthelme) 218

Sapolsky, Robert M. 104
satire 209–10
Saturday Evening Post, The 383
Saussure, Ferdinand de 201, 202
Save the Narmada Movement, India 443n
Scarlett Letter, The (Hawthorne) 297
Scholes, Robert 211, 220, 232
School Daze (Lee) 346
Scribner, Charles 157
Sears 411
secondary revision, dreams 19
Second Sex, The (de Beauvoir) 89, 92
Sedaris, David 319
Sedgwick, Eve Kosofsky 321, 322, 341n
*Selections from the Letters of Geraldine Endsor
     Jewsbury to Jane Welsh Carlyle* (Ireland) 341n
selective memory 15
selective perception 15
self: definitions 407–8; fragmented 244, 408;
     human identity, deconstructing 243–4;
     insecure/unstable sense of 16; *see also*
     subjectivity
"Self as Other: The Politics of Identity in the
     Works of Edmund White" (Radel) 318
self-esteem, low 16, 17; in *Great Gatsby* 41
self-made man, American dream image 70
self-regulation, and structure 200
semiotic language vs. symbolic language
     (Kristeva) 99
semiotics 220; semiotic codes 207; of
     restaurant menus 207; of wrestling 205–6
Sense and Sensibility (Austen) 133
separatists, lesbians as 310–11
sequences, in structuralist narratology 214
settings, in *Great Gatsby* 153–5
sexism/sexist ideology 54, 85, 125, 308, 311
sexual difference 95, 97, 98
sexuality: activity 309, 311; continuum of
     possibilities 320; desire 309, 313; and
     dreams 19; and gender 104; and identity
     24, 327; imagery 312; meaning 23–5;
     romantic/sexual relationships 17–18,
     41, 47; transgressive 326, 328, 334;
     and Victorian society 24, 25; of women
     85, 86, 87
Shakespeare, William 130–1, 209, 210,
     302, 424
Shelley, Mary 6, 35–6, 48, 64, 113–14, 179,
     210, 265, 402, 440–1
Shelley, Percy 114
Shilts, Randy 319
Shockley, Ann Allen 314
Shuffle Along (musical comedy) 385–6
Shulman, Sarah 314

sibling rivalry 11, 14
sign-exchange value 59, 60; in *Great Gatsby*
     70, 71
significance, rule of 219
signified and signifiers 202, 237, 238–9
signifyin(g), in African American
     criticism 370
Signifying Monkey, The (Gates) 369, 370, 371
signs 237, 325, 329–30
sign systems 205, 206, 207
Silko, Leslie Marmon 408
similes 135, 137
Simon Called Peter (Keable) 384
Simpsons, The 316
Sinha, Indra 445n
sisterhood, and feminism 101
slavery/slave resistance 344, 348, 350
"Sleeping Beauty," and feminism 85
Smith, Barbara 313
Smith, Bessie 385
"Snow White and the Seven Dwarfs," and
     feminism 85
social class: in *Great Gatsby* 44, 72, 119, 253–4,
     436; LGBTQ people 308, 309, 313; in
     United States 52–5, 57, 86–7; *see also*
     Marxist criticism/Marxism; socioeconomic
     class
social constructionism 82, 92, 306, 321; social
     construction of race 352, 353–8
social reader-response theory 164, 176–8
socioeconomic class, in Marxism 52, 53, 71
Something Happened (Heller) 226
"Song of Myself" (Whitman) 6, 219, 318,
     322–3
Song of Solomon (Morrison) 374
Sons and Lovers (Lawrence) 226
Sophocles 210
Souls of Black Folk, The (DuBois) 346, 442n
Sound and the Fury, The (Faulkner) 325–6
Soyinka, Wole 408
Spade, Joan Z. 105
Spenser, Edmund 209
spiritual themes, in African American criticism
     371–2, 393
Spivak, Gayatri 424
spring, mythos of 210
Springfield, Dusty 316
Stadler, Matthew 319
states, in structuralist narratology 214
Stefancie, Jean 351, 352, 355, 359–60, 362,
     364, 365
Stein, Gertrude 80, 302
Steinbeck, John 76, 209, 232, 298
Stoddard, Theodore Lothrop 383, 436

Stonewall/Stonewall Inn bar, Greenwich Village 304
"Storm, The" (Chopin) 76, 125–6, 135, 158, 193, 264
Streetcar Named Desire, A (Williams) 319
structuralism/structural criticism 129, 198–234, 243, 448; components of a structure 201, 202; definition of "structure" 200; formulaic description, reliance on 231; goal 208; *Great Gatsby*, structuralist reading 208, 212, 213, 215, 221–31; literary interpretation, structure of 217–20; literary texts, questions asked by structuralist critics 220–1; and literature 207–9; narrative, structure of 212–17; other literary works, structuralist approaches to 231–2; and reader-response criticism 161, 208, 219–20; rules and codes 217, 218, 219; as science of humanity 231; semiotics 205–7; structural anthropology 203–4; and structuralist activity 198; structural linguistics 201–3; structure of literary genres 209–12; surface phenomena 199, 200, 201, 208; *see also* deconstruction/deconstructive criticism
structuralist narratology 212–17
Structuralist Poetics: Structuralism, Linguistics and the Study of Literature (Culler) 195n
St. Vincent Millay, Edna 80
stylistics, affective, reader-response theory 166–9
subjective reader-response theory 164, 169–73
subjectivity 90, 100, 243; and new historicism 269–70, 275, 276; *see also* self
suicide: and fear of death 23; of LGBTQ adolescents and young adults 341n
Sula (Morrison) 313, 325
summer, mythos of 209, 210, 226, 230
superego 24, 25, 48
surface phenomena 199, 200, 201, 208
Survival International 444n
"suspended woman," in African American literature 373, 393
Swift, Jonathan 209
symbolic language vs. semiotic language (Kristeva) 99
symbolic objects 170
Symbolic Order, Lacanian psychoanalysis 27, 28, 30, 31, 32, 37, 48
symbolization 170
symbols 135, 136; theory of 233n; *see also* dreams/dream symbols and phallic symbols
syncretism/hybridity 404, 426

Tate, Allen 386
"Teaching Black-Eyed Susans" (Washington) 373
Tebtebba: Indigenous Peoples' International Centre for Policy Research and Education 444n
"Tell-Tale Heart, The" (Poe) 142
Tempest, The (Shakespeare) 209, 424
Tender Is the Night (Fitzgerald) 117, 390, 393
tense, in structuralist narratology 216, 217
tension, in literary texts 134, 138, 145, 246, 248, 250
testosterone 104
thanatos (death drive) 21
Their Eyes Were Watching God (Hurston) 373, 393
thematic unity, rule of 219
themes 135, 140, 169; and deconstruction 248–9; identity 175, 176; spiritual 371–2, 393
The Nature Conservancy (TNC) 419
theoretical jargon 1–2
"There Is a Girl Inside" (Clifton), New Critical reading of 137–41; closing lines 139; metaphors 139; parts of speech 138–9; punctuation 138; slang and humor 140, 141; theme 138–9, 140; tone 140; youth and age 139–40
thick description 274, 285
Things Fall Apart (Achebe) 440
Third World 401, 404, 405, 407, 413, 416, 419, 420, 443n; multinational activity 410–11
Third World Network (TWN) 415
Thomas, Brook 278–9
Thomas, Clarence 367
Thoreau, Henry David 416
"Those Winter Sundays" (Hayden) 193
Tiffin, Helen 424–5
Tillyard, E. M. W. 299n
Todorov, Tzvetan 212, 214–15, 217, 221
To Have and Have Not (Hemingway) 375–6
Tom Jones (Fielding) 210
Toomer, Jean 371, 386
To the Lighthouse (Woolf) 226
tourism, global 412–16, 443n
tourist companies 443n
Toyota 409
tragedy, in structure of literary genres 210
transactional reader-response theory 164, 165–6
transactive analysis 173
transformation, and structure 200
transformation mode, in psychological reader-response theory 175
transgender 341n; activists 108–9; *see also* LGBTQ (lesbian, gay, bisexual, transgender and queer) people

trauma, in psychoanalysis 21; of the Real 31–2
Troy, William 294
Tsui, Kitty 314
Tucker, Hazel 408
Turnbull, Andrew 391
Turn of the Screw, The (James) 339
Twain, Mark 209–10, 307, 325

unconscious: and anxiety 17; and fear 20;
　language, structured as 29; origins 12–15;
　portrayal in literature 35–6; and repression
　28–9; *see also* consciousness
undecidability 245, 251
underclass, in United States 53–5
under erasure, words 239
Underground Railroad 343
unhomeliness 403, 435, 443n
United Nations Permanent Forum on
　Indigenous Issues 444n
United States: American Civil War (1861–65),
　and African American history 358, 366, 368;
　American Revolution (1775–83), and new
　historicism 273; Census Bureau 356, 357;
　classification of Americans according to race
　356–7; class system in 52–5, 57, 86–7;
　Constitution 352, 366, 439; cultural
　hegemony of white America 343–4; Federal
　Bureau of Investigation, definition of hate
　crime 124; First World War, effects on
　1920s America 381, 382; homosexual
　immigration, imposing of restrictions (1952)
　304; judicial system, and African American
　history 355–6; millionaires 287, 291, 293;
　modern world, depicting spiritual poverty of
　in *Great Gatsby* 145, 226–8, 252–6, 258,
　261, 262; New York City *see* New York
　City; patriarchal oppression, differences 101;
　position of women prior to World War One
　116; and postcolonial criticism 406; women's
　movements 100; *see also* African American
　criticism/African Americans; African
　American history; American dream; Marxist
　criticism; racial issues; racism
United States Agency for International
　Development (USAID) 415
universalism, Eurocentric definition 345, 401
universalizing views of homosexuality 306, 341n
universal significance concept, New Criticism
　134, 141, 159n, 448
Unquiet Woods, The (Guha) 442–3n
unresolved conflicts: in dreams 20–1; with
　parental figures 13, 14, 18
upper classes, in United States 53, 56–7
use value 59

Valdez, Luis 264
Valentine, Catherine G. 105
value, in Marxist theory 59–60
Vanatinai (New Guinea), people of 106
Vanderbilt, Emily 385
Van Vechten, Carl 389, 391
verbs, in structuralist narratology 217
Victorian period: on femininity 101;
　"good-girl/bad-girl" attitude 86; sexuality
　24, 25; women writers in 85
video games, and cultural criticism 284
Vindication of the Rights of Woman, A
　(Wollstonecraft) 10n, 89
voice: in structuralist narratology 217; of color
　353, 361

Walcott, Derek 408, 445n
Walker, Alice 102, 345, 371, 373, 374, 393
Waller, Fats 385
Wal-Mart 411
Waring, Laura Wheeler 387
Washington, Mary Helen 373, 393
wastefulness, global 419–20
water, dreams about 20
Waters, Ethel 385
Weltner, Peter 319
West, Mae 385
Western philosophy, and deconstructive
　theory 242
Wharton, Edith 133, 209
Wheatley, Phillis 348
White, Brian 195n
White, Edmund 318, 319
white nationalist/supremacist groups
　351, 403, 440
White Noise (DeLillo) 226
white privilege 361–3, 367
white settler colonies 407, 426
Whitman, Walt 6, 219, 302, 306, 317, 322–3
wholeness, and structure 200
Wideman, John Edgar 345
Wide Sargasso Sea (Rhys) 424
Wilde, Dolly 338
Wilde, Oscar 302, 324
wilderness areas 416–17, 418, 419, 420;
　Wilderness Act 1964 417
Wildlife Conservation Society (WCS) 419
Wildman, Stephanie M. 363
Williams, Patricia 361
Williams, Sherley Anne 345
Williams, Tennessee 302, 318, 319
Wilson, August 345, 392–3
Wilson, Edmund 337, 391
Winfrey, Oprah 283

winter, mythos of 210, 226, 230
Winterson, Jeanette 314, 339
Wittig, Monique 314
Wollstonecraft, Mary 10n, 89, 114
woman-identified women 310, 313
womanspeak 97, 98
Women in Love (Lawrence) 226
women's work 93–4
Woolf, Virginia 89, 96, 226, 302
Wordsworth, William 130
Worldwide Fund for Nature (WWF) 419
wrestling, semiotic analysis 205–6

Wright, Richard 178, 209, 226,
    370, 371
W   rley, William 210

Yeats, W   406
"Yellow Wa.   er, The" (Perkins Gilman)
    32, 125
"Yet Do I Marvel   llen) 346
Yosemite National Pa.   West Coast 417–18,
    420, 444n

Zack, Naomi 356–7